Europe and the Maritime World

Europe and the Maritime World: A Twentieth-Century History offers a new framework for understanding globalization over the past century. Through a detailed analysis of ports, shipping, and trading companies whose networks spanned the world, Michael B. Miller shows how a European maritime infrastructure made modern production and consumer societies possible. He argues that the combination of overseas connections and close ties to home ports contributed to globalization. Miller also explains how the ability to manage merchant shipping's complex logistics was central to the outcome of both world wars. He chronicles transformations in hierarchies, culture, identities, and port city space, all of which produced a new and different maritime world by the end of the century.

Michael B. Miller is Professor of History at the University of Miami. He is the author of *The Bon Marché: Bourgeois Culture and the Department Store, 1869–1920* (1981) and *Shanghai on the Métro: Spies, Intrigue, and the French between the Wars* (1994). Professor Miller serves on the board of the *International Journal of Maritime History*.

Europe and the Maritime World

A Twentieth-Century History

MICHAEL B. MILLER

University of Miami

CAMBRIDGE
UNIVERSITY PRESS

CAMBRIDGE UNIVERSITY PRESS
Cambridge, New York, Melbourne, Madrid, Cape Town,
Singapore, São Paulo, Delhi, Mexico City

Cambridge University Press
32 Avenue of the Americas, New York NY 10013-2473, USA

Published in the United States of America by Cambridge University Press, New York

www.cambridge.org
Information on this title: www.cambridge.org/9781107659629

First published 2012
First paperback edition 2013

A catalogue record for this publication is available from the British Library

Library of Congress Cataloguing in Publication Data
Miller, Michael B. (Michael Barry), 1945–
Europe and the maritime world : a twentieth-century history / Michael B. Miller.
pages cm
Includes bibliographical references and index.
ISBN 978-1-107-02455-7
1. Merchant marine – Europe – History – 20th century.   2. Shipping – Economic
aspects – Europe – History – 20th century.   3. Europe – Commerce –
History – 20th century.   I. Title.
HE821.M55   2012
387.5094′0904–dc23   2012006481

ISBN 978-1-107-02455-7 Hardback
ISBN 978-1-107-65962-9 Paperback

Once again, for Mary

Contents

Tables, Figures, Maps

Tables

Figures

Maps

Acknowledgments

To turn Tolstoy on his head, all books are happy in their own fashion. For this I wish to thank the staff of the Hamburg Staatsarchiv, particularly Dr. Klaus-Joachim Lorenzen-Schmidt, who was supportive in many ways; the staff of the Commerzbibliothek der Handelskammer Hamburg; the staff of the Gemeentearchief Rotterdam, especially the exceptional support from Dr. R. H. Krans; Henk Torenvlied of the Havenbedrijf Archief of the Port of Rotterdam; Internatio-Müller N. V. in Rotterdam for allowing me to consult the Internatio archives, and Annelies Tol who oversaw my visit; the staff of the Nationaal Archief in The Hague; the staff of the Gemeentearchief Amsterdam; Virginie Saverys of the Compagnie Maritime Belge for allowing me to consult its archives in Antwerp, and Riet de Block who helped guide me through them; the staff of the Antwerp Stadsarchief; the staff of the Antwerp Havenbedrijf Bibliotheek; Albert Himmler and G. Thues of the Antwerp Havenbedrijf's Technische Dienst; Dawn Littler, Gordon Read, and the staff of the Merseyside Maritime Museum; the staffs of the University of Liverpool Archives and the Liverpool Record Office; the staffs of the British Library, the National Archives of the United Kingdom, the Guildhall Manuscripts Collection – now in the London Metropolitan Archives – the National Maritime Museum in Greenwich, the School of Oriental and African Studies Archives, and the Docklands Library and Archive, especially Bob Aspinall; Lord Sterling and Stephen Rabson of P & O for graciously allowing me access to house materials and arranging interviews; Elementis; Jean-Paul Herbert of the Archives de l'association French Lines in Le Havre; the staff of the Centre des archives contemporaines in Fontainebleau; and, in Paris, the staffs of the Archives nationales, the archives of the Ministère des affaires étrangères, and the Service historique de la marine, with special thanks to the staff of the Bibliothèque nationale de France during difficult teething moments in 1999.

I would also like to thank all the individuals who granted me interviews, many of whom showed me additional kindnesses, which I shall never forget. Their names appear in the bibliography. In addition, I am grateful for the introductions or other support shown me by many maritime professionals and their organizations. For Belgium these are the Antwerpse Scheepvaartvereniging and Frank Boogaerts of the Vereniging der Expediteurs van Antwerpen. For France: Madame Auguste of the Banque Indo-Suez and Madame Collet of COFRALI. For Germany: Hans-Jürgen Capell of Hapag-Lloyd; Herbert R. Schmidt and Robert Völkl of the Verein Hamburger Spediteure e. V.; P.-J. Schönberg of Behn Meyer Holding A. G.; and especially Wilhelm Michels of C. Illies & Co., who over much correspondence answered many questions about his company for me. For Great Britain: Charlotte Bleasdale of the John Swire and Sons archives; Mrs. B. Fletcher of the Institute of Chartered Shipbrokers; and R. G. S. Johnston of the United Kingdom Major Ports Group Limited. For the Netherlands: S. S. Balgobind of Nedlloyd; M. S. B. Duin of the Vereniging van Rotterdamse Cargadoors; Fenex; Ton de Graaf of ABN-AMRO Bank; and A. C. Snelleman of HAL Investments B. V.

Generous support for this project came from the Deutscher Akademischer Austauschdienst, the National Endowment for the Humanities, the John Simon Guggenheim Memorial Foundation, the American Council of Learned Societies, and the German Marshall Fund of the United States. Syracuse University twice allowed me leave time to accept these fellowships. I am also appreciative of the research support I have received from the University of Miami and its College of Arts and Sciences, which supported the production of maps and the reproduction of pictures that appear in this volume. I would also like to thank all those who invited me to present earlier versions of this research and offered valuable feedback. These include university presentations at Carnegie Mellon, Cornell, Ghent, Memorial (St. John's), Miami, Rice, and Princeton (the Shelby Cullom Davis Center for Historical Studies), as well as invitations to the following focused conferences or workshops: the Comparative and Cross-National History conference at the University of Cincinnati; the Internationaal Instituut voor Sociale Geschiedenis workshop in Amsterdam; the Marine marchande française de 1850 à 2000 conference in Paris; the Resources and Infrastructures in the Maritime Economy, 1500–2000 conference in Hull; the Seascapes, Littoral Cultures, and

Trans-Oceanic Exchanges conference in Washington, D.C.; and the New Horizons in Maritime History conference at King's College, Cambridge.

Earlier versions of some material in this book appeared in "Ship Agents in the Twentieth Century," in Gordon Boyce and Richard Gorski, eds., *Resources and Infrastructures in the Maritime Economy, 1500–2000* (St. John's, 2002), 5–22, used here with the kind permission of the International Maritime Economic History Association; "The Business Trip: Maritime Networks in the Twentieth Century," *Business History Review* (Spring 2003): 1–32; "Comparative and Cross-National History," in Deborah Cohen and Maura O'Connor, eds., *Comparison and History* (Routledge: 2004), 115–132; "Pilgrims' Progress: The Business of the Hajj," *Past and Present* 191 (May 2006): 189–228; "L'Enigme de la marine marchande française au XXe," *Revue d'histoire maritime*, 5 (2006): 119–134; and "Steamships," in Akira Iriye and Pierre-Yves Saunier, eds., *The Palgrave Dictionary of Transnational History* (Palgrave Macmillan: 2009), 976–979, reproduced with permission of Palgrave Macmillan.

Others who in one way or another helped me through this project are John Barzman, Lenny Berlanstein, Marie-Françoise Berneron-Couvenhes, the late Frank Broeze, Vicki Caron, Bernard Cassagnou, Roland Caty, Alice Conklin, Lorraine Coons, Marcel Courdurié, Ferry de Goey, Torsten Feys, Skip Fischer, André Frémont, Patrick Fridenson, Donna Gabaccia, Wendy Goldman, Jean-Michel Harel, Renate Hauschild-Thiesen, Jean Heffer, Poul Holm, Stéphane Hoste, Franklin Kopitzsch, Andrew Lambert, Michel Lescure, Maurice Lévy-Leboyer, Reginald Loyen, Patrick Malcor, Roy Mankelow, Rory Miller, Sarah Palmer, Keetie Sluyterman, Paul van de Laar, Hugo van Driel, Stephan Vanfraechem, Alex Varias, and Birgitte Wolf. Tom Cairns Clery prepared the special-made maps in this book. Thanks as well to David Tenenbaum for his help on these. I would also like to thank my editor, Eric Crahan.

Finally, there is Mary Lindemann, without whom this book, and everything else during the years I researched and wrote it, would have been less rewarding.

Abbreviations

Company names presented in abbreviated form in the text appear below. Source abbreviations can be found in the bibliography.

APL	American President Lines
BI	British India Steam Navigation Company
CGT	Compagnie Générale Transatlantique
CMB	Compagnie Maritime Belge
CNCO	China Navigation Company
COSCO	China Ocean Shipping Company
CP	Canadian Pacific
DADG	Deutsche-Australische Dampfschiffs-Gesellschaft
DSR	Deutsche Schiffsreederei Rostock
ECT	Europe Container Terminus
HAPAG	Hamburg-Amerikanische Paketfahrt-Actien-Gesellschaft/ Hamburg Amerika Line
H & C	Harrisons & Crosfield
JCJL	Java-China-Japan Lijn
JNL	Java–New York Line
JPL	Java-Pacific Line
K-Line	Kawasaki Kisen Kaisha
KNSM	Koninklijke Nederlandsche Stoomboot Maatschappij
KPM	Koninklijke Paketvaart Maatschappij
KWIM	Koninklijke West-Indische Maildienst
NDL	Norddeutscher Lloyd
NOL	Neptune Orient Lines
NYK	Nippon Yūsen Kaisha

OCL	Overseas Containers Limited
OOCL	Orient Overseas Container Line
OSK	Osaka Shōsen Kaisha
PLA	Port of London Authority
P & O	Peninsular & Oriental Steam Navigation Company
RIL	Royal Interocean Line
SMN	Stoomvaart Maatschappij "Nederland"
SSC	Straits Steamship Co.
TMM	Transportacíon Marítime Mexicana
UASC	United Arab Shipping Company
VNS	Vereenigde Nederlandsche Scheepvaart Maatschappij

Introduction

We know a great deal about how Europeans sailed in ships to the far reaches of the world, set in motion a process of world integration, and, from the fifteenth to the eighteenth centuries, established extended maritime empires. Strangely, we know much less about how Europeans circulated goods and people across the seas in the twentieth century, even though industrial societies, consumer societies, overseas empires, and mass travel could not have developed as they did without the European steamship lines, European ports, European merchant companies, European markets, and European intermediaries that made these things possible. Europeans did not monopolize the sea lanes, but they did control them for almost the entire century. Americans constructed formidable numbers of merchant ships during the two world wars, but the sum of the American merchant marine in sheer numbers belied its significance on the seas. Not until containerization in the last third of the twentieth century did American shipping pose a serious challenge to European lines. Japan built a very large merchant marine, but Japanese shipping integrated into a European-led shipping system, so that powerful growth made the Japanese fleet simply one of the largest of the world's fleets, but a modest one when set alongside the combined numbers of European ships. Only in the last decades of the century did Asian shipping reverse this relationship, although even then, at century's end, the largest containerized shipping fleet was still European (Denmark's Maersk), and the largest shipowning nationality was equally European (Greek). Europe's ships sailed to ports around the world, but most called at a European terminus, and in many cases at a series of harbors along the northwest or Mediterranean-European littoral. No continent possessed such a number of great ports as did Europe in

I

London, Liverpool, Hamburg, Bremen, Rotterdam, Antwerp, Le Havre, and Marseille. Many of the world's other ports were built or expanded by Europeans, who then directed traffic through them. This was most true of imperial ports in the British, French, and Dutch empires, including world hubs such as Singapore or Hong Kong.

Moreover, whereas these ports functioned as entrepots of regional trade, many of the goods that shipped out were mined or logged or grown on properties controlled and managed by Europeans, traded with or through Europeans, brokered by Europeans, and, at some point, marketed by Europeans. The river and coastal companies that carried people and goods into and out of these ports, and that joined local to world traffics, were mostly European. There were vital local and regional traffics run by non-Europeans, and at no point did Europeans possess exclusive ownership over the transport and commerce of foreign lands. Increasingly we are coming to realize the extent to which the medium of Asian economic development was Asian-conducted intra-Asian trade.[1] Chinese merchant networks, in particular, controlled short-sea or inland trading in eastern waters, and were persistent shipping competitors, trading partners, or organizers of migrant flows. One of the arguments of this book is that world transport and trade functioned largely through the overlay of one network on another. Generally, however, it was Europeans who assembled or interlocked those networks on a transoceanic scale.[2] If ports outside the imperial ring – in Latin America, for example – differed in sovereign details, shipping, import-export trading houses, foreign capital, and overseas markets and networks remained heavily European. Asian traders, including intra-Asian commerce, relied on a Western infrastructure of steamships and ports.[3] Even the North Atlantic was dominated by European shipping. Maritime history, or the overseas history of travel and trade, was, deep into the twentieth century, a European history. Even when things changed, the history continued to be in large part European, either because the reversals were caught up with the withdrawal from empire, because of legacy investments and networks,

---

[1] Kaoru Sugihara, ed., *Japan, China, and the Growth of the Asian International Economy, 1850–1949* (Oxford: Oxford University Press, 2005).

[2] For an exception, see Adam McKeown's discussion of Chinese overseas emigration networks in Hong Kong, although even here European (British) rule, as McKeown acknowledges, established the basis for this trade: Adam McKeown, "Conceptualizing Chinese Diasporas, 1842–1949," *The Journal of Asian Studies* 58 (May 1999): 313–321.

[3] Sugihara, *Japan*, 9–10, 270; Claude Markovits, *The Global World of Indian Merchants, 1750–1947: Traders of Sind from Bukhara to Panama* (Cambridge: Cambridge University Press, 2000).

or because the reverberations in Europe altered older shipping and port hierarchies.

This book seeks to restore the sea to the center of how we think and write about modern history. It is a book about how "maritime" Europe ordered the flow of peoples and things around the world, but it is also, implicitly, about how Europeans lived, because little of what Europeans made, sold, or consumed in contemporary times was independent of overseas markets or sources of supply. At its basic level, then, it asks readers to take one step backward and ask not what mass industrial and consumer societies represented for European life and culture, but what infrastructures of trade and transport were essential for Europeans to create and run such societies in the first place. It thus denies an old but enduring tendency to particularize between maritime and interior – or continental – Europe.[4] It recalls that some of Europe's greatest cities were, and remain, port cities, and that far from peripheral, these functioned as national and transnational connectors. All were outward looking, but no less inward oriented, because all survived off hinterlands that reached deeply inland not only along the spines of waterways and railways, but also along the fashioned networks of human exchange. Ports were accumulated infrastructures, but also conduits and wealth generators. They were, too, bases for merchant fleets and merchant trading houses by which Europeans spread their influence, power, and grasp outward. They and the passenger ships that called at their harbors were no less the means – until late in the century nearly the only means – that enabled Europeans to travel across bodies of water. The history of migration, business, empire, and leisure in the twentieth century can no more be written without the history of maritime infrastructures than can the history of work, production, and possession. Not even the great-event history of the twentieth century, although much of it was acted out on the European landmass, operated independently of the sea. This book also argues that the ability to manage the complex logistics of merchant shipping was central to the outcome of the two world wars.

"Maritime" implies all things related to the sea, and although it is deployed broadly in this study, its use is not intended to be all encompassing. Left out are navies and sea power, as well as certain nonmilitary sectors such as fishing or oceanography. Dockworkers appear only infrequently, not because they were unimportant to the central subject of

---

[4] Paul M. Hohenberg and Lynn Hollen Lees, *The Making of Urban Europe, 1000–1950* (Cambridge, MA: Harvard University Press, 1985); Edward Whiting Fox, *History in Geographic Perspective: The Other France* (New York: Norton, 1971).

this work, but because the material on them is potentially so vast that to include them would have made a long book much longer still. The central subject is those sectors engaged in transport and trade across the oceans, and for these purposes the net has been widely cast. The sectors begin, of course, with ports and shipping, but cannot be understood without including trading companies; the harvesting enterprises they created and operated abroad; the riverboat and coastal shipping lines that connected hinterlands with forelands at both ends of the great trunk routes; an appreciation of commodity chains and markets; and the extensive range of intermediaries – ship agents, forwarders, warehousers, migrant labor and commodity brokers, dealers, insurers, compradors, tasters, the water-front services that included master porters and stevedore companies, but also local specialities like Antwerp's *naties* or Rotterdam's *vemen* – who provided essential services but also, in the case of agents and forwarders, acted as the essential coordinators in a well-constructed yet fragmented global system. Each of these, in its own right, requires exploration of how it worked, but the interest is in the combined effect, or the systematic cal-ibration of all sectors into an infrastructure for moving people and goods around the world. Reconstructing how this occurred, how a maritime world operated and coordinated world flows, is one of the two principal goals of this study.

The other is to examine the exchanges between maritime history and the larger currents of the twentieth century. That is a somewhat lofty presump-tion, as this is a century still awaiting its "long," "short," or 100-year history. Indeed the project has scarcely been taken up,[5] because nearly all work has divided with the Second World War. This study, by contrast, begins with a maritime system in place at the start of the century and runs to the year 2000. There is no claim that maritime history explains twentieth-century history. Frankly, it cannot. Nevertheless, war, depression, empire and its disintegration, the circulation of people and their ideas, the rise of a new leisure society, the evolution of modern business, and globalization are also maritime themes, so the overlap is considerable. One result, therefore, is to cross between the hard and soft halves of the past century in order to understand impacts and influences. Mostly the flow is in the direction of the maritime: how the fates of port cities, or of trading companies, or of

---

[5] There are indications that this tide may be turning: Charles S. Maier, "Consigning the Twentieth Century to History: Alternative Narratives for the Modern Era," *The American Historical Review* 105 (June 2000): 807–831; Victoria de Grazia, *Irresistible Empire: America's Advance through 20th-Century Europe* (Cambridge, MA: Harvard University Press, 2005).

passenger travel, or of the way the system worked altogether were determined by the broader historical turnings of the century. Yet it is also an intention to interrogate how maritime business communities could shape the way in which twentieth-century people lived their lives. Such influences are implied in the basic premise of this work, that a commercial maritime world provided the infrastructure for modern production and consumption societies. But the effects came also from other directions, such as the circulations or transfers made possible by systematic sea communication, or the revolutionary ramifications of containerization.

It is also the objective of this study to present a European history. That objective can be met only partially, because not all of Europe was "maritime," nor can all of its maritime peoples fit easily or equally into a single monograph. Mainly, research for this book was conducted in the collections of five nations – Great Britain, Germany, France, the Netherlands, and Belgium – because within these countries could be found the main ports of the continent as well as a very steep percentage of Europe's merchant fleets and overseas trading houses. For other significant shipping communities, such as the Norwegians or Greeks, I have relied on secondary literature in accessible languages. Some histories, therefore, will predominate over others, but in sum the approach has been to write about maritime Europe as the overall actor in this text. At multiple points this has meant gravitating toward comparative history, or the effort to explain influences, staying power, or declines by setting one experience against another. The comparative fates of ports, for instance, has been one challenge to explain, and one means of measuring the temporal outcomes of historical change. Antwerp and Rotterdam retained main port status throughout the century, Hamburg demonstrated remarkable resiliency in the face of crippling losses after both world wars, London and Liverpool dropped out of contention following containerization, and Le Havre and Marseille, while experiencing ups and downs, never fulfilled the promise of positions established toward the middle years of the nineteenth century. To understand why, this study sets one port's history against another's to investigate how national contexts – but also the tensile strength of individual port networks – account for differences in port city destinies.

Throughout, however, I favor a transnational approach to a strictly comparative one.[6] The transnational history of the seas is almost

---

[6] See the discussion of both approaches in Deborah Cohen and Maura O'Connor, eds., *Comparison and History: Europe in Cross-National Perspective* (New York: Routledge, 2004).

redundant in its expression, but an additional purpose of this book is to underscore the degree to which even in this most nationalistic of centuries European history was cosmopolitan. Europeans ran the maritime world and that world ran on transnational connections. Its basic component, networks, nearly always ignored land or sea borders. Shipping companies and ports were incessant assemblers of transnational linkages. Freight forwarders could not organize shipments without correspondents in distant lands. Trading houses, by tradition, sent their sons to train with other firms, often in foreign countries, so that professional cosmopolitanism was built into formational experiences. Expatriate merchants and agents had one foot planted in their new host territories, the other in their home communities. After several generations abroad some possessed dual national identities and could be as Brazilian, say, as they were German. Shipping conferences institutionalized private, transnational governance. At interfirm levels they and shipping networks exhibited the cosmopolitan, trans-state behavior today customary for NGOs.[7] Maritime culture, while national in one regard, was no less cosmopolitan in another. British houses competed with German ones, but old ties also prevailed in the resurrection of German shipping and trading firms after their obliteration in two world wars.

This book, therefore, is about European businessmen interacting with each other or with multiple other parties, including non-Western business communities, rather than about competing national outcomes. Built into its narrative will be the dynamics of cross-national exchanges such as the dissemination of Western tourism and consumerism, or the transport of populations to harvesting centers in tropical lands, or the entry of European profit-seeking companies into the Hajji carriage trades. At a broader level, its transnationalism will capture the common European experience that cannot be contained within a purely comparative approach. The aim is to understand how Europeans, not necessarily British, French, Germans, or Dutch, organized and managed world flows.

The transnationalism of global transport, however, cannot be separated from local and national identities or realms of action. Port networks, if multinational, also coalesced around home interests and civic engagement. Shipping and trading companies were well connected abroad, but no less embedded in home communities. Maritime culture, while strongly cosmopolitan, was simultaneously impregnated with national affinities.

---

[7] Wallace J. Campbell, *The History of CARE: A Personal Account* (New York: Praeger, 1990), 40, 93–94, 175, 177, 183, 203–204.

The transnationalism that appears in this book will therefore be a transnationalism of interplay, indeed complementarity, between local and global that could be found within companies, port communities, and personal experiences, and that accounted for the ability of each to organize and manage world flows. A critical argument is that hybridity of identities and realms of action translated not into rootlessness, but connectedness and the ability to mobilize networks and resources at both ends of the local-global spectrum.

Such a perspective passes perforce into the history of globalization, and in this book I hope to clarify how a globalizing process did in fact proceed over the course of the last hundred years. Chronologically, I begin with the commonly held presumption that at the turn of the nineteenth into the twentieth century it is possible to speak of a highly coordinated world. The most recent statement to this effect is Jürgen Osterhammel's monumental work on the nineteenth century. Although our books are very different in time and focus, there are a number of parallels between Osterhammel's approach and mine. Both concentrate on globalizing patterns and the networks through which they occurred. Both see European centrality as a basic fact of globalization, even if they might dispute when that centrality faded away. Both insist, nonetheless, on the indispensability of non-Western networks in the globalizing process, and both stress the significance of port cities, shipping, and merchants in carrying it out.[8]

In this regard the current, almost endless literature on globalization is a source for considerable reflection,[9] but within it there are strains with

[8] Jürgen Osterhammel, *Die Verwandlung der Welt. Eine Geschichte des 19. Jahrhunderts* (Munich: C. H. Beck, 2009), 13–17, 20, 112, 381–384, 402–412, 1011, 1031–1037. A second fundamental work on global connections in the nineteenth century is C. A. Bayly, *The Birth of the Modern World, 1780–1914* (Oxford: Blackwell, 2004).

[9] This is a very large literature. Those works that have been particularly useful for this study are: Manuel Castells, *The Rise of the Network Society*, 2nd ed. (Oxford: Blackwell, 2000); Jeffrey A. Frieden, *Global Capitalism: Its Fall and Rise in the Twentieth Century* (New York: W. W. Norton, 2006); David Held et al., *Global Transformations: Politics, Economics, and Culture* (Stanford: Stanford University Press, 1999); Paul Hirst and Grahame Thompson, *Globalization in Question: The International Economy and the Possibilities of Governance*, 2nd ed. (Cambridge, UK: Polity Press, 1999); A. G. Hopkins, ed., *Globalization in World History* (London: Pimlico, 2002); Harold James, *The End of Globalization: Lessons from the Great Depression* (Cambridge, MA: Harvard University Press, 2001); Geoffrey Jones, "Globalization," in Geoffrey Jones and Jonathan Zeitlin, *The Oxford Handbook of Business History* (Oxford, UK: Oxford University Press, 2008), 141–168; Michael Lang, "Globalization and Its History," *The Journal of Modern History* 78 (December 2006): 899–931; Kevin H. O'Rourke and Jeffrey G. Williamson, *Globalization and History: The Evolution of a Nineteenth-Century Atlantic Economy* (Cambridge, MA: MIT Press, 1999); Jürgen Osterhammel and Niels P. Petersson,

which I must disagree. It is not a foregone conclusion that expanding transnational bodies or networks have obviated the significance of either state power or national experiences. In nearly every instance where globalizing processes can be identified, it is possible to locate a state presence or the advancement of the state. Again, what strikes one repeatedly in the history of maritime communities was the synergy they manufactured from world and home connections.[10] It is difficult, moreover, to comprehend how one can write transnational history in modern times without first being conversant with national historiographies. Furthermore, there is no advantage in distinguishing between "international" and "global" as a means of explaining what globalization was or is. Such distinctions simply return us to the national-transnational dichotomy at the expense of focusing on interconnectedness.

In particular, I break with the definition of globalization as market integration on a worldwide scale. Nor am I sympathetic to the consequent static view that measures globalization in the twentieth century strictly against a Belle Epoque equivalent, or its dynamic doppelgänger that defines globalization as the world of difference by the 1990s.[11] The market integration approach, largely posited and held by social scientists, has the advantage of a systematic and time-ordered understanding of what can be labeled as true "globalization." Where capital, labor, trade, and information moved fluidly across the world, as occurred in the decades before the First World War – "the closest thing the world had ever seen to a free world market for goods, capital, and labor"[12] – we can glimpse the arrival of globalization. When substantial barriers made such flows difficult, at times even impossible, we can identify an era of deglobalization. When a reconstruction process restored integration of global markets, or so rapidly surpassed all earlier levels of global interchange to

---

Globalization: A Short History (Princeton, NJ: Princeton University Press, 2005); Saskia Sassen, *The Global City: New York, London, Tokyo*, 2nd ed. (Princeton, NJ: Princeton University Press, 2001); Pierre-Yves Saunier, "Globalization," in Akira Iriye and Pierre-Yves Saunier, eds., *The Palgrave Dictionary of Transnational History* (Houndsmills, Basingstoke: Palgrave Macmillan, 2009), 456–462.

[10] This is not quite the same point as made by Alan Milward about European integration, but the consequences were not dissimilar. Alan S. Milward, *The European Rescue of the Nation-State*, 2nd ed. (London: Routledge, 2000).

[11] The framework is pervasive. See, as examples, Michael D. Bordo, Alan M. Taylor, and Jeffrey G. Williamson, *Globalization in Historical Perspective* (Chicago: University of Chicago Press, 2003); Frieden, *Global*; Held et al., *Transformations* (especially pp. 422–425); Hirst and Thompson, *Globalization*; O'Rourke and Williamson, *Globalization*; and Osterhammel and Petersson, *Globalization*, although with some interesting hedging.

[12] Frieden, *Global*, 16.

create something distinctively new, we can grasp what is implied when one speaks today of "globalization." That cohesiveness of perspective has made market integration and its chronological procession – the first global economy to 1914; deglobalization between the two world wars; and the second global economy from the 1970s/1980s to the present – the paradigm, or "master narrative,"[13] by which we chart globalization across our times.

This view of globalization is not altogether as tidy as it might at first seem. Cultural historians and postmodernist critics, keenly attuned to globalizing influences, may align their arguments with economic transformations. Yet their concentration on identity, "de-territorialization," time-space hierarchies, compression, modernity, or homogenization versus heterogeneity frame globalism within a perspective that ranges far beyond market integration.[14] Moreover, market compression in the interwar years runs counter to the unrelenting reach, at world levels, of cinema or advertising, or the intensified circulation of ideologies such as communism, or the exchange of knowledge and culture that accompanied refugee movements, or continued population flows, or the growth of transnational and nongovernmental organizations that persisted through the 1920s and 1930s. Even a strictly economic approach produces a more complex picture of the supposed march of deglobalization. Business historians have already remarked the resiliency of international business in the face of closing markets. Mira Wilkins's work on multinationals not only has pointed to the continued expansion of multinational investment throughout the interwar years, but has shown how the very act of restriction generated responses – jumping tariff walls, opening triangular trades for supplying markets – that increased as well as contracted world presence.[15]

[13] Saunier, "Globalization," 458. James, *End*, 1–2, 7 provides a good example of how the narrative has been adopted by historians.

[14] Alys Eve Weinbaum et al., *The Modern Girl around the World: Consumption, Modernity, and Globalization* (Durham, NC: Duke University Press, 2008); Mike Featherstone, *Undoing Culture: Globalization, Postmodernism, and Identity* (London: Sage, 1995); David Harvey, *The Condition of Postmodernity: An Enquiry into the Origins of Cultural Change* (Cambridge, MA: Blackwell, 1990).

[15] Jones, "Globalization," 141–142, 148, 161; Saunier, "Globalization," 458; Adam McKeown, "Global Migration, 1846–1940," *Journal of World History* 15 (2004): 155–190; Akira Iriye, *Global Community: The Role of International Organizations in the Making of the Contemporary World* (Berkeley: University of California Press, 2002), 20–36; Mira Wilkins, *The History of Foreign Investment in the United States, 1914–1945* (Cambridge, MA: Harvard University Press, 2004); idem, *The Maturing of Multinational Enterprise: American Business Abroad from 1914 to 1970* (Cambridge, MA: Harvard University Press, 1974); Weinbaum et al., *Modern*.

I join with those who have sought to complicate the paradigm by offering a different interpretation of what we mean by globalization and its progression over the past century. My treatment of globalization begins, therefore, as a more expansive one, where globalization entails primarily global interchange and connectedness, for which integrated markets can be fundamentally constructive but not indispensable. Globalization, in this view, is about the exchange of ideas, people, and goods across oceans and civilizations; mounting world presence; and the hybridity that comes when local and overseas are coupled on a global scale.[16] The degree or intensity of that connectedness, to use the formula of one major contribution to the literature,[17] may change over time, but globalization from a historical point of view is about linkages that have a long pedigree, and that cannot be conflated with the workings or effects of what we call globalization today. Most of all I seek to return historical thinking about globalization to historians, rather than leaving it to the social scientists who have dominated the production of thought on this topic.

In this book, the history of globalization occurs in two ways. First, globalization is presented not as a meta-narrative with "globalizing" (in the French sense of the word) explanatory powers, but as a reality of relationships – in this case by sea – that formed the building blocks of modern societies. Those that I identify were not the only ones, but they were, as I argue, essential to the making of modern material culture. Regardless of how far one projects back into time the sighting of globalization, shipping and commerce lie at the center of that vision. If globalization preceded the Europeans, then a Muslim ecumene spread and cohered through mercantile networks on sea and land.[18] If the origins of globalism are dated to the sixteenth century, then it was the voyages of discovery and conquest, creation of seaborne trading monopolies, and overseas migrations – voluntary and forced – that initiated the process. To place the first true global moment in the nineteenth century is to write about the effects of the steamship and its business organization into world-ranging liner networks. As one leading study of this period has argued, "The globalization that took place in the late nineteenth century cannot be ascribed to more liberal trade policy. Instead, it was the falling transport costs that

---

[16] In the context of globalization this book therefore uses the term "hybridity" somewhat differently from those who use it to rebut global homogenization. See, as an example, Jan Nederveen Pieterse, *Globalization and Culture: Global Mélange*, 2nd ed. (Lanham, MD: Rowman & Littlefield, 2009).

[17] Held et al., *Transformations*, 15–16, 433.

[18] Amira K. Bennison, "Muslim Universalism and Western Globalization," in Hopkins, *Globalization*, 74–97.

provoked globalization."[19] Even globalization as we speak of it today, in an era of jet travel and real-time global communication, emerged no less from containerization. Globalization as a historical phenomenon must therefore be rooted in its day-to-day realities of shipping and trading. There were other dimensions to globalization that elude this reduction, but showing how a maritime world functioned to create global interconnectedness substitutes historical action for abstraction.

Second, I reconsider how we historicize globalization in the twentieth century. I agree with other historians that some form of global interconnectedness reaches back at least four centuries, and that we can identify different stages in its history.[20] I do not, however, agree with the argument that the First World War detonated deglobalization. My argument is that globalization, viewed from a maritime perspective, remained deeply entrenched throughout the century and took on new forms as the century progressed. Even as markets contracted, there were widening exchanges on other fronts. Thus in this analysis the First World War is seen as a stimulus to greater globalism in multiple ways. It confirmed the interconnectedness of trade. Its outcome was not only the rise of new world centers in the East and West, but also the expansion of European-driven routes and trades. War needs forced investments in ports that formerly had been backwaters on world circuits.

Between the wars, restrictive laws and economic crisis depressed older immigration traffic in the West, but to a certain extent this was replaced by refugee flows or the aggressive marketing of tourist traffic, while strong eastern passenger trades persisted. People and goods still circulated over the seas in high volumes. Trading companies transferred consumer goods to non-Western societies. Tellingly, Japanese penetration of Asian markets followed the same network patterns deployed earlier by Western firms. In Singapore and South Asia, indigenous entrepreneurs, like Marwaris, increasingly encroached on expatriate markets. Some shipping lines went over to imperial preferences in their home and colonial markets, but simultaneously introduced round-the-world services. Despite controls, global flows remained the norm and began to outline the shape to come.[21] The Second World War set still more globalizing forces in motion. It put paid to empires but in so doing realigned globalism as

[19] O'Rourke and Williamson, *Globalization*, 35.

[20] Hopkins, *Globalization*, 3; Osterhammel and Petersson, *Globalization*, ix–x. Held et al., *Transformations* also underscores historical dimensions, 414–436.

[21] For an interesting parallel: Hopkins's remarks about the interwar years in A. G. Hopkins, "The History of Globalization – and the Globalization of History?" in Hopkins, *Globalization*, 29.

less Eurocentric. Circuits diffused. Asians established an increasing presence in transoceanic markets. Shipping lines, once anchored to imperial trunk routes, shifted to cross trades that broke with homeland identities. Before the technological revolutions and deregulation of the late twentieth century, volumes and vectors of world trade reconfigured and expanded enormously. Supertankers and bulk carriers came close to eradicating distance as an economic factor. Containerization slashed transportation costs much like the steamship revolution of the nineteenth century, but it also systematized world flows and global logistics to the point that it was possible to create a new order of globalization.

For if globalization did not come to a crashing halt in the middle decades of the century, it also did not remain the same. At the end of the twentieth century it was considerably different from what it had been at the century's beginning. That difference was partly to be found in levels of intensity, but equally in how global connectedness was structured and functioned. For the first two-thirds of the twentieth century, the globalism of sea exchanges was Eurocentric, strongly imperial, and fragmented. Major termini began or ended with European ports. Routes, trade (manufactured goods for commodities), and expatriate firms were closely allied to imperial patterns. Few shipping lines or trading companies operated in more than one hemisphere or over two oceans. There was a world maritime system, but it was the composite of partial networks coordinated through ports and intermediaries, especially ship agents. Transnationalism was still anchored to local affiliations. By the 1980s and 1990s, the look, but also the internal workings, of sea exchanges had changed. Once Eurocentric, they were now multipolar, with three major centers in North America, Europe, and East and Southeast Asia. Former subjects reinvented themselves as trading partners, rivals, global initiators, and predators. Fragmentation gave way to global operators. Container logistics and global sourcing reorganized global flows. Liner ships that once had sailed between two fixed points with ports of call along the way now circulated containers through the cheapest points of production and assemblage before final transport to points of sale. Intermodality of land and sea transport, global presence, and flags of convenience reordered transnational identities.

Global interconnectedness, so interwoven with a maritime history in a century that advanced and often defined it, is therefore better told as a story of progressions and mutations than one of interruptions and new beginnings. The historical trajectory of this study will reflect this pattern: a global system of flows, in place at the start of the century, that remained constant and widespread while also metamorphosing until it ceded to an altered system of connections and exchanges at the end of the century. This is not the history that presently dominates our understanding of globalization. But it is the history that best represents the twentieth-century maritime world.

This book, in part, is also an imperial history. For millennia long-distance travel and trade benefited from the stability, protection, uniformity, and cosmopolitanism of empire, and global flows in modern times, until recently, did not much differ.[22] This perspective should not obscure the fact that a considerable proportion of twentieth-century commerce occurred within European waters or across the Atlantic to North America. Yet global maritime circuits were, down to decolonization, just as highly structured within a system of formal or informal empire. At a basic level this arrangement was unavoidable, as European empires were dispersed across seas and oceans and accounted for a very large portion of the world's land surface.[23] In the two leading cases, seaborne power projected across all the hemispheres, North and South, East and West; maritime empire by the start of the twentieth century was inherently global. In addition, despite multiple motivations, modern empire was, from the start, conjoined with trade. The Dutch empire in the East Indies was, in significant ways, a commercial project. The French empire had religious, military, administrative, but also merchant origins, and the French increasingly came to concentrate their maritime commercial connections on their empire. The British empire, as has been cogently argued, operated largely as an expression and extension of a gentlemanly capitalism whose "main dynamic was the drive to create an international trading system centered on London and mediated by sterling."[24] Coalesced around a common public school formation, the directors of British overseas influence and power harbored in Whitehall, but no less in the City's service industries: banking, shipping, merchant houses, and insurance. If there is a flaw to that argument, it is that in its urgency to emphasize the City over "Manchester," it understates the role of other British service sectors, especially among the Scots or in Liverpool.[25]

[22] See Niall Ferguson's reminder of this to economists fixated on markets in "Panel," in Bordo, Taylor, and Williamson, eds., *Globalization*, 558.

[23] David Abernethy, *The Dynamics of Global Dominance: European Overseas Empires, 1415–1980* (New Haven, CT: Yale University Press, 2000), 8, 87.

[24] P. J. Cain and A. G. Hopkins, *British Imperialism: Innovation and Expansion, 1688–1914* (London: Longman, 1993), 44.

[25] Ibid.; idem, *British Imperialism: Crisis and Deconstruction, 1914–1990* (London: Longman, 1993). A review of the index for Liverpool will turn up only "Liverpool, Lord" in the first volume and nothing in the second. See also Andrew Porter, "Gentlemanly

Structured linkages between maritime business and empire were therefore manifold. In the nineteenth century steamships had encouraged migration to settler economies, provided long-distance bulk commodity carriage, and set in motion the globalizing dynamic by which settlers opened new lands for production, shipped primary commodities back to Western urban centers, and imported manufactured goods from the homelands. Steamships had also made practical the development of mines, plantations, and timbering enterprises in tropical colonies; the transport of large, cheap labor forces from Asian lands to work these; and thus another dynamic of tropical commodity shipments homeward to imperial centers in exchange for the requisite shipments of machinery and tools. Underpinning these dynamics had been the sizable export of capital to formal or informal empire; in 1914 more than half of world foreign direct investment had gone to Latin America and Asia.[26] In still more symbiotic ways the expansion of maritime business had gone hand in hand with the expansion of empire. Transoceanic, coastal, and riverboat companies had built their route structures out of public service contracts, but these had also served to advance imperial power, influence, extension, and linkage. Trading companies had justified imperial claims and had developed the exportable resources of colonial dependencies. In return they had received protection, stability, infrastructure investment, and property rights.

The maritime world of the twentieth century (until empires fell apart) was thus, in good part, an elaboration on these earlier developments. Hub ports abroad concentrated among imperial harbors such as Hong Kong, Singapore, or Batavia, seconded by the construction of plantation ports like Belawan or the imperial rehabilitation of faded ports like Makassar. Passenger liners east of Suez carried colonial administrators; colonial officers; engineers, planters, and settlers; family members who accompanied them or who traveled out and returned each year for home visits; educators traveling outward, but also children sent to schools in colonial homelands; commercial travelers to imperial markets; missionaries; or labor emigrants, returning migrants, and pilgrims. Transoceanic travel to and from Latin America retained a quasi-imperial flavor: travel to European consumer centers or carriage of immigrants, seasonal laborers, and expatriate businessmen. Cargo flows were heavily colonial in

Capitalism and Empire: The British Experience Since 1750," *The Journal of Imperial and Commonwealth History* 18 (1990): 277–278, 287.

[26] Geoffrey Jones, *Merchants to Multinationals: British Trading Companies in the Nineteenth and Twentieth Centuries* (Oxford: Oxford University Press, 2000), 8.

their patterns: primary commodities homeward to Europe, manufactured or processed goods outward to the rest of the world. Cross trades ran counter to these harmonics, but they too serviced colonial economies by shipping food to monoculture or mining communities or carrying jute bags for sugar. Imperial regional, feeder, and trunk lines thus reinforced the Eurocentric and fragmented element to globalization. When empires broke apart after the Second World War, one of the first indicators of the transition to a new kind of transnationalism and globalism was the shift by former imperial shipping companies to cross trades independent of home port connections.

These shipments to and fro were managed by an expatriate maritime business community that was deeply embedded in formal or informal imperial territories. The principle purpose of European banks overseas was to finance "the movement of commodities and minerals around the globe." Their names, such as the Bank of British West Africa or the Banque de l'Indochine (whose activities spread to China and throughout Southeast Asia), disclosed the regions they served. So intertwined were they with the cultivation or harvesting of regional export products that some banks were colloquially referred to as the nitrate bank or the sugar bank. Expatriate banks financed export trades, but they also poured in capital to develop port facilities or rail networks to transport goods to the harbors.[27] Closely allied were a host of shipping and trading companies, again imperially ensconced; their presence fills the pages that follow. All three – imperial banks, shipping companies, and trading companies – were in bed with each other, participating as founders, customers, and agents. Their interconnections with empire were legion. The fortunes of the shipping and trading company Mackinnon Mackenzie, to take one example, evolved out of a close personal relationship co-founder William Mackinnon developed with Sir Henry Bartle Frere, a senior figure in the Indian government and desirous of using Mackinnon's steamship line to advance British imperial interests. Frere granted Mackinnon access to mail contracts and to other power brokers in London and India. From these beginnings, Mackinnon built the British India Steam Navigation Company, which sailed along the Indian coast and throughout the Indian ocean, and which became one of the world's largest shipping companies at the time of its absorption into the P & O Group in 1913. Mackinnon's

[27] Idem, *British Multinational Banking, 1830–1990* (Oxford: Clarendon Press, 1993), 32, 37, 83 (quoted); Marc Meuleau, *Des pionniers en Extrême-Orient. Histoire de la Banque de l'Indochine, 1875–1975* (Paris: Fayard, 1990).

trading interests grew to include a network of managing agencies engaged in trading, ship agency, plantation, cotton mill, riverboat, and wharfage operations based in India and distributed across British imperial outposts from the Persian Gulf to East Africa and Singapore. Mackinnon's successor, James Lyle Mackay, subsequently Lord Inchcape, became one of the most important figures in British shipping and trading circles and was at one time considered for the viceroyalty.[28] The composite of relationships such as these dominated the world's north-south or east-west sea lanes, excepting principally the United States. Even maritime business culture was heavily laden with the imperial connection, exuding the clubbiness of expatriate communities, their oscillations between national identities and cosmopolitan associations, their territoriality, their paternalistic attitude toward the organization of the world's sea transport, and their virtues of trust that lubricated the networks and personal transactions of all nations' gentlemanly capitalism.

Yet in this globally interlocked world, the networks mattered more than their colonial connections, even if the latter often determined the vectors they took. The problem with focusing too restrictively on empires is the danger of compressing the picture within a frame it only partially fits. Smoothing out the wrinkles that result is not so easily accomplished. Germany after 1914 possessed no colonies, but its maritime commitments were worldwide and extensive. Many of these can be ascribed to informal empire, but that concept too wore increasingly thin over the course of the century. The global flows that dominate this account cannot be separated from the colonial context that for the first half of this narrative encased so many of them, but their real history lies in the business networks at home and abroad that circulated peoples and goods across the seas. More than empire, transnational relationships and their principal medium – networks – are the motor of this study.

That too is an old story. Fernand Braudel, in his classic work on the Mediterranean, argued that the sea constituted a human unit "created by the movements of men, the relationships they imply ... 'the sum of its routes,'... an immense network of regular and casual connections,"

---

[28] J. Forbes Munro, *Maritime Enterprise and Empire: Sir William Mackinnon and His Business Network, 1823–1893* (Woodridge, Suffolk: Boydell Press, 2003), 46–51, 105, 237–244; Stephanie Jones, *Trade and Shipping: Lord Inchcape, 1852–1932* (Manchester: Manchester University Press, 1989), 68, 86–87; idem, *Two Centuries of Overseas Trading: The Origins and Growth of the Inchcape Group* (Houndmills, Basingstoke: Macmillan, 1986).

and the "the infrastructure of all coherent history."[29] By the twentieth century the unit was global, but its infrastructure was still the sum of its routes, or the port, shipping, and trading networks that added up to world integration.

The networks were protean. Port networks were geographical, physical (railroads, waterways), and human, and the latter split into business networks, port community networks, or port operatives stationed in hinterlands and markets abroad. Shipping networks were route networks but also agency networks, or networked ties with shipyards, railroads, exporters and importers, port directors, harbor captains, custom houses, travel agencies, government officials, and other shipping companies. Trading company networks divided among multihouse networks, station or branch networks, distribution networks, route networks, financial networks, management networks, supplier and buyer networks, broker and dealer networks, networks of sources of information, and network links with indigenous businessmen who ran their own sets of networks. The overlap between shipping, trading, and port networks was so great that it was possible to speak of networks within networks.

The common element to all these networks was that individually, and in their ensemble, they processed the world's flows. What was transnational, global, and imperial to this history was therefore ultimately a story of maritime networks and how they worked. This story has in fact been intimated throughout this Introduction, and it is the builders and operators of networks who appear as the central actors in this book, their creations as its central mechanism. The task has been not simply to invoke or identify networks, but to catch the architects in the act of networking, to show how maritime firms and communities constructed, sustained, and expanded networks, and then to seek the concatenation of networks, their gathering within specific centers, that explain the lines of force or nodal points – to remain within Braudel's way of thinking –[30] that concentrated flows and directed them to focal cities or maritime hubs such as Hamburg, London, or Singapore. Power, wealth, and influence in the twentieth century were, to a very large measure, an outcome of commanding networks on a globalized scale. Because concatenation required synchronization, it is also necessary to follow the intermediaries

---

[29] Fernand Braudel, *The Mediterranean and the Mediterranean World in the Age of Philip II*, vol. 1 (1966; reprint, Berkeley: University of California Press, 1995), 276, 282. "Sum of its routes," was originally formulated by Lucien Febvre.
[30] Ibid., 277.

who coordinated networks and created a world system out of its frag-
ments. Since maritime culture was constructed largely out of the cultural
presumptions of network culture – trust, cosmopolitanism, shared identities, and codes – it has again been necessary to concentrate on networks.
Networks too were the great conduits of knowledge, almost certainly
the critical resource in the twentieth century. Historians and economists alike have recognized the fundamental role that learning capacity, knowledge transfer, or informational flows have played in innovation
and market power. Maritime enterprise, strung out across the world, was
always knowledge based. All the great historical switchboards – from
Amsterdam to London to New York – assembled vast arrays of services
and infrastructures, but at their core they functioned primarily as hubs of
intelligence. Without access to information, modern shipping and trading
companies would have withered on the vine, and global exchange with
them. Therefore it will be necessary to return repeatedly to networks as
sources of knowledge, and the means for passing it on.[31] Finally, it has
been necessary to follow the networks because when these changed, so
too did nearly everything else about the maritime world. A history of the
maritime world, this book is foremost about maritime networks and how
they functioned.

Research for this book was primarily conducted in Hamburg,
Rotterdam, The Hague, Antwerp, London, Liverpool, Le Havre, and
Paris. Long ago I learned the value of business collections for excavating
the processes of modern life. Maritime history is no different. For the
worldwide circulation of people and things, the records of shipping and
trading companies are unsurpassable, and in some cases close to insur-
mountable; the best preserved shipping company archives fill hundreds
of linear meters of shelf space. The peculiarities of running an enterprise
extended over thousands of sea miles have resulted in extraordinary
quantities of correspondence and reports, especially the reports of business trips, and these I have mined as best I could. Ports, more spatially
confined and verbally accessible, were, comparatively, less "document
productive," but their records too have been essential for grasping the
history of global flows contained in these pages. House histories, often

---

[31] Gordon Boyce, *Information, Mediation, and Institutional Development: The Rise
of Large-Scale Enterprise in British Shipping, 1870–1919* (Manchester: Manchester
University Press, 1995); Jones, *Merchants*; Oliver Williamson, *Markets and Hierarchies:
Analysis and Antitrust Implications* (New York: Free Press, 1975); idem, *The Economic
Institutions of Capitalism: Firms, Markets, Relational Contracting* (New York: Free
Press, 1985).

scorned by historians, have offered incomparable information on firms whose records, in many cases, have long disappeared and perhaps never existed. I have also conducted more than forty interviews with port directors, shipping company executives, and especially with ship agents and forwarders. Through the retelling of their experiences, I have been able to re-create the lived history of maritime business, its culture, the histories of professions rarely preserved in archival collections, and the immense changes of the past thirty to forty years. Needless to say, the wider secondary literature for a project of this scope has been indispensable. To be frank, my best materials are Dutch, German, and British, and, even though I am a historian of France, the subjects of these sources dominate.

The book is divided into two parts. Part One reconstructs how the maritime world worked until the 1960s; that is, until containerization revolutionized not only shipping, but ports, professions, identities, and hierarchies. This part is divided into chapters on the four key sectors – ports, shipping, trading, and intermediaries – and a fifth chapter on the maritime culture that pervaded and held that world together. Throughout, Part One has deliberately treated the first two-thirds of the century as a whole, because systems or patterns established at the beginning of this period did not change substantially until containerization and jet air travel swept them away. By concentrating on the static side to these years, and leaving underlying dynamics to Part Two, it is possible to bore into how each sector contributed to local-global connectedness, and how, combined, they did so in interlocking but also parallel ways. Part Two presents the chronological progression of maritime affairs and their historical exchanges since 1914. In this part, narrative fuses with war, depression, and decolonization, and most of all the history of globalism over the past century. Here is where I lay out my arguments about globalism's steady advance on the seas and its gestation toward a new stage that emerged as the century closed. The final chapter, then, takes up the great transformations, the end of passenger crossings by sea – save a new concept of cruises – and the breakthroughs but also eviscerations resulting from the shipping of goods inside a container.

PART ONE

NETWORKS

I

Ports

Ports and shipping were the two bases of the maritime world. Shipping provided the means of movement. Ports were the points of entry and exit for travelers and trade. At the basic level, then, ports were physical places identified by their location between land and sea. Nearly all the great European ports, save Le Havre and those on the Mediterranean, were situated on tidal rivers: Hamburg on the Elbe, Bremen on the Weser, Rotterdam on the Maas, Antwerp on the Scheldt, London on the Thames, and Liverpool on the Mersey. Rivers offered shelter from seaborne weather and linkages to hinterlands. Yet tidal rivers also limited the times of arrival and departure, and often required elaborate docks and locks to maintain depth levels at low tide. There was the constant problem of clearing out silt and, as ships increased in size, dredging to deepen and widen channels became an unending fact of life. Human-created needs, but also the effects of nature, forced engineers and city officials to turn ports into places of incessant manipulation and improvement.

Ports were, therefore, also the creation of history and human activity and thus far more than mere physical places. They were infrastructures, conglomerations of installations and services that signaled the power, scale, and value of city – or harbor – output. To make these water stations productive, states, cities, and businesses invested in dredgers, docks, quays, warehouses, sheds, cranes, grain suckers and elevators, cold storage houses, and elaborate transportation facilities: canals, railroads, drawbridges, and locks. Gathered in an around great ports were shipping companies, ship agents, ship brokers, freight forwarders, insurance companies, exchanges, importers and exporters, stevedore companies, warehousing companies, lighter and barge companies, towage companies, salvagers, shipyards, elevator companies, ship chandlers, ships' painters, boiler cleaners, fumigation companies, bunkering companies, commodity dealers, and customs houses. Among the multitudes that worked these facilities could be found stevedores, dockers, lightermen, crane drivers, tally clerks, sack and bag sewers, transporters, warehousers, and all the engineering, mechanical, construction, and clerical workers who worked in shipyards or port business houses.[1] Until containerization, such an environment, as André Vigarié put it, "could not, in any case, be improvised," but was "a local patrimony transmitted from generation to generation."[2] Only a select number of ports could offer such a range of facilities and services. Over time these became the main ports of the continent, and they competed largely with each other. Although theoretically a ship could be

---

[1] Even when reduced to the core of harbor workers, the sheer numbers betray the labor intensity of ports before containerization. In 1925 there were 54,558 registered dockers in London; there were 33,774 in 1938. Perhaps 22,000 showed up weekly for work in Liverpool in 1913, and 16,464 dockers were registered in 1938. There were 21,000 in Hamburg in 1925, perhaps 14,000 to 18,000 in interwar Antwerp. Transshipment and storage workers at Rotterdam in 1909 came to 23,000. Rotterdam's interwar figures appear too low and may reflect the absence of casual laborers among those counted or a higher percentage of mechanized bulk cargo. On the eve of containerization registered workers numbered 16,706. A 7,500 figure for Le Havre in 1913 likewise appears short of comprehensive. The casual character of much labor before the Second World War seriously interferes with the calculation of comparable figures across the range of main ports: Gordon Phillips and Noel Whiteside, *Casual Labour: The Unemployment Question in the Port Transport Industry, 1880–1970* (Oxford: Clarendon, 1985), 94, 178, 215 (precise numbers on London and Liverpool); London, Public Record Office (PRO)/ Ministry of Transportation (MT) 63/203/Report by Mr. Frank Pick on his Visit to the Port of London, n.d.; Liverpool, Merseyside Maritime Museum (MMM)/Mersey Docks and Harbour Board (MDHB)/PEC (Port Emergency Committee) 14/2; Klaus Weinhauer, *Alltag und Arbeitskampf im Hamburger Hafen. 1933: Sozialgeschicte der Hamburger Hafenarbeiter, 1914–1933* (Paderborn: Ferdinand Schöningh, 1994), 19; Karel van Isacker, *De Antwerpse dokwerker, 1830–1940*, 2nd ed. (Antwerp: De Nederlandsche Boekhandel, 1966), 185, 204; idem, *Afscheid van de havenarbeider, 1944–1966* (Antwerp: De Nederlandsche Boekhandel, 1967), 128; Stephan Vanfraechem, "The Antwerp Docker between Militantism and Pragmatism, 1900–1972," *International Journal of Maritime History* 14 (December 2002): 172 (with slightly lower figures than van Isacker's); Paul van de Laar, *Stad van formaat. Geschiedenis van Rotterdam in de negentiende en twintigste eeuw* (Zwolle: Waanders, 1999), 164–166, 346; Erik Nijhof, "'Dock-work Is a Skilled Profession': Decasualization and the Rotterdam Labour Market (1945–1970)," in Reginald Loyen, Erik Buyst, and Greta Devos, eds. *Struggling for Leadership: Antwerp – Rotterdam Port Competition Between 1870–2000* (Heidelberg: Physica-Verlag, 2003), 277; Hugo van Driel, *Samenwerking in haven en vervoer in het containertijdperk* (Delft: Eburon, 1990), 55; Paris, Archives "nationales" (AN)/F12/7746/3 July 1915; John Barzman, *Dockers, métallos, ménagères. Mouvements sociaux et cultures militantes au Havre (1912–1923)* (Rouen: Presses Universitaires de Rouen et du Havre, 1997), 32, 34.

[2] André Vigarié, *Les grands ports de commerce de la Seine au Rhin. Leur évolution devant l'industrialisation des arrière pays* (Paris: S.A.B.R.I., 1964), 21–22.

directed to any harbor large enough to enter, the abundance of firms and features were the twentieth century's sirens, and they concentrated traffic on the great ports of Europe. Retaining and building out the infrastructure was a life-and-death condition of remaining in the front rank.

But ports were also generators and intersection points of networks, and rank fell to those that converted connections into the global arteries of the twentieth century. It is above all in this light that Europe's main ports must be comprehended. All great ports possessed three sets of networks to varying degrees. Hinterland networks were the collectors, the gatherers of travelers and production for world distribution and the conduits through which people and goods found their way to interior centers. Foreland or overseas networks established world linkages of shipping and trade and turned ports into global hubs of information exchange. City or harbor networks made ports coherent and efficient operation centers and so powered port interests that the local and global welded together. All three, while serving home port advantages, were thereby in one way or another amplifiers of world exchange. To begin the history of the maritime world with its ports is thus to begin as well with their networks: how these were constituted and how they operated; how they sustained or undercut main port rank; how a European network system was replicated abroad; and how, in all cases, port networks commanded world flows.

NETWORKS

A port's size and significance were, first of all, determined by the radius (and value) of its interior connections. Ports with relatively poor hinterland extension, like Marseille, lagged behind ports whose hinterlands opened to them the vast flows generated by producer and consumer territories. To a certain extent hinterlands were a fact of nature, particularly for ports located on rivers. Traffic along the Elbe flowed through Hamburg. But traffic along the Rhine could run, via waterway connections, through a number of possible ports. Hinterlands were thus constructed relationships, most notably but not exclusively, out of transportation networks that exploited or overcame nature and joined interiors to desired points.

Inland waterways offered superb opportunities to elaborate zones of influence. Combining main rivers (engineered for navigability), tributaries and branches, and, where nature had failed, connecting canals, Europe's water networks by the twentieth century resembled vast circulatory systems through which coursed the lifeblood of trade. Enormous advantages

accrued to those ports that were well endowed with waterway connections to the great urban and industrial heartlands. Rotterdam made its
fortune through building its New Waterway to the sea and because of its
unparalleled water ties to the Rhine and the Ruhr, from which wider penetration of southern Germany and the Danube was possible along branch
rivers and canals.[3] In contrast, Le Havre and Rouen suffered from the
failure to create a comparable Seine canal system that would have locked
northeastern French traffic within their sphere of influence. Problems of
terrain and hydrology posed considerable obstacles, but there was also
no concerted effort to construct an integrated water network converging on Norman ports. Too often, local canals were constructed to satisfy local electorate desires, leading to a situation in which 220 locks
extended across a 391 kilometer distance.[4] Additional contrast can be
drawn with Antwerp, whose Rhine waterway connections were no match
for Rotterdam's, but compensated by creating the densest port railroad
network in Europe.

Such a division into waterway or railway harbors could have other
impacts on ports, because freight generally divides into two categories –
bulk cargo and general cargo – each with preferred methods of transportation. Bulk cargo refers to heavy, unpackaged materials that are primarily
shipped in great quantities and single loads, for instance, coal, ores, grain,
or oil. Low in unit value, bulk cargo is most readily transported through
interior waterways, where costs are low and time is relatively inconsequential. Bulk cargo adds weight to port turnover figures and was more
easily mechanized, leading to installation of transporter cranes and floating coal elevators, or the floating grain sucker, a monstrous-looking
device with drooping pipes that made a disproportionate contribution to
uglifying ports but which cut turnaround time dramatically. Where bulk
cargo predominated, ports did not require complex handling or sorting, but they did demand heavy equipment investment and broad harbor basins where ships could be worked on both sides simultaneously.[5]
General cargo on the other hand, in its classic form, applies to goods

[3] J. Ph. Backx, *De haven van Rotterdam. Een onderzoek naar de oorzaken van haar econo-
mische beteekenis, in vergelijking met die van Hamburg en Antwerpen* (Rotterdam: N.V.
Nijgh & Van Ditmar's, 1929), 81–112.
[4] Vigarié, *Grands*, 299–301.
[5] Hugo van Driel and Ferry de Goey, *Rotterdam: Cargo Handling Technology 1870–2000*
(Eindhoven: Stichting Historie der Techniek, 2000), 36–42; Van Isacker, *Antwerpse*, 68;
N. Th. Koomans, "The Port and Its Equipment," in J. Schraver, ed., *Rotterdam: The
Gateway to Europe: History of the Port and Trade of Rotterdam* (Rotterdam: A. D.
Donker, 1948), 107–109, 116; Backx, *Haven*, 10–12.

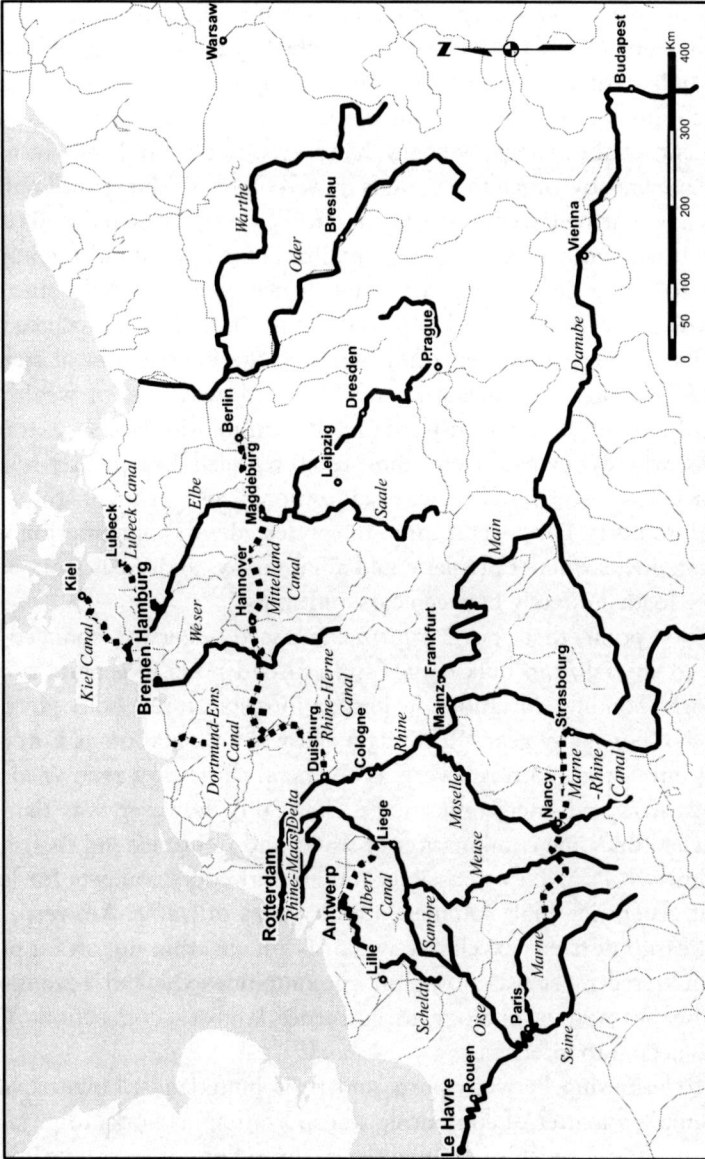

MAP 1. Hamburg–Le Havre range and its waterways.

packed in barrels, crates, cases, chests, bales, and so forth. Cargoes of heavy, bundled goods such as steel or paper also fall within a more open-ended definition of general cargo, as does grain when shipped in sacks. More valuable, general cargo often shipped on railroads (later, trucks), where higher transport costs were outweighed by the advantage of speed. Unlike bulk cargo, its handling remained a physical, labor-intensive process well into the century. For all the investment in infrastructure and equipment, chains, slings, winches, handcarts, hooks, and muscle were the instruments by which most goods moved on or off ships, until pallets and then, in particular, containerization broke bottlenecks, reduced turn-around time, and altered ports forever. But labor intensity also entailed greater handling and service costs, and hence greater added value for ports. General cargo, off-loaded, tallied, weighed, scribed, sorted according to its marks, warehoused, and requiring the intervention of freight forwarders or agency canvassers, was the lead generator of wealth in ports. Moreover, ocean transport of bulk cargo was largely a tramp business, whereas general cargo most often traveled on regularly scheduled liner services, whose heavier organizational costs brought still more money into ports. For general cargo the preferred port configuration was long, thin docks where rail lines could adjoin quays and sheds and goods could be loaded directly between cars and ships.[6]

Up to a point, then, ports with unsurpassed waterway connections tended to specialize in bulk cargo, and railroad ports in general cargo, with corresponding variations in harbor infrastructures, both physical and social. For many years Rotterdam enjoyed a reputation as Europe's leading bulk cargo port, Antwerp as a general cargo port renowned for its forwarders and liner connections. The reality, however, was that all ports relied on some combination of water and rail to extend their hinterland networks as far as possible, and no port could compete for long without generating high volumes in both forms of traffic. Antwerp, the general cargo port par excellence was also a huge grain-importing port. What mattered most was how port communities exploited advantages in landscapes and technology to construct land-sea connections that reached deep into interiors.

The relationship between ports and their hinterlands, however, was never simply a matter of contouring transportation networks to physical geography. Power intruded on hinterland connections or rearranged them

[6] Gordon Jackson, *The History and Archaeology of Ports* (Kingwood, Tadworth Surrey: World's Work Lt., 1983), 75–75, 151; Backx, *Haven*, 12.

wholesale. Railroads projected port influence inward but equally radiated authority from alternative command centers. Le Havre had terrible battles with the Western Railroad, which refused to build a second line into the port and blocked efforts by another company to do so.[7] Marseille's fate was largely determined by deep conflicts that arose between port business interests and railroad strategies emanating from Paris.[8] German state subsidies to railroads, in the form of artificially low freight rates, the *Seehafenausnahmetarif*, diverted traffic, whose natural outlet was Antwerp or Rotterdam, to Bremen and Hamburg. Efforts to tap hinterlands thus nearly always entangled in a tissue of competing interests, because new rail or canal lines were almost certain to interfere with someone else's trade, whether that belonged to rival ports, barge companies, other transport systems, or way stations along preestablished routes.[9]

History and political geography had still greater impacts on the configuration of hinterlands. The most notable case was the unification of Germany, whose export-driven economy paradoxically drained flows into the water and rail networks of the Low Countries. Both Antwerp and Rotterdam rose to front-rank status on the coattails of German industrial expansion. Just as decisive was the detachment of Alsace-Lorraine from France in 1871, whose political consequences are well known but whose geoeconomic effects were perhaps more critical. An important source of import-export traffics and pivotal to routes converging eastward, this region was subsequently integrated into a German rail system that tapered toward Dutch and Belgian ports at the expense of France's channel harbors. State formation thus determined pathways, with multiple transnational effects, bringing Danubian, Italian, Swiss, French, and German flows within Rotterdam's and Antwerp's orbit. Half a century later, following French victory in the First World War, efforts to reverse these trends would founder on built-up advantages and entrenched networks, but also on concerted efforts by the port of Antwerp to retain and widen its French connections.[10]

On a grander scale, the twentieth century as a whole represented a long-term, structural shift in port-hinterland relationships. Once

[7] Vigarié, *Grands*, 319–321.
[8] René Borruey, *Le port moderne de Marseille du dock au conteneur (1844–1974)* (Marseille: Chambre de Commerce et d'industrie Marseille, 1994), 173; Marcel Roncayolo, *L'imaginaire de Marseille. Port, ville, pôle* (Marseille: Chambre de Commerce et d'Industrie Marseille-Provence, 1990), 169–170.
[9] Backx, *Haven*, 35.
[10] Vigarié, *Grands*, 265–266, 287–288. See also Chapter 7.

merchant command centers, ports ceded the initiative to the interior. This metamorphosis from entrepot to transit hub is a thread that runs through the literature on twentieth-century harbors. Vigarié placed the story of the triumph of the port *de l'horizon terrestre* over the port *de l'horizon marin* – "the center, pulsator of exchanges and sovereign authority in deciding matters of transport, is seated in the hinterland" – at the center of his remarkable study of Channel and North Sea ports. The triumph was practically a revenge for a continent that had governed port life in medieval times only to lose the initiative in the sixteenth century when "the ocean assumed decisive weight."[11] Gordon Jackson caught the same dislocation when he wrote of British harbors that "by 1980 the ports had gone full circle.... Once again ports are trans-shipment centres for inland towns, and inland merchants and manufacturers.... Apart from the grain and timber trades, the ports appear to have slipped back to a position they held in the early Middle Ages."[12] The physicality of the shift could be seen in the routinization on quays of the shed or hangar – the anti-warehouse – minimalist structures of roof and sides, designed for the orderly movement of freight through a port as rapidly as possible.

Transit, however, still confirmed the underlying and most endur-ing feature of ports: their cosmopolitanism conjoined to a local sense of presence. The milieu Thomas Mann captured in *Magic Mountain*, a transnational gathering of home identities, also defined Europe's har-bors. In these spaces local pride and connections coexisted side by side with foreign communities or continental agents. Hinterlands, regardless of conversions they underwent, could not erase the fact that ports were transnational nexus points built out of established home bases. That position intensified with overseas links that combined local power with connections on a global scale.

This second set of port networks can be likened to a perspective in which ports functioned as the vanishing points of lines of influence radi-ated overseas by markets and firms. We are talking here about home fleets or home-based trading companies, which projected the reach of great mercantile centers like Hamburg and Liverpool across all seas and to all continents. This was not simply a matter of routes and traffics, although their importance cannot be minimized, especially the direct linkage these assured to large parts of the globe. Both were compulsive networkers, whose aggregate effect was to spin out webs of influence for their home

[11] Ibid., 344–345, 410–411, 531, 534, 597–598.
[12] Jackson, *History*, 166–167.

ports as well as for themselves. Shipping companies established organizations in every port of call. On business trips, their directors visited offices, exchanges, gave and attended lunches, threw cocktail parties, and met with importers and exporters, rail companies, port officials, and local chambers of commerce. They thus sold services but also the harbors from which they had emanated. As in the nineteenth century, when corps of agents, working for shipping companies, had steered emigrant traffics their way, these companies functioned as the forward representatives of port cities, through which they then washed great volumes of people and goods. Trading companies went a step further: They were effectively home ports' foreign bases across the globe. They too were great generators of networks, especially when they linked up with networks of indigenous businessmen to project the same zonal influences as accrued from the cultivation of hinterlands.

Moreover, these forward maritime firms created synergies for their port cities. As command centers of overseas networks they summoned not only traffic, but also markets, exchanges, and that full range of business and harbor services or local patrimony that could not be improvised. Even more, they were sources of knowledge: of possibilities, dangers, goods, and traffics, all of which passed through their networks back to their ports of origin. The congeries of dealers, brokers, agents, forwarders, buyers, and sellers who gravitated to ports were drawn by the information that circulated in these centers, but they too trucked and bartered in intelligence and added still more harbor networks of their own. London, thanks to the proximity to the port of one of the world's two premier business centers, was the prime knowledge market in Europe, but every major port developed an interchange between its marketing and shipping services. All the great ports were thus headquarters or hubs of information, transportation, and business services that bestowed tremendous power and wealth, but that also served as switchboards of global connectivity.

The synergies were themselves founded on close collaboration between ports and their overseas instruments. The ties between home shipping and trading companies were intricate and dynamic. It was not unusual for trading houses to participate in the founding of lines to open service to distant but potentially productive markets they wished to prospect or had already penetrated. Nor was it unusual for them to receive appointments as agents once the new services opened. There was intermarriage of sons and daughters, and it was common for each sector to apprentice its sons in the offices of the other. In merchant cities shipping and trading circles thus intertwined through ownership, family relations, or first-choice business connections that spanned the world. In such cities, the tradition was to ship on local carriers via home ports. Meanwhile ports too stationed representatives abroad to build contacts and sell their harbors. The port authorities of London and Liverpool each placed staff in Australia and South Africa. Liverpool's first agent in Sydney was H. W. Richards, who previously had worked for fifty years with Dalgety, wool brokers and stock and station agents, and one of the most powerful firms in the Australian export trades. As former head of Dalgety's shipping organization, Richards was a man with vast connections in the country. When Herbert R. Young succeeded him at the end of the 1940s, Richards took Young around from office to office and initiated his membership in the New South Wales Club, an essential base for further networking in the capital. Young, however, also leaned heavily on what he called "the Shipping fraternity," or the local agents of Liverpool shipping companies, who provided the same services when top Mersey Docks and Harbour Board officials made their own voyages to Australia and called on chambers of commerce, editors, and leading commodity shippers or boards.[13]

There was then what can be considered a third set of networks that brought together port authorities and port users, adding to these local government and business powers. This third network was especially active at local levels in which ports sought to create communities of interest to minimize differences or to secure investment and attract traffic. Such communities could not be taken for granted. Ports were jumbles of conflicting interests that required reconciliation. In just one Hamburg harbor basin, the Kuhwerderhafen, there were running battles during a nearly forty-year period over encroachments into the basin, or its approaches, by the huge Hamburg shipyard Blohm & Voss, by elevators and cranes of receiving companies on the far side at the Grevenhofkai, or from lighter companies whose barges lined up in rows of twos and threes alongside ships in berth and interfered with free passage, all the while ignoring signals from passing pilots or tugs to clear away. All of these

[13] MMM/MDHB/Management Files/Australian Trade/14 August 1947, 15 March, 2 April 1948 (quoted), 5 April 1949, January–September 1948 report; MMM/MDHB/ Management Files/1/Visit to Australia, 1922; ibid., Tour of South Africa, Australia and New Zealand, 1950…; London, Docklands Library and Archive (DLA)/Port of London Authority (PLA) 441/Report of Research Committee/Docks and Traffic Managers Office, 1934; DLA/PLA 2096/12 October 1928. See also Adrian Jarvis, *In Troubled Times: The Port of Liverpool, 1905–1938*, Research in Maritime History 26 (St. John's, Newfoundland: International Maritime Economic History Association, 2003), 195–204. Jarvis refers to Harold Davies as the MDHB's representative in Australia in 1938, but the 14 August 1947 and 5 April 1949 documents seem to contradict this.

parties regarded their rights as sacred, as did the passing ships that were Hamburg's bread and butter, and which would go elsewhere if harbor authorities did not mediate solutions, which they did tirelessly, year after year.[14] Anything affecting a port's cost competitiveness – high harbor fees or poor labor relations – or the indirect costs produced by port congestion or poor river approaches that were financially dead time to shipping companies or shippers (exporters and importers), were especially pressing causes for rallying the troops.

Especially vital was the need to mobilize local communities to invest massively in their harbors and to cooperate in winning contracts. Individual port histories in the twentieth century often read as a narrative of channels dredged and widened, new basins carved and new docks erected, equipment purchased, or as the quantitative measurement of basin acreage and linear quay space. These investments were immensely expensive and could have riven port communities in two because revenues in part derived from user fees. Yet harbor authorities in nearly every main port rallied local businessmen behind them to commit to expansion and where possible, to lobby for state subsidies. If ports were welters of differences, users nonetheless bonded with port authorities and invested in home shipping lines or provided mutual support at home or abroad. Labor relations were often a more intractable problem, but because nearly every port suffered from the same conflicts, especially the persistence of casual labor, and evolved along the same lines, the competitive impact of labor costs was often mitigated, at least until the 1960s.[15] In the long run the leading ports were those where overseas interests were affixed to home identities, so that the switching mechanisms between

---

[14] Hamburg, Staatsarchiv/Deputation für Handel, Schiffahrt, und Gewerbe (DHSG) II/S VI B 1.53.2/Kuhwärderhafen, 1921–1930, 7 March, 21, 27 July, 28 September, 10 October, 20 December 1921, 26 March 1930; Hamburg, Staatsarchiv/Bureau für Wirtschaft und Verkehr (BWV) I/1994/Kuhwerderhafen 1951–1960, 7, 10, 12, and 31 October 1955, 2 November 1955, 28 September 1959, 4, 16 November, 9, 11 December 1959.

[15] Increasingly the prevailing trend was toward some form of a three-class system: workers guaranteed employment; workers without guarantee but the next to be hired; and the thoroughly casual who were hired when categories one and two did not suffice: Weinhauer, *Alltag*, 38–48; Roy Mankelow, "The Effects of Modernisation and Change in the London Docks: With Particular Reference to the Devlin Reforms and Events since 1967" (Ph.D. diss., Cambridge University, 1994), 13; Jean Legoy, *Le peuple du Havre et son histoire. Du négoce à l'industrie, 1800–1914* (Le Havre: Le Cadre de Vie, 1982), 207; Van de Laar, *Stad*, 163; Nijhof, "'Dock-work,'" 276–277; Van Isacker, *Antwerpse*, 200. Decasualization in Antwerp was slower than in Hamburg and Rotterdam; a strike in 1936 raised labor costs and undercut Antwerp's reputation as a cheap port. On Antwerp differences: Stephan Vanfraechem, "Why They Are Tall and We Are Small! Competition between Antwerp and Rotterdam in the Twentieth Century" (work in progress).

global and local could engage smoothly together. Where home cohesiveness was inherently weaker, as was the case for French ports, or where
they frayed, as occurred in London and Liverpool by the late 1960s,
competitive positions attenuated, or even unraveled. But local networks,
when sustained, endowed Europe's harbors with relentless growth and
increasing efficiencies, and with a base for fanning out across the world,
with the net result – as was true of all port networks – of greasing the
wheels of world commerce.

Port networks were, therefore, doubly meaningful. They determined
hierarchies, or competitive rankings. But combining local solidarities and
cosmopolitan connections, they also mediated between the interior and
abroad, or between the local and global, which is how a world economy functions. In their sum, port networks thus processed world flows
of people, goods, and information, even as they channeled these through
one nodal point or another. As ports expanded their hinterlands, com-
mandeered forelands, built out their infrastructures, vaunted their services, and honed their efficiencies, they extended the wider capacity for
global exchange. Rarely was competitiveness a strictly zero-sum matter;
one port's growth invited imitation and added to the world's total. What
is essential, then, is to examine the great ports' networks up close and
measured against each other, so as to comprehend what made for individual port power, but also world circulation.

MAIN PORTS

Port hierarchies change over time, but in the twentieth century Europe's
greatest ports were Hamburg, Rotterdam, Antwerp, London, and
Liverpool, with Bremen, Le Havre, and Marseille forming a second, outer
circle. All eight ports competed with each other, and it must be remembered that competition within nations was often as fierce as among
national harbors. The measurement of success was in the eyes of behold-
ers, but size, rank, and status were set by comparative statistics, and these
require a short excursion into the somewhat arcane realms of tonnage,
numbers, and interpretations of what these mean.

It should be understood at the outset that there is no clear conclusion
that can be drawn from any set of statistics. None is necessarily accurate.
Numbers vary by source. Series for some ports are incomplete. Some sets
of figures concentrate on numbers of ships, but this says nothing about
tonnage unloaded or charged within a particular port. Calculations by
tonnage often include the full tonnage figure for a ship, not the actual

amount of cargo unloaded in a port.[16] As if this were not complicated enough, there are three major tonnage figures for ships – deadweight (dwt), gross registered tons (grt), and net registered tons (nrt) – and these vary not only by how they are determined but by their very unit of measurement: weight or volume.[17] Add to this that Belgium had its own net tonnage measure, and it is possible to see the built-in futility to any search for exactitude. Moreover, a ton of coal and a ton of diamonds are not equal in the wealth they pass through a port. Ports with a preponderant tonnage in bulk cargo have a built-in advantage in tonnage figures. On the average, however, the added value that general cargo brought into a port – in other words income for port authorities and port companies, wages for employees – could run from three to fifteen times its weight in bulk cargo.[18] Huge traffics in coal or oil, therefore, skewed still further the meaning of raw tonnage numbers. In the mid-1960s, on the eve of containerization, Rotterdam's throughput was more than double Antwerp's, but the value-added figure for Antwerp was higher.[19] Still, ports competed by their numbers, and, on their own terms, the following tables (1, 2, and 3) provide some indication of where they ranked on the eve of the two world wars. On the whole, cargo-handled statistics were likely to be the most meaningful of the three, but the best indicator of power and wealth remained the networks they constructed.

Hamburg, Rotterdam, and Antwerp

Hamburg

Hamburg, Rotterdam, and Antwerp were the continent's greatest harbors in the twentieth century. Each offered a variation on the successful port model, where networks made ports global command centers. Of the three, Hamburg, on the eve of the First World War, was arguably the

---

[16] Backx, *Haven*, 15.

[17] Deadweight tonnage is calculated by weight (one ton = 2,240 pounds) and represents the carrying capacity of a ship down to its load line. Gross and net registered tonnage are calculated by volume (one ton = 100 cubic feet). Gross registered tonnage represents the entire interior space of the ship, including nonproductive areas such as machinery or crew quarters. Net registered tonnage represents passenger or cargo space.

[18] Helmut Nuhn, "Der Hamburger Hafen. Strukturwandel/und Perspectiven für die Zukunft," *Geographische Rundschau* 41 (1989): 651; Reginald Loyen, "From Register Tonnage to Added Value: The Cautious Advent of a New Performance Indicator," in Ferry de Goey, ed., *Comparative Port History of Rotterdam and Antwerp (1880–2000): Competition, Cargo, and Costs* (Amsterdam: Askant, 2004), 216.

[19] Reginald Loyen, *Haven in de branding. De economische ontwikkeling van de Antwerpse haven vanaf 1900* (Leuven: Universitaire Pers Leuven, 2008), 282.

TABLE I. *Seaborne Cargo Traffic Handled in Metric Tons*

Port	1913	1938
Hamburg	25,458,000	25,741,628
Bremen	7,166,956	8,966,878
Rotterdam	28,145,046/c. 32,000,000[d]	42,370,990
Antwerp	18,871,935	23,578,949
London	–	42,078,000/44,600,000[d]
Liverpool	–	11,586,000
Le Havre	3,847,000/4,395,137[b]	6,588,000/8,580,000[c]
Marseille	9,044,968[c]	9,955,000

[a] The range between the statistics cited in HAPAG/1411 and those in Paul Th. van de Laar, "Port Traffic in Rotterdam: The Competitive Edge of a Rhine-port (1880–1914)," in Loyen, Buyst, and Devos, *Struggling*, 72–73. Van de Laar suggests his newer figures may, however, be too high.
[b] Vigarié/SHM.
[c] From Olivesi and Perrein. The figure they give for 1938 – 8,830,400 – does not correspond to Koomans's 1938 figures, so some adjustment for 1913 may also be necessary.
[d] Koomans/DLA. It is not certain whether these figures cover more than the PLA's docks.
[e] Vigarié/Koomans.
Sources: Hamburg, Staatsarchiv 621/1/Firma HAPAG-Reederei (HAPAG)/1411; Koomans, "Port," 113 (for 1938 figures); Havenbedrijf der Gemeente Rotterdam/Jaarverslag 1938, 7 (also for 1938 figures for Hamburg, Bremen, Rotterdam, and Antwerp; the Koomans figures correspond to these); Antwerp, Bibliotheek Havenbedrijf (BH)/National Institute of Statistics/Goederenverkeer, Goederenverkeer ter zee sedert 1860; DLA/Trade of the Port of London (charts with no further indications); Vigarié, *Grands*, Atlas, Document XI; Paris, Service historique de la marine (SHM)/1BB3/61/Le développement du Port autonome du Havre, 1931; A. Olivesi and L. Pierrein, "Marseille contemporaine," in Edouard Baratier, ed., *Histoire de Marseille* (Paris: Privat, 1973), 456.

leading harbor, with unparalleled hinterland, foreland, and home-based networks, and so it is the port city with which to begin.

Lying on the Elbe, approximately sixty-five miles upriver from the North Sea, a town of waterways and rail bridges and Germany's second largest city, Hamburg's port traditions reach back to the fourteenth century. During that long history, Hamburg enjoyed numerous special connections, with the Baltic, with Spain and France, and with Britain, who twice in the twentieth century (with its allies) massacred Hamburg's shipping and trade, but with whom Hamburg trading companies established close commercial and financial ties that proved often the means to revival after 1918 and 1945. But one relationship was distinctive: that with Bremen. Both members of the Hansa, both city-states, both homes to great fleets and trading companies, their rivalry in the twentieth century was intense. Mostly it was expressed through the competition of

TABLE 2. *Incoming Ships and Ship Tonnage (nrt): 1913*

Port	Incoming Ships	Ship Tonnage
Hamburg	15,073	14,185,496
Bremen	–	4,509,000[e]
Rotterdam	10,203	12,785,861
Antwerp	7,056	14,146,819 Bnt/c.12,000,000
London	25,470[d]	20,000,000[d]
Liverpool	15,000[b]	15,100,000[b]
Le Havre	5984/6536[c]	5,406,000/9,954,461[f]
Marseille	9,588[d]	10,606,560[d]

[a] DLA's chart and Bell list these as "Vessels that Arrived and Departed." The figures in the table are thus divided in half; they also include coastwise shipping.
[b] From 1914.
[c] Legoy/SHM.
[d] The same cautions regarding Olivesi and Perrein's figures listed in Table 1 pertain here. Their figures almost certainly count departing as well as entering ships; I have divided these, and their tonnage, in half.
[e] From Vigarié.
[f] Vigarié/Legoy. Legoy does not identify his choice of tonnage measurement.
Sources: J. De Keuster, *La concurrence entre les trois grands ports nord-européens: Hambourg, Rotterdam, Anvers* (Antwerp: Groll, 1930), 7; H. C. Hazewinkel, J. Schraver, and J. M. Pattist, "Rise and Growth of Rotterdam," in Schraver, *Rotterdam*, 33; BH/National Institute of Statistics/Zeeverkeer; DLA/Trade of the Port of London; Alan Bell, *Port of London, 1909–1934* (London: Port of London Authority, 1934), 64; Francis E. Hyde, *Liverpool and the Mersey: An Economic History of a Port, 1700–1970* (Newton Abbot (Devon): David & Charles, 1971), 143, 169; Vigarié, *Grands*, Atlas, Document XI; Legoy, *Peuple*, 421; SHM/1BB3/61/Le trafic du Port du Havre; Olivesi and Pierrein, "Marseille," 456.

their major shipping companies, the Hamburg Amerika Line (HAPAG) in Hamburg and the Norddeutscher Lloyd (NDL) in Bremen. Nearly every step the one took was matched by the other. Yet Hamburg and Bremen were too close physically, and in maritime traditions, not to cross networks with one another. Hamburg trading companies were also NDL agents. Hamburg merchants and shipping men sent their sons to train in the offices of their Bremen counterparts. Throughout the century, shipping rivalry alternated with collaborative ventures.

On neither score, however, was it ever a meeting of equals. Bremen's trumps in the nineteenth century were its connections to North America and its initial lead in transatlantic migration; by the 1870s Bremen was second only to Liverpool (and first on the continent) in cotton imports. Bremen merchants traveled the world and set up large trading houses overseas like Melchers & Co. in China. The city's home fleet included

TABLE 3. *Incoming Ships and Ship Tonnage (nrt): 1938*

Port	Incoming Ships	Ship Tonnage
Hamburg	18,595	20,833,176
Bremen	9,143	10,138,912
Rotterdam	15,306	24,744,472
Antwerp	11,762	19,979,743
London	29,835	30,777,000/31,450,000[a]
Liverpool	–	16,600,000/17,628,000[b]
Le Havre	–	10,867,000
Marseille	6,450	15,490,000/16,031,000[c]

[a] Koomans/DLA.
[b] Hyde/Koomans.
[c] Olivesi and Perrein/Koomans.

Sources: Havenbedrijf der Gemeente Rotterdam/Jaarverslag 1938, 3; Koomans, "Port," 111; BH/National Institute of Statistics/Zeeverkeer; DLA/Trade of the Port of London; Hyde, *Liverpool*, 169; Vigarié, *Grands*, Atlas, Document XI; Olivesi and Perrein, "Marseille," 456.

not only the giant NDL, but also the Hansa and Roland lines. Some of the largest freight forwarders in the world – Kühne & Nagel, J. H. Bachmann – were Bremen based. In nearly every category, however, save certain commodities, Hamburg outstripped Bremen. The city on the Weser was hampered by a river that was short and difficult to navigate and that commanded no great hinterland. Hamburg siphoned off traffic to the east, and to the west Bremen competed directly with Rotterdam and Antwerp. Hamburg was the larger, more industrialized city. Despite their similarities, between the two there was always a difference. Bremen was indisputably a great port, but Hamburg was the greater one.[20]

Endowed with excellent river, canal, rail, and short-sea services, Hamburg harvested a wide share of German but also central European and Baltic traffics. A city nearing 2 million by the 1930s, Hamburg was, moreover, its own mass market, and one of Germany's most industrialized cities, although the smelting of tin and copper from Southeast Asia and Chile, the crushing and milling of vegetable oils from the tropics, and mammoth shipyards all testified to the unity between industry and overseas trade. After the Second World War, Rotterdam built a port industrial

---

[20] Karl Löbe, *Seeschiffahrt in Bremen. Das Schiff Gestaltete Hafen und Stadt* (Bremen: H. M. Hauschild, 1989); Rolf Engelsing, *Herm. Dauelsberg Schiffsmakler, 1857–1957* (Hamburg: Verlag Hanseatischer Merkur, 1957), 41–88; Backx, *Haven*, 25–26, 100, 167.

structure to capture flows through the harbor. Hamburg already possessed one a half century earlier.[21] Thus even after the great transatlantic emigration trades waned in the 1920s, Hamburg continued to drain
voluminous quantities of bulk and general cargo through its port. On any
given day in the early 1930s, despite severe economic depression, nearly
100 barges and 2,500 railway cars arrived in the city. Ironically, its greater
distance through the North Sea was also its good fortune, because calling
at Hamburg extended the sea route to the interior, where railroad carriage rates were considerably higher than the charges on ocean freight.

But it was Hamburg's overseas networks – where local and transnational so intertwined they were difficult to disentangle – that powered
global connectedness and constituted the lifeblood of the city. At a micro
level, the house of Vorwerk (founded 1832) stands as an example of how
business networks at home and abroad soldered civic identities to merchant affairs, but also made Hamburg a world port. The Vorwerks were
Hamburg traders, merchant bankers, agents, and, initially, shipowners. In
1847 a branch house was established in Valparaiso, and from this point
on Vorwerk concentrated its business in Chile, although it continued to
trade, in lesser ways, worldwide. By the 1890s it was the leading German
firm in Chile and before the First World War a leading house in Chilean
saltpeter commerce. In 1933 the family closed the Hamburg house and
made its Chilean branch, Vorwerk & Co., its base of operations. Forced
to liquidate in the Second World War, the firm returned in the late 1940s.
By the 1990s the fifth generation of Vorwerks, or their offspring, were
still running the business.

Vorwerk's ties were therefore equally extensive within Hamburg and
Chile. Georg Friedrich Vorwerk (1793–1867), the founder, married into
a Hamburg sugar refining family, was active in community and philanthropic life, and for many years served as a member of Hamburg's
Commerzdeputation. His eldest son, Friedrich, (1837–1931) married
the daughter of a Hamburg magistrate; assumed, like his father, civic

---

[21] L. Wendemuth and W. Böttcher, *The Port of Hamburg*, 2nd ed. (Hamburg: Meissner
& Christiansen, 1932), 1, 7–9, 22–31, 37–48. See also the long list of city firms at the
back of the book. Backx, *Haven*, 7, 23–54; Arnold Kludas, Dieter Maass, and Susanne
Sabisch, *Hafen Hamburg. Die Geschichte des Hamburger Freihafens von den Anfängen
bis zur Gegenwart* (Hamburg: Ernst Kabel, 1988), 143; Charles Wilson, *The History of
Unilever: A Study in Economic Growth & Social Change* (London: Cassell & Company,
1954), vol. 2, 104–105; Commonwealth Economic Committee, *Vegetable Oils and
Oilseeds: A Summary of Figures of Production, Trade, and Consumption* (London: Her
Majesty's Stationery Office, 1952), 111–112; Katharine Snodgrass, *Copra and Coconut
Oil* (Stanford: Stanford University Press, 1928), 98, 130.

positions; and occupied seats on the boards of the Bank für Chile und Deutschland and the Sloman saltpeter works. His brother Adolf (1839–1919) apprenticed with a Hamburg firm trading with Mexico, spent nearly fifteen years working with the house in Chile, and then returned to Hamburg where he too took up civic and philanthropic obligations and presided over the supervisory board of the city's Norddeutsche Bank. His son, Carl (1875–1949), perhaps the most talented of his generation, was vice president of the Hamburg Chamber of Commerce and sat on the boards of two Hamburg shipping lines, a saltpeter works, and the Norddeutsche Bank. Even nonfamily partners in the Chile business, such as Carl Heinrich Pini, the son of a Hamburg merchant and married to the daughter of a Hamburg senator (and granddaughter of a Hamburg burgomaster), were deeply fixed within the Hamburg establishment.

Yet, from 1850 on it was also tradition that a Vorwerk partner serve as Hamburg consul in Valparaiso, and over the generations Vorwerks continued to work in both Hamburg and Chile. Between Chile and Hamburg, the Vorwerk house was often the central intermediary, and thus played as active a role in developing Chile's as Hamburg's overseas relations. The Vorwerks participated in the founding of the Dampfschiffahrts-Gesellschaft "Kosmos," Hamburg's shipping line to the west coast of South America, and acted as its general agent for Chile. Later they held the same position for HAPAG when it took over the line. Beginning in the late 1920s, Vorwerk acted as the intermediary, and at times consortium participant, for the huge Hamburg smelting company Norddeutsche Affinerie in its business dealings in Chile. After many years in Chile, the house had cemented superb ties to Chilean business circles and often introduced Hamburg principals to its own clients. Thoroughly wedded to the Hamburg establishment, increasingly the Vorwerks became Chilean minded and based, until subsequent generations were just as thoroughly Chilean in birth, education, and domicile.

Hamburg's strength, in good part, thus rested on its merchant community being embedded in multiple world communities. Whether Vorwerks by the third decade of the twentieth century considered themselves more Hamburg or Chilean was beyond the point; they were both, with additional, transept lines to Britain and America. The Vorwerks trained with British firms, held British insurance representations, and were tied financially to the London merchant banker, J. Henry Schröder & Co., whose own family ties led back to Hamburg. When these networks broke in the First World War, Vorwerk opened new trading relations with the American Warburgs, they too of Hamburg origins. They were a relentlessly networked firm whose connections both at home and abroad sustained world reach and exemplified the local-global dynamics that created and ran a world economy and at which Hamburg excelled.[22]

The Vorwerk story could be retold, with variations, for other Hamburg trading companies, such as Albrecht & Dill (West Africa and South America), Behn, Meyer & Co. (Southeast Asia), Bernard Buschmann (Middle East and Asia), C. Illies & Co. (Japan), and Theodor Wille (Brazil). The dynamics were just as relevant for Hamburg's home fleet, the greatest on the continent. These houses too, thanks to their networks of routes, agents, and contacts, were crossbreeds of Hamburg and the world. Hamburg shipping tonnage in 1930 totaled more than 2 million tons grt. About half belonged to HAPAG whose networks were worldwide, but there were several dozen other companies, among these Hamburg Süd, which sailed to South America, and the Deutsche Levante Line and the Woermann Line, which sailed to Africa. Hamburg's forward networks, anchored by home trading and shipping firms, impressed by size but also globalism.

Consequently Hamburg evolved into an extraordinary agglomeration of installations and enterprises by the twentieth century. In the interwar years the port area spread across thirty-two miles of quay walls and covered 10,000 acres. In Blohm & Voss, the city possessed Europe's largest shipyard. On the Speicherstadt, Hamburg's main warehousing district, the buildings of the Hamburger Freihafen-Lagerhaus-Gesellschaft stretched close to a mile, but, immense as the company was, it represented only two-thirds of Hamburg's warehousing volume. Downriver at Cuxhaven, Hamburg had its auxiliary port on the sea to dock the big North Atlantic passenger liners. In town, the exchange combined a financial and commodities bourse and functioned as a general merchandise mart. Its showrooms and transaction halls; its corps of brokers, agents, and dealers; and its futures markets compounded the commercial energy, and freight drawing power, of the shipping and trading community.[23]

[22] Renate Hauschild-Thiessen, *Zwischen Hamburg und Chile* (Hamburg: Vorwerk y Cía., 1995).

[23] DLA/PLA/1540; C. Prange, "The Development of the Port of Hamburg in the 19th and 20th Centuries: The Process of Decision and Execution," in L. M. Akveld and J. R. Bruijn, eds., *Shipping Companies and Authorities in the 19th and 20th Centuries: Their Common Interest in the Development of Port Facilities* (Den Haag: Nederlandse Vereniging voor Zeegeschiedenis, 1989), 11–13; Wendemuth and Böttcher, *Port*, 15–20, 23, 54–82, 193–197, 254; Kludas, *Hafen*.

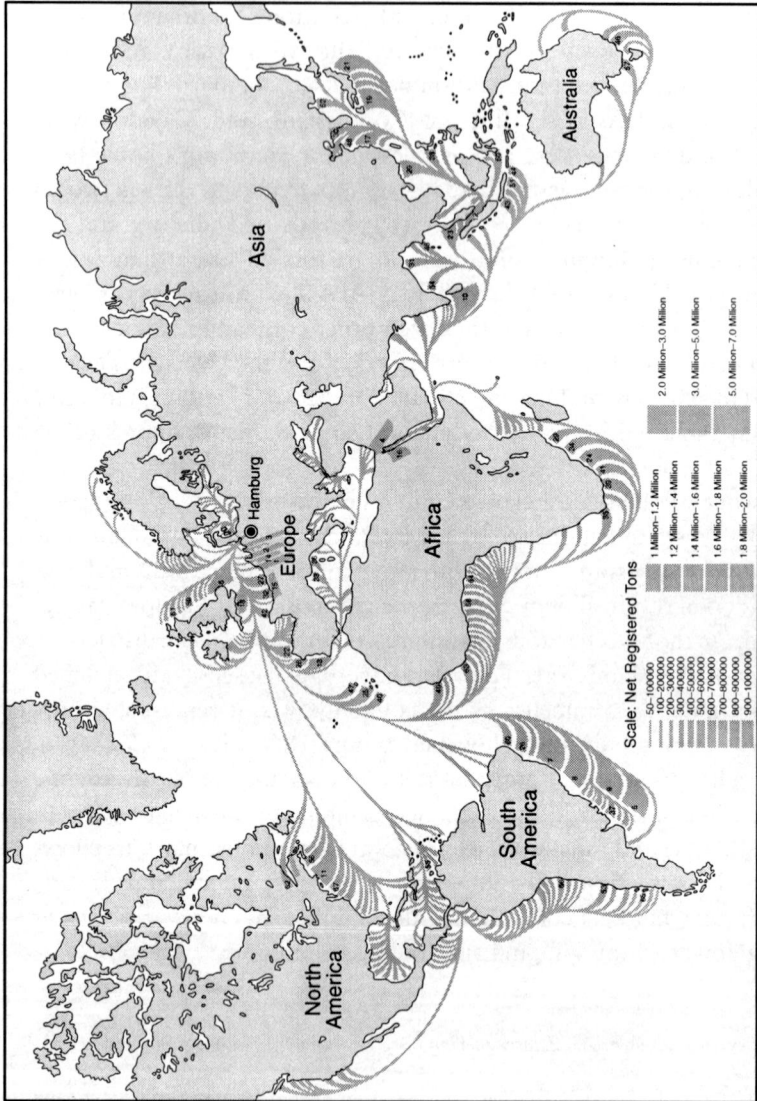

Created in the cartography office of Baubehörde Strom-u.Hafenbau Hamburg

Printed by Jagdmann u. Bohm. Hamburg 8.

MAP 2. Ocean-borne goods traffic, in net registered tons, between Hamburg and its world ports, including intermediate ports of call. Reprinted from L. Wendemuth and W. Böttcher, *The Port of Hamburg* (Hamburg: Meissner & Christiansen, 1932), p. 46, with the permission of the Hamburg Port Authority.

42

Holding it all together was the port's third network of interlocking commitments with city authorities and the business community. The Vorwerks were one striking example, but another was shipowner Adolph Woermann, an aggressive promoter of Hamburg's merchant interests and a member of the city parliament from 1880 to 1914.[24] He was also president of the chamber of commerce, whose own activities were typical of the close relationship between business and harbor. The chamber possessed a seat on the city committee that governed the harbor, and it maintained the Commerzbibliothek, a superb collection that functioned as an informational clearing house for harbor business and is still critical today for research on the port. Senators, shipping men, and leaders of other local firms sat together on official inquiry boards into harbor affairs and turned to still other businessmen as expert consultants.[25] In Chapters 2 and 3 we will see further evidence of how Hamburg's powerful shipping community interbred with the port and its trading interests. Here, it is sufficient to acknowledge how powerful hinterland, foreland, and home networks combined into an equally powerful engine of world trade. Hamburg, however, was only one leading example.

Rotterdam

Rotterdam, after the First World War, traded places with Hamburg. If Hamburg was Europe's top continental port at the beginning of the century, Rotterdam was the kingpin for its remainder. Both ports had extensive inland waterway networks. But Rotterdam's led to the western European heartland, whereas much of Hamburg's led east, to rural lands and, after the Second World War, partly forbidden ones. Ironically, both were essentially German ports, but the one located in Holland fared better for longer than the one located in Germany. On the other hand, if both ports were home to major steamship lines, Hamburg's were greater, even if German shipping men admired the audacity of the Dutch and regarded them as clever as pirates (*schlitzohrig*).[26] Both benefited from the outreach of home trading companies abroad, but Amsterdam, more than Rotterdam, was the colonial port in the Netherlands, and consequently Hamburg's forward networks were more extensive. The trade-offs probably could go on forever. At the end of the century people in Hamburg

---

[24] Prange, "Development," 15.
[25] HAPAG/1411.
[26] Otto J. Seiler, interview with author, Hamburg, 6 August 1996. Seiler had worked for HAPAG.

admired and feared Rotterdam's power and go-getter mentality, but
Rotterdamers saw in Hamburg a greater bastion of maritime tradition.

Rotterdam started its ascent from far more modest beginnings. The city
derived its name from the Rotte, which flows into the Maas, and from
the dam or dyke erected to protect its medieval settlement from flooding.
Not until the seventeenth century did it grow into a mercantile link in
trans-European traffic, and not until late into the nineteenth century did
two overlapping developments set it on its course to be the giant of the
future. The first was the cutting of a new waterway to the sea, endowing Rotterdam with an open, direct, short, deep, unbridged, and lockless
channel, and Europe's finest river approach.[27] A century later, giant tankers and ore carriers still navigated the (deepened) channel, accounting for
Rotterdam's explosive growth into the largest port in the world.

The second development was German unification, and the subsequent
industrialization of Rotterdam's natural hinterland. The effect was that a
vast share of German imports and exports passed through Rotterdam's
harbor, but at the cost of concentrating German power over Rotterdam's
flows. In certain ways, Rotterdam was, even more than Hamburg, a
transnational port because of the foreign hinterland's command over its
trade. In Hamburg, business networks radiated outward from port-based
traders and shipping companies. In Rotterdam, business networks frequently radiated inward to and from Germany. As the French geographer
Vigarié remarked, the near dependency of Rotterdam's flows on German
industry led to a certain Germanization of the harbor. In the late nineteenth century, German grain traders took up residency in Rotterdam.
Much of the traffic in coal and ore that passed through Rotterdam lay in
the hands either of German companies or their Rotterdam subsidiaries.
Large German fleets, some controlled by the big coal concerns, dominated Rhine barge traffic. Magnified into a German gateway, Rotterdam
was the model of a modern transshipment harbor.[28]

So predominant was the German trade and the bulk cargoes it elicited
that it tended to overshadow the multivariate character of maritime life
in the city. Rotterdam was home to a sizable fleet, including the Holland
Amerika Line and the Rotterdamsche Lloyd, the latter being one of the

---

[27] W. F. Lichtenauer, "The Economic Position of Rotterdam," in Schraver, *Rotterdam*, 240;
Hazewinkel, "Rise," 7–16.
[28] Vigarié, *Grands*, 282, 485, 540; Van de Laar, "Port," 76; idem, *Stad*, chapters 2, 3;
W. F. van Gunsteren, "Netherlands Rhine Shipping," in Schraver, *Rotterdam*, 195;
Backx, *Haven*, 110–112. Ilmari Wäänänen, *Rotterdam als Seehafen unter Besonderer
Berücksichtigung des konkurrenzkampfes mit Antwerpen* (Weida i. Thür.: Thomas &
Hubert, 1930), 98–99, as well on the Dutch barge fleet.

two great trunk lines to the East Indies. The largest East Indies trading company, Internatio, was a Rotterdam firm. Nevertheless, it was
Rotterdam's superb inland waterway connections that effectively shaped
its destiny: as feeder and outlet for German industry. Along its network
of rivers and canals, ideal for bulk cargo transports, sailed the preponderance of Europe's coal, ore, and grain shipments. Later, massive oil traffics
would generate still greater bulk tonnage figures.

Such heavyweight concentrations on waterborne bulk – on the eve of
the Second World War, nearly four-fifths of the tonnage moving through
the port was bulk cargo, three-quarters of this transit traffic –[29] brought
still further consequences. Port layout dictated the carving of capacious
basins where ships could moor midstream for discharge along both
sides of the vessel. An entire village disappeared for the Maashaven, surpassed by the gargantuan Waalhaven of nearly 800 acres and designed to
accommodate more than a hundred ships at one time. Having wrestled
land from the sea over centuries, the Dutch now gave it back in massive
fell swoops to reap other, sea-given prizes. The trend toward gigantism
continued after the Second World War with the Botlek and Europoort/
Maasvlakte projects out to the sea.[30] Oil, bulk, and industrialization ultimately stretched the port the full length down the river. The living image
of the modern transit port, Rotterdam became also the epitome of the
divorce between harbor and city.

Rotterdam too generated forceful local networks, but these also
bore the imprint of its bulk trades. More than any other main port,
Rotterdam evolved into a stevedore's port. Large stevedore companies,
favored by the susceptibility of bulk to mechanization, and by city policy
that granted long-term rentals of quays, invested in physical plant and
equipment that made Rotterdam an innovator in the mechanical handling of shipments.[31] In Rotterdam terminal operators were instrumental in draining traffic through their harbor. At wider levels, a consensus
emerged among Rotterdam's business, political, and bureaucratic circles
that civic culture should mirror the city's port-centered function, and this
held until the 1970s by which time Rotterdam was already far ahead of
any competitor,[32] including its perennial Low Country rival, Antwerp.

[29] Havenbedrijf der Gemeente Rotterdam/ Jaarverslag 1938; Lichtenauer, "Economic,"
243. For the nonetheless considerable general cargo trade, see de Goey, *Comparative*,
especially p. 40.
[30] Van Driel and de Goey, *Rotterdam*, 43; Hazewinkel, "Rise," 24–25.
[31] The indispensable work on Rotterdam's stevedores is van Driel, *Samenwerking*.
[32] Han Meyer, *City and Port: Urban Planning as a Cultural Venture in London, Barcelona,
New York, and Rotterdam: Changing Relations between Public Urban Space and*

Antwerp

Between Rotterdam and Antwerp there was no love lost, but there were also striking similarities. Both ports rose with German industrialization, both organized for huge transit trades, both were prolonged success stories throughout the twentieth century. Antwerp received greater state aid for port development, but both ports were deemed central to their national economies and were well looked after in international negotiations. Rotterdamers were known as resourceful negotiators who went extra lengths to grab business. The Rotterdam forwarder, Charley Dietvorst, told the story of receiving a fax from the United States to bid on beer ship-ments from Strasbourg. He could have sent back a fax, or a letter, but he flew directly to JFK Airport in New York and called from a phone, saying he had an offer to make and would be there in an hour. In his opinion, this was a typically Dutch response, and others would not do it the same way.[33] But Antwerpenaars also fashioned a self-image out of their flexibil-ity and daring. Both ports measured themselves against the other.

Antwerp, however, was a third variation of the successful port. For practically its entire history water was an issue. The approach from the sea is long and potentially difficult.[34] Tidal ranges from fifteen to eigh-teen feet on the average have created delays and forced the construc-tion of large and expensive locking systems. Water access, ever since the Dutch closed the mouth of the Scheldt in 1572, and then again in 1585, loosed even greater complications. Deep into the twentieth century the Dutch resisted Belgian efforts to open desired Scheldt-Rhine connections, and they relented only when the Common Market and the signing of a Benelux Economic Union promised to reward Rotterdam's traffic as well as Antwerp's.[35] For four centuries after 1572, the basic fact governing Antwerp's water links was their passage in nearly every instance through rival Dutch territory.

Large-Scale Infrastructure (Rotterdam: Han Meyer, 1999), 305–308; Ferry de Goey, Ruimte voor industrie. Rotterdam en de vestiging van industrie in de haven, 1945–1975 (Delft: Eburon, 1990), 53; Van de Laar, Stad, 350–351.

[33] Charley L. M. Dietvorst, Internationale Expediteurs Alfons Freriks Rotterdam b.v., inter-view with author, Rotterdam, 15 July 1997.

[34] Etienne Schoonhoven, Anvers son fleuve et son port. Coup d'oeil sur les principales étapes de son histoire économique et maritime (Antwerp: Lloyd Anversois, 1958), 14; Backx, Haven, 129; Klaus Bültjer, interview with author, Hamburg, 21 June 1996.

[35] F. Suykens et al., Antwerp: A Port for All Seasons, 2nd ed. (Antwerp: MIM, 1986), 464–469; Lode Hancké, "The Controversial Success of a World Port: Antwerp's Port in the 19th Century until 1914," in Jan Blomme et al., Momentum: Antwerp's Port in the 19th and 20th Century (Antwerp: Pandora, 2002), 29; Frank Seberechts, "The Political Influences on the Port of Antwerp in the Twentieth Century," in ibid., 36.

The solution was the railroad, and its ability to reverse the grip of political geography. Antwerp came to possess the densest port rail network on the continent to complement its position as the most westerly situated North Sea port and the one closest to northwestern Europe's population and industrial centers. Antwerp rail lines threaded through Belgium and Luxembourg, western and southern Germany, northern and eastern France, Switzerland, Italy, and the Danube basin. There were always large cargo volumes that traveled nonetheless by water,[36] especially following the First World War, and enormous shipments of grain passed through the harbor. But the initial rise came via the railroad, and on this Antwerp built a reputation as a rail, liner, and general cargo port.[37] Far from the vast basins Rotterdam cut into polders and riverbanks, Antwerp's port came to resemble a series of inland canals, self-contained behind locks, through which fingerlike quays projected – a port designed for rail movement and tidal flows and for a more diverse traffic.

Antwerp was, of course, Belgium's greatest port, and thrived off of Belgian heavy industry exports. That more steel shipped out of Antwerp than anywhere else in Europe provided the city with one of its trumps: ready export cargoes for shipping companies suffering from an imbalance of incoming freight in nearly all other harbors. In Antwerp ship captains could almost always find a cargo to load. Yet Antwerp's identity was semi-Belgian at best. A mere sixteenth among world ports in 1840,[38] its penetration into the front ranks came, like Rotterdam's, off the German transit trade. This made Antwerp too both a Belgian and German port, and not only in regard to the source of its cargoes. Before the First World War the numbers of Germans active in Antwerp ran into the thousands, by one count the tens of thousands. These migrants were instrumental in the city's efforts to attract German shipping companies to the harbor; close to one-third of all incoming tonnage in 1913 was German.[39] After the war, hostile sentiment drove most of them out, but what was lost in German trade was compensated for by new markets in northeastern France, which made Antwerp a French port as well. City traders were no less multinational. The networks of the Bunge group, responsible for a major share of the grain shipped through the harbor, extended to the

---

[36] Loyen, *Haven*, 167–210, but see also p. 358 on railroads.

[37] Antwerp, Stadsarchief (SA)/MA 35/Haven 63347/1 June 1951.

[38] Löbe, *Seeschiffahrt*, 250.

[39] DHSG II/S XX1 D1.24/15 September 1937 (c. 30,000); Vigarié, *Grands*, 362–363; Greta Devos, "German Ocean Shipping and the Port of Antwerp: An Introduction," in C. Koninckx, *Proceedings of the International Colloquium "Industrial Revolutions and the Sea"* (Brussels: Collectanea Maritima V, 1991), 217–218, 226.

capitals, financial centers, and port cities of Europe, and across the seas
to South America, the Congo, and Southeast Asia. In Argentina, its affiliate, Bunge & Born, emerged as the largest dealer in Argentinian cereals.
Partners in South America were a mix of Belgians and Germans, some
of whom took out Argentine citizenship, so that even before the second
and third generations, Bunge & Born's national identity was a matter of
interpretation.[40]

Unlike Hamburg or Rotterdam, Antwerp never possessed much of a
home fleet. But what it lacked on the seas it more than made up for in its
access to general cargo and export traffics and by the virtuosity of its local
user networks. The city was famed for its forwarders, who collected the
diverse, high-value freight that lured liner ships into Antwerp.[41] They sold
the harbor by keeping shipper rates low, and they glided goods through
customs.[42] The city abounded too in ship agents who were the local powers for their principals and equally adept at pulling in customers. Indeed
between port authorities and all user sectors – forwarders, agents, cargo
handlers, maritime factory agents, city representatives, the chamber of
commerce, and representatives from the Belgian railroads and customs –
there developed a local culture of pulling together to lobby the state for
port expansion projects or to harvest business for the harbor.[43]

At the heart of the culture was a reputation for being a nimble, swift,
flexible port.[44] Antwerp cultivated that image through a strategy of
"freight attracts freight." The dynamics were simple. Create favorable
conditions for shippers (importers/exporters), and freight will pour into
the port. Create a port with bountiful general cargo, especially exports,
and liner companies will flock in as well. Create a port with superb liner
opportunities and more freight will gush in, until the process becomes

[40] Stéphane Hoste, *Bunge in de Lage Landen: Twee eeuwen maritieme handel vanuit Amsterdam,
Antwerpen en Rotterdam. Bunge in the Low Countries. Two Centuries of Maritime Trade
from Amsterdam, Antwerp, and Rotterdam* (Tielt: Lannoo, 2006), chapter 2.

[41] At the end of the 1950s there were about 200 forwarders active in Antwerp: SA/MA 36/
Havenbedrijf 63337/67 page report c. 1958–1959.

[42] Philip Durot, A. Durot N.V./Boekmans N.V., interview with author, Antwerp, 18
November 1997; Jan de Bie, De Keyser Expeditions, interview with author, Antwerp,
25 November 1997; Jean-Pierre Bosteels, Ziegler, interview with author, Antwerp,
12 January 1998; Vigarié, *Grands*, 249–250; Backx, *Haven*, 222–223, 227; Suykens,
Antwerp, 513.

[43] SA/MA 35/Haven 63347; SA/MA 36/Havenbedrijf 24279 (Contact Commissie); Jacques
Damster, Compagnie Générale Maritime Benelux n.v., interview with author, Antwerp,
13 January 1998.

[44] Durot (interview); Leon Rijckaert, General Maritime Services, interview with author,
Antwerp, 18 November 1997; DHSG II/S XXI D1.24; Suykens, *Antwerp*, 521–523.

self-sustaining. Concessions and subsidies, especially at the ignition stage, were therefore liberally dispersed. Fast railroads and favorable landing clauses produced a reputation for "quick dispatch" or rapid turnaround time. More subtly, flexibility together with quick dispatch became a style or way of thinking and doing, a reputation that Antwerp clad as its persona. Clearing goods through customs was rarely a problem in Antwerp, where "the local services have always demonstrated a broad comprehension, and a great suppleness in the interpretation of texts, in regard to maritime operations."[45] Not surprisingly, Antwerp was the port of preference for gunrunners in the years before the First World War.[46] In larger dimensions it reflected Antwerp's self-image as a can-do port. That was one more epithet to add to all the others: railroad port, general cargo port, liner port, forwarders port. The net effect was to make Antwerp everybody's port.

Antwerp thus offered a third way. But parallels also balanced distinctions, and none more clearly than the enduring quality of networks. All three ports were locally and globally connected. The transnational dimension of each is not simply a matter of historical curiosity. Vorwerks in Hamburg and Chile, Bunges in Antwerp and South America, and Germans in Rotterdam and Rotterdamers abroad captured the essence of how these ports worked. Bundles of relationships across borders and oceans gave these ports drawing power. All three were international cities and incessant globalizers. Yet all three were locally cohesive. Over the course of the century, these reciprocal networks paid big returns, mustering prodigious numbers of ships, amassing mountains of wealth, and rendering all three world centers of travel and trade. Networks cashed into leadership and infrastructure and demonstrated how big ports could anchor world flows.

London and Liverpool

Across the channel, London and Liverpool were testimonies to what networks created but also, when they withered, took away. London was, after New York, the world's top port at the beginning of the century and probably still Europe's largest up until the 1950s.[47] Its pride was

[45] Vigarié, *Grands*, 406.
[46] Paris, Archives nationales (AN)/F7/12836.
[47] Jameson Doig, *Empire on the Hudson: Entrepreneurial Vision and Political Power at the Port of New York Authority* (New York: Columbia University Press, 2001), 27; R. Douglas Brown, *The Port of London* (Lavenham: Terence Dalton, 1978), 115; Bell,

the Royal Dock complex, which covered 245 water acres; but this was only one of five Port of London Authority (PLA) dock systems that in 1960 offered 35 miles of quay walls.[48] And the PLA accounted for less than one-third of the traffic in London's harbor. The remainder landed at private wharfs – known as wharfingers – that lined the riverfront, and that ranged from small frontages where the owners might toil alongside their workers, to big commercial operations like Hay's Wharf, which extended along the south bank from London Bridge to Tower Bridge and specialized in dairy shipments. In the late 1960s, shortly before its closure, its labor force numbered more than a thousand.[49] Some sense of this extraordinary complex of installations can be gleaned from the materials prepared for war measures in April 1939:

> Mr. Burgin then displayed a chart showing the position of every ship in the Port of London area. It covered a distance of some 70 miles and showed that, although there was considerable concentration in the Dock areas, only a very small percentage of the total ships were situated in those docks and the rest were scattered over a large number of quays and jetties or at moorings throughout the whole 70 miles or moving up and down the river.[50]

Liverpool, on the other side of the country, cleared as many ships as Hamburg in 1914. Located on the Mersey, where tides can vary by thirty feet and currents are strong, its harbor was sheltered in locks and docks behind massive walls, but these extended in nearly a straight line for more than six miles along the Mersey. There were more docks at Birkenhead, across the river, and still more – private docks, such as Lever's Port Sunlight and the London and North Western Railway docks at Garston – whose sizable freight and ship movements evaded Liverpool's port statistics. The cold storage facilities on the Alexandra Docks and the grain silos of the Liverpool Grain Storage Company were the largest of their kind in Europe. The tobacco warehouse at Stanley Dock, covering nearly thirty-six acres, was considered the largest warehouse in the world.[51]

Port, 64; James Bird, *The Major Seaports of the United Kingdom* (London: Hutchinson & Co., 1963), 24; Koomans, "Port," 111, 113. PLA statistics on shipping and throughput were compiled differently from how they were handled on the continent, and it is difficult to get clear comparative measurements.

[48] Jackson, *History*, 124, 145; D. J. Owen, *The Port of London Yesterday and Today* (London: Port of London Authority, 1927), 44–48; Bird, *Major*, 366, 379–384, 418.

[49] Bird, *Major*, 388, 391, 396–405, 409; Brown, *Port*, 90; Mankelow, "Effects," 53, 57; Greenwich, National Maritime Museum (NMM)/P & O series/4/71/Agents' Reports 1957/Import Freight Department.

[50] PRO/MT 63/94/20 April 1939.

[51] Bird, *Major*, 320–324; Hyde, *Liverpool*, 133–134; Mersey Docks and Harbour Board, *The Port of Liverpool*, 4th ed. (Liverpool: Littlebury Bros., 1923), 50, 52, 82–86, 101;

Both ports were therefore equipped as bases for massive overseas circulation, but neither fit easily into categories or templates. The Thames, Joseph Conrad tells us at the beginning of *Heart of Darkness*, was a conqueror's river, the way outward to the world, in contrast to the dark, penetrable, inner-leading Congo.[52] In fact, the great fleet-gathering conduit was, by the turn of the century, more an inward-directed port, Britain's leading import harbor until it surpassed Liverpool in exports just before the Second World War.[53] It was a unique port, the only main port of Europe that was equally a political, cultural, and financial capital. Within Britain a certain complementarity developed between London as the leading import port and Liverpool as the leading export port. Nevertheless, both processed huge volumes of each and handled all kinds of cargoes.

Hinterland was an especially amorphous concept, located as they were on an island laden with ports and where no city lies very far from the water. It was, however, possible to speak of certain interior networks. Liverpool grew in tandem with the industrial mills of Lancashire, Bradford, Leeds, and the engineering plants of the Midlands, which explains its leading role in exports but also its vast imports of industrial raw materials and foodstuffs.[54] London's captive hinterland was southeastern England, a slice that included 9 million people within 25 miles of the docks and that formed one of the world's most concentrated consumer markets. Each was a transnational collector port, despite being attached to an island. London retained many of its entrepot functions, even if these had shrunk considerably with the advance of European overseas shipping lines in the nineteenth century.[55] The warehousing space of the PLA alone customarily squirreled away half a million tons of goods, from all over the planet, at any one time. In the 1920s, several hundred thousand passengers landed or debarked at London, even if Liverpool's best days as an emigration port were largely behind it.[56]

Quentin Hughes, *Seaport: Architecture and Townscape in Liverpool* (London: Lund Humphries, 1964), 7–15; Edward P. Cotter, *The Port of Liverpool* (Washington, DC: U.S. Government Printing Office, 1929), 108.

[52] Joseph Conrad, *Heart of Darkness* (1902; reprint, London: Penguin Books, 1989).

[53] Hyde, *Liverpool*, 164.

[54] Cotter, *Liverpool*, 262–263, 297, 303; Hyde, *Liverpool*, 98–99.

[55] Kurt Wiedenfeld, *Die nordwesteuropäischen Welthäfen: London – Liverpool – Hamburg – Bremen – Amsterdam – Rotterdam – Antwerpen – Havre in ihrer Verkehrs- und Handelsbedeutung* (Berlin: Ernst Siegfried Mittler und Sohn, 1903), 273–274.

[56] Owen, *Port*, 29, 51; Brown, *Port*, 94–101, 124–125; Bird, *Major*, 368–406; J. Grosvenor, *The Port of London* (London: Staples Press Limited, 1957).

The three network system thus made as much sense for these ports as it did for Hamburg, Rotterdam, and Antwerp, particularly when it came to forward or port-centered networks. No port so closely approximated Hamburg's trading and shipping community as did Liverpool's. Cotton and grain traders typified the merchant ethos of the city,[57] but Liverpool houses in a variety of trades fanned out across the world. Liverpool was even more a shipowners' port. The great companies were Alfred Holt (also known as Blue Funnel and Ocean Steam Ship), Bibby, Booth, Brocklebank, Cunard, Elder Dempster, Harrison, Lamport & Holt, Pacific Steam Navigation, and White Star. Set up in 1858 as the Liverpool Steamship Owners' Association, shipping men were by far the most powerful force in the port, with ample justification. They represented one of the largest agglomerations of shipping tonnage in the world. Their power reflected a deep identity with their city, and they endowed Liverpool with local networks that sustained its trade at home and abroad. Of Holts, Britain's premier shipping line to East and Southeast Asia and arguably Liverpool's flagship company, Andrew Crichton, a leading figure in London's P & O, wrote:

[They] were a closely knit clan and had a very high opinion of themselves. There was some justification for this since they had bred and trained a series of most competent people. They possessed that faith in themselves which was the strength of our commercial forbears, and this was expressed in the certainty that they were superior to everyone else. For them, shipping-wise, Liverpool led the world and they led Liverpool.[58]

Holts viewed itself, and was viewed by others, as a local institution. Richard Holt, senior partner, dedicated himself to the successful reorganization of Elder Dempster when the failure of its parent group – Royal Mail – rocked the Liverpool shipping community at the beginning of the Depression.[59] At Holts it was incumbent on managers to participate in

---

[57] D. M. Williams, "Liverpool Merchants and the Cotton Trade, 1820–1850," in J. R. Harris, ed., *Liverpool and Merseyside: Essays in the Economic and Social History of the Port and Its Hinterland* (London: Frank Cass, 1969), 181–211; Graham L. Rees, *Britain's Commodity Markets* (London: Paul Elek Books, 1972), 98, 129–145; Graeme J. Milne, *Trade and Traders in Mid-Victorian Liverpool: Mercantile Business and the Making of a World Port* (Liverpool: Liverpool University Press, 2000).

[58] London, Peninsular House, P & O Archives (P & O)/INF/465/P. A. Tobin, "OCEL: The Early Years, 1965–1980" (OCEL): Recollection of Sir Andrew Crichton.

[59] Peter N. Davies, *The Trade Makers: Elder Dempster in West Africa, 1852–1972* (London: George Allen & Unwin, 1973; reprinted as *The Trade Makers: Elder Dempster in West Africa, 1852–1972, 1973–1979*, Research in Maritime History 19 (St. John's, Newfoundland: International Maritime Economic History Association, 2000), 213–235.

the civic life of the city and to serve their term on the Mersey Docks and Harbour Board (MDHB), the port authority that operated the harbor on both the Liverpool and Birkenhead sides of the river. Richard Holt was himself a chair. None of these activities, however, was exclusive to the Blue Funnel line. In 1929, half of the MDHB members were shipping company men, and others represented commodity import interests.[60] MDHB networks abroad, with the support of Liverpool shipping companies and agents, were simply an extension of port and user collaboration at home on a daily level.[61]

London's networks were yet more powerful. The home fleet included P & O, for a time the world's largest shipping company, but practically every British shipowner found it necessary to run services through the port.[62] British trading companies led the world and the majority were London based or maintained a London partnership. Many utilized their access to London's financial markets to float rubber, timber, or mining enterprises in Asia, Africa, and South America. Their advantage for London in overseas contacts and worldwide networks was magnified by the fact that London offices frequently determined routes and shipping decisions abroad.

Like Liverpool, the PLA possessed its own overseas networks, with agents in Australia and South Africa, but it also ran networks in London and up-country to capture traffic for the port. Fourteen canvassers in the interwar years worked by commodity. F. D. Rowlstone, the number one salesman, covered sugar, coffee, and cocoa. Fifty-two years old in 1934, Rowlstone spent most of his time at the London Commercial Sale Rooms chatting up importers, brokers, and buyers, and he was on friendly terms with a large number of traders. His colleague for meat, C. W. Oakley, roamed the Smithfield Market. Three more canvassers solicited for business out of a PLA Birmingham office in a radius that extended to Manchester, Bradford, and Bristol. In Birmingham the office paid the cost of a weekly lunch for the canvasser-in-charge at the local Rotary Club.[63]

---

[60] Malcolm Falkus, *The Blue Funnel Legend: A History of the Ocean Steam Ship Company, 1865–1973* (London: MacMillan, 1990), 14, 328; Adrian Jarvis, "The Members of the Mersey Docks and Harbour Board and Their Way of Doing Business, 1858–1905," *International Journal of Maritime History* 6 (June 1994): 123–139; Jackson, *History*, 122; Cotter, *Liverpool*, 15–16; Boyce, *Information*, 147.

[61] See, for instance, MMM/MDHB/Files of Supporting Papers/Traffic Committee/96/2, 8, 9 March 1923.

[62] Boyce, *Information*, 298–299.

[63] DLA/PLA 2096/Dock and Warehouse Committee Reports, 23 March 1928; ibid., 441/ Report of Research Committee/Dock and Traffic Managers Office, 1934.

London's central network, however, was the City, or the thick knot of markets and services that wound together within it and governed flows of money, insurance, commodities, and information throughout the world. In 1911, 364,000 people, the equivalent of an entire urban port's population elsewhere, were employed in the City. Here financial and merchant power converged with political and imperial power, the four held together by common interests, upbringing, lifestyle, and personal codes of behavior. All were outward looking and had been pronouncedly so since the seventeenth century. What would at the dawn of the twenty-first century be trumpeted as a "global city" was already in place in London at the dawn of the twentieth.[64] This confluence of expertise, organizational headquarters, knowledge, and money within one tightly packaged center was London's trump network, and combined with trading and shipping, overseas networks made London's port nearly unchallengeable. "Out here [Australia]," wrote a representative of Liverpool's MDHB, "London dominates the whole trade export position … I cannot reiterate too strongly that it is markets which rule the destination of goods, not dock or distributive facilities."[65]

Yet, for all these glories, there were two twentieth-century port narratives to London and Liverpool. The first was about the extraordinary infrastructures they created for world trade and flows. The second was about their stunning decline. At the end of the twentieth century the dominant feature of Liverpool was the contrast between past and present. Downtown mercantile architecture reflected the riches that had once washed through this shipping and trading center; but at the end of the century Liverpool was one of Europe's poorest big cities, and most of these buildings were no longer occupied by maritime firms, nor, in large part, companies of serious international standing. Jesse Hartley's celebrated docks had signaled the commercial power of the port but now housed museums and archives and denoted the vestigial quality of Merseyside harbor. In the late 1990s Rotterdam, Antwerp, and Hamburg were moving millions of containers; Liverpool handled 150,000. Cargo tonnage was approximately a third of Antwerp's total and just about

---

[64] Youssef Cassis, *Capitals of Capital: A History of International Financial Centres, 1780–2005* (Cambridge: Cambridge University Press, 2006), 83–84, 144, 161, 167; Cain and Hopkins, *Innovation*, 62–63, 67, 104, 127; Sassen, *Global City*; Sir Russell Kettle, *Deloitte & Co., 1845–1956* (1958; reprint, New York: Garland, 1982) as an example of overseas branches, even in accounting.

[65] MMM/MDHB/Management Files/1: Visit to Australia, 1922.

one-tenth Rotterdam's.[66] London's fate was no better. Between 1968 and 1981, all the dock systems save Tilbury closed down, with nearly all the wharfingers in between. At the start of the twenty-first century, London port was no longer a competitor for main port status, and the once inimitable installations were better known as office and residential blocks, an airport, and a venue for the swim events of the London Triathlon.

To a certain extent the angle of slide was deceptively gentle; it had begun as early as the first years of the century when White Star transferred its express line from Liverpool to Southampton. In a larger sense, however, the crisis that engulfed each port in the 1960s and 1970s and hurled them from great port status was network generated. Withdrawal from empire, the rise of new economic centers, altered trade and transport patterns, mutations in overseas trading and banking, and the decline, then disappearance, of all but a handful of Britain's most venerable shipping firms, reversed or attenuated older foreland networks. Location, which once had worked for both ports now worked against them. In London railroad interests had influenced dock building in the nineteenth century, and established the mode of linkage between port and hinterland. The changeover to motor transport in the twentieth century, absolutely critical once containerization prevailed, left London poorly equipped to move goods effectively between harbor and distribution centers.[67] Both ports were abandoned by their local network structures. Liverpool's simply faded away, metamorphosed into other business, or moved to London. The City remained a global market center, but without a clear commitment to London harbor. Hamburg, Rotterdam, and Antwerp had always been adept at building networks with the state and harnessing public money and power to their cause; in an island nation, London and Liverpool were denied national port status.

London and Liverpool therefore rose and fell with their networks. Like the three great continental ports they demonstrated how networks vaulted ports to top rank status and made them command centers of a world economy. But whereas Hamburg, Rotterdam, and Antwerp either sustained or reconfigured their networks over the course of the century, London and Liverpool's plunge from grace exposed the dispensability of even the greatest of harbors when their networks frayed, and unwound, and finally failed them.

[66] P. T. Furlong, The Mersey Docks and Harbour Company, interview with author, Liverpool, 15 July 1998; Gemeentelijk Havenbedrijf Rotterdam, *Haven in cijfers* (Rotterdam, 1997).
[67] Frank J. A. Broeze, "Paradigm of Britain: The Port of London in the 19th and 20th Centuries," in Akveld and Bruijn, *Shipping*, 72.

Le Havre and Marseille

In the early nineteenth century, no port on the northwest littoral of Europe offered more promise than Le Havre. With prosperous trade lines to the Americas, business connections to Rouen and Paris, and railroad lines east to Alsace and Germany, Le Havre was poised to become the first port of Europe.[68] By the end of the nineteenth century, however, Hamburg, Rotterdam, and Antwerp had passed Le Havre by. Marseille, then France's largest port, experienced the same, comparative drop. The third port of Europe in 1870, it fell to sixth by the turn of the century.[69] On the eve of the Second World War, the rankings had altered little, and in some categories had even deteriorated.[70] Big oil imports swelled Marseille's totals late in the century, but while Rotterdam, Hamburg, and Antwerp ranked, respectively, fourth, ninth, and tenth among the world's largest container ports, neither Marseille nor Le Havre made it into the top twenty.[71] Here then was a third trajectory that fell between that of the great North Sea ports on the one hand and the spectacular crash of British ports on the other, and that reflected the long-term limits to power when networks were bounded.

There can be no question of the importance of these harbors. Both were giant combines of basins, quays, and port business services, one oriented primarily toward the Atlantic, the other toward Africa, the Levant, and East Asia. Between 1820 and 1913, more than 2 million emigrants shipped through Le Havre,[72] the home port of the French Line. Colonists, administrators, troops, and tourists crossed to Africa, the Mediterranean, or Indochina from Marseille. But if the decline of the two was scarcely comparable to London's and Liverpool's, the lag set in early and was all but irreversible. What then kept their networks in check?

To begin with, neither port was well sited for seizing traffic from others. Both were sea links to a country less industrialized and less export driven than Britain or Germany. Le Havre counted the enormous Paris basin as its hinterland but divided this traffic with Rouen. Waterway linkages

---

[68] Vigarié, *Grands*, 177–183.
[69] Roncayolo, *L'imaginaire*, 165.
[70] Koomans, "Port," 111, 113.
[71] Gemeentelijk Havenbedrijf Rotterdam, *Haven in cijfers*, 1997; Frank Broeze, *The Globalisation of the Oceans: Containerisation from the 1950s to the Present*, Research in Maritime History 23 (St. John's, Newfoundland: International Maritime Economic History Association, 2002), 169.
[72] Legoy, *Peuple*, 274, 422.

eastward to the Rhine were poor – those 220 locks – and by the second half of the twentieth century the railroad, with only one line, had turned into one of the city's worst enemies. Both railroad and Rouen interests blocked efforts to construct additional lines.[73] Marseille's hinterland was even more restricted. Far from the production and consumer centers in northwestern Europe, the Mediterranean became a second-tier setting for global movements of goods and people. Beyond Lyon, no major industrial center fell within its orbit, and the poorly navigable Rhone was a weak competitor to the Elbe, let alone the Rhine.[74] Paulin Talabot, one of the grand system builders of the nineteenth century, envisioned Marseille as the key link in a north-south transport network to pivot, ultimately, on Suez. But Marseille's port interests fought him tooth and nail because he was an outsider – worse, a quasi-Parisian – and because they feared, correctly, his designs to transform Marseille into a transit port. Winning the battle, they lost the one opportunity to redress historical demography with infrastructure.[75]

Such resistance signaled an attenuating business spirit that filtered through to other networks. For the first two-thirds of the nineteenth century, Marseille's trading and shipping community was vibrant and explained its standing as Europe's third port.[76] Greek grain merchants,[77] home-grown traders such as Victor Régis and Charles-August Verminck (of Belgian origins), both pioneers of West African supply chains, and

[73] Backx, *Haven*, 7; Vigarié, *Grands*, 139–140, 287–288, 300–302, 319–321; Legoy, *Peuple*, 268–269.

[74] L. Pierrein, "L'Introduction," in Baratier, *Marseille*, 5–8; idem, "Du Négoce aux industries 'classiques' (1870–1940)," in ibid., 360; Borruey, *Port*, 37–40, 232; Xavier Daumalin,' *Marseille et l'Ouest africain: L'Outre-mer des industriels (1841–1956)* (Marseille: Chambre de Commerce et d'Industrie Marseille-Provence, 1992), 47; Roncayolo, *L'imaginaire*, 144–146, 161–163, 251–253; Jean Ritter, *Le Rhône* (Paris: Presses Universitaires de France, 1973), 59–68.

[75] Borruey, *Port*, 37–40, 86–90, 150–154, 172–174, 231–240, 290–291, 351–352; Roncayolo, *L'imaginaire*, 169–170; Pierrein, "Du Négoce," 361.

[76] Daumalin, *Marseille*; Hubert Bonin, *C.F.A.O. Cent ans de Compétition* (Paris: Economica, 1987); Paul Bois, *Armements marseillais. Compagnies de navigation et navires à vapeur (1831–1988)* (Marseille: Chambre de Commerce et d'Industrie de Marseille-Provence, 1988).

[77] Gelina Harlaftis, *A History of Greek-Owned Shipping: The Making of an International Tramp Fleet, 1830 to the Present Day* (London: Routledge, 1996), 7–98; P. Guiral, "Marseille de 1814 à 1870," in Baratier, *Marseille*, 314–320; Guy Durand, "Marseille, l'Indochine et la crise. De la riziculture à l'industrialization," in Marcel Coudurié et Jean-Louis Miège, *Marseille colonial face à la crise de 1929* (Marseille: Chambre de Commerce et d'Industrie Marseille-Provence, 1991), 368; Stanley Chapman, *Merchant Enterprise in Britain: From the Industrial Revolution to World War I* (Cambridge: Cambridge University Press, 1992), 155–156, 163.

local shipping houses like Cyprien Fabre radiated city influence outward. Creative urges in the city, however, began to sputter by the turn of the century. Command of markets in key soap and vegetable oil trades shifted to Britain, Rotterdam, and Hamburg. Local shipping companies took on an increasingly fossilized look. "Between 1888 and 1929 one searches in vain for a twentieth-century Verminck or a Marseillais William Lever." In the twentieth century, Marseille's overseas networks were increasingly content to remain circumscribed within captive colonial markets.[78] Certain Le Havre houses such as Raoul-Duval or Interocéanique remained enterprising well into the century.[79] But here too a flagging has been noted. "There resulted a lack of cohesion and logic, while it was Antwerp's great fortune to have had, almost unceasingly, a unity of conception and decision making in the management of its interests." Few sentences sum up more succinctly the difference between a port on the rise and a port on the slide.[80]

When forward networks atrophied there was little at the local level to pick up the slack. In France, port network systems converged on the center. Le Havre and Marseille were home ports, respectively, for France's two largest shipping companies – the Compagnie Générale Transatlantique (CGT) and the Messageries Maritimes – but both were Paris headquartered. In other countries forwarders and agents concentrated in ports. In France they were just as likely to locate in the capital, "because ships call in ports but many deals go down in Paris."[81] Stripped of a powerful local base, France's main ports thus fell back on state spending and protection, but the relationship was double edged. The state invested in harbors, but high tariffs and high port charges made French ports expensive for users. State subsidies or protected colonial markets provided assistance, especially in troubled moments, but they could also brake drives and limit

---

[78] Daumalin, *Marseille*, especially 247–261 (quoted 261); Fontainebleau, Archives nationales/Centre des archives contemporaines (CAC)/800544/3/March 1938 (Etude sur la situation de la flotte marchande desservant l'Afrique Occidentale Française); Jean-Louis Miège, "Le Maroc, Marseille et la Crise," in Coudurié and Miège, *Marseille*, 41–76; Marcel Coudurié, "Marseille colonial," in Coudurié and Miège, *Marseille*, 24–25; Roncayolo, *L'imaginaire*, 200, 226–228.

[79] Claude Malon, *Le Havre colonial de 1880 à 1960* (Mont-Saint-Aignan: Publications des Universités de Rouen et du Havre/Caen: Presses universitaires de Caen, 2006).

[80] Vigarié, *Grands*, 383–384 (quoted), 390–392; Wiedenfeld, *Nordwesteuropäischen*, 278–279.

[81] Edouard de Clebsattel, G. Feron-E. de Clebsattel S.A., interview with author, Paris, 5 March 1999. Feron-Clebsattel, too, was headquartered in Paris. See also CAC/810740/95/March 1965.

horizons.[82] Decolonization came as a serious blow to Marseille: "The end of privileged exchanges, the closing of subsidiaries, the drying up of traffic currents, the rapid surge back upon the metropole."[83]

Perhaps the most debilitating effect of Paris-centeredness was that state networks only occasionally coincided with those of the ports. Eastern shippers who preferred Antwerp were just as likely to be favored. Ultimately, the problem was that state networks were critical, but the reigning mentality in Paris was more continental than turned toward the sea.[84] Le Havre and Marseille were thus big international ports, but less so than their main port competitors. Hinterlands, business inhibitions, colonial preferences, and the preponderance of Paris kept them focused on France, curbing greater possibilities.

Ports, then, lived and died by their networks, and among Europe's main ports three network experiences predominated. Those ports with superb networks that held or reconstituted – Hamburg, Rotterdam, and Antwerp – retained top rank status over the century. Those ports with networks that were constrained early on – Le Havre, Marseille – remained great ports, but at a notch below the others. Those ports whose once exemplary networks unwound in the years of containerization – London, Liverpool – fell stunningly to second-rank status, or below. Networks were essential port mechanisms, but not just for interport competition. The network systems this section has elaborated must also be understood as the means by which ports functioned as collectors, distributors, and hence coordinators of a global economy. Ports were junctures where hinterland and foreland networks converged, and where information circulated with such intensity that ports came to act as switchboards of connections on a truly global scale. To that end we must also take into account both the gathering and dispersal of diasporic elements – the Greek trading communities of Marseille and London, the Vorwerks and Bunges who went out to Chile and Argentina – because they clarify much about the intersection of local and global within these ports. In

---

[82] Borruey, *Port*, 37–40; Legoy, *Peuple*, 273; Vigarié, *Grands*, 274, 322–323, 368, 385–387. Malon, *Le Havre*, offers valuable counter-examples, but he too acknowledges the attraction to protected markets: 73–76, 221.

[83] Coudurié, "Marseille," in Coudurié and Miège, *Marseille*, 24–25; Daumalin, *Marseille*, 293–342; Roncayolo, *L'imaginaire*, 200, 226–228; Olivesi and Pierrein, "Marseille," 451–452 (quoted); Antoine Frémont, *La French Line face à la mondialisation de l'espace maritime* (Paris: Anthropos, 1998).

[84] Vigarié, *Grands*, 156, 619; Pierrein, "Négoce," 383; de Clebsattel (interview); Jean Lerbret, Lerbret et Cie S.A.M., interview with author, Paris, 29 January 1999.

still another sense, one must keep in mind a man like Richard Holt, who
was embedded in the local culture of Liverpool, but at the same time led
an international shipping company operating across thousands of miles
of oceans, with agents in foreign stations who lived a large part of their
professional lives in distant lands. The crisscrossing of local and transnational networks, an everyday occurrence within port cities, interbred
home with cross-world orientations. Port networks may have been vital
for port survival and abundance. But they were also vital for the day-to-
day functioning of world movements and explained how main ports not
only acquired that ranking but fulfilled it.

WORLD PORTS

There remain the world ports, the feeders, gateways, and hubs across the
globe, whose linkage to Europe's main ports made a world system possible. Their range was truly extraordinary. At one end were behemoths like
New York, for a time the world's largest port. Half of the United States'
international trade sailed into or out of New York in 1915.[85] Buenos
Aires was the gateway to South America's richest and most Europeanized
culture. In 1948, eighty-three steamship lines called at the harbor.[86]
Calcutta, in the last years before the Second World War, handled 10 million tons annually, a figure that placed it ahead of Marseille, Bremen, and
Le Havre.[87] Shanghai, situated halfway between northern and southern
China, was at the intersection of all the great sea lanes of East Asia. It
had access to a watershed covering half of the Chinese interior, housed
several million people – including a large foreign contingent – and commanded approximately half of China's foreign trade before the Second
World War.[88]

   At the other end were the backwaters. Along the north Colombian
coast the small harbor of Ríohacha, a town of 5,000 inhabitants, lacked
any pier facilities. Hides carted overland by mules or wagons were carried by canoes out to the ships. The salt port of Manaure, forty miles

[85] Doig, *Empire*, 27.
[86] Rotterdam, Gemeentearchief Rotterdam (GAR)/Holland-Amerika Lijn Collection
(HAL)/Directie 952.
[87] PRO/MT 63/256.
[88] Rhoads Murphey, *Shanghai: Key to Modern China* (Cambridge: Harvard University
Press, 1953), 2–3, 45–55; Robert Y. Eng, "The Transformation of a Semi-Colonial
Port City: Shanghai," in Frank Broeze, ed., *Brides of the Sea: Asia from the 16th–20th
Centuries* (Honolulu: University of Hawaii Press, 1989), 132–133.

to the northeast, was a still smaller dot, inhabited by 200 Indians and a Colombian official. Infrastructure was nonexistent. Ships anchored four to five sea miles out. Nine "rather dilapidated" canoes brought the salt to the boat, except during the first four months of the year, when heavy swells made loading dangerous and ships were in peril of grounding.[89] Before the Second World War, most ports along the West African Coast could take lighters only, or required anchorage off the coast and canoe or small-boat transfer to the beach.[90] In the late 1940s, copra off Sangir Island north of Celebes (Sulawesi[91]) was still being loaded by thousands of people marching with huge bags on their heads to loading boats off-shore. Most unforgettable of all was the turn-of-the-century description by Captain Brown of entry into Klang (Kelang), thirteen miles up the Sungei Klang along the west Malayan coast:

In my time you rushed your ship up the stream on top of the flood tide, with par-rots screaming among the rigging, and the crocodiles lying like a guard of honour on either shore. The river was too narrow for a ship to turn. The manoeuvre, if that is not too neat a word, necessary to bring the ship's head round for the return journey, was to charge the mud bank, then, with the bow fixed, let the tide sweep the stern round, and back out. When the water was high the bow went far into the jungle amid the protesting monkeys and parrots, and the look-out men skipped and squeaked as hornets' nets, dislodged from the trees, fell on the deck.[92]

Yet all these far sides were integrated one way or another into global networks, whether by coastal carriage to Barranquilla or Santa Marta for transshipment to New York and Hamburg (Ríohacha's hides), or transfer to oceangoing vessels farther out in the bay (Sangir's copra). Even tiny Manaure shipped out roughly 300,000 sacks of salt a year in the early 1930s.

It is difficult to miss the imperial character to many of these ports, or that it was Europeans who interlocked them into a system on a global scale. The result was connectedness, but largely in Western-oriented ways. Ports that had once straddled major trade routes but were off the European sea lanes turned into backwaters. Others became hubs, gate-ways, or transshipment points of Western production and consumption.[93]

---

[89] HAPAG/3127/5, 8 December 1931.

[90] Davies, *Trade Makers*, 301–303.

[91] Where place-names have changed in ways that may be uncertain, the current name will hereafter be placed in parenthesis.

[92] Quoted in K. G. Tregonning, *Home Port Singapore: A History of Straits Steamship Company Limited, 1890–1965* (Singapore: Oxford University Press, 1967), 31.

[93] Frank Broeze, "The Ports and Ports Systems of the Asian Seas: An Overview with Historical Perspective from c. 1750," in *Puertos y sistemas portuarios (siglos XVI–XX): Actas del*

A good number were structured for one big commodity export: Santos for coffee, the later oil ports in the Middle East, or Rangoon, an insignificant port in the mid-nineteenth century, but the outlet for huge rice exports in the twentieth. In 1926 and 1927, more than 3,000 vessels moved through the Rangoon harbor.[94] On the other hand, non-Westerners learned how to exploit the system, and its routes, for their own ends.[95] Moreover, without preexistent networks, the European ones would have been incomplete. Singapore presents a fine example of how all these things came together in the overseas counterpart to Liverpool or Antwerp: a global hub, imperial in construction but transnational in practice, no less diasporic in its mode of collection, and where an equivalent tripartite set of networks explained its ability to tie Southeast Asia into a worldwide system of flows.

Singapore

Located on the southern portal of the Straits of Malacca, astride the sea channel between South and East Asia, Singapore was destined for superior port status. Only the Sunda Straits offered an alternative corridor, but this passage was more distant from the great coaling station of Colombo and uncompetitive once the Suez Canal opened east-west traffic to coal-burning steamships. At the confluence of regional and global exchange, Singapore enjoyed three other assets: a fine natural harbor, an administratively free harbor, and British imperial backing as the outpost between the Indian Ocean and the South China Sea. Yet the stupendous potential that Stamford Raffles first identified in 1819, when he acquired control of the island, was only realized through a fourth: Singapore's networks, both Chinese and European, and their intersection within the city.[96]

The core of maritime commerce in Singapore was the resident Chinese business community and its control of trade throughout Southeast Asia. Singapore lay just off the Malay peninsula, and for 150 years it was under British rule, but massive immigration made it into a Chinese city. Three-quarters of Singapore's population in the twentieth century

---

Coloquio International el sistema portuario español, Madrid, 19–21 October 1995, Madrid: 1996, 106–110.

[94] London, Guildhall Library (Guildhall)/Steel Brothers/MS 29, 557/Brief History of the Company.

[95] Markovits, *Global*; Sugihara, *Japan, China*, 9–10.

[96] W. G. Huff, *The Economic Growth of Singapore: Trade and Development in the Twentieth Century* (Cambridge: Cambridge University Press, 1994), 8.

were of Chinese origin, "the world's biggest concentration of overseas Chinese."[97] Their commercial power lay in their numbers but also in the spread of compatriot communities to Burma, Malaya, Siam, the Dutch East Indies, Sarawak, North Borneo, and Indochina. Many migrated in the nineteenth century to work the tin mines or newly founded plantations. Others, of longer standing, developed traditions as traders or farmers of export crops.[98] Whatever their origins, they were linked by Singapore-based merchant networks that encompassed the region and made Singapore island the central market of Southeast Asia.

Trading relations with the Dutch East Indies (DEI) reveal the ethnic, credit, and shipping ties through which this occurred. On the Borneo coast, Singapore branch houses advanced credit to local traders and shipped the pepper, gambier, sago, copra, rubber (by the 1920s), and upriver forest products such as rattan and birds' nests they collected for sale in Singapore. On the east coast of Sumatra, personal or financial ties bound Chinese exporters to Singapore markets, and nearly all interisland commerce, save large Deli plantation production, moved through Singapore. Makassar, for centuries a regional transshipment center for the eastern spice islands, but where a large Chinese merchant class again traded for the account of Singapore firms, fell equally within Singapore's orbit at the turn of the century. Even Arab and Malay merchants active in Makassar traded through Singapore channels.

The linchpin that held these chains together was the Chinese shipping fleet based in Singapore. Near the turn of the century there were perhaps as many as fifty companies active throughout the East Indies, collectively nicknamed the "mosquito fleet" because their merchant ships swarmed over the entire archipelago. Most were shoestring operations with low costs and good connections. Many were formed as joint shipping and trading ventures with merchants in Singapore. Traveling with the ships was a *tjintjoe*, or loading clerk, who functioned as the go-between with local traders. The *tjintjoe* knew his customers personally, conferred with them regularly, and, most important, lent them money. These mobile, credit-bearing intermediaries were the wheel-greasers of interisland trade and bound shippers and importers to their Singapore networks. Joining them were some sizable undertakings, like Wee Bin & Co., shipowner, trader, and merchant banker. Wee Bin ships by the 1890s covered Indonesian

---

[97] Huff, *Economic*, 24–25 (quoted); C. M. Turnbull, *A History of Singapore, 1819–1988*, 2nd ed. (Singapore: Oxford University Press, 1989), 92, 95.
[98] Rajeswary Ampalavanar Brown, *Capital and Entrepreneurship in South-East Asia* (New York: St. Martin's Press, 1994), 13–20.

waters and sailed between the Straits and China. It too developed close
relations with local traders and shopkeepers or maintained agents, like
the Tiong Tjioe on Bali, who operated the only local cattle boats and was
well positioned to deliver export trade.

So thoroughly was archipelago trade centered on Singapore that
when the Dutch feeder line – the Koninklijke Paketvaart Maatschappij
(KPM) – was created for the purpose of concentrating East Indies traffic
on East Indies ports, the KPM recognized no alternative than to organize
its first routes largely through the British port colony. By the interwar
years, KPM efforts to redirect trade to Dutch colonial ports shook loose a
fair portion of the Chinese traffic. But what was lost was more than made
up by rubber production in Malaya and Sumatra, or by Chinese networks duplicated throughout the rest of the region. A very large part of
the tropical commodity commerce of Southeast Asia, excepting European
plantation output, passed through the hands of Singapore Chinese merchants, while Singapore lodging–house keepers and shipping agents were
essential intermediaries in the flow of immigrant Chinese to Malaya. The
Ho Hong Steamship Company, Wee Bin's successor by the early twentieth
century, transported rice from Burma on the outward run and coolies on
the return. Eventually British and Dutch shipping prevailed; but in the
1930s, of nine coastal shipping services run out of Singapore, six were
Chinese.[99]

With the 1920s, rubber trading and export sustained Singapore's
role as a regional hub. Plantation cultivation came to be dominated by
Europeans, but the marketing of smallholder production, or "native rubber," widespread in Indonesia, Siam, and Sarawak, was managed primarily through Singapore Chinese networks. Clan, kin, and credit relations,
especially in the DEI, again contributed to making Singapore the shipping
point of 40 percent of the world's rubber exports in the interwar years
and the largest rubber milling site in the world. Of five rubber "magnates" in the city, four were from the same village or locale in Fukien

[99] M. G. De Boer and J. C. Westermann, *Een halve eeuw paketvaart, 1891–1941* (Amsterdam:
Koninklijke Paketvaart-Maatschappij, 1941), 58, 221–223, 292–293, 314–344; J. N. F.
M. à Campo, *Koninklijke Paketvaart Maatschappij. Stoomvaart en staatsvorming in de
Indonesische archipel, 1888–1914* (Hilversum: Verloren, 1992), 172–185, 359–379;
Huff, *Economic*, 24–25 (quoted), 63–66, 84, 103, 154–156, 225; G. C. Allen and Audrey
G. Donnithorne, *Western Enterprise in Indonesia and Malaya: A Study in Economic
Development* (1954; reprint, New York, Augustus Kelley, 1968), 243–244; Tregonning,
Home, 33, 63–68, 123–130, 138, 150; Peter Pugh et al., *Great Enterprise: A History
of Harrisons & Crosfield*, ed. Guy Nickalls (Harrisons & Crosfield, 1990), 165–168;
Sugihara, *Japan, China*, 259–260.

province, and three got their start working for the fourth, Tan Kah Kee. The city thus grew on and prospered from the broad-based networks Singapore's Chinese excelled in creating. Such business relations spun out of the port were infectious among its Asian communities. Singapore was an eastern hub for Sindhi merchant networks. Islamic intellectual networks throughout the region centered on Singapore. The city was headquarters for Japanese trade with Siam and Indonesia. Nothing, however, compared to the power of Chinese business networks, except those the Europeans constructed.[100]

Chinese networks were Singapore's link to its hinterland, but the overseas connections that turned Singapore into a world port were the work of Europeans. Although always a small minority – the European population in 1871 was fewer than a thousand and in 1912 approximately 5,700 in a city of more than 300,000 inhabitants – Europeans quickly gravitated to Singapore as their shipping, trading, and banking base in Southeast Asia.[101] Two of Singapore's three principal exports – tin and petroleum – were firmly in the hands of European or American producers and merchants by the early twentieth century. Westerners shared in the production of the third, rubber, and completely controlled its overseas marketing until the 1930s. As the rubber business magnified, dealer and broker networks extended among Singapore, London (the world's largest rubber market until Singapore surpassed it in the 1940s), and the United States (the world's largest rubber consumer).[102]

European agency and shipping houses were at the heart of these developments. The agencies began as general merchants but expanded into rubber trading, estate flotation, and estate management. Big expatriate houses such as Bousteads and Guthries, or the German firm Behn, Meyer, had partnerships or branch establishments in London and Hamburg. The agencies made fortunes from rubber, but their position in Singapore was enhanced by their ship agency work for the European shipping companies that tied Singapore to distant ports and gave it its raison d'être as a global hub. Nearly every major liner company transiting eastern waters

[100] Huff, *Economic*, 20–21, 76–79, 96, 180, 190–195, 204–234, 265; Austin Coates, *The Commerce in Rubber: The First 250 Years* (Singapore: Oxford University Press, 1987), 171–181; Markovits, *Global*, 148–149; Mary Byrne McDonnell, "Patterns of Muslim Pilgrimage from Malaysia, 1885–1985," in Dale F. Eickelman and James Piscatori, eds., *Muslim Travellers, Pilgrimage, Migration, and the Religious Imagination* (Berkeley: University of California Press, 1990), 122.
[101] Emil Helfferich, *Behn, Meyer & Co. – Arnold Otto Meyer*, 2 vols. (Hamburg: Hans Christians Verlag, 1957–1967), I, 28; II, 36.
[102] Coates, *Commerce*, 188–190, 286, 337; Huff, *Economic*, 195–201.

called at Singapore; more than fifty lines put in there regularly in the 1920s. Like Antwerp, the sheer availability of connections and scheduled sailings drained passengers and freight into the port. Ship tonnage figures in 1910 were 7 million, 16 million in 1929, and 17 million in 1937.[103]

European shipping effects in the region were potentially double edged. The KPM succeeded in detaching large chunks of the East Indies archipelago from Singapore's sphere of influence. But the Straits Steamship Company (SSC), founded in 1890, also shows how European packet shipping focused maritime networks on Singapore. SSC services extended along the Malaya coasts and to Burma, Sumatra, Thailand, and Sabah and Sarawak on Borneo island. All routes concentrated on Singapore, where the company was headquartered. Its intercoastal line to Sabah, or North Borneo, was a microcosm of how its network operated. Sabah's shore villages and upriver settlements completely depended on small coastal vessels or riverboats to trade with each other or with the nearby Sulu Archipelago. The largest local operator was the Sabah Steamship Company, founded by Harry Pfort, a former Blue Funnel ship captain. Regularly scheduled Sabah Steamship boats, stationed in the port cities of Sandakan or Labuan, plied coastal waters or steamed up the Kinabatangan River carrying labor and supplies to tobacco estates in the interior and bringing down tobacco, rattan, and birds' nests for transshipment to Singapore. A branch line, the South Philippines Steamship Company, added trade routes to Jolo, Puerto Princesa, and Zamboanga in the southern Philippines. Thus the interisland service operated in the following manner: SSC ships would steam across to Sandakan and arrive on Saturday afternoons with passengers and supplies. These would then transfer to the small vessels of the Sabah Steamship Company on their Monday sailings south along the coast or their fortnightly routes north to Kudat, Jesselton, and Labuan or over to Jolo and Zamboanga. On their return they would collect timber, tobacco, hemp, rubber, and other tropical produce in Sandakan for transshipment on the next SSC boat's homeward voyage to Singapore. In this way, a feeder chain was set into motion. The little steamers of the Sabah Steamship Company (taken over by the SSC in 1926), fed commodity production in the North Borneo-Sulu range to the slightly larger SSC ships. SSC ships in turn fed their cargo to the big overseas liners in Singapore, which then transported it to the main ports

[103] *Bousteads* (n.p., n.d.); Helfferich, *Behn*; Jones, *Merchants*, 69–70; Pugh, *Great*, 83–87, 165–168; Huff, *Economic*, 102, 120–121, 131–137, 182–187, 201, 245; Coates, *Commerce*, 113–121, 175–176; NMM/P & O/4/57/Agents' Reports/Singapore, 31 July 1937.

of America and Europe, where further hinterland connections completed the linkage with producers and consumers. Passengers traveled along the same chain, and to the south, on Sarawak, the SSC worked the same arrangements through the Chinese-run Sarawak Steamship Company, which the SSC also subsumed into its group in 1931.[104]

We think of the SSC as a British Company. It was closely tied to Holts (or Blue Funnel) in Liverpool, and after the First World War, Mansfields, Holts' Singapore agents, managed the firm. But the Straits Steamship Company was founded by a Dutchman, Theodore Cornelis Bogaardt, in conjunction with Chinese investors and partners to gain entrée to Chinese tin-mining interests. Three members of the board were Straits Chinese, and company networks were equally transnational, with European, Chinese, or in some instances Malay trading firms selected to represent it at ports of call because of their superior contacts with local producers and shippers. All of this is a reminder that Singapore's force lay in the intersection of its two networks. European shipping companies and trading houses relied on Chinese to distribute the manufactures they imported and to feed in a large portion of the commodities they exported. Chinese business networks predominated because in Singapore they had access to European imports and overseas shipping connections.[105] At the juncture emerged a third set – local networks – through the exchanges that transpired between Europeans and Chinese. The Chinese Produce Exchange was founded in 1911 for the express purpose of bringing the two business communities together. Significantly, the most successful by far of all the Chinese rubber magnates was Lee Kong Chian, who was shrewd and talented enough to marry Tan Kah Kee's daughter, but whose real power derived from his westernized training as a civil engineer and his ease in negotiating both Chinese and European (and then also Japanese) business circles. Not surprisingly, Harrisons & Crosfield, another big trading house, still maintained a comprador as late as the post–World War II years, so thick was the trading between the two networks and the dependency of Europeans on Chinese commodity sources.[106]

In the fifty years following the Second World War, Singapore underwent substantial changes. Decolonization, the departure of agency houses, and regional political turmoil disrupted older mercantile patterns, while rubber exports suffered from synthetic production abroad. The city's

---

[104] Tregonning, *Home*.
[105] Ibid., 6–17; Huff, *Economic*, 93–96, 258–259; De Boer and Westermann, *Eeuw*, 315.
[106] Huff, *Economic*, 98, 221–222; Pugh, *Great*, 165–168; De Boer and Westermann, *Eeuw*, 319–320; Coates, *Commerce*, 350–354; Meuleau, *Pionniers*, 292.

economic identity metamorphosed, first into a production site for multinational firms and then as a financial and transport services center. What
stands out, however, is how older network relations – close ties to the U.S.
market, traditions as a market center, and deep penetration of Indonesian
markets (still the source of much rubber handled in Singapore and of the
city's huge spice and pepper trade) – could contribute to Singapore's postwar transition or continued affluence from commodity traffics. Similarly,
the expansion of world commerce, containerization's concentration on
hub and spoke ports, the growth in Asian economies, and the availability
of bunker fuel from Singapore's refinery industry, converted Singapore's
old location and entrepot advantages into leverage for the future. As the
century came to a close, Singapore harbor vied for the rank of world's
largest port in either containers or overall cargo handled, and Singapore
remained a network hub for the entire region.[107]

What made busy ports busy, then, returns us to where this chapter began:
the networks and networking skills that propelled them into main port
status. Ports in the twentieth century were formidable material creations.
But their true architects were the network builders who combined continental and global reach with home identification, and thus, at either level,
engineered their ability to function within a world system. Machinery,
infrastructure, and technique were all important, but a transnational
community of interests counted still more in processing the incessant
flows on which sophisticated economies depended. Yet ports could not
do this alone. Often the first line of action when a ship entered a harbor required the initiatives of shipping lines and their agents. How ports
worked, therefore, as world nodes also hinged on what shipping companies did, just as all of port history fused into the history of shipping and
its networks.

---

[107] Gemeentelijk Havenbedrijf Rotterdam, *Haven in cijfers*; Huff, *Economic*; Coates,
Commerce.

2

Shipping

Ports were nothing without ships, and world ports only integrated into a global system when shipping chains tied them together. From the beginning of recorded history people and goods had traveled by ships, but millennia later, in the twentieth century, that carriage was routinely transoceanic and, moreover, inexpensive, comparatively efficient, finely patterned, and increasingly regular. Even when air travel eliminated surface passage, 90 percent of world commerce continued to cross the seas by ship.[1] Twice in modern times shipping revolutionized world transport and trade in ways that knit the world more closely together. The second of these, containerization, occurred merely a half century ago and rewrote, in part, the meaning of globalization. The first, conversion from sail to steam, dated back two centuries, but it, too, quickened global connectedness with effects that carried into the twentieth century.

The steamship brought to ocean carriage the same revolutionary possibilities railroads introduced on land at approximately the same time: regular, safer, all-weather, rapid, and increasingly lower-cost transport across vast bodies of water. Linked together – the first rail lines often converged on ports – the two created a global infrastructure for high volume circulation of people and goods between any two points. Abetted by the Suez Canal, which cut steaming time while increasing access to bunkering ports, the steamship all but swept the commercial sailboat from the seas. In the half century following its widespread adoption – that is, from

---

[1] Hartmut Rübner, *Konzentration und Krise der deutschen Schiffahrt. Maritime Wirtschaft und Politik im Kaiserreich, in der Weimarer Republik und im Nationalsozialismus* (Bremen: H. M. Hauschild, 2005), 12.

the mid-nineteenth century until 1914 – ocean freight rates fell dramatically while the value of world trade increased nearly tenfold. After that, the motor ship, powered by diesel fuel, increased shipping efficiency still further, but although the source of power had changed, this was but an advance on what the steamship had wrought.[2]

Steam however was only a means. Business organization converted it into an instrument of global interconnectedness. Shipping men quickly perceived the advantages over sail and created the liner company, a shipping firm that sailed as a common carrier according to fixed schedules rather than as a tramp in search of single voyage opportunities. Nearly all the great names in shipping before containerization – Cunard, Holt, P & O, HAPAG, Norddeutscher Lloyd, Compagnie Générale Transatlantique, Holland Amerika, and so on – were liner companies that dated from the age of steam. What exporters wanted, as late into the steam age as the 1920s, "is ships which *sail on time and keep to their schedules* … All exporters expect an increase in shipments as soon as a regular direct service is started."[3]

Liner companies in turn coordinated global exchange at completely new levels. Many were sizable enterprises. Medium-sized companies such as the Rotterdamsche Lloyd or Amsterdam's Stoomvaart Maatschappij "Nederland" (SMN) ran several dozen ships each with fleet tonnages roughly between 250,000 and 300,000 tons grt on the eve of the Second World War.[4] In the late 1920s France's CGT (100 ships), Japan's NYK (92 ships), and Britain's Holts (81 ships) were all about a half million tons, or slightly larger; Cunard (100 ships) and Ellerman (219 ships), after acquisitions, were more than a million tons; P & O (438 ships) was well over 2 million tons.[5] Far more than all previous modes of sailing, these liner firms required transoceanic organizations. Operating ships on fixed schedules, sailing empty or full, they set up agents in every port of

[2] C. Ernest Fayle, *A Short History of the World's Shipping Industry* (London: Allen & Unwin, 1933), 230, 239–240, 247–248; Daniel R. Headrick, *The Tools of Empire: Technology and European Imperialism in the Nineteenth Century* (New York: Oxford University Press, 1981), 142–148; Max E. Fletcher, "The Suez Canal and World Shipping, 1869–1914," *The Journal of Economic History* 18 (1958): 556–573; Boyce, *Information*, 14–19.

[3] GAR/Rotterdamsche Lloyd Collection (Lloyd) 2/S2016/JCJL Reisrapport, 28–29 April 1925.

[4] F. W. G. Leeman, *Van barkschip tot 'Willem Ruys'. 120 jaar zeevaart* (Rotterdam: Willem Ruys & Zonen, 1961), 231; Daniel Delprat, *De reeder schrijft zijn journaal. Herinneringen van Mr. D. A. Delprat* ('s Gravenhage: Martinus Nijhoff, 1983), 15, 206; C. Vermey, "Tramp Shipping," in Schraver, *Rotterdam*, 162–163.

[5] Rübner, *Konzentration*, 179–180.

call to turn around vessels and to canvas for traffic. These organizations moreover were extraordinarily elastic. Agents built out connections to shippers, port authorities, customs officials, and inland transport companies. If expatriate trading companies, they possessed broad connections up-country or across a region. Liberally networked, they came to enjoy access to the world's most valuable commodity: information. In their totality liner companies thus came to function as transnational switching mechanisms for moving anything point-to-point around the world. Because they were expensive to sustain, liner services also placed demands on investment in port facilities and inland transport. They gravitated to ports that met their needs, thereby setting the grids of deep-sea transport but also amplifying world infrastructure.

Practically all liner companies started with the passenger trades; this was the first big business for which speed and regularity really mattered. Over time, they increasingly became freight carriers, particularly once migration flows slackened in the twentieth century. But in both spheres they set in motion dynamics – settler and labor migrations, the harvesting and mining of tropical commodities, supplies to each, and all in high volumes[6] – that again furthered global connectedness. It was not simply the consequence that the size of world trade and intercourse magnified. The content of daily life in Western societies changed as these came to depend on steady massive flows of grain, metals, rubber, mineral and vegetable oil, meat, and practically any other consumable commodity.[7]

Meanwhile, the combination of liners and tramps intensified the interdependence of world commerce. Food supplies offer just one example. At basic levels, grain grown in North America or Argentina shipped to European ports, and rice grown in Burma and Indochina shipped to rice-consuming regions such as India. None of these commodities, however, traveled without the outward flow of trampers lugging coal from producing regions (for instance, Wales) to coal-hungry or bunkering ports. In addition, tramp steamers transported nitrates from Chile to Egypt, where wheat, corn, and rice were grown for home consumption but also for export to other regions in the Middle East. Australia imported phosphates from South Pacific islands a thousand miles distant, and shipped the grain it produced to Indian Ocean or more distant ports.[8] Most grain traveled in bulk, but commodities such as sugar, coffee, and flour were

[6] See Introduction.
[7] Fayle, *Short*, 251.
[8] C. B. A. Behrens, *Merchant Shipping and the Demands of War* (London: Her Majesty's Stationery Office, 1955), 230, 239.

shipped in gunnysacks woven on the Indian subcontinent and then carried on regularly scheduled liners to the Caribbean, Brazil, Argentina, or Java for the next wave of transport to consumers in the West.

This was not yet the global sourcing of the late twentieth century. Traffic lines remained largely Eurocentric and only a handful of shipping companies were more than one- or two-ocean operators. The British merchant marine, far and away the most powerful in 1914, with 8,587 steamships, nearly 19,000,000 tons grt, and comprehending two-fifths of world tonnage,[9] sailed in every trade – North America, Latin America and the West Indies, the Mediterranean, Africa, and east of Suez – but probably no line, save tramps, was in all of them. It was in their totality, or the sum of their routes, inclusive of all other seafaring nations, that steamship lines created a global transport net.

The reciprocity between shipping and empire also remained highly pronounced. The string of ports that came to monopolize shipping east of Suez consisted of Japanese harbors plus those of the British, Dutch, and French empires. Empires subsidized steamship lines, enlarged their harbors, and fattened their traffics. Liner companies routinized colonial lines of communication, begot settler communities, and drove non-European shipping from all but the short seas. The extensive role of Dutch shipping in these waters typified the imperial connection. The two trunk lines, the Rotterdamsche Lloyd and SMN, collectively known as the Dutch Mails, spawned a series of daughter or affiliated companies pivoted on Batavia: the interisland KPM, the Java-Bengal Line, and the Java-China-Japan Line (JCJL). When the First World War interrupted transit traffic via the Netherlands to America, they set up the Java-New York Line (JNL) and, to the West Coast, the Java-Pacific Line (JPL). After the war, and profiting from the absence of German shipping, the Dutch established more lines under the umbrella of what was known as the Vereenigde Nederlandsche Scheepvaartmaatschappij, or VNS. All were embedded within imperial structures. The Rotterdamsche Lloyd conferred its East Indies agency work to the largest trading company in the colony. Its clientele list read like a compendium of trading and commodity production in Indonesia. Mails' ships and the KPM carried Dutch colonial administrators, traders, and planters between the various East Indies islands and the mother country. Together with Liverpool's Holts they operated the Kongsi Tiga, the premier pilgrim transport company from Southeast Asia to the

---

[9] C. Ernest Fayle, *The War and the Shipping Industry* (London: Humphrey Milford/Oxford University Press, 1927), 2–4.

Hajj.[10] At regional levels, the Mails and their spin-offs tied the archipelago into an economic and administrative unit and validated the economic development of the colony. The companies in turn became powerful home and colonial enterprises. Effectively the two histories marched in tandem. The steamship became a vehicle of penetration, conquest, and communication, and in routinizing travel to the tropics it altered the very nature of the colony. By reducing the meaning of the "remote," it created the means by which people in one part of the planet had their lives transformed by the desires or needs of people in another part, thousands of miles away. But Dutch steamships and their services also abetted the spread of new ideologies, pan-Islam and communism, and thereby helped undermine imperial rule, including their own base of operations. In multiple ways the imperial bond ran very deep.

Yet, it did not embrace all of global shipping. The North Atlantic remained the most heavily contested route in the first half of the century. Even in imperial seas, shipping history was as much about networks and company connections to promote services and trades as it was about the construction or deconstruction of colonialism. In 1923, P & O, after mergers and acquisitions with the British India Company, the New Zealand Shipping Company, the Strick Line to the Persian Gulf, and several others, was running hundreds of ships, nearly all east of Suez in one manner or another, which made it the world's premier imperial steamship company.[11] Liners such as the *Viceroy of India*, built in the 1920s, served practically as official transport for imperial travel. The steamers of British India (BI) sailed Indian Ocean trunk lines, but also coastal routes or across to tiny ports in the Persian Gulf whose names "can only be found in a good atlas," carrying coolie laborers, pilgrims, troops to fight Britain's small imperial wars, and animals (151,267 in 1927).[12] BI, however, also brought into P & O its founder and manager, Mackinnon Mackenzie, which came to function as "the nerve centre of the P & O's and the BI's operations overseas."[13] Mackinnon Mackenzie's power and success emanated from its networks. Agencies spread P & O/BI influence and traffic throughout the Indian Ocean. Holts' Shanghai agents in the 1920s noted that Mackinnon's agency in Colombo was so

[10] Rotterdamsche Lloyd activities can be traced across their large archives in the GAR.
[11] Jones, *Trade*, 68, 98, 102, 149–150; David Howarth and Stephen Howarth, *The Story of P & O*, rev. ed. (London: Weidenfeld and Nicholson, 1994), 124.
[12] George Blake, *B. I. Centenary 1856–1956* (London: Collins, 1956) 99–106 (quoted 102), 179; NMM/P & O/4/47/Agents' Reports/1927 Statistics.
[13] Jones, *Trade*, 113. On Mackinnon Mackenzie, see Introduction.

powerful that nearly all transshipments through Hong Kong were sent
on P & O rather than Blue Funnel ships.[14] Its East Africa affiliate, Smith
Mackenzie, did business for BI with imperial mining firms, but it also
built up trade with local houses such as Shah and Company, brokers and
commission agents in Kampala, or Matrudas Kalida, who owned several sisal estates and was a major shipper on BI freighters out of Lindi.[15]
Where shipping clients proved difficult, interhouse networks within the
larger Mackinnon Mackenzie group offered ways of creating alternative
streams of traffic.[16]

The imperial focus does get right the primacy of Europeans. But the
underlying factor to world flows was their organization by shipping companies. Shipping lines exploited opportunities but they also unfettered and
orchestrated them. The history of global shipping therefore returns to the
basics of the steamship revolution: how business organization converted
technology into an instrument of global interconnectedness. Behind that
conversion were two operative realities. The first was that global shipping rested on the networks that shipping companies constructed. The
network relationship was essentially inbred, even incestuous. Not only
could shipping companies not function without representatives and connections in foreign ports, but many lines were in fact established with the
participation, often the leadership, of home ship agents or trading houses,
which then took up the agency work. Liner companies consequently were
hardwired to build, sustain, expand, and operate through their networks.
The byproduct was the enlargement of world shipping grids and a solder-
ing of the local to the global.

The second was the exponential power of shipping expertise, which
was braided into maritime culture. Alan Bott, who spent forty years with
P & O, his last twenty as director for Australia/New Zealand P & O
and chairman of all conferences concerned with New Zealand, Australia,
and South Africa, displayed supreme levels of confidence when discussing
scheduling, commodities, or fleet requirements. He too had been hardwired for the role. The son of a shipping man, he read history at Oxford,
but joined P & O through family contacts and spent his first five years

---

[14] London/School of Oriental and African Studies/John Swire and Sons Ltd Papers (SOAS)/
JSS II 2/5/Box 41/11 October 1926.
[15] Guildhall/Smith Mackenzie & Co. Ltd/MS 28,124/Managing Director's Report on His
Visit to East Africa, 1938; Jones, *Two*, 113, 116.
[16] NMM/BIS [British India Steam]/10/8/Travel Report, January–February 1958; NMM/
BIS/10/10/Travel Report, September–October 1959; NMM/BIS/10/13/Travel Report,
January–February, 10 March, 3 July 1961.

with the firm in various London-based departments learning the basics, before setting out for Australia and New Zealand to learn all the ports, some fifty in all:

And I went around looking at them all seeing the country, seeing the cargoes, meeting the farmers, meeting the producers so that you knew the business. We're only carriers, but if you do know about the man's business you will be much more sympathetic or tough or whatever you like.... You went out and met the hides men, and the skins men, and the meat men, the butter men and all that ... we were canvassing.[17]

Merchant shipping ran on organizations, but organizations ran on knowledge of logistics, of commodities, of ports, of the right people to get things done, or of simply how to load a ship in time. In two world wars, shipping men applied their experience in running global transport chains to keeping sea lanes charged for Allied victory. The rest of the time, they simply made it possible to move millions of passengers and hundreds of millions of tons of cargo all around the world as their matter-of-fact task for the day. Globalization, at its nub, moved through shipping networks and the expertise to run them.

LOCAL TO GLOBAL

Fleet Histories

Every company history tells a larger story. The history of HAPAG, founded in 1847 and the world's largest shipping company before 1914, was about many things: the emerging power of German shipping on the seas, the encroaching concentration of big shipping lines, annihilation in two world wars and rebirth after each, how world shipping services were created, or about how home ports gave birth to great and enduring shipping companies. But mostly it was about how shipping companies were such superb globalizers because their own networks spun outward across the world, but also recoiled homeward to local connections.

This was truly a world company. In possession of a fleet of more than a million tons grt in 1914, back up to 900,000 tons by the late 1920s, despite the ruination of the First World War, HAPAG was one of the few steamship lines to call at all continents in the first half of the twentieth century. But its globalism existed in more than its routes. Wherever it

---

[17] Alan Bott, New Zealand Shipping Company, interview with author, Milford, 16 September 1998.

went, a string of foreign agents attended its ships – Wambersie & Zoon in Rotterdam, Sudden & Christensen in Seattle, Juan H. Krüger in Ecuador, the Swiss Volkart Brothers in India, Poppe, Schunhoff & Guttery in Capetown, Gilchrist Watt & Sanderson in Sydney – to make HAPAG a truly transnational firm.[18] These were, moreover, only the tip of the iceberg. A business trip two HAPAG executives – Marius Böger and J. H. F. Loepthien – made to the United States in 1928 exposes the greater depths of network connections. In New York Böger and Loepthien visited commodity exchanges and pursued an incessant round of meetings with importers, exporters, department-store buyers, customs brokers, freight forwarders, and custom-house officials. In Philadelphia and Baltimore they visited ports and lunched with Pennsylvania Railroad officials, whose control over through freight, shipping, port traffic, and even port real estate made them powerful people to know. Traveling west, Böger, vice chairman of HAPAG's management board, continued to visit harbors and exchanges and call on current or potential shippers. Arriving at the San Francisco Chamber of Commerce, Böger was invited to attend a working luncheon on cold-storage facilities in the harbor. Seizing on the occasion, Böger worked the room, making the acquaintance of the chamber's foreign trade manager, the manager of United Fruit Company, the traffic manager of the Admiral Line (a Pacific Coast shipping company), the head of a harbor tugboat company, and the foreign trade manager of the Southern Pacific. Two days later, the chamber of commerce arranged a breakfast in Böger's honor, presided over by the president of its Foreign Trade Committee. "I had," Böger wrote in his report, "the opportunity to know the following people," among whom figured representatives of Standard Oil, Union Oil, the Paraffine Company, Douglas Fir Exploitation and Export Company, Western Pacific, the Southern Pacific, and various steamship lines. In Chicago, Böger lunched at the Bismarck Hotel in the company of Armour's vice president in charge of exports and its general traffic manager, Swift's vice president for foreign sales, and other foreign shippers.[19] On a similar trip a decade later to the west coast of South America, another director, A. Stephenson, began to piece together a network of agents, travel bureaus, railroad executives, and government officials to lay the groundwork for tourist travel.[20]

---

[18] HAPAG/397, 2988, 67, 1264, 401, 2805, 3127. The list is based primarily on interwar representations.
[19] HAPAG/1263; ibid., 1264.
[20] HAPAG/444.

This intensely global firm was, however, no less an intensely local one, in which close-knit ties among home shipping, agency, and trading houses were an abiding source of identity and power. Abroad it was just as ready to fasten its global expansion, where it could, to Hamburg merchant firms, many with impeccable Hamburg pedigrees – the Vorwerks in Chile, Theodor Wille in Brazil, Behn, Meyer in the Straits, or Richard Eversbusch, the German consul in Mexico City – all of whom received overseas agency assignments. HAPAG supplied the transportation network; the merchants reciprocated with trading connections between home port Hamburg and world markets. At home, HAPAG was Hamburg's flagship company, and a city institution. At the turn of the century, nearly a quarter of the port of Hamburg concerned HAPAG operations.[21] Company headquarters, smack on the Inner Alster, occupied – and continue to occupy – one of the commanding buildings of the city center. Embedded in Hamburg and economically and psychologically committed to it, HAPAG worked hard to bring in port business. It invested heavily in the largest transport company operating on the Elbe and Oder. It hammered out agreements and arrangements with Baltic feeder lines, and it established freight departments in inland German cities.[22] It networked abroad for imports and exports shipped through Hamburg. Engaged in a struggle for dominance with its archrival Norddeutscher Lloyd – the two heavyweights stalked each other around the globe – its high-seas contention simply projected globally older traditions of city rivalry.[23] When in the mid-1920s a union was proposed between the two companies, but the NDL insisted on traffic parity for Bremen as a condition, HAPAG's Wilhelm Cuno responded that "no prize, not even collaboration, was great enough to sacrifice Hamburg interests in favor of Herr Glässel's demand for Bremen's interests."[24] But all this is what its creators, mostly Hamburg men, had intended it to do, even if HAPAG must have exceeded their wildest dreams.

If the power of shipping was thus its routine capacity for bringing together local and global, that consequence flowed from each company's

[21] Susanne Wiborg and Klaus Wiborg, *1847–1997. Unser Feld is die Welt. 150 Jahre Hapag-Lloyd* (Hamburg: Hapag-Lloyd AG, 1997), 126–127.

[22] Heinrich Meyer, *Hamburg als Güterumschlagsplatz vor und nach dem Kriege* (Hamburg: Schroedter & Hauer, 1930), 49–51; Wendemuth and Böttcher, *Port*, 9, 244–245; Backx, *Haven*, 31.

[23] Frank Broeze, "Albert Ballin, The Hamburg-Bremen Rivalry and the Dynamics of the Conference System," *International Journal of Maritime History* 3 (June 1991): 4.

[24] Wiborg and Wiborg, *Unser*, 231.

own balancing act between the two. Fleet histories were complex ones in which city, nation, and world all took part. Hamburg's second most celebrated shipping line, the Hamburg Süd Dampfschiffahrts-Gesellschaft (nearly 400,000 tons grt in 1939),[25] better known as Hamburg Süd, was no different. Founded in 1871 to provide regular service between Hamburg and the east coast of South America, Hamburg Süd too awarded its Brazilian agency to Theodor Wille, the largest German coffee exporter in Brazil and a Hamburg house. Out of this relationship, but also because of its "powerful support" in scheduled services and the favorable terms it provided to shippers and receivers, it loaded its steamers full with coffee and helped turn Hamburg into one of the two greatest coffee ports in Europe. Yet in Argentina it assigned its agency to Antonio Delfino, a man of unparalleled contacts in business and government circles, and secured another traffic stream, in grain and beef, from the Plate region. Three generations later, Hamburg Süd was still benefiting from the Delfinos, whose connections to grain and cattle exporters were the best in the country. It too, consequently, was both a world and home company, and like HAPAG became an instrument for the development of both South America's and Hamburg's economies. Its luxury liners carried businessmen and travelers across the South Atlantic, but Hamburg Süd ships also transported emigrants and seasonal workers from Spain and Portugal to Argentina or to Brazilian coffee plantations. In the 1930s, as coffee, wheat, and passenger trades waned, it worked with Brazilian state and business interests and with Hamburg's port to develop traffic in tropical fruits on its fast refrigerated ships.[26]

Remarkable about these Hamburg firms was how readily they ensconced themselves abroad but were no less interwoven into their home merchant communities. Repeatedly one sees the same Hamburg figures, or the same concatenation of Hamburg firms present at the founding of Hamburg shipping companies and serving thereafter on boards, in management, or as company agents. Prominent in the establishment of Hamburg Süd were August Bolten, Heinrich Amsinck, Carl Woermann, Carl Laiesz, and

[25] Herbert Wendt, *Kurs Südamerika. Brucke zwischen zwei Kontinenten* (Bielefeld: Ceres, 1958) 157, 230, 319; Anne-Marie Thede-Ottowell, *Hamburg vom Alsterhafen zur Welthafenstadt* (Hamburg: Otto Heinevetter, 1988), 379–380.

[26] Wendt, *Kurs*, 139–140, 176–187, 193–195, 313–315; Otto J. Seiler, *Südamerikafahrt: Deutsche Linienschiffahrt nach den Länden Lateinamerikas, der Karibik und der Westküste Nordamerikas in Wandel der Zeiten* (Herford: E. S. Mittler & Sohn, 1993), 113–116, 150–153; Backx, *Haven*, 224–225 (quoted on "powerful support").

the Commerz- und Disconto-Bank, which was, in part, a Theodor Wille creation. Bolten also participated in the founding of HAPAG (he bought the largest number of shares) and owned one of the most important ship agency firms in Hamburg; Bolten subsequently would hold HAPAG and Hamburg Süd agencies. The Amsincks were an establishment Hamburg family, had originally made their money in sugar refining, but were also shipowners. Woermann ran a prominent steamship line to West Africa. Carl Laiesz's father, Ferdinand, established what became Hamburg's most successful sailing ship company, F. Laiesz, and he too (Ferdinand) was a founder of HAPAG. Carl was deputy chair of the HAPAG board and its ruling figure. His support for Albert Ballin in his early years with the company was decisive: it was Ballin who would turn HAPAG into the largest shipping company in the world before 1914. Between 1883 and 1901 Carl also held the chair of Hamburg Süd. Both father and son equally participated in the founding of Hamburg's Kosmos Line. Joining them were other Hamburg houses: Knöhr & Burchard (another powerful ship agency firm), H. H. Eggers (coffee importers), and Vorwerk. Ferdinand Laiesz, Knöhr & Burchard, Adolph Woermann (Carl's son), and Albert Ballin turn up as well among the founders of Hamburg's Deutsche-Australische Dampfschiffs-Gesellschaft Line (DADG) line.[27] Hamburg's shipping companies were transport mechanisms, but they also became the central actors in a maritime merchant community that begot powerful synergies from its interlocked import, export, and shipping activities.

In all this Hamburg was merely an exemplar. Bremen enjoyed the same global and local combinations. Hermann Heinrich Meier, who was the leading force behind the founding of the NDL, was the continental head of family trading houses located in Bremen and New York. Bremen's C. Melchers & Company, a prominent trading house in China, became general representative for NDL operations in East Asia, while a Melchers was among the founders of the NDL, and Melchers or partners held seats

---

[27] Siegfried Zimmermann, *Theodor Wille, 1844–1969* (Hamburg: Hanseatischer Merkur, 1969), 70; Seiler, *Südamerika*, 82, 88, 95–98; Lamar Cecil, *Albert Ballin: Business and Politics in Imperial Germany, 1888–1918* (Princeton, NJ: Princeton University Press, 1967), 22; Wiborg and Wiborg, *Unser*, 79; Mary Lindemann, *Patriots and Paupers: Hamburg, 1712–1830* (New York: Oxford University Press, 1990), 42; Richard Evans, "Family and Class in the Hamburg Grand Bourgeoisie, 1815–1914," in David Blackbourn and Richard J. Evans, *The German Bourgeoisie: Essays on the Social History of the German Middle Class from the Late Eighteenth to the Early Twentieth Century* (London: Routledge, 1991), 124–125; HAPAG/3156.

on the NDL board well into the twentieth century. NDL too operated as a Bremen institution, but also as a world company.[28] Marseille's Cyprien Fabre Cie., which sailed the Mediterranean and to the west coast of Africa, and ran a passenger line to New York, was the eponymous creation of the president of the Marseille Chamber of Commerce and a figure who, alongside his brother, the chief harbor engineer, was instrumental in the development of the port of Marseille.[29] Holts was a Liverpool firm but its satellites, as we shall soon see, placed it equally on the other side of the planet.

All these shipping companies therefore told a story of how local and global networks harvested, but also fomented transoceanic traffics, and how ports, shipping communities, and the world alike fed off these relationships. These were plot lines that could be writ large for European shipping as a whole. Even the HAPAG directors' road show through North America, or Hamburg Süd's trade stimuli, were conventions.[30] For all there was a mix of cosmopolitan and fiercely local identities, with a sense of perhaps "Germanness" or "Britishness" in between. Home rivalries were fought around the world, but it was not unusual for Hamburg and Bremen firms to rely on each other. In particular, what stood out were the bookends of these arrangements, the ability of steamship lines to mobilize both home and transnational networks. Implanted overseas they were engines for their ports; implanted in their ports, they were equally capable of turning these into engines for them. Pendulum-like in their purpose, they swung naturally and rhythmically between the harbor cities of Europe and all the markets and resources in the rest of the world. In this way they matter-of-factly connected the local and global, so connected were they themselves with the one and the other.

Coastal and Riverboat Feeders

Local and Global, it should now be obvious, were relative terms in shipping. The tug and salvage company, Smits, began along the southern

[28] Georg Bessell, *Norddeutscher Lloyd 1856–1957. Geschichte einer bremischen Reederei* (Bremen: Carl Schünemann, c.1957), 7; Wilhelm Treue, "Die Geschichte des Bremer Handelshauses C. Melchers & Co. von seiner Gründung bis zum Ende des Ersten Weltkrieges," in Friedrich Prüser and Wilhelm Treue, *Beiträge zur bremischen Firmen-Geschichte* (München: F. Bruckmann, 1966), 33–46; *150 Jahre C. Melchers & Co. Bremen. 90 Jahre Melchers & Co. China* (Bremen: 1956); Wiborg and Wiborg, *Unser*, 267, 304; Meyer, *Güterumschlagsplatz*, 50–51.

[29] Daumalin, *Marseille*, 97–99, 122–130; Borruey, *Port*, 188, 194, 199.

[30] GAR/HAL/Viamar/MMPH 4/Reis Naar Amerika, 29 August–27 October 1936.

Dutch coast, but expanded into ocean towage, hauling dredgers, dry docks, and later oil rigs to South America, Singapore, and the Persian Gulf.[31] Tugboat operators were emblematic of local harbor operations, but Smits's boats also crossed the high seas and with equipment that advanced the integration of distant harbors.

Global connectedness, then, was a complex shipping process in which many kinds of shipping participated. This was especially true of coastal and riverboat companies, which in the history of global shipping may appear small beer, but were actually indispensable links in the creation of global chains of traffic. The development of the Assam tea gardens, which turned tea cultivation into a controlled, mass-production industry vital to class and industrial culture in Britain, occurred in a distant, heavily forested, fluvial, navigably opaque, and labor-short area along the upper Brahmaputra, into which it was necessary to move, on an annual basis, engineers, administrators, and estate supplies, plus tens of thousands of migrant laborers, and to move downstream to the port of Calcutta millions of pounds of tea. Later, when rail transport captured a large share of the tea trade, jute shipments picked up the relay. This task was carried out by the Joint Steamer Companies. In the 1930s, the company operated a river fleet numbering close to 1,200 vessels over 5,000 miles of waterway with calls at 324 river ports.[32]

There were many Joint Steamer Companies. Joseph Conrad, who made the Congo synonymous with imperial riverboat journeys, departed Kinshasa in 1890 as second in command of the *Roi des Belges* for one of the enterprises running craft up the river and bringing out rubber and ivory. Here, in the 1930s, the Union Nationale des Transports Fluviaux controlled 40,000 tons of riverboats covering nearly 9,500 kilometers of waterways. It was on the Congo (and the Mississippi) that push-tug convoys, which would transform barge traffic on the Rhine, were pioneered.[33] This combination of exotic otherworldliness and modernity was one of the qualities that would adhere to riverboat travel far into the century. Gabriel García Márquez's born-to-love president of the River Company of the Caribbean may have voyaged up the Magdalena nearly a half century after a first emotive experience, only to discover the jungle

---

[31] Lels (interview); Murk Lels, "Ocean Tugs," in Schraver, *Rotterdam*, 170–192.

[32] Guildhall/River Steam Navigation Company/MS 27,953/1938; Percival Griffiths, *A History of the Joint Steamer Companies* (London: Inchcape & Co. Limited, 1979), especially p. 77 for statistics.

[33] André Lederer, *Histoire de la navigation au Congo* (Tervuren (Belgique): Musée Royal de l'Afrique Centrale, 1965); Headrick, *Tools*, 196–197.

pared back, the riverbanks deforested, wood stocks depleted, the mana-
tees, alligators, and parrots all gone.[34] At what would have been roughly
the same time, however, Harold Braund, an employee for the British trading company Steel Brothers, recalled his 1930s voyage to oil fields far up-
country along the Irrawaddy, the great spinal river running a thousand
miles through the center of Burma, as a leisurely, nostalgically romantic
voyage. The Irrawaddy Flotilla Company, on which he traveled a large
part of the way, worked a fleet of more than 600 boats between the delta
and Bhamo, close by the Chinese border. It functioned as a principal connecting line for the harvesting outposts of foreign trading houses, and
in the 1920s transported 9 million passengers and 1.25 million tons of
cargo per year.[35]

The voluminous flows of human beings and commodities that passed
up and down these river lines were little different from the massive barge
traffic distributed along Europe's elaborate inland waterways system or
the coal, sand, bricks, ore, and grain hauled by coasters along the littorals. The scale of this business should not be underestimated. The Rhine
barge fleet alone in 1914 comprised 11,689 boats and measured 5 million
tons. At the beginning of the century the water surface of the river-dock
basins in Duisburg Rurhort was double that of the port of Antwerp.[36]
Without all these small craft, from the Brahmaputra to the Seine, it would
not have been possible to form the integrated system of trunk lines and
feeders that joined peripheries to centers, making possible the capacious,
scheduled flows of people and goods on which sophisticated Western societies depended in the twentieth century, no matter how far from major
sea lanes and ports sources or destinations might lie.

What, in fact, made maritime chains fully global was their ability
to integrate any "remote" corner of the world with transport circuits
an ocean away. It was not, however, merely the end-game functionality that mattered. Coastal and riverboat companies overseas, as Conrad
understood, were also empire builders and consolidators. They too took

---

[34] Gabriel García Márquez, *Love in the Time of Cholera* (New York: Alfred Knopf, 1988),
331–337.

[35] Guildhall/Steel Brothers/MS 29,556/Harold Braund/"'But the Melody Lingers On': A
Personal Story," 1969; Alister McCrae and Alan Prentice, *Irrawaddy Flotilla* (Paisley, UK:
James Paton, 1978), 128.

[36] Vigarié, *Grands*, 294–295; Bird, *Major*, 394; John Armstrong, "Coastal Shipping: The
Neglected Sector of Nineteenth-Century British Transport History," *International Journal
of Maritime History* 6 (June 1994): 175–188; John Armstrong and Andreas Kunz, eds.,
Coastal Shipping and the European Economy, 1750–1980 (Mainz: Philipp von Zabern,
2002), 249–250.

initiatives to expand world services or production for world markets. Despite their "remoteness" they were central to the process by which globalism evolved because, through their hookups, European networks overlapped with indigenous ones, and influences or relationships flowed in both directions. In this regard, they were intrinsically transnational, a quality enhanced by their carriage of local and international traffics that served the dual role of advancing the interconnectedness of regional migratory cultures while incorporating these into European world ones.[37] Yet they, too, were umbilically tied to the cultures and enterprises that created them, which also enhanced their ability to bring local and global together. All this we can see in an examination of two leading examples, the Dutch interisland KPM in the East Indies, and the Holts-connected Chinese Navigation Company, which operated riverboat services on the Yangtze and coastal services as far southeast as Bangkok and Singapore.

The KPM

The Koninklijke Paketvaart Maatschappij, or KPM, began its business life in 1891 as the issue of the Dutch Mails (Rotterdamsche Lloyd and the SMN), with the mission to create and run a feeder service covering an island archipelago that extended over several thousand sea miles. This required assembling an agency organization throughout its territories, contracting with local prau and lighter owners to ferry goods in the large number of harbors where even KPM ships could only anchor offshore, establishing its own harbor services where none existed, and arranging for bunkering stations, especially for a widely scattered fleet in distant archipelago waters. To reach an almost endless variety of harbors or anchorages, the KPM also had to construct a fleet of varying designs and dimensions. Yet within one year of operation the KPM had put together an interisland network and a half century later was running 64 lines, 130 ships, and calling at 250 "ports." From its start it was the model colonial business enterprise, a dazzling demonstration of technical and organizational abilities, but concentrated on marshaling island resources for European import and consumption.[38]

---

[37] See also T. N. Harper, "Empire, Diaspora, and the Languages of Globalism, 1850–1914," in Hopkins, *Globalization*, 141–166, although I do not see World War I as a breaking point.

[38] À Campo, *Koninklijke*, 393–442, 467; De Boer and Westermann, *Eeuw*, 304–307, Bijlage 9.

Those imperial overtones were more tightly drawn as the KPM fulfilled a second mission: to disconnect what it could of island trade from the markets of Singapore and redirect it to the Java ports where the Mails' route structure was centered.[39] To filch business from the mosquito fleet, the KPM shrewdly combined the best of the European and Chinese systems, reflecting how colonial business, as it imposed Western manners and practice, was nearly always in turn infiltrated by local habits. In particular the KPM incorporated the *tjintjoe* and credit system that formed the core of Chinese shipping relationships. Like its Chinese competitors, KPM boats became traveling banks, with captains required to be as knowledgeable about shippers, markets, and prices as they were of navigation hazards.[40]

Victory was clinched, however, through close coordination between company and state. From its origins, the KPM was conceived as an instrument of imperial rule: to advance the expansion and consolidation of Dutch authority across the archipelago as well as to create a Dutch-centered economic unit in the Indies. Such intertwining was common in the history of imperial river and coastal trades, but few arrangements matched the tango danced between the KPM and the Dutch imperial regime. The KPM supplied boats for expeditions and pushed out services as Dutch stakes in the water. The state reciprocated with subsidies and the closure of coastal harbors to non-Dutch vessels. In the classic moment, the company made possible the mounting of an expedition against Lombok in the Lesser Sunda islands and was rewarded with a state crackdown against Wee Bin & Co., its principal rival. In company circles, the Lombok War and the huge profits it generated were considered a turning point, and well into the future the years with top returns were known as "Lombok years."[41]

Probably no routes captured so vividly the workings of the KPM system as those it sailed out of Makassar along the extended Celebesian coast, with its long scorpion-like tail that whips around the Gulf of Tomini and then points north, at the tip, in the direction of the Philippines. Once the bastion of the VOC spice trade, but suspended for two centuries in the torpid zones of seaborne commerce, the salty coastal plains by tropical

[39] Leeman, *Barkschip*, 124–125; À Campo, *Koninklijke*, 65, 233–234, 459, 478–479; Allen and Donnithorne, *Western*, 216–221.

[40] On practices: De Boer and Westermann, *Eeuw*, 325, 332; À Campo, *Koninklijke*, 246, 366–375; The Hague, Nationaal Archief (NA)/Koninklijke Paketvaart Maatschappij Collection 2.20.58.01 (KPM)/123/Dienstreizen #41.

[41] À Campo's *Koninklijke* superbly shows how this was done. On Lombok, 172–185 (quoted 177).

seas that characterized the Groote Oost, or outer islands of the East Indies, were ideal for planting and cultivating the coconut palm. The fruit of these trees, when cracked and dried, yielded copra, one of the most widely used sources of vegetable oils and fats in the world. Of all tropical exporters of copra, the East Indies led the way, and within the colony the Groote Oost came to dominate the trade, particularly the island of Celebes, which in the 1940s was alone responsible for 200,000 tons, or 40 percent of all East Indies copra dispatched abroad. Neither capital nor labor intensive, the commodity was easily harvested by individual small-holding families. Their connection to the consumer markets in the West were the transport and trading links established by Chinese traders, the conversion of Makassar into a deep-sea port, transshipment via overseas steamers, and, in between as the basic linkage, KPM coastal collectors.[42]

KPM ships plied up and down the coast. On outward voyages they carried sundry items such as sugar, benzine, roofing metals, or old gun-nysacks for the following copra harvest. On the return they brought back rattan, ebony, cloves, sea cucumbers, but, most of all, copra sold to Chinese merchant houses whose representatives traveled with the KPM ships. Where no banks were available the ship's captain (or KPM agent if in residence) dispensed credit to the dealers. Gathering the copra was no easy matter. Scenes of copra bearers, human ropes strung out from shore to ship, could still be seen in the late 1940s. The Tominibocht was one extended collection point; in 1938 KPM ships called at fifty-eight separate "harbors" along its coast. On the other hand, big ships sailed into the bay of Gorontalo. One of the most frequently reproduced KPM pictures from the interwar years – a sizable vessel anchored in the bay, amid lush surrounding hills, with praus and other craft swarming to and from the landing stage – captured the absorption of the tropics into European-driven commodity chains. To gather cargo from the remotest regions of north Celebes or its outer islands, the KPM, with Arab and Chinese investors, established its own feeder company, the Cekumij. At the other end of the scale, KPM ships connected with oceangoing liners awaiting their feeder haul in the port of Makassar.[43]

[42] De Boer and Westermann, *Eeuw*, 226–252; Snodgrass, *Copra* 1–11, 33–34, 231–232; International Institute of Agriculture/Bureau of Statistics, *Oleaginous Products and Vegetable Oils: Production and Trade* (Rome: International Institute of Agriculture, 1923), xxiv–xxvi; Great Britain/Empire Marketing Board, *Oilseeds and Vegetable Oils: A Summary of Figures of Production and Trade* (1933), 15.

[43] De Boer and Westermann, *Eeuw*, 221–271; NA/KPM/371/18 June 1946; I. J. Brugmans, *Tachtig jaren varen met de Nederland, 1870–1950* (Amsterdam: N.V. Stoomvaart

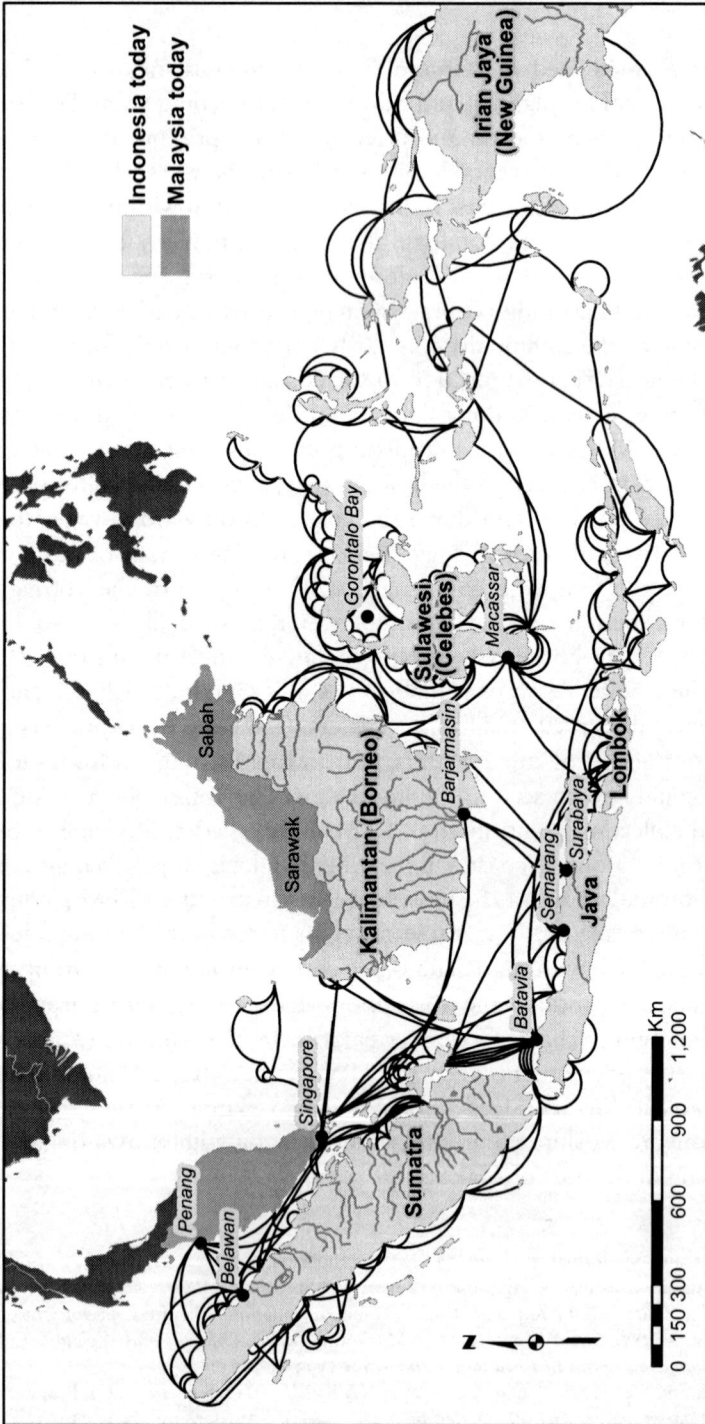

MAP 3. KPM routes circa 1940.
Source: De Boer and Westermann, *Eeuw,* Bijlage 6.

KPM business life thus shuffled between the poky, small-time world of island culture and the larger domains of global commerce. The same collector ships that steamed throughout the Groote Oost conveyed inter-island passengers and Chinese peddlers, who hawked their petty wares, perhaps knickknacks and cigarettes, to village folk. The arrival of a KPM steamer was a local event that brought contact with the outside world – mail, dealers, a traveling market, ship's officers – and a great deal of excitement for a brief few hours or perhaps a day. In outposts scattered along the remotest fringes of the empire, KPM agents experienced a daily routine a galaxy removed from their colleagues in the world ports. Way up in Sigli (in Aceh), in 1917, the agent managed the company's prau service, developed relations with merchants in the Chinese quarter, handled petty complaints about theft from poorly packed cases, and, in "the considerable free time, which the agency allows him," repaired praus or learned the local language. The agent in Lho Seumaweh (Lhokseumawe), down the coast, was locally celebrated for never failing to boat out to an arriving ship, no matter how miserable the weather, and for the many times he had fetched the mail, even under the most wretched conditions, despite the cost of periodically capsizing on the return and being forced to swim ashore. Whereas termites had eaten to pieces the new customs warehouse, the agent had given orders to his clerks and oarsmen to keep chickens in the company godown because these would seek out and destroy the termites' larvae. Satisfied with his lot, he was the perfect man for "these peaceful surroundings." On an inspection tour, the president-director empowered the agent to settle a claim from two local merchants, Ee Liong and Tieng Hoat, that had been pending for two years. The sum was all of twenty gulden.[44]

Yet agents like this, in the agglomerate, accounted for how large parts of the world were integrated into a Western-driven global economy. In its home waters, the KPM was essential to the functioning of the Dutch East Indies as a unit, but inevitably that coordination tied into world patterns. In 1930 the company transported more than 1.2 million people.[45] Many of these were islanders shuttling back and forth or European administrators. But there were also merchants and planters, whose business was

Maatschappij "Nederland," 1950), 78–80; Allen and Donnithorne, *Western*, 219, 241; Reuchlin, "Handelsvaart," 237; H. W. Dick, *The Indonesian Interisland Shipping Industry: An Analysis of Competition and Regulation* (Singapore: Institute of Southeast Asian Studies, 1987), 10–11.

[44] NA/KPM/123/Dienstreizen #41, 1917.

[45] De Boer and Westermann, *Eeuw*, Bijlage 11.

never strictly local, and a large coolie trade that supplied the labor for mass plantation export production.[46] KPM feeder services, the collector freighters winding along the copra coasts or the river lines running into central Sumatra, created chains comparable to those the Straits Steamship Line implemented with Sabah. The child of the Mails and the imperial state, the KPM grew into what they had ordained it to be. But in so doing, it also forged indispensable links between the sleepy, humdrum, back-of-beyond universe of colonial shipping and the vast commodity flows into Western harbors.

China Navigation Company

The China Navigation Company was the shipping arm of Butterfield and Swire, an old, well-established China trading house whose networks were riverine, littoral, but, because it was joined to Liverpool's Holts, also transoceanic. Here too global-local links operated on multiple levels: overseas systems tied into feeder systems, interwoven or cross-national networks, and individuals and firms embedded at home and abroad.

Its waters were not easy to navigate. Captains and pilots encountered on the Yangtze some of the widest fluctuations on the planet between high and low water levels. When the river rose, it carried down heaps of silt that erased existing navigation channels and created wholly new ones. River shipping was plagued by boycotts, bandits, civil war, and invasion. Hazards along the coast were typhoons, monsoons, and piracy. Pirate attacks in the South China Sea were so endemic that most ships encased their engine room and bridge behind locked iron grills, and voyaged with armed guards.[47] The piracy that infests certain shipping lanes today is but a variation on what has never fully disappeared as a modern shipping problem.

Nonetheless, these were some of the most heavily traveled waters in the world. Japanese, Chinese, British (Jardine Matheson's Indo-China Steam Navigation Company), and, until the First World War, Germans provided stiff competition. Nearly always, however, the leading or second company was China Navigation.[48] Company steamers ran between

---

[46] NA/KPM/363/1022/23 April 1938.

[47] Christopher Cook, *The Lion and the Dragon: British Voices from the China Coast* (London: Elm Tree Books, 1985), 76–87, 126–127; SOAS/JSS III 1/7/Box 66; PRO/Admiralty/116/2706.

[48] William D. Wray, *Mitsubishi and the N.Y.K, 1870–1914: Business Strategy in the Japanese Shipping Industry* (Cambridge: Harvard University Press, 1984), 341–357,

Shanghai and Chungking (Chongqing) and along the Canton River system carrying goods such as salt, wood oil, eggs, cotton, pig intestines, or European manufactured and piece goods – and also a great number of passengers. Up and down the China coast and to the Philippines and Indochina, the trades divided between freight and passengers, but other routes, to Singapore and Bangkok, consisted primarily of migrant labor for plantations and mines. Some river craft measured only several hundred tons, but the largest riverboats carried their own cranes and could load up to 40,000 pieces of cargo. Ships to Singapore were equipped to carry a thousand people, mostly as deck passengers.[49]

Much of China Navigation's power emanated from its relationship with Holts. Less of a household name than P & O or Cunard, Alfred Holt and Company, also known as Blue Funnel or Ocean Steam Ship, was often viewed within maritime circles as the Rolls Royce of British shipping. In 1930 it carried nearly half of British exports via British lines to Singapore, China, and Japan, and in 1938 Holts was second only to NYK (and only by 500 tons) among major lines operating in the Far East. More Holts ships sailed to Australia, across the Pacific to North America, and, in the pilgrim trade, to Jiddah. In the late 1960s it possessed 125 ships combining 1 million tons plus. Its reputation, however, came from more than its freight statistics. Holts built its ships to a higher standard than Lloyd's AI classification, and called this designation, "Holts Class." Recruiting from family, but also from men with firsts at Oxford and Cambridge, to whom it gave a superb training, it possessed a top management corps known for its tremendous shipping knowledge, its superior mental talents, and its tremendous faith in itself.[50] None of this it was reluctant to express to its peers. Richard Adams, who rose to the top of P & O, remarked that "they did rather tend to tell you what the form was.... Blue Funnel did run their ships extremely well. They did run an absolutely splendid service to the East. But they did unfortunately have the view that nobody else could

388–397; Zhang Zhongli, Chen Zengnian, and Yao Xinrong (Zhang), *The Swire Group in Old China* (Shanghai: The Shanghai People's Publishing House, 1990), 114, 156–159, 173–188; SOAS/JSS III 2/6/Box 87/China Navigation Company, 22 April 1927.

49 Charlotte Havilland, *The China Navigation Company Limited: A Pictorial History, 1872–1992* (N.p.: John Swire and Sons, 1992); Cook, *Lion*, 70, 81–82, 129–131; Zhang, *Swire*, 170, 173.

50 Falkus, *Blue*, especially 9–25, 147 – this book is excellent throughout on the cultural ethos of this firm; HAPAG/1246/17 October 1938; NMM/P & O/4/62/Agents' Reports/ Singapore, 1947; MMM/OA 4A/554; Francis E. Hyde, *Blue Funnel: A History of Alfred Holt and Company of Liverpool from 1865 to 1914* (Liverpool: Liverpool University Press, 1956), 134–135.

do it and that what they did was right."[51] This quintessential Merseyside firm, rooted in the shipping, trading, home-centered "non-Conformist, London Hostile"[52] traditions of that port, yet lavishly cosmopolitan in its projection, was one more globalizing agent where local-global connections were the essence of its own internal dynamic.

Holts was also celebrated for its string of agencies in the East, of which two stood out: Mansfields in Singapore and Swires in China. The association with the latter was perhaps the most famous of all shipping and trading company relationships. So powerful was the connection that John Samuel Swire, whose trading house was the mother company of Butterfield and Swire, and hence China Navigation, has been seen as second only to Alfred Holt in the construction of the Blue Funnel Line. From Holts, Swires gained agency commissions, but even more the prestige and business that flowed from identification with Britain's premier line to China. In return, Swires was Holts' ticket into the China trade. Practically all of Holts' operations in East Asia were in the hands of Swires. Swires' Taikoo Sugar Refinery, with its own extensive network of up-country agents, offered access to inland markets. China Navigation provided the essential feeder service, plus its own string of agencies along the Yangtze and in the coastal ports of China and Japan. But what Swires offered most of all was its second source of influence and power: its entry to Chinese networks.[53]

Those networks were historical and deeply entrenched. Within China, the bulk of cargo shipments was controlled by shipping *hongs*. Roughly equivalent to freight forwarders, hongs arranged transport, but their range of services, from banking to documentation, was so comprehensive that few shippers were prepared to save on commissions and negotiate directly with foreign shipping companies. There were also residential shipping hongs that functioned in ways reminiscent of *khans* or *funduqs* along eastern Mediterranean trade routes hundreds of years earlier. Such hongs, located in major trading centers, provided business services and connections. Across the South China Sea, in what became known as the Nanyang, much of local trade was in the hands of Chinese merchants and dealers. In port cities, Chinese forwarding hongs commanded shipments to and from

[51] Richard B. Adams, interview with author, Henley-on-Thames, 24 September 1998.
[52] Falkus, *Blue*, 11.
[53] Hyde, *Blue*, 32–36, 56; Falkus, *Blue*, 58–59, 60–70; Sheila Marriner and Francis E. Hyde, *The Senior John Samuel Swire, 1825–1898: Management in Far Eastern Shipping Trades* (Liverpool: Liverpool University Press, 1967); SOAS/Elizabeth Hook, "A Guide to the Papers of John Swire and Sons Ltd.," 1977; Cook, *Lion*, 35–46; Jones, *Merchants*, 111.

China. The huge migratory trades passed largely through more Chinese chains of recruiters, dealers, brokers, and lodging–house keepers. Business in China was unimaginable without Chinese network connections. "No shippers at all," as one China Navigation report put it, "ship direct in our Northern or River berth trades, everything is done by Shipping Hongs, while to Southern ports fully 90% of the business is transacted through brokers."[54] All European firms active in China scrambled to cultivate relations with hongs and coolie brokers. Few, if any, rivaled the network interchanges that Swires and China Navigation constructed.

The hinge on which Swires swung open the door, was, as for all the others, the comprador, a man of money, reputation, and extensive connections who acted as go-between with the Chinese business community. That functionality, however, tells us little about Swires' connections without looking more closely at just who its men were, and what they could deliver. Chun Koo Leong, who held the post of Shanghai comprador from 1884 to 1920, to be succeeded in turn by two family members, had a merchant background and possessed high social standing as a founder of hospitals and schools for people from his home province of Guangdong, encompassing Guangzhou, or what was then Canton. Both the Shanghai comprador and the shipping comprador, who coordinated shipments from hongs, appear to have invested substantially with Lee Tai Chong, a residential hong and valuable contact for Swires. Mok Se Ou, who established a family dynasty in the Hong Kong office of Swires, was an importer and exporter with strong ties to Chinese merchant circles. His son, Mok Tso Chun, founded his own trading hong, Nan Tai, to expand relations with Chinese shippers on the mainland.[55] S. Y. Ching, Swires'

---

[54] SOAS/JSS III 2/6/Box 87/16 December 1927 (quoted); SOAS/JSS III 2/13/Box 94/1 April, 1 July 1932; SOAS/JSS III 1/18/Box 77/19 August 1938; Deborah Howard, *Venice & the East: The Impact of the Islamic World on Venetian Architecture, 1100–1500* (New Haven, CT: Yale University Press, 2000), 114–115, 120–121; Sugihara, *Japan*, 35, 257–260; Brown, *Capital*, 13–20; Persia Crawford Campbell, *Chinese Coolie Emigration to Countries within the British Empire* (London: Frank Cass & Co., 1971; first published 1923); Yen Ching-Hwang, *Coolies and Mandarins: China's Protection of Overseas Chinese during the Late Ch'ing Period (1851–1911)* (Singapore: Singapore University Press, 1985); McKeown, "Conceptualizing," 306–337; François Gipouloux, *La Méditerranée asiatique. Villes portuaires et réseaux marchands en Chine, au Japon et en Asie du Sud-Est, XVIe–XXIe siècle* (Paris: CNRS, 2009), 175–177.

[55] Zhang, *Swire*, 217–240, 323–326; SOAS/JSS I/Box 15/2 May 1930; SOAS/JSS III 1/21/ Box 408/12 April 1948; SOAS, JSS III 1/22/Box 511/5 March 1948; Jones, *Merchants*, 221–223. Mok-Kou Sang (third generation), caught manipulating dealings for Taikoo sugar, was forced to resign. In the 1930s Swires began a changeover to a Chinese manager system, but continuities outweighed ruptures with the older arrangements.

Newchang comprador, was financially allied to at least one, and perhaps both, of two hongs, Tung Tai Shun and Chi I Hsin, each in charge of Swires' marketing in the north.[56] The shipping comprador position at the river port of Hankow in the early 1920s went to W. F. M. Woo. Thirty-five, Woo had attended Boone University in Wuchang, had worked for four years in the Hankow comprador department of the German trading company Carlowitz & Co., and for four years more as the assistant to Jardine Matheson's Hankow export comprador. His principal qualifications were "his close relationship with the Ningpo group of shippers," and "his experience of the grain trade, and intimate knowledge of these shippers."[57]

In the south, China Navigation's freight brokers were Kao Seet Chee (Amoy and Swatow) and Kwei Kee (Hong Kong and Canton). Their connections to the dominant forwarding hongs in Haiphong would prove useful as war closed in by the late 1930s. Nam Kee, a branch of the comprador Moks in Hong Kong, was China Navigation's biggest broker in the migrant labor trades. Nam Kee was well established in Swatow, and maintained branches in its two biggest markets, Bangkok and Singapore. The association with China Navigation lasted nearly sixty years.[58] After the Second World War, Maurice Ching, who almost certainly was the son of Swires' Newchang comprador, made a bid to grab the business for himself. The dilemma posed by this choice revealed the strengths of Swires' Chinese connections. Ching was a bundle of energy and ambition. J. K. Swire, to whom Ching pitched his takeover, was struck by his bravado, but also his credentials:

> He knows all the shippers and lodging houses, as they have been friends of his father's for years. He would be quite prepared to cut Nam Kee right out straight away and take it all over himself.... He is certain that in a very short time he would kill Nam Kee stone dead.

Swire, moreover, had to admit that Nam Kee, whose most promising young men had disappeared in the war, were at present a rather unimpressive lot. But Nam Kee was still "delivering the goods," and if cut out

---

[56] SOAS/JSS II 2/13/Box 94/1 July 1932; SOAS/JSS I/Box 17/18 October 1940; SOAS/JSS I/Box 15/2 May, 22 June 1930.

[57] SOAS, JSS II 2/1/Box 37/24 November 1922. Ningpo bankers and merchants formed a powerful clique in the Shanghai business community: Meyer, *Hong Kong*, 71–73.

[58] SOAS/JSS III 1/21/Box 408/12 April 1946; SOAS/JSS III 2/6/Box 87/11 February 1927; SOAS/JSS III 1/18/Box 77/31 October, 19 November 1938; SOAS/JSS I/Box 17/18 October 1940; SOAS/JSS III 1/22/Box 511/5 March 1948; SOAS/JSS III 1/1/Box 60/3 June 1921; SOAS/JSS I/Box 15/28 March 1930; Zhang, *Swire*, 227–236.

would take their Singapore and Bangkok organizations with them. Other postings would have to be found to satisfy the energies of Ching *fils*.[59]

All of which returns us to the not-so-small beer of these companies. Nothing more than a river and coastal affair, China Navigation nonetheless worked at the confluence where the networks of Liverpool and London flowed into the networks of Shanghai and Hong Kong. Like KPM's lazy backwater steamers, it too maneuvered between two worlds. Its beancaker freighters hugged the China coast and its Yangtze steamers, some fewer than 300 tons, hauled local cargo and passenger trades between upriver ports. But it also ferried prodigious numbers of laborers to Southeast Asia where they produced the tropical commodities that satisfied demand in Western cities, and as a feeder to Holts' transoceanic liners, it supplied the crucial back end between markets and trades on both sides of the world. Once again that function was performed by a company that was, itself, East and West. British in ownership, home office, managing personnel, and national identity, an imperialist intruder resented as such by the Chinese, it was also an expatriate firm with a century of residence in China, where it adopted the name Taikoo and allied itself with Chinese collaborators. When the First World War came, large numbers of staff returned to fight in Europe.[60] Yet F. R. Lamb, a highly regarded figure in Swires' eastern organization, also described himself three decades later as a "great personal friend" of Wong Kwei Kee and noted of his son, Wong Pao Hsie, and of Kao Yung Lien, the successor to Kao Seet Chee (all of these China Navigation's southern freight brokers) that "I have known them and their fathers for many years past ... I have (as it were) grown up with them in the Southern trades ... my wife and children have been on terms of intimacy with them and their families for a long time."[61] Global and local were binary terms. Riverboat and coastal companies that should have proved this as a rule demonstrated, to the contrary, they were anything but.

Where liner-feeder combinations did not go, tramp vessels did, wrapping the world in still more sea lanes. Little has been said about the tramping trades so far. In the popular mind there was something romantic attached to tramp shipping, an image no doubt encouraged by the vessels' activity

[59] SOAS/JSS III 1/22/Box 511/5 (quoted), 12, 19 March 1948. Nam Kee remained Swires' Swatow broker until 1951, when the firm ended its shipping line from the city: Zhang, *Swire Group*, 228, 234.
[60] SOAS/JSS I/2/25/Box A35/17 May 1915; Zhang, *Swire*. 149.
[61] SOAS/JSS III/1/21/Box 408/12 April 1946.

in distant commodity ports, as if all tramp steamers corresponded to their appearance in W. Somerset Maugham short stories. In reality, tramp business concentrated in bulk cargoes, often dirty, where speed was inconsequential and shipments of one commodity filled their holds. The classic tramp cargoes were grain (especially the River Plate trade), ore, sugar, timber, and most of all coal, which, despite its thoroughly prosaic character, was the tramper's freight par excellence, because it was nearly always available as a starter shipment outward from Europe. Tramp trades lost ground to liner shipping after the First World War, but they still were essential to world transport. The tramps hauled much of the world's food and fuel supplies, they responded to seasonal trades that could not necessarily be worked into a liner company's tight schedule, and they called at out-of-the-way ports or ports where loading was notoriously slow. They also constituted a large part of the cross-trades, sailing between ports that could not sustain regular liner traffic. Like liners, they too were local-global trades. Tramps could crisscross the oceans for a year or longer before returning home, but the companies that ran these were often family firms that spanned generations of ties to home ports and whose networks thrived on local connections or on home communities dispersed among the world's harbors.[62]

The sum of all three was a steady progress toward a single world, even if the consequences could be as fractious as they were unifying. Through the complex of circuits coursed passengers and trade, but also parallel forms of globalism. Global transport at these levels made many things happen. Diasporas magnified not only in number but in perception of their interconnectedness. The flow of peoples and ideas produced a global cosmopolitanism, but also subsets of cultures and communities that were transnational in new and differently shuffled ways. European transnationalism, meanwhile, had powerful home affiliations from which it drew strength and to which it drew traffics. Globalism therefore also became, and primarily so, European or Western access to what it needed in the world, impeded only by political or macroeconomic developments. The vector lines were heavily Eurocentric and concentrated on those ports with which shipping companies most identified. What all these globalizing forces held in common was a closer interpenetration of global and local, effectively the definition of globalization.

---

[62] Ioannis Theotokas and Gelina Harlaftis, *Leadership in World Shipping: Greek Family Firms in International Business* (Houndmills, Basingstoke: Palgrave Macmillan, 2009), 76–91.

Shipping's contribution to this lay largely in the filaments it spun out and its networks of overseas services. It also lay in companies' own dual character. Intensely local and global, and well connected at both levels, they turned world shipping into a larger image of themselves. But there was a third factor, the ability to manage global shipping, to make it work. Command of logistics, of networking, and of how to turn a ship around on time were also building blocks of global connectedness.

EXPERTISE

It makes little sense to write about shipping on a grand scale without discussing how shipping companies actually managed to ship an item from one part of the world to another, undamaged, and quite possibly on schedule. World flows required organization, but also knowledge, skill, and execution. John Hobhouse, a Holts cousin and senior manager, described the job of running a shipping company as both terribly demanding and practical:

We ... have to solve the problems of receiving the cargo from the shipper, stowing it safely on the ship, landing it at the right port and delivering it intact to the right consignee. We had got this up to about 99½% success before the war, but we slumped badly and have not yet completely recovered. You may think this does not sound very difficult. No more it is for one package, but we have to deal with millions of all shapes and sizes, and not always too well packed, and with contents, which often require special treatment, or are liable to damage other cargo.[63]

Neither tramp nor liner shipping were simple enterprises to run. Tramping was its own world apart from the big business regularity of major liner companies. Whereas a liner schedule was fixed, a tramp's itinerary was open-ended in regard to destination, time out of home port, and profits earned or losses incurred. Once underwater cables supplied worldwide market information, it was possible to direct tramp vessels from an office in London or Oslo. Even with global communication, however, tramping was a constant struggle to position ships where freight was abundant and competitors' ships were not, where rates therefore were high not low, where voyages contracted would not undercut arrival in time for seasonal trades, where going for a "spot loading" was better than fixing a cargo in advance, where cargoes were quick loads or discharges (such as coal or grain whose handling was mechanized), where ballast

---

[63] MMM/OA 4A/671/8 December 1950.

voyages were kept to the bare minimum, and where destination ports were equally good loads. Running a tramp company was thus much like playing snooker or chess: Each move was calculated in regard to moves to come. Knocking a red ball flush into the pocket only to end up with no following shot at the other colored balls was of scarce, if any, advantage. Innate abilities to think ahead provided an edge, but experience and knowledge of many things – commodities, seasonal traffics, competitors' ships and their positions, ports, and seas – determined the margin between profits and losses.[64]

Increasingly shipowners came to prefer the alternative of time charters, where vessels were placed at the disposal of a charterer for a specified period of time. Time charters, like bonds, as opposed to equities, traded off speculative returns for secure ones. In the culture of the tramping business, where consecutive negotiations encouraged initiative and risk taking, time chartering was seen as the mark of a lazy owner. Still, time chartering required the ability to read markets correctly and judge whether rates would be falling (good for time charters) or rising (bad). Moreover, if arranged in advance of construction, time charters were a means for securing loans to finance the building of ships to be chartered. Norwegian shipowners used time charters to stage an oil tanker coup after the First World War.[65] After the Second World War, Aristotle Onassis, Stavros Niarchos, and Hong Kong's Y. K. Pao largely built their shipping empires out of loan guarantees secured on long-term time charters.[66] Then again, Onassis – who had attempted to break Aramco's hold over Saudi oil shipments, had failed, and was shut out of time charters with the majors as his punishment – reaped a king's fortune when Suez suddenly closed in 1956 and oil companies outbid each other for any available ship on the spot market. Luck and improvisation all figured into the

---

[64] Gordon Boyce, "Edward Bates and Sons, 1897–1915: Tramping Operations in Recession and Recovery," *International Journal of Maritime History* 23 (June 2011): 20–24 (Boyce also uses the chess analogy); Charles D. MacMurray and Malcolm M. Cree, *Shipping and Shipbroking: A Guide to All Branches of Shipbroking and Ship Management*, 3rd ed. (London: Sir Isaac Pitman & Sons, 1934), 4, 133–135.

[65] S. G. Sturmey, *British Shipping and World Competition* (London: Athlone Press, 1962), 75–81.

[66] F. J. A. Broeze, "Rederij," in R. Baetens, Ph. M. Bosscher, and H. Reuchlin, eds., *Maritieme geschiedenis der Nederlanden. Tweede helft negentiende eeuw en twingtigste eeuw, van 1850–1870 tot ca. 1970* (Bussem: De Boer Maritiem, 1978), 167–168, 215; Sturmey, *British*, 75–81, 258; Fayle, *Short*, 266–267; J. Bes, *Liner and Tramp Shipping: Practical Guide to the Subject for All Connected with the Shipping Business* (New York: W. S. Heinman, 1966) 28; Harlaftis, *Greek*, 187, 204–205, 262–264; Nicholas Fraser et al., *Aristotle Onassis* (Philadelphia: J. B. Lippincott, 1977), 86–90, 136–156.

tramp trades. Skill was just as significant, however, and on a long-term basis accounted for tramp owners' ability to position ships where they were needed, and without which the intricate cross exchanges of a global economy could not have functioned.

The foundation for liner companies was having the right ships for the right trades in the right numbers. Fleet investments were the most critical decisions liner owners or managers made, because the outlays were so high. But even for well-traveled routes there were always design options to select from. What about power (coal or oil)? What about speed (dependent on fuel costs, but also scheduling needs and the relative value of time in each trade)? What about size (dependent on ports of call, operating costs, and the prospect of seasonal traffics)? What about schedules (how many ships would be needed for a rotation)? The history of shipping was littered with wrong choices and, occasionally, the company crash that followed. The CGT's decision to build the *France* when it was already obsolete was notorious. Even Malcom McLean, who pioneered container shipping, built the wrong ships at the wrong time in the early 1980s and sunk United States Lines. Overall, however, global shipping got the ships that it needed, in numbers, sizes, and kinds, and at requisite levels of productivity.

As shipowners gained practical knowledge in building ships they also learned with increasing adroitness where to place them and how to use them. Global commerce thrived on the initiation of new lines and routes. Often this was the spigot that opened up the flows.[67] What is striking is the prodigious research that preceded such moves, and, just as impressive, the way entire organizations were mobilized to investigate potential services. Holland Amerika's inquiry into opening a U.S. East Coast service to South America in the late 1940s produced files crammed with reports, statistics, and charts covering volumes of exports broken down by countries; imports and exports broken down by ports; information on existing liner services broken down by company; and port details (facilities, harbor fees, quay lengths, warehousing possibilities, numbers of cranes, stevedore rates). To collect this data, company representatives traveled to South America and to the outports along the North American East Coast. They queried the U.S. Maritime Commission, the Dutch shipping agency in Buenos Aires (Lirosa), and their Gulf Coast representative. They met

[67] Adam McKeown, *Chinese Migrant Networks and Cultural Change: Peru, Chicago, Hawaii, 1900–1936* (Chicago: University of Chicago Press, 2001), 45, 146–147 – in this case on opening a shipping line between China and Peru.

with their insurance brokers. They planned conference memberships. One of their number traveled to the outports to identify suitable agents.[68] The same meticulous planning that filtered through into logistical command, or came to reflect it, went into the complex drafting of schedules[69] or, at micro levels, into the drafting of ships' voyages. For one voyage between Hamburg and South Africa in the summer of 1939, the instructions to the captain of the HAPAG steamer *Dortmund* ran twenty pages. Calculating "circa 288" sea miles daily steaming range, it was to arrive in Cape Town precisely on 22 August, Mossel Bay on 25 August, Port Elizabeth on the 26th, East London on the 27th, and Durban on the 29th.[70] The precision with which a voyage over thousands of sea miles with multiple calls was to be conducted was striking in its routineness. So was HAPAG's presumption of the organization it could summon on a regular basis to make this happen. Behind the voyage of the *Dortmund* or a thousand journeys like it, were agents; the floating staff of captains, ship's officers, engineers, and crew; nautical services to advise on navigational matters; inspectors or marine superintendents in frequent ports of call; and dock and warehouse staffs, all the way down to night watchmen in ports.

What I wish to argue here is that, in the end, expertise at all these levels made global shipping work. Despite the nearly anal list of details for the *Dortmund*'s captain, for perhaps 50 percent of the time everything rested on his skill because at sea, captains, or masters, possessed absolute authority over their companies' millions of pounds of investment. Some were legendary, such as Holland Amerika Line's Roggeveen, who, advised that his infected finger required amputation and a four-day rest, chopped it off in the doctor's office and, without missing a beat, said, "OK doctor, it's gone. Now bandage me up, because I have to sail in four hours."[71] Nearly all who served with major liner companies were highly skilled, if for no other reason than it took them years to reach the master position. Hendrik van Manen joined the Rotterdamsche Lloyd in 1918 as a fourth mate, advanced to third mate in 1920, but took another eight years to reach the second officer position and then another ten before promotion to the rank of first officer. Not until 1947 did he receive command of

[68] GAR/HAL/Directie 123, 130, 951, 952, 953, 954; A. D. Wentholt, *Brug over den oceaan. Een eeuw geschiedenis van de Holland Amerika Lijn* (Rotterdam: Nigh & Van Ditmar, 1973), 299. Even then, disappointed in the results, Holland Amerika withdrew its ships a decade later.

[69] GAR/HAL/Directie 773/13 February 1947; GAR/Lloyd 1/218/Dienstregling, EL Mailschepen 1924–1934, 11, 28 August 1930, 2 April 1931.

[70] HAPAG/215/"Reisebrief für D. DORTMUND 35. R. nach Südafrika."

[71] Wentholt, *Brug*, 88–89.

his first ship, although later he captained several passenger liners for the company. Ernst Passehl went to sea as an ordinary seaman on a sailing vessel, served as a steersman, and obtained certificates from the nautical college in Stralsund before joining DADG in 1913 as a third officer. By 1925, at the age of thirty-seven, he had advanced to the position of first officer, but he held at this rank for the next eleven years before his promotion to captain with HAPAG in 1935. In smaller ports captains and first officers oversaw loading and unloading. This was a chore, but also a matter of pride. Stunned by his poor performance charging logs in the Philippines, the captain of the Rotterdamsche Lloyd's *Salatiga* requested the same assignment on his next eastbound voyage "as he would very much like to prove that the loading of logs is merely a matter of experience rather than a complicated problem." Their greatest responsibility, however, was to convert uncertainty and vigilance into effortless routine. In the 1970s Tom Wolfe described how test pilots fashioned a style of studied boredom that filtered down to standard airline pilot communications. Voyage reports, however, show that the original honor belonged to sea captains.[72]

For all the economic theories of the firm, the day-to-day ruled. Shipping companies' files were filled with the records of shipments or schedules gone wrong. More interesting, however, was the daily problem solving that set things right. As in loading a ship. Otto Brix, HAPAG's inspector in Antwerp in the 1920s, ascribed 75 percent of all loading irregularities to the difficulty of working at night, and sent in his own chilling details. On the other hand, inspectors like him possessed the technical knowledge and experience to fix the screwups. Brix's own performance in loading the *Brasilia* explained why global flows ever moved with any semblance of the regularity promised by liner shipping. The *Brasilia* arrived in Antwerp harbor on the 27th of November 1925 in cold, black ice, and what would develop over the next several days into driving snowstorms. It was forced to tie up at a post the first night because its quay berth was not vacated until the next evening. Because of the miserable weather, a loading lighter was unable to come. Having already assembled work gangs, Brix put them to work moving auto frames loaded in Hamburg onto the deck to make way for stowage of heavier cargo. Several days into the job the stevedore workers demanded more money. An official labor representative

---

[72] GAR/Lloyd 2/S1305/6 October 1955 (Van Manen), 12 December 1953; HAPAG/3492/31 October 1937 (Passehl); Tom Wolfe, *The Right Stuff* (New York: Farrar, Straus & Giroux, 1979).

was summoned. He ruled the workers out of line and they settled down, but the friction caused a day's slowdown. Much of the cargo loaded was heavy cargo, up to five-ton crates, which demanded great time and effort to stow and secure in the holds. Loading from lighters in the cold and snow was not too difficult, but land transport in the port was scarcely moving, and this delayed loading cargo from quayside. With all the heavy cargo charged, it was necessary to sort out the lighter cargo and shift it to the back of the ship to keep the vessel from lying too low in the water. Working days and nights, the ship was close to turnaround within one week, even under the "unbelievable conditions at the quay," as Brix described them. It was still necessary, however, to replace the auto frames below, and heavy cargo now occupied their original place in the second hold. The only place for the frames to go was between decks, if they would fit. Brix, the first officer, and the stevedore measured the hatches and decided it was worth a try, even though there were only millimeters to spare. Thwarted, Brix then had the carpenter saw off the end of the cases – this was possible without damaging the frames – to get them through. There remained the problem of what to do with crates of mirrors two meters high. The only space where they would fit securely was designated for another large box. Brix recommended leaving the mirrors behind, but smaller boxes in the shipment had already been loaded and the agent insisted that they all go together. The only thing to do with the other large box was to lash it on deck, but this required approval from the shipper and time had run out. The box was left behind. Brix, in his report, regretted he had not advised the agent of this possibility earlier, but hoped the company would understand that the loading of the *Brasilia* was in every which way "*eine aufregende Sache.*"[73]

The greater value of a Brix was the replication of his kind in all parts of the world. Juan H. Krüger, HAPAG's agent in Guayaquil, alerted at nine in the evening that the *Amasis*, not due until the next morning, was arriving in an hour, managed to "drum up" the necessary port authorities and unloading services, even though "in nine times out of ten this is impossible." By 11:30 that evening Krüger had four lighters and four gangs ready to work, keeping them going through the night and the next day, and thus holding turnaround time to about twenty hours. To prepare for a smooth reception at the next port, Puerto Bolivar, Krüger had been in contact with the principal consignees for more than a week. When a promised tug to tow extra lighters to Puerto Bolivar was not forthcoming

[73] HAPAG/2917/UA 1/1 June, 18 December 1925.

(there were only three in the port and one was always out of service), Krüger fired off a telegram to the director of Public Works and got the necessary boat.[74] There were also the exceptional efforts of Diethelm & Co., Rotterdamsche Lloyd's agents in Bangkok, to compensate for the on-and-off promises of a company steamer to make an unscheduled stop at the southern Thai ports of Phuket and Kantang to take on rubber. When one ship's arrival was canceled, Diethelm fired off cables to Batavia to get a replacement, the *Salatiga*, to rescue shippers who had already contracted with buyers in the United States. When an urgent cable arrived in Bangkok on the 30th of November, announcing the *Salatiga*'s arrival for the 2nd of December (not the 6th as promised), Diethelm suddenly faced the challenge of getting its men to Kantang in time to organize and supervise the ship's loading. The only efficient means of transport from Bangkok was by air, but the next flight to the nearest airport, still a thirty-six hour motorboat ride away from Kantang, was not until the 3rd. Taking this route would result in a three-day delay for the *Salatiga*. The alternative was to catch the 5:30 AM flight to Singora (Songkhla) on the far side of the Thai peninsula. From Singora they would then have to take a taxi or bus to Haadyaai thirty-five miles away, then connect by train to Patalung, another seventy miles distant, and then, "by any obtainable vehicle," voyage through the jungle, avoiding "the frequently occurring holdups by bandits and gangsters in this area," to Trang just north of Kantang. Seeing no other option, the agents spent the entire night hunting all over Bangkok for officials of Siamese Airways to arrange tickets to Singora, only to learn that there were no seats on the plane. "We succeeded, however, in securing these passages after some negotiations," and managed to make it to Kantang late on the night of the 2nd, where they loaded 825 of the promised 900 tons on board the *Salatiga* (the remaining 75 tons were lost when the wooden lighter carrying them out to the ship hit a submerged rock and sank: another of the standard perils of calls at little-frequented ports).[75] Again global and local figured within shipping companies, this time as resourcefulness and expertise.

Perhaps what shipping men did best, however, was what their passengers and cargo did: They traveled, constantly, to every point in the world. Böger and Loepthien's voyage to the United States for HAPAG in the 1920s inspecting agencies, visiting exchanges, meeting with shippers, working luncheons and receptions, "schmoozing" with railroad companies

[74] HAPAG/3127/25 January 1937.
[75] GAR/RL/Correspondentie/1948/1453/1, 8, 18, 27 December 1948.

and customs officials, was only one of hundreds, probably thousands, of networking trips undertaken by shipping executives of all companies of all dimensions. In older world economies, it was often the intermediary between two worlds who bridged cultures and advanced world trade. In the highly globalized context of the twentieth century, it was frequently the businessman on the business trip that fulfilled the connecting role. Such incessant travel served myriad functions. One inspected. One canvassed. One studied port facilities. One smoothed out rumpled feathers. One of course learned a great deal. Decades before Alan Bott set out to learn his trades, W. G. Leeman of the Holland Australia Line journeyed to Australia for eight months to study sheep stations, wool auctions, wool consignments, and loading techniques – anything that could inform him about how the voluminous business in wool exports operated.[76]

Mostly, however, one networked. The personal approach to travel built ties, but it also allowed companies to infuse familiarity and trust – the oxygen of networks – into their relationships. The first order of business for L. P. D. Op Ten Noort in 1890, when he arrived in the Dutch East Indies to run the newly created KPM, was a trip across the islands where he met personally with European, Chinese, Arab, and Indonesian traders to inquire into their needs and to sell his service. In letters to the board in Amsterdam he wrote of these talks: "I have no hesitations in saying that all these conversations will contribute, in spacious measure, to securing a favorable reception for our company's trade in the outer islands; they have delivered up a treasure house of information which we could never have gained in any other way."[77] Interestingly, as the world bureaucratized more, global interchange continued to run on face-to-face contacts. The better part of a century later, the near oxymoronic intimacy of global business remained an effective strategy. André André-Dumont, of Belgium's Armement Deppe, expressed exactly this sentiment when he described how he had won an American Gilsonite contract for his firm, taking it away from the competition at the last moment by traveling from Antwerp to the middle of the American continent:

I was able to expose, *in person* [author's italics] Antwerp's advantages in general from the point of view of storage and forwarding, [and] the advantages of the CMB-DEPPE quays in particular where they would secure storage at the water's edge practically for nothing and a limitless possibility of forwarding by truck, rail, or water, without other expenses aside from loading. I was able to

---

[76] GAR/Lloyd 2/S2014/Reisrapport, 21 March 1922.
[77] De Boer and Westermann, *Eeuw*, 53–60 (quoted 54).

demonstrate that we live neither by warehousing nor by forwarding but by transporting, and the rest is for us only "*services rendus*" to our clients practically without cost to them.... As a result of all this, a first allotment of 1,000 tons has just been booked, and there is every reason to expect that these movements will be regularly confided to us.

Then, at the end of this report:

The annexes of this report show that personal contacts are productive and indispensable and that the Americans like it when one takes the trouble to go and see them.[78]

Ports required massive installations, but their importance to a global economy was the quality of the networks they constructed. The same pertained to shipping. Companies built ships in profuse numbers, but it was their skill in forming and running networks that determined how and why world transport operated.

Fifteen years before his tour through the United States, Marius Böger traveled to Australia, New Zealand, the Dutch East Indies, and South Africa, where he met with countless exporters and shippers. In Melbourne alone he visited the offices of fifty-eight companies. A handful were banks or shipping firms, but the remainder were general merchants, traders, or manufacturers concerned with import and export.[79] Their sheer number testified to the breadth of a world economy fueled by shipping connections across the seas, but also to how thickly trading houses had populated the widest reaches of the globe. The history of maritime globalism in the twentieth century begins with ports and steamship lines. Invariably it moves on to trading companies. Expatriate firms, they too were about Europeans projecting out into the world, but also home based, and building networks, and thus mediating between local and global.

[78] Antwerp, Compagnie Maritime Belge Archives (CMB)/D 13/2/19 February–20 March 1962.
[79] HAPAG/3477.

3

Trading Companies and Their Commodities

Internatio, the largest trading company in the East Indies on the eve of the Second World War and shorthand for the more cumbersome Internationale Crediet- En Handelsvereeniging "Rotterdam," was, like other commercial juggernauts Europeans scattered throughout the non-Western world, an archly imperial firm. Founded in 1863, its office personnel in the East in 1939 numbered more than 1,300, of whom more than 200 had been sent out from Europe, and its seventeen branches covered mostly colonial territory. Dutch owned and run in a Dutch domain, it was favored by Dutch legal conditions for trade, ownership, or simply presence in a distant territory, and its principal transactions were the exchange of harvested goods for European manufactures. It was the East Indies' largest trader in pepper and sold vast quantities of sugar, although its export trade encompassed close to the full range of tropical commodities. Between the two wars, it opened mills and factories, but its closest production ties were to the world of estates or plantations. On Java the company owned tobacco, coffee, tea, rubber, and cinchona plantations, and it invested and managed the affairs of still more estates that consigned their products to Internatio and were operated under its superintendence. Since 1878 it had held the ship agency for the Rotterdamsche Lloyd, another pillar in the colonial business establishment, and for the remainder of their mutual time in the archipelago, Internatio ran the Rotterdamsche Lloyd's business in the East. Like Swires and Holt or Mackenzie and BI, the Rotterdamsche Lloyd founded its operations east of Suez on the networks that Internatio built. Internatio's personnel thus came to see themselves as old hands and at home in the little Hollands they constructed abroad. Initiates of a clubby, informal community, where first names were used, they forever linked colonial society and commercial purposes in what they did. J. J. Noorduyn, who worked for the ship agency department on Sumatra in the 1940s, recalled week-end invites to the big estates, including Goodyear's Wingfoot. He played sports, he danced and was shown around, "and then you get to know the people and you see how actually a rubber plantation works." Thoroughly immersed in Dutch colonial culture, Internatio turned into an institution of it. House photographs of prominent office buildings in Batavia or Semarang, or of office staff, Europeans dressed in white and seated on chairs, Indonesians in indigenous clothing with legs curled on the ground in front of them, bore, as much as the pepper Internatio shipped back to Europe, the imperial scent of a former world.

This was, however also a global company where Eastern relations were as transnational as they were imperial. Worldwide purchasing was done through Rotterdam, but also through a correspondent house in New York and a branch in Kobe. The head office in Rotterdam dealt with Batavia, but also Europe and America. Offices in the East Indies sold directly to Australia, China, and the Middle East. On the islands, Internatio depended on Chinese middlemen for its local distribution networks. J. J. Noorduyn traveled to the big estates, but a large part of his day was also taken up with visits to Chinese traders during which he learned a very different way of operating. As shipping agent Internatio oversaw the imperial transportation networks by which European personnel in the East transited back and forth between Europe and the colony. But it also ran the Rotterdamsche Lloyd's pilgrim trades, where European shipping prowess intersected with Islamic religious practice to advance the integration of a very far-flung Muslim world. Wider globalizing processes were implicit in the establishment of these houses. Alongside Dutch trading companies the East Indies trading world was populated by Japanese, Hadhrami Arab, Armenian, Indian, and Malay merchant firms. To the formulaic tropical-commodities-for-manufactured-goods exchange pattern must be added the degree to which trading companies came to function as intermediaries for the spread of Western consumer culture to populations in other lands. Attached to the home base in Rotterdam, Internatio personnel passed long stages in Indies ports and were no less identified with their prosperity. Like the shipping companies it served, Internatio too was a local and global firm, and the very name – Internationale Crediet- En Handelsvereeniging "Rotterdam" – captured nicely the dual identities enclosed within. This was a company clearly operating between two

Two Examples of Maritime Architecture, Imperial and Home Port

FIGURE 1. Internatio's Batavia office building. With the permission of Internatio-Müller NV.

worlds, both in terms of its own identity and network formation, but also as a mediator between Europeans and the "overseas."[1]

---

[1] A. C. Mees, N. V. *Internationale Crediet-En Handels-Vereeniging 'Rotterdam'. Gedenkboek uitgegeven bij het vijf-en-zeventig jarig bestaan op 28 Augustus 1938* (Rotterdam: N.V. Internationale, Crediet- En Handelsvereenigning 'Rotterdam,' 1938); Rotterdam, N. V. Internatio-Müller/Archiven van de Internationale Crediet-En Handelsvereeniging 'Rotterdam' (ICHVR)/168/June 1944, 24 May 1946; ibid., 172/1954; J. W. Noorduyn,

FIGURE 2. Hamburg's Chilehaus. Denkmalschutzamt Hamburg-Bildarchiv, Germany Willi Beutler, 1940.

One Internatio would have been a phenomenon, a multitude of Internatios capture in good part how a world of connections proceeded. Big and small, in all quadrants of the globe, their stark imperial identities in non-Western domains cannot be denied, and need to be explored. Of all maritime enterprises they were the most colonial in terms of where they clustered and how they functioned. Here is where empire most visibly intersected with globalism. It was, however, their transnational character, and their facility for crossbreeding home and abroad that, like ports and shipping, revealed a global world in action.

Ruys & Co., interview with author, Antwerp, 11 February 1998; F. A. van Brouwershaven, ex-Internatio, interview with author, Rotterdam, 4 September 1997; Joost Jonker and Keetie Sluyterman, *At Home on the World Markets: Dutch International Trading Companies from the 16th Century until the Present* (The Hague: SDU, 2000) 202–214, 230, 245–249 (where they cite higher figures for personnel in 1939); G. E. Sipos, "Expansie, crisis, en aanpassing. De geschiedenis van het handelshuis Internatio in Nederlands-Indië voor de Tweede Wereldoorlog en de mate waarin de aanpassing aan de crisis van de jaren dertig effectief was" (Ph.D. diss., Rijksuniversiteit Leiden, 1992); William Gervase Clarence-Smith, "Middle Eastern Entrepreneurs in Southeast Asia, c. 1750–c.1940," in Ina Baghdiantz McCabe, Gelina Harlaftis, and Ioanna Pepelasis Minoglou, *Diaspora Entrepreneurial Networks: Four Centuries of History* (Oxford: Berg, 2005), 222–223.

HOUSES

From the start it should be understood that trading houses, though
entwined with shipping, were something other than shipping companies. Many served as agents for shipping lines or were themselves shipping operators, as was the case with Swires (China Navigation) or even
more so Mackinnon Mackenzie (British India Steam Navigation). The
identity – trading house – was in fact often a misnomer, so diversified had
many companies become by the middle of the twentieth century. Besides
shipping, trading companies moved into planting, mining, milling, timber harvesting, manufacturing, real estate, insurance and brand product
representations, or some combination of these. Some houses all but abandoned traditional import/export activity. Yet so ingrained was trading
in their traditions that it could never fully be separated out from everything they did. From trade flowed knowledge, experience, contacts, and
information, so that even if trading was no longer always a core activity
the trading company label remained fixed and represented an accepted
sense of themselves.[2] Perhaps the best definition of a trading company
was therefore a house, such as Internatio, that retained its merchant origins and that, despite diversification, was still implicated in one way or
another with international commodity trades.

The number and range of trading companies by the beginning of
the twentieth century were truly striking. Some, like the Sassoons, who
carved out trading, banking, cotton mill, and real estate empires in India
and China, and numbered among their ancestors the oldest, wealthiest,
and most prominent of Jewish families of Baghdad, were steeped in centuries of merchant wealth and storylike in their origins.[3] By contrast, in
the backwater Caribbean port of Ríohacha, where hides were carted in
by mule and taken out by canoe to ships, two German trading firms –
Enriquez & Cia and Moises Enriquez – and several small Colombian
houses eked out an import/export business.[4] In between the numbers
were legion. Europe's port cities would have spawned thousands of small
and medium import and export houses such as Hüpeden and Company,
which shipped textiles to East Asia and whose roots ran back to the nineteenth century.[5] At the other side of the world, an advertisement by the

---

[2] Jonker and Sluyterman, *Home*, 120, 149–151. On the difficulty of definitions, see also
Jones, *Merchants*, 13–14.
[3] Stanley Jackson, *The Sassoons: Portrait of a Dynasty* (London: Heinemann, 1989).
[4] HAPAG/3127/5 December 1931.
[5] Peter Hüpeden, Hüpeden and Company, interview with author, Hamburg, 27 June 1996.

Borneo Company – a large British trading house in Southeast Asia – for companies for sale turned up a dozen and a half replies. These included G. H. Slot & Co., a venerable Penang and Singapore house dating back to the 1880s, and H. Bolter & Co., "a one-man show literally," but also Sim Ah Kow, whose connections extended to Europe, Egypt, India, China, America, and Australia.[6]

Not to be forgotten therefore were the numerous non-Western merchant firms, many sustaining sizable volumes of trade, whose commercial networks looped through those of European shipping and trading companies and constituted a wider transnational connection within the more formal relations of empire. Claude Markovits has described how Sindhi merchants fanned out along the steamship routes to market Asian silks and curios to a mounting Western imperial clientele and tourist trade, a reverse side to the transfer of Western consumer culture described further on in this chapter. Some were present as far west as Panama; others as far east as Japan.[7] Less well known, but also sizable were Allibhoy Chagla & Co. in Colombo, or H. S. M. Kazrani & Sons, a Bombay house engaged in Persian Gulf trade and working often with the Sassoons.[8]

All were part of a global web of commerce, but there were so many firms at the top that it makes the most sense to concentrate on those. Geoffrey Jones, in his study of British trading companies, identified more than seventy large enterprises operating abroad.[9] For all these companies, and their German, Dutch, French, Swiss – and so forth – counterparts, perhaps the standout feature was how alike they were. Nearly all were imperially based, either within home empire or within an informal imperial relationship. Nearly all too had wider cosmopolitan linkages. Individually, their histories are endlessly fascinating, but they nearly always added up to a much of a muchness.

What Internatio set up on the East Indies was therefore simply the Dutch variation on a common experience throughout Southeast Asia. This chapter could just as easily have begun with Britain's Harrisons & Crosfield, no less a huge trader and producer of tea, rubber, and palm oil in India, Malaya, and the Dutch East Indies, with later investments in timber harvesting in the forests of British North Borneo, and also a holder of steamship agencies. This too was a huge company, thriving on

---

[6] Guildhall/Borneo Company LTD (BCL)/MS 27,259/Box 1/18, 24, 26, 29 August 1955, 1, 3 September 1955; GAR/Lloyd 2/2024/#219/17 August 1946.

[7] Markovits, *Global*, 110–155.

[8] GAR/HAL/Directie 785/1912.

[9] Jones, *Merchants*.

empire but also active on the world scene with branches, partnerships, or interests in Kobe, China, Australia, and North America.[10] Or it could have begun with the German version, Behn, Meyer & Co., founded in 1840 in Singapore by two Hamburgers, or the French version, Denis Frères, established in Saigon in 1862, huge sellers of rice, and described by Swires right after the Second World War as "probably the largest general merchants and estate agents in Indochina." They too were ship agents and, like Swires, ran a coastal affiliate, the Compagnie Côtière de l'Annam.[11] Such multiple pairings could be tracked around the world.

All were properly the descendants of the VOC and East India Company, even if they lacked the monopolistic and parastatal qualities of such forebears. Geographically they still captured the metropole-colonial nexus. Nearly all required a European base, which functioned as their liaison with home markets. With few exceptions they located in the great port cities of the west European continent. At the other end they tended to cluster within their respective empires, and remained identified with these even after the firm opened offices elsewhere: Denis Frères in Indochina; Internatio in the Dutch East Indies; Steel Brothers in Burma; Rallis, Finlays, and Mackinnon Mackenzie in India; United Africa Company and CFAO in West Africa. The imperial connection was not all they were about, but it was conspicuous. Group portraits before impressive colonial structures were a business cliché, but they also signaled a special kind of embedment, connectivity, and, most fundamentally, a bundle of world trade built out of a colonial paradigm. That business fact of life, and milieu, is inescapable.

Imperial Enterprises

Empire was built into the economic framework inherited from the late nineteenth century. Newly settled lands, or the extraction of raw materials by cultivation, mining, or logging in the conquered territories of Africa and Asia triggered massive seaborne flows of people and goods. Colonial harvesting in all its forms became a big business central to how a global economy functioned through the first half of the twentieth century. Although the largest share of trade was still within and between

[10] Pugh, *Great*; Guildhall/Harrisons & Crosfield [Harrisons]/Spheres of Operation, 1917; Jones, *Merchants*, 166–169.
[11] Helfferich, *Behn*; *La Maison de Denis Frères à l'occasion de son centenaire. Histoire depuis sa fondation en 1862 jusqu'à nos jours* (Denis Frères: Bordeaux: 1963); SOAS/JSS III 1/21/Box 408/16 July 1946 (quoted).

Western countries, commerce with formal or informal empire accounted for a very considerable share of the "global" in global exchange. Much of the rubber, copper, tin, tea, coffee, cocoa, rice, spices, fruits, meats, skins, wool, tropical woods, and mineral or vegetable oil – as well as prodigious quantities of grain consumed by Westerners – emanated from these overseas lands.

The orchestrator of these flows was an imperial business structure nearly as expansive as the trades it handled. Imperial banks exported capital for infrastructural development and provided the credit for international trade. As Cain and Hopkins have argued, capital export launched a dynamic by which outward flows of money financed inward flows of products to service debt.[12] The maritime business sectors with which this book is engaged – ports, shipping companies, trading companies, and other service intermediaries – then became the enabling mechanisms that made this happen. Well into the twentieth century shipping and trading networks were an economic and institutional presence in Western empire and the means by which colonies were harnessed for global exchange. Even in the case of Germany, where empire was never extensive and was obliterated by the First World War, sizable German overseas "colonies" of trading companies, estate owners, agents, and brokers functioned in a comparable way. Up until 1914 the imperial world was a fairly open one. Melchers, a German house in China, held memberships on the board of directors of the Hong Kong and Shanghai Banking Corporation, the Hong Kong and Kowloon Wharf and Godown Co., and the Hong Kong and Shanghai chambers of commerce.[13] Much of this openness disappeared with the war and the Depression, giving way to systems of imperial preference or import substitution. Colonial markets never closed entirely, however, and even import-substituting nations needed foreign machines, parts, and materials. Throughout networks remained the key instrument of shipping and trading, and nearly always they transcended purely imperial connections. Nevertheless they found in the colonies, especially those of their home nation, favorable shelter in which to nestle. Dutch trading and shipping companies concentrated in the East Indies, and British companies concentrated in British South and Southeast Asia. Imperial rule favored network formation and, in doing so, often set the vectors by which flows moved.

[12] Cain and Hopkins, *Innovation*, 233, 302.
[13] Allister Macmillan, *Seaports of the Far East: Historical and Descriptive Commercial and Industrial Facts, Figures, and Resources*, 3rd ed. (London: W. H. & L. Collingridge, 1926), 226.

Within this process the central intermediary became the trading company. These were the companies most deeply set within imperial lands. They were present through their trading posts, their multiple office holdings, their overseas staffs, but especially through their exploitation of imperial rule and property law, as well as the security that came with empire, to invest in and manage the great harvesting concessions that poured modern colonial commerce upon the world's markets.

Plantations had accompanied colonization across the Atlantic, and become, in part, synonymous with it. In modern empire, estates or mining and logging operations were just as much a defining feature. There was no one model for how these commercial enterprises developed, nor did they need to be strictly colonially sited. Coffee plantations in Brazil bridged slave- and free-labor economies, and even in Malaya there were large estates under Chinese ownership.[14] Elsewhere, in Western-held Africa and Asia, big corporate multinationals laid out estates at considerable scale. But two other developments preoccupy us here. One was the creation of independent – yet often very large – tropical plantations inseparable from the empires that produced them. The Assam Company was an offspring of botanical gardens research, grand imperial designs, and daring missions to transplant tea from China to India. Nearly a hundred years after its founding, India and Ceylon together accounted for 275,000 of the approximately 400,000 tons of world teas on the export markets.[15] The Michiels-Arnold lands on Java, dating back to the days of the VOC, possessed even more impeccable colonial bloodlines. Encompassing close to 115,000 hectares on which it cultivated rice, coffee, cinchona, sugar, tobacco, and rubber, its headquarters were in The Hague, with a small corps of thirty administrators and planters on Java in 1937. On the Selawangi tea estate alone, however, monthly figures included more than 20,000 laborers.[16] Still larger, and supremely imperial, was the Deli My, a huge tobacco grower in northeast Sumatra. J. T. Cremer, the man most responsible for the company's success, was also to serve as colonial minister.[17] Such estates were obviously rooted in colonial

[14] GAR/Lloyd 1/1545/19 July 1952; Huff, *Economic*, 219–222.
[15] H. A. Antrobus, *A History of the Assam Company, 1839–1943* (Edinburgh: T. and A. Constable, 1957); DLA/PLA 445/Tea 1933.
[16] NA/Michiels-Arnold, Cultuur-en Handelsmaatschappij te Amsterdam 1887–1957, 2.20.02.02 (MA)/Inventory; ibid., 133/Jaarrapporten 1921–1937; ibid., 128/Jaarslagen 1936 (Selawangi). E. C. Godée Molsbergen, *Maatschappij tot exploitatie van rijstlanden op Java. "Michiels-Arnold" N.V. 'S-Gravenhage, 1887–23 Juli–1937* ('S-Gravenhage: Mouton, 1937).
[17] NA/N.V. Deli Maatschappij/2.20.46/N.V. Deli Maatschappij en daarmee gefuseerde bedrijven 1869–1967 (Firm history); Allen and Donnithorne, *Western*, 79–81, 95–98; Anna

rule, but they also gravitated into close relationships with trading companies that they used as agency houses for their exports. In the Michiels-Arnold case, one of the partners in the merchant house Reynst & Vinju, through which it traded, was both a close adviser and, later, head of the board. After the Second World War, Michiels-Arnold would itself evolve into a trading firm.[18]

For the first half of the century, however, it was the reverse that obtained: estates evolving out of trading house initiatives. Across South Asia, Southeast Asia, and Africa, and true as well of Latin America, trading companies owned, floated, and managed plantations, mines, logging concessions, oil exploitations, and sheep farms. In most instances they preferred agency control to wholesale possession. Even large firms such as Internatio and Harrisons, which invested heavily in plantation development, managed far more estates than they owned outright. Either way, however, their role was assured by the drift toward bigness in many commodity groups, and the resources trading companies could marshal in return. There were numerous sources of this trend: price fluctuations, standard grading that favored scaled-up uniform production, increasing global competition, and entry and equipment costs.[19] In multiple commodities the gestation period was often years. Rubber trees only begin to produce in their fifth year, with no money coming in before that time.[20] Cinchona trees required fifteen before maturity. The Assam Company took years to learn how to produce tea correctly on the hillsides of India, and for the sheer struggle to wrestle tea plantations into productivity, few accounts can match Hella Haasse's tale of Rudolph Kerkhoven's endeavor on Java.[21] Breeding-up programs on Argentinian ranches – in effect, a plantation for animals – took several years, and required five to ten times as much land as did fatteners.[22] Teak, legendary for its durability and resistance to insects, and lumbered in great quantities by Westerners for use in shipbuilding or rail ties in India, required girdling and then

Laura Stoler, *Capitalism and Confrontation in Sumatra's Plantation Belt, 1870–1979* (New Haven, CT: Yale University Press, 1985), 16–17.

[18] Godée Molsbergen, *Maatschappij*, 57–77.

[19] J. W. F. Rowe, *Primary Commodities in International Trade* (Cambridge: Cambridge University Press, 1965), 13–27; Stoler, *Capitalism*, 17–18; Allen and Donnithorne, *Western*, 139.

[20] Coates, *Commerce*, 108–109; Huff, *Economic*, 75, 79.

[21] Antrobus, *History*, 75–90; Hella S. Haasse, *Heren van de thee* (Amsterdam: Querido, 1992).

[22] Colin Crossley and Robert Greenhill, "The River Plate Beef Trade," in D. C. M. Platt, ed., *Business Imperialism, 1840–1930: An Inquiry Based on British Experience in Latin America* (Oxford: Clarendon Press, 1977), 293, 311–312.

three years for sap to dry out and render the log floatable. It then had to be hauled by elephants or buffalos to where it could be launched downstream. "All this means years of waiting for any return on the necessarily large capital placed at risk.... Obviously, no small firm ... could afford to engage in this exacting trade."[23]

But trading companies could. Knowledgeable on the ground and headquartered in financial centers, they could convert reputation, experience, and contacts into mobilization of capital for commodity production. They did not need to own many shares themselves. Through interlocking directorates they could exert control and appoint themselves managing agents, with all the agency fees and insider commissions that came with that sweet assignment. In effect, as managers they could enhance every profit center in their enterprises: purchasing and selling through their trading divisions; shipping and insurance commissions through their in-house representations.

So immersed, in fact, was trade with empire, that imperial culture – life experiences, expectations, forms of expression in language or dress, enabling mechanisms, and ways of relating – as well as commerce came to be mediated by these companies. As good an introduction as any to this basic in imperial life can be found in Harold Braund's memoirs of his early career with Steel Brothers, one of the great Burma trading houses. Born in Colombo as the son of a tea taster, and living the first seven years of his life in Calcutta, Braund packs his account with the tropes and ingrained habits of service in the colonial tropics. Braund in 1932 interviews with Steel Brothers in London where he must list on a written exam the four main ports of Burma. "Down went Rangoon and then, ten pen-sucking minutes later, I remembered that the summons to the ordeal was in my pocket and that the letter-head catalogued the lot." Meetings with directors are about as challenging, a few "monosyllabic indications of interested attention," as old men reminisce about "what happened in Bhamo in 1910" (one senses that he had read George Orwell's *Coming up for Air* before writing up his own story). For the next two years he works in Steel's Rice Department under the direction of senior managers known as "the Bo-gyis,"

men who having completed an oriental stint of twenty-five years or more had returned Home as Departmental Managers, with a possible Directorship as their

[23] Guildhall/Steel Brothers/MS 29,557 (quoted); Henry Longhurst, *The Borneo Story: The History of the First 100 Years of Trading in the Far East by the Borneo Company Limited* (London: Newman Neame, 1956), 73–77; Malcolm Falkus, "Early British Business in Thailand," in R. P. T. Davenport-Hines and Geoffrey Jones, eds., *British Business in Asia since 1860* (Cambridge: Cambridge University Press, 1989), 133–146; Jones, *Merchants*, 255–256.

remaining goal. The hallmarks of these demi-gods tended to be the Burma cheroot, a duodenal ulcer and a habit of absence at funerals of Eastern contemporaries who had died from one or other of these causes.

Poorly paid and living at home at Guildford, in Surrey, Braund studies Burmese in the evenings at the School of Oriental Languages at company expense. "Weekends were devoted to bird watching in the summer ... and, in the winter, to rugby football, and the subsequent pub crawl, with the Guildford R.F.C." All of this will make him a success when he goes to Burma.

That chance comes two years later when "Kep" Brown slips and falls "to his rocky death in the remoteness of the upper Chindwin," and Braund is rushed out as his replacement. He catches the Bibby Line's *Cheshire* in Marseille (Steel Brothers held the Bibby ship agency), joining mostly a passenger list made up of the Sudan Political Service (as far as Port Sudan). Nearly everyone is male. At Colombo he is met by a relative who carts him off to Hirdiramani's, where he is measured for two white drill suits tailored by evening time. At his arrival in Rangoon, Braund is greeted by five chums from his London office days. "After a suitable intake of brandy and ginger ale," at the ship's bar, they take him to Steel Brothers' office where he makes the rounds and is introduced to the Bo-gyis. His accommodations are in a sixth floor chummery, or company bachelor housing, which he shares with five other assistants. This is a dump, and junior assistants with more time in Rangoon board in a somewhat more regal chummery known as "The Gin Palace." Drinking figures largely in this portrait.

Yet Braund works hard. He is at his office desk by six in the morning, stops at about nine to bathe, shave, and eat, then goes from ten to 5:30 in the afternoon with only a fifteen-minute lunch break. The routine repeats on Saturday for most of the day, and then again on Sunday morning, although he does not have to begin until seven. Braund nevertheless finds time to become "a regular worshiper at the Anglican Cathedral." During his off-hours he studies for the Government exam in colloquial Urdu, and is not allowed to join a club until he has passed. Then he has to prepare for the Lower Burmese Commercial exam, including in written script. His greatest relief comes from playing rugby for the Steels' team. He is good enough to be one of only two Steel Brothers players making it onto the Burma fifteen for the All-India tournament in Calcutta, which he sails to in a BI steamer.

Upon his return, Braund is posted to Steel Brothers' oil fields in the north, and travels upriver on an Irrawaddy Flotilla steamer, a slow, romantic voyage whose "enchantment ... I was never to lose." His first assignment is near a larger Burmah Oil Company field with an Anglo-American contingent numbering close to 150, so he has access to a hospital, church, and most important of all, a club with swimming pool, golf course, and cricket and football grounds, with polo available forty miles south at Yenangyaung. Later, when he transfers to Indaw further up-country, the staff is much smaller and the facilities more primitive, but there is still a club with a bar, a library, a billiards table, and a tennis court. Conditions are nonetheless exacting. Temperatures reach 100 degrees by midday. There is an attack on their line of communication by a tiger and a rogue elephant, both of which are hunted and shot, but the greatest threat is the Anopheline mosquito, and Braund's American driller, Jimmie McMurtrie, dies of malaria. Later, Braund too catches malaria. He also gets a new posting, in Steel Brothers' tin dredging works at Tenasserim Archipelago, sailing there again in an old BI steamer. Here he is still more isolated, and swimming waters are infested with crocodiles, although on weekends he can get to Mergui, "Somerset Maugham country, a haunt of beachcombers." This brings to an end his Asian years in the 1930s. During the war, Braund serves behind the lines in occupied Burma. In England on leave at war's end he reunites with Maxine Strong, an American he knows from Burma (her father is an oil-field driller) and whom he will later marry. Back in Rangoon in 1946, he is posted to Steel Brothers' oil fields in India, where he will work for the next two decades.[24]

Nearly everything about this story, and how it is told, echoes life in the late imperial overseas firm. Braund's rush to outfit himself at Hirdiramani in Colombo recalls the long lists of "Outfit for Assistants" prepared for recruits in the tropics: three dozen socks, a dozen short pants, a half dozen white button-up suits, two dozen Indian gauge singlets, but also dinner jackets and shirts "suitable for daily wear & Tennis."[25] The chummeries, and Braund's late marriage, were no accident at all. Nearly everyone he met traveling East in the summer was male. Nearly all his young colleagues were bachelors, because they were cheaper, or because companies feared up-country postings were too severe for Western women, or because, despite the abundance of other women, companies worried about how their men would fit in. Most forbade marriage to indigenous

[24] Guildhall/Steel Brothers/MS 29,556/Braund/"Melody." This was later published as *Distinctly I Remember: A Personal Story of Burma* (Mount Eliza, Victoria: Wren Publishing, 1972).

[25] Guildhall/Harrisons/Correspondence/Kuala Lumpur/Box 1/1910–1920, 22 August 1912 (this box was not yet catalogued when consulted).

women, or to those who were "too local" or "too much of the country," code words for mixed-race descendants.[26] Illness was a banality, and "old Asian hands" were not so old after all. The overwhelming majority of employees in these companies were in their twenties or thirties.[27] Turnover on plantations was potentially severe. At one Michiels-Arnold estate, a supervisor departed, his successor withdrew at the last moment, and a third man was temporarily brought in until a fourth, Philipp, could take the job. But Philipp was found wanting and dismissed five days after his arrival, to be succeeded by Lorm, until he was assigned to another post and succeeded in turn by Doorman, who soon asked for a transfer because the estate was too isolated and his wife's health was poor.[28]

From these conditions trading companies helped fashion a certain imperial way of life. Its habits were reflected in dress styles, bachelor quarters, gin drinking, racial segregation, and practices of a system of home leaves that accounted for the constant movement of Europeans and their families between metropoles and imperial outposts. But all these things – and the tale Harold Braund recounts – emanated from a still deeper immersion in the culture of gentlemanly capitalism whose values, personnel, and purposes permeated the expansion of Europeans overseas. The interweaving of business and empire on these planes was exceptional. Gentlemanly values of trust, character, duty, leadership, fitting in, reputation, face-to-face relationships, and the informality of transacting that carried over into the management of empire were also the operative attributes of the networks by which maritime enterprise functioned. The fundamental, unassailable supposition of gentlemanly behavior – a man's word is his bond – was taken up as the motto, "Our Word Our Bond," by the Baltic Exchange, where ships and cargoes were sold, chartered, and brokered in London. Cain and Hopkins have shown how traditional and merchant elites blended together within the City to form a common service class, and how the mechanisms of public schools, "ancient universities," clubs, and service cultures acculturated a wider personnel for the

---

[26] Guildhall/BCL/MS 27,259/Box 2/19 December 1955, 19, 31 November 1958; Robert G. Greenhill, "Investment Group, Free-Standing Company or Multinational? Brazilian Warrant, 1909–1952," *Business History* 37 (1995): 98; Pugh, *Great*, 87–88. On the real-life dangers of bringing out a spouse on low pay, see the sad story of Hertslett in Guildhall/Harrisons/Kuala Lumpur/Box 1/1910–1920, October 1919–December 1920.

[27] CMB/E 28/33–38/Rapport voyage M. Cattier, 3 September 1941; GAR/Lloyd 2/S1091/11 August 1944; Guildhall/Binny & Co./MS 27,160/Box 7/26 November 1938.

[28] NA/MA/49/27 September 1926, 17 January 1927, 11 June 1928; ibid., 133; Jaarverslag Menteng, 1920.

expanding needs of each, leading to an interchangeability between imperial and merchant circles.[29]

The influence they identify with Sir Ralph Furse is suggestive. For the
better part of the first half of the twentieth century, Furse almost sin-
glehandedly recruited the British colonial service. "Furse's method of
recruitment favoured selection by interview from a pool of candidates
created very largely by his own actively cultivated contacts at Oxford and
Cambridge, and his experience as an undergraduate gave him a 'keen eye
for the merits of that admirable class of person whom university examin-
ers consider worthy only of third-class honours.'" Team games, most of all
cricket, were seen as the right formation.[30] Recruitment by trading houses
of public school graduates and, after the First World War, increasingly of
college graduates, could be remarkably similar. Swires relied extensively
on the recommendations of R. Truslove, the secretary of the Appointments
Committee at Oxford University. "He has found us about fourteen fellows
in the last four years.... He frequently comes to see us in London, has got
the exact stamp of man we want clearly in his head and very seldom wor-
ries us with candidates who are unsuitable." J. K. Swire, a graduate of Eton
and Oxford, also took the lead in selecting overseas staff from the rolls of
Oxbridge, and, occasionally Edinburgh. Harrisons & Crosfield relied as
well on Truslove ("you know the type we want"), but they also canvassed
widely, corresponding with Cambridge, Liverpool, Birmingham, and
Manchester, visiting universities and public schools alike in Glasgow and
Edinburgh, or corresponding with other public schools and with societies
of chartered accountants. Most of the men they dealt with knew whom to
forward on. Responding to an inquiry, Cambridge's secretary sent in three
names: Lathbury ("a pleasant athletic Rugbian, who, although he has not
particularly distinguished himself in Examinations, is, we think capable
and eminently suited for life in the East, and where he would get on well
in all circles"); Thompson ("he is spoken of very highly by his College;
energy and force of character are particularly noted"); and Smallwood
("a prominent man in his College, and as you will see from his War record likely to do well wherever he goes"). Even in the 1950s an application
form used by the Borneo Company still carried as categories "History in
Athletics" and "What games do you play?" In all these cases the real training was still going to occur with the firm.[31]

[29] Cain and Hopkins, *Innovation*, 23–36, 67, 122–127 ("ancient universities" 122), 465.
[30] Cain and Hopkins, *Crisis*, 25–26.
[31] SOAS/JSSXI 1/6/Box 57/28 July 1926; Jones, *Merchants*, 208–210; Guildhall/
Harrisons/845.2/7 April 1920 (Truslove), 14 June 1920 (Cambridge), 17 November 1919
(Liverpool), 4 December 1919; Guildhall/BCL/MS 27, 259/Box 2/19 December 1955.

The other cohering institution – the club – was a mainstay abroad. Historians have pointed to the close correlation between these givens of imperial gentlemanly culture and the business needs of companies overseas. Conformity in background and personality, and a common education followed by in-house training, backed by socializing quarters such as clubs and chummeries, induced identification with business firms whose central management was thousands of miles away. Likewise, a value system that stressed service, "character," and personal honor were of considerable use when agents were distributed across distant postings. Sports and drinking furthered social bonding. They provided outlets for men in isolated surroundings, and in the case of sports, were an antidote to the general unhealthiness of the tropics. Sportsmen in fact were deemed to possess all the right qualities: character, aggressiveness, authority, yet also skill at fitting in. Male camaraderie, buttressed by adherence to a common code, held the firm together, engendered trust within, and provided a reputational face without. In addition, clubs were perfect venues for making contacts and culling information. Nearly everyone who traveled around the world on a business mission – harbor board emissaries, shipping men looking for traffic lines, trading company men setting up a new operation – headed to the clubs. It was not much different from J. J. Noorduyn's weekend invites to big commodity estates, as if he were making country house rounds, where you played sports, you danced and were shown around, "and then you get to know the people and you see how actually a rubber plantation works."[32]

What one got, or aimed for, was, therefore, much akin to what the directors of Smith Mackenzie had to say about their branch personnel in East Africa as they swept through on inspection trips. Morton, the senior shipping assistant in Mombasa, was "very popular with the Mombasa public, the Captains of ships and his Staff. He has a very cheerful disposition, is a good mixer and, when time permits, can knock up 50 or 60 runs for the Mombasa Sports Club ... he should be one of the first for future promotion." Moxon, in Uganda, "is a live wire and I should think will get business." Hodgson in Tanga, who joined Smith Mackenzie after working for another firm, "has an excellent knowledge of the cotton piece goods trade being Manchester trained. He has an excellent knowledge of

[32] Jones, *British*, 49–53, 169–172; Jones, *Merchants*, 206–221; Maria Misra, *Business, Race, and Politics in British India c. 1850–1960* (Oxford: Clarendon, 1999), 45–52; Frank H. H. King, *The History of the Hong Kong and Shanghai Banking Corporation* (Cambridge: Cambridge University Press, 1987–1988), vol. 1, 570–578; vol. 3, 315–347; Cain and Hopkins, *Crisis*, 27; Noorduyn (interview).

Swahili and knows the bazaars of East Africa very well indeed." He was also "a likeable man, good at games and musical. He is well known in East Africa and popular." On the other hand, Malaher, also in Tanga, "is very painstaking and hardworking but rather a recluse and inclined to be a trifle abrupt with customers. He is not a good 'mixer' as he plays no games but keeps very fit by taking long walks alone."[33]

If such a correlation most closely approximated the British model from whence it came, the lives of other European businessmen abroad were not wholly different. For them too, club life was a fixture,[34] and the Dutch phrase "*een man een man, een woord een woord*" or roughly "an honest man's word is as good as his bond" – constituted Dutch shipping circle doctrine.[35] What gentlemanly capitalism transplanted to empire, the trading company replicated to the point that it too represented, and reproduced, an imperial lifestyle, of which Harold Braund, sportsman, club man, good mixer, hard worker, company man, church man, long-term expatriate, a recruit with no particular aptitude for his profession except his formation, his personality, and his desire to go East, was one express product.

The close alliance between business and empire set in motion a number of things, beginning, literally, with human beings, myriads of migrant laborers up rivers or overseas to Southeast Asia or the West Indies, but also Europeans whose far smaller numbers were still impressive. Trading company investment brought infrastructure. The companies dug mines, laid out estates, built office buildings and company houses, erected exchanges, and advocated for harbor facilities and inland transport systems. The frequent connection between trading companies and riverboat or coastal companies in Asia, and also Africa, was far from coincidental.[36]

Their history was interwoven with the creation of botanical gardens and agricultural research stations. Rubber and tea cultivation transferred to South and Southeast Asia through the mediation of botanical gardens in Buitenzorg, Kew, Calcutta, Heneratgoda (Ceylon), and Singapore. The career of Eric Macfadyen represented one telling side to this experimentation. Macfadyen arrived in Malaya in 1902. He served for three years with the Colonial Service and then quit to become a rubber planter.

[33] Guildhall/Smith Mackenzie & Co. Ltd./MS 28,124/1947, 1938.
[34] Bonin, C.F.A.O., 187–188; Brouwershaven (interview); Seiler (interview).
[35] Van Driel, *Samenwerking*, 45.
[36] Broeze, "Ports," 12–13; Huff, *Economic*, 14–25; D. K. Fieldhouse, *Merchant Capital and Economic Decolonization: The United Africa Company, 1929–1987* (Oxford: Clarendon Press, 1994), 194–197 (Niger River Transport Company).

Working up his own estate, he managed, with the backing of a family friend, to float the New Crocodile River (Selangor) Rubber Co. for the development of more rubber plantations. An expert in rubber cultivation, Macfadyen carried that mastery over to Harrisons & Crosfield in 1918. He was an early proponent of the bud-grafting experiments to produce higher yielding trees that were being carried out on the Prang Besar estate, and in 1925 Macfadyen convinced Harrisons & Crosfield to purchase Prang Besar and make it a research center for all of the company's rubber operations. At Golden Hope estate, Macfadyen supported the reintroduction of ground covers to produce healthier rubber trees. Under Macfadyen's leadership, Harrisons also became a pioneer and leader in the collection and shipment of liquid latex. At nearly the same time, he led the company in the mass production of palm oil on its Malayan properties. His prestige and influence within Malayan planter circles was therefore immense. When after the Second World War the Malayan Emergency began to take its toll on planters' lives and nerves, Macfadyen, now in his seventies, came out from London and visited every estate to create an air of unwavering commitment.[37] His life history was, however, merely a leading footnote in the collaboration between agency houses and colonial states to rationalize tropical production for home consumption.

The developmental effects of trading companies upon empires were thus very powerful. Trading companies brokered the world's commodities and created the commercial networks that circulated the world's goods between producers and consumers. As investors, floaters, managers, recruiters, and researchers they were even more instrumental in bringing colonial products onto world markets and orienting the necessary resources – labor, capital, and crop transfers – back upon empire. But all the effects they set in motion, so many human beings on the move, so much globally powered investment, so much time spent between two worlds, can be seen in a wider light and deserve a second scrutiny. Return to Braund for a moment. If he appeared fresh off an imperial assembly line, he was also both Easterner and Westerner, a man of either world. His England was establishment territory: the southeast, Surrey, commutes into the City. He pub crawled. He played rugby. He bird-watched. So colonial in one sense, he was so impeccably British in another. His London time at Steel Brothers he called his "period of preparation for

---

[37] Pugh, *Great*, 46–49, 109–110, 155–156, 175–176, 196–197; D. J. M. Tate, *The RGA History of the Plantation Industry in the Malay Peninsula* (Kuala Lumpur: Oxford University Press, 1996), 418–419, 428.

exile," implying that England was his only true home. Yet he also studied Burmese and Urdu well enough to pass the exams, and he opened his memoirs in an Eastern key: "Child and man I was Asia-based for thirty-eight years. I did not expect ever to return." Sailing to Calcutta to play in the All-India rugby tournament, he recalled his childhood years there. His company, Steel Brothers, could stand for any British imperial company. But it also had entered the cotton and produce business through an association with A. S. Jamal Brothers, an Indian merchant firm in Burma, and Braund's division, the Indo-Burma Petroleum Co., stemmed from another Jamal-Steel Brothers partnership.[38] Like Braund, Steel Brothers carried the traits of crossbreeding. Macfadyen, who went back out to Malaya to quiet fears during the guerilla Emergency, merits a similar retake. Oxford educated, a ruler of sorts, he funded his first venture by calling on an old family friend in Manchester to round up investors. But the first two decades of his career were Malayan: He was fluent in Malay,[39] his crossover from colonial to private service abroad began with a partnership with a Chinese friend,[40] and it was his tropical experience as much as his Western know-how that drove his innovative practices. Transfers, in his case, were more circular than linear. Western science filtered through Eastern formation led to research breakthroughs at his estates, and from these discoveries in Asia, as from the Botanical Gardens in Calcutta or Buitenzorg, came benefits for the West. Imperial enterprises these trading houses were, like ports and shipping companies, balancers between two halves of the world. They too were home and world companies, and need to be placed on this global plane.

Transnational Enterprises

Imperial connections were vital, but they also obscure how global – and local – these companies truly were. The attentions of the London & Kano Trading Company, a short-lived affair dealing in hides and skins from northern Nigeria and whose historical memory was only wrested from oblivion when a graduate student rescued its records from the Cunard House trash in the early 1970s, fluctuated between the intensely micro

---

[38] Guildhall/Steel Brothers/MS 29,557/Brief History of the Company, 1970.

[39] Violet S. Macfadyen, *Eric Macfadyen, 1879–1966* (Barnet, Hertfordshire: Stellar Press, 1968), 3.

[40] Guy Nickalls, "Macfadyen, Sir Eric (1879–1966)," in *Oxford Dictionary of National Biography*, see online ed., ed. Lawrence Goldman (Oxford: Oxford University Press, 2004), http://oxforddnb.com/view/article/34722 (accessed 1 March 2009).

realm of herders and flocks on the central Sudan and world market and production levels.[41] No matter how abridged, traders lived among the world.

Those broader transnational implications cohered to even the most imperial of trades or business houses. The Hajj tells us a good deal about this imperial-transnational relationship. The overseas pilgrimage to Mecca by the turn of the century was circumscribed within the affairs of empire. Colonial powers required passage through quarantine stations, issued passports, and set shipping regulations.[42] Most Hajjis from the two great overseas sending regions – South Asia and Southeast Asia – traveled on the purpose-built pilgrimage ships of Western imperial companies. For the Kongsi Tiga condominium, which controlled the largest of the maritime pilgrimages and was run by the Dutch Mails and Holts from the Straits and East Indies, this was in many regards another imperial trade, a complement to their commodity transports or their passenger trades in migrant labor. Holts entrusted its pilgrim business in Singapore to its agent, Mansfields (which also supplied migrant workers to tobacco estates on Sumatra and Borneo), while the Rotterdamsche Lloyd's Dutch Mails' share was managed through its eastern alter ego, the trading company Internatio.[43]

The Hajj, however, had always been a transnational as well as a religious phenomenon. Centuries earlier, Hajjis had carried the taste for coffee across the Muslim world and begun its dissemination that would, in modern times, make it the second or third most valuable commodity on world markets. For centuries too the Hajj provided the convergence point for pilgrims and merchants crossing and mixing from the far parts of the Muslim ecumene. The intrusion of Western steamship companies in the nineteenth century represented in one sense the encroaching reach of Western imperialism, but in another sense it simply stirred in one more transnational ingredient. Western steamship companies conquered the

[41] Liverpool, Liverpool Record Office/Records of the London Office of the London and Kano Trading Co. Ltd./380 Lon/2/5.

[42] William R. Roff, "Sanitation and Security: The Imperial Powers and the Nineteenth Century Hajj," *Arabian Studies* 6 (1982): 143–160; Mary Byrne McDonnell, "The Conduct of Hajj from Malaysia and Its Socio-Economic Impact on Malay Society: A Descriptive and Analytical Study, 1860–1981," (Ph.D. diss., Columbia University, 1986); MAE/Levant 1918–1929/Arabie-Hedjaz 33/Pèlerinage à la Mecque/21 August 1923; Government of India, *Report of the Haj Enquiry Committee* (Calcutta: Government of India, 1931).

[43] The following is based on Michael B. Miller, "Pilgrims' Progress: The Business of the Hajj," *Past and Present* 191 (May 2006): 189–228.

bulk of the Hajji carrying trade in part because they won the favor of their imperial regimes, but far more because they brought to Hajji transport the logistical, recruiting, and shipping management skills they had hammered out in a century of global migratory transport. The Hajj was a complicated business trade. Scheduling required coordination with feeder services, positioning ships in a highly seasonal traffic, fitting tight windows for arrival in Jiddah, and, once the pilgrimage ended and Hajjis crammed back into the port in a rush to get home, the provision of return vessels without the loss of too much dead time in berth. All of this had to be done across thousands of sea miles. Western steamship companies, however, having mastered global flows, turned this complexity into matter-of-factness. The effects of their intrusion upon the overseas Hajj were therefore considerable. In the mid-nineteenth century, perhaps 2,000 Indonesians had embarked for the Hajj, journeying on small craft of 300 tons or fewer. Following the introduction of Western steamship service the numbers of Indonesian Hajjis increased to 10,000 by the turn of the century, and topped 50,000 in 1927. The great bulk of these traveled on Kongsi Tiga ships, just as nearly 20,000 of the 36,000 Hajjis arriving from India in the same year sailed on Mogul Line ships managed by the British agency house Turner Morrison. Other factors such as rising commodity prices or matters of Islamic identity contributed to these numbers. But the role of the Kongsi Tiga and its confreres was indisputable.

Particularly effective were Kongsi Tiga network linkages with preexistent Muslim ones. Long before the Europeans entered the trade, the business of the Hajj had been run by guides who, on travels of their own or through agent networks, recruited pilgrims and then provided the indispensable services of translation, explaining ritual, and organizing lodging and camel hires (often with exorbitant kickbacks) for the progress to Mecca and Medina (Al Madinah). The genius of the Kongsi Tiga system was to weave these Muslim networks into its larger operation, converting both guides and guides' agents into local brokers. In this way it interposed Islamic intermediaries between a European enterprise and Hajjis traveling to a sacred place from which Europeans were excluded. Within the East Indies, the brokers and their interior networks made up of village chiefs, mosque officials, and religious teachers, coordinated recruitment and the flow of information vital to Kongsi Tiga scheduling, particularly as many pilgrims in outlying regions were transported in KPM feeder ships to collection ports where the larger pilgrim ships docked. Traveling to Makassar in 1948, when everything after the war and occupation was in transition, agent Jacobsz Rosier reported to the Kongsi Tiga on the confusion that now governed pilgrim affairs, in contrast to the old system it had operated through its Muslim agents. Paperwork was a mess, and the precise information that the companies had regularly received before the war on arrivals, numbers, and connections was nowhere to be had. "Nothing," he concluded, "about this [new] organization is going to make us forget our well-tested brokers."[44]

The European or colonial era of the Hajj was thus most notable for the way it amplified cross-national influences on multiple levels. The Dutch and British Kongsi Tiga introduced Western shipping methods into a Muslim sacred event and routinized overseas Hajji transport. It succeeded, moreover, by subsuming Muslim international networks into its own. In its Westernizing manner, it applied to these the same organizational techniques that had served it so well around the world. Business trips glued these networks together, and the reports of Internatio representatives read no differently from those its agents filed after networking visits to plantations on Sumatra. The results were not only to magnify passengers but also the numbers of Eastern religious travelers and the power of the Hajj to shape Muslim cultures. As Westerners moved east, Easterners moved west (as far as Arabia), and as Westerners made profits, the integration of the Muslim world advanced substantially. That transnational dynamic continued even after Muslims reclaimed the trade following decolonization. Then Muslim entrepreneurs or national administrations turned Western co-option of Eastern networks on its head by absorbing the Kongsi Tiga broker system into their own. Yet in the ultimate transnational irony, they would also retain, within their control of their most holy event, the practice and logic of Western enterprise.

It was difficult, perhaps impossible for "colonial" trading companies to elude such transnational consequences, so cosmopolitan were they in their own make-up and business relations and so implicated were they in passing the world's goods around the world. Their imprint, in this regard, was notable in the transfer of Western consumerism to the East. It is now clear that a globally linked consumer culture, in film, beauty, and other products, was radiating outward by the third and fourth decades of the twentieth century.[45] Multinationals, but also trading companies as marketers

[44] GAR/Lloyd 1/1207/20 October 1948 (attached to 14 December 1948).

[45] Kristin Thompson, *Exporting Entertainment: America in the World's Film Market, 1907–1934* (London: British Film Institute, 1985), 137–147; Geoffrey Jones, *Beauty Imagined: A History of the Global Beauty Industry* (Oxford: Oxford University Press, 2010), 121–134; Weinbaum et al., *Modern*; Rory Miller, "Latin American Consumers, British Multinationals, and the Merchant Houses, 1930–1960," MS, 2004; Peter N. Stearns,

and exclusive representatives of branded goods in their distant territories,[46] were among the prime agents of this process, a trail we can pick up in the business travels of H. F. A. A. Behrens for the Batavia trading house G. Hoppenstedt. On a long swing in 1937 through China and Japan, and then through the United States and Europe, completing a round-the-world trip before returning to Java, Behrens was on the hunt for new product lines to sell in the Indies. In Shanghai he was struck by the Warner-Hudnut cosmetics lines he saw in a visit to department stores and in the factory Warner-Hudnut had set up for the Shanghai and Asian markets. "The spending of the modern Chinese woman on lipsticks, powder, and rouge," he wrote in his report, "is greater than I had ever expected," and although he acknowledged that Java was a far different market he wondered what might be accomplished once he had access to a complete sample collection. In New York he mapped out with the Vick Chemical Company a marketing strategy for Vicks VapoRub and Vicks Cough Drops on Sumatra and Java. Vick would ship tens of thousands of samples and Malay inserts, the former to be "distributed from house to house, so that they will reach the homes of Europeans and the better class of Chinese natives," the latter to dealers on the two islands. In other meetings in San Francisco, Chicago, and New York, Behrens spoke with representatives of Bauer and Black, Chesebrough (Vaseline hair tonic), Upjohn, and Mennen. None of this was a novelty for Hoppenstedt. Five years earlier, another Hoppenstedt traveler, P. Blumenthal, had captured the Wrigley's chewing gum account for the colony, speculating on "whether the natives will not like the mint [Spearmint] flavor much better than the peppermint." Blumenthal even had conversations about marketing Cream of Wheat in the Indies.

The potentially endless transfer of goods from one targeted market to another, no matter how distant culturally and geographically the one was from the other, was undoubtedly abetted by the fact that facilitators like Hoppenstedt swam effortlessly within either. Founded in Batavia in 1892, with a German partner, until it decamped from Hanover to Amsterdam in the midst of the First World War, Hoppenstedt from its beginnings juxtaposed Dutch with transnational relationships, and carried this over into nearly everything it did. First stops for Behrens in Kobe, Shanghai, and Hong Kong were invariably Dutch import/export houses.

Consumerism in World History: The Global Transformation of Desire, 2nd ed. (New York: Routledge, 2006), 96–105, 112–113, 118, 128–133.

[46] For a sampling, the list of ninety-seven agencies held by Borneo Co. on Sarawak before World War II: Guildhall/BCL/MS 27,441/Typescript history by T. C. Martine. Also: Jones, *Merchants* 108–110, 246–248; Jonker and Sluyterman, *Home*, 237.

He especially relied on the shipping agencies of the Dutch Java-China-Japan Line for information and introductions through their compradors. Yet his trading partners and networks were Japanese, Chinese, American, and European, including, in Shanghai, C. H. Tang, the manager of the ABC Underwear Weaving and Dying Mill who was of the same ilk and had just returned from a study trip to America. Almost thirty years later, another Hoppenstedt traveler, J. Van Dijk, this time to the Middle East, would start with the same sorts of home networks, albeit now with KLM, and enlarge these into Lebanese ones.[47]

All of these intersections recall just how transnational these trading houses were even within their own colonial sphere. Some were mixed ventures. Sime Darby, one of the largest agency houses in Malaya and Singapore, was a joint Chinese and European firm.[48] Mansfields' management of the Straits Steamship Company (SSC) involved it in an array of cross-national relationships, especially as the SSC acquired three Chinese shipping companies: Eastern Shipping Company of Penang in 1922, the Sarawak Steamship Company in 1931, and the Ho Hong Steamship Company in 1932. The SSC introduced new Western management, but these companies remained to a considerable degree Chinese in character. Chinese were directors, agents, board members, and investors. Board meetings of the Sarawak Shipping Company were conducted in three languages: English, Chinese, and Malay. Bousteads were SSC agents at Tumpat, and Harrisons & Crosfield at Sandakan, but Teck Guan were agents at Brunei, the Hokkien Guild at Kuantan, Yat Fong Brothers at Kudat, Ali Mohammed at Bachok, and Choon Seng, "large copra traders," at Tandjoeng Balei on Sumatra's east coast. From the reverse end, Kian Gwan, the trading and shipping firm assembled by Oei Tiong Ham of Semarang, reputedly the richest man on Java, shipped large quantities of sugar to Volkarts and E. D. Sassoon in India (Volkarts was itself a Swiss firm operating in the British Empire). Its shipping arm, Heap Eng Moh Steamship Co., encountered difficulties in the late 1920s and sold controlling interest to the Dutch KPM, but this company too continued to be operated as a joint European-Chinese concern.[49] Still more common

[47] NA/N.V. Handel-Maatschappij v/h G. Hoppenstedt 2. 20. 56 (Hoppenstedt)/47 (Behrens), quoted 15 April, 22 July 1937; ibid./45 (Blumenthal), quoted 20 June 1932; ibid./56 (van Dijk); ibid./Sri Handajani, "Inventaris van het archief."

[48] Tate, *RGA*, 243–244; Allen and Donnithorne, *Western*, 57; Macmillan, *Seaports*, 470; GAR/Lloyd 2/S2018/#78/8 July 1930.

[49] Tregonning, *Home*, 53–66, 89–94, 112, 117, 130, 139, 150; SOAS/JSSII 2/17/Box 53/19 January 1939; Huff, *Economic*, 147; NA/KPM/127/Rapport Straatemeier, 1924 (quoted); À Campo, *Koninklijke*, 377–378; GAR/HAL/Directie 785/v. d. Linde, 1912.

were the interlocking trading networks between Europeans and non-Europeans: Swires in China and Vorwerks in Chile, certainly, but also French traders in West Africa or in the ports of Morocco, British trading houses working with Marwari dealers in India, or Melchers forming a buying organization with Chinese friends to purchase camel, goat, and sheep wool in inner China.[50]

Ultimately, it boiled down to the same inbred linkage between local and global identities we have found with ports and shipping companies. The instinctive clinging of Hoppenstedt's Behrens to home networks on the start of a journey of ever-widening dimensions captured the hybridity of nearly all these enterprises. The fusion was probably deepest at the edges of empire, where the imperial reach was at best informal. Over generations Vorwerks came to see themselves as both Hambourgeois and Chilean, with the full resources of each community at their disposal. Theodor Wille was a Hamburg-Rio-Santos-São Paulo company, founded in Santos in 1844. Like the Vorwerks its Hamburg connections were flawless, but the roots were just as deep on the other side of the Atlantic, indeed so deep that British Black List attempts to weed it out of existence in the First World War were doomed to futility, and even the definition of German versus Brazilian was impossible to disentangle.[51]

Yet the more typically "colonial" houses were not really different. The Denis brothers' relationship to home port Bordeaux and Indochina discloses a comparable pluralism. Etienne Denis, who founded the firm, was born at Blaye, in the Gironde estuary, and despite the concentration of the Maison Denis Frères' activities in Saigon, Cambodia, Laos, and Tonkin, the head office remained in Bordeaux. Eventually all four Denis sons went out to Indochina, but all inevitably gravitated back to the family seat, the home site of identity. Etienne, grandson of the founder and head of the firm after 1933, was well entrenched within Bordeaux business and social circles, where he served as an *administrateur* with Maurel et Prom, another important Bordeaux trading house, and was elected to the Bordeaux Academy of Sciences and Fine Arts. Identifications with Indochina, however, were nearly as strong. In 1906, when he was seventeen, Etienne traveled with his parents to India, Indochina, and Hong Kong. In 1919, following demobilization from the army and recently married, he went out again (with his wife) on a study trip and to build personal ties to local businessmen. He was in Indochina again in 1926,

[50] Bonin, *C.F.A.O.*, 225–226; Miège, "Maroc," 54; Jones, *Merchants*, 107; *150 Jahre Melchers*, 16.
[51] See the discussion of Theodor Wille further in this chapter and in Chapter 6.

and still again at the beginning of the 1930s for another eighteen-month stay. Once he succeeded his father in 1933 as head of the firm, his trips were frequent, culminating in a decision in 1941 to debark for Haiphong, and later Saigon, where he stayed until 1946 (although the length of this sojourn may not have been altogether voluntary). During the last decade of his life he spent several months every year in the East. His ties to both Bordeaux and Asia, where his associations were Vietnamese as well as French, were thus close and intense.[52]

Most trading companies, in colonies or outside them, straddled home and overseas identifications. They were still Liverpool or Bremen or such-like companies, a home port house that drew on local resources and connections, functioned as a base abroad, mustered forward networks, and channeled an unending flow of goods and services back to the source from whence they had come. Yet as they took up residence in foreign ports, they also came to have the fullest stake in luring liner and commodity traffic to these second-home harbors. Thus, in near perfect imitation of themselves, they turned local or regional connections into world ones. Their twin identities were sustained through partnership houses in Europe and empire, but also by overseas doppelgängers. While founding families or directors returned home, both frequent voyages out and long-serving representatives abroad – such as Lamb, the "great personal friend" of Wong Kwei Kee – solidified dual residencies. At the family firm of Illies, a big Hamburg-Japan trading outfit, Rudolf Hillmann entered in 1920, was sent east from Hamburg in 1924, made junior partner, and subsequently ran the business at the Japanese end. When Carl Illies, Jr. died at the age of fifty-nine, Hillmann took charge. He became the senior figure in the house and effectively guided the firm until he died in 1958, when a third-generation Illies – Carl Jürgen – resumed leadership. Illies was thus a very Hambourgeois but also a very Japanese house.[53] Innately home oriented, the overseas trading firm congruently was unrestrainedly cosmopolitan. Its networks crossed ethnic, religious, national, and power divides, and Steel Brothers was far from alone in attempting to breach the language barrier.[54] The multilateral directions of these firms should therefore not be discounted. Denis Frères ran along the Bordeaux-Indochina axis, but

---

[52] *Denis Frères*, 7–18.
[53] Käthe Molsen, *C. Illies & Co. 1859–1959. Ein Beitrag zur Geschichte des deutsch-japanischen Handels* (Hamburg: Verlag Hanseatischer Merkur, 1959), 84–89.
[54] Jones, *Merchants*, 214–215; SOAS/JSS1 4/7/Box A35/18 November 1916; Guildhall/Binny & Co./MS 27,160/Box 2/17 April 1919; ibid., Box 4/29 April 1926; Guildhall/Smith Mackenzie & Co. Ltd./MS 28,124/1938 (Tanga); NA/MA/Inventory; NA/N.V. Deli Maatschappij/Firm history.

also took on ship agency representations for British and Japanese shipping lines.[55] In this light, the enclaves that Europeans set up abroad – the
little Englands and Hollands – that customarily have been regarded as a
distancing mechanism between occupier and occupied, might instead be
understood as the continued attachment to home within a larger global
identity, empire serving in this instance as the bridge between the two. At
least that coalescence informed the inner as well as outer associations of
trading companies, and enabled them to knead cross-world commitments
into a world trading order.

Articulations

Trading thus dovetailed with ports and shipping to build out world maritime systems. Ports provided docking, handling, coordinating and information centers, and processed mass movements inland and overseas.
Shipping companies offered transport, speed, regularity, and organization that lowered rates and magnified trade. Trading companies added
commercial know-how, conduits for exchange, and promoted the production and distribution of commodities and migrant labor. Each sector thoroughly interlocked with the other. Global chains were formed
of hub ports and feeder ports, or of liner companies and collector lines,
that then followed commodity production around the world. From the
start, however, estate growth depended on adequate transport links with
deep-water harbors through some combination of rail or riverboat feeders and regular, timely connections across oceans to markets and sources
of supply. Comparably, home ports provided city trading conditions and
resources for investment; trading and shipping companies directed massive shipments back to them. The three sectors therefore complemented
one another, but they also created synergies of growth.

By now it should be clear that these happy junctions were far from
circumstantial or the work of providence. Networks accounted for global
flows, and maritime networks aggregated into three great sets – port,
shipping, and trading – each coiled around the others. Main port networks overseas were symbiotic with shipping and trading networks, and
these were often caduceus-like in their own relationships.

A key convergence point was markets, or the venue of trading.
Markets altered profoundly following the introduction of steamships
and overseas cables. The former promised high-volume delivery of

[55] MMM/OA 4B/192.

distant commodities with relative dispatch and on-time arrival. The latter effected near instantaneity in communications between regions of supply and regions of demand. Under these conditions, it was possible to replace scattered, local markets with large formal exchanges that communicated with each other and set world prices. If harvests or supplies failed in one corner of the world, it was possible to offset these with information about substitute shipments from another. In particular, steamships and cable encouraged the rise of futures trading, where contracts merely promised purchase and delivery at some later date. Whether futures speculation evened out price differentials across world markets is debatable. But future markets did lower the threshold of stockholding and thus its accompanying carrying costs. Moreover, by signaling the trends prices were liable to take, they set indicators by which manufacturers could plan their strategies. They also made possible "hedging" – the practice of covering, for example, a contract to sell with a futures contract to buy – which raised comfort levels in high-volume commodity trading by reducing risks of serious loss. Lower risks lowered profit margins and, in turn, lowered costs of commodities for high-volume consumption. Thus the circle was completed. Modern shipping expanded markets; modern markets greased flows and amplified demand for overseas cargoes carried by shipping.[56]

Ports and markets were still more conjoined. Ports were natural sites for commodity trading for three basic reasons. First, they were the physical location where goods were landed, broken in bulk, or transited, and where ownership was transferred from exporters to importers.[57] Second, the congregation of shipping, merchant, brokering, and insuring services made ports nerve centers of information. Markets thrive on intelligence, and on the trust that accrues through a concentration of face-to-face transactions, both of which port cities supplied in abundance. In many European ports, the bourse, or exchange, combined a variety of markets because its primary purpose was simply its existence: a meeting place for anyone engaged in international commerce. Third, the convergence of services in ports made them reservoirs of skill and expertise, without which complex markets cannot operate.

---

[56] Rowe, *Primary*, 43–51; Rees, *Commodity*, 89–90, 103, 133–136, 169–170, 414–416, 434–438; Alston Hill Garside, *Cotton Goes to Market: A Graphic Description of a Great Industry* (New York: Frederick A. Stokes, 1935), 137, 206–226; Robert Greenhill, "Merchants and the Latin American Trades: An Introduction," in Platt, *Business Imperialism*, 172–174.

[57] Rowe, *Primary*, 38.

But there was also a fourth factor that located markets in the great harbors, and that was the networks of these port cities. Liverpool's shipping and trading connections with North America and its proximity to Manchester and Lancashire's mills made it Europe's largest cotton market, just as Le Havre's transatlantic networks resulted in futures trading in cotton, coffee, River Plate wool, indigo, cocoa, sugar, and hides.[58] London's market position derived from its special networks as capital of the world's largest trading and shipping nation and the world's largest foreign direct investor. Shipping, trading, banking, and insurance congregated within the City of London and superimposed layers of service, expertise, and knowledge upon the port. So networked was the City itself that it was possible to buy and sell commodities, hedge these on the London futures market, broker freight carriage at London's Baltic Exchange, and insure these with Lloyd's, without the actual commodity ever passing through London or any other part of Britain.[59] At the same time, these networks turned London into a huge physical market renowned for its public sales in the London Commercial Sale Rooms in Mincing Lane, also located in the City. Despite many contrary factors – the displacing of markets to extra-European ports, direct purchasing by manufacturers, or government controls – port exchanges remained an integral part of maritime systems, at least until the dispersal of port user businesses in containerized harbors.

In *Cotton Goes to Market*, Alston Hill Garside described the peculiarities of trading at Liverpool's Cotton Exchange, Bremen's Bremer Baumwollbörse, and Le Havre's Palais de Bourse. But two things characterized all three. First was the large number of trading and brokering firms concentrated around each exchange. In Liverpool in 1935, 225 cotton trading houses possessed offices either in the Liverpool Cotton Exchange Building or within walking distance, and 115 firms congregated in the Bremer Baumwollbörse or nearby. Second, none was able to make its trades independent of the quotations on the others. One world cotton market existed, joined by cables and banks of telephones.[60] Markets too were local and global, and they functioned like ports, shipping, and trading companies as connectors on a world scale. When all four then worked together and integrated into a common network, they not only marshaled but directed world flows. Commodity chains in two mass consumer goods – wool and coffee – show how.

[58] Vigarié, *Grands*, 207–211.
[59] Rees, *Commodity*, 178.
[60] Garside, *Cotton*, 95–102, 115–169.

COMMODITIES

Wool

The wool trade is one of the oldest, and most prosperous, in the world. Phoenician merchants traded in wool and woolen cloth in the seventh century BCE. Woolen exports to Flanders in the Middle Ages were a major source of wealth, and explain today the solid, glowing beauty of Cotswold villages or the remarkable wool churches of Suffolk. In early modern times, Spanish merchants in Burgos exported abroad millions of pounds of coveted merino wool. In the nineteenth and twentieth centuries, however, industrialization, population growth, and the mechanization of wool manufacture multiplied the volume of wool consumption and export to hitherto unimaginable figures and altered the geographical structure of the trade. In the early 1930s the world's sheep population was estimated to number close to 700 million, and world exports of wool, now counted in tons, climbed above the 1 million mark. Five countries, all in the Southern Hemisphere – Australia, New Zealand, South Africa, Argentina, and Uruguay – accounted for approximately nine-tenths of that commerce. This represented an extraordinary turnaround. As recently as the first half of the nineteenth century, most wool for European consumption had still been grown domestically. What drove wool production overseas were two developments, each occurring about mid-century. One was the growing need of urbanizing societies to convert land use to food crops or meat production. The other was the realization that good quality wool could be raised in the southern temperate zones where pastureland was abundant and rainfall amounts appropriate to expansive sheep ranching. Wool thus developed into a globally traded commodity dependent on sophisticated business arrangements among merchant traders, processors, market operators, and ocean transport companies to secure its movement from inland sheep farms to mills an antipode away. Toward the second half of the twentieth century, wool ranked eighth in export value among the world's traded goods.[61]

---

[61] H. S. Bell, *Wool: An Introduction to Wool Production and Marketing* (London: Pitman & Sons, 1970), 2–4; Carla Rahn Phillips and William D. Phillips, Jr., *Spain's Golden Fleece: Wool Production and the Wool Trade from the Middle Ages to the Nineteenth Century* (Baltimore: The Johns Hopkins University Press, 1997); Imperial Economic Committee (Intelligence Branch), *Wool Production and Trade, 1928–1934* (London: His Majesty's Stationery Office, 1935), 8, 53; A. Barnard, "A Century and a Half of Wool Marketing," in Alan Barnard, ed., *The Simple Fleece: Studies in the Australian Wool*

Its most prized producer was the merino sheep, whose soft, fine fleece can contain up to 8,000 fibers in a square centimeter. An additional attribute of the merino is its hardiness and its aptness for drier pasturelands suitable for little else than sheep ranching. Other breeds, such as the Lincoln or Romney Marsh, yield varying degrees of coarser quality wool, but are better suited for mutton and, especially in the case of the latter, thrive in wetter environments. Among the great Southern Hemisphere producers, different strategies consequently prevailed. Argentina, the world's third largest wool-producing country and second largest exporter, saw its absolute export figures decline as more land was turned over to grain and cattle use, and the huge market in chilled and frozen meat encouraged sheep ranchers to cut back on their stocks of merinos and raise crossbreeds that could be sold for mutton as well as their wool. In New Zealand, where there are "bags of water," ranchers also focused on meatier animals and lamb and mutton production. New Zealand wool was therefore tough and better suited for carpets. By contrast, the drier Australian climate produced a wool that grew more slowly and was more deeply sprung and hence desirable for garments that would hang out in the morning. In South Africa, where merino sheep represented the major portion of the flock, wool was equally of a higher quality. The result was that on world markets South Africa ranked just behind Argentina as a wool exporter, while Australia emerged as the unquestionable leader.[62]

The first European settlers arrived in Australia in 1788, and nine years later a ship sailed in with the first merinos. The fate of the first cleaved to the second as Australian wool developed into the country's leading export and the world's greatest source of supply. From 1928 to 1929, the United Kingdom imported close to 120,000 tons of Australian wool, and tens of thousands of tons more went to France (89,000), Germany (52,000), Belgium (53,000), and Japan (50,000).[63] The wool trade's needs gave rise

Industry (Carlton: Melbourne University Press, 1962), 476–477; Rowe, *Primary*, 5. In the early 1930s, the United States also possessed one of the world's largest flocks, but nearly all American wool was consumed domestically.

[62] DLA/PLA/439/1931; Fernand Maurette, *Les grands marchés des matières premières* (Paris: Armand Colin, 1922), 68–82; A. F. Du Plessis, *The Marketing of Wool* (London: Pitman & Sons, 1931), 2–8, 94–99; H. Munz, *The Australian Wool Industry* (Melbourne: F. W. Cheshire, 1964), 129–134; Paul Link, *Sheep Breeding and Wool Production in the Argentine Republic* (Buenos Aires: 1934); Imperial Economic Committee, *Wool*, 18–27; Bell, *Wool*, 72–84; Bott (interview, quoted).

[63] Simon Ville, *The Rural Entrepreneurs: A History of the Stock and Station Agent Industry in Australia and New Zealand* (Cambridge: Cambridge University Press, 2000), 2–3; Imperial Economic Committee, *Wool*, 14–18.

to what was initially Australia's biggest business enterprise: the stock and station agent. These agents financed farmers' short- and long-term capital needs, sold them livestock or other farm equipment, advised on new scientific methods and veterinary matters, and handled nearly every facet of marketing, from brokering or consignments to arranging transport, insurance, and storage. The Australian auctions that superseded those in London were initiated and run by the stock and station agents. Their historian, Simon Ville, has described the embedment of these firms in local sheep farmer life. Branch managers set up shop on local main streets, transacted business in public houses, traveled or dispatched subagents to isolated ranches, and sponsored local social events. But a number were among Australia's largest enterprises. Their vast inland networks connected with overseas shipping companies and buyers to ensure the transmission of the world's greatest source of fine wool from interior grasslands deep in the Southern Hemisphere to textile mills in northern England and western Europe. For all express purposes they were simply an Australian version of trading companies with local-global rootedness turned inside out.[64]

The progress of wool to market in Europe thus began on the sheep ranches of Australia in early summer, with shearing and bundling of wool into bales. The wool was then confided to a stock and station agent for its descent upon the ports of Australia and, increasingly, the auctions that were held in Sydney, Melbourne, Brisbane, and Geelong. The pastoral agents collected lots in their wool stores, prepared catalogs, and like selling brokers in London ran the sales. Then the shipping companies took over. Their agents intensively canvassed for contracts and assigned the wool to a dumping plant, where it was marked by ship and destination, hydraulically compressed for shipment, and sorted by port of arrival. Not surprisingly, the two central actors, stock and station agents and shipping lines, created their own chains to market, the one frequently serving as the shipping agent for the other.[65]

Two great markets dominated the sale of international wool, the auctions in London and Australia. Up until the turn of the century, the London auctions held in the amphitheater at the Wool Exchange on Coleman Street in the City monopolized the wool trade. Later they ceded leadership to auctions in Australia, although in 1929 wool was still the most

---

[64] Ville, *Rural*; J. D. Bailey, *A Hundred Years of Pastoral Banking: A History of the Australian Mercantile Land & Finance Company, 1863–1963* (Oxford: Clarendon Press, 1966).
[65] GAR/Lloyd 2/2014/Leeman.

valuable commodity in the United Kingdom entrepot trade.[66] In either case the essential link remained the sea. Australian auctions concentrated in port cities and served as a sorting station for transoceanic delivery. Liners brought buyers in for the auctions and carried out bales of wool to British or continental harbors. During wool season, ships came and went in a seemingly endless stream to transport the clip to distant harbors, where it was consigned to buyers, or to markets for further sales.

How and where wool moved through all these processes highlights the further importance of networks. London's position, for many years, was fortified by them. Geographically set between Britain's northeast and the North Sea, London was the convergence point for the big re-export markets in Yorkshire and Europe. Within its home base, the harbor and the City, local business networks joined wool traders to a massive capital, service, and informational infrastructure, and to nearly inexhaustible supplies of selling expertise. In London it was easy to finance consignments, warehouse bales, or obtain credit for unsold wool. Moreover, British financial and maritime relations with Australia and South Africa primarily ran through London. The majority of British shipping routes to Australasia were operated by London firms, especially the combine of companies within the P & O group. Two of the largest stock and station agent companies – New Zealand Loan and Mercantile Agency Company (NZLMA) and Australian Land and Finance Company (AMLF) – originated as London companies, and nearly all the others became in some way London related. By far the largest import and export trade between Australia and Britain passed through London. Shipping men traveling to Australia heard the same refrain: Have your London agents talk to ours.[67] By contrast, Liverpool's shipping and trading networks were more pronounced with North America, which was excellent for cotton imports but not wool; with West Africa, which did not produce wool; and with Latin America, which exported a great deal of wool, but whose clip shipped primarily to Europe. Harbor representatives stationed abroad and shipping agents for Holts and White Star were successful in securing traffic, but London remained paramount in Britain's wool trade. Yet what networks gave they also took away. City allegiances were to profits not to London, and City connections did not prevent Sydney from supplanting

---

[66] DLA/PLA/439.

[67] Cain and Hopkins, *Crisis*; Maurette, *Marchés*, 84–85; DLA/PLA/439; Rees, *Commodity*, 322–323; Ville, *Rural*, 19, 45; MMM/MDHB/Management Files/1, Australia 1922; GAR/Lloyd 2/2014, Leeman.

London in Australian wool sales. Eventually all the big wool brokers, even the London-associated ones, participated in the Australian sales. Similarly, managerial control gradually devolved to Australia.[68] London's networks, which once made the city the center of the wool trade, were not adverse to shifting it elsewhere. Trade in wool therefore also foreshadowed the larger fate for London harbor, especially after decolonization and containerization overturned its once impregnable supremacy.

Networks across the channel were no less determinant. By all rights, Antwerp should have been the leading port of entry for French-imported wool. But that role fell to Dunkirk, despite its second-tier status, its underdeveloped hinterland liaisons, and its lack of internal cohesiveness among port users. Dunkirk, however, possessed two other resources that trumped Antwerp's. First, around the 1880s, mill owners in the nearby wool centers of Roubaix and Tourcoing began sending buyers to Argentina and Uruguay to purchase wool on the spot and arrange shipments to France. They also established buying counters or offices in these countries, and began to invest in other South American enterprises, including *estancias*. More buyers fanned out to Sydney, Melbourne, and Punta Arenas in far southern Chile. Preferring the cheapness of Dunkirk to Antwerp these wool industrialists made it their importing harbor of choice. None of this would have come about, however, without a second networking source, this one emanating from the political influence peddling of a local merchant, Jean-Baptiste Trystram, who held important positions in the chamber of commerce, on local councils, and in the national parliament. From these political bases he succeeded in winning funding for new harbor basins and for clearing a channel that was so treacherous that ships entering Dunkirk suffered from insurance surcharges. Shipping companies with state subventions found it practical, in ways that are not too mysterious to plumb, to add Dunkirk to their ports of call. Most notably, in 1886, Messageries Maritimes ships returning from Australia began discharging in Dunkirk. While Trystam did his work, the Northern Railroad wooed the Chargeurs Réunis' South American terminus from Le Havre. The methods may have been ungainly, but in one way or another trading, shipping, and market networks concentrated wool shipments on Dunkirk.[69]

[68] Ville, *Rural*, 166–179, 198.
[69] Vigarié, *Grands*, 341, 428–437, 556–557; Maurette, *Marchés*, 85–88; Michael Stephen Smith, *The Emergence of Modern Business Enterprise in France, 1800–1930* (Cambridge, MA: Harvard University Press, 2006), 112–113, 150–151.

Raised, sheared, bundled, carted, auctioned, and dumped in profusion in the Southern Hemisphere, but marketed, woven, and consumed in still greater quantities in the Northern, wool was therefore a truly global commodity whose progress from one side of the world to the other resulted in considerable wealth for both. As it traveled, it passed through networks that ports, shipping companies, trading companies, and markets constructed with one another to execute the movement of so much wool across so much space and to determine where it went. Shipping company and stock and station agent liaisons, which linked inland and transoceanic circuits, made it possible for wool to journey, relatively easily, from deep within the Australian interior to ports thousands of sea miles away. A second set of networks, predicated on port hinterlands and exchanges, took it to the mill towns and factories of Europe. At the center of both conduits were port networks, composed of home fleets, trading company connections, markets, and hinterland connections, which explained why far more wool journeyed to London rather than to Liverpool, or why so much wool transited through Dunkirk. Between sheep farmers on remote Queensland stations or on grazing lands in Patagonia, and wool-clad Europeans, were therefore local-global chains that maritime business built. That local-global connection can be drawn still more tightly for another commodity – coffee – where we can see with greater precision how transnational networks within one port community orchestrated cross-ocean flows.

Coffee

Coffee, more so than wool, has always been an export crop. In modern times, it has often been the second or third most valuable commodity on world markets. The original arabica trees from which coffee beans were taken grew wild in Ethiopia, but trading ties spread their use to Yemen, and from there Hajjis carried the taste for coffee across the Muslim world. Beginning around the middle of the sixteenth century, Yeminis began to cultivate coffee for export. Over time, Indian and Arab commercial networks traded coffee between India and Jiddah, while merchants in Cairo organized the carriage and marketing of coffee from Jiddah north. Marseille merchants through their commercial links in Alexandria tapped into these networks and spread the trade to Europe. Gradually, however, the center of gravity in the coffee economy shifted beyond the Muslim world to a Western-dominated global business with production centered on Latin America. By the twentieth century Latin

America accounted for nine-tenths of the world's supply, more than three-fifths coming out of Brazil, much of the remainder from Colombia and Central America.[70]

During the first half of the twentieth century, more than 20 million bags of coffee shipped annually to consuming lands. To illustrate the dimensions of world coffee drinking, William Ukers produced a sketch in the mid-1930s of a coffee cup measuring 6,360 feet in diameter and 40 feet deep, in which a tiny *Normandie* floated in the middle.[71] The transposition of the world's biggest ship in the midst of the world's biggest coffee cup was intended for effect, but it also conjured the indispensability of maritime services in sustaining flows at such a massive level. Here the familiar network relationships abounded. In Colombia, where most coffee-growing regions were high up in the interior, the same riverboat/steamship linkages developed as happened earlier for moving tea down from Assam to London. In the upland coffee districts of Giradot, Honda, Tolima, Manizales, and Medellin, coffee shipped by rail to the river ports of the Magdalena River and then hundreds of miles downstream to the ocean port (by 1935) of Barranquilla. Coffee beans grown in the still more isolated region of Cíucuta wound their way to New York via thirty-five miles of rail to Puerto Villamizar on the Zulia River, then by flat-bottomed lighters on several days' journey to Puerto Encontrados on the Catatumbo River, and then again by river steamer to the Venezuelan port of Maracaibo where, loaded onto liners, they made the transoceanic passage.[72] In the United States, San Francisco became one of the major spot markets in coffee because of initiatives by local merchants to build coffee-buying networks in Central America and the decision of the W. R. Grace shipping line to concentrate Central American coffee imports on San Francisco. Aggressive marketing strategies by these merchants extended distribution lines all the way to St. Louis and Cincinnati.[73] Nowhere, however, were the articulations so prevalent, and visible, as

[70] Steven C. Topik, "Coffee," in Steven C. Topik and Allen Wells, *The Second Conquest of Latin America: Coffee, Hennequen, and Oil during the Export Boom, 1850–1930* (Austin: University of Texas Press, 1998), 42, 53–56; William Gervase Clarence-Smith and Steven Topik, eds., *The Global Coffee Economy in Africa, Asia, and Latin America, 1500–1989* (Cambridge: Cambridge University Press, 2003); Suraiya Faroqhi, *Herrscher über Mekka. Die Geschichte der Pilgerfahrt* (München: Artemis, 1990), 272–274; William H. Ukers, *All About Coffee*, 2nd ed. (New York: The Tea & Coffee Trade Journal Company, 1935), 500–510.

[71] Ukers, *All*, 501.

[72] Ibid., 331–344.

[73] Ibid., 423–425.

in Hamburg, one of the two great coffee-importing ports, alongside Le Havre, on the European continent.

Hamburg's advantages began with its markets. Coffee consumption in Germany was the highest in Europe before the First World War, and second only to France after 1918. Hamburg was also the gateway for coffee shipments to northern and eastern Europe, and even after 1918 when the transit trade to Scandinavia fell away, this business remained considerable.[74] In addition, Hamburg, since 1887, possessed a futures market in coffee. Not only did this market increase trading options; the need to cover commitments with large stocks of all grades on hand sucked shipments into the port and increased spot market trades. Intermediaries – importers, dealers, commissioners, agents, and brokers – clustered at Hamburg's bourse, or general produce exchange. Address books from the beginning of the century indicate 325 firms engaged in coffee trading and another fifty-seven listed as roasters.[75]

However, Hamburg's drawing power, as might be expected, lay principally in its home port–overseas networks. The Hamburg-Rio-Santos-São Paulo coffee trading company Theodor Wille provides a good entry into how these worked for the import of coffee. In Hamburg, Wille was very much a home port house. Its headquarters were in Hamburg, its founder was one of the men instrumental in creating the city's Commerz-und Disconto-Bank for investing in Hamburg-generated affairs, he was equally a founder of Hamburg's coffee futures market, and from Hamburg headquarters radiated networks of Wille correspondents and agents in all the leading coffee ports of Europe. Hamburg was also the base for Wille's national and continental coffee marketing, which Wille carried out through vehicles such as Kaiser's Kaffeegeschäft, a German roaster and seller of coffee, chocolate, and cakes with more than 1,600 outlets in Germany and Switzerland in 1939. Beginning at the turn of the century Wille secured a special relation with Kaiser's.

Upstream however, Wille, if anything, was even more a Brazilian firm, where its business and civic contacts within local business circles were

---

[74] Katharina Trümper, *Kaffee und Kaufleute: Guatemala und der Hamburger Handel 1871–1914* (Hamburg: Lit Verlag, 1996), 55, 63; Ukers, *All*, 521–528; Meyer, *Güterumschlagsplatz*, 57–58; Backx, *Haven*, 229.

[75] Vigarié, *Grands*, 211, 391–392; Hugo van Driel, "Uitschakeling van Nederlandse koffie-handel in de negentiende en twintigste eeuw?" *NEHA-jaarboek voor de economische bedrijfs-en techniekgeschiedenis*, 60 (1997): 172; Zimmermann, *Wille*, 105; Ursula Becker, "Entwicklung und Organisation des hanseatischen Kaffeehandels im 19. um 20. Jahrhundert" (Ph.D. diss. University of Münster, 1995), 108–109; Wendemuth and Böttcher, *Port*, 15–20.

yet more expansive. Operating as a general trading house, Wille imported standard European products such as textiles and beer, and represented German machinery and aircraft works. The firm invested in Brazilian enterprises. Its core business, exporting coffee, entailed widespread linkages to all local sectors – producers, intermediaries, state officials – engaged in the coffee trade. Wille ran its own Commissário-Abteilung, which suggests it performed the same services of supplying *fazendeiros*, advancing them credit and marketing their crops, as did the Brazilian factors or brokers who went under the name of *commissários*. By the 1920s Wille was buying directly from estates up-country. It invested in estates and controlled its own plantations. Leading members of the firm held positions in local chambers of commerce. So well-connected was the house of Wille in Brazil that it was entrusted with central responsibilities in carrying out Brazil's first valorization scheme (to sustain prices by withholding supplies), and it was protected from Allied pressures during the First World War. Still more transnational, Wille spun out a third set of networks in the huge North American coffee market. In doing so it received considerable assistance from Hermann Sielcken, a dominant figure on the New York coffee scene and himself Hamburg born (not unlike the Hamburg banking connections of Vorwerks in Chile). A series of critical business trips by Otto Uebele, partner and head of the Santos house, consolidated and expanded these contacts in the 1920s and 1930s.[76]

The two ends fused through Wille's massive coffee exports – it was Brazil's leading exporter before the First World War and still sizable, if smaller, after 1918[77] – but equally via steamship connections that were intrinsically Hambourgeois. Wille, and the Commerz- und Disconto-Bank he helped found, played a leading role in the creation of Hamburg Süd, the home line expressly formed to cull South American traffic. Heinrich Diederichsen, a Wille partner, was an influential member of the Hamburg Süd supervisory board in the 1920s and 1930s. Wille's European-bound coffee thus poured onto Hamburg Süd ships, for which Wille in Brazil also functioned as agent. Until the Nazis reorganized trades and gave Hamburg Süd a monopoly on the east coast of South America, HAPAG also did a huge carrying business in coffee from Brazil. It too made Theodor Wille its agent.[78]

[76] Zimmermann, *Wille*.
[77] Robert Greenhill, "The Brazilian Coffee Trade," in Platt, *Imperialism*, 208; Zimmerman, *Wille*, 115–116, 178–179.
[78] Zimmermann, *Wille*, 70, 114, 125–129, 161–164; Wendt, *Kurs*, 138–140, 326; Seiler, *Südamerika*, 114, 124.

The same shipping, trading, and port commercial networks were sewn into Hamburg's coffee connections in Mexico and Central America. Often grown on richer mountain soils, and processed through the superior "wet" method, coffees from this region tended to ship to more discriminating European markets. Although far behind Brazil in absolute export figures, the place of coffee in the Central American economies could reach hegemonic levels of 80 or 90 percent, as occurred in Guatemala and El Salvador. And Hamburg merchants all but controlled the foreign exports of Guatemalan coffee. Hamburg-owned plantations in Guatemala produced one-third of the coffee output before the First World War and two-thirds afterward. Approximately half of the coffee crop was dispatched over Hamburg. There were houses such as Hockmeyer & Rittscher, or Schlubach, Thiemer & Co. where German overseas traders, with Hamburg backgrounds, established export houses in Guatemala and diversified into plantation cultivation, and then opened home offices or branches in Hamburg. In other instances, Hamburg trading houses opened branches in Guatemala and invested in coffee estates. As the nexus of credit, the trading companies used Hamburg financial ties to lend money to *fincas* and claimed the marketing of crops in exchange. German merchants were also heavily active in El Salvador and made inroads into what had once been a British monopoly of the Costa Rican trade.[79] Farther north, German planters with Hamburg connections, or Hamburg trading firms, were highly prominent, perhaps even dominant, among coffee producers in Chiapas.[80]

That coffee was also lifted on Hamburg carriers: HAPAG and the Kosmos Line, which merged into HAPAG in the 1920s. Here too relationships were incestuous. Among the founders of Kosmos were Ernst Rittscher of Hockmeyer & Rittscher, Theodor Eggers of H. H. Eggers, a big Hamburg coffee importer, and Ferdinand and Carl Laiesz, of Hamburg's most successful sailing ship firm. Ferdinand also figured among the founders of HAPAG and Carl served as deputy chair on the HAPAG board. Both father and son had trading house interests in Guatemala. Adolf Kirsten, yet another Hambourgeois with ships in these waters (his company fused with Kosmos at the turn of the century), sat on the board of the Hanseatische Plantagen-Gesellschaft Guatemala-Hamburg, a

[79] Trümper, *Kaffee*; Ernst-Günther Küsel, *Die Kaffeehandelsorganisation in Zentralamerika und Kolombien* (Hamburg: Friederichsen, De Gruyter, 1939), 32–86; Michael J. Biechler, "The Coffee Industry of Guatemala: A Geographic Analysis" (Ph.D. diss., Michigan State University, 1970), 35–49.
[80] Trümper, *Kaffee*, 33; Topik, "Coffee," 66, 82; Seiler, *Südamerika*, 144.

Hamburg-controlled coffee estate.[81] Between Hamburg trading and shipping there thus developed a relationship of mutual support and respect. HAPAG's West Indies and Central American section won a reputation for top-notch service. In the post–World War II years the department ran dozens of vessels, including charters during coffee season, to meet shippers' needs. Otto Seiler, who was in charge of inward traffic in HAPAG's West Indies or Central American service, remarked that "if they had a very urgent shipment where they needed an urgent ship, we just got one, you know." Great care was taken to see that coffee arrived in excellent condition. Captains received precise orders on measures they should take, such as fastidious cleaning of the holds, as fertilizers were a common cargo outward.[82]

But the ties were most tightly wound through the transnational connections and identities that pervaded Hamburg houses. In Central America, HAPAG agents who worked to meet exporters' needs enjoyed close social and personal ties with them. The two joined the same clubs, they played tennis together, they visited and knew one another's families. Recalling their talents, Seiler remarked that "they all made a fortune," but that "the whole business stood or fell on their personalities, on their genius, on their ability to … get as much cargo as possible in competition against the international other lines."[83] Such relationships were pivotal for recovery from the twin disasters of two world wars. In the 1920s, as the city's shipping and trading companies struggled to climb out of the hole in which they had been buried since 1918, HAPAG's Mexico agent, Richard Eversbusch, a Mexican of German origin and brought up in Germany, traveled with Harald Schuldt, whose Ocean Line ran a joint service with HAPAG, to the coffee *fincas* in Chiapas to win shipping contracts from the big German planters, Lüttmann, Edelmann, and Giesemann.[84] After 1945, when the hole was still deeper, C.-A. Hoffmann, HAPAG's director of Central American, Mexican, and Caribbean services, traveled across the Atlantic to meet with El Salvador coffee shippers, a number of whom were Jewish. Hoffmann was fluent in Spanish and had been in Venezuela and Cuba before the war. Placed in a staggeringly difficult situation that must have made for bed-sweat nights, Hoffmann succeeded, probably

---

[81] Trümper, *Kaffee*, 41, 75–76; Hildegard von Marchtaler, *Geschichte der Kaffee-Import und Reederei-Firma H. H. Eggers Hamburg* (Hamburg: 1953), 14, 35; Seiler, *Südamerika*, 89–91.

[82] Seiler (interview).

[83] Ibid.

[84] Seiler, *Südamerika*, 135–136, 140.

because of his considerable personality and HAPAG's earlier traditions of serving these clients, but also for his ability to fall back on his on-site agent, Curt Nottebohm, himself a large plantation owner and personally friendly with many of the leading shippers. Through Nottebohm, Hoffmann was able to meet with Don Heriberto de Sola, the dean of exporters, and this greased the wheels with other merchants. Once successful in getting its foot in the door, HAPAG went on to reestablish its coffee service and benefited from still more in-grown connections, such as the Cia. Mercantil Intercontinental S. A. San Salvador, which provided customs clearance and dispatch services in port, and belonged to the Nottebohms.[85]

Such commodity chains can be constructed for nearly any world commodity. Trade in edible oils and fats could trace through West African caravan trails; European trading company posts; coastal collectors operated by the same trading companies; transoceanic shipping companies like Elder Dempster, which invested in wharfage facilities and surf boats to carry oils and seeds to waiting vessels at sea along the mostly inhospitable stretches of West African coastline; and then to the gluttonous milling and crushing plants of Merseyside, Marseille, Rotterdam, and Hamburg. These were ports with shipping and trading traditions in the producing regions where large, integrated mass marketers such as Unilever or Henkel transformed the commodity into consumer goods and distributed them via their sales divisions across the continent and back out into world.[86]

For a bulk trade, such as grain, drawn from North and South America, Australia, North Africa, Russia, and the Danube, the articulations and transnationalism that have featured in this chapter became second nature. Dominant firms including Continental, Louis Dreyfus, and Bunge & Born evolved into global traders and integrated forward to owning their own fleets. In the interwar years Louis Dreyfus was probably France's leading tramp shipper, and at the end of the century was the country's premier bulk carrier.[87] Internally, these companies often mimicked the

---

[85] Ibid., 195–196; Seiler (interview).

[86] Bonin, *C.F.A.O.*, 77–80, 225–226; Fieldhouse, *Merchant*, 197; Davies, *Trade*, xxxi, 79–81; Martin Lynn, "From Sail to Steam: The Impact of the Steamship Services on the British Palm Oil Trade with West Africa, 1850–1890," *Journal of African History* 30 (1989): 227–235; Wilson, *Unilever*, vol. 2, 348.

[87] Dan Morgan, *Merchants of Grain* (Harmondsworth: Penguin, 1980), 129–130, 138, 237–238; Bernard Cassagnou, *Les grandes mutations de la Marine marchande française (1945–1995)*, 2 vols., 349, 644, 881, 901–993.

itinerancy of their trading connections. Continental was owned by a family that came from Metz, set up in Antwerp, moved to Paris, and then migrated to New York. The company was rife with Egyptian traders, and its New York agent, Joseph Feuer, was a Pole who had traded in Antwerp, Romania, and Argentina and was at home in at least six languages. During a family interregnum after the Second World War, the company was run by a Dutchman, a German, and an American. Traders in Argentina often began as German or Belgian, but then became naturalized Argentinians or Americans. Personal multiculturalism paralleled the firms, and explained in good part their success at worldwide trading.[88]

Two constants therefore governed and made possible the global movement of goods and people through the first two-thirds of the twentieth century. The first was network linkage between ports, shipping, trading, and markets that created world conduits but also directed who dominated trades and where things went. The second was the internalization of home and abroad within each one of these sectors. Latched into local and overseas connections, and identifying with each, the companies that made up these networks constructed a system whose transnationalism reflected, in the end, their own fluency in navigating across multiple worlds, and making them one.

[88] Morgan, *Merchants*, 19, 63, 106–110, 129, 140. On nationalities in Argentina, see Chapter 6.

4

Intermediaries

Thus far intermediaries have been alluded to more than discussed, yet the maritime world was powerless to move anything without them because they were providers of essential services that coordinated between one sector and another. Effectively they were defined as middlemen or go-betweens, but their range of services was extensive. They included classic middlemen such as brokers, dealers, compradors, agents, forwarders, insurers, warehousers, stevedores, and receivers, but also specialist services like auction houses or tasters. Some worked as branches or subsidiaries of shipping firms, others were independent contractors. In certain trades their traditions and identities varied from port to port, a legacy from earlier formation. But all mediated between one activity and another and possessed specialized knowledge without which neither ports, nor shipping companies, nor trading houses could function.

It has been presumed that their position weakened with the globalizing and concentrating trends of the second half of the nineteenth century. Wider access to information, standard grading, or vertical integration and direct buying all narrowed the number of intervening parties. Increasingly intermediaries appeared on the way out, as witnessed by the fading of *commissários* in the Brazilian coffee trade once exporters established buying organizations and integrated upstream.[1] The reverse, however, was just as frequently the case. In the interwar years, the marketing of tea, the leading commodity in value auctioned in London's Mincing Lane Sales, was entirely in the hands of expert brokers. Estate managers

---

[1] David Kynaston, *The City of London*, vol. 2, *Golden Years, 1890–1914* (London: Pimlico, 1996), 15–16; Jones, *Merchants*, 50.

in India and Ceylon consigned their tea to correspondents in London, who contracted selling brokers to organize its sale. These brokers possessed insider knowledge of auction practices, but they also mediated sales because they were experts at evaluating the marketable qualities of tea, which was inconstant from season to season and varied not only by species but by tea garden. They sampled every break (a consignment by species from the same plantation) for flavor, strength, and color and assigned a worth in catalogs they prepared for buyers. Dealers and blenders, who purchased the tea and were often middlemen marketers in their own right, hired buying brokers to represent them in the sales.[2] Experts who knew how to handle tobacco, another commodity notoriously difficult to sort into standard grades, remained in demand throughout the century. A company as large as the Deli My marketed its output through brokers in Amsterdam.[3] As late as the 1990s, specialist "leaf managers" and tobacco dealers continued to travel the world assessing tobacco tillage, color, moisture, leaf, and nicotine content in lands as widespread as the United States, Brazil, Turkey, Thailand, and Zimbabwe. These men could spend eight months of the year inspecting sources abroad. In Antwerp, the middleman firm Tabaknatie still stored and arranged documentation and transshipment of nearly all the tobacco shipped through the port. Conscious that expertise was its prime asset, it offered seminars for recruits on the proper treatment of commodities and sent them to producing countries to see how tobacco was grown and packed.[4]

In truth, it was the advent of modern shipping and trading that produced intermediaries in their classic professional form. Once shipping became a specialty of shipowners, others specialized in providing services for them. Shipbrokers negotiated charters. Forwarders "recognised the growing divide between those selling cargo space and those wanting to fill it, and set themselves up as brokers, making their living by connecting the two." Ship agents organized bookings and turnaround and handled arrangements for liner companies abroad. Insurance agents brokered insurance. Once steamships – with less rigging – required fewer crew members, stevedores replaced ships' crews in the loading and discharge of cargo.

[2] DLA/PLA 445/Tea 1933; F. W. F. Staveacre, *Tea and Tea Dealing* (London: Pitman & Sons, 1933), 66–69. On the persistence of middlemen in the coffee trade up until the Second World War, van Driel, "Uitschakeling."

[3] NA/Deli Maatschappij firm history; Jonker and Sluyterman, *Home*, 181–182.

[4] Jules de Maeyer and Erik Van Nueten, Tabaknatie, interviews with author, Antwerp 23 December 1997. I am especially indebted to Mr. Van Nueten, who provided me with a tour of the company's state-of-the art warehouses in the port. During this tour I was able to meet one of the traveling buyers who discussed his business with me.

New commodity markets increased the demand for specialty brokers. The growth of transit trades through ports opened more opportunities for specialist warehousing and transshipment firms. Modern processes thus called forth middlemen services as much as turned these into casualties.[5]

Even more, the imperatives of globalization, at least before its reconfiguration at the end of the twentieth century, accounted for the indispensability of middlemen. Globalism in this earlier stage, as we have seen, was the sum of multiple networks, many confined to one or two ocean zones, but whose interconnected aggregate formed a world system. Middlemen under these circumstances were not only useful but absolutely necessary, because they were the ones who did the connecting. Switching mechanisms, to employ a nineteenth-century metaphor, or search engines, to employ a contemporary one, they joined one network to another and enabled anything, or anyone, to move point-to-point around the world. Ship agents and freight forwarders best fit this definition of world coordinator, but in less complete ways the others performed some connecting function. As they did so, moreover, they took on the attributes of the globalizing process they empowered. Home port based, and often encased in local traditions, they too became innately transnational, either through their mediating between one culture and another or through their participation in transnational networks. Expertise, similarly, was defined by how this globalism worked. Knowledge of rates and routes, whom to call, or the logistics of creating point-to-point service where practically none existed, the very stuff of their raison d'être, was a byproduct of globalism's oxymoronic, but real, fragmented connectedness. In turn, having inscribed themselves within a transnational order and calibrated their knowledge to its needs, their capacity for mediating at global levels was all the greater. The next stage of globalism, and especially its henchman, containerization, would compress these realms of maneuver. Even then, however, there would always be a place for middlemen, albeit at the cost of former identities.

COLONIAL TRADES

In empire, the quintessential go-between was the comprador. Identified with China, but also found in Japan, the Philippines, and throughout

---

[5] Milne, *Trade*, 96–97 (quoted); Van de Laar, *Stad*, 89; Boyce, *Information*, 28; Van Isacker, *Antwerpse*, 41–42; Vigarié, *Grands*, 413–414; Williams, "Liverpool," 197; Jonker and Sluyterman, *Home*, 181–185.

Southeast Asia, wherever a sizable Chinese merchant community existed, the comprador was simply the most familiar of a common imperial phenomenon. Counterparts in India were known as banians, in Persia as mirzas, and in Ceylon as shroffs. Wherever Western and non-Western networks converged, one or another was usually the connector.[6]

Compradors did many things for their European employers. They recruited and managed local staff; acted as house treasurer; handled insurance on shipments; ran stevedore, godown, and tallyman services; and extended the credit that was a necessary and commonplace method of doing business in non-Western lands. Mostly, however, they were company liaisons with the indigenous merchant and political communities. In this capacity they canvassed for passengers or cargo for steamship companies, established financial connections for foreign banks, provided networks of information and sales for all enterprises doing business in Asia, and provided entry to inner political circles. The general take on compradors is that they were necessary to pierce the barriers of language and kinship or native-place ties, or to navigate the peculiarities of Chinese banking customs, and that either through foreign efforts to internalize their transactions, or through nationalistic reaction at home, the practice withered over the first half of the century. Neither half of this picture is entirely correct. European firms encouraged, and sometimes required, their staff to learn local languages. Even when compradors were reinvented as Chinese managers, they did mostly the same things as before, and the position died a very slow death. Harrisons & Crosfield retained a comprador in its Singapore office until the late 1970s. British-American Tobacco pitted a traditional comprador-organized sales network against its own internal sales organization; the traditional system won hands down.[7]

Compradors were hard to shake because they were such highly networked figures. If language had been the principal issue, a mere interpreter would have done. Companies were careful to select as compradors

[6] Jones, *Banking*, 91; Misra, *Business*, 53–56, 110–112.

[7] Yen-P'ing Hao, *The Comprador in Nineteenth Century China: Bridge between East and West* (Cambridge, MA: Harvard University Press, 1970); Howard Cox, Huang Biao, and Stuart Metcalfe, "Compradors, Firm Architecture, and the 'Reinvention' of British Trading Companies: John Swire & Sons' Operations in Early Twentieth-Century China," *Business History* 45 (April 2003): 15–34; Jones, *Merchants*, 221–223; Zhang, *Swire*, 236–240; Pugh, *Great*, 165–168; King, *Hong Kong and Shanghai Banking Corporation*, vol. 1, 503–520, vol. 3, 347–354; Sherman Cochran, *Encountering Chinese Networks: Western, Japanese, and Chinese Corporations in China, 1880–1937* (Berkeley: University of California Press, 2000), 44–69.

men of social status and connections. Most were established businessmen in their own right. Often they invested in the Chinese firms with
which they traded. Once selected, they tended to establish a comprador
dynasty within the house they served. But choices were geared to function
and suitability. The Banque de l'Indochine's preference for comprador
in Peking (Beijing) was Soun Che Hsun, a man with little business clout
but the protégé of a powerful and rich former minister and thus capable of wining railway concessions.[8] Swires selected men with strong ties
to Chinese merchant circles and who were well established within their
communities. Nearly always they were wealthy, to bear the social costs of
their position.[9] In what is probably destined to become the defining quo-
tation on the social duties of the comprador, the Swire agent in Nanking
stated it this way:

The Comprador makes compassionate allowances to our staff when their parents
die, if the Hong Kong Comprador's business friend comes to Nanking he takes
him out to Sun Yat Sen's tomb, if a sugar dealer's son dies he sends a scroll to the
funeral, if a big shipper's nephew is married he sends a present, if the manager
of a piece goods hong insured with us wants to get to Shanghai the Comprador
pays his passage. He greases the palms that need greasing, he gives a few dollars
to the police, the postman and the telephone man, he supports local charities,
he gives tips where it is wise to give them. It may seem unnecessary but it is the
Chinese way of doing things and it is all for Taikoo's good and it helps to get and
retain clients.[10]

Compradors stood out as a near-institution, but mediating between
Western and Eastern business circles was common in tropical commodities such as rubber. Whereas European agency houses controlled the production and export of plantation rubber, most native rubber (produced
by smallholders throughout the region) meandered through a series of
exchanges involving brokers, dealers, shopkeeper commission agents, and
subsequently packers. The chain can be wound backward from the final
marketing end. London dealers sold to Western factory owners and purchased from export merchants or other dealers in Singapore. Singapore
dealers divided among European specialist traders in rubber, representatives of agency firms, large Japanese trading companies, and Chinese
houses. The latter often worked through local dealers up-country or in
the East Indies, whereas the commission houses frequently interceded as

[8] Meuleau, *Pionniers*, 201, 203.
[9] NA/Koninklijke Java China Paketvaart Lijnen (KJCJL)/2.20.58.02/409/5 February
1940.
[10] SOAS/JSS I/Box 15/28 March 1930. The quote appears also in Jones, *Merchants*, 222.

the connecting mechanism between the two. If the dealers were European, they purchased either through their own up-country buyers or from other dealers, including Chinese ones, on the Singapore market.

At the heart of the trading in Singapore was the rubber exchange founded in 1911. Here the two worlds of Europeans and Asians physically joined as Chinese and European brokers negotiated deals. These were figures of some local color, identifiable by their knee-length tunics and accustomed to moving about the business quarters of the city looking for sellers to match with buyers. On long business days when Singapore dealers could not locate the up-country rubber they needed, brokers were available to broker sales. Despite the picturesque veneer, these brokers survived because they acquired a mastery over the qualities of different grades of rubber and their applications for various users. As the rubber industry became more scientifically complex in the 1960s, brokers updated their expertise. Pressures on their business did not, therefore, push them over the edge because, like dealers, they too were handy go-betweens in a city built upon overlapping Chinese and European circuits. Moreover, their daily business life simply wrote small, like compradors, the transnational and networked workings of the rest of the maritime world.[11]

ON THE WATERFRONT

When a ship arrived in port, its cargo was unloaded, either into lighters or onto the quay. If the quay, then the freight was tallied, weighed, and sorted to marks. If goods did not then ship directly to the interior, or transship onto another vessel, they were transported to consignees or stored in warehouses in the port area. These operations occurred in every port, every day, and were seamless in their execution except for the fact that separate middlemen companies carried them out. Divided by tradition and guildlike jurisdictions, all fell into the category of goods handlers. Over time, especially after containerization revolutionized the method of shipping cargo, they reinvented themselves as terminal operators and emerged as harbor powerhouses. Until then, however, they were mostly the port's muscle, and low men on the totem pole. But they too were experts at what they did and were connectors between the three main sectors: ports, ships, and merchant traders.

[11] Coates, *Commerce*, 172–173, 180–189, 255–256, 335–354; Huff, *Economic*, 22, 201–202; Allen and Donnithorne, *Western*, 242–248.

The principal division that prevailed among them was between those who handled goods shipside – stevedore companies – and those who handled goods quayside, whatever their incarnation: master porters in London and Liverpool, *naties* in Antwerp, *vemen* in Rotterdam, *Quartiersleute* in Hamburg, *brouettiers* in Le Havre, and cargo superintendents throughout. The carryover of guildlike traditions, revamped but alive and well after the premature notice of their death in the French Revolution, was striking. In Hamburg's harbor, once a crate was suspended from a crane hook overside, the longshoreman handlers took over. In Antwerp, a blue stone marker at the quay wall set apart the realm of the stevedores from the realm of the *naties*. The latter took their names from the goods they specialized in or the provenance of the traffic they handled. There was a Wijnnatie, a Katoennatie, a Tabaknatie, a Noordnatie, an Amerikanatie, a Cubanatie. Hamburg's landside equivalent, *Quartiersleute*, referred to earlier centuries when partnerships of four men – one to man the hoist, one to work the doorways, and two to stack – took charge of bringing goods from ships to warehouses. By the twentieth century, however, these hand-me-downs had also worn very thin. Stevedores and reception firms constantly intruded upon each other's domain, and some stevedores now worked as an in-house service to integrated shipping lines. Jurisdictions or defined operations were constantly in flux. A 1929 manual of the Port of Liverpool listed twenty activities that master porters, the descendants of men enlisted by merchants to come to waterside and take care of their goods, now performed. Just before the Second World War, Blaauwhoedenveem, with one of those quaint names ("Blue Hats") that carried over from centuries earlier, set up stevedoring and grain elevator companies in the port of Rotterdam, but only as a countermeasure to the invasion of its warehousing territory by some of Rotterdam's big stevedoring firms. In the 1950s, its rival, Pakhuismeesteren, diversified into stevedoring, forwarding, Rhine shipping, and even ship agency work.[12]

Thus past traditions were not written in stone and could only partially explain distinctions between stevedores and the others. Identity, power, function, and growth were very much products of each port's peculiar development. Divisions between stevedore and PLA dock services in London varied from dock to dock and replicated the quirky conventions worked out piecemeal throughout the nineteenth century. In Rotterdam

[12] Gustaaf Asaert, Greta Devos, and Fernand Suykens, *De Antwerpse Naties: Zes eeuwen actief in stad en haven* (Tielt: Lannoo, 1993); Van Isacker, *Antwerpse*, 66; Wendemuth and Böttcher, *Port*, 197–200; Thede-Ottowell, *Hamburg*, 221–224; Cotter, *Port*, 132–137; MMM/MDHB/148/21 August 1928; Hugo van Driel, *Four Centuries of Warehousing:*

and Antwerp, differences in legal governance were decisive. Beginning at the turn of the century, Rotterdam granted long-term leases, which stevedore companies turned into platforms for large-scale investment in physical plant, equipment, and cargo services, and explains why Rotterdam became known as a stevedore's port. Antwerp moved fairly late in this direction; not until the interwar years and really only after the Second World War did the city relinquish control of quayside superstructure. Instead, liner companies and their agents dominated Antwerp's pecking order and leased, short-term, most of the berths. In Antwerp, *naties* retained a certain local power that positioned them to make the leap to terminal operators and swallow up stevedores when containerization arrived.[13] Consequently, waterfront companies mimicked and reproduced the same qualities that distinguished one great port from another before containerization turned them all into variations on a parking lot.

The most singular dockside group were Antwerp's *naties*, who descended from medieval guilds – the earliest recorded mention of a *natie* in Antwerp is 1448 – and whose cooperative structure remained at least until the Second World War. *Naties* took charge of goods; sorted, weighed, and drew samples from them; and transported the goods to consignees, railroads, or their own storage rooms above their offices. They elected a dean to represent and administer the firm, but *naties* were cooperative ventures in which the other members held shares. Known as *natiebazen* (or bosses), these were generally men from the countryside, rough-hewn types who had amassed sufficient capital to buy into a house. Despite a market in shares by the late nineteenth century, many passed through family members or individuals from the same village. The trend in modern times was for *natiebazen* to oversee foremen and work crews, but there were still a fair number who swung a hook alongside the rest of the men. Such conditions created a bond between *natiebazen* and

Pakhoed, the Origins and History, 1616–1967 (Rotterdam: Royal Pakhoed N.V., 1992), 119, 139.

[13] A. E. Jeffery, *The History of Scruttons: Shipbrokers and Shipowners, 1802–1926; Stevedores, Master Porters, and Cargo Superintendents, 1890–1967* (London: Scrutton, 1967), 24–35; conversation with Bob Aspinall, DLA, summer 1998; Greta Devos and Hugo van Driel, "Local Government and Port Business in Antwerp and Rotterdam in the 19th and 20th Century," in Anne-Marie Kuijlaars, Kim Prudon, and Joop Visser, eds., *Business and Society: Entrepreneurs, Politics, and Networks in a Historical Perspective, Proceedings of the Third European Business History Association (EBHA) Conference* (Rotterdam: 2000), 79–89; Hugo van Driel and Irma Bogenrieder, "Memory and Learning: Selecting Users in the Port of Rotterdam, 1883–1900, *Business History* 51 (September 2009): 649–667.

their workers that was difficult to replicate in other kinds of firms. Often those recruited on to crews, or as fixed workers, were fellow villagers of the boss. Antwerp was not immune to severe strike action, but stevedores were far more militant than *natie* dockers. Their esprit de corps and local political clout were therefore sufficient to keep the wolves from the door. In the interwar years there was some diversification and intrusion from competitors, yet things remained largely as they had been. In some regards the most drastic change in their traditions was to adopt the use of the internal combustion engine at the expense of their beloved horses, which appear in practically every *natie* image from before the war. Rarely has a photograph been more revealing than the one taken (and this as late as 1937) of four *natie* workers sitting on a cart eating their lunch with casks stacked behind them, while at a cart alongside stand their horses with muzzles deep into feed bags.[14] These very provincial, very turf-oriented, atavistic organisms, whose daily life was nevertheless to handle the world's commerce, provided, ironically, another take on the role of ports as mediators between the local and the global. Certainly they call into question the presumption that globalization was automatically a tradition killer.

On the other hand, guild traditions did not preclude modernization. Rotterdam's *vemen* acquired barge fleets to move goods from the harbor to their warehouses, and the "Blue Hats," in the interwar years, went international and set up subsidiary operations in Antwerp, London, Basel, Hamburg, and the East Indies. In Hamburg, warehousing developed into a big business with state-of-the-art facilities.[15] Even the *naties*, if some were dragged kicking and screaming, made the transition under containerization to big terminal operators or special service providers like Tabaknatie. Hessenatie grew into the port's largest terminal operator and was so advanced that by the 1980s it was taking initiatives to construct a new riverside container harbor.[16]

Stevedores in particular reflected the expertise required of modern maritime systems. A byproduct of the demise of sailing ships, they were also an outgrowth of liner companies and their need for a professionalized service to guarantee rapid turnaround in ports. A number of shipping lines consequently organized their own stevedore companies or invested

[14] Asaert, Devos, and Suykens, *Naties*; Van Isacker, *Antwerpse*, 38, 65–66; De Maeyer (interview).
[15] Van Driel, *Four*, 79, 95, 110–113, 136; Wendemuth and Böttcher, *Port*, 195–200, 254–256.
[16] Antwerp, Havenbedrijf/Technische Dienst Archives/7281/27 April 1992.

FIGURE 3. *Naties* and friends at lunch. City Archives, Antwerpen.

in subsidiary outfits. More common, however, were the stevedoring companies founded by former captains, sailors, or waterfront workers to take advantage of these new opportunities when entry was easy – "at that time the only material needs were a few ropes, chains, shackles, and wires."[17] Gerd Buss, whose company developed into one of the very largest in Hamburg, was a sea captain who came ashore in 1920 and started up a stevedoring outfit. Melchior Venkeler, at sea for close to a decade, set up his venerable Antwerp stevedoring firm in 1864. T. F. Maltby, a former ship captain, carried out stevedoring work for a London dock company before creating his own business in 1868, one of the two largest independent stevedoring firms (alongside Scrutton) in London. Peter Thomsen, the founder of Rotterdam's largest and most famous stevedoring company, was a Danish sailor paid off in Rotterdam in 1860. Leendert Swarttouw, whose two sons ran the remainder of Rotterdam's big three, began as a mere warehouse man, and then did manual stevedore work before scraping his way into running his own company. Most of these men were raw, tough competitors. Their physical force, as well

[17] John Hovey, *A Tale of Two Ports: London and Southampton* (London: The Industrial Society, 1990), 8.

as their leadership skills and initiative, propelled them to boss status. Management retained the characteristics of its origins. Photos of shipboard operations before containerization distinguish bosses from workers by their topcoats and fedoras, but the size and look of these men suggest they were rough customers to deal with. Gorillas in suits could be the caption for a picture taken from Venkeler's seventy-fifth anniversary in 1939. The competitive culture was ingrained and hard to shake. Swarttouw's elder son, Cornelis, pushed his brother out of the business following the death of their father in 1886, despite an agreement between them. Frans, only eighteen, began his own company, Quick Dispatch, but for a long time he was left out in the cold and the rivalry between the two brothers was a bitter one. Van Driel recounts one story in which a stevedore spit on the bread of another, boasting, "You won't eat this one anymore," although the man gulped it down just to get the better of his competitor. Even when Rotterdam's big three formed common pooling arrangements after the First World War, and when more sophisticated types such as J. Ph. Backx (of Thomsen) occupied top management, they remained deeply suspicious of each other. Backx was the most respected man in Rotterdam stevedore circles and a leader in promoting cooperation, but he also sent a boat around the harbor every day to see if the two Swarttouws were violating their agreement.[18]

Local firms, stevedores were also absorbed into the worldwide networks of shipping companies. Every company had its string of stevedores in its ports of call, Jarka Corporation on the U.S. East Coast and Texas Transport & Terminal Corporation in Gulf ports for the Holland Amerika Line, for example, plus the Havana Docks Corporation in Cuba – until the local agent, Dussaq & Torral, organized its own stevedoring service. In-house or subcontracted, they could replicate the culture of repeated ties upon which these networks thrived. HAPAG was in the habit of utilizing two stevedore companies in a port to exert greater control, and in Antwerp it contracted with Venkeler and August Pays, both family firms. But both these relationships were long-term affairs. On the eve of the Second World War, Venkeler had worked for HAPAG for more than fifty years and continued to do so after 1945.[19]

[18] Lutz Ehrhardt, Gerd Buss (AG & Co.), interview with author, Hamburg, 6 August 1996; Van Isacker, *Antwerpse*, 41–43; Jeffery, *Scruttons*, 111–112; van Driel, *Samenwerking*, 72–74; idem, "Collusion in Transport: Group Effects in a Historical Perspective," *Journal of Economic Behavior & Organization* 41 (2000): 394–395; HAPAG/3066/12 August 1939 (Venkeler photo).

[19] HAPAG/3072, Beschäftigung unserer Stauerei-und Ladungskontroll Firmen in Antwerpen, n.d.; ibid., 3066/21 November 1939; ibid., 1577/2 February 1959.

The significance of stevedore companies in advancing global circulation has typically been overlooked,[20] but many of these were big, powerful firms upon whose skill liner schedules, costs, reputation, and even ship safety rested. John Hovey, whose stevedore firm went back four generations, described how the "life-and-death" affair of stowing securely in sailing days carried over into a professional ethic in the age of steamships: "The stevedores' pride in their work and the expertise which this engendered persisted long after the demise of the sailing ships. The art of stowage – for it was an art – was passed down from father to son within the stevedoring families."[21] For the best firms, proficiency spilled over into innovation. Scrutton in the mid-1930s was a company handling more than 3 million tons of cargo for ships of more than two dozen lines, including P & O and Cunard. A repository of skill and knowledge, it played a critical role in setting up an emergency port on the Clyde in the Second World War. In the 1950s, Elder Dempster brought it in as a consultant on how to speed up port operations in Lagos. Thomsen held a dominant share of the transshipment work in Rotterdam, and handled more than 2 million tons before the Depression. It too was a pioneer, in the mechanization of cargo handling. Along with other big stevedores, Thomsen turned Rotterdam into a model fast harbor. Later, in the early days of containers, both it and Quick Dispatch undertook study trips to the United States. In Hamburg, Gerd Buss, Jr. experimented with new kinds of slings to increase capacity as well as control. He was perhaps the first handler to introduce a forklift in Hamburg, even though he had to lock it away in the evenings so the old man wouldn't see it because he didn't believe in "all these funny modern things." When containers took over, Buss, Jr. continued to experiment with how to pack goods inside metal boxes. His equivalent in London was Claud Scrutton, who pushed through designs for the mechanical unloading of chilled beef and for electric-powered platform trucks on the quays.[22]

Their trajectory after containerization only magnified their importance. The one exception was Scrutton, which collapsed with much of the rest of the port of London in the 1970s. Other, smaller firms fell by the wayside. In the early 1970s there were still perhaps as many as thirty

[20] The recent work of Hugo van Driel, and his collaborative book with Ferry de Goey, have gone far to provide the corrective.
[21] Hovey, *Tale*, 16. For things that could go wrong with a shoddily managed firm, see GAR/ HAL/Directie/622/26, 29, 31 March, 15 April, and 12 May 1937 on Holland Amerika's Gulf port operations.
[22] Jeffery, *Scruttons*, 46–59, 99; Van Driel, *Samenwerking*, 68, 185–186; Ehrhardt (interview, quoted).

stevedore companies in Hamburg; by the end of the century only two or three remained. But the big ones, such as Buss, or the Rotterdam firms who created Europe Container Terminus at the dawn of the changeover, or Gylsen, which emerged as one of the top terminal operators in Antwerp, were very large operators indeed, and at the top of the pile in their home ports, whatever their origins as musclemen and bread spitters.

INSURERS AND REGISTERS

The history of insurance far transcends the history of shipping, but without marine insurance few ships would sail. In the First and Second World Wars the British government intervened to provide affordable insurance; otherwise both war efforts would have ground to a standstill. Risk coverage through third parties dates at least back to early fourteenth-century Italy. In the sixteenth century, Italian and German banking houses provided the insurance for Spanish treasure fleets across the Atlantic. A century later, the center of the insurance world was gravitating to London, and in 1914 perhaps as much as three-quarters of the world's marine insurance was written by the City. No institution was more instrumental in shaping modern marine insurance than Lloyd's, whose origins are well known. Toward the late seventeenth and early eighteenth centuries, merchant shipowners gathered in coffee houses – the Jamaica (for West Indies traders), "Sam's next the custom house," and Lloyd's – to exchange information and conduct their business. At the last the proprietor, Edward Lloyd took to posting news useful to shipping. The bait took. In the eighteenth century, Lloyd's coffee house became the venue where individuals interested in selling or obtaining marine insurance gathered. Decamping to other premises in the 1770s, Lloyd's developed over the next two centuries into the premier organ of marine insurance in the world, although it worked primarily as an underwriters' market.

The insurance industry, its brokers, underwriters, surveyors, and adjusters, thus formed another corps of intermediaries, although industry influence was still greater through two publications – *Lloyd's List* and *Lloyd's Register* – both spinoffs from Edward Lloyd's original postings. The *List*, with information of shipping arrivals and departures in British ports, first appeared at Lloyd's in 1734. By the First World War, benefiting both from the reports of 1,400 Lloyd's agents distributed among the harbors of the world and from the instantaneous communication of arrivals, departures, wrecks, and salvage operations picked up by 150 signal stations, it had developed into the world's clearinghouse of shipping information. The *Register* can be traced back to 1760, although its modern series dates from 1834. It listed and classified all ocean tonnage, identifying ships by name, owner, place of registration, and by those physical features of interest to insurers: age, size, and condition of the vessel and its equipment. Without classification by the *Register* or one of the two other institutions that, like Lloyd's, came to enjoy semi-official status as a setter of standards – Bureau Veritas (founded in Antwerp in 1828 and relocated to Paris in 1833) and The British Corporation for the Survey and Registry of Shipping (established in Glasgow in 1890) – insurance at affordable rates was all but impossible. High classification was the ticket to low-cost insurance, but it came at a price: construction, maintenance, and periodic surveys that conformed to *Register* criteria. In 1890 the Board of Trade delegated to three agencies the authority to set load lines for British ships. Lloyd's and other marine insurers and registries thus had enormous impact upon shipping, and the choice by continentals of company names – Norddeutscher Lloyd, Rotterdamsche Lloyd, Lloyd Triestino – identified the industry leader with the very meaning of modern sea transport. Insurance companies and registers minimized risk, forced safer construction and maintenance, and, to meet industry needs, circulated vast amounts of shipping intelligence. Their concentration most notably in the market of London added to that city's role as a maritime command center. But Lloyd's and Bureau Veritas were also transnational organizations; early NGOs, with agents strewn across the world; international in their reach; standards setters for all nations' vessels; and hence characteristic too of the globalized context in which shipping operated throughout the entire century.[23]

FREIGHT FORWARDERS

With forwarders we return to the middleman as a world connector. But they were not always as self-explanatory as their name implied. Pierre Bauchet wrote of forwarders, "They are the best-known auxiliary, but also the hardest to define by their activities."[24] In good part that was because forwarding companies did many things besides classic forwarding. Hernu Péron were important French *transitaires* (or forwarders),

[23] Fayle, *Short*, 79, 134–135, 209–210, 281–285; idem, *War*, 6, 25–26; Godfrey Hodgson, *Lloyd's of London* (New York: Viking, 1984); Behrens, *Merchant*, 96–97.
[24] Pierre Bauchet, *Le transport international dans l'économie mondiale*, 2nd ed. (Paris: Economica, 1991), 326.

but they also were ship agents and insurance agents. G. Feron-E. de Clebsattel, another French firm, were ship agents, but also forwarders and stevedores.[25] Belgium's Ziegler were forwarders, but also the biggest transport company in Belgium.[26] Germany's J. H. Bachmann started business in 1775 in Bremen as a merchant house dealing in cotton and silk goods. When its founder, Johann Christoph Bachmann, was unable to fill his own wagons with goods, he set up as a transporter for others. The Dubbers, who took over the company (Johann Christoph married a Dubbers), developed Bachmann into a big forwarding house with a major branch in Hamburg and other branches in Rotterdam, Antwerp, and northern Germany. The Dubbers, however, were also wine traders and investors in Bremen shipping companies. They expanded Bachmann into a storage and handling company with more than seventy warehouses and sheds by the mid-1920s. Bachmann also ran its own quay installations with cranes, elevators, lighters, and railway cars. Its rival, the equally colossal Kühne & Nagel, founded in 1890, also in Bremen, was Germany's largest privately owned forwarder in 1965, with thirty-eight branches or affiliates and twenty-four representatives in Europe and overseas, and 3,000 employees. It too diversified into warehousing and cargo handling (particularly for bulk cargo shipments), and added travel bureaus.[27]

Nevertheless, forwarding proper could be bordered by a number of precise functions: coordinating among different modes of transport (trains, trucks, and ships), possessing a thorough knowledge of rates or ready access to this knowledge, assuming responsibility for customs clearance, handling documentation from transit papers to insurance, and overseeing packing and storing. All of these fell under the rubric of managing individual shipments of goods from senders to receivers. Bolko Graf von Pfeil, a Hamburg ship agent, cut closer to the heart of the business when he described forwarders in this way:

[Sometimes] principals believe a forwarder is somebody who runs a truck and he delivers cargo to the port, but this is not the case. If you, for example, are the producer of a type of machinery and you have your factories somewhere in the south of Germany and you have exports to the United States, to the Far East, to Africa,

---

[25] NMM/New Zealand Shipping Co. Ltd. (NZS)/20/1/17 May, 12 June 1967 (by this time, Hernu Péron were part of the Danzas Group); PRO/MT 63/28/21 August 1940; De Clebsattel (interview).

[26] Bosteels (interview).

[27] *175 Jahre J. H. Bachmann Bremen. 20 August 1775–1950* (1950); *1890–1965. Kühne & Nagel 75 Jahre* (Bremen, 1965).

to South America, to Central America and all over the place, if you were trying to organize transportation yourself, that means permanently being aware of freight rates available in the market, the different systems available in the market, conference, non-conference, container, break-bulk ... air freight, sea freight, getting the cargo from the factory to the seaport, on the ship, from the point of destination to the site where you need the cargo, let's say somewhere in the jungle of the Amazon, you would need [your] own shipping department ... and therefore most of German exporters or manufacturers have decided to give their transport requirements to a forwarding agent.

Or as Walter Stork, a Hamburg forwarder, put it in a sentence: "[The] freight forwarder is the architect of transport."[28]

A forwarders' manual written around 1940 by Mathieu Adriaens, an Antwerp freight forwarder and vice president of his professional organization, was still more precise, blocking out point by point just what a forwarder did to effect a shipment. In Adriaens's example, an exporter in Brussels, Durand, sells fifteen tons of machinery (dismantled and packed in twenty cases) to his client, Taplos, in Cairo. Durand, however (just to introduce more nuances into the case), is himself a middleman, having purchased the machinery from the Zurich manufacturer Rütli. The question involved is how to get the twenty cases from Zurich to Cairo. The contract between Durand and Rütli provides for shipment at the latter's expense of the cases from Zurich to Basel. From this point, it is Durand's responsibility to get the cases to Cairo. To get a rate, Durand calls Peeters, a freight forwarder in the port of Antwerp, who now takes over responsibility for arranging the shipment. Peeters first contacts his correspondent in Basel, Ruesch, to determine the rate of transport from Basel to Antwerp. He then adds the freight charges for handling and clearance in Antwerp plus the freight rate from Antwerp to Alexandria to Ruesch's figure to provide his principal, Durand, with a through rate for Basel–Alexandria. Taplos, the purchaser in Cairo, will then take responsibility for the cost of the final leg of the shipment, although Peeters, as point-to-point forwarder, is still in charge of orchestrating transport all along the way from Zurich to Cairo. To do so, he arranges overseas shipping (probably through a ship agent) with a liner firm calling in Antwerp. Peeters then writes Ruesch (his Basel correspondent) to send Rütli, in Zurich, instructions for getting the cases from Zurich to Basel, and he writes Rütli to follow the instructions that Ruesch is going to send him.

---

[28] Bolko Graf Von Pfeil, Detjen Schiffahrtsagentur, interview with author, Hamburg, 13 June 1996; Walter Stork, Navis Schiffahrts-und Speditions Aktiengesellschaft, and Wolfgang Piehler, formerly of J. H. Bachmann, interview with author, Hamburg, 22 July 1996.

He also requests Ruesch to arrange transport from Basel to Antwerp. Once the cases arrive in Antwerp, Peeters draws up the proper bill of lading papers that must accompany the shipment, he sees to it that the insurance is in order, and he handles the other transit paperwork. He pays ocean freight to the shipping company in advance for Durand, and he makes certain the cases are in the loading docks in time to be hauled aboard ship. He also contacts now a new party, Lakil, his correspondent in Alexandria, to organize transport from Alexandria's harbor to Cairo in conjunction with any instructions from the purchaser, Taplos. Peeters's final responsibility then is to assure that Lakil receives all the necessary paperwork for reception and clearance in Alexandria, including the essential bill of lading.[29]

The most revealing thing about these examples was less their demonstration of what forwarders did than how they did it by reproducing within their middleman world the same local-global hybridity as their principals, the traders and shipping companies. Bachmann, for instance, was a deeply embedded Bremen house. Johann Christoph Dubbers, the founder of the family line, was a member of the Bremen City Council and active in harbor affairs. His son, Edouard, numbered among the founders of the DDG Hansa Line, Bremen's second largest shipping company. Edouard's son, August, born in 1873, partner in 1900, and still with the firm fifty years later, sat on the Bremen City Council, chaired the chamber of commerce's Railway Committee, and sat on the boards of numerous Bremen companies. At the same time, he presided over a company that relied on correspondents across the world to carry out its forwarding obligations. Before taking up his place as a home port establishment figure, his career had begun with training in Bordeaux, London, and Liverpool, followed by a world tour to North America, Japan, China, Java, and India where "old relationships were then strengthened, valuable new ones struck up."[30]

Nearly all forwarding firms fit this transnational pattern in one way or another. Adriaens's fictional Peeters was based in Antwerp but could command support in Basel or Alexandria. Von Pfeil's imagined forwarder was a Hamburg man who spent his day organizing shipments to America, Africa, or the Amazon. In real life, forwarders incessantly networked to build out their connections. The Kühne brothers, Alfred and Werner, sons of founder August Kühne, based themselves in Bremen and Hamburg but eventually assembled representatives or branches that covered most

[29] Mathieu Adriaens, *Le commissionnaire-expéditeur au port d'Anvers*, 3rd ed. (Anvers: Editions Lloyd Anversois, c. 1940), 96–97.
[30] *175 Jahre*, 20–27.

of the world. Hernu Péron's London office listed on its letterhead correspondents in Sydney, Singapore, Bombay, South Africa, Alexandria, New York, and Montreal. Jan de Bie, a local Antwerp boy who boasted that Antwerp forwarders did not know the meaning of "impossible," built up in Antwerp a circle of contacts among importers and exporters, ship agents, bankers, and chamber of commerce officials, all of whom funneled him information on business possibilities in exchange for the information or favors he passed on to them. Yet he too traveled widely and set up networks overseas. Ziegler's Bosteels, another Antwerp man, traveled all over the world to find good agents. These were all worldly men, yet they were also locally connected with strong home port loyalties. So renowned were Antwerp's forwarders for steering traffic the Scheldt's way that Antwerp became known as a forwarders' port.[31]

There was, in addition, something of an art to successful forwarding. The best forwarders had the rates in their heads and knew cargo, how it should be packed, how it should be stowed, and how it should be sent. A clever forwarder understood that the most direct route was not always the fastest nor the cheapest. Goods from Hamburg to Manchester, for instance, were better sent via Goole, on the Humber, because English railroad companies held large leaseholds in the port, ran their own shipping lines, and, eager for rail, shipping, and port business, offered better rates than direct service through the ship canal.[32] But what forwarders offered most was expertise, or knowledge converted into resourcefulness – which perhaps explains why they were also such master storytellers. Walter Stork of Hamburg, who sealed a bid with a ten-pfennig piece pulled out of his pocket; de Bie, who, to avoid a factory shutdown, overcame a strike and a driving snowstorm in England to shepherd home a special valve; and Charley Dietvorst of Rotterdam, the forwarder who flew to New York to put in a bid firsthand, and who explained how, as the son of a Shell executive, he ended up in freight forwarding – "They kicked me out of school. I had to find a job. My father gave me two days to find a job" – recounted tale after tale of risk taking and improvisation, for themselves and for their clients, yet always succeeding because they were so grounded in the fundamentals of what they did.[33]

[31] *1890–1965*, 10, 18–31; PRO/MT 63/28/21 August 1940; de Bie (interview); Bosteels (interview).

[32] Claus Friedemann, *Der Speditions-Fachmann* (Hamburg: Verlag Hans A. Blum, 1932), 67–68.

[33] Stork (interview); de Bie (interview); Dietvorst (interview). The same resourcefulness turned up in the stories Hans Hentzen, a Rotterdamer forwarder, told of his father,

Middlemen in modern times have often been seen as an impediment, but freight forwarders like these created efficiencies. Through their contacts and their performance skills, they gathered goods, identified best possibilities in rates and routes, cleared customs, and managed point-to-point coverage. None of this is meant to glamorize them, but to catch the infinite possibilities that middlemen assembled into a clear, articulated series of connections. As P & O's Alan Bott remarked, before the era of container logistics and one-stop shopping, when no shipping company was in all the trades, it was forwarders who organized the dispatch and reception of crates and cases on a global scale.[34] They too, like stevedores, were rough and ready characters when need be, but they were also global coordinators, an identity, however, they shared with ship agents.

SHIPBROKERS AND AGENTS

Before containers, ship agents managed world flows; literally, they made the world go round. Their specific duties were to see to the arrival and departure of ships from a port, but that scarcely begins to capture their role or their significance. They were port representatives, but also sources of traffic, channels of information, local managers, advisers, initiators, network builders, and, at an earlier stage in their history, not infrequently the founders of shipping lines. In certain cases the history of the shipping companies they served was also their history. The history of Holts could not be written independent of the history of Swires and Mansfields. The history of British India began with the history of Mackinnon Mackenzie. The history of the Rotterdamsche Lloyd was often written on the letterhead of Internatio. Agents inhabited the first circle of the shipping world. In their ports they were men of status, suit wearers and officeholders, lunch givers and exchange partners, independent professionals, but also the face of the big, international shipping lines they handled. In the East, they were often business mandarins, the hubs of their own far-reaching networks. Most of all, they were the key maritime node, the point where shipping and all the other sectors converged to produce out of many parts and pieces, or multiple networks,

Henk: Hans Hentzen, Henk Hentzen Beheer B.V., interview with author, Rotterdam, 29 July 1997.
[34] Bott (interview).

a truly global system. All the themes of this chapter thus replicate in the history of ship agents: a fragmented globalism coordinated through middlemen; a repetition, at the intermediary level, of home and transnational identities and connections that made this possible; and the expertise that translated desire into performance.

It is necessary to begin with their differentiation from shipbrokers, who mediated the sale and chartering of ships and cargoes. Nearly every language distinguishes between the two: *agence maritime/courtier maritime, scheepsagentuur/cargadoor* or *scheepsmakelaar*, and so on. The disentangling, however, is not an easy chore. Many of the oldest firms began as shipbrokers and then developed ship agency business with the rise of liner service. Some continued to combine both functions, even if regularly scheduled liner work was their cardinal trade. In some shipbroking firms it was also necessary to maintain an agency department to handle the outward agency work for a vessel during a charter party. Nevertheless, during the twentieth century the two professions drifted apart, like branches from a common ancestor. Important shipbroking firms in the City of London, such as Clarkson or Gibson, considered themselves operating in wholly different lines of business.[35]

Shipbrokers could be found in any significant port, but they also possessed a world hub, the Baltic Exchange on St. Mary Axe in the City. Here was the transnational world of shipping in a microcosm. Shipbrokers of multiple nationalities gathered face-to-face and mediated the world market in ships or fixed cargo charters, the means by which vital commodities such as grain and coal, and later oil, crossed the oceans. The Baltic's power lay in its centralizing the two foundations of maritime business: knowledge and networks. The expertise of its members was of necessity encyclopedic. Simply to fix charters to the best advantage of its principals, a broker needed to know the conditions of freight markets around the world, port-specific customs and dues, the average running costs of steamers, the reputation of owners and ships, all the conditions specific to the loading and stowing of various commodities, and turnaround rates and obstacles in ports on six continents.[36] Brokering the sale of a ship could take months, but as Eric Shawyer, who began in the business after

[35] Hugh O. McCoy, Clarkson and Baltic Exchange, interview with author, London, 20 April 1998; Eric Shawyer, E. A. Gibson Shipbrokers Ltd. and Baltic Exchange, interview with author, London, 21 April 1998.
[36] MacMurray and Cree, *Shipping*, 4, 33, 133–148.

FIGURE 4. A Scrutton's office in London's Royal Docks. Courtesy Museum of London, Scruttons Collection.

FIGURE 5. Internatio's ship agency office, Batavia, c. 1912–1913. With the permission of Internatio-Müller N.V.

the Second World War, described it, "If [you came to me] in the morning and said 'I want to be a shipowner,' we could take you from the cradle to the grave. We could find out what you were thinking of; we could find out the ship you wanted; we can get it inspected for you. We can buy it for you. We can arrange the finance for you. We could then arrange for it to be managed for you, and we could then arrange employment for it."[37] All of this Shawyer could do out of his office in London, because the nearby Baltic (which Shawyer would chair), gave access to a concentration of information and fellow brokers and proximity to the world's greatest marine insurance market. More than a meeting place, the Baltic was a thick agglomeration of contacts held together by a reputation in fair dealing. Even away from London, shipbrokers lived off their entry to its knowledge banks and connections.[38]

Shipbrokers were therefore very different business animals than ship agents, whose world was liner shipping. The typical transaction for a shipbroker was fixing a buyer with a seller, and all the bargaining that took place in between. The first line of business for a ship agent on the other hand was to oversee the arrival, unloading, and dispatch of ships for a regularly scheduled shipping line. This meant, upon receipt of a telegram that a company liner was arriving, notifying harbor authorities; arranging a berth assignment; arranging for tugboats and pilots if necessary; arranging for stevedore services; arranging for a grain elevator if loose grain was on board; arranging with harbor medical authorities if debarking passengers were on board; notifying consignees of shipments listed on the manifest; notifying freight forwarders that the ship would be accepting shipments for its following ports of call; and so forth. When the steamer arrived, the agent's job was to coordinate the scheduling of various operations, prepare an unloading plan with stevedores, meet the ship and its captain, handle damage claims, countersign the release of cargo (and decide the element of risk when not all the paperwork was available), arrange for through-cargo, and assure the smooth debarkation of passengers. Comparable chores accompanied the other end of preparing the ship's departure. Throughout, there was a mountain of paperwork to

[37] Shawyer (interview).
[38] Lewis R. Fischer and Helge W. Nordvik, "Economic Theory, Information, and Management in Shipbroking: Fearnley and Eger as a Case Study, 1869–1972," in Simon P. Ville and David M. Williams, eds., *Management, Finance, and Industrial Relations in Maritime Industries: Essays in International Maritime and Business History*, Research in Maritime History 6 (St. John's, Newfoundland: International Maritime Economic History Association, 1994), 1–29.

process: stowage charts, bills of lading, declaration manifests, payments for harbor services, bookkeeping for the shipping company, and correspondence regarding three bales of this or one crate of that, which were not unloaded and turned up in the next port.[39]

Such manipulations only scratched the surface. The personal trajectory of Diedrich Döhle, a Hamburg agent, provides a better introduction to what went into the prowess of these men. Döhle, like most of his generation of ship agents, came from a maritime family. Returning from a POW camp at the end of the Second World War, he trained with Bachmann and then joined his father's shipbroking firm, Euge Cellier. In 1957 Döhle entered Paul Günther, a substantial Hamburg agency house founded in 1891 by its namesake, the son of a shipbroker. The firm had a long history as agent for Hamburg shipping lines sailing to South America and the East, but it also represented foreign flagged firms, including Mitsui. Once at Günther, Döhle pioneered in leading the company into the computer and container age. His real home, however, was the traditional world of ships and quays, waterfront expertise, and personal relations that had characterized ship agency work for a century. As an apprentice he worked half a year as a stevedore and then half a year as a tallyman so that he could explain to someone in southern Germany why their cargo had to be packed a certain way. He sold service and bookings, and in the early 1950s traveled nearly half the year, from Buenos Aires to Tokyo or overnight from Hamburg to Hanover, sleeping in cheap hotels, to cement the relationships that brought in business. His forte was to get to the traffic managers at 7:30 in the morning, before anyone else, and to court these relatively low-ranked company officials who nonetheless decided which carrier to use. He excelled at building contacts; knowing the business; knowing ship captains, their wives, and their girlfriends; knowing cargo; loving the tangible, physical contact of the business, the scent of cargo, the fact that "cargo smells!"; knowing what was in the hatch simply by sticking one's nose down into it; and especially, closing a sale. Even in the modified world of the 1970s, now partner and one of the two men running the company, he could recall standing smashed outside the Hapag-Lloyd building after a whiskey-drinking session during which he had won an important share of

[39] I have relied heavily here on Hermann Reincke, *Schiffsmakler-Kompass* (Hamburg, 1939), 137–157. The text appears to have been written by Franz Guido Caulier-Eimbcke; see the second edition under his name (Hamburg: Cram, De Gruyter, 1954) 7, 9, and 127–141.

their containerized agency business. "You have to drink like a lion," was another Döhle aphorism.[40]

Ship agents were thus strong blends of fiercely proud practical men, local powers, and cosmopolitans. Deeply knowledgeable in the ways of cargo and ships and harbors, they loved the challenge of working out problems. As Rolf van den Wall Bake described his work in Sydney harbor, "You were always a 'Mr. Fix-it,'" a rubric that took in troubleshooting but also a fair degree of quay smarts.[41] Yet they were also courtly figures, a trait that pertained, especially for the older generation including Döhle, or Hans Killinger, another Hamburg agent, or Philip Durot in Antwerp, up until the end of the century. As yet another agent put it, "Stevedores, with all their equipment, are men on the spot. They are very much local, but a ship's agent represents a foreign ship owner.... You are a man of the world."[42]

They were, in effect, both, men of their harbors and men of the world. At home they shared in the prestige of the companies they represented, or in some cases, had founded. Along with shipping companies they leased quays in ports such as Antwerp and Rotterdam.[43] Many made a good living off their commissions and their short-term terminal leases. They mingled with their principals, and the apprenticing of agents' sons, merchants, and ship owners to the offices of one another was an old maritime tradition. Their firms were local institutions, firmly rooted in the power structures of their ports. Killinger's house, Aug. Bolten, had been among the founders of HAPAG and Hamburg Süd. In Antwerp, Randaxhe-Bally dated from 1862. Jean Randaxhe, third generation, acquired the representations of the big German firms, HAPAG, NDL, and Hamburg Süd, and in 1939, Randaxhe-Bally was handling 450 ships in a year and covering destinations or arrivals from around the world. P. van Doosselaere, an associate of Randaxhe's by marriage, until he parted ways after the Second World War and founded his own ship agency, was later chair of the Antwerp Shipping Federation, the powerful lobby of shipping interests in the city and dominated by agents.

[40] Diedrich Döhle, Paul Günther, interview with author, Hamburg, 4 July 1996; Gert Uwe Detlefsen, *1891–1991, Paul Günther: A Century of Dedicated Service*, Norbert Bellstedt, trans. (Hamburg: Paul Günther, 1991).

[41] Rolf H. A. van den Wall Bake, Mitsui O.S.K. Lines (Nederland) B.V., interview with author, Rotterdam, 23 July 1997.

[42] Noorduyn (interview).

[43] Hugo van Driel, Reginald Loyen, and Stéphane Hoste, "Cargo-Handling Costs: Competition in the Break-Bulk Sector," in de Goey, ed., *Comparative*, 179–180.

Maurice Velge, son of old family friends and Jean Randaxhe's successor when he died in 1965, also became president of the Antwerp Shipping Federation, and for ten years chaired the Promotion Association of the port.[44]

Still, they were incorporated into the transnational networks of their principals so easily because they were themselves such international creatures. Their purpose was to arrange the flow of shipments across the seas. They traveled extensively. Döhle traveled to Buenos Aires and Tokyo, and represented Hambourgeois, Japanese, South American, and South African shipping companies. Knöhr & Burchard, founded in 1814 and as old-line Hamburg as they came, held the agencies of Hambourgeois, Scandinavian, Japanese, British, American, and Greek lines. Its long-standing relationship with Britain's Currie Line proved to be its lifeline in the critical "resurrection" years following the Second World War.[45] Randaxhe-Bally represented German firms in Antwerp. When a Holland Amerika official toured the eastern Mediterranean in 1923 on the hunt for refugee traffic in the wake of the mass slaughters and deportations of the previous six years, he fastened on W. F. van der Zee, a Dutch, but Piraeus-based company with "a preponderant position in Smyrna [Izmir]" and a network of correspondents throughout the Greek mainland and islands: Allalouf & Cie in Salonika, J. N. Chaidopoulos in Patras, E. D. Chamarakis on Crete, Fraraki Frères on Rhodes, Cardassilari Frères on Khios, and their own office on Samos.[46]

Overseas, agents were by definition transnational: expatriates who had set up abroad or local powers such as the Delfinos or Jimmy Dodero, the twenty-five-year-old son of a former Argentinian shipping magnate to whom the Compagnie Maritime Belge confided its Buenos Aires agency. Funch, Edye, a big American ship agency with a large number of European representations was founded by the son of the Danish consul in Algiers, later joined by a Scot who had lived for some time in Hamburg. East of Suez were the trading companies, although the Silver Java Pacific Line, in search of a Persian Gulf agent, took a chance on Yusuf Bin Ahmed Kanoo, a small-time operation in the port of Bahrein in the 1930s, that

[44] SA/MA 36/Havenbedrijf 63337/14 December, 1962; SA/MA 36/Havenbedrijf 24283/2 October 1933; Maurice Velge, Grisar & Velge, interview with author, Antwerp, 8 January 1998.

[45] Friedrich Jerchow, *Knöhr & Burchard NFL. Hamburg, 1814–1989* (Hamburg: Hanseatischer Merkur, 1989).

[46] GAR/HAL/Passage 8/14 July 1923.

paid off. Thirty-plus years later, a Kanoo advertisement noted that the firm handled 2,400 tanker and 800 dry cargo ships annually.[47]

It was in particular the long-term insertion of these men "of the world" within home or regional communities that mattered. The advantage of the locally powerful and well-connected firm was its ability to secure cargo, passengers, and extraordinary amounts of information. Agents were far more than harbor rats. Their first responsibility was to acquire and get to know clients "to establish a continuous working relationship with your customer so that he contacts you whenever he has a cargo."[48] The prime commodity they traded in was knowledge. Ports spilled over with information that agents "hoovered up" through their links to customs officials, port authorities, club buddies, entrée with local consuls or embassies, lunches and drinks with colleagues, chats with trading company connections, telephone calls to people in the know, exchanges of favors, conversations with clients, and their own regional networks within networks. J. J. Noorduyn, who went out to the Dutch East Indies right after the Second World War and worked for the next forty years with various agencies of the Rotterdamsche Lloyd, described how information exchange was an essential part of his business. Every morning between ten and twelve he visited clients to canvass for business, but he was also "in the meantime, picking up ... information." The best way to get this intelligence was to listen well, but also to supply intelligence in return on markets and commodities the client was interested in by tapping the resources of his own organization's wider network. In this regard, one network functioned as a platform for the creation of another.[49] Functionally, shipping companies could not operate without an agent to turn over their ships in each port; but service as listening posts for their principals was inestimable. From the loneliest of outposts agents dispatched opinions and judgments. Agents in major stations sent in voluminous amounts of information, sometimes compiled in long, end-of-the-year statistical reports.[50] Ship

[47] CMB/C7/17/P. Scraeyen, Voyage en Amérique du Sud, 20 March–16 April 1965; *A Century of Ship Agency and Brokerage: The Story of Funch Edye & Co, Inc. 1847–1947* (New York: Business Biographies, 1947); Delprat, *Reeder*, 133, 150–151; *Fairplay*, 18 June 1970.
[48] Hans H. Killinger, FA. Aug. Bolten Wm. Miller's Nachfolger, interview with author, Hamburg, 11 June 1996; Von Pfeil (interview, quoted).
[49] Noorduyn (interview).
[50] This was particularly true of in-house networks. See the Messageries Maritimes annual reports in AAFL/MM/Rapports d'activité, and the P & O agent reports in NMM/P & O/ Agents' Annual Reports.

agents who were not part of a network but who wanted in, often supplied free information to build up good will and demonstrate their usefulness. In the head offices of shipping companies, from Hamburg to Marseille, all this data was then sifted and filtered into decisions about investments, routes, schedules, traffics, and the opening of new markets.[51]

For many shipping companies, then, the most crucial decision was not what ships to build but what agencies to secure. Entries into new trades or markets began with a search for the proper representative. To make that choice shipping companies again turned to conduits of information. They consulted with banks and maritime colleagues, and they visited offices and quays.[52] Sometimes they picked real clunkers, indifferent or shoddy types, or the CGT agent in a Latin American country who was indolent only in his work habits, and whose "*idées donjuanesques*" and "adventures *d'ordre galant*," were an embarrassment.[53]

The reverse, not infrequent, was the pick of a lifetime: Alfred Holt's choice of Swires, or the Harrison Line's selection of Alfred Le Blanc & Co. as their New Orleans agent, the means by which they "broke into the cotton and wheat trade of the Mississippi basin."[54] Just how good a good agent could be can be seen in what Hansen & Tidemann, Gulf port agent for Belgium's Armement Deppe, could do in return for its commissions. Hansen & Tidemann were a big operation. They were headquartered in Houston and employed more than 150 people spread across ten branches, including New York, Havana, and Mexico City, so that they were able to coordinate canvassing, contacts, shipments, and intelligence across the United States and into the Caribbean. The firm's contacts with banks, consul generals, port authorities, and shippers made its services virtually indispensable. It built its canvassing organization upon close personal connections to its customers. Wayne White, the firm's general sales manager, was himself a former traffic manager with W. D. Felder, one of the leading cotton shippers. His contacts with traffic managers and cotton shippers out of Dallas was close to comprehensive. The president of the ship agency, Svend Hansen, personally knew the heads of many of the companies with whom he did business and was an investor in the American Cotton Cooperative Association, whose shipments via Deppe

---

[51] See, for instance, HAPAG/3007. Boyce, *Information*, throughout, is essential on the value of information flows.

[52] GAR/HAL/Directie 123/3, 14 September 1948.

[53] MMM/B/BROC/5/2/1/1908 (Shire Line); Ministère des affaires étrangères (MAE)/ Amérique 1918–1940/Dossiers Généraux/103/CGT 1923–1929, 31 March 1926.

[54] Hyde, *Liverpool*, 57.

increased accordingly. In the special culture of the cotton business, these connections counted for everything, so that when a ship was half-empty, a phone call – "'Do me a favor, will you?'" – secured extra cargo, just as when a ship was overbooked and there was better-paying freight, a phone call could push back a shipment until the next sailing. As business through its Mexico City correspondent flagged, Hansen & Tidemann established its own agency in the capital,

having the wisdom to reserve the presidency for Monsieur le docteur ALFARO, former San Salvador ambassador to Mexico, a resident of this city for twenty-five years, and married to a direct descendant of the Emperor Iturbide. Monsieur Alfaro has the best relations with government circles…. His brother-in-law, Monsieur Annibal de Iturbide, is the President of the Banco Commercial de Mexico. Monsieur Alfaro was able to secure the presence of the Minister of the Navy … at a cocktail party I gave in Mexico City for 60 importers and exporters considerably surprised by the Minister's coming since it is unusual for him to attend this sort of reception.

The local director assigned to handle day-to-day matters was Mario Garcia, who was from the north of Mexico and well connected with clients.

The power of Hansen & Tidemann to command traffics, even to pioneer routes and capture markets, and thus, potentially, to advance regional economic shifts and international consumer preferences, was demonstrated by a campaign Belgian shipping waged in 1967 to win transatlantic citrus juice shipments. Mobilizing all three of the agencies involved – Hansen & Tidemann in the Gulf, the Belgian Line in New York (this was the affiliate of the Agence Maritime Internationale, a very large Antwerp agency that managed the Compagnie Maritime Belge's commercial operations; the CMB had taken over Deppe in the early 1960s[55]), and Deppe's Paris agent, the Comptoir Maritime Franco-Belge – the Belgians drew on canvassing skills, intelligence networks, personal contacts, and marketing resources on both sides of the Atlantic. The agents conducted market research on demand in Europe for bottled juices and their annual selling cycle in France. They met with juice company executives, forwarders, railroad company managers, trucking companies, and lawyers to put together a package they could sell. They demonstrated why shipping either via Norfolk or Gulf services was superior to shipping juice out of New York, as was standard for southeastern exporters. They coordinated

[55] Deppe, before its World War II losses, had been Belgium's second largest shipping line. It continued to run routes under its own name to the Gulf ports and Mexico.

with other business interests in the region to promote transport through these ports. They forwarded extensive information on port facilities and methods of shipping. They gathered meticulous, insider information on their competitors' experiences and costs. By 1968 Deppe had its contract with Tropicana.[56] Of the three, Hansen & Tidemann were especially aggressive in every facet of this campaign. At one point early in its takeover of Deppe, the CMB had contemplated reassigning representation to its in-house Belgian Line agent. Needless to say, after closer experience it abandoned that project. Any other decision would have been comical.[57]

Ship agents were thus the fulcrum upon which everything else turned. They were the building blocks of shipping networks, but they were equally instruments through which still wider networks came to be assembled and worked. They managed world flows by carrying out the basic operational services in every port of call, but they succeeded because they were world-oriented professionals, cosmopolitans in their own right yet also so locally entwined that they could provide the contacts, intelligence, and legwork through which most networking was done. At nearly every conjunction they were the key connectors. They coordinated the services of stevedores, dockers, warehousers, and forwarders. They coordinated between shipping companies and between shippers and destinations, serving as the mechanism by which shipping networks buckled together. Their mediation, consequently, was not simply between persons and firms, but between dual realms, the local and the global to be sure, but also between the incompleteness of single company coverage and what summed up into a world-enmeshing system. The arch-coordinators, they were therefore paradigmatic and indispensable. Until, that is, the system changed, and displaced them from the center of the maritime universe.

That universe, we have seen, broke down into its basic sectors: ports, shipping, trading, and mediators. But we have also seen how three things bound them together. First, and self-evidently, all collaborated to transport everything, and everyone, that traveled by sea. A world maritime system began with these harmonics. Pianos ship from Leipzig to Rosario. The order processes through a trading house. The trading house engages the services of a freight forwarder who also works through a ship agent.

[56] The victory, however, proved ephemeral; several years later Tropicana rerouted the traffic via New Jersey.
[57] CMB/D13/2/Gulf, 28 March 1961 (quoted on cotton shippers); ibid., Mexico/USA, 19 February–20 March 1962 (quoted on Mexico); ibid., Mexico/USA, April 1968; CMB/ D13/59.

The pianos transit in crates to Hamburg where they are loaded and stored by stevedores. They ship out and cross the Atlantic on a regularly scheduled liner. The shipping company orchestrates the basics of ocean transport but relies on the harbor services and infrastructure of the port authority. In Buenos Aires the pianos are off-loaded and transited through the services of ship agents, forwarders, stevedores, and landside or lighter services, for travel by rail or riverboat up the Plate and the Paraná. Having arrived in Rosario, they are warehoused by the trading company until delivery to the final consignee. They are paid for by a shipment of grain back across to Antwerp. Human passage would perhaps be simpler, but the underlying collaboration of sectors still pertains: All work together or nothing works at all. Second, all sectors worked (and joined) through networks. Ports were the spatial crossroads of networks. Shipping lines were the assemblers of networks, route networks, and overseas networks, into which they incorporated other sectors, mostly trading companies and ship agents, but also sometimes stevedores. Trading companies, forwarders, and agents additionally constructed their own, not infrequently, extensive networks, to produce the synergistic effect of networks within networks. Agents, although parts of networks, acted, with forwarders, as switchboards that connected one network to another. The pursuit of contacts, or the action of networking, broadened networks to include port and government officials, travel agents, railroad companies, importers and exporters – anyone who had an interest in overseas transport and could grease its wheels. Networks and networking were thus, at once, vehicle, lubricant, and bridge by which maritime commerce happened. Third, permeating all were local and global engagements. A fundamental argument that has run through the discussion of all of these sectors is that the management of world flows occurred because at so many levels the maritime men and firms responsible for making them possible were themselves locally embedded yet globally connected. The globalism of the century was a product of this internalized fusion.

There was, however, a fourth cement that explained or consolidated the first three: the business culture that infused life in ports and on the shipping lanes. This culture was itself a product of a maritime system built upon networks and home and overseas identities; but it was most of all what bound the maritime world together and made it function, until it too was remade by containerization.

5

Culture

When Julian Taylor, one of the fast-tracked officers at Holts, was sent out to Singapore in 1960, he spent his first few weeks traveling to ports of call in the East. To orient him for the trip, Kerry St. Johnston, a manager with many years of experience in Blue Funnel's East Asian operations, wrote a long letter, because "anything that can be done to lay a foundation of useful knowledge is to your advantage." In Bangkok, Taylor was told to watch the draft of vessels going up the river. The wharf was also worth inspecting closely, as its working rate was high. If Taylor overlapped with a Holts ship in the port, then he must definitely go on board where he would "probably see some brilliant pilfering going on, as I did myself." But scenically, Bangkok was also "superb, and it is well worth trotting around the various temples and getting up one morning early and going off up one of the Klongs in a boat to the floating market." The stock questions to ask, as St. Johnston always did when he was in a harbor, were "speed of discharge, speed of loading, size of gangs, hours worked, hours ships were able to come and go, approximate port charges, etc. I still find this information most useful in my little notebook." As for personnel, he would find the shipping manager, Alistair Greelees, "a particularly nice chap.... He is a personal friend of mine, and has taken on the invidious task of replacing an 'institution,' a man called Marr who knew a great deal about shipping but was too old to have much energy left."

At Hong Kong the thing to watch was the "speed of work" by lighters loading on both sides of the ship. To understand how Hong Kong functioned as a port, St. Johnston advised Taylor "to ask to be taken to the back street factories in Hong Kong or Kowloon in order to see just how tiny the premises are, with no storage space and with packages of cargo standing on the pavement half filled, with the balance still coming off the production line although the ship it is marked for is probably sailing that afternoon." Jackie Tarr, the shipping manager, could probably arrange this. He should also observe all of Swires' (Holts' agents) operations in the port carefully, and he should meet with Mr. Choy, the Chinese manager, "with whom it is worth spending as much time as you can to get an idea of how the Department works."

In Japan, the man to meet was Tony Raynor, manager of Swires' Kobe office. But the Kobe office concentrated on harbor business alone, and Taylor should also spend several days hanging out with the canvassers in Osaka, and the Osaka manager, Tada-San. In Swires' Tokyo head office, the Japan shipping manager, Pat McCabe, was "an extremely nice experienced man who will tell you some of the complexities of doing business in Japan." Taylor should also try to get someone to explain the Zaibatsu to him. What Taylor especially needed to be cognizant of was that "the most difficult job so far as we are concerned in Japan, is estimating what cargo is going to be available for a particular ship. Canned goods ebb and flow with bewildering rapidity and you may come into the office one morning and find that 6,000 TS has dwindled to 3,500 TS overnight. Nothing but experience and hunch can give you the right answer."

When Taylor arrived in Labuan, in Sabah, St. Johnston recommended that he catch a plane if he could to Sandakan, the main homeward port for North Borneo. "The cargo moving is mainly logs and sawn timber.... Our vessels normally need four days to cover Borneo/Boheyan/Tawau/ Wallace Bay as the quantities are fairly small." Significant quantities of sawn timber were also loaded further south in Sarawak. "If you go there by sea as you will, it is important that you should travel up the Rejang River to Sibu with the agent in order to meet the Shipping Manager there, Pat White, and he will be able to put you in the picture very quickly on the situation." It was equally "worth paying a visit to the Saw Mill of Montague Meyer nearby where there is a charming Anglo-Burmese Manager called Hector Sword, whose sons are in Blue Funnel" (another letter in 1962 to Peter Nelson added that "the run up the Rejang River is unforgettable"). The two operational matters to keep in mind "are the way weather affects the supply of lighters full of timber from along the coast and congestion which occurs if more than a few vessels are there at once."

There was more, on Manila, Indonesia, and Singapore – the letter ran nine closely printed pages, and St. Johnston himself referred to it apologetically as "this enormous thesis" – but the above is sufficient to render its substance and, even more so, to catch what it tells about the culture or *mentalité* of maritime businessmen. The letter is all about networks: men on the spot and local connections. Its traits are those of a letter-writing culture. It is literate, chatty, presumptive of shared values, yet attentive to detail, and deliberately personal. In St. Johnston's world, contacts, knowledge, and experience are everything. Letters are mailed across oceans, but relations are face-to-face, or at the least, between individuals. This is how things get done. Agents serve principals, but their relations are close, respectful, and reciprocal. The milieu is competitive, yet cosmopolitan and clubby. Mixed in with all the old-boy jargon – Jackie, Tony, Pat – is a thorough grounding in trades and ports. St. Johnston's counsel – walk the commercial alleys of Hong Kong, observe how things are done in the harbors, talk to the engineering people, travel up the river to the sawmills, get to know our local insiders – is that of the expert, or the old shipping hand. This is schooling the old way – travel, meet, observe, learn. In the end, all judgments boil down to experience and hunches, or the ways of someone who has spent a lifetime in the shipping business.[1]

Yet, even this "thesis" cracks only the surface in a business culture that defined who businessmen were, what they did, and how they should do it. The idea of a business culture should therefore not be construed as the appropriation of cultural studies for the purpose of writing business history. Identities were simply one facet of the cultural context in which businessmen operated, and even then they were linked to concrete developments in the histories of firms and the world's commerce. Nor would it be correct to see in business culture the remains of the day: Business history with business left out. Culture as a set of patterns of behavior, or as unwritten rules, or as the things businessmen presumed about themselves and their profession, and thus inscribed into the common elements of their lives, informed how shipping, trading and middlemen conducted their daily affairs. Action was predicated on styles of relating, or the formation of professional identity. The networked structures of maritime enterprise engendered particular cultural forms but relied as well on specific cultural values in order to function. Culture thus established frameworks and contoured how maritime business worked. It was, in short, what the maritime world took for granted about itself.[2]

---

[1] MMM/OA 4B/1064/3 February 1960, 9 January 1962.

[2] For excellent introductions to business and culture, see Jeffrey R. Fear, "Constructing Big Business: The Cultural Concept of the Firm," in Alfred D. Chandler Jr., Franco Amatori, and Takashi Hikino, eds., *Big Business and the Wealth of Nations* (Cambridge: Cambridge University Press, 1997), 546–574; Ken Lipartito, "Business Culture," in Jones and Zeitlin, *Handbook*, 603–628.

DICHOTOMIES

The unmistakable thing about this culture was how riven it was with dichotomies: cosmopolitan yet enclaved; cooperative and clubby yet competitive; hierarchical yet closely personal and often a meeting of equals within the latticework of its relationships. The third trait was distinctly visible in the relations between principals and agents, especially those of shipowner and agent. Shipping circles took seriously strictures against agents working for competitors. Principals brooked no conflict of interest. HAPAG policy required that agents seek their permission when other agencies were contemplated, and they would not grant it if the company in question was an outsider (nonconference line). "Please," they would say, "this is ... not correct. We want to be first class."[3] This was typical of nearly all regular carriers, and self-restraint on the part of agents revealed how deeply they internalized the rules that subordinated them to their principals. Even now the relationship remains power driven, or as one agent confided, "We have to execute everything they ask."[4]

But the Durot experience with the Johnson Line tells another story. Father and son represented the Swedish firm in Antwerp for more than fifty years, beginning in 1936 when Durot senior set up as an exclusive agent for Johnson. During the war, when shipping through Antwerp all but dried up and the house had no business, the Durots sold off family possessions simply to keep from starving. But the Johnson Line also sent them assistance and placed them under the protection of the Swedish consulate. When the elder Durot died in 1961, his son, Philip, took over the firm and received permission to represent other lines, but remained principally an agent for Johnson Line. Over the years the Durots established an extremely close rapport with the company, a "feeling we [were] part of the family." They knew the owning family well and traveled to Stockholm several times a year for discussions. Meetings were always cordial, very gentlemanly, very friendly. Johnsons always consulted the Durots on anything that might affect their position in Antwerp. When consortia services following containerization forced a consolidation of agencies, the Durots opted to go it alone, but the separation proceeded like the old relationship: amiably, gentlemanly, and with efforts by Johnsons to make the transition as smooth as possible.[5]

[3] Killinger (interview). See also HAPAG/402/4 June 1969, letter to Baquera, Kusche y Martin S. A.
[4] Rijckaert (interview).
[5] Durot (interview).

Geniality, and even intimacy, thus characterized these circles as much as hierarchy. If the relation was formal and contractual, expectations were reciprocal and predicated on the assumption that representations, if possible, could go on forever. Something of old-fashioned paternalism saturated these relationships. Both sides expected loyalty and a family-like connection. Taking on an agency entailed commitments for the long run. The reality was of course often more brutal. Yet long-term associations were frequently the norm. The idea was that one signed a contract but joined an enterprise. Consequently the severing of relations met with hurtful, almost violated responses.

Selected for their local knowledge and connections, agents were business partners as much as underlings. Probably no association quite compared to the one constructed by Swires and Holts. The two houses invested in each other, and Holts' business in China was practically entirely in the hands of its agent. In 1879 it was John Swire who founded the first China shipping conference to stabilize the trade and protect Holts' interests.[6] Letters from John Samuel Swire to Alfred and Philip Holt, if read blind, would leave one hard put as to who was the superior.[7] Richard Holt, who would succeed to running the company, was educated at Oxford, but also spent a long training stint with Swires and Mansfields in the 1890s before returning to Liverpool and partnership in the firm. Such apprenticeship exchanges, as we shall see, would continue into the twentieth century.[8] Neither Swires nor the British, however, were unique in developing such long-term "affairs." Internatio's bonds to the Rotterdamsche Lloyd were roughly equivalent. Throughout the first decades of the century Bernard Ruys (B. E. Ruys, Sr.) fired off opinions and complaints to his agents in the East. They, with some measure of politeness, were no less inclined to hold forth on fleet and trade policy. Ruys, meanwhile, found it perfectly natural to entrust Internatio's top man in Batavia with the education of his son in the Indies for a year.[9]

First encounters with this culture thus immediately reveal a world of split personalities, and it is difficult to imagine how it could have been otherwise for a business community so transnational and yet so home affiliated. Cosmopolitanism, we have seen, was inscribed into the way figures and firms did business. When Böger and Loepthien voyaged to

[6] Marriner and Hyde, *Senior*, 116–117.
[7] SOAS/JSSXI 1/1–2, 4/Box 1173.
[8] Falkus, *Blue*, 17.
[9] Correspondence between Ruys and A. Tigle Wybrandi in GAR/Lloyd 2/1550/ 1910–1918.

America for HAPAG in 1928, they met with their American representatives, toured American ports, visited the offices of American exporting firms, called on the offices of American railroad and shipping companies, and were feted by American chambers of commerce. HAPAG, in fact, had restored its transatlantic business after the First World War through an alliance with American shipping interests. In the maritime world, one did business abroad, often in person as much as on paper. For many shipping men, from Böger to St. Johnston, life memories were like beads, strung out along a necklace of harbors.

Their cosmopolitanism found supreme expression in the shipping conference system. All the majors subscribed to it. The first conference, established in 1875, covered the homeward trade from Calcutta, and by 1914 there were more than 300 conferences,[10] often divided between inward and outward services. It was not unusual for individual companies to participate in half a dozen conferences or more. The system originated as a creation of liner economics, where the central fact of life was that ships sailed on schedule, full or not. Fixed costs in vessels, crew, shore staffs, and port facilities could not survive excessive tonnage ("over tonnage" in shipping parlance) or its spilling over into mutually destructive rate wars. To tame the ruinous side to competition, the industry's answer, like railroads, was to apportion traffic and sustain rates through pools and conferences.

Yet culture as much as economics drove conferences. Networks built cosmopolitan partnership into the quotidian habit of doing business on an international scale. Their currency, trust, lessened the cost of transacting business across borders and oceans, and fostered a shipping culture in which collaboration was highly regarded, much sought after, and daily practiced. In this regard, conferences were networks writ large, or, as Gordon Boyce has argued, the networks that pervaded maritime business "conditioned" the cosmopolitan, cooperative spirit of conferences. It would be difficult to deny, moreover, that once set in motion, the effects could just as often run in the opposite direction.[11]

Consequently conferences, with their multinational membership, international confabs, globalized perspectives, and insider tone of communication epitomized the transnational ethos of liner shipping. They were open institutions. The welcoming of former enemy firms back into the fold following world wars signaled a return to normal (read: cosmopolitan)

[10] Broeze, "Rederij," 187.
[11] Boyce, *Information*, 162–163, 173.

times in the industry. Although initiated by Europeans, conferences incorporated any serious challenger from other sea-trading nations. Within the system there remained plenty of competition. Members periodically revised allocations based on performance and traffic lifted. Nearly all, at some point, cheated. Brocklebanks' agent in Antwerp compiled a forty-two page dossier of drawbacks or falsified bills of lading designed to bypass conference charges on specific shipments in the Antwerp-India trade alone.[12] All jockeyed for the best position, and there was always a bit of the black widow spider mentality in these companies.[13] To counter the ever-present danger of unfriendly incursions by outsiders, conferences granted deferred rebates to shippers who kept the faith or formed "fighting committees"[14] to attack with rate wars. But mostly their preference was to co-opt a particularly nettlesome challenger into the conference, which was also often exactly what the challenger was after.[15] By and large, shipping people were comfortable with the idea that they were all in the same boat together. Their goal was to order and regularize trades, and they treated the oceans as shared dominions.

Paradoxically, however, these showpieces of transnational attachment were no less instruments of national power politics. The state has often been a powerful globalizing agent,[16] and this current too ran deeply through maritime culture. To a certain extent, the British created and ran the conference system to prolong their hegemony in liner shipping. In certain conferences, chairmen were always drawn from British firms. John Swire initiated the Far Eastern Freight Conference and following him, every chair until 1963 was a P & O man, to be succeeded for the next three terms by people from Holts. The conferences serving Australia, New Zealand, and South Africa always had a British chair. British empire ties gave British firms precedence: "The British were going to be there and it would be played according to British rules." In the Dutch empire the Dutch Mails occupied a similar position in Java-based conferences; here too it was customary for one firm (SMN) to monopolize the chair.[17]

---

[12] MMM/B/BROC/5/1/15/42 page report (n.d.) running from 27 February 1927 through 2 March 1930.

[13] For example, Broeze, "Rivalry," 8.

[14] NMM/P & O/4/62/Agents' Reports/1947 Statistics.

[15] On this strategy, but also how it could misfire: CMB/C7/17/1 February 1963.

[16] Bayly, *Birth*, 237–238, 247; Osterhammel and Petersson, *Globalization*, 70.

[17] Falkus, *Blue*, 128; Bott (interview, quoted); Alan G. Jamieson, "An Inevitable Decline? Britain's Shipping and Shipbuilding Industries since 1930," in David J. Starkey and Alan G. Jamieson, eds., *Exploiting the Sea: Aspects of Britain's Maritime Economy since*

There was nothing unassailably innate about maritime cosmopolitanism. Repeatedly, at quotidian levels, Europeans doing business abroad sought out their own for first connections.

Dutch networks in the East provide as good an example as any of the national cliques into which global business could disaggregate. The Dutch Mails trunk lines, SMN (Amsterdam) and the Rotterdamsche Lloyd, participated in international conventions and consortia, but from their earliest years they settled into the preferred habit of collaborative ventures. Bernard Ewoud Ruys (great-grandson of Willem, Lloyd's founder) noted of his time as a Lloyd director that "I had contact on a nearly daily basis with Amsterdam regarding freight and sailings." The SMN's Daniel Delprat remarked that "we had an arrangement with the Lloyd not to expand our packet lines without informing the other and to undertake things jointly as much as possible." Every Monday before the Second World War representatives of the two companies met in one of their boardrooms, the first three weeks of the month in Amsterdam and the last week on the Veerhaven in Rotterdam.[18]

Samenwerking – literally, "working together" – was built into Dutch shipping as it fanned out across the Indian and Pacific Oceans. The Mails created the KPM, held shares in the company, and possessed seats on its board. These three then created the Java-Bengal Line and were key in setting up the JCJL between Java, China, and Japan. All three were shareholders, and for nearly half a century B. E. Ruys (of Lloyd) sat on the board. Laurens Pieter Dignus op ten Noort was more representative still of this inbred world. After a naval career he joined the SMN, and then, with the formation of the KPM, transferred over to serve as its first general agent. His celebrated business trip around the islands of the archipelago laid the basis for the company's start-up traffic and service lines.[19] Later he returned to the SMN and led the company after the death in 1904 of Jan Boissevain, the SMN's dominant figure in the first quarter century of its history. In 1912 he left the directorship but continued to serve as a board member and then as chairman of the SMN board. All the time he remained on the managerial board of the KPM and held the chair of that shipping line from 1909 until his death in 1924. He was also

[18] *1870* (Exeter, U.K.: University of Exeter Press, 1998), 88; Sturmey, *British*, 354; Delprat, *Reeder*, 300–301; Brugmans, *Tachtig*, 54–55.

Leeman, *Barkschip*, 99–100, 120; Bram Oosterwijk, *Op één koers* (Rotterdam: Koninklijke Nedlloyd Groep N.V., 1988), 47 (quoted), 68–69 (quoted).

[19] See Chapter 2.

instrumental in the creation of the JCJL and chaired its board from 1902 till 1924. As late as 1920, at the age of seventy-two, he journeyed on a business trip east. The night before he died he was still doing paperwork for the JCJL.[20]

The significant sum of all of these ventures, including more collaborative lines opened during and after the First World War, was the self-contained world they created within the larger confines of international maritime culture. Intuitively, Dutch shipping and trading men relied on each other for their first line of connection. The Amsterdam companies – SMN, KPM, and JCJL – kept offices in the Scheepvaarthuis at the intersection of Prins Hendrik Kade and Kromme Waal. Delprat, in his memoirs, recalled how this made for close cooperation. In another set of recollections he remembered in the 1930s watching out his office window as "the *heren* Ruys, old Bernard and old Willem [of the Lloyd], came walking down from the train station. After meeting to discuss all the affairs that concerned both our companies, Bernard climbed a floor higher to the KPM, where he also served as a board member."[21] In the same way, Dutch shipping and trading companies turned to each other as their business partner or source of information in the East.[22] None of this was in any way exceptional. German shipping lines, even if clear of imperial attachments, apportioned their agency representations to German expatriate firms, almost as if Hanseatic stepping stones pointed the way across the seas. Just as maritime business was both home and globally centered, it offered no clear divide between national and global histories. Cosmopolitan to the core, its culture nonetheless subdivided into separate inner sanctums. Constantly one navigated between the two, but then navigation, for most of these people, was part of the job description.

Comportment so commodiously balanced, shaded into a third dichotomy. Cooperative to a fault, these men and their companies pulled out the competitive stops when circumstances dictated. The Lloyd could forgive the SMN a half million guilder debt at one point in their relationship,[23] so mutually supportive were the two, but none of this precluded keen rivalry for passengers and freight. Not for nothing did

[20] I. J. Brugmans, *Van Chinavaart tot oceaanvaart. De Java-China-Japan Lijn, Koninklijke Java-China-Paketvaart Lijnen, 1902–1952* (KJCPL: 1952), 33–54, 129; idem, *Tachtig*, 28–29; De Boer and Westermann, *Eeuw*, Bijlage 1.

[21] Delprat, *Reeder*, 16; Oosterwijk, *Op*, 69.

[22] GAR/Stout Papers/79/16 April 1928, in addition to Internatio managing Lloyd affairs and the Hoppenstedt business travels.

[23] Oosterwijk, *Op*, 72.

the Dutch shipping umbrella VNS locate its headquarters in the Hague, roughly halfway between Amsterdam and Rotterdam.[24] In a still more famous rivalry, Bremen's NDL and Hamburg's HAPAG moved in point-counterpoint around the world. "Lloyd was hunted everywhere," was one verdict on Albert Ballin's expansionist strategy before the First World War,[25] yet through all the years until the Second World War the two oscillated between razor-edged wariness and pursuit of working arrangements.[26] Even a blue blood like P & O was perfectly content to bludgeon its way into a call at Genoa, despite opposition from "the so-called 'Conference.'"[27]

Richard Adams, who came up the BI side of the company, betrayed this tension when, on being asked to identify his principal competition in Singapore, he began to say Blue Funnel, but then thought for a second and phrased it this way: "It's difficult, when you are running in a conference with other people, OK they are opposition, but they are not enemies ... one treats them as partners rather more than as competition."[28] It was, indeed, a very clubbable world where all took for granted a common membership provided one played by the rules. HAPAG had no hesitation writing Bremen's Hansa Line for details about water depths in Calcutta's harbor (HAPAG had no agent in Calcutta; Hansa did), and it would have been very bad form for Hansa not to have complied.[29] Maritime business, as in conferences, was conducted within one big network. Buss' Lutz Ehrhardt caught the interconnect with club culture. You buy a man a drink, and perhaps he will tell you something important in exchange. You give information to a contact one day, and that contact reciprocates another day. "This is how it works. And if you have a problem and want to learn something you know who to ask and who you can trust. And there's a sort of network which works."[30]

The similitude began with close-quarters sociability, the thick agglomeration of merchant houses, business offices, exchanges, chambers of

[24] GAR/Lloyd 2/S2014/Volkenhoven and Baart de la Faille, 27 June 1922; ibid., S2023/ van Vugt en Giel, 26 January 1938; ibid., S2032/den Dulk and Pot, 2 February 1959, pp. 11–13; GAR/Lloyd 1/1550/12 January 1918; NA/KPM/366/12 September 1928, 9 January 1929. Van Driel notes a cooling of relations after 1945: *Samenwerking*, 129.

[25] Broeze, "Rivalry," 16.

[26] Wiborg and Wiborg, *Unser*, 128–131, 195, 231, 257, 322, 327, 350; Seiler, *Century*, 49–50, 62; HAPAG/1263, 443, 444.

[27] NMM/P & O/4/62/1947/Freight Department.

[28] Adams (interview).

[29] HAPAG/2805/14 February 1933.

[30] Ehrhardt (interview).

commerce, restaurants, cafés, pubs, hotels, and clubs themselves in downtown business sectors that were often a short walk from the harbor. Those
who worked in port cities around the world remarked on the seamless
flow between places of business and places of leisure. Business moved in
and out of offices and exchanges; exchanges and bars; clubs, restaurants,
and office buildings. In Batavia, frequent contact between men who knew
each other was unavoidable. "The business district was not extensive, we
knew each other well and it was the tradition to drop in on each other
informally." At lunchtime, directors and partners in shipping and trading
houses congregated at the same lunch club on one of the side streets off
the Kali Besar.[31] In Antwerp, traders, brokers, dealers, agents, forwarders,
shippers, *naties*, and stevedores put in a daily appearance at the Bourse to
meet and talk business, often spilling over to the cafés nearby.[32] The many
restaurants and pubs in the business heart of Rotterdam were "the meeting
centers for the fraternity."[33] Antwerp's Meir, Liverpool's India Buildings,
and Hamburg's Chilehaus were famous place-names, but they were also
synonymous with the concentration of great shipping and mercantile
houses in the heart of their cities. Without necessary intent or design, maritime culture was physically structured for viscous encounters.[34]

Central to this milieu was the club, the indispensable institution for
mixing and establishing a local presence, but also the cultural tone setter.
Perhaps the gentlemanly culture of British merchant capital spilled over
into the maritime world at large, given Britain's world predominance in
shipping and trade. Certainly that culture's values, predicated on a world
of insiders – men of common background, men who were good mixers
and capable of getting along, men of trust and abiders of rules – were
the values by which maritime business operated. The Burmese world in
which Harold Braund moved, for example, was not simply the encrus-
tation of empire but defined an element woven into how all these men
transacted their affairs.

The binders – homogeneity, trust, codes – were the same. In the next
section we will see how alike in training, expertise, or professional experience connected to the sea most of these maritime figures turned out
to be. Trust, which was intrinsic to club life, reached into every corner
of maritime business, including the identities businessmen clung to. In

---

[31] Delprat, *Reeder*, 27–28.
[32] Durot (interview).
[33] J. J. Hordijk, Vinke & Co., B.V., interview with author, Rotterdam, 16 July 1997.
[34] Cocktail parties also doubled the progression of business trips. For instance, GAR/HAL/
Viamar/MMPH 4/Reis naar Amerika, 29 August–27 October 1936.

a milieu where business began at exchanges and ended in pubs, or was conducted over the phone, and thus where little or nothing was written down, the system was grounded in taking a man's word for his bond.[35] Alston Hill Garside probably summed it up best when he created a fictional model of a successful cotton shipper firm:

The real assets of Smith, Brown & Co. are not to be found in their capital funds or other tangibles, but in their knowledge of cotton and the cotton trade and of how to merchandise cotton economically, and in the good will and confidence which spinners feel toward them because of satisfactory dealings with them over a long period of years. Smith, Brown & Co., like all other shippers, often enter into agreements for the purchase or sale of cotton to a value of scores of thousands of dollars simply by word of mouth, to be confirmed later by written contracts, and those from whom they buy and those to whom they sell know that their word is as good as their bond. These intangibles are the most essential assets of Smith, Brown & Co.[36]

Trust, therefore, began with one's word, but it implied a wider internalization of club rules that, if mostly unwritten, spelled out the dos and don'ts of acceptable business conduct and in which this maritime world operated. They were many. Agents did not work for competitors. Poaching – of territories or personnel – was very bad form. Competition was acceptable, but aggressive, sharklike competition was trouble for all. Established companies had a particularly heightened sense of rights or *droits acquis*. One basic rule was that companies that had operated a reliable service for a substantial period of time had built up a privileged claim to that trade. The P & O, which was not above bludgeoning its way into someone else's trade, was a great defender of rights. It could get away with that contradiction because its character, over time, as a senior club member with a record for constructive leadership had been well established. When the Ben Line, not a new firm, but a minor operator before 1945, increased its market share in the East Asian trades by berthing newer and faster ships, both P & O and Holts (through its Glen Line) took umbrage. The language in which the terms of the conflict were framed was revealing. For Glen's chair, Herbert McDavid, Ben Line were upstarts, former "operators of a semi-tramp service," with all the pejorative implications that came with a liner man's use of that phrase. Their berthing of extra services was "the last straw."[37] Back when Ben first

---

[35] Stork and Piehler (interview).
[36] Garside, *Cotton*, 195.
[37] MMM/OA/4A/1696/Box 1/East Coast Rationalization, 19 March 1963, 24 January 1961.

began to make its move, a Holts person acknowledged that "one must not grudge them the fruits of their undoubted enterprise," but added, "I do not think that a Conference dominated by the Ben Line will be a good one.... I do not think they have any grasp of the proper balance to be maintained between regular and reliable services on the one hand and a willingness to go anywhere on the other."[38] P & O's Andrew Crichton all but confided to McDavid that Ben was not one of them, and therefore not to be trusted.[39] Trying to understand the behavior of Ben's Douglas Thomson, and his rejection of their overtures for all three to reduce services and "rationalize" the berth, both P & O and Glen men could only attribute it to the wounded pride and gaucheries of a man outside their circle:

As regards Douglas, it was suggested that he may be suffering from "amour propre" in that he feels he has not been seriously considered as a responsible shipowner by the Seniors in London. This was thought to be possible because of his infrequent appearances at Chamber of Shipping meetings, which, when he does attend, he on occasion makes comments that can only be considered irrelevant or unhelpful, and sometimes rather childish.[40]

In club terms this was not, as Thomson saw it, a matter of classical economics, but a classic divide between insiders and outsiders. The real premise of this gentlemanly world was less compliance than common understandings and fitting in.

Reinforcement came from a business culture that remained dedicated to face-to-face relations and the personal touch. So ingrained was networking as a method of doing business that little passed outside the realm of personal connections. Managers traveled long distances on business trips to meet their agents and talk to clients. They took a personal hand in organizing visits by their counterparts from other lines, arranging hotels, teas at their clubs, tours of the docks, and dinner out. Even in up-country tea gardens on the far side of the world, the Joint Steamers agent was "on excellent terms with the 'Nazira' planters, and the personal factor counts for a good deal in retaining the Assam Company's traffic."[41]

At bottom, this was a salesman's culture. Shipping and trading people prided themselves on their operational skills, but they were also charmers, pleasers, persuaders, or comprehensive personality machines, with a talent

---

[38] Ibid., Box 2/24 August 1950.
[39] Ibid., Box 1/24 January 1961.
[40] Ibid., Box 1/22 March 1963.
[41] Guildhall/Rivers Steam Navigation Company/MS 27,953/vol. 1, 1938.

for making others feel important and comfortable in their presence. If their houses were venerable firms, city institutions, their business was still to sell a service and, most often, a long-term relationship. J. J. Hordijk, a Rotterdam ship agent, said that a good salesman can sell anything, but he also took for granted the world of business sociability, the codes of trust, the fitting in, and the dense personal interchanges that made it possible for deals to go down. Hordijk described his typical day as "look[ing] after all the sales and marketing aspects of the group ... maintaining contacts with our main principals." Explaining how he won the agency for the Brazilian shipping line Transroll, he talked about the presentation he put together, his market knowledge, but mostly how through the years he and his firm had preserved contact with the line. To close the deal, he had flown to Rio to make his pitch face-to-face. Moreover, as he put it, once Transroll began its search for an agent he had to move quickly because "shipping is a fairly small circle ... [where] people have friends and the friend has a friend and then before you know it half the market knows it."[42]

The letter-writing culture that lasted through at least the first half of the century, and with which this chapter began, must also be seen as simply the continuation of face-to-face communication across the abyss of space. Letters were conversations on paper.[43] They commingled personal news, gossip, and flourishes of literacy with information, orders, advice, and requests, and the one was never just a diversion from the other. Letter writing stressed intimacy, but also adherence to form. In this way it resembled the style and structure of personal calls. Its language was the shared language of common experience, the repertoire of those who fit in. Like any other encounter, it was a medium of exchange and for getting things done. The long letter was thus of a piece with the long lunches and business talks that carried over to restaurants and bars. Both were about the ability to connect, and the familiarity that came with working with each other for a long time or inhabiting a common milieu. Both thrived in the gregarious world of shipping and trading. Both consequently captured its cooperative style and, in so doing, reaffirmed it. Both also depended on it. Cooperation created comfort zones; it also did wonders for transacting business.

[42] Hordijk (interview). Walter Friedman, *Birth of a Salesman: The Transformation of Selling in America* (Cambridge, MA: Harvard University Press, 2004), 56, 61, 66, 256 on salesmanship and face-to-face relations.
[43] Martha Hanna has called these "conversations from afar." Martha Hanna, "A Republic of Letters: The Epistolary Tradition in France during World War I," *American Historical Review* 108 (December 2003): 1339.

But these were still profit-driven organizations, and the original ambitions that had sent them out into the world to conquer markets and reap rewards were primordial traits outed with each successive generation. One need only look to the great rivalries of maritime communities – Hamburg versus Bremen, or Rotterdam versus Antwerp – to recall how pugnacious this culture could be. The interesting thing, however, at least up until the final third of the century, was how readily one sought to confine the roughhousing within the codes, even if these were honored largely in the breach.

The peculiar to-and-fro and catlike mentality, in which long bouts of cozying-up drowsiness were interspersed with fierce fights over territory, can be seen in a decision of Swires' China Navigation Company to invade the East Indies-East Asia trade immediately following the Second World War, and the Dutch JCJL's dilemma over how they should respond. This was a standard fighting situation in which, nonetheless, all the civilized conventions came into play. What stands out in this episode was thus the atavistic return of combative reflexes, and yet the discomfort of straying too far from the club rules. Competitiveness there was aplenty, but it was not always the desired affect.

The motivations of China Navigation to attack were unambiguous. British fortunes, in retreat all along the China coast, mandated a search for new markets. Where better to seek them than in Southeast Asian waters, where they possessed experience, potential bases, and a vulnerable Dutch opponent in the aftermath of Japanese occupation? The decision to move was made at a meeting at Mansfields' Singapore office in May 1946, attended by people from Mansfields, Swires, and MacLaine Watson – Holts' agents on Java. In effect, Holts' eastern network was being mobilized to plan China Navigation's strategy. There could not have been any illusions about what they were about to do nor that the established line would greet this move as "an unfriendly act." Growing concerns over Dutch encroachment into British territories in the last years before the Japanese invasion had produced from China Navigation precisely the sense of violation that they were about to inflict on the Dutch. Then the British position had been that "it is out of the question to admit any such argument as lack of cargo in any outsider's own trades as a reason for letting them into ours.... Besides, these Dutchmen, much as we like them personally, are always trying to creep forward and the only treatment is to stop them firmly on every occasion." Enjoying "the whip hand," the inclination had been "to treat our Dutch friends rough when it suits us," and "there is no object in arguing with the JCJL. The only thing the

Dutchman understands is being hit on the head, so, if and when you get the chance, do so and keep him in his place." Codes are never so useful as when one occupies the high ground. Short memories help as well.[44]

Complicating matters further was the fact that the JCJL and China Navigation had a long history of working together, despite the periodic battles over territory. One of the JCJL's biggest trades was sugar export, and Swires' Taikoo Sugar Refinery had been a major shipper. In view of this business, the JCJL had assigned ships in need of repair to Swires' Taikoo Dockyard and had also given representations in Amoy and Swatow to Swires, even though elsewhere it preferred to contract with Dutch agents. Only when Swires was unable to carry out its agency functions as a result of Chinese boycotts in the 1920s did JCJL replace them with its own agents.[45]

Consequently, when Swires made its move, it approached the JCJL as an old friend, couching its aggression in terms acceptable to old-boy shipping circles. C. N. Howard, partner at MacLaine Watson, was dispatched to inform the JCJL personally, and his discomfort during his visit to JCJL offices could not have been more palpable. Howard was "exceedingly friendly," "made many excuses for having to bring such unpleasant news," and tried to rationalize the decision on the grounds that "Messrs. MacLaine Watson & Co. were formerly agents for Japanese lines [read: *pre-existing rights*] and that the entrance of the China Navigation Co. Ltd. into the trade was not a threat at Java-China-Japan Line but was merely taking the place of Japanese lines which were no longer in a position to participate nor would be likely to do so in the future." Howard made it clear that the decision was irrevocable, but he also cobbled together the argument that together the two companies "would fulfill shippers' requirements and thereby be able to keep out outside competition [read: *look, we are really doing you a favor*]." Leaning over backward to defuse the situation, he emphasized that China Navigation "should very much desire to work closely with the JCJL in the future." Even the JCJL had to acknowledge that the pressures on China Navigation had made its actions "understandable," that Swires' conduct could not be more "diplomatic," that they had placed a stress on "our old and friendly relationships and expressed the wish that these would continue," and that any decision about how to respond must take into consideration that Swires was "an

[44] SOAS/JSSIII 1/18/Box 77/2 September 1938; SOAS/JSSIII 1/20/Box 80/15 August, 31 October 1941.
[45] Brugmans, *Chinavaart*, 58, 80, 135.

old and friendly relation of ours." A couple breaking up amicably over lunch would have been hard pressed to do better.[46]

Although the JCJL pondered the benefits of compromise – China Navigation, they remarked, was unlike any other competitor they had trounced in the past, and its China coast experience was "second to none" – ultimately they donned their battle armor. As much as anything else the clinching argument was the fear that to let one company in without a fight would be to invite in all the others. In the end, the JCJL behaved with the same aggressiveness that would have characterized any of its peers in the same situation. As the head man in Batavia summed it up in a letter, "We can argue all we wish over old rights, but in practice, old rights are only valuable if we can defend them." Politely, and deploying the same language of the codes, the JCJL informed Swires that "the pre-war interest of the Japanese flag in the China/NEI trade was only of nominal importance so that there can be no reason for a third party to take the place of the Japanese [read: *going by our conventions, you have no rights*]." As for East Indies–Japan traffic, the JCJL was "in a position to handle this … without any outside assistance." Then the company, after some vacillation, came out swinging. By November 1946, there had been a "Council of War." Plans were made to launch a counterstrike against China Navigation territories. In Hong Kong JCJL's Shanghai man, Carriere, accused China Navigation of "poaching," and told Swires that "we should get out and stay out of the NEI. If we do not, they should fight us tooth and nail there, in our own sphere, and elsewhere, whatever this last may mean." Probably most revealing of the culture that produced these remarks is that they were exchanged over informal social gatherings ("Socially we have seen … a good deal of Carriere"), and that Swires' response to this tough talk was that "Carriere, as you well know, is about the most pugnacious of all of them and can bluff better than most, but we can still say of him that he does not sulk. In some ways it is a pity that, as he has just told us, he is retiring in a year's time." War was one thing, the loss of good club men another. In any event, both sides, as they acknowledged, were simply gathering bargaining chips for the inevitable accommodation. Two years later, there was stiff competition between the two lines. However, in a letter from Batavia to Swires in Hong Kong, MacLaine Watson's H. A. Vinke noted that "as agents of the Blue Funnel Line I am of course in regular, and by the way in very friendly contact with the KPM [which had merged its long-distance lines with the

[46] NA/KJCJL/409/3 June 1946; SOAS/JSSIII 1/21/Box 408/31 May 1946.

JCJL after the war] and I often say to Hens: 'When are you going to give me 50% of your through cargo, making it plain to him that if I only could fill my ships to Hong Kong and Japan I would not bother him so much by carrying sugar to Singapore.... Next week I am to lunch with Iken, a new KPM Director." On the surface of things, relations were frosty, but day-to-day, there was plenty of the familiar give-and-take. As for the JCJL directly, Vinke also did his best to wear down his counterpart, A. H. Veltman, and crack into the passenger trade, which for China Navigation thus far had "been a flop." "Mind you," Vinke wrote to Hong Kong, "all these conversations are unofficial and in a friendly tone." Maritime business always had plenty of fight in it, but its heart was in clubland.[47]

It is not difficult to see how appropriate this culture was to the management of world maritime flows through the first two-thirds of the twentieth century. The dualism of global and local, built into sectors and firms, found legitimization and a means of expression in a culture that blithely juggled cosmopolitan and national values, or the urge to cooperate and the urge to compete. This was a cultural universe in which the definition of one's own – the international milieu of shipping and trading, we Brits or we Dutch, port-centered circles – was as malleable as circumstances dictated. In this sense the cultural juxtaposition of territories and enclaves within a broader construct of cosmopolitanism, fit a globalism that remained fragmented, imperial, and Eurocentric. The Dutch, Germans, French, British, and all the others who banded together but formed easy, working relationships across their national communities reflected a tightly inter-connected global order, yet one still composed of powerful nation-states with far-flung empires and a perception of acquired rights and territo-ries to defend. Their clubbiness was the transnationalism of a maritime community in which Europeans of a common formation predominated; their rules the cozy arrangements of companies that had parceled out routes and spheres over one or two oceans. This was very much too a net-work culture, where connectedness depended on coordination. All sides of the dichotomies spoke to these needs. Hierarchies assured cohesion and command centers. Intimacy assured information flows and suited an assemblage of local powers. Clubbiness was the oxygen of networks. Competition soldered them and defined their purpose. Cosmopolitanism fostered network building across peoples and oceans. Nationalism gave

[47] NA/KJCJL/409/3 June 1946; ibid., 410/10 June, 6 November 1947; SOAS/JSSIII 1/21/ Box 408/3 June, 8 November 1946; SOAS/JSSIII 1/22/Box 511/19 April 1948.

them stiffer bindings. Indeed in a maritime system that brought together men and companies of multiple worlds and identities, it was not unnatural that there should emerge a culture consisting of varying elements and yet resolutions between them. The dichotomies, or their balance, however, were also time bound; and although the transition to national mergers and international consortia in the age of containerization would owe a great deal to a long-practiced spirit of cooperation, the arrival of new men, new leaders, new methods, and a new globalism would explode this culture along with most everything else in the maritime world.

LIVES AND EXPERIENCE

It is all well and good to write about values, but culture was also ingrained into lives and experience. The best introduction to comprehending these men is to let their biographies speak for themselves. No two lives were ever the same of course, but the repetitiveness factor is nonetheless striking and explains the material foundations – backgrounds, training, expertise – of cultural agreement. Cooperation, cosmopolitanism, and clubbiness came easily enough among men who were so alike in professional ways.

Ary Lels, one of the two guiding figures at the Holland Amerika Line in the late 1960s and 1970s, descended from a family of shipping men, and throughout his life he capitalized on connections to Rotterdam shipping circles. But he also learned the business from the bottom up. He worked in a shipping department in Indonesia right after the Second World War and then in the copra trade on the outer islands of Celebes. Returning to Holland after three years, he joined Smits, the big tug and salvage company that his great-grandfather had helped found. In 1956 Smits sent him out to Suez to help clear the canal. There he picked up ideas about offshore oil platforms as the way of the future, and he convinced his bosses at Smits to send him to Texas, Louisiana, and Venezuela to build contacts and learn what he could about offshore towing. Later, in 1968, he moved on to run the freight division at Holland Amerika, at the invitation of its managing director, Nicholas Van den Vorm, a close friend Lels had known since childhood.[48] Such a personal history differed little from the preceding generation's. John Hobhouse, a senior partner at Holts until he retired in 1957, was the son of Mary Heyworth Potter, sister of Beatrice, but also of Lawrencina Potter, who married into the Holt shipping family

---

[48] Lels (interview).

and whose sons were the second-generation leaders of the firm. Educated at Eton and Oxford, Hobhouse joined Blue Funnel in 1912. He was among those fast-tracked into managerial ranks, but only after he served an eighteen-month stint with Mansfields in Singapore, which prepared him to be the firm's expert in Southeast Asian matters for the rest of his career. Across the channel his counterpart was Bernard E. Ruys, Jr., who was born in 1900 in a house on Rotterdam's Westerkade, by the Maas, and was the great-grandson of the founder of the Rotterdamsche Lloyd. As a boy he was taken to see ships in the harbor, or on visits to shipyards by his father, B. E. Ruys, himself a senior manager of the Lloyd. Ruys, Jr. would also become a director at the Lloyd, a position he would hold for decades, but only after an initial training year in Lloyd's agency in Hamburg; then three more years overseas where he booked freight in Batavia and got to know clients, the harbor, and key commodities such as tea and tobacco that shipped on company vessels; and time in Sydney to learn the wool trade. In 1925 he was recalled to the Rotterdam home office, but even then he did "anything and everything, in all the departments" for another four years, before being named director in 1929.[49]

Neither Richard Adams of P & O group, Job (Jacob Paul) Kruseman of the Koninklijke West-Indische Maildienst (KWIM) out of Amsterdam, or Eric Shawyer of Gibson had quite the same pedigree, but that was about all that differed in their life histories. Adams was the son of a barrister, and he was educated at Winchester and then read history at Oxford until he left for the Western Desert in the Second World War. Looking at war's end for something that did not require a completed degree and assuming that shipping "looked a slightly more gentlemanly occupation," he managed an interview with a P & O director, who passed him on to Mackinnon Mackenzie. Thus began a long career that culminated with Adams occupying the top position as P & O's chief executive, or managing director – about as high as one could climb in British shipping ranks. Along the way he made all the familiar stops. He was sent to India to work in Mackinnon's ship agency division for British India, where he rose to run BI's Far East services out of Calcutta. From there he was given charge of BI operations in Hong Kong, where he worked twelve-hour days, "An extraordinary life really because you visited your ships and probably you would be down there at 7:00 in the morning to see ships." After three years in Hong Kong, four more back in India, and then three more in Singapore, he returned to London in 1966 as a

---

[49] MMM/OA 4A/671; Falkus, *Blue*, 144, 282–283; Oosterwijk, *Op*, 46–49.

director, familiar with nearly every facet of the company's cargo business in the East.[50] Kruseman's father was a high-ranking Amsterdam magistrate, but he preferred a shipping career. Joining the KWIM right after the First World War, he learned the ropes of the shipping business in the company's agency in Paramaribo from the docks up, handling coffee, sugar, cocoa, and tropical wood cargoes. After more postings in Port au Prince and Curaçao, he returned to Amsterdam to take charge of the company's West Indies general affairs. Eventually he would rise to the position of managing director, and would spend nearly half a century in the shipping profession.[51] Shawyer, who became chairman and chief executive of the shipbroking firm E. A. Gibson and chairman of the Baltic Exchange, began work as an office boy. His sole old-boy network into the firm was an alumnus of the local central school he attended where he learned commercial affairs; the alumnus was secretary of Gibsons. Like Andrew Carnegie a century earlier, he began by delivering letters in the City which he learned intimately. His introduction to shipbroking was on-the-job training. "You learned from the man you were with. You were his dogsbody. You ran, fetched, and carried, answered the phone, and gradually learned the job on the floor so to speak." When he became a full-fledged shipbroker he benefited from Gibson's connections in the oil tanker chartering business and had the good fortune to hold the Shell account, the "big account," which meant his name began to circulate through chartering circles. He had fabulous success when Suez closed twice, but he also built his rise on his ability to network. He got to know Onassis and Niarchos on a first-name basis, and when Shell or other companies desperately needed ships, "I could get them tonnage by the old boy networks."[52]

Biographies like these are nearly inexhaustible: men who learned their trades from the ground up, developed an expertise from hands-on practice, seesawed between home and overseas, were locally and transnationally connected, and who spent their entire professional lives in shipping or trading. The one inconstant was family background, although even here there was not much variance. A very large number of shipping men came from families with maritime traditions. Trading houses such as Vorwerks, Denis Frères, Swires, Buschmanns, or Illies passed through generations of the same families. In C. Melchers & Co., there were multiple Melchers

---

[50] Adams (interview).
[51] Oosterwijk, *Op*, 166–169. In 1927 KWIM was taken over by Amsterdam's KNSM.
[52] Shawyer (interview).

over the years, but also an Adalbert Korff, Jr. and an Eduard Michaelson, Jr., each sons of earlier partners.[53] The older generation of ship agents, still active toward the end of the twentieth century, frequently descended from shipping or ship agent families. Diedrich Döhle's father had been a shipbroker. Maurice Velge, of Antwerp's Grisar & Velge, grew up in shipping circles. His father had been with the Lloyd Royal Belge, one of the predecessors to the CMB. Jean Randaxhe was a close personal friend and frequent visitor to the Velge home in Antwerp or at their house in France. When Maurice finished his university studies he joined Randaxhe-Bally, where he made partner after three or four days. Grisar, with whom he merged in the 1960s, was another Antwerp family ship agency. Edouard de Clebsattel, head of the French ship agency, stevedore, and forwarding company, G. Feron-E. de Clebsattel, was third generation. Philip Durot started in his father's ship agency as an office boy, although he later confided, "Actually I started in the shipping business when I was born."[54]

Those who had no maritime family connections often possessed the same middle-class credentials. Educational levels differed, with firms establishing their own homogeneous internal cultures. What bound them all was that they were, through and through, studied in their trades. Shawyer was a self-made man, but practically no one, especially the family scions, rose to the top without first learning the basics. Velge was truly an exception. De Clebsattel, who read law and then commercial studies at the Haute Etudes Commerciales in Paris, did an apprenticeship with foreign shipping and ship agency firms in Britain, Germany, Denmark, Spain, and the United States. Connections opened doors, but after that, class or family mattered no more than formation. There were various degrees of "insidership," but all began with knowing the business from the inside out.

Apprenticeship was therefore customary, regardless of background or level at which one entered. Some trained in-house, but there was also an older tradition, especially among trading, agency, and forwarding houses, to farm sons out to correspondent firms. Often the choice was to send them abroad, where they could learn ports and markets and make contacts. Carl Illies, Jr., son of the founder of the trading firm C. Illies & Co., was born in Yokohama, but was sent by his father back to Hamburg for schooling followed by an apprenticeship, before entering the family firm at the level of salaried employee. He then spent more than three

---

[53] *150 Jahre Melchers.*
[54] Velge (interview); De Clebsattel (interview); Durot (interview).

years in France, England, and the United States, after which he returned
to Yokohama in 1901. There he worked for another fourteen months,
before his appointment as partner in his father's house. Both his sons, Carl
Jürgen Illies and Herbert August Illies, did an apprenticeship in Hamburg.
The Ruys sons, beginning with the second generation, spent part of their
leertijd in Antwerp, London, and the East Indies. The practice of training-
up was nearly universal and was not limited to family members. Holts,
despite its preference for university graduates, seconded nearly all the
"crown princes" – recruits groomed to rise to the top – to Swires or
Mansfields so they could familiarize themselves with business in the East.
R. S. (Stewart) MacTier, a graduate of Eton and Cambridge and recruited
for Mansfields, where he would spend many years and eventually run the
house before returning to top management in Liverpool, was first trained
on the London docks to learn the homeward side of the trade. A Captain
Mackellar, to whom he was assigned, was instructed that he "should go
through every stage of discharging, tallying and delivering cargo, check-
ing claims, etc.... In short I want him acquainted with all your routine."
Even Frits de Koe, a twenty-six-year-old lawyer who joined the KPM in
1930 to work in their legal department in the Indies, was required to
learn the ropes of the shipping business. Initially he spent eight months
with Ruys & Co., the Ruys family's ship agency business, and another
half year in the KPM office in Amsterdam. Sailing to Batavia in 1931,
he was assigned for a year to the KPM's special trades in coal, salt, and
petrol, before at last moving over to legal affairs. The tradition lasted
well through the century. Klaus-Michael Kühne, born in 1937 and heir to
Germany's largest privately owned forwarding company, worked his way
through practically every department, and accompanied his father on a
series of business trips before he was granted the position of partner.[55]

Constant in the lives of all of these men was their immersion, from
the start, in the daily, transnational world of ports, ships, trading, and
brokering houses. Practically all of them spent the sum of their professional careers working as maritime businessmen. Lels banged around as
a copra purchaser, wire trader, and then towage and salvage specialist
before joining Holland Amerika, but rarely, if at all, did he operate outside
the worlds of shipping and overseas commerce. Adams built up years of
experience as a cargo man with Mackinnon Mackenzie and then British

[55] Molsen, *C. Illies*, 50, 80, 87; Leeman, *Barkschip*, 61; Falkus, *Blue*, 17, 59–60, 93,
277, 284; SOAS/JSSXI 1/6/Box 57/25 January (quoted), 21 May, 25 September 1928.
Oosterwijk *Op*, 119; *1890–1965: Kühne & Nagel*, 20.

India, and he had firsthand knowledge of the ports and business communities in Calcutta, Bombay, Hong Kong, and Singapore. Kruseman hopped around from Paramaribo, Port au Prince, Curaçao, and Amsterdam. Each man knew company operations but also shipping circles in their territories inside and out long before they reached the time of retirement. Overseas or cross-national contacts were bred into their personal experience. Lels was closely allied to Rotterdam circles, but he picked up ideas from people in Egypt, Texas, and Venezuela. Eric Shawyer stayed put in London, but his business clients were Greek tanker tycoons or anyone else on the planet interested in moving oil. Identities obviously varied – by company, family, specialty, or territory – but overriding all of these was the lifetime they spent steering ships, goods, and people around the globe.

Expertise for these businessmen meant more than a command of business techniques in general. What they held on to throughout their lives, and prized as part of their persona, was their mastery of all the ins and outs of running a maritime company. They were at home on docks or in the holds of ships. They knew commodities and specialized markets. They knew how to add up the figures in their heads, what rates were for such and such goods to such and such ports. They knew how to load ships. They knew how to broker the best deal, how to sell, or how to figure out markets based not on print runs of statistics, but on the day-to-day experience of working their trades. Later, maritime businesses would be run by people who had never loaded a ship or rarely, if ever, visited a port, but that was uncommon through at least the 1960s. Expertise was sewn into training and lifelong experience, and hence into professional identities. It too defined who was an insider.

Old hands were quite vocal on the role of expertise in building their careers. They defined it in terms that linked it to apprenticeships and their years in their trades, but also in ways that captured their own sense of self-worth, and pleasure in executing their jobs. Walter Stork stressed how essential it was for forwarders to know all realms of the business; not just how to get goods from point A to point B, but how ports and shipping companies worked. He was proud that he had learned the business the old-fashioned way, from the ground floor up. He had started as a messenger boy for Bachmann running papers to ships, and then was seated next to forwarders and told to observe, until he knew how to fill out forms. He was instructed in commodities, and had to handle them, get to "*know*" them, until he developed an expertise in fibers, steel, New Zealand apples – everything that Bachmann shipped. He learned all kinds of secret rates, which he stored in his memory, and he taught himself to convert British measurements into metric ones so well that he could do the conversions in his sleep. All his future successes, which he delighted in telling and related with gusto, he traced back to his supreme confidence in how to perform the job. Jan de Bie, in Antwerp, who also started as a messenger boy and had worked alongside an older forwarder, had been on waterfronts, and had been on ships, delighted in his sense of an edge, and his ability to take on the "impossible," because he knew the basics: "We had a knowledge of merchandise. We knew what we were talking about."[56]

This was a world that belonged to experts. There were tobacco dealers, tea brokers, coffee tasters, or hide buyers – all experts in grading and assessing the goods in which they traded. Wool buyers judged the fineness, softness, shortness, color, spinning property, prospective yields, and market value of the wool they purchased.[57] Pursers were expert in local market conditions and sources of supply.[58] Power, in fact, derived from expertise. D. K. Fieldhouse listed five skills that rendered United Africa Company men irreplaceable and assured them autonomy from home-office meddling by Unilever people: knowledge of African produce and trading; knowledge of European manufactures that would sell in Africa; knowledge of running river and coastal boats in African waters; knowledge in world produce markets dealing in African goods; and knowledge in running the company's oceangoing fleet.[59] Those who fell behind in expertise fell out of market share. In the 1960s Pakhuismeesteren surpassed Blaauwhoedenveem ("Blue Hats") in its dockside operations, not least because its director of dry cargo handling, Van Beuningen, personally observed the loading and unloading of ships in the evening, whereas the leading person at Blaauwhoedenveem, H. J. W. Brouwer, was a finance man interested in real estate deals and cared little about the day-to-day work of a terminal operator.[60]

Even then, after all the correspondence or the interviews, it is difficult to fathom just how much these men must have known, or the numbers of people they had met and filed away in black books, or the recesses of memory. Their long histories of growing up in the business, training with other firms, shuttling from one port assignment to another, traveling overseas on business trips, business lunches and dinners, club gatherings,

[56] Stork (interview); De Bie (interview).
[57] Du Plessis, *Marketing*, 69–71.
[58] NMM/P & O/4/71/Pursers' Department, 1957.
[59] Fieldhouse, *Merchant*, 4–5.
[60] Van Driel, *Four*, 144–146.

or congregating at the exchanges, meant a lifetime of contacts with men like themselves. Networking was part of that formative process, but it too was shaped, or at least made easier, by a milieu so globally similar in its professional histories. At some point in their careers, they probably knew, or had met, practically everyone who mattered in their end of the business. This too contributed to the ability to make things work, to create transoceanic circuits. It also explains a culture in which home inclinations surrendered so easily to cosmopolitanism, and where competitiveness shaded, like colored strips of paint samples, into the softer tones of a clubby world.

CULTURE IN ACTION

But how did it actually happen? Rarely was maritime culture so manifest as during the business trip. Conventions, dualities, and the ambient familiarity of a milieu where career experiences were largely the same, came to the fore in the networking agenda of these voyages. One such trip – P. (Philip) J. Clarke's voyage to Brazil in 1944 – illustrates how culture facilitated and circumscribed daily encounters, and, in turn, how businessmen reproduced it in the networks they built all over the world.

Clarke was a director of Gibbs & Co., the Chilean partnership of the British merchant and banking house, Antony Gibbs & Sons. For years Gibbs had been active as an agent, importer, exporter, and banker on the west coast of South America, especially Chile. In 1944 Gibbs planned expansion to Brazil, where a subsidiary house would coordinate trade within Southern Cone countries and conduct agency business from Britain. Clarke's trip during the summer of 1944 was to set these plans into motion. His brief was to visit prospective clients, discuss financial matters with bankers and legal matters with law firms, and to chat up local business executives on the ins and outs of doing business in Brazil. His primary objective, however, was to select a head manager for Brazil. Because Gibbs was entering into this project as a joint venture with two other British trading firms in South America – Williamson Balfour and Roberts, Meynell & Co. – joining Clarke were the former's John Irvine and the latter's John Phillimore, Henry Roberts, and Hartley E. Clisby.[61] All five were to play a role in what followed.

---

[61] Guildhall/Antony Gibbs & Sons, Ltd./MS 16,897; W. Maude, *Merchants and Bankers: A Brief Record of Antony Gibbs & Sons, 1808–1958* (London: Antony Gibbs & Sons, 1958). Williamson Balfour was the Chilean partnership of Balfour Williamson. Roberts, Meynell was a Buenos Aires trading house: Wallis Hunt, *Heirs of Great Adventure: The*

As Clarke confided in his travel diary,[62] "The success of the new company would depend to a very great extent, on the nomination of the *right*
man as manager, [thus] it was considered that this nomination should be
very carefully studied before final decision." Much of his trip would indicate how one set about identifying "the *right* man," and what codes governed his selection. What would also stand out from this search is how
enclaved British expatriate life was in Brazil, and yet how transnational it
could be in terms of birth, residence, and judicial status.

At the time of Clarke's arrival in Rio de Janeiro, the leading candidate was Arthur Freeland. Until his retirement to Wimbledon in 1934,
Freeland had run the import and export departments of Davidson, Pullen,
a British trading house in Rio in which he was a partner. Married to a
Pullen, Freeland had returned to Rio in 1938 on the urging of his wife,
who wished to be nearer to her mother. Since 1940 he had been the secretary of the British Chamber of Commerce in Rio. He was consequently a
man of considerable trading experience, and well connected in expatriate
Brazilian circles, but the local word on Freeland was less than encouraging. On the evening of Saturday, 1 July, Clarke and Phillimore had a drink
at the Hotel Glória Bar in Rio with René Berger, a French businessman
whom Phillimore knew from Buenos Aires. The three then dined at the
Palacio Cristal, and Berger may well have raised doubts about Freeland,
because at a chat over a nightcap back at the hotel, Phillimore told Clarke
he "was not too enthusiastic about the nomination of Arthur Freeland,"
and began to suggest other possibilities for the position. On Monday
the 3rd, Clarke called on S. McAllister C.B.E., manager of the Royal
Bank of Canada. McAllister thought that Freeland "was a good man, but
not likely 'to set the Thames on fire.'" The following day Clarke and the
others spoke with F. Whittle, the manager of the Banco de Londres, who
recommended another man, W. E. McGregor, for the job. On the 5th,
Clarke visited Richard Norman Davis, the general manager of the City
of Rio de Janeiro Improvements Co., who agreed that Freeland was no
"go-getter." That evening, Clarke, his wife, and Irvine dined at the home
of Mr. and Mrs. George S. Benedict, of Price Waterhouse Peat & Co.,
"who thought that Freeland was not the man for us. He did not know
Freeland even by sight, but based his opinion on the argument that a man
who was contented to work as the Secretary of the British Chamber of

History of Balfour, Williamson and Company Limited (Norwich: Balfour Williamson,
    1960), vol. 2, 236–237. Its London Associate was Leng, Roberts.
[62] The following discussion is from Clarke's travel diary, Guildhall/Antony Gibbs & Son,
    Ltd./MS 16,897/August 1944. The section on Brazil runs more than fifty pages.

Commerce for four years, should be considered a failure as far as business was concerned." Freeland never did fall out of contention, but it is clear that from early into their quest Clarke and his colleagues began to look for someone better.

For much of the rest of July the hunt for "the *right* man" continued, in government and business offices, in hotel room gatherings, over meals at Mappins' restaurant in São Paulo, and over at least half a dozen lunches more at Rio's Santos Dumont Airport. They spoke with Kilian E. Bensusan, who was British and the son of a fairly prominent figure in the mining industry in Brazil. Bensusan had lived at various times in many parts of South America and, during the last twelve years, had acted as the representative of an English engineering company specializing in the manufacture and export of mining machinery. They looked at H. Broadhurst, Gilbert Durward, L. L. Coxwell, and Alexander McLeod Pain. Broadhurst had lived in Brazil for more than twenty years and "had experience in the export of coffee and cotton." Durward had been in Brazil since the mid-1920s in trading and shipping. Coxwell had experience with Brazilian Warrant, a large coffee exporter with plantations, warehouses, and agency representations in Brazil.[63] Pain was another old Brazilian hand. Still another possibility was Gordon Fox Rule. Born in Brazil, Rule had worked with British banks in Brazil, served in the RAF, and, since 1924, had been second in charge at Brazilian Plantations Ltd., later named the Cia. de Terras norte do Paraná. There was initial excitement over C. O. Kenyon, a former Wilson, Sons employee. Kenyon said he was a personal friend of the chairman, C. F. Cruickshanks, "with whom he stayed when he was in England." He had also managed the São Paulo branch of Brazilian Warrant. For twenty years he had run his own firm, Kenyon & Cia, an orange-export business, and had acted as agent for a steamship operated by the family of Oscar Drummond Costa, which ran between Brazil and South Africa. But vetting Kenyon raised questions about his record for success. Kenyon, as we will see, would continue to figure in this story, but not in quite so favorable a way as Clarke first presumed. Another early enthusiasm was Osborne Wilson Jeans, who was "recently released from the army in India to carry on the business [a family insurance firm]. He was educated at Cranleigh, is a first class cricketer, and impressed us very favorably." The family "had been for many years in Rio de Janeiro." For a time the group toyed with the idea of making the offer to Wilson Jeans, but in the end decided that he was too young

---

[63] Greenhill, "Investment Group."

(or too involved with the family business) for the posting. One more possibility they spoke to, but at that time for a different position, was Hans Blas Gomm, a Brazilian national with business interests in Curitiba. He was energetic, "a good mixer," but Clarke was dubious. Introductions to these men and others came from the same sorts as they had talked to in regard to Freeland: Davis of the City of Rio de Janeiro Improvements Co.; George Benedict of Price Waterhouse; R. C. Stevenson, C.B.E., the British Consul General in Rio; George Mulford, Arthur Balfour & Co.'s South American representative; C. G. Hayes, manager of the Royal Bank of Canada in São Paulo; and G. A. Last of the British Chamber of Commerce in São Paulo.

Ultimately their choice was Robert S. Harvey of Wilson Sons, a large expatriate house in Brazil since 1835. Harvey was thirty-three, a Glaswegian who had begun his career with Butler, Brodie & Co. in London, handling imports from Brazil. In 1932 he emigrated to Brazil, worked briefly for a firm in Santos, then for three months with the Brasileira de Cimento Portland, and then, in 1934, moved to J. R. Williams & Co., shipping agents for the Donaldson Steamship Line. A year later he joined John Gatis, a cotton house in Pernambuco, and since 1940 he had been working at Wilson, Sons in São Paulo, running their export business. Having lived in Brazil for more than ten years and sired children born in the country, he was "considered as of Brazilian nationality as far as Brazilian Social laws are concerned."

Clarke's first meeting with Harvey was over dinner at Harvey's home on the Rua Atlantica in São Paulo. At this point, Harvey was just another local expatriate to consult, but it is not difficult to see him positioning himself for the offer from the beginning. At the dinner, Harvey dismissed one potential candidate, proposed another, and then "strongly recommended a trip in the train from São Paul to Campinas, to see a bit of the country and some coffee and cotton fazendas. He said that one could leave São Paulo at 8 a.m. and be back by 1:20 p.m. and offered to go with me if I should decide to make the trip," an offer Clarke took him up on the following Wednesday. When Wednesday came, Harvey picked up Clarke, took the 7:55 train to Campinas, picked up a car there, and then took Clarke to a fazenda where "the Brazilian Manager was very attentive and drove us throughout the farm." His appetite whetted, Clarke, on the train ride back to the city, began to broach the possibility of Harvey as a candidate.

But Harvey came with a price. He worked for a fellow trading company and any attempt to lift him without their approval, or any offer that he could use as a lever to jack up his salary, would violate the cultural codes against poaching. Clarke, an insider and painfully conscious of the professional risks, had to proceed cautiously. He felt he had. Before going to São Paulo, he and his team had lunched at the Santos Dumont Airport with the Wilson manager in Rio, A. D. Sharpus, who had been "all out to help us." The Wilson manager in São Paulo, B. S. Coxe, was an acquaintance of Clarke. He too "said that he would be pleased to help the new company in any way he could." On the train ride back from the fazenda, Clarke was circumspect in how he raised the subject with Harvey, simply mentioning that Harvey's name had been proposed for the position, but that "due to our long friendly connections with Wilson Sons & Co. Ltd I had not spoken to him about the matter." Harvey played it well, acknowledging that "he was interested in the post," but had not said anything because he liked working with Wilson, had been with them for four years, and, would not like to leave them until suitable arrangements had been made to replace him." He said that he would consult with his manager, B. S. Coxe, later that afternoon. The following day, Clarke had a critical meeting with Coxe during which he couched the situation in the most culturally acceptable terms: "We did not want to make Harvey any offer before first talking to him [Coxe] ... we did not wish our friendly association with Wilson ... to be disturbed in any way on that account." Coxe, speaking more frankly, gave Clarke the green light to proceed, although just to be on the safe side, he said he wanted to consult with Innes Gent, the firm's general manager, who was currently in London. Coxe then invited Clarke, his wife, Irvine, and Harvey to lunch at Mappins.

Back in Rio, however, Clarke suddenly found himself forced to maneuver through cultural shoals. Kenyon, the orange-exporting candidate, had overheard talk in the Club Central de São Paulo that "we had definitely fixed up with R. S. Harvey," and had repeated this to his friend Sharpus, the Wilson manager in Rio, over lunch at the Santos Dumont Airport. Sharpus, "rather 'put out' over what had taken place ... considered that we were 'pinching' one of their Staff," a rebuke that struck at Clarke's sense of professional honor. Sharpus's attitude stiffened when he received a cable from London "advising that ... they definitely considered our approach to Mr. Harvey as an unfriendly act towards their Company." Clarke, insisting that he had behaved properly all the way through, told Sharpus that if Wilson thought they were pinching Harvey he was prepared to drop the matter immediately. Then he came upon safe water. In a phone call with Coxe in São Paulo, Clarke learned that the telegram from London had been incorrectly transcribed and should be ignored. Coxe was still friendly and said Harvey was once again clear for the position. Ready to leave for Buenos Aires, there was little more for Clarke and Irvine to do than resolve the Harvey matter. Stopping in São Paulo, they made it clear to Harvey that they were prepared to make an offer, but to avoid any more appearance of poaching, they insisted that Harvey first resign from Wilson so that he could apply for the manager position as a "free" man. Over the next week, as negotiations hung fire and Harvey dithered, they held to this line, until finally, on 19 August, a cable from Harvey announced that he had resigned his position with Wilson and would be free by the middle of November. "Hereby make formal application position your Manager Brazil on terms already indicated." Clarke's notation following this in his diary was "very satisfactory." On Sunday morning Clarke telephoned Harvey formally to offer him the job. The next day he flew back to Chile.

The Harvey "affair" clearly dominated the voyage, although only an insider would have seen it as such. At stake was not just identifying "the *right* man," but the honor of Clarke and his firm and their future relations with Wilson when cultural codes forbade poaching or initiating a bidding war. Getting Harvey was not difficult; it just required more delicate strategies than might have been deployed in other milieux. At the very least it demanded the appearance of adhering to club rules. Consequently, when Wilson people began to reproach his behavior, Clarke was stung to the quick. He thought he had danced all the right steps and had avoided treading on anyone's toes. In the end, it was not necessary to abandon the pursuit of Harvey, but Clarke would have done so without hesitation if he believed that to proceed would compromise his, and Gibbs's, reputation. Even when things were already far gone, and they knew they wanted Harvey, Clarke did a nifty two-step (insisting on Harvey's prior resignation) to retain an aura of absolute propriety. On larger terms, Clarke's dancing was about a culture of trust that permeated far-flung networked relations, and without which the system would have worked less efficiently. Strictures against poaching were intended to protect firms' resources, but they reflected, on a wider scale, a reliance on unwritten rules to promote reciprocity, shore up confidence, and minimize faulty judgments in a working world where firms interlocked on a daily basis and, when possible, face-to-face. At no point did Clarke contemplate subverting an honor code he subscribed to. It is interesting how frequently the word "honest" recurred in Clarke's notes when assessing the qualities of the men he interviewed. Following the rules to the letter, he revealed himself a creature of the culture that had spawned him. Equally, he inscribed it into the networks he and his partners were assembling.

But why did he select Harvey? In Harvey's favor were his years of experience in trading and shipping. He had been in Brazil since the early 1930s. For four years he had been with Wilson, Sons and had "organized their export business." Yet nearly all the men considered as strong candidates for the position had comparable trajectories. Freeland had been a partner "in charge of the import and export departments" of Davidson, Pullen. Kenyon had been in trading all his life and had previous experience with Wilson and Brazilian Warrant. Coxwell too had worked for Brazilian Warrant, and Broadhurst "had experience in the export of coffee and cotton." Durward's career spanned exports, imports, shipping, and insurance. Pain and Bensusan were candidates with long careers in the trade. They were all men with the right kind of background and expertise. Practically all, like Harvey, had lived in Brazil for many years, thereby meeting Brazilian employee laws, but also possessing a wealth of knowledge and local contacts. Obviously there were certain intangibles – personality, what Clarke picked up in his conversation with Harvey during their fazenda outing – that made him stand out above the others. It is also difficult, however, not to see in Harvey's victory an element of default. Pain asked for terms the partners were not prepared to meet. Broadhurst was reported to be difficult to get along with. The partners were much taken with young Wilson Jeans, but either his youth or commitment to family affairs eliminated him from further consideration. Other candidates were simply gambles. Kenyon had many so-so ventures behind him. Moreover his imprudence in repeating rumors he heard in São Paulo was a breach of club rules and identified him as a violator. Freeland was, from the start, the front-runner, but repeatedly the word on him was that he was not a "go-getter."

Everything about the choice of Harvey therefore brought into play the cultural dualities of cooperation and competitiveness. Clarke and his partners were after a "go-getter," someone with energy, experience, ambition, and contacts. But their "*right* man" was also someone who would fit in. In addition, he would have to be a "good mixer," a phrase whose multiple connotations brought together salesmanship and cultural acceptance. Competitiveness was thus an essential ingredient for these companies, but typically the gambits for making this happen – building contacts, starting up connections, identifying and vetting candidates – fell to the practices of clubland. Information was gathered over lunches and dinners. Even disagreements were handled over dining tables. Whoever held the concession for the Santos Dumont Airport restaurant must have thanked heaven for British businessmen. Clarke worked a very long day – the meetings recounted in the above narrative are only a fragment – but his progress throughout was face-to-face, and with familiars. Intent on building a network, he also relied on networks in place to get what he wanted. Insider confidences flowed freely for a man who understood the conventions and was considered one of their own. Easy entry to banking and business circles was guaranteed a partner in a venerable expatriate firm. In a number of cases Clarke already knew the men with whom he was dealing. The gentlemanly capitalism Cain and Hopkins identified for Britain's financial and imperial elite carried over to its maritime service firms. Young Osborne Wilson Jeans, who was educated at Cranleigh public school and was a first class cricketer, "impressed us very favorably."

This world of insiders in far-off Brazil points straight at other dualities. It is not possible to miss the transnational element pervading this entire story. Clarke, Harvey, Kenyon, and all the others were men with considerable overseas experience. An ocean away from home, they were links in global business chains. Many had been in South America for decades, had perhaps married Brazilian women, and had raised their families abroad. Legally, they were *equiparado*, or in possession of Brazilian nationality as far as employment laws were concerned. Freeland had not only worked for many years in Rio but had returned from retirement so his wife could be near her mother. The Jeans family "had been for many years in Rio de Janeiro." Gordon Rule had been born in Brazil and, aside from his RAF service, appears to have spent all his life there. Broadhurst had lived in Brazil for more than twenty years. Durward had been in Brazil since the mid-1920s, Kenyon probably just as long, Harvey since 1932. There is no reason to assume that they had not developed the same contacts with the Brazilian or international merchant community in Brazil as their German counterparts, the Willes. Harvey was apparently on personal terms with the Brazilian fazenda manager who showed Clarke around. In his early stages of playing coy, he recommended to Clarke Hylton John White, the Rio manager of an Argentine company. Kenyon had served as agent for a steamship company run by the family of Oscar Drummond Costa. At several points Clarke and his partners spoke with Hans Blas Gomm, a Brazilian. One of the first social meetings Clarke and Phillimore held in Rio was a drink with René Berger, a Frenchman with business in Buenos Aires, at the Hotel Glória Bar, with all three going out to dinner afterward.

Yet the Clarke team also operated within a highly circumscribed world of fellow nationals. All the men Clarke interviewed for the position of manager were either British or British Empire/Commonwealth in their origins. With the exception of Gomm and Berger, the same qualification held for the men Clarke consulted. In Brazil for more than a month, Clarke seems to have seen primarily little Britain. Home identity, as well as position and experience, gave him his card of entry. One wonders whether the menus ever changed at Mappins in São Paulo or the Santos Dumont Airport restaurant, or whether it mattered to men who were accustomed to business life within enclaves. But then it was also this combination of worldly firms with home attachments that, as we have seen, lay at the heart of how a global shipping and trading system operated.

Business culture thus embedded itself into everything maritime businessmen did. Strictly, it was neither cause nor effect, but nothing would have happened quite the same without it. Probably its most salient quality was how well it fit both networks and globalism, at least of this part of the century, and thus became their facilitator. Of course when either of these – or both – changed, then so too would the culture.

The final thought on how Europeans organized seaborne passage in the twentieth century returns to the basic fact of its globalism. This narrative began with European harbors but quickly expanded to include hub ports and networks spread many thousands of miles distant. The networks it has been at pains to describe were Eurocentric in their construction but joined in every sea with indigenous shipping and trading circles. All through this account we have come across expatriate firms and Europeans who lived and worked overseas for extensive periods of their lives. Many retained home or national attachments, but their careers were also bounded within transnational experience. In their capacity to orchestrate flows, they depended on their command of markets, commodities, and ports in distant parts of the world. Their expertise, often overlooked as a critical factor in how modern processes work, or the identities that make these possible, was grounded too in knowledge on a global scale.

Part Two of this book will follow this global history through the course of the twentieth century and look at the interaction of maritime spheres with larger historical trends or events. Throughout, four arguments will pertain. First, that maritime history was highly globalized throughout the entire century. Second, therefore, that globalization advanced as well as contracted in years often viewed as ones of retreat. Third, that globalization was nonetheless a process rather than a fixed entity, and that change was thus inherent and constant. As the century drew toward a close, new technology and practice combined with the reversal of encounters to produce a different and new stage of globalization, and consequently a deeply altered maritime world. But that new stage was also brought about, and implemented, by maritime change – especially containerization – so that a fourth argument will be that interaction was always reciprocal and in this way shaped the world we live in.

PART TWO

EXCHANGES

6

World War I

The Allied nations prevailed in total war because they were able to control and marshal world resources while denying the Germans access to them. No other factor, military or ideological, could be as decisive once the fighting forces deadlocked on the western front. Even American intervention required the means to ship 2 million men across the seas, supply them, and all the time retain sufficient transport to feed, fuel, and sustain civilian populations and mass armies in the field. The maritime history of the war thus emerges, ironically, as the pivotal factor in a conflict centered on colossal land battles and casualty figures in the millions. Few other moments have so starkly illuminated the paramountcy for contemporary societies of international transport and trading networks or the global interconnectedness that informed them. Alongside the mobilization (and undermining) of imperial structures, it was the war at sea, in all its dimensions, that defined an essentially European clash as a world conflagration. Three dimensions in particular stood out. One was the mastery, or at least muddling through, of global shipping logistics. Allied victory depended not simply on controlling sea lanes and access to world provisions, but on getting sufficient numbers of ships, directing these to crucial resources, turning them over in bearable times, and maintaining supply lines in the face of daunting circumstances, including the ruinous threat of submarine warfare. Maritime infrastructures, but also experience and professional expertise, made the difference. A second dimension was the waging of economic warfare through blockades and blacklists to cripple German overseas connections and to undermine the Central Powers' means to persist. Again, transnational, transoceanic affairs were a pivotal domain of the war. The third was the configuration maritime warfare bequeathed to world relations. Trade and transport networks altered with the war in ways that rearranged older hierarchies and that enlarged, as well as constrained, twentieth-century globalization. A fourth dimension, naval command of the oceans, although essential throughout, extends beyond the compass of this study and must, in its details, be presumed within the other three. Uniting all dimensions, however, was their international, transoceanic scope, or the indispensableness of daily seaborne flows.[1]

WAR AND LOGISTICS

On 1 August 1914, Louis Dreyfus & Cie, one of the world's largest grain traders, had commitments totaling several hundred million francs, "dispersed through all the countries of the globe: merchandise rolling on the railroad tracks of the five parts of the world or floating on all the seas, in the process of reception in the purchasing countries or in the process of delivery in the countries that sold, in storage in faraway lands." Its very expansiveness, representative of the commercial chains wound round the world over the previous half century, left it vulnerable to the interruption general war would introduce into peacetime routines. Thus on the same date, 1 August, fifty million francs of goods were in the hold of 114 ships that in days would sail under enemy flags or head to enemy ports. A year later most of these matters were still under litigation. Louis Dreyfus's war would be in certain respects typical. The French firm was accused of profiteering and of trade with the enemy. Its Jewish ownership, central European attachments, and participation in world markets subjected it to an increasingly nationalistic environment superimposed over previously cosmopolitan relations, although such problems also stemmed from the power and profits the war offered to traders in what was to become the most precious wartime commodity. Its troubles in August 1914 concentrated in the experiences of one worldwide firm the severe disruptions the war was to bring to quotidian patterns of trade, once the division of Europe into opposing camps split apart a hitherto seamless system for moving goods and peoples across the oceans. Merchants and markets in all parts of the world were affected by battles

---

[1] The critical role of shipping is a theme that runs through the maritime histories of the war: Fayle, *War*, 320–321; idem, *Seaborne Trade* (New York: Longmans, Green & Co., 1920–1924), vol. 3, 454; J. A. Salter, *Allied Shipping Control: An Experiment in International Administration* (Oxford: Clarendon Press, 1921), 1–2, 5.

on the killing grounds of Europe. Still, the momentum of the war was less to dismantle than to rearrange and, in some ways, to augment global interconnectedness.[2]

What happened to Louis Dreyfus shipments therefore repeated across the world. Australian wool brokers, facing the loss of German, Austrian, and Belgian markets, as well as the key French markets in Roubaix and Tourcoing, curtailed by a third the clip brought to auction.[3] For want of credit from German financiers, themselves separated from their sources of capital, Argentinian shippers could only watch as their maize sat stranded in port. Interference in global credit flows affected cotton shippers in India. In China, "Merchants found their capital locked up in the rich cargoes of German liners blockaded in Far Eastern ports, and were thus obliged to reduce their own orders in Europe and America."[4] For months shipments from the Dutch East Indies were thrown into disarray.[5]

When a certain equilibrium was reestablished, its basis increasingly rested on the location of new routes, new markets, and new sites of supply.[6] The greatest shift substituted seaborne materials for staples formerly shipped via the continent. The war not only highlighted the significance of world trade, it extended it. Sugar provides a good example. In peacetime, Britain imported all of its sugar. Two-thirds of the supply came from beet sugar cultivated within the Central Powers. Forced to resort to alternative sources, the British expanded their purchases around the world. They bought in Java, Cuba, Mauritius, Peru, the British West Indies, and North America. At the height of the sugar harvest, sixty to seventy ships were allocated to sugar transport. The French, large producers of beet sugar, but in their northern provinces, also imported more heavily from abroad. So critical was the need for substitute supplies from the first days of the war that government regulation of commodity shipping began with sugar. To be rendered effective, however, the exceptional nature of government control required collaboration with existing networks and trading mechanisms available across the globe. Familiar names in shipping, agency, trading, and brokering circles turn up as sugar charterers, purchasers, and facilitators. Circumstances of war distorted

---

[2] SHM/SSEa 335/Dossier Dreyfus & Cie, "Juillet 1915" (quoted).
[3] A. Barnard, "Wool Brokers and the Marketing Pattern, 1914–1920," *Australian Economic History Review* 11 (1971): 2–3.
[4] Fayle, *War*, 44–45 (quoted 45).
[5] GAR/Lloyd 1/1550/7 May, 21 June 1915; Leeman *Barkschip*, 160–161.
[6] Fayle, *War*, 72; AAFL/Compagnie Générale Transatlantique (CGT)/1997 004 5191/ Conseils d'Administration/26 August, 3 November 1914.

world commerce, yet they also sustained or amplified the channels by which it operated.[7]

Once world markets overcame their initial jitters, the greatest threat to trade lines was the prospect of chasing shipping from the seas. In the first phase of the war this was never serious, for two reasons. First, coal-driven German surface raiders were limited in number and utterly dependent on bunker supplies. It has been estimated that at least one-half of the cruisers' time was eaten up in search of fuel. In addition, the paraphernalia of world commerce – wireless communication, international cables, the presence of Lloyd's agents and signal stations – favored merchant steamers and provided their naval protectors the means to hunt down their predators. As Paul Halpern summed up the cruiser phase of the war, "The general law of the sea that big fish eat small fish and are in turn eaten by bigger fish appeared to have been demonstrated once again."[8]

By far the greater threat from the raiders – and a wider objective of cruiser strategy – was a crippling rise in insurance rates that would drive merchant shipping from the seas. But this danger too was countered by the introduction of a State Insurance Scheme. The British government assumed 80 percent of the risks on every voyage. Norwegian shipping companies introduced their own mutual plan, the Krigsforsikring. Whereas skyrocketing premiums in the first days of the war had immobilized the large Norwegian fleet, nearly all ships were back in operation by the end of August.[9]

Even the impact of the submarine was at first largely contained. First World War submarines were limited in their range, speed, and depth, but they could do what surface raiders could not. Against a superior navy raiders could operate with impunity only in distant seas, where their impact would never be critical. Submarines could strike in the enemy's home waters, where traffic was densest. In sheer tonnage terms, the first wave of unrestricted submarine warfare produced impressive results. Yet international rules of engagement were written for surface ships capable of issuing warnings in advance and distinguishing between neutrals and

---

[7] PRO/MT 25/86, pp. 343–355; ibid., MT 23/390/T20832/1915/5 June 1915; Fayle, *War*, 163–164; Michel Augé-Laribé and Pierre Pinot, *Agriculture and Food Supply in France during the War* (New Haven: Yale University Press, 1927), 34, 199, 201.

[8] Fayle, *Seaborne*, vol. 1, 21–27 (on coal, 22); Paul Halpern, *A Naval History of World War I* (Annapolis, MD: Naval Institute Press, 1994), 65–100 (quoted 100).

[9] Fayle, *War*, 35–36, 57–63; SHM/SSEa 380/20 December 1918; Kaare Petersen, *The Saga of Norwegian Shipping: An Outline of the History, Growth, and Development of a Modern Merchant Marine* (Oslo: Dreyers, 1955), 57.

foes, and they required the safe evacuation of passengers and crews. They thus turned potential war winners like submarines into outlaws in the eyes of much of the rest of the world. Threatened by diplomatic ruptures with neutral states, especially the United States, Germany shut down its first experiment in unrestricted attacks on merchant shipping in less than a year. Moreover, despite losses, throughout the first year and a half of the war no dramatic interference with shipping in fact occurred. Tonnage in mid-1915, through replacement or captured ships, was nearly what it had been in August 1914. Import volume into Britain between August 1914 and December 1915 was down 12 percent, a manageable level and far from a life-and-death situation.[10]

Not until 1916 did continued losses, prolonged steaming times, and the unending strains of war turn getting ships into an overriding concern. The German decision to return to unrestricted submarine warfare at the start of 1917 propelled this state of affairs into outright crisis. The trade-off between almost certain entry of the United States into the fray and a bid to break the supply lines of the Allies now seems a grave miscalculation, but looked at from the perspective of summer and fall of 1917 it appeared to have a chance of succeeding. Compared to all previous periods of the war the losses were breathtaking: more than 2.5 million tons sunk between February and May alone. Everywhere in the Allied camp there was a sense that supply lines were buckling.[11]

In a larger sense, however, the emergency conditions of 1917–1918 were the consequence of the global and structural character of shipping and trade by the twentieth century, and the effect that world war had on it. As wartime priorities contracted, distended, or rearranged interlocked systems, the logistical management of flows became tougher and tougher. Like a tsunami, the concussive impact of the war rushed outward in waves from the epicenter; or, as the leading historian of seaborne transport in the First World War acknowledged, "The crisis of 1917–18 was the result of a cumulative deficit dating back almost to the beginning of the war."[12] The problem, historically, is therefore to identify first why war in the twentieth century challenged so completely the global supply lines of the Allies, and second, why those challenges were nonetheless

[10] Halpern, *Naval*, 287–303; Fayle, *Seaborne*, vol. 2, 1–4, 37–38, 127, 173; idem, *War*, 103; Salter, *Allied*, 2–4, 46–47.

[11] Halpern, *Naval*, 335–341; Salter, *Allied*, 3–4; Fayle, *Seaborne*, vol. 3, 30–31, 91; idem, *War*, 278; Henri Cangardel, *La Marine marchande française et la guerre* (Paris: Presses Universitaires de France, 1927), 85.

[12] Fayle, *Seaborne*, vol. 3, vii.

met, and surmounted. If shipping was the key to victory, what was there about world maritime systems that allowed them to reconstitute in the midst of total war?

The starting point for understanding both problem and solution is to comprehend how thoroughly dependent Europeans had become on overseas supplies of basic materials, including food. In the years immediately preceding the conflict, Britain imported 100 percent of its sugar, cocoa, and chocolate; 79 percent of its grain; 64.5 percent of its butter; and 40 percent of its meat. Nearly two-thirds of the British people's caloric intake came from abroad. Supplies of industrial materials such as cotton, oil, or rubber were completely dependent on imports. Imports provided a large share of the ore, metals, and wool worked or woven by British factories. France was more self-sufficient, yet the war distorted previous sources of supply and invasion and massive mobilization pared back domestic production of nearly everything, including basics like grain. Already before 1914, a majority of French imports traveled on ships. In both quantity and proportion those figures mounted throughout the war. Germany, like France, produced much of what it consumed, but it also imported considerable quantities of coffee, cotton, wool, copper, rubber, animal fodder, and nitrates, which were essential for maintaining soil productivity. Imports accounted for one-third of Germany's wheat and flour. Approximately half of the barley consumed came from Russia, a source eliminated with the war. In value, about 70 percent of these imports traveled on ships.[13] All three combatants, to varying degrees, relied on a world economy.

For those nations to whom the sea lanes remained open, the imperative was to find sufficient ships to bring in sufficient resources from abroad. Beginning in the first year of the war, and absolutely preoccupying strategic thinking by the third, Allied staying power distilled down to tonnage. The Allies began the war with an overwhelming percentage of the world's shipping supply, most of this British. In 1914, out of a world steamship fleet of approximately 45,000,000 grt, about two-fifths were British flagged, 45 percent (20,524,000 tons) if Dominion and other imperial-flagged shipping are added in. The French steam fleet represented close to another 2,000,000 tons; the Japanese and Italian fleets, respectively, 1,700,000 and 1,430,000 tons; the Russian 852,000 tons. When war broke out, diligent efforts on the part of the Admiralty to warn British captains of impending war prevented the capture of sizable numbers of

---

[13] Idem, *Seaborne*, vol. 1, 3–13.

ships in enemy harbors. On the other hand, 223 German steamers and 35 sailing ships amounting to 650,000 tons either found themselves in Allied ports at the start of the war or sailed in unawares over the next several days. On the surface of things, the Allies possessed sufficient shipping for their war needs. The numbers, however, were in some ways misleading. Less than half of the British tonnage figure grossed more than a thousand tons, which was the floor suitable for ocean work, and as markets and sources closed on the continent, overseas transport consumed a heavier share of the load. Moreover, Admiralty demands were exacting. By the end of 1915 more than 6 million tons had been removed from normal international carriage to serve as troop transports, mine carriers, fleet messengers, war supply ships, and hospital ships. France's situation was still more vulnerable. Only 30 percent of French imports and exports were carried in French bottoms, and nearly all imported coal sailed on foreign ships. The question throughout the war was therefore whether shipping supply could balance with shipping demands and shipping losses.[14]

German submarine warfare, if the clearest source of crisis by 1917, was therefore only one of a series of obstacles Allied planners had to overcome beginning in the first days of the war. Distance too became critical; once in pursuit of alternative sources of supply, ocean voyages doubled or tripled in length. When the shipping shortage hit crisis levels in 1917, the only resort was to abandon the most distant routes whenever possible and concentrate every available ship on transatlantic cargoes, despite the long-term maritime consequences.[15] Daunting too were the bottlenecks war brought to even the most efficient ports. Ships suspected of carrying contraband to Germany were directed to ports where their cargo was meticulously unloaded and reloaded, a process that could take weeks. Damaged ships limped into ports lacking the equipment to discharge their cargo or remove it from the harbor area, adding to still more congestion. In France, traffic through Le Havre paid the price of dependency on a single rail line, and suffered from the call-up of large numbers of stevedores and dockworkers. Genoa was in a near perpetual state of blockage.[16]

---

[14] Fayle, *War*, 2–8, 39, 102; idem, *Seaborne*, vol. 1, 54–57; Brian Dyson, "The End of the Line: Oswald Sanderson, Sir John Ellerman, and the Wilsons of Hull," in Starkey and Jamieson, *Exploiting*, 59; Behrens, *Merchant*, 17; Cangardel, *Marine*, 9.

[15] Fayle, *War*, 114, 226–228, 279; PRO/MT 25/86, pp. 347–350; Halpern, *Naval*, 304–310, 381–388; NMM/P & O/4/37/Agents' Reports/Yokohama, 31 July 1917.

[16] PRO/MT 25/6/#72073/19 March 1918; ibid., MT 25/62/Final Report, Part II, 15 March 1921; ibid., MT 25/86, pp. 217–218, 365–366; MMM/MDHB/17/11 May 1915; Vigarié,

The great crippler was the breakdown in inland transport networks and its repercussions for harbor turnover. Although Liverpool and London possessed massive storage installations, the fundamental principle governing the working of ports in peacetime was rapid distribution of goods from harbor to markets. In the war this became impossible. The problem thus turned into the following: Troop trains, supply trains, and shipment of locomotives and cars overseas for service in France, strained the railroads. As transport lines clogged, goods piled up in transit sheds. As goods piled up, quays became unworkable. As quays became unworkable, ships sat in harbor waiting for berths to clear. Port turnaround times increased 50 to 100 percent. The condition became a global one. Mediterranean ports with limited facilities were suddenly designated bunkering, transshipment, or assembly points. The situation at distant Basra, a staging point for Middle East operations and where twenty ships at one point sat in the harbor awaiting berthing or anchorage space, typified how global warfare in the twentieth century catapulted backwater harbors, never designed to handle more than the occasional passing steamer, to first-class status.[17] Even great ports like New York, encumbered by war demands, functioned poorly.[18]

The litany of circumstances culminating in the tonnage crisis by the third year of the war can be extended almost indefinitely. British shipyards lacked the men and steel to match prewar production rates. French shipyards went over to munitions production and constructed no new ships.[19] France and Italy would have frozen and starved if they had relied solely on their merchant marines. Still hundreds more of British ships were assigned to carry coal, wheat, and meat to allies. U.S. entry into the war promised to solve all tonnage problems, but initially the inadequacy of the American merchant marine to transport soldiers and supplies across the Atlantic compounded existing shortages. J. A. Salter, who served as director of ship requisitioning, summed up the urgency of the situation in 1917 when he described how every possible ship had been allocated, how "every sea had been swept, every trade denuded, to obtain

---

Grands, 450; Fayle, *War*, 41–42, 319; idem, *Seaborne*, vol. 2, 62–64, vol. 3, 418–419; Salter, *Allied*, 53–54; AN/F 12/7746/3, 6 July 1915.

[17] PRO/MT 25/62/Final Report, Part II, 15 March 1921; ibid., P48/#46174/28 March 1918; ibid., MT 25/14/Basra Papers/26 July 1917; ibid., Basra Papers/#52624/11 September 1917; Guildhall/Gray, Mackenzie & Co./MS 27,734A, Noble Transcript, pp. 4–6; Cangardel, *Marine*, 54.

[18] GAR/HAL/Correspondentie/V-122/23, 24 March, 23 May 1916, 18 January, 30 April, 10 May 1917; AN/F12/7792/19 May 1918.

[19] Salter, *Allied*, 81–84, 199; Cangardel, *Marine*, 49; Barbance, *Histoire*, 215.

every possible ship," and yet "all the importing departments and combatant services were crying out for more ships, each with the menace of an imminent breakdown which would be fatal to the continued prosecution of the war."[20]

Yet, somehow the Allies managed to find the ships they needed and, even more miraculously, to rebuild and preserve their lines of supply throughout the war. Mostly that story has been told as a victory of convoys over submarines, and there is no question that the introduction of a convoy system stemmed the hemorrhaging of shipping losses and broke the back of the U-boat offensive. The story has been told often enough that it can be reduced to its essential outlines. Convoys had been attempted on some short sea routes, but for the first three years of the war the British navy steadfastly refused to countenance them. The Admiralty had a cupboard full of arguments against instituting convoys. Convoys would waste time to assemble. The use of wireless to do so would tip their hand to the enemy. Merchant ships could not keep station. Slow ships would impede faster ones. There were not enough escort ships to go around.

All but the last of these arguments proved to be without foundation. Perhaps one reason why more pressure was not brought to bear earlier was that many shipowners and shipmasters were also loathe to sail in convoys. Even after the initial trials succeeded, a number of them remained skeptical. "Keeping station with ships of slow speed is nothing less than suicide," wrote one captain in a letter forwarded by the Canadian Pacific's Maitland Kersey, a persistent gadfly, to N. A. Leslie, the Ministry of Shipping's liaison with the Admiralty. Leslie's reply summed up the reality of the situation: "If it were not for the shortage of tonnage, I should like the experiment [letting ships sail on their own] to be made, though I should be sorry for the men. I feel sure that in a few weeks you, together with such Masters as were not taken prisoner or drowned, would implore the Admiralty to include the remnant of your fleet in any convoy that might be available." By November 1917, when Leslie wrote these words, the loss figures were already in steep decline. Gradually the number and range of convoys expanded, until by the end of the war nearly 17,000 ships had sailed under escort with only 1 percent sunk. Into 1918 there remained a shipping shortage, but the peril of too few ships and failing supply lines was receding as an issue.[21]

---

[20] Salter, *Allied*, 77–78.
[21] Halpern, *Naval*, 351–370; Fayle, *War*, 285–286; PRO/MT 25/47/#46140/6 June 1917, #46158/12 December 1917, 7 February 1918, #46156/29 January 1918; PRO/MT 25/48/#46179, 30 October, 1 November 1917 (quoted).

Those numbers, however, were only possible because the Allies had also managed to supplement their merchant navies with those of the neutrals. Scandinavian and Dutch merchant marines alone amounted to about another 5.5 million tons,[22] but few of these ships could be taken for granted. The Dutch had heavy overseas home needs and were subject to German pressure. Norwegian ties were counterbalanced by the danger of submarines. By hook or by crook, the Allies nevertheless got what they needed. They relied on pro-Allied sentiments of the Norwegians, but they also reinsured Norwegian ships when heavy losses threatened to sink the Krigsforsikring too. They cut a deal with Norwegian shipowners to guarantee sufficient coal imports and carry these to Norway in armed ships, in return for placing vessels under British charter or under British command.[23] The default reflex, however, was to fall back on coercion. In control of bunker supplies on all the great sea lanes, save in East Asian and North American waters, the Allies apportioned coal as they wished. By 1916, no ship loaded fuel coal unless it carried Allied cargoes. No neutral tramp received coal cargoes in U.K. ports unless it brought back preferred commodities or could prove that no such cargoes were offering. The more desperate they were, the more ruthless they became. Frustrated with the inability to negotiate a deal over Dutch ships, the Allies force-chartered Dutch vessels in U.S. and British harbors, bringing another 140 ships and hundreds of thousands of tons into the fold. The same tactic was used against idle Scandinavian ships, while cutbacks in exports of cotton, phosphates, and oil were used to tighten the screws on the Swedes.[24]

Even then, ships were only the means of carriage. Just as important was figuring out how to deploy them in the midst of total, and global, war. In many respects it was the reconstruction of worldwide logistical systems, adjusted to the constraints of war, that brought the victory at sea. Before 1914 Europeans had created infrastructures to direct world flows, but the war warped or rearranged these. Certain trades were minimized while others were flooded. Shipping was requisitioned, rationed, and diverted. Troop transports and expeditions created new traffics out of scratch. These, in turn, required hastily constructed supply lines. Improvisation was the rule at a time when turning around ships and running them full

[22] Behrens, *Merchant*, 17.
[23] Pro/MT 25/87/IV, chapter III, pp. 47–53, 62; Petersen, *Saga*, 59, 67–69.
[24] PRO/MT 25/87/IV, chapter III, pp. 29–37, 79–84; Salter, *Allied*, 103–107; Leeman, *Barkschip*, 169; Louis Guichard, *Histoire du blocus naval (1914–1918)* (Paris: Payot, 1929), 111–113, 144–156.

took on a whole new imperative. Finding ships or even keeping them afloat was one thing; working them to maximal advantage, particularly as crisis conditions mounted, was something else altogether. In effect the war had always been about logistics.

Again, this story has largely been understood as a matter of state intervention and inter-Allied cooperation. From the first steps of insurance supports and sugar regulation, the war was a steady march toward state organization of supply lines. As of 1916 no British ship was completely outside government control.[25] The French followed suit, although not until the start of 1918, after British pressure and embarrassing lapses – one ship, it was disclosed, had sailed with a hold full of rhododendrons (surely not intended for flower power) – did the French requisition all ships for the war effort.[26] Grain, the one commodity absolutely critical to staying power, was bought, transported, and distributed through a Royal Commission on Wheat and a Wheat Executive, both established in 1916. Together, the two wheat programs formed a template for subsequent inter-Allied coordination of purchasing and rationing essential resources, including the allocation of shipping. According to Salter, Britain's director of requisitioning, it was this inter-Allied shipping and supply apparatus that, alongside the embrace of convoys, ultimately overcame the effects of unrestricted submarine warfare and likely staved off Allied defeat.[27]

Thus the war was also won through organizational virtuosity. At home, but also overseas, new, large bureaucracies requisitioned, directed, diverted, purchased, rationed, and allocated. In 1918 the British mission in New York to coordinate rail, port, and shipping operations occupied more than 600 persons. Wheat-, sugar-, and meat-purchasing organizations extended to all the continents. A Port and Transit Committee broke harbor logjams by mobilizing labor reserves, pooling wagons, creating incentives for more coastal traffic, and forcing companies to clear out sheds. To break congestion at Basra, government engineers undertook construction of a completely new harbor. The Ministry of Shipping concentrated voyages on the North Atlantic to shorten runs and economize

[25] Salter, *Allied*, 29, 49–50, 70; Fayle, *War*, 157–166, 199–213, 223–225; idem, *Seaborne*, vol. 3, 6–11.

[26] Cangardel, *Marine*; Barbance, *Histoire*, 219–220.

[27] PRO/MT/25/86, pp. 356–361; Salter, *Allied*, 5–6 (on overall significance), 91–93, 149–150, 283; Fayle, *War*, 193–195; idem, *Seaborne Trade*, vol. 3, 21; Elizabeth Greenhalgh, *Victory through Coalition: Britain and France during the First World War* (Cambridge: Cambridge University Press, 2005), 102–132; Avner Offer, *The First World War: An Agrarian Interpretation* (Oxford: Clarendon Press, 1989).

on tonnage. At New York, shipments of grain, oats, steel, and bulky but light cargoes for American troops were so fine-tuned that ships were loaded down to their marks while utilizing all of their hold space. The shipping tonnage sailing into French ports declined by a quarter, but the weight of goods carried in increased by more than half.[28]

But none of these things would have been possible without the mobilization of experts, so that a fourth, indispensable factor returns us to the practice and culture of maritime enterprise, where global logistics were a matter of daily routine. The state did not know how to manage coordinated global systems, but shipping and port men did. They were the ones who ran nearly all the improvised bureaucracies. Britain's shipping controller, with the power to assign ships to any route deemed necessary for national interests, was Joseph Maclay, a partner in a Glasgow shipping firm. Nunzi, the first head of France's Maritime Transit Section, was a shipbroker. Ashley Sparks, who headed the Ministry of Shipping's operations in New York by the last year of the war, had worked for the American ship agency Funch Edye, before joining Cunard, where he rose to the position of chief representative in the United States in 1917 (a position he then held for more than three decades). The chair of the Port and Transit Committee was Lord Inchcape of British India (and P & O). L. A. P. Warner, the Ministry of Shipping's liaison with the Port and Transit Committee, was the deputy general manager of the Mersey Docks and Harbour Board (and later its general manager). Frederic Scrutton, partner and manager in one of London's largest stevedore firms, was sent to the French channel ports to inspect port-handling procedures. Alex Monteath, a P & O director, traveled on a similar mission to Bombay and Basra. The entire shipping and purchasing bureaucracy co-opted maritime experts into its executives. The sugar and wheat commissions bought through experienced traders and brokers and assigned their agencies abroad to shipping agents long familiar with local ports. Clerks in the Wheat Commission, "under the supervision of shipping men ... kept records of itineraries, noted delays, sent ... instructions on such matters as coaling, routes, and ports of discharge ... noted cases of casualties, inefficiency ... arranged for discharge ... dealt with demurrages." The Admiralty quickly added shipowners and managers to its staff. When

---

[28] PRO/MT 25/87/Part VI, chapter II, 39–43; ibid., MT 25/62/#36260/Final Report, 15 March 1921; ibid., MT 25/14/Basra Papers/77326, 2 November 1917, 52624, 11 September 1917; ibid., MT 25/86/362–363; Salter, *Allied*, 31, 91–92, 214; Guichard, *Blocus*, 100.

the decision was made to concentrate shipping on the North Atlantic, operations were handed over to lines with established networks on this route. To keep from bidding up the price of neutral charters, the Allies agreed to centralize chartering and assigned the brokerage to Furness Withy, one of Britain's largest shipping firms. Even after the Inter-Allied Chartering Committee was established in January 1917, it continued to operate largely through Furness Withy offices. French shipping companies managed neutral charters carrying cargoes for France. A committee of five French shipowners or directors advised the Sous-Secrétaire d'Etat, which was, roughly, France's equivalent to the Shipping Controller. Thus shipping, purchasing, chartering, brokering, trading, and port operations were entrusted to men who did this for a living. As much as tonnage, it was maritime business resources – expertise, experience, overseas networks, the knowledge of how to run a global system – that carried the Allies through the supply war.[29]

ECONOMIC WARFARE

Germany failed to choke off Allied access to overseas food and material. But as the Allies kept their sea lanes open they shut off the oceans, and world resources, to the Central Powers. Their means for doing so were threefold. First, they erased German and Austrian merchant shipping from all but local seas. Second, they blockaded Central Power sea coasts and expanded the definition of contraband to include practically any item to keep body and soul together. Third, they destroyed where they could German overseas investment and blacklisted trade with their enemy. Behind the third strategy lurked a grandiose project to secure German markets for their own, and to threaten Germany into submission by menacing its prospects for postwar recovery. Although this proved elusive,[30] there was no question about the outcome of economic warfare.

---

[29] Fayle, *War*, 203–205, 213–232; idem, *Seaborne*, vol. 3, 168; Salter, *Allied*, 33, 41–42; Liverpool, University of Liverpool/Cunard Steam-Ship Company Archives/Frederick A. Bates Papers/C4/8/20 February 1950; PRO/MT 25/87/VI, chapter II, 39–43; ibid., MT 25/86, pp. 343–352 (sugar), 356–363 (wheat, quoted on Wheat Commission); ibid., MT 25/62/#36260/Final Report, 15 March 1921 (Inchcape); ibid., MT 25/14/26 July 1917 (Monteath); Hyde, *Cunard*, 163; Jeffrey, *Scruttons*, 38, 59; Cangardel, *Marine*, 29; Barbance, *Histoire*, 219–220.

[30] Phillip Dehne, *On the Far Western Front: Britain's First World War in South America* (Manchester: Manchester University Press, 2009), 40, 75, 211–218; Richard A. Smith, "Britain and the Strategy of the Economic Weapon against Germany, 1914–1919," Ph.D. diss., University of Newcastle upon Tyne, 2000.

The Germans waged it with submarines and lost. The Allies waged it with sea and trading power and won.

There are two issues here that need to be addressed. The first concerns the tactical effectiveness of the blockade and its strategic outcome. What could the Allies do to cripple Germany's capacity to sustain total war, and how well did they succeed? At the most direct level of cutting the Central Powers off from their overseas markets, save for what neutral tonnage could carry in, Allied sea power was unqualifiedly successful. Germany's merchant marine in 1914 was the world's second largest. More than 5 million tons sailed under the German flag, and another million tons were Austrian registered. But the surface seas belonged to the Allies, and by the end of the first five months of war – subtracting ships detained in Allied ports, captured on the high seas, and hundreds more holed up in neutral harbors – only about 2 million tons remained available, and practically none of these dared venture into open waters.[31] The scattering of the German fleet, like its networks, was worldwide. A HAPAG tabulation from 1916 showed that aside from ships in government service, sunk, sold, or requisitioned after Italian entry, thirty-four sat in Hamburg; ten in Portuguese harbors; eight in Atlantic island harbors; twenty-four in American ports from New York to Honolulu; twenty-one in ports up and down the South American coasts; and fifteen in Asian ports, mostly those of the Dutch East Indies.[32] German tonnage trapped in South American waters alone was impressive: a minimum of a quarter million tons. There were some breakout attempts. Hamburg Süd's *Rio Negro* made it safely back. A converted river steamer, the *Vasco de Gama*, tried and failed. Generally, life for a once-grand merchant marine abroad turned mostly safe and listless.[33] The only sphere of operations where German merchant shipping continued to serve a purpose was the Baltic, or in safe, close-in areas of the North Sea. Ore traffic from Sweden may have occupied as many as 200 ships in late 1916. Otherwise, the German merchant fleet was a negligible factor in the war. Estimates culled from German sources in late 1916 indicated that since the beginning of the war, 152 ships (452,000 tons) had been destroyed, 276 ships (807,000 tons) had been seized, 621 ships (from 2,100,000 to 2,340,000 tons) lay in neutral harbors, and 490 ships (2,410,000 tons) were bottled up in home waters.

[31] Guichard, *Blocus*, 13–14.
[32] HAPAG/1135/UA 7/5 January 1916.
[33] AN/F 12/7798/German Merchant Shipping July 1916 to July 1917 (from Mission Anglaise to Ministère de la Guerre), p. 37; HAPAG/1135/UA 6/Heinrich Green; Wendt, *Kurs*, 231, 233.

Of those sitting idle in neutral ports, about another million tons fell into Allied hands when the United States, Cuba, and Brazil declared war.[34]

Yet no clear advantage could be reaped from sweeping enemy shipping from the seas unless foreign-flagged vessels were also prevented from making up the difference. To this end an increasingly rigorous blockade was imposed to seal off imports and exports altogether. If carried through successfully, its impact was potentially devastating. Germany was far less dependent on the seas than Britain for its economic survival, but it could not fight a long war on home resources alone. It has been seen that a long list of raw materials – cotton, wool, rubber, copper, and many metals necessary in industrial processes – were, in their majority, shipped in from abroad. German food production was largely self-sufficient, but there were three crucial gaps that forebode danger if outside supplies dwindled practically to naught: fats and vegetable oils, artificial fertilizer essential for sustaining food yields, and animal feed. If feed supplies tumbled, so too would supplies of milk, meat, and butter, as well as manure.[35]

In theory the weapons of blockade were relatively simple. Navies set up choke points at the Downs in the Channel, at Kirkwall in the Orkneys, and at Alexandria and Gibraltar in the Mediterranean to prevent contraband, which came to mean any good destined for Central Europe, from getting through. To identify suspect importers or exporters on ships' manifests, and to scare off neutral and rogue companies from trading with the enemy, a Black List supplemented the physical stranglehold. Any firm that landed on the Black List was debarred from commercial, transport, or financial transactions under Allied jurisdiction, and its goods fell automatically into the category of contraband. Insurance too was denied to blacklisted traders.

In practice, none of this was simple. Circumvention of blockades had a venerable history. No system could be watertight, especially when money was involved. During the French revolutionary and Napoleonic wars, Dutch merchants looking to run the blockades had turned to the tiny east Frisian states of Kniphausen and Papenborg (landlocked and about two kilometers square), whose enterprising rulers had trafficked in papers ("antedated upon request") for cargoes, captains, and crews alike.[36] The Central Powers thus did not have to look far to figure out

[34] AN/F12/7798/German, pp. 34–41; Fayle, *Seaborne*, vol. 2, 159–160. Rübner, *Konzentration*, 62, 67, 116, provides different figures: 126 ore ships in summer 1916, about 845,000 tons sequestered by former neutrals.
[35] Fayle, *Seaborne*, vol. 2, 163–165, vol. 3, 37–38; Guichard, *Blocus*, 14–15; Offer, *First*, 63.
[36] Jonker and Sluyterman, *Home*, 133–137.

ways to get goods through, although they were no less imaginative than their predecessors. Large shipments were broken down into many small ones, shipped on big, neutral liners that were least likely to be detained, and scattered among a host of consignees in neutral countries, most of them phoney. In addition, ships left American harbors with two sets of papers – and these were just a few in a very large bag of tricks.[37]

Two stratagems – re-exports via neutral countries and the use of cloaks – exploited the biggest holes in the blockade. Massive quantities of goods crossed over from neutrals bordering on Germany, and commodities that neutrals exported in normal years suddenly appeared on their import columns. As long as the blockade was limited to enemy seacoasts, it was impossible to cut off all avenues of trade between Germany and the outside world.[38] Moreover, Black List targets fought back by cloaking themselves under bogus identities in a cat-and-mouse game played out all over the world. The French consul general in Shanghai dispatched a list of enemy firms in the city, but did not forward their "*prête-noms*" because "these change as soon as they are unmasked, and it is difficult to establish a list exact in any permanent way."[39] Cloaks and intermediaries melted into one another, so that it was difficult to tell the difference. Hamburg's Grapow & Wellman commissioned Busch & Co., located at 14 Rua Conselheiro Mafra in Florianopolis (Brazil), to secure the release of goods on board an interned ship and to forward the bill of lading to Germany, but via Salmon Davidsen, at 3 Brogade, Copenhagen. Berringer & Co., bankers and rubber merchants in Pará, shipped rubber aboard Brazilian steamers in the name of Suter & Co., a local Dutch commission agent.[40] Others, like the Lord of Kniphausen, saw their opportunities and took them. At some point the Hamburg freight forwarder A. Hartrodt figured out that there was good money to be made out of the blockade and began to expand as widely as he could. He set up a business in Göteburg using Gustav Holm & Co. as his cover. More negotiations were opened with houses in Christiania and Bergen. As of March 1916 he was reported to be in South America "with the object of opening agencies in Chile, Bolivia, Brazil, &c., and intends to return to Germany *via* the United States after enlarging his branch in New York."[41] The task of

---

[37] Fayle, *Seaborne*, vol. 2, 137–153, 302–303; Guichard, *Blocus*, 46–50, 122–127.

[38] Guichard, *Blocus*, 36–37; Fayle, *Seaborne*, vol. 1, 296; AN/F 12/7979/Guatemala 1916–1918/1 September 1917; SHM/SSEa 74/Brésil, 2 February 1915.

[39] AN/F 12/9669/Chine 1911–1917, 23 August 1915.

[40] SHM/SSEa 339/Who's Who, 5th issue (Busch); SHM/SSEa 340/Who's Who, 16th issue (Berringer).

[41] SHM/SSEa 340/Who's Who, 16th issue.

ferreting out all the cloaks was thus a Sisyphean one. When the German firm A. Trommel & Co. of Brazil was blacklisted, it continued to do business under the name J. P. Chaves & Co. When J. P. Chaves was blacklisted, it used the cloak Eduardo Oliveira. When the Allies caught up with Eduardo Oliveira, it used the cover J. da Silva Barroso. Bogus firms were like hurricanes in a bad season. As soon as one passed another name was on the horizon.[42]

Plugging the neutral gaps in the blockade was full of its own challenges. Before the war, the keenest arguments against a blockade strategy had hit precisely on this problem.[43] No degree of Allied duress could compel neutral states to close down all their exports to Germany. The Netherlands depended on Germany for much of their coal, and Dutch exports of domestic dairy products to Germany had been an important trade before the war. Any pressure the Allies could bring to bear on Denmark was countered by Germany's ability to mount a credible threat to invade should Danish exports be cut to the bone. The Allies and Central Powers alike negotiated agreements with the Danes in which they recognized some measure of collaboration with the enemy. Switzerland was an almost impossible nut to crack. German and Swiss engineering companies, including Swiss watchmaking firms, had closely integrated production processes, and the Swiss state was determined to protect these relations at all cost. The Swiss too depended on coal imports from Germany. Swedish resistance was just as tough. The Swedes feared Russia and had long trading relations with Germany. The Baltic, through which most of this trade was conducted, was beyond the reach of Allied ships. Germany, moreover, could not do without Swedish ore imports and placed Sweden under intense counterpressure. Trespass on Swedish neutrality alone was sufficient to produce a backlash, and when the Allies squeezed the Swedes harder, the Swedes squeezed back, bottling up British ships in the Baltic and holding up passage of goods to Russia.[44]

Slowly, however, the Allies accomplished their primary objective: to quarantine the greater share of Germany's overseas trade. The greatest victory came relatively early when Dutch businessmen, dependent on overseas trade, constructed the Netherlands Overseas Trust (NOT), an umbrella consignee for overseas imports, and guaranteed that certain goods would

[42] SHM/SSEa 74/13 March 1917.

[43] Offer, *First*, 285–292.

[44] Guichard, *Blocus*, 105–134, 158–176; A. C. Bell, *A History of the Blockade of Germany and of the Countries Associated with Her in the Great War, Austria-Hungary, Bulgaria, and Turkey, 1914–1918* (London: Her Majesty's Stationery Office, 1937), 245, 525–536.

not transit across the border to Germany. The Swiss set up a comparable organ in the spring of 1915. The NOT model could not be so easily applied to the Scandinavian countries where, for example, Copenhagen served as a regional transit and distribution center, so that imports into Denmark were often destined for Norway and Sweden. Early in the war, however, the Allies had forged agreements with American exporters, and in some cases importers, to limit the shipment of strategic materials to clear-cut domestic needs, and in 1915 and 1916 a series of similar conventions were signed with Scandinavian merchant associations and shipowners. When all else failed, the Allies fell back on the default option of force majeure and simply seized ships. The longer the war wore on, the less reluctant they were to resort to coercion; and the entry into the fray of the largest and most self-righteous neutral of all in 1917 then plugged the largest loopholes and put paid to any overreaching thoughts of neutral power.[45] There is no question that by the third year of the war seaborne flows to and from Germany had slowed to a trickle. Neutral re-exports were considerably abated. Reports from around the world charted the drying up of German imports and exports. Black List entries noted firms whose business had been brought "to a standstill" and were prepared to abjure trade with the enemy.[46]

But if tactics over time proved fairly successful, what about their strategic impact: How effective was the blockade as a decisive weapon in winning the war? The most complete studies of this question present a complex, and at times, mixed picture. Despite serious food shortages in Germany, there was no generalized famine. Germans were not starved into submission. Preferred food rations were distributed to soldiers and war industry workers at the expense of other civilians; those who suffered most directly from food shortages were those least integral to the war effort. Moreover, as body weight fell, there was a corresponding fall in the body's daily need for calories. The blockade was therefore very successful in stressing German food supplies, but not correspondingly so in stressing nutritional intake. It is not even certain that the figure of three-quarters of a million German civilian dead, often attributed to the blockade, has any evidentiary substance.

Nevertheless, if diets did not fall below essential needs, the drain on time, energy, and morale cut very deep indeed. Food was to be found in

---

[45] Guichard, Blocus; Bell, History, 256–257; Fayle, Seaborne, vol. 2, 144–155.
[46] AN/F 12/7979/Hollande/1 January, 13 May 1916; ibid/Guatemala, 1 September 1917; AN/F 12/7951/Indes néerlandaises/11 August 1916; SHM/SSEa 9/14 June 1917; SHM/SSEa 339/Who's Who, 12th issue (Markt & Hammacher); ibid., SSEa 340/Who's Who, 16th issue (Amsinck G. & Co.); Molsen, C. Illies, 81.

queues, and if not there, on the black market, but the time spent standing in line or scrounging in the countryside was terribly wearing. The
psychological impact of severe cuts in sugar, coffee, meats, and fats was
sustainable only so long as victory seemed likely or imaginable. In fact
it was precisely in these foods where the cuts fell the hardest. Not only
was Germany largely deprived of its huge prewar imports of animal fodder by the blockade, but home supplies of cereals or potatoes or turnips
that went into fodder before the war were devoted to direct human use
to make up for shortages elsewhere, resulting in acute shortages of meat,
milk, and butter. Thus, as Avner Offer has pointed out, there occurred
the paradox of "a relatively sufficient diet combined with a sense of deep
deprivation." A thriving black market made up much of the difference,
but its power, inequities, and very existence undermined respect for legal-
ity or official authorities, as did the failed and unequal distribution of
official food supplies. Moreover the corrosive impact of the blockade
cannot be limited simply to food. Nearly everything was short, including
cotton and wool; lack of warm, or even decent clothing further sapped
energies and morale. Coupled to this was a running down, at last, of the
war machine. Motor oil stocks could be sustained through the war, but
the blockade closed off import of lubricants. Sweden may have provided
sufficient iron ore, but there were severe scarcities in tungsten, nickel, and
tin. Engines and machines in the thousands were inoperative for lack of
materials necessary for parts or repairs. Even food supply systems for the
army unraveled from spring to fall 1918. In the spring of 1918, Germany
could still mount potentially decisive offensives. Their failure, however, at
this stage in the blockade, exhausted the country's will to continue. In the
end, the blockade alone cannot be said to have won the war, but it was,
alongside American intervention and Allied access to world resources,
critical once war on the western front settled into stalemate. Even U.S.
entry into the war, provoked by unrestricted submarine warfare, was in
part a product of Germany's desperate gamble to break the stranglehold
of economic warfare by unleashing its full impact on the British. What
might have resulted in the First World War if the seas had remained as
open to the Central Powers as they were to the Allies can only be imagined. That they were not underscores how vital maritime flows were in
the determination of the difference.[47]

---

[47] Offer, *First*, 1–78 (quoted 66), concludes that although it was not sufficient to bring
about defeat, it nevertheless produced deep disaffection and unraveling at home by summer 1918. For Offer, the home front was as crucial as the battlefront in determining

The second issue in this story concerns globalization. Did economic warfare herald an end to the global interconnectedness that prevailed in 1914? The Black List was itself an affirmation of the dense transnational commercial life Europeans had spread overseas and the world-encompassing architecture of merchant relationships. The sheer number of business houses, large or small, scattered across the globe and engaged in world trade, was astonishing. But the rippling effects of war were no less engulfing, and touched big commodity traders like Louis Dreyfus, but also jewelry dealers in Havana or shipping agents in Yokohama.[48] There is no doubt that the easy cosmopolitanism of prewar years fell into the casualty column. A Portuguese firm such as Jorge, Martins & Co. of Pará, Brazil, importers of jute yarn from Moore & Weinberg of Dundee, whose selling agent in Pará was a German named Schumann, found itself under pressure by late 1915, even though the partners were listed as "of good status and reputation, and may be trusted."[49] The impact of the blockade and submarine war was felt keenly by Dutch merchants in the East Indies cut off from their markets in Europe.[50] At home, Rotterdam's seaborne traffic fell by 70 percent between 1913 and 1917, and its international Rhine traffic was off 80 percent in the same period. By the third year of the war there were severe shortages and labor troubles in what had been one of the world's greatest ports.[51]

Yet strangely, the Black List testified as well to the vitality and protean character of cross-national networks, even as they were being whittled down. The closing of one outlet led to the opening of another, often through markets or intermediaries where no geographical liaisons had existed before. Thus Burnay, Henry & Co., a Belgian-Portuguese-German firm based in Lisbon, and another example of the cosmopolitan trading

surrender. A similar conclusion about disaffection informs Belinda Davis, *Home Fires Burning: Food Politics, and Everyday Life in World War I Berlin* (Chapel Hill: University of North Carolina Press, 2000); Roger Chickering, *Imperial Germany and the Great War, 1914–1918*, 2nd ed. (Cambridge: Cambridge University Press, 2004), 41–46, 138–148. The fuller impact of the blockade can be traced in Fayle, *Seaborne*, vol. 2, 145–146, 160–162, 404–408; ibid., vol. 3, 37–38, 177–181, 427–430; Bell, *History*, 671–676. For the contrary view, Niall Ferguson, *The Pity of War* (New York: Basic Books, 1999), 248–281.

[48] SHM/SSEa 340/Who's Who, 16th issue, "correct to April 30th, 1916" (Carlos Böhmer, Havana); NA/KJCJL/22/26 May 1916.

[49] SHM/SSEa 339/Who's Who, 12th issue, "corrected to December 31st, 1915" (Martins and Schumann).

[50] AN/F 12/7951.

[51] Van de Laar, *Stad*, 315–321; Havenbedrijf der Gemeente Rotterdam/Verslag van den toestand der Gemeente Rotterdam over het jaar 1916.

house that squared so ill with a warring world, exported "enormous quantities of cocoa to Germany *via* Holland and Scandinavia." Or Costa & Ribeiro, Hamburg and Brazilian merchants and major importers of tobacco and cocoa, set up a "temporary office" at the Palads Hotellet in Copenhagen to continue their business.[52] Eventually the Allies did shut most of these down, particularly after American entry into the war, but the repeated disclosure of "cloaks" pointed to the irrepressible ingenuity of global commerce, and its ability to connect across oceans and borders. Before multinationals such as Brown, Boveri, a Swiss company with branches in France, Germany, Austria, and Britain, the blockade was stymied. Switzerland, whose economy was integrated with those of surrounding nations, was a conundrum for the prosecutors of economic warfare. The Compagnie des Aceries in Schaffhausen was the affiliate of a German concern, but it was also such an important supplier of Allied munitions that the War Office eschewed any large-scale interference, "thinking it preferable that a certain proportion of British metals should go on to Germany, than that any part of their own contracts with the company should be unexecuted."[53]

The Argentinian grain trade typified the futility of forcing established trading patterns to conform entirely to wartime categories. Grain was the most coveted commodity for either side, but the great international grain traders, who controlled its export and sale, were multinational companies with links to all sides. Their networks, or even identities, defied procrustean definitions of friends and foes. Nearly all the largest firms were highly cosmopolitan. Louis Dreyfus had thousands of collaborators, "disseminated across the globe." Bunge & Born, the largest dealer in South American cereals, had been founded in 1884 by Ernest Bunge and his brother-in-law Jorge (or George) Born, both of whom emigrated to Buenos Aires in the late 1870s, while Ernest's brother Edouard remained in Antwerp where he ran trading operations at home and managed investments in Africa and Asia. By 1915 its managing director in Argentina was Alfred (or Alfredo) Hirsch, an Argentinian citizen of German birth who had joined the company in 1897. Jorge Oster, also German-born, was, in 1915, in charge of London operations and, like Hirsch, a naturalized Argentinian citizen. Both Hirsch and Oster were partners in the firm, which gave it a Belgian-German cast, or a Belgian-Argentinian cast, depending on who

---

[52] SHM/SSEa 339/Who's Who, 5th issue, through at least July 1915 (Costa & Ribeiro); ibid., 12th issue (Burnay, Henry); SHM/SSEa 74/Brésil, 2 February 1915.
[53] Bell, *History*, 300.

was doing the gazing. In addition, there were Bunge mother houses in Antwerp and Amsterdam and sales affiliates in London, Hamburg, Genoa, Paris, and Copenhagen. Herman Weil, chairman of Weil Brothers (or Weil Hermanos), the third great Argentinian grain exporter, was equally a German-turned-Argentinian. Sam Weil, a director in Argentina, was likewise German but a naturalized American. The manager of Weil Brothers' London branch was British. Edelstein, who had run the Antwerp branch but was now a director in London, was an Austrian-turned-Argentinian. Another director in Argentina, Garde, was German. Still another big firm, General Mercantile Company, confounded all the boundaries. Founded in Belgium but incorporated in Great Britain, its principal and possibly sole shareholder was Wm H. Müller, a shipping, ore, and stevedore company based in Rotterdam. Müller was a German, but control of his firm had devolved to A. G. Kröller, a Dutchman who (as any art fancier will know) had married Müller's daughter. Kröller, moreover, had been the founding spirit behind the blockade-accommodating NOT. General Mercantile's London manager was Rogenhegen, of Russian background but naturalized British. The manager in Buenos Aires was Alberto Zeller, another German who had become an Argentinian many years earlier.

In the wartime clash between nationalist, exclusionary politics and prewar internationalism there would thus be an inevitable bloodletting of sorts, but little likelihood that well-entrenched multinationals like these, even if suspect, could be driven out of the grain trade altogether. Forced to place a label on firms, the Allies did hack away at the open cosmopolitanism of prewar years. In the cases of Bunge & Born and Weil Brothers, both of whom employed many Germans (although possibly these too were naturalized Argentinians), the decision was to regard them as German or German sympathizers. Even Louis Dreyfus, a French firm, but also Jewish, for a time fell under suspicion. Yet General Mercantile tied the British into knots; into 1916 there was no clear policy on how to treat this company. There were no clear means either of dealing with those firms the Allies found suspect. The Allies blacklisted them, denied cable and insurance and credit facilities to them, and requisitioned ships chartered to them, but with only partial success. The one unqualified victory came only when they succeeded in shutting off grain imports to Germany at the source of entry. Efforts in particular to cripple Bunge & Born, however, were a dismal failure. As Phil Dehne has shown, no offensive by the British within Argentina could undermine Bunge & Born's extensive purchasing, credit, storage, milling, and marketing networks, nor its Argentinian identities. Through cloaks or intricate marketing schemes, the company operated almost with impunity. Even British dealers could not avoid purchasing Bunge & Born grain. In fact, in 1915 Bunge had set up a new affiliate in Paris under the name of P. van Hinderdael & Co., which carried out purchases for France, further muddying the exclusionist waters. In the 1920s Bunge & Born still controlled one-third of the market in Argentinian grain and was developing wider connections in North America. In this realm of international commerce, the nationalist impact of war was nil.[54]

It cannot be said, therefore, that economic warfare automatically turned globalization into a casualty of war. Even in 1914 there had been a tension between cosmopolitan and national currents, reflected in business cultures, or the overlap between international flows and empire, or in impinging restrictions on the free circulation of goods and people. Whereas internationalism had dominated without suppressing its alternative, the reverse dynamic would operate during the war. Even in its bluntest application, economic warfare could not eradicate all the cosmopolitan connections established over preceding decades. Instead there would be compromise and negotiation, stimulus of alternative markets, subterfuge, and rebound once hostilities were over.

BALANCE SHEETS

British merchant marine losses in the First World War totaled at least 7,240,000 grt and perhaps as much as 9,032,0000 grt, depending on the computation. The lower figure represented approximately 37 percent of the fleet in 1914. At the end of 1918, taking into consideration all forms of losses and the addition of replacement ships or captured vessels, British tonnage had slid 16 percent from its prewar total. French and Italian shipping losses ranged into the 30th and possibly 50th percentiles, respectively. Norway, a neutral country, but one that placed its shipping largely at the disposal of the Allies, lost, by one accounting, 829 ships comprising 1,239,283 grt or nearly 50 percent of its prewar tonnage. As usual, statistics vary with the source consulted, but none is short of staggering.[55]

[54] Hoste, *Bunge*, chapters 2 and 3; Philippe Chalmin, *Négociants et chargeurs. La saga du négoce international des matières premières* (Paris: Economica, 1983), 26, 204; PRO/MT 23/540/T42028/1916, especially 14 October 1914, 1 January, 7 October, 9 November 1915, 2 January, 1–2 March 1916; SHM/SSEa 339/Who's Who, 5th and 12th issues (Bunge & Born); Dehne, *Far*, 149–156, 205–206.

[55] Differing figures are offered by Rübner, *Konzentration*, 443; Fayle, *Seaborne*, vol. 3, 436, 439; Harlaftis, *Greek*, 185; and Petersen, *Saga*, 67, 69.

These are, however, raw figures that capture little more than the destructiveness of the war at sea. The war's effects appear quite different when broken down to company level. Ships sank, but their loss was balanced by new acquisitions during and immediately following the war. Some companies made a great deal out of the war, and avoided paying excess profits taxes by rolling over profits into capital investment. Foreclosed from ordering new ships by government control of shipyard construction, large British companies swallowed up smaller ones. By the same token, inflated values encouraged smaller firms to sell.⁵⁶ Losses were therefore poor indicators of company fortunes. Cunard, Ellerman, CGT, and P & O all suffered big losses, one-third of CGT's prewar fleet, eighty-one ships or nearly half a million tons for the P & O group. Nevertheless all emerged considerably larger after the war, and with extended route structures. Cunard's acquisition of the Commonwealth and Dominion Line in 1916 expanded its operations to Australia and New Zealand. P & O, which purchased companies through the early postwar years, possessed 500 steamers by the early 1920s. What had essentially been an Indian Ocean and East Asian shipping company now added transpacific services and was only one ocean shy of being truly global.⁵⁷

Postwar inventories must therefore take into account measurements other than losses to convey the longer-term consequences of the war. More far-reaching were the effects of logistical warfare. The British strategy of husbanding shipping resources for essential wartime uses and concentrating a preponderance of shipping on the North Atlantic denuded the cross-trades, undercut business networks, and forced the abandonment or scaling down of service to markets once a British preserve. A very large percentage of American forces had been transported across the Atlantic on British ships, but to do this meant stripping services on South American and other routes.⁵⁸ As a seafaring nation, Britain never recovered from this wartime experience. In 1914 British steamers and motor ships constituted 41.6 percent of the world's total, only 30.8 percent in 1924, and only a quarter of the world fleet on the eve of the Second World War. Before the war slightly more than half the

⁵⁶ Boyce, *Information*, 127, 144. This merger or buyout trend had begun before the war.
⁵⁷ Ibid., 128; Hyde, *Cunard*, 159–170; James Taylor, *Ellermans: A Wealth of Shipping* (London: Wilton House Gentry, 1976), 68–73, 87; Barbance, *Histoire*, 176–177, 208–228; F. A. Hook, *Merchant Adventurers, 1914–1918* (London: A. & C. Black, 1920); Howarth and Howarth, *P & O*, 124.
⁵⁸ Fayle, *War*, 238, 284; Smith, "Britain," 84–85; Blake, *B.I. Centenary*, 188–189.

value in world trade had traveled in British bottoms; far less was carried after 1918.[59]

In most, if not all respects, the war was a gift to Allied trading companies. Vast quantities of materials were dispatched overseas, and German markets were invaded or simply liquidated. Again companies not only reaped in the profits but diversified and expanded in the process. CFAO turnover from West African trading was up 43 percent between 1913 and 1918. Lacking men, it recruited Swiss, Belgians, Swedes, and even some English.[60] The London-Shanghai firm of Dodwell's saw its huge trade in Chinese tea to Moscow go up in smoke after 1917, but Dodwell then pioneered new markets in Tunisia and Morocco, and it made a bundle off of its charter business in Japanese steamers. Steel Brothers advanced to the position of largest rice miller and exporter in Burma, perhaps in the world, following its purchase of confiscated German milling concerns. Troops sailed from India to Europe or to Mesopotamia on British India ships, as did horses from Australia, with all of these shipments managed, turned over, and supplied by Mackinnon Mackenzie. Balfour Williamson in Chile prospered and opened new operations in Bolivia, Ecuador, Colombia, and Chicago.[61] Only the longer-term effects of the war on international commerce, mixed in with postwar developments, adversely influenced these companies' fortunes.

The question of gains and losses proves still more complex when shifting to Germany. Half of Germany's merchant marine disappeared in the war. The other half disappeared in the surrender.[62] Once Germany had accounted for 11 percent of the world's merchant fleet. At the beginning of the 1920s German shipping represented less than 1 percent. HAPAG, NDL, and Hamburg Süd possessed barely a seaworthy vessel among them. Yet all of these companies possessed everything needed to run ships – expertise, networks, personnel, wharves, even cash – and it was only a matter of time before they got their hands on the one thing they lacked. Despite the colossal loss in capital assets, companies turned tidy profits on the Swedish ore trade or by converting their facilities to war-

---

[59] Fayle, *War*, 415; Jamieson, "Inevitable," 80; Sturmey, *British*, 22, 34; Harlaftis, *Greek*, 189.
[60] Bonin, *C.F.A.O.*, 245–248.
[61] *The House of Dodwell: A Century of Achievement, 1858–1958* (London: Dodwell & Company, 1958), 38, 100; Guildhall/Steel Bros./MS 29,557/Brief History; Jones, *Two*, 56, 58; Hunt, *Heirs*, vol. 2, 100–132.
[62] By the Treaty of Versailles, all German ships grossing more than 1,600 tons and half of all ships grossing between 1,000 and 1,600 tons were ceded to the Allies.

contracted business. During and after the war they received voluminous state handouts. Banks and steel companies invested in them. The most striking aspects of their recovery, however, were the joint arrangements they negotiated with firms from countries that had been out to savage them only a year or so earlier. Only the cosmopolitan, highly networked culture of maritime business can explain the rapidity with which they rejoined the club. Holts, Ellermans, and NYK awarded their Hamburg and Bremen agencies for Far East services to HAPAG and NDL, respectively. Both companies were almost immediately back on the North Atlantic thanks to joint services they set up with U.S. shipping interests. Purchases, mergers, and new constructions filled in the gaps. NDL acquired the Roland Line, HAPAG the already merged Kosmos and DADG. By 1926 HAPAG was back to 879,000 grt, NDL to 613,000 grt, Hansa to 230,000 grt, and Hamburg Süd to 152,000 grt – and they kept growing after that. Once ships were sailing again, network resources assured that all else fell into place. Discussions of agencies or of other basic matters in Böger and Loepthien's 1928 business report from America would have been difficult to distinguish from those preceding the war. Elder Dempster's reconstructed relationships with Woermann on west African routes shows that these cross-national connections occurred across the board.[63]

Trading company experiences express still better the global effects of economic warfare. Behn, Meyer saw its Singapore headquarters confiscated and liquidated and its employees shipped to Australian internment camps. By 1915 all its houses were blacklisted, and when Siam and America entered the war, branches in Bangkok and the Philippines also disappeared. Yet the company managed to sustain operations throughout the war. To get around the Black List, two Swiss employees, Eugen Engler and J. M. Menzi, took over the business in Manila and Bangkok, and when these houses were liquidated Menzi continued to buy and sell on his own account in the Philippines. Managers in the East Indies created a new, Dutch-registered firm and used this cover to conduct business, and harvest profits, for the remainder of the war. Black List entries of cloaks testify to the impossibility of shutting the company down altogether. Within a few years of the end of the war, Behn, Meyer had rebuilt its trading, agency, and estates operations throughout Southeast Asia,

---

[63] Witthöft, *Hapag*, 60–64; Wiborg and Wiborg, *Unser*, 212; Lars Scholl, "The German Merchant Marine in the Inter-War Period, 1920–1932," in Lewis R. Fischer and Helge W. Nordvik, eds., *Shipping and Trade, 1750–1950: Essays in International Maritime Economic History* (Pontefract, West Yorkshire: Lofthouse, 1990), 191; Seiler, *Century*, 81; HAPAG/1263, 1264; Davies, *Trade*, 178–185.

even if it had to return to Singapore under new nomenclature (Straits Java Trading Company). All the while, Arnold Otto Meyer, its partner firm in Hamburg, expanded to Shanghai, Japan, and across the Pacific to Argentina, Chile, Colombia, Peru, and Brazil. Recounting a speech by Adolf Laspe, one of the directors, on business operations in the 1920s, house historian Emil Helfferich remarked that these comments "read as if there had never been a war."[64]

In Brazil, Theodor Wille also had a rough war. Allied estimates in early 1917 place Wille coffee shipments at little more than 1 percent of the total. Yet the firm carried on, under cloaks and through its U.S. networks that functioned until American entry into the war. Its extensive business and state connections within Brazil won it protection from the worst of Allied machinations. When the war was over, business networks in Brazil, the United States, and Europe, including with former enemy houses, enabled the firm to regain its role as the leading shipper of coffee. Especially valuable were the connections of its Le Havre agent, George Lafurie, in reestablishing trade through that port. By the mid-to-late 1920s Wille was shipping 13 million sacks of coffee per annum out of Santos and Rio. In the decades that followed the war, the company rebuilt but also extended its buying and marketing networks, particularly within the United States – by far the largest consumer of Brazilian coffee.[65]

Remarkable in these histories was therefore the enduring role of networks in the lives of maritime firms. Before the war networks were the means of building, expanding, and sustaining transoceanic business. During and after the war they were the means of survival, reconstitution, and renewal. Significantly, the cosmopolitan, highly networked culture that prevailed in shipping and trading overrode wartime divisions, so that frequently it was formerly "enemy" connections that provided the crucial postwar jumpstart. Wille's, NDL's, and HAPAG's experience was a trope in the postwar history of German overseas firms. Buschmanns, which had ground to a halt in the war and languished for another year or two, received its first orders from a British West Indian importer, T. R. Evans, with whom Franz Buschmann had developed a close personal relationship. Shortly after, "old friends" such as Alex. Ross & Co. in Hong Kong sent in orders from Asia, and the firm was up and running again.

[64] Helfferich, *Behn*, vol. 1, 152, vol. 2, 140–169 (quoted 164); SHM/SSEa 339/Who's Who, 5th issue, 12th issue; SHM/SSEa 340/Who's Who, 16th issue.
[65] Zimmermann, *Wille*, 134–164; SHM/SSEa 74/30 July 1916, 9 February, 13 March, 5 May, 6 June 1917.

C. Illies & Co.'s old connections were the platform for rebuilding business in Japan. Melchers rebuilt its business in the East through the support of "loyal, longtime Chinese friends." Vorwerk's Chile house opened or enlarged U.S. contacts during the war and these aided in recovery after 1918.[66] Just as remarkable were the broadened geographical patterns that emerged from the war in ways not dissimilar to what occurred for the British. Behn, Meyer, a Southeast Asian firm in 1914, diversified to China and South America by the 1920s. Wille and Vorwerk, with Europe shuttered, extended their lines in North America. To these effects could be added the way port networks altered or rebounded following the war, but that story belongs more properly to Chapter 7.

What still beggars consideration is the worldwide impact of the war. Nearly 8 million people died in the First World War, nearly all on narrow strips of ground in western and eastern Europe. But the effects of the war were, from the start, felt around the world. Yokohama shippers of silk piece goods could not find sufficient carriers for all the markets clamoring for them. Planters watched commodities sit idle in East Indies warehouses for want of shipping assigned to North American grain shipments, dispatched on longer Cape routes, or, in 1918, requisitioned by the Allies. When war broke out, panic struck pilgrims already in Mecca, fearful that they would be stranded for the duration of the hostilities. All of the pilgrims actually made it home (the Government of India put on extra ships), but there were no further East Indies pilgrimages for the remainder of the war, and the overseas flow from India was but a fraction of its former number. Half a world away, shippers in the Ecuador cocoa trade, or in the coastal trade between Guayaquil and Panama, could not find ships to lift their cargoes. Meanwhile, New York Harbor strained to move the glut of traffic entering and clearing the port. So tight was shipping that French importers of nonessential goods, like Paris's Vve Chanudet & Fils, makers of bone and horn for corsets, could not get authorization to load their materials, even though these were paid for and often sitting in docks across the Atlantic.[67]

---

[66] Hans Krieg, *Bernhard Buschmann. Die Geschichte eines Ostasienhauses* (Hamburg: Verlag Hamburgische Bücherei, 1952), 40; Molsen, *C. Illies*, 81; *150 Jahre Melchers*, 14; Hauschild-Thiessen, *Zwischen*, 204–232.

[67] NMM/P & O/4/37/Agents' Reports/Yokohama, Kobe, 31 July 1917; Leeman, *Barkschip*, 164, 168; GAR/Lloyd 1/1550/21 June 1915; *Records of the Hajj: A Documentary History of the Pilgrimage to Mecca* (Records), 10 vols. (Slough: 1993), iv, 781–803, v., 70–71, 105–107; PRO/MT 23/581/T4848I/19, 22 April 1916; Fayle, *Seaborne*, vol. 1, 166; AN/F 12/7752/Transports internationaux.

Generally we think of the war as ushering in an era of deglobalization, one in which flows of trade, money, and people, which had circulated virtually unimpeded before 1914, were constrained by protectionism, exchange and immigration restrictions, and bilateral trade agreements. Yet, as this chapter has argued, there was equally an unrelenting global-izing effect to the war. All the world, in one way or another, was brought into this war. The closure of one source of supplies forced the creation of other, more extended supply lines. Logistical and economic warfare dem-onstrated the interconnectedness of world trade. Winners and losers alike emerged from the war with company networks more far-flung than those with which they had begun. The trend for British shipping was relative decline and shrinkage – another piece in the postwar paradigm – but indi-vidual companies such as P & O, Cunard, and Ellermans extended their route and market structures.

The experience of neutrals or of marginal combatants confirms still further the globalizing patterns advanced by war. Companies from these lands made out like bandits. The freight rate for Indian jute, hemp, and cotton, for example, less than 18 shillings per ton in summer 1914, was at 322s 6d in 1917 and 400s in 1918.[68] Navigating the submarine-infested Mediterranean waters, Greek ships sank in droves during the war. But, excepting the men who went down with their ships, the war, with its scar-city of tonnage and its skyrocketing freight rates, was a boon for Greek shipping. Profits in 1914–1915 alone were double the capitalized value of the fleet. After the war Greek shipowners, perhaps the most highly networked of all, rapidly made up losses, and continued to grow; by the late 1930s Greek shipping ranked ninth among world fleets and consti-tuted the world's second largest collection of dry-cargo trampers. It was also a far more global fleet after the war. Traditionally Greek vessels had plied the Black Sea and Mediterranean bulk cargo trades with northwest Europe. The war sent the fleet to all parts of the world, and even though it regrouped on its traditional routes after 1918 it also continued to expand worldwide. Whereas the Greek fleet had at one time represented zero per-cent of the Argentinian grain trade, more than a million tons of Greek shipping steamed to the Plate in the 1920s and half again as much in the 1930s. More than a quarter of the postwar fleet operated in the Atlantic, Pacific, and Indian oceans.[69]

---

[68] Hook, *Merchant*, 295–296.
[69] Harlaftis, *Greek*, 181–199; PRO/MT 25/87/Part IV, chapter III, pp. 88–89; Sturmey, *British*, 44.

Global extension was also carried out by the Dutch, who opened new routes and increased world infrastructure in shipping and trade. Forced to search for new outlets or sources of supply, East Indies trading companies branched out to New York, Japan, South America, and China, while American farm machinery manufacturers moved into the vacuum left by the exit of German exporters. The huge expansion in the U.S. automobile industry created a voracious market for East Indies rubber and oil. These were the years when the Dutch Mails inaugurated the Java-New York line and the Java-Pacific line to San Francisco.[70] Dutch shipping interests were bloated with cash. Holland Amerika dividends in 1912 and 1913 were 15 percent. These were looked on as banner years, but the 1915 dividend climbed to 50 percent, and the 1916 dividend to 55 percent, before profits tailed off to a still stunning 25 percent in 1917 as harder times beckoned. The Rotterdamsche Lloyd's dividends were far more modest, but during the same period large deposits were made to the company's reserve fund (even though only three ships, or less than 10 percent, of the fleet were sunk in the war). Flush as the war came to an end, and with German competition driven from the seas, Dutch shipping companies collaborated in the creation of a new shipping combine – the VNS – to operate routes to British India, Australia, East Asia, and to the east and west coasts of Africa. Even though they started from a far wider base than the Greeks, by 1920 Dutch shipping and trading too were more globally oriented than they had been in 1914.[71]

Japan's world maritime presence by 1919 was still more striking. So profitable was the war for Japanese shipping that P & O representatives, whose own company had engorged itself on war traffics, spoke of "phenomenal" prosperity, and the Dutch, who did very well themselves out of the war, reported on fortunes raked in by Japanese shipping companies; both braced for strong competition at war's end. The advances were impressive. Net earnings for each war year averaged ten times what they had been before the war. Japanese shipyards constructed nearly a million and a half tons of new ships during the war. Huge shipping concentrations – Suzuki, Kokusai, Yamashita – emerged from the war to rival, and

[70] Leeman, Barkschip, 161–168; Brugmans, Chinavaart, 95–99; ICHVR/76–127/ Jaarverslag 1917; Mees, Internationale, 33, 35; Leonhard Huizinga, "*Take Your Jacket Off:*" *The Chronicle of a Merchant House as Seen against 75 Years of World History* (n.p.: Hagemeyer N.V., 1975), 112, 117; Jonker and Sluyterman, Home, 223–224; AN/F 12/7949/Hollande/13 May 1916; ibid., 7951/Indes néerlandaises/May 1917.

[71] GAR/HAL/Viamar/MMPH 4/Winst- en Verliesrekening, 1912, 1913, 1915, 1916; Wentholt, *Brug*, 148; Leeman, *Barkschip*, 335; Reuchlin, "Handelsvaart," 247–248.

in some cases surpass, NYK and OSK, even though these two liner companies also came out of the war greatly enlarged. The Japanese fleet in 1914 stood at 1,700,000 tons. In 1919 it was up to 2,790,000 tons and surpassed 5 million by the end of the 1930s, at which time it counted for 9 percent of the world's fleet, compared to 4 percent in 1914. More meaningful was the range of services it ran across the world after the war. Before the conflict the largest company, NYK, was sailing to major world markets, and even small tramping charterers, known as *shagaisen*, were venturing across the oceans. But services magnified in number and coverage during and following the war. OSK opened routes to San Francisco, New York, South America, European ports, and Calcutta. In search of cargo for all legs of the journey, it extended its east Africa–Brazil line up to New Orleans and then home via Panama, thus traversing the globe. The new, big combines sent steamers to harbors around the world. Driving this expansion were not simply the vast profits from freight rates and the scarcity of shipping outside of war channels, but denser, and more global, penetration of vacated export markets by Japanese trading companies. As early as 1916 it was apparent that "the European Export Trade of Japan is more and more passing from the Foreign Merchant to the Japanese." Enlarged shipping and trading networks thus complemented and fed into each other, and as a result, global networks expanded but also altered in their configuration. World routes became less Eurocentric. Trading patterns became more geographically heterogeneous. It would take another half century or more before the division of the world into three trading blocs was firmly sketched out; but that pattern, a cornerstone of late-twentieth-century globalization, was already underway by 1918.[72]

The First World War did great damage to European economies, but it is questionable whether it ground prewar globalism to a halt. It is undeniable that market integration broke apart with the war, and where that serves as the definition of globalization then it can be said that an era of deglobalization ensued. If, however, globalization is understood to encompass broader levels of interconnectedness, and consciousness, as this book argues, then the world-circulating effects of the war were nearly endless.

---

[72] NMM/P & O/4/37/Agents' Reports Yokohama, Kobe (quoted on export trade), 31 July 1916, 1917; GAR/Lloyd 1/1550/3 August 1918; Sturmey, *British*, 39; Keiichiro Nakagawa, "Japanese Shipping in the Nineteenth and Twentieth Centuries: Strategy and Organization," in Tsunehiko Yui and Keiichiro Nakagawa, eds., *Business History of Shipping: Strategy and Structure* (Tokyo: University of Tokyo Press, 1985), 1–31; PRO/Ministry of Reconstruction/279/9 August 1917; HAPAG/1135/UA 6/Abschrift. Geschäftslage Brasiliens, p. 3; NA/KJCJL/22/2 June, 10 August 1916.

New infrastructures were created, not only in the elaboration of trade routes between different regions of the world, but also in the engineering of new harbor structures across the seas. Cosmopolitan companies became still more globally inflected. Immigration laws severely tightened the vast voluntary movements before 1914, but far less so outside the Atlantic, while the war introduced waves of refugee flows in which the twentieth century would excel, beginning with a million Russian émigrés dispersed to all parts of the globe. The Russian Revolution, which sent them flying, espoused a world-focused ideology. Indeed it is here that one is reluctant to confine globalism to open flows of trade, people, and capital. In market integration terms, the Soviet Union catches, in dramatic form, the postwar trend toward closed economies. But in ideas, challenges, and agent networks, that revolution contributed to a far more appreciable perception of global linkages in everyday affairs than had been the case before 1917. Undoubtedly the most forceful globalizing consequence of the war was to disperse or widen the centers of transoceanic relations. Cut off from their traditional sources of supply, lands that had previously functioned largely as commodity exporters emerged from the war as processors and incipient manufacturers. Japan and the United States, an ocean or two removed from Europe, now rivaled Europe as organizers of world flows. In this sense, the world after 1914 was a more global domain than the world it replaced.

7

The Time of Troubles

When the First World War ended there remained, for a time, a shortage of shipping. Across the globe, exporters hunted for space on freighters. As late as March 1920, more than 2,000 people in Batavia waited for passage.[1] Shipping companies, anticipating a long, pent-up demand and a rapid return to prewar trades, opened new lines and deluged shipyards with orders. Quickly they were subjected to a rude awakening. Although the 1920s saw world consumption surpass 1913 levels,[2] the ruling conjuncture for two decades was more often marred by contraction. For thirty years before the First World War, per capita rates of growth in world trade averaged close to 35 percent. Between 1913 and 1937, that figure dropped to 3 percent. Europe's share in this trade, formerly two-thirds, fell to half. With 1913 as the index year of 100, trade flows climbed to 135 by 1929. Thereafter they fell steadily and hard. World trade volume in 1932 was down by a quarter, its value by three-fifths. In the second half of the 1930s there was an upward turn in the curve, close to 1929 volume levels and, in seaborne trade, even beyond.[3] But the two-decade figure, compared to the past, remained dismal. Marking the era, and the source of the problems, were warped exchange and capital flows, protective tariffs and imperial preference zones, import quotas, policies of import substitution, and drops in demand relative to productive or

[1] GAR/HAL/Directie 787/9, 20 August 1919, 26 March 1920.
[2] Brugmans, *Tachtig*, 93.
[3] Jonker and Sluyterman, *Home*, 220; Sturmey, *British*, 65; Charles H. Feinstein, Peter Temin, and Gianni Toniolo, *The European Economy between the Wars* (Oxford: Oxford University Press, 1997), 104, 170. Hirst and Thompson, *Globalization*, 54, give still more dire statistics. Sturmey's figures are for world seaborne trade.

carrying capacity. Even earlier, gates had shut on the massive immigration flows across the Atlantic. The defining narrative for these years must be, therefore, one of troubles.

Yet maritime history between the wars cannot be told solely in terms of adversity. In the midst of loss there was adaptation. Beneath restrictive political economies remained an underlying global connectedness; indeed contraction was often accompanied by processes of global extension. The trick is to capture the impact of crisis without missing the elements of resiliency and transition. No maritime sector was left unbuffeted by the Depression. In writing about shipping, ports, and overseas traders, however, it will be important to see how all remained linked with world flows, and how their histories overlapped with wider changes underway since the war.

SEA FLOWS

Private – Watching – Service – Captain – A. Van Heetvelde
For Shipdecks – Holds and Quays
Reliable Unemployed Shipsofficers Supplyed

Letterhead announcing a quayside watch service organized among unemployed ship captains and officers in Antwerp in the 1930s, some of whom had not worked for more than three years and all of whom "no longer had the slightest hope of finding work with the Belgian fleet becoming ever smaller."[4]

Trade

Under any circumstances world shipping after the First World War was going to change. The United States had launched a massive building program during the war. From a fleet of 2 million grt in 1914 it had grown to 10 million tons in 1919 and was only slightly off that figure in the late 1930s. If these elephantine proportions failed to translate into effective deep-sea transport, there were nonetheless more ships, and more American ships, than there had been before the war.[5] The Japanese fleet almost doubled by the beginning of the 1920s and practically tripled by the end of the 1930s. Norway's fleet rose from 2 million tons on the eve of the First World War to nearly 5 million tons on the eve of the Second. The trend continued nearly across the board, propelled by war profits,

---

[4] HAPAG/3065/20 February 1936.
[5] René De La Pedraja, *The Rise and Decline of U.S. Merchant Shipping in the Twentieth Century* (New York: Twayne, 1992), 59–129.

war construction programs, war traffics, and postwar expectations. Even after paring in the 1930s the world's fleet was still some 20 million tons larger than what it had been in 1914.[6]

The central shipping issue after the war was therefore surplus tonnage in respect to trade. Add to this the conversion to motor ships and faster ships in the interwar years. Diesel-powered ships required less bunker space, leaving more for cargo. Faster ships made more voyages per year. Together the two multiplied the effects of over tonnage.[7] The celebrated markers from the interwar years were the great ocean liners, but more appropriate would have been all the ships laid up in harbors or sent to scrap. The second half of the 1920s was a generally prosperous time for world trade and shipping, but on the eve of the Depression more than 3 million tons of ships nevertheless sat in ports.[8] During the depths of the Depression in the summer of 1932, that figure would comprehend only the mothballed tonnage of British ships, approximately 17 percent of the national fleet. Thirty percent of the German fleet was idle in 1932. On the 1st of January 1932, more than a third of Dutch shipping was going nowhere. It is estimated that, at the worst moments of the 1930s, 14 million tons of ships may have lain idle in the world's ports. In 1937, when conditions had improved, 2 million tons still remained laid up.[9] There were other markers, particularly during the brutal first years of the Depression. Freight rates fell as much as 25 or 30 percent, loading rates per ship perhaps more so.[10] Trades collapsed. The Dutch had created the Java-Bengal shipping line expressly to carry Java sugar to India, but indigenous production in India backed by tariffs in the 1930s corroded this trade and did the same for the return carriage of gunnysacks.[11] Human misery was widespread. Ship's officers turned watchmen or sailed as ratings.[12] In his memoirs of the family agency in Merseyside, Edward H. E. Turner described how "at one time there were over seventy ships laid [up] in the river Dart alone and more laid up in other places....

[6] Sturmey, *British*, 38, 75, 91, 117–120, 139; Behrens, *Merchant*, 17; Petersen, *Saga*, 92–93, appendix.
[7] Sturmey, *British*, 74; Petersen, *Saga*, 79–89; Falkus, *Blue*, 173–174.
[8] Petersen, *Saga*, 79.
[9] Falkus, *Blue*, 203; Sturmey, *British*, 67; Wiborg and Wiborg, *Unser*, 260–261; Brugmans, *Tachtig*, 120; Petersen, *Saga*, 79.
[10] Falkus, *Blue*, 203; HAPAG/223/16 September 1937.
[11] GAR/HAL/Directie 785/Brits-Indië reisverslag, 1912, Bombay section; MMM/OA 4B/192/ MacTier reports 1937–1939, Sourabaya; Leeman, *Barkschip*, 143, 212; Brugmans, *Tachtig*, 14, 122; idem, *Chinavaart*, 137–158.
[12] P. M. Heaton, *Lamport and Holt* (Risca, U.K.: The Starling Press, 1986), 55–56.

In 1931 the strain of keeping the business going told so heavily on my Father that he had a nervous breakdown."[13]

In nearly every maritime nation, states were obliged to intervene to rescue or subsidize their national fleets. So touch-and-go were the finances of France's CGT in 1931 that only a state bailout saved the company. Only with British state supports could Cunard build its *Queens*. Rotterdam businessmen rallied to save the Holland Amerika Line, but here too, in the Netherlands, and also in Weimar and Nazi Germany, there was state intervention. All of this came with a price. The French state became majority shareholder and sat on the CGT's board. Cunard agreed to take over the failing White Star Line.[14] Nazi intrusion into shipping affairs was pervasive. The Third Reich reordered routes and set the terms of trading. Its racist ideology, aggressive church policies, and foreign exchange restrictions drove away international passengers.[15] Interference with company organizations was worse. Jews within HAPAG were forced to go, and Jewish identity was purged from the collective memory of the firm, although the firm would have had no meaningful history without it. Progressively there was party pressure to break off all Jewish relations outside the country, accompanied by efforts to Germanize its representations abroad.[16] Where it could, HAPAG fought back hard to preserve its agents and its reputation for trust. The war had demonstrated that companies could survive the worst of conditions, even without ships, but without their networks they were nothing.[17]

Politics and economics thus tore away at older shipping structures; but these were also years of opportunities and new beginnings, as well as crisis, and the creative realignments or advances should not be obscured by the more generalized pall. The CGT, for instance, under Henri Cangardel, made the necessary economies, divested of losing propositions, applied tramping methods, booked cruises, and saw its fortunes rise by the second

---

[13] MMM/Edward W. Turner & Son Collection /F/34, Typewritten history of the firm/74–75.

[14] Barbance, *Histoire*, 259–272; Hyde, *Cunard*, 188–218; Wiborg und Wiborg, *Unser*, 254–275; Wentholt, *Brug*, 172–196, 347; Brugmans, *Tachtig*, 152–156; Reuchlin, "Handelsvaart," 252–253.

[15] HAPAG/3553/Die Lage in nordamerikanischen Passagiergeschäft/30 May 1938.

[16] HAPAG/166/Band 19/24 May 1938; ibid., 3553/Vertraulich Notiz über Personalfragen, 28 April 1936; ibid., 67/Neumann, 14 November 1936; Wiborg and Wiborg, *Unser*, 267–269; Ron Chernow, *The Warburgs: The Twentieth-Century Odyssey of a Remarkable Jewish Family* (New York: Random House, 1993), 274, 286–291, 380–381. Although, despite intense party insistence, the liner *Albert Ballin* was not renamed until fall 1935.

[17] HAPAG/403/2, 5 November 1936 (Ivers & von Staa); HAPAG 454/3 October 1938 (Jamal); HAPAG/3492/Bericht über Australien, 30 April 1938, p. 15.

half of the 1930s.[18] One of Cangardel's winning strategies was to deploy a banana boat fleet in the West Indies trade. Despite the collapse of other commodity traffics, fruit imports to Europe rose sharply after the war and especially in the Depression years. In the mid-1920s the French were importing a scant 62,000 tons of bananas, but that figure close to quadrupled by the early 1930s thanks to initiatives by shipping companies to invest in refrigerated ships and special gear and facilities at the port of Nantes. Britain and Germany saw parallel increases, here too because of initiatives by shipping companies and ports. At roughly the same time that Cangardel was developing the Antilles trade, Hamburg Süd was constructing refrigerated ships, investing in its terminal in Hamburg, and working with Brazilian state and business interests to diversify into fruit and frozen meat exports.[19]

Elsewhere creative strategies emerged amid the aggregate bleakness. British shipping never fully recovered from abandoned networks and markets during the war. Sharp declines in coal exports pared away as much as 1.5 million tons of British tramp shipping. There were also missed opportunities, most famously a pass when Shell put a large part of its tanker fleet on the market.[20] Yet Liverpool's Harrisons, hurt by declines in its cotton and Indian business, refocused its Indian traffic on gunnysack exports to sugar, coffee, and flour shippers in the Caribbean and South America. It also reorganized its route structures to concentrate on more profitable traffics to South America and the West Indies.[21] The poster child of interwar shipping was the Norwegian merchant marine, which invested in fast ships, tanker ships (the Shell ships), and motor ships, and more than doubled its tonnage. Like the Greeks, it too established a worldwide presence after the war, calling at more than 2,000 foreign ports, whereas in 1914 Norwegian ships had been largely concentrated on intra-European trades.[22]

---

[18] Barbance, *Histoire*, 262–276.

[19] SHM/1BB3/61/Le Trafic bananier des colonies et l'aménagement des ports français, 1934; Peter N. Davies, *Fyffes and the Banana: Musa Sapientum, A Centenary History, 1888–1988* (London: Athlone, 1990), 261; Meyer, *Güterumschlagsplatz*, 60. The French banana fleet benefited from Depression-era flagging restrictions, but this appears to have simply encouraged investment. On flag requirements: Wilkins, *Maturing*, 196.

[20] Sturmey, *British* 61–89, 103, 118–129, 386; Wardle, *Steam*, 175–176. On tankers, see Chapter 2.

[21] Hyde, Liverpool, 151–159; idem, *Shipping Enterprise and Management, 1830–1939: Harrisons of Liverpool* (Liverpool: Liverpool University Press, 1967).

[22] HAPAG/1434; Petersen, *Saga*, 74–110; MAE/Asie 1918–1940/Affaires Communes/69/ Messageries Maritimes/29 July 1938.

The scope for expansion, with wider societal and geopolitical effects, was particularly visible in the huge growth in transoceanic oil shipments between the wars. Oil's history in several ways requires some rewriting of these years. Like other industries it too was caught in a cycle of restrictive trade policies, following American implementation of the Smoot-Hawley Tariff Act, but U.S. producers circumvented these by shipping Venezuelan rather than American oil to their European markets.[23] The invention of such "triangular" trades shows how even a choking off of once-open markets generated still more intense forms of global connectedness rather than stifling it altogether. Oil too defied the general conjuncture of collapse and continued to grow as a global industry. Conversion from coal to oil for heating and propulsion, and the rise of a mass automobile market, multiplied oil consumption by as much as sixfold between 1913 and 1937. At the same time oil fields scattered still farther to Latin America, the Persian Gulf, and Southeast Asia. Thus as overseas trade entered an era of constriction the sea became ever more critical to oil flows. Only by building out global maritime infrastructure – tankers, port off-loading and storage areas, and inland distribution networks – was it logistically possible to bring oil drilled an ocean or two away to its ever-voracious sites of consumption. The first steps were taken before 1914, but the interwar years were a period of expansion or maturing on all fronts. Ten million of the world's additional tonnage was composed of tanker fleets. The largest Dutch fleet in 1939 was Shell's Bataafsche Petroleum Maatschappij. Companies developed greater experience and expertise in inland transfer. In Europe, but also overseas, ports constructed special installations to handle and store the highly inflammable material. Significantly the gateway complex at Palembang, in southern Sumatra, consisting of pipelines, storage tanks, a refinery, and jetties, was the East Indies' leading export harbor by the 1930s.[24] Even before the great explosion in oil transport after the Second World War that would have colossal effects on life and politics, but also the shape of shipping and ports, the interchange between oil and the sea was operative on a global scale.

It was thus the tug and pull of national and global impulses, rather than a closure of globalism, that best captures these years from the perspective of shipping. The Dutch may have abandoned free trade and gone

[23] Wilkins, *Maturing*, 210–211.
[24] Petersen, *Saga*, 75, 109–110; Sturmey, *British*, 73–85; Reuchlin, "Handelsvaart," 266–267; Broeze, "Rederij," 204; Van Driel and de Goey, *Rotterdam*, 16–19; Jackson, *History*, 144; De Boer and Westermann, *Eeuw*, 337–338.

over to imperial preferences in their East Indies colony in the 1930s, but just as barriers were going up the Dutch Mails were busy expanding their Java-Pacific line into a round-the-world service.[25] Here was encapsulated the dual edge to the period. Along its route the new Silver-Java-Pacific line sailed in and out of protected market zones, struggling for cargoes, all the while pushing out the global networks of trade. Toward the end of the decade the Mails were prepared to extend service to the Persian Gulf and were contemplating additional calls at South American west coast harbors.[26] The coastal KPM, beneficiary of the imperial preference system, fell into the same pattern. Forced during the Depression to cut services at home, it sent a ship on an exploratory voyage to sound out markets in South Africa, Réunion, Mauritius, and Madagascar. On board were representatives of East Indies trading companies with sample cases. The voyage proved a stunning success, and the KPM in the early 1930s inaugurated a regular line connecting the Indies with the African coast from Mombasa to Capetown. Eastward it prolonged service to Hong Kong and Shanghai and, by the last years of the 1930s, it was linking its African service to the east coast of South America.[27]

As the period drew to a close, Kho Tjiauw Tek, a merchant in Silboga on the far coast of Sumatra, may have been obliged to file for exchange clearance with the Crisis Export Bureau in the Hague. Still, the request, handled through his bankers, the Nederlandsche Handel Maatschappij, concerned fifty cases of gum benzoin (Sea Gull brand) shipped to Galatz in Romania.[28] Strangely, despite world depression, restrictive policies, and gathering war, the world remained a highly connected place.

Passengers

How far did the interwar years go in shutting down the free and overseas circulation of people? It is generally understood that U.S. anti-immigration laws, followed by the economic effects of the Depression, ended the prewar era of massive flows. Adam McKeown, however, has recently described the late 1920s as "one of the high points of global migrations," pointing

[25] The SJPL was a joint venture with the Kerr Line.
[26] Brugmans, *Tachtig*, 132–140, 174–175, 189–193; Jonker and Sluyterman, *Home*, 242–244; Brugmans, *Chinavaart*, 146–147; Delprat, *Reeder*, 134–135; GAR/Lloyd/274/20, 22 March 1939.
[27] De Boer and Westermann, *Eeuw*, 202–207, Bijlages 5, 8; NA/KPM/127/Amstel Travel Report, 1935; ibid., Reisverslag, 22 September–19 October 1938.
[28] NA/Nederlandsche Handel-Maatschappij Collection/7526/30 August 1937.

to the 1.25 million migrants to Southeast Asia in 1927 and another 1.5 million to North Asia in 1929.[29] No less problematical is the irony that the era of foreclosure has also come to represent the last great age of "travel" and an opening toward an age of mass tourism to run riot after the Second World War.[30] There can be no unequivocal answer to the question. In the peak years before the First World War, more than 2 million people had crossed both ways between Europe and America, 2.5 million when Canada is included. Only 10 percent had traveled first class.[31] The great bulk of the trade had been among immigrants, and that traffic was reduced in the 1920s by a very large fraction. The Depression slashed further what remained of business and tourist traffic. French Line totals, for instance, dropped by half between 1929 and 1933.[32] Still, perhaps the more striking fact about sea passage between the wars is not how few but how many people continued to sail the oceans, despite the legal and economic prescriptions against them, and how fundamentally complicit steamship companies were in making this happen.

The numbers first. Voluntary immigration in the West fell fast and hard, but replacing it, to a point, were hundreds of thousands of refugees emanating from Turkey, Russia, and, in the 1930s, central Europe. Migrant flows receded, but did not disappear altogether, and certainly not on all runs. Just one emigration agent claimed to have booked more than 32,000 passengers to South America in the nineteen years he worked as general representative in the Balkans for Hamburg Süd and HAPAG, and then thousands more after 1937 for the Compagnie Maritime Belge.[33] Where old immigrant passage faded, new tourist traffics blossomed. Passenger traffic on the North Atlantic crashed early in the 1920s, falling from 2,578,000 in 1913 to 785,000 in 1924, following the application of strict quotas; but in 1929 it was back up over a million.[34] The 1930s were a golden age for cruises, and not to be forgotten were the several hundred thousand Germans who traveled on Strength through Joy ships between 1934 and 1939.[35]

---

[29] McKeown, "Global," 167, 172 (quoted), 175–176.

[30] Paul Fussell, *Abroad: British Literary Traveling between the Wars* (Oxford: Oxford University Press, 1980); A. J. Norval, *The Tourist Industry: A National and International Survey* (London: Sir Isaac Pitman & Sons, Ltd., 1936), 8, 45.

[31] Drew Keeling, "The Transportation Revolution and Transatlantic Migration, 1850–1914," *Research in Economic History* 19 (1999): 61–62. Rübner, *Konzentration,* 455.

[32] Barbance, *Histoire,* 266.

[33] CMB/E/28/5–12/2 March 1942.

[34] Rübner, *Konzentration,* 455.

[35] Shelley Baranowski, *Strength through Joy: Consumerism and Mass Tourism in the Third Reich* (Cambridge: Cambridge University Press, 2004), 134–154; Wiborg and Wiborg, *Unser,* 284–285.

East of Suez, millions of Asians continued to migrate through the 1920s but also into the 1930s, when the outward flows of Chinese to Southeast Asia, excepting 1932 to 1933, were close to those before the war, and the return flows often heavier.[36] Throughout the 1920s close to 2 million British also emigrated overseas, which was comparable to prewar numbers, except that a far greater percentage headed to white settler lands such as Canada or Australasia. Far fewer – 335,000 – emigrated overseas in the 1930s, but between 1920 and 1939, 854,000 nationals emigrated back to Britain from the empire.[37] Moreover, the East retained its special imperial and expatriate traffics. If Dutch business trip figures are to be believed, all ocean travel to and from Hong Kong in 1934 totaled more than a million.[38] There were also pilgrim ships to Mecca, and, in the most obscene variation on travel, the NKVD prison ships sailing between Vladivostok and Gulag camps in northeastern Siberia.

Millions therefore continued to sail the seas, in all kinds of trades. None of this occurred without the shipping companies. Where there were refugee streams, there were steamship lines, not only as carriers but also as negotiators or intermediaries with help committees. Some sprang into existence for the express purpose of transporting desperate people for money. Hamburg's Arnold Bernstein, who built a highly successful business out of shipping Ford automobiles and tractors to Europe, created the Palestine Shipping Co. in 1935 to carry Jews to Palestine, a short-lived venture but one followed by the shadier voyages of Greek, Turkish, and Balkan vessels with the outbreak of war.[39]

One way the companies coined new traffics was by building new, bigger, and sleeker ships. The most remembered of ocean liners were the generation of fast, supersized transatlantic vessels nearly all conceived – and in some cases first laid down – in the 1920s, but mostly launched in the Depression era of the thirties: NDL's *Bremen* and *Europa*, Italia's *Rex* and *Conte di Savoia*, the CGT's *Normandie*, and Cunard's *Queen Mary*, the latter two nearly twice the size of the *Titanic*. These ships have

[36] Sugihara, *Japan*, 247–250; McKeown, "Global."

[37] Stephen Constantine, "Migrants and Settlers," in Judith Brown and W. M. Roger Louis, eds., *The Oxford History of the British Empire* (Oxford: Oxford University Press 1999), vol. 4, 163–167, 177.

[38] GAR/Lloyd 2/S2021/Reisrapport #159.

[39] GAR/HAL/Passage 8/14, 24 July 1923; Arnold Kludas, *Die Geschichte der deutschen Passagier-Schiffahart*, vol. 5 (Augsburg: Weltbild, 1994), 100–103, 106–109; Wentholt, *Brug*, 207; Witthöft, *HAPAG*, 83; Wiborg and Wiborg, *Unser*, 292–295; Bernard Wasserstein, *Britain and the Jews of Europe, 1939–1945* (Oxford: Clarendon Press, 1979), 53–57, 60–67.

largely been seen as emblems of modernity for their revolutionary engi-neering and the replication of streamlined features in their exterior and interior design. From the inside, however, the view was very much that of a business proposition.[40] The obsession with size and speed was driven by flagship prestige considerations, but also by the realization that two fast, giant ships on the North Atlantic run could do the work of three. Cunard decided to stake its future on "the laying down of new ships of immense size and power which would at one and the same time sustain prestige and increase trading capabilities." Twins were planned for the Cunard's and the French Line's premier liners, the *Queen Elizabeth*, which was only finished in time to begin its career as a troopship, and the *Brittany*, which was never built because of the war. Still, both the *Normandie* and the *Queen Mary*, when put in service, increased market share and abso-lute number of passengers.[41]

At the same time all these companies marketed a new mass concept – tourist third cabin, as it was labeled – to create or cater to a new class of traveler in the hope of replacing lost immigration trades.[42] Whereas the new superliners divided between first class and tourist cabins, generating higher passenger numbers in each, some slower vessels were converted to single, tourist class as an added inducement.[43] If not fully able to match previous totals, tourist passage was the great breakthrough in the inter-war years.

Increasingly, steamship lines veered wholly into the tourism business. The history of travel between the wars cannot be written without their initiatives. Drawing on expertise, global positioning, and their ability to create or creatively use networks, steamship companies were among the great fomenters of tourism's spread between the wars. HAPAG organized series of what it called "study trips" for German professional groups to North America and more adventurous tours to Cuba, Mexico, and Central America.[44] Where no networks existed HAPAG assembled them. In a 1937 trip to the west coast of South America HAPAG's Stephenson met with shipping agents, travel bureaus, railroad executives, and gov-ernment officials to lay the groundwork for greater tourist travel. In

---

[40] See, for example, the mundane details – baggage difficulties, passengers hurt by medi-cine balls, comment on the cheese delivery – in AAFL/CGT/1997 004 5116/*Normandie* Rapport Général de Voyage, 25 May to 6 June 1938.
[41] Hyde, *Cunard*, 190 (quoted), 234–255; Barbance, *Histoire*, 266, 276, 291–294.
[42] See Keeling, "Transportation," 49–50, for pre-1914 precedents.
[43] Hyde, *Cunard*, 236; Lorraine Coons and Alexander Varias, *Tourist Third Cabin: Steamship Travel in the Interwar Years* (New York: Palgrave Macmillan, 2003), 25–53.
[44] HAPAG/188/Liste der Reisenden, 1938, pp. 33–37; HAPAG/190.

Valparaiso Stephenson conferred with the Department of Tourism to ease visa applications and entry conditions. He discussed fare reductions and special cars with the Chilean state railway. In Arequipa he had a long talk with the director of the International Railroad about developing European tourist traffic through southern Peru. In Lima, exploiting good relations between HAPAG's agent, Ostern & Co., and state authorities, Stephenson hosted a breakfast for government ministers who promised support. Further conversations with Touring Club managers, in possession of excellent ties to the president, led directly to state initiatives to expand the number of modern hotels at tourist sites.[45]

In empires, liner companies built or sponsored hotels and promoted tourist services. The CGT established a chain of hotels across French North Africa and tied these together with a motor pool of touring cars; a French ministry official later attributed to the line the "opening of North Africa to international tourism."[46] In the East, the Dutch Mails routinely canvassed among the big estates, oil and mining companies, government residents, religious orders, and every other expatriate circle to collect home-leave bookings, although in big cities such as Bombay and Shanghai they also worked with travel agents to sell regional tourist trade. On Java and Bali, and then on Sumatra, the Mails, the KPM, and the Dutch travel agency Nitour, with which they were closely associated, developed extensive plans to create an East Indies tourist industry.[47]

Probably the most successful way shipping companies lured people onto the seas was to sell cruises. The history of cruises extended well back into the nineteenth century and had developed substantially since the 1890s, but in these overtonnaged years all liner companies entered the cruise business and made it a regular part of their slow-season schedule. In the 1930s practically any cruise was cheaper than laying-up costs.[48]

---

[45] HAPAG/444 (Stephenson report). Stephenson's trip was occasioned by a new liner, the *Patria*, beginning service on this route in the late 1930s.

[46] Barbance, *Histoire*, 241–244, 263; CAC/800115/3/"Note sur la Société des Voyages & Hôtels Nord-Africains," n.d. (quoted); Miège, "Maroc," 65, on Paquet doing the same in Morocco; Ellen Furlough, "*Une leçon des choses*: Tourism, Empire, and the Nation in Interwar France," *French Historical Studies* 25 (Summer 2002): 451.

[47] GAR/Lloyd 2/S2021/Reisrapport #148; GAR/Lloyd 1/1575/26 June 1930, 6 October 1931; GAR Lloyd 1/1577/29 May 1934, 26 May 1937; GAR/Lloyd 1/1571/25 May 1949; GAR/Lloyd 1/814/Herstelplan, 14 October 1948; De Boer and Westermann, *Eeuw*, 177–193; 389–393.

[48] Arnold Kludas, *Vergnügungsreisen zur See: Eine Geschichte der deutschen Kreuzfahrt* (Hamburg: Convent Verlag, 2001), vol. 1; Ferry de Goey, "De Holland Amerika Lijn, Carnival Cruises en de cruise industrie in de twintigste eeuw," *Tijdschrift voor zeegeschiedenis* 26 (2007): 17–38; HAPAG/3305; Wardle, *Steam*, 152; Seiler, *Südamerika*,

Company dossiers on cruises attest to their growing importance and again to how organization, expertise, and networks were the fundament of world circulation. Everything passengers came to take for granted – schedules, ports of call, arrivals, local arrangements, and excursions – were meticulously worked out in advance through consultations with agents, nautical departments, travel agencies, and ship captains, especially over the question of accessibility and anchorages in rarely frequented ports.[49] The wealth of information Swires sent Cunard about berthing options, river conditions, local transport, and provisioning in Hong Kong and Shanghai for the round-the-world cruises of *Laconia* and *Samaria* in 1922 could only come from professionals with years of on-the-spot experience.[50]

Just how hard steamship companies worked to sell overseas passages, and the networks they could deploy to accomplish this, can be seen in the extensive travels Holland Amerika canvassers made through the United States. Almost certainly they called on an organization originally constructed for prewar immigration trades.[51] Canvassers visited (among many others) H. W. T. Searle in Port Arthur Texas, "a most enthusiastic sub-agent," with many contacts throughout the region and prepared "on the slightest provocation" to show HAL promotional films to schools, colleges, club meetings, and "gatherings of all sorts"; Ona Brown and Ela Hockaday (of the Hockaday School) in Dallas, both "organizers" of groups traveling to Europe; Fred L. Haskett Travel Service, "one of our most active ones in Dallas," who contributed $7,798.71 worth of business for a North Cape (Norway) cruise; W. T. Yohn of the Missouri Pacific Railroad in Joplin, with whom the HAL canvasser visited a Mr. L. P. Buchanan, "veteran traveler," and sold him two cabin bookings on the *Rotterdam*'s South American cruise, one for himself and his wife and one he planned to "dispose of" to friends; Alta Ruffin, Joplin's clerk of the court, who received all applications for passports, although as an "agent" she had been inactive for some years; J. F. De Young in Orange City, Iowa, a town of only 1,700 inhabitants, but 90 percent of Dutch origin with more Dutch towns in the vicinity, because De Young was "well

---

150–158; Wentholt, *Kurs*, 262; Wiborg and Wiborg, *Unser*, 280–285; Coons and Varias, *Tourist*, 53–62.

[49] See especially HAPAG 2797, 2805; GAR/HAL/Passage 793, 821.

[50] SOAS/JSS II 2/1/Box 37/25 May, 25 July, 2 November, 21 November 1922.

[51] Torsten Feys, "A Business Approach to Transatlantic Migration: The Introduction of Steam-Shipping on the North Atlantic and Its Impact on the European Exodus, 1840–1914" (Ph.D. diss., European University, 2008), 345–346.

known in this county and ... is very faithful to our Line," having turned over $2,200 worth of business for HAL that year alone; Joe Folkman of Akers, Folkman, Lawrence Company, travel agents in Cleveland who put up the HAL representative, Elliot Liman, at his home and introduced him to "Mrs. Kirtz, whom I am pleased to state will go on the Volendam cruise (a party of four)," a sale quite likely made by Liman at the home; Carl Giesse of the Central Trust Bank in Cincinnati; Mr. Southwell of the Merkle Bank and Trust Co. in Hazelton, Pennsylvania, who organized local radio broadcasts featuring HAL cruises; Professor Bradley at Cornell, who "is also our agent.... He is desirous of obtaining the college business and is going to appoint an undergraduate as our representative"; the president's assistant, Roberts, at Hobart College, "who promises to select a good organizer for us"; Dr. J. C. Lyons, "our agent," at Chapel Hill; contacts at William and Mary and the University of Virginia; and Ethel Winterfield in the Spanish Department at Randolph-Macon Woman's College, "who expects to organize a party of from ten to fifteen girls for next summer. We talked over plans for an itinerary using the sailing of the s.s. VOLENDAM."[52]

Across the Atlantic the slogs of HAL canvasser Van Dongen revealed the same dogged efforts:

Wednesday 7 October: This morning I was with Dr. van der S ... and Mr. McGillevray of the Canadian trade delegation ... among other things to view films that might suitably be used for emigration purposes. After that I visited the Travel Bureau "Hilversum" in Hilversum and the Travel Bureau "Bussum" in Bussum.

Tuesday 8 October: In Nimegen I visited the Travel Bureau Centropa. At Mook I visited Heer Hendriks, agent. At Gennep I visited Heer v. Riet who is going to emigrate with his family (12 or 15 persons) early next year to Canada, probably Ontario.... At Mill I visited Heer Gierzen, agent there.[53]

The HAL went after all possible traffics. In 1937 its Brussels agent was convincing the Société Verviétoise de Voyages, a Catholic travel agency in Verviers specializing in excursions by coach, to convert to cruises and sea travel.[54] A decade earlier, thwarted by the U.S. immigration laws, the line opened a passenger service to Cuba and Mexico and ordered four combination freight and passenger ships, each designed to carry nearly a thousand people in third class during the seasonal flux. Agent Dussaq in

[52] GAR/HAL/Passage 725 (1933–1937) and 614 (1928).
[53] GAR/HAL/Passage 842/Reisrapporten van Van Dongen, 1935–1938.
[54] GAR/HAL/Passage 899/7 April 1937.

Havana converted its ground floor into a "steerage office," and hired a porter to work the cafés where Spanish migrants hung out.[55] At roughly the same time Manoil Spiegler, a recruiting agent in Jassy and Bucharest, and almost certainly a prewar emigrant agent for the company, was prepared to deliver peasants from Zevenburg, or Siebenburg, for settlement in Canada. Technically, this traffic was inadmissible. Canadian preferences were limited to Hungarian, Yugoslav, or Czech farmers only, and although Zevenburg had originally been settled by Germans and lay in a part of Transylvania formerly Hungarian, it was, after the war, handed over to Romania. Holland Amerika, however, persisted, selling the Zevenburgers' qualities to a Canadian immigration official in Antwerp: "These peasants know their work, are Christian, are hardened against heat and cold, wish to leave their land for good because they hate the Rumanians." The overture produced the desired effect.[56]

The bipolarity of restrictive policies and economic crisis, yet mass travel on the seas, becomes, then, less paradoxical when set against the efforts of shipping companies to fill their ships. By mobilizing their transnational networks, they made possible, for others, transnational experiences. If anything, tourism or refugee dispersal simply shifted connectedness into a new key. The presence of agents in Arequipa, Peru, or in southern Sumatra, or in Joplin, Missouri, all for the purpose of selling ocean travel, captures the urgency of closures in these years, but also the abiding openings to world passage.

PORTS

No main port of Europe was untouched by the war. The extreme case was Antwerp, where stiff resistance, then fall and occupation, produced four years of closure and penury. Time series on traffic through the port simply skip over the years 1914 to 1918. Hamburg handled more than 25 million tons of cargo in 1913. Blockade, and the scattering, sequestration, or annihilation of its fleet and trading connections, drove that figure down to 1.3 million tons in 1915, a loss approximately of 95 percent of its prewar traffic. For the remainder of the war, the best the port could do was to double output to 2.6 million tons. Dutch shipping reaped huge profits during the better part of the war, but the port of Rotterdam saw

---

[55] Wentholt, *Brug*, 111, 156, 159–160; GAR/HAL/Passage 266/13 August 1921, 3 November 1921.
[56] GAR/HAL/Passage 8/30 March 1924.

its Rhine and seaborne traffic drop precipitously. At the other end of the spectrum, Le Havre's infrastructure was overwhelmed by war traffic. Four times as much grain as ever before was off-loaded at Le Havre. But so disorganized were conditions, particularly through the rail choke point, that at certain moments it was necessary to close down the stations. War revealed how structurally unsuited Le Havre was to assume a leading role on the continent. Liverpool and London were also clogged through the war, but only because of the disruption in normal loading and discharge patterns. With less tonnage available for seaborne commerce, and other ships sunk shy of safe haven, both ports recorded a significant decrease in prewar traffics.[57]

In one sense, then, the interwar history of ports begins with the recovery that followed the war. The revival of Hamburg, a port starting so low, and losing so much, shows this well. At war's end, this was a city with a toy fleet and overseas trading networks in shreds, yet within a decade harbor traffic was denser than ever.[58] Rarely has the idea of the main port as "a local patrimony transmitted from generation to generation" proved more a truism. The resurgence was driven by beneficial rail rates and export-favoring hyperinflation,[59] but no less by the deep investment in knowledge and skills, and by the extraordinary comeback of HAPAG, Hamburg Süd, and Hamburg-based merchant firms around the world. Recognizing how closely its fate was tied to its harbor, HAPAG worked hard to funnel in traffic.[60] In adversity perhaps more than in affluence, port networks proved their intrinsic value.

But conditions had changed, and these disadvantaged the port as much as favored it. The city's big emigration flows wilted. There were losses to Danzig and Gdynia.[61] The spectacular success in synthetic nitrogen production during the war brought Hamburg's big Chilean nitrate trade to an end, and the re-export coffee trade with Scandinavia was lost.[62] Although in many ways still the model port, Hamburg now battled

---

[57] BH/National Institute of Statistics/"Zeeverkeer" and "Goederenverkeer statistics; Kludas, *Hafen*, 148; Vigarié, *Grands*, 449–468; PRO/MT 25/6/#72073/19 March 1918; Bell, *Port*, 64; Hyde, *Liverpool*, 142–143.

[58] Hamburg, Staatsarchiv/DHSG II/S VI B1.53.11/Vulcanhafen, 28 September 1928, 9 March 1929; Wendemuth and Böttcher, *Port*; Keuster, *Concurrence*, 67.

[59] HAPAG/1411; Meyer, *Güterumschlagsplatz*, 25–27, 41.

[60] See Chapter 2.

[61] SHM/1BB3 61/6 March 1935.

[62] Hauschild-Thiessen, *Zwischen*, 221, 225; Peter Hayes, *Industry and Ideology: I. G. Farben in the Nazi Era* (Cambridge: Cambridge University Press, 1987), 10–12; HAPAG/1411; Backx, *Haven*, 223–226; Meyer, *Güterumschlagsplatz*, 57–58.

Antwerp for second place on the continent, both well behind Rotterdam in total throughput figures.[63]

So in another sense the interwar history of ports began with deep structural changes bequeathed or advanced by the war. No one who wrote about ports in the interwar years failed to notice the altered environment. Of the ruptures and deviations, three in particular ate at the foundations of Europe's main ports. First was the displacement of capital, marketing, and trading functions beyond the Old World. Second was import substitution. The war's interruption of flows encouraged home industry development, and Depression-era politics pushed the trend further. Third was direct purchasing by manufacturers. Port income from entrepot functions increasingly receded to the hinterland. The process reached back to the transportation and communication revolutions of the nineteenth century, but the war speeded it up by undermining merchants' power to extend credit to suppliers, and also there were bigger industrial combines by 1918.[64] Lurking in all three were globalizing tendencies that would reach beyond Eurocentrism, even if future decentralization was masked by compressions in trade.[65]

The compressions hit hard, especially in basic trades, but in no way did they fall evenly across the board. Coal exports slumped after the war but oil imports grew. Britain's export of cotton textiles was permanently damaged, but automobile export created new traffics, while greater use of refrigerated ships made possible wider consumption of meat, fruits, and vegetables from distant sources. Port statistics crashed in the early 1930s, but by the end of the decade the numbers had rallied (see Table 4).

What is necessary, therefore, is to see how this roller-coaster ride, with steep plummets over the top, yet grinding, steady climbs back up the incline, played out in different ports to grasp the interaction between networks and history. Three experiences – those of Le Havre, Antwerp, and Liverpool – provide three different versions of the exchange. Le Havre first, because it shows the contractions inherent in postwar forces where networks were already bounded. Antwerp second, because it provides the

---

[63] Horst Sanmann, *Die Verkehrsstruktur der nordwesteuropäischen Seehäfen Antwerpen, Rotterdam, Amsterdam, Bremen und Hamburg und ihre Wandlungen von der Jahrhundertwende bis zur Gegenwart* (Hamburg: Schiffahrts-Verlag "Hansa," 1956), 49, 83–101.

[64] SA/MA 36/Havenbedrijf 63337/Lenssens, pp. 1–13; Vigarié, *Grands*, 448–449, 521–534, 558; Backx, *Haven*, 8–10, 219–221; Meyer, *Güterumschlagsplatz*, 35–37.

[65] A. G. Hopkins, "History," 29, on import substitution, has made this same point.

TABLE 4. *Seaborne Cargo Traffic Handled in Metric Tons between the Wars*

Ports	1913	1929	1933	1938
Hamburg	25,458,000	28,800,000[d]	19,580,000	25,741,628
Bremen	7,166,956	c. 6,500,000	c. 4,300,000[c]	8,966,878
Rotterdam	28,145,045	37,831,643	c. 23,000,000	42,370,990
Antwerp	18,871,935	26,066,683	18,952,897	23,578,949[e]
London	–	–	34,300,000	42,078,000[f] 44,600,000[f]
Liverpool	–	–	–	11,586,000
Le Havre	3,847,000[f] 4,395,137[d]	4,215,000[f] 5,471,919[d]	5,966,687[d]	6,688,000[f] 8,580,000[g]
Marseille	9,044,968	9,151,000	8,321,421[d]	9,955,000

See Table 1, Chapter 1 for information and caveats about sources.

[d] Vigarié/SHM documents. For 1933, and probably for 1913 and 1929, the figures include riverborne goods traffic.

[b] Harburg Wilhemsburg and Altona were included in statistics beginning with 1929.

[c] This figure is for 1932.

[d] This figure is from 1932.

[e] Antwerp turnover in 1937 was 28,367,858 before a strike raised port costs. See discussion of interwar Antwerp, below.

[f] Koomans/DLA.

[g] Vigarié/Koomans.

Sources: HAPAG/1411; De Keuster, *Concurrence*, 141; BH/National Institute of Statistics/ Goederenverkeer; DLA/Trade of the Port of London; SHM/1BB3/61/Le développement du Port autonome du Havre, 1931; ibid., Le trafic du Port du Havre en 1933; ibid., Mouvement des ports maritimes, 1929, 1932; Vigarié, *Grands*, Atlas, Document XI; Olivesi and Pierrein, "Marseille," 456; Weinhauer, *Alltag*, 29; Frank Broeze, "The Political Economy of a Port City in Distress: Hamburg and National Socialism, 1933–1939," *International Journal of Maritime History* 14 (December 2002): 3; Loyen and van de Laar, "Cargo-Handling," 78; Havenbedrijf der Gemeente Rotterdam/Jaarverslag 1938, p. 7; Koomans, "Port," 113.

alternative perspective, even as war and depression unsettled the strongest of ports. Liverpool third, as a port in between, because it was beset by serious problems yet possessed the networks and resources to cope.

Le Havre's experience between 1914 and 1939 was largely encapsulated in what became of its trading position. Before 1914 Le Havre led all French ports in the value of tonnage that passed through its harbor. Its merchant functions, and the wealth these injected into the city, were reflected in its futures markets in cotton, coffee, cocoa, pepper, sugar, hides, and copper. Among European ports it was a leader in cotton and coffee imports. All of these trades, however, depended on overseas connections that were hammered, then constricted, by the war and its economic consequences. Despite the heavy flows that overburdened the harbor, wartime conditions were inimical to trading. Overseas there were "amputations." Connections within Europe shut down or were expropriated by unfettered neutrals. To dampen speculation in formerly mundane but now increasingly scarce commodities, state controls of exchanges, and obligatory quotas, discombobulated markets and depleted stocks. At war's end, Le Havre's merchant structures were in sorry condition, yet this in itself should not have accounted for the difficulties that followed. Other ports were battered worse by the interregnum. Key commodity markets in the city in fact rebounded with the rest of maritime commerce in the best years of the 1920s. The problem was that Le Havre's state-charged networks left international trading prospects especially vulnerable to structural changes and Depression trade wars, and that even creative adaptations were written into this dynamic.

Le Havre's coffee trade tells this story best. Before the First World War, Le Havre and Hamburg were Europe's greatest coffee-importing ports. At war's end, stocks were down to about 6 percent of their prewar norms, but during the 1920s they rebuilt to the point that Le Havre surpassed Hamburg as the leading coffee importer on the continent. Prewar positions, however, were not regained. Re-exporting markets had disappeared in the course of the war, and so much traffic had transferred to Amsterdam and Rotterdam that the two Dutch cities combined had edged past Hamburg and were challenging Le Havre for first place in Europe. Worse followed in the 1930s when Brazil raised tariff rates on French imports and France retaliated with a tripling of charges on Brazilian coffee imports, despite the fact that the nation's second port was the world's second leading entrepot for the distribution of Brazilian beans. In 1934 commercial relations with Brazil were broken altogether, forcing Havre merchants to purchase their coffee stocks on the New York market. In the same year, additional entrepot surcharges were piled on. Not until 1936 were relations regularized with Brazil. In that year, however, the government turned its guns on Haiti for nonpayment of loans and cut commercial relations, again despite the fact that more than half of the Haitian coffee crop traded over the Havre market. For nearly a decade, then, national policies had a punishing effect on the port. Between 1910 and the 1930s, French consumption of coffee grew by nearly 60 percent while Havre stocks dropped to approximately one-eighth of what they had been at the beginning of the century. Whereas coffee re-exports had averaged close to 50,000 metric tons in the first decade of the century, between 1936 and 1938 the port's re-exports were a paltry 2,675 tons. Part of the loss was made up by new imports from the French empire. It has been argued[66] that an increasing turn to colonial sourcing provided Le Havre firms a shelter in the crisis and a platform for greater international engagement following decolonization. Yet the lure of colonial coffee was its protected market and price supports, a preference symptomatic of French maritime trajectories in the century; and if later initiatives resulted in more expansive trading between former colonies and third parties, this often came at the cost of bypassing Le Havre's harbor altogether.

The coffee wars were representative of how vulnerable port interests were in a state more continentally than maritime focused and where networks tended to center on Paris. From the beginning of the postwar years, a series of government restrictive measures corroded the bases on which Le Havre fortunes had been built before 1914. The state restricted export of capital. In certain commodities entrepot operations were hampered. With the Depression came licensing controls that could have been devised by Joseph Heller. Importers were licensed to import the same quantities as the previous year, but with no distinction between the original or intermediate source of purchase. Consequently, importers who had exploited momentarily favorable conditions to buy x amounts of y over competitor markets, were licensed in the next year to buy the same amounts of y *but* in the same markets regardless of circumstances. Smart trading required flexibility, but this was denied. In the late 1930s, the port's traditions as an international entrepot simply were crumbling away. In 1913 five commodities alone – coffee, cotton, cocoa, pepper, and skins – produced 104,996 metric tons of re-exports, with all the wealth this bestowed on in-city operations. Between 1936 and 1938, the average for *all* re-exports, excepting bulk cargoes of grain, coal, and oil, amounted to 9,736 tons. Le Havre became the classic case of the subordination of the *horizon marin* to the *horizon terrestre*.

Home networks, meanwhile, were weak reeds on which to lean. Hinterland connections had always been comparatively constrained, and efforts to reel in Alsatian traffic after Versailles, as we shall see, came largely to naught. There remained little in the way of local ship ownership after the Panama Canal wiped out the Havre sailing fleet. Along France's Atlantic coast there was competition from Rouen and Dunkirk, but also smaller ports that possessed "rights" accorded by state-subsidized shipping. Ironically, so powerful was port labor that no strike wracked the city during the great strike movement of 1936. Nevertheless all the

---

[66] Malon, *Le Havre*, 66–79, 221–238, 356–362, 597–607.

accoutrements of 1930s politics – mass protests, workers' actions, higher wages and benefits in the Popular Front era, employer counteroffensives, and international intrigues – were present in Le Havre, and these produced a turbulence and added costs that the port could ill afford.

The *bilan* was not altogether negative. There was serious interwar investment in the port, endowing it with a modern petroleum harbor and state-of-the-art passenger installations. As a passenger port, Le Havre outshone all rival continental harbors west of the Rhine. But deeper trends were not encouraging. Tonnage figures, which in 1933 actually exceeded 1929 levels, reflected a rise in oil imports rather than the more valuable general cargo trades of the Belle Epoque. Investments positioned Le Havre for passenger and oil business, but the one possessed too little of a future and the other too much, presaging the role that oil imports, or bulk cargoes in general, would play in supporting its international rankings over the second half of the century. As an entrepot, the city's best days were behind it. Without superior networks, Le Havre's postwar adjustment was toward less rather than greater radius, at best toward a "*bourse nationale*."[67]

The corrective was offered by Antwerp, although one would have been hard put to imagine this in 1918, or in the crushing first years of the Depression. No main port was more victimized by the war than this seaport. Attacked, fired, and occupied, Antwerp during those four epic years might just as well have been some memory from antiquity, asleep beneath the sands until war's end scraped away the veils and disclosed basins, docks, quays, installations – a complete harbor once used but fallen silent. Not even the Germans could do anything with it, since the exit to the sea traversed Dutch, hence neutral, territory. Their departure was not without consequence. Before 1914 there had been thousands of Germans residents in the city, many key to the shipping and merchant business of the port. Anti-German fury for the years of hardship and destruction led to resolutions, expulsions from the chamber of commerce, plundering of German establishments, and a mass exodus of people, capital, knowledge, expertise, market skills, and connections. As German merchants left the port German preferential railroad rates took more cargo away from the Scheldt and the Maas and up to the Weser and the Elbe. Antwerp,

[67] Vigarié, *Grands*, 452–474, 493–534 (quoted "amputations," 452, "*bourse nationale*," 458); SHM/1BB3/61/Havre reports 1931, 1933; ibid., Mouvement des ports maritimes/1929; Backx, *Haven*, 225, 229; John Barzman, "Port Labour Relations in Le Havre, 1928–1947," *International Journal of Maritime History* 9 (December 1997): 83–106.

like Rotterdam, had risen on the German tide, but with its ebbing those ties would have to be reconstructed or compensated for by other hinterlands. That would not be easy. Trade in other sectors suffered from the war. South American exports, once 14 percent of goods shipped out of Antwerp, were to peel back to 8 percent.[68]

No less afflicted by economic collapse and Depression-era politics, Antwerp saw its port throughput fall by a third between 1929 and 1932, from more than 26,000,000 tons to 17,383,000 tons, or less than 1913 figures.[69] This was moreover a city with perhaps 14,000 to 18,000 dockers, a tough-minded employers group that preferred negotiations from strength, and intractable problems of inadequate wages, casual labor, and recruiting abuses despite periodic reforms, all magnified by the crushing yet volatile climate of the 1930s. An explosive strike in 1936, settled by higher wages, had a powerful effect on the port's attractiveness. Port authorities were besieged with visits from Swiss firms or their Antwerp forwarders and representatives describing the tremendous pressure they were under to take their business elsewhere, because *"Antwerp is too expensive."*[70] Port throughput, which had climbed back up to 28,368,000 tons in 1937, fell back roughly 17 percent in 1938.

Still, twice between 1918 and 1937 Antwerp clawed its way out of the hole, both times ascending to all time highs. Resilience, borne of strategies, initiatives, and entrenched networks, contrasted boldly with the marionette-like movements on the Seine. If sliding coffee markets told Le Havre's story, Antwerp's bid for the postwar Alsatian trade, pursued with brazen single-mindedness, was a far different tale. In search of new traffics, Antwerpeners all but wrote the script for Belgian economic negotiations right after the war. Seconded by industrialists in eastern France, who preferred to import and export through Antwerp, they won an exemption from surtaxes for goods cleared and transited through Belgian harbors but destined for Alsace-Lorraine. Thus bolstered by the state networks so often denied Le Havre, and by networks to the recovered

[68] Vigarié, *Grands*, 485–486; DHSG II/S XXI D1.24/15 September 1937; Seberechts, "Political," 34–35; Loyen, "Shipping Movements and Cargo Flows: A Quantitative Analysis of the Momentum in the Seaport of Antwerp (1860/1900–2000) in Blomme et al., *Momentum*, 107; Ilmari Wäänänen, *Rotterdam als Seehafen unter besonderer Berücksichtigung des Konkurrenzkampfes mit Antwerpen* (Weida i. Thür: Thomas & Hubert, 1930), 104–113; Backx, *Haven*, 226–227.

[69] BH/National Institute of Statistics/Goederenverkeer; PRO/FO 371/18786/Document 1325/18 February 1935.

[70] SA/MA 36/Havenbedrijf 24272/Leeman to C. [Camille] Huysmans, Burgemeester, 8 October 1937.

territories, the port achieved customs parity with the northern French harbors – although this was no parity at all, as Antwerp's superior liner connections, its reputation for cheap and fast service, its suppleness, its geographical position, and its favorable national rail rates made it no match for its French rivals.

In the years to come those networks were repeatedly called on to solidify Antwerp's position. The state subsidized barge transport costs when an agreement to open rapid waterway access to the Rhine was scuttled by Rotterdam interests. Better yet, city networks rallied to win a huge contract for Alsatian export of potash. Both Dunkirk and Le Havre made overtures but were met with rebuffs. Neither could compete with Antwerp's locational and cost advantages. "Be cheaper than Antwerp and we will come," Dunkirk was told, a challenge it could not meet. Le Havre could not sell the slow creep through all the locks that lay between it and Alsace, nor its rail line. Antwerp held better cards, but it also broke with traditions and agreed to long-term rental concessions and to building a special terminal to bag its game. Some 400,000-plus tons of potash in one direction, grain in the other, moved up and down the Rhine between Antwerp and Strasbourg in the late 1920s. As a bonus, trade with Strasbourg opened a gateway to Switzerland and helped renew German ties.[71] The strategy of rallying local networks and building new ones continued deep into the 1930s. Opened in 1939, the Albert Canal joined Antwerp to Liège and the Meuse, and hence one more gateway into eastern France. When threatened with the loss of French steel exports to Dunkirk on the eve of the war, the port mobilized every contact it could – local forwarders, Belgian rail officials, port representatives abroad, the Belgian consul in Dunkirk – to hold on to the trade.[72]

Comparisons with archrival Rotterdam are meaningful. On the surface of things, Rotterdam was by far the more successful port. Between the wars Rotterdam shot well ahead of its continental rivals and may even have surpassed London by the late 1930s to become Europe's largest port in terms of seaborne cargo. Bigger and more technologically advanced, Rotterdamers should not have had to worry about Antwerp in these years, yet that was exactly the reverse of the matter, and for good reason. Antwerp's capture of Alsatian traffic came largely at Rotterdam's

[71] Vigarié, *Grands*, 485–504 (quoted 500); Frank Seberechts, "Le port d'Anvers et le trafic des potasses d'Alsace, 1920–1950, *Revue Belge d'histoire contemporaine* 29 (1999): 91–143; AN/F 14/16427/Concurrence Dunkerque-Ports Belges, 24 October 1935.

[72] SA/MA 36/Havenbedrijf 24272; AN/F 14/16427/24 October 1935, 2 July 1937, 2 August 1938.

expense. Between the interwar years, Antwerp invested heavily where it was weak, especially in inland waterway connections and in building up its bulk cargo traffic. Rotterdam invested where it was strongest, in bulk cargo handling, with superb results but paradoxically counter to what it had identified as its greatest need: increasing the higher-value general cargo proportion of its throughput mix. Antwerp was therefore a far more diverse and balanced port by 1939 than Rotterdam. Rotterdam's throughput figures, if staggering, mostly represented transit traffic to and from Germany. The autarchic policies of National Socialism drove home the vulnerability of the port to command centers over which it possessed little control. To be sure, both ports, if periodically battered, were effectively winners after 1918, as the balance of power in northern Europe shifted in their direction. Still, if one were looking for a success story in challenging times, Antwerp was the better port to turn to.[73]

Liverpool was anything but, yet it too demonstrated how ports coped after the war, even when pressure was especially severe. This was a port against which practically every card in the deck was stacked. Liverpool had been Britain's premier emigration port, but that trade was largely gone, and much of the newer tourist business reoriented on Southampton's deep-water port south of London. Liverpool was Britain's premier export port, but British exports declined in most markets after the war. In terms of value, Liverpool's top trade by far was cotton goods, but cotton exports were wracked by import substitution, drops in purchasing power among customers abroad, competition from Japan, or disruption of key markets like India, where boycott of British goods and devaluation of the rupee hit cotton manufacturers hard. Decreases in exports in turn meant decreases in imports of raw cotton, another massive Liverpool trade. Liverpool was a shipping company's port, but seven major Liverpool firms were caught in the Royal Mail crash, Britain's biggest shipping demise between the wars. This Job's tale was not unrelenting. Liverpool was also an imperial port, and thus it benefited from imperial preferences. The bald reality was nonetheless full of sorrows. Between 1914 and 1938 Liverpool's share of Britain's seaborne trade fell from nearly one-third to nearly one-fifth. Long Britain's greatest export port, Liverpool lost that ranking to London in 1938. For those statistics held on Liverpool, the numbers throughout the period are fairly flat. There was less growth by the end of the twenty-year

---

[73] Suykens, *Antwerp*, 449; Reginald Loyen and Paul van de Laar, "Cargo-Handling, Technology, and Competition during the Interwar Years," in de Goey, *Comparative*, pp. 77–98; Van de Laar, *Stad*, 334–336; Backx, *Haven*, 80; Vigarié, *Grands*; 504.

period than in nearly any other main port, and practically no growth when shipping was booming in the mid- to late 1920s. Unemployment in Merseyside in the 1930s was never less than 18 percent.

Still, Liverpool held on as a great port because of its residual strengths. Cotton markets plunged, but Liverpool's shipping and trading connections to the West Indies, South America, West Africa, and Southeast Asia sustained large incoming streams of sugar, fruit, meat, vegetable oil, oilseed, and tin. In the nineteenth century Liverpool had emerged as Europe's greatest grain and milling port. Part of that traffic in the twentieth century diverted to continental ports and London, but between 1935 and 1937 the Liverpool Grain Storage Company constructed a huge new storage complex on the Brunswick Docks, capable of loading directly from ships to quayside silos, and Liverpool held on to its position as Britain's top grain port and the world's second largest milling center. Farther south the port invested in petroleum tank farms, and northward it completed the capacious Gladstone Dock system with its three miles of quays.

Most remarkable of all is how, under pressure, home networks held and expanded. Cunard, Booth, and Harrison lost trades but added new ones or shifted resources to more profitable centers. Steeped in local identities, Richard Holt's leadership went a long way toward minimizing the effects of the Royal Mail disaster. These were also years when the Harbor Board sent out emissaries to Australia to lobby for the port, and when Australia's contribution to port revenues doubled.[74]

Chronology, or the idea of interludes, stagnation, crisis, even roller coasters, cannot, therefore, be the only way to grasp what was occurring in ports between the wars. Better to identify where networks expanded and contracted, were useful or constricted in exercising options, and thus to see how successfully individual ports held on to their central role as collectors and coordinators in what remained a seaborne world economy. Perhaps most overlooked in these years are the advances in building out the world's transport infrastructure. Despite serious financial difficulties, every main port constructed larger, more flexible harbors. London carried out a vast modernization program – giant dock projects, deeper basins, newer machinery – often in the face of daunting technical difficulties.[75]

---

[74] Hyde, *Liverpool*, 126, 142–177; Jarvis, *Troubled*, 161–204; Phillips and Whiteside, *Casual*, 180; Cain and Hopkins, *Crisis*, 39; MMM/MDHB/Management Files/1/Visit to Australia, 1922.

[75] Jackson, *History*, 145–147.

All along Europe's seafront there were acres of newly engineered water surfaces, miles of new quays, better sheds, more specialized facilities, and superior lifting equipment. Terminal operators refined and took to a new state of the art earlier breakthroughs in bulk cargo handling.[76] These were also the years when ports geared up for serious intakes of mineral oil and built huge, new, and distant installations for the reception and storage of this highly inflammable commodity now pouring into harbors in the millions of tons.[77]

The basic reality of ports around the world remained their role in processing what were still immense flows of people and goods, regardless of economic uncertainties and crises. If anything, the world's harbors testified to a further globalizing of world transport. Ships sailing into Hong Kong in 1918 totaled 8,500,000 tons but, in the depths of the Depression, that tonnage had risen to 20,000,000, which made Hong Kong by this measurement the sixth largest port in the world. Singapore saw its net registered tonnage of merchant ships (of more than 50 nrt) rise from 8,618,000 in 1913 to 15,631,000 in 1938. Over the same period the throughput over Singapore Harbour Board wharves went from 2,576,000 tons to 3,296,665 tons, a figure that excludes goods loaded and unloaded in the roads. The Singapore Harbour Board undertook major expansion between 1908 and 1917, and then added another 25 percent of wharfage capacity between 1934 and 1937. Much of this was necessary to handle the sensational growth in rubber exports that climbed to 254,000 tons in 1929 and then to 316,000 tons in 1934, paralleling the ascent of Singapore's rubber market to one of the world's big three alongside New York and London. Buenos Aires remained a congested mess, but these were also the years when HAPAG freighters scrounged for business along even the most unlikely backwaters of South America's western coast, while petroleum complexes were constructed at Palembang. Farther up the Sumatran east coast, along one of the greatest plantation complexes in the world, lay Belawan. Before the First World War a ship needed a draft of eight feet or fewer to tie up at its modest quay. Most cargo transshipped over Penang and Singapore. Then, between 1918 and 1921, "after super-human difficulties and prodigal expenditure of money," the Dutch built a modern deep-water harbor to fix this overseas traffic to a home imperial port. By 1938 more than 1,100 liners were tying up at its

[76] Koomans, "Port," 110; Van Driel and de Goey, *Rotterdam*, 34–53.
[77] Jackson, *History*, 144; Koomans, "Port," 124–127; Van de Laar, *Stad*, 339–341; Marcel Coudurié, "Face à la crise de 1929," in Coudurié and Miège, *Marseille*, 462–463.

quays, an interesting commentary on the juxtaposition of national interests and international connectedness.[78]

WORLD TRADING

One must be careful in talking about deglobalization when referring to world trade between the wars. The Bunge group, heavily invested in one of the centers of interwar protectionism, offers a rather different take on these years. In the 1920s and 1930s, Bunge expanded to North America, Australia, China, and Japan. Although headquartered in Antwerp, the engine of operations increasingly gravitated to Buenos Aires and to managers Alfredo Hirsch and Jorge Oster, both naturalized Argentinian citizens. Joining them was Jorge Born II, himself born in Argentina and very likely of Argentinian citizenship. One of the world's biggest grain traders, Bunge's answer to tariffs and import substitution was to become still more transnational by investing in South American industrialization. Bunge & Born held flour, paint, textile, and chemical plants in Argentina, chemical plants in Uruguay and Peru, and flour mills and more chemical factories in Brazil, where they were also the nation's largest cotton exporter. At the same time, the rise of Robert Werner to top management ranks in the 1930s reaffirmed the local-global identities inherent in maritime globalizing processes since at least the mid-nineteenth century. Werner, an Antwerpener born into a merchant family of German descent, seriously wounded fighting with Belgian forces in the war, immersed in local Antwerp civic and cultural life, and married to Jorge Born I's eldest daughter, led a career that alternated between Buenos Aires and the Scheldt. The first half of the 1930s he spent in Argentina. Returning to Antwerp in 1935 he coordinated the Bunge group's European operations. With the threat of German occupation rapidly approaching in 1940, he was back in Buenos Aires. After directing Bunge's expansion in the United States and Canada during the war, he returned to Antwerp following the liberation to rebuild Bunge's European networks, although he also labored to create still larger trading networks around the world. Like his company he was deeply rooted in his Antwerp origins, but he

---

[78] SHM/1BB3 61/Port of Hong Kong, 9 January 1935; Huff, *Economic*, 76–77, 139–144, 195, 236–237, 398–399; De Boer and Westermann, *Eeuw*, 346–354; Straits Settlements Trade Commission, *Report of the Commission Appointed by His Excellency of the Governor of the Straits Settlements to Enquire into and Report on the Trade of the Colony, 1933–1934* (Singapore: Government Printing Office, 1934), vol. 4, appendix 4, 36 (quoted).

was also a man of two continents with commitments or connections on another four.[79]

This is not to deny the crisis conditions and formidable obstacles that traders confronted after the war, and particularly in the 1930s, and that made reconstruction of pre-1914 trading conditions all but impossible. The precipitous fall in world trading figures with which this chapter began was the basic fact all companies struggled against during the Depression. The end of free trade, the creation of trading blocs, and the curtailment of international capital flows created a very new, and difficult, trading environment. Even before the crash world traders had to struggle with the oversupply and fluctuating price levels of commodities. Every commodity had its own history in these years, but a widespread vicious cycle prevailed. Surplus production drove down price levels. Depression then compressed Western demand, dropping prices and exports to still lower levels. Import substitution and efforts to bolster prices by restricting production depressed trade further. All these things then lowered demand in commodity-producing territories, thereby completing the contracting cycle.

The travails of the rubber trade illustrate the dynamic and its effects. A tropical plant transformed into a mass commodity for tire manufacture half a world away, rubber typified the coordination between contemporary human wants and maritime resources on a global scale. Initially harvested in the wild in Brazil and Africa, but increasingly cultivated on estates in Southeast Asia where production could be converted to a factory regimen, rubber passed through planters, trading companies, brokers, dealers, agency houses, markets, ports, and shipping companies, all of whom melded into a chain to connect tree fluids to motorists. Europeans, through their command of imperial territories and maritime infrastructures, assured the flow of Latin American-turned-Asian raw materials to essentially American purchasers.

But whereas about 65,000 acres constituted world rubber cultivation in 1905, and dividends could reach a whopping 325 percent, the consequent rush to invest brought close to 8,000,000 acres under production by 1930.[80] In the 1920s rubber suffered from all the warped consequences of overproduction, falling prices, and a restriction scheme destined to fail because it did not include East Indies production. Global

[79] Hoste, *Bunge*, chapters 3 and 4.
[80] Allen and Donnithorne, *Western*, 111, 117; Helffereich, *Behn*, vol. 2, 26–27; P. T. Bauer, *The Rubber Industry: A Study in Competition and Monopoly* (Cambridge, MA: Harvard University Press, 1948), 25.

depression was still more disastrous. In Malaya there were wholesale dismissals of planters and workers. Perhaps several hundred thousand Asians left the Peninsula. Out-of-work planters squatted on land outside the Kuala Lumpur Anglican Church. This time a more inclusive restriction scheme proved fairly successful; and in the 1930s experiments with tapping, planting, grafting, and processing, while increasing yields, also lowered cultivation costs. Rubber planters and traders thus managed to survive the worst of the crises, but their history was a troubled one.[81]

This history of crisis and control, repeated over other commodities, meant that trading and estate companies struggled between the wars. Most companies were in and out of profits through the two decades. Many showed little gain for much of this period and venerable companies like Jardine Matheson had excessive numbers of red-ink years.[82] But crisis also engendered creative strategies. Wille moved up-country in Brazil and aggressively reinforced networks in the world's largest coffee market, the United States. Its volumes and market share of exports rivaled all but its most spectacular years preceding 1914. Balfour Williamson deepened relations with Chilean companies. Buschmann moved into Syria, Iraq, and Iran in the 1930s. Steel Brothers expanded into Cuba and Palestine. Melchers diversified into Malaya, Thailand, South Africa, and Iraq. Dutch traders, beset by Japanese competition in the East Indies, leapfrogged their buying to the home islands. Going one better, Rallis, big cotton traders in India, set up a joint British-Japanese company for trading with Japan and widened their distribution networks to include Marwari dealers.[83]

There was therefore the paradox that as globalization in terms of market integration collapsed, globalization in other senses advanced.

---

[81] Tate, *RGA*, 320–385, 468–478; Coates, *Commerce*, 207–227, 271–278; Pugh, *Great*, 106–107; Allen and Donnithorne, *Western*, 120–127; Huff, *Economic*, 194; Bauer, *Rubber*, 26, 67, 217–233, 254–267; NA/MA/133/Jaarverslag 1929, Menteng, Aanplant Hevea.

[82] Jones, *Merchants*, 91–93; Jonker and Sluyterman, *Home*, 244; Sipos, "Expansie," 43, 52, 82–83; Mees, *N.V. Internationale*, 51, 66.

[83] Zimmerman, *Wille*, 115–116, 141–145, 156; Jones, *Merchants*, 100–115, 303–304; Hunt, *Heirs*, vol. 2, 169–212; Krieg, *Buschmann*, 43–59; H. E. W. Braund, *Calling to Mind: Being Some Account of the First Hundred Years (1870 to 1970) of Steel Brothers and Company Limited* (Oxford: Pergamon Press, 1975), 37–38, 44, 94; *150 Jahre*, 16–17; NA/Hoppenstedt/47 (Behrens 1937); Jonker and Sluyterman, *Home*, 243; for a more conservative or critical view of these years, focusing on British companies, see, B. R. Tomlinson, *The Political Economy of the Raj, 1914–1947: The Economics of Decolonization in India* (Houndmills, Basingstoke: Macmillan, 1979), 48–52; Misra, *Business*.

Closed and failing markets forced trading companies to become more transnational. This was a pattern with parallels beyond maritime business. Multinationals jumped tariff barriers and set up production abroad. Restrictions on remittance of profits deepened their investment in the host countries. Triangular relationships, by which American overseas affiliates invested in a third part of the world, multiplied webs of connection and scrambled identities.[84] It has been noted too that the damming of certain flows could not prevent breaching by others, and that we can trace the emergence of a global consumer culture to the "closure" years of the 1920s and 1930s.[85] Truly remarkable was the simultaneous appearance worldwide of the modern girl phenomenon, a certain look and presumed lifestyle disseminated by globalizing film and cosmetics industries.[86]

Moreover, European losses were balanced by American, Brazilian, Argentinian, Japanese, Indian, and Chinese gains. Signs that often appeared as contraction were instead premonitory signals of rival contenders on the scene, or the decentered, global connectedness that would edge forward after 1945 and then spill over all banks toward the end of the century. The classic case, perhaps, was what became of the jute industry. Indian jute was milled into bags and shipped all over the world, where in turn it was used to package grain shipments from Argentina and Egypt; corn shipments from Australia; sugar shipments from Cuba, Java, and the Middle East; or cotton shipments from America. It was in this sense a thoroughly globalized commodity, grown in one part of the world, shipped to nearly all others, and then utilized thrice over for cross-world transport. In the interwar years its industry too transformed, but not in any way that lessened its global dimensions. Calcutta jute mills, dominated by British agency houses at the start of the interwar years, were controlled by Marwaris at the end. Marwari ownership in the Calcutta mills rose to about two-thirds in the interwar years, and by the 1940s Marwari business houses controlled three-quarters of jute exports from India. They were but the leading edge of a more expansive drive by Indian business groups.[87]

What Indians accomplished in South Asia, Chinese business magnates repeated in Singapore. Tan Kah Kee, who amassed a fortune in rubber, is often cited, but more important was his son-in-law, Lee Kong Chian, who

[84] Wilkins, *Foreign*, 136, 160–162, 217, 395–436; idem, *Maturing*, viii, 138–146, 172, 196–211.
[85] See Chapter 3.
[86] Weinbaum et al., *Modern*, especially 2–5. See also Jones, *Beauty*.
[87] Guildhall/River Steam/MS 27,953/vol. 2, 1938, Narayanganj Section; Gordon T. Stewart, *Jute and Empire: The Calcutta Jute Wallahs and the Landscapes of Empire* (Manchester:

picked up the pieces following Tan's crash and over the next decades built Lee Rubber Company into one of the world's leading rubber firms. Lee was a leader in a new generation of Singapore Chinese businessmen that as early as the 1930s was integrating forward into international rubber trading. Significantly, Lee utilized not only his Western banking connections, but credit from big Japanese trading companies and new shipping services from Japanese steamship companies to expand and market directly to the United States. The Japanese, in return, used the Chinese to expand their presence in rubber buying and trading. Significantly too, when Tan failed it was Japanese and Hong Kong competition that moved in on his rubber-soled canvas shoe trade.[88]

Japanese, of all non-Westerners, made the most aggressive global moves; their rivalry, like import substitution, has typically been lumped in with Depression-era deglobalizing patterns, even though both represented a prelude to the globalism of the future. Already in the 1930s the Japanese possessed the world's third largest shipping fleet, and their trading companies marketed globally in Asia, the Americas, the Middle East, and the USSR. In certain markets their presence was overwhelming. Before 1914 Japan had held only 1 percent of the market in manufactured imports in India, but by the end of the 1930s that figure was approaching a third. In the early 1930s Japan dominated textile imports in the East Indies.[89] The telling thing about this penetration is how like it was to the Europeans': The Japanese too linked up with indigenous networks. Connections nurtured over the years with Chinese traders were used to market in Indonesia. When anti-Japanese boycotts threatened to crack these apart, exporters formed new networks with Indian and Hadhrami Arab houses on Sumatra and Java.[90] In Burma, half of

Manchester University Press, 1998), 4–26; Misra, *Business*, 55, 107, 123–124; Omkar Goswami, "Then Came the Marwaris: Some Aspects of the Changes in the Pattern of Industrial Control in Eastern India," in *The Indian Economic and Social History Review* 22, 3 (1985): 225–249; B. R. Tomlinson, "British Business in India, 1860–1970," in Davenport-Hines and Jones, *British*, 100.

[88] Brown, *Capital*, 112–122, 158–159; Huff, *Economic*, 206, 218–235, 312.

[89] Jones, *Merchants*, 87, 100; Brugmans, *Tachtig*, 175; ICHVR/76–127/Jaarverslag 1938, p. 7; Brown, *Capital*, 197–202.

[90] Masako Sakamoto, "Diversification: The Case of Mitsui Bussan," in Shin'ichi Yonekawa, *General Trading Companies: A Comparative and Historical Study* (Tokyo: United Nations University Press, 1990), 66–91; Nobuo Kawabe, "Overseas Activities and Their Organization," in ibid., 174–176; Peter Post, "Chinese Business Networks and Japanese Capital in South East Asia, 1880–1940: Some Preliminary Observations," in Rajeswary Ampalavanar Brown, *Chinese Business Enterprise in Asia* (Routledge: London, 1995), 163–170; Clarence-Smith, "Middle," 222–223.

the Japanese textiles sold were marketed through Indian networks; in the Straits Settlements, nearly two-fifths.[91] Global connectedness since at least the beginning of the century had always been about local-global interchanges. In the 1930s, Europeans and non-Europeans alike were drawing these tighter. The one looming threat to both sets of networks was the intrusion of multinationals into foreign markets, but this too had the look of the future.

Transnationalism, therefore, was not seeping away. What was on the brink of turning inward, and then imploding, was the colonial world of Harold Braund, whose perfect cocoon moment was about to burst. In its 1938 year-end report, Internatio noted that "rumors of war were the order of the day," and that this "could not fail to leave a mark on our business affairs ... where increasingly greater hindrances were placed in the way of import and payment possibilities."[92] Seven years later, when the survivors straggled out of the internment camps, or the Braunds returned from the jungles of Burma, far more than international payments and profits would be on their minds. Defeat and occupation, coming before victory, bore with it the end of an older global order and the beginning of a new one.

[91] Brown, *Capital*, 210.
[92] ICHVR/76–127/Jaarverslag 1938.

8

War and Remaking

1939–1960s

By the late 1930s, Swires, in China, could feel war closing in on them. Maurice Ching, their man in Newchang (the same young man full of energy who at the end of the 1940s was certain he could "kill Nam Kee stone dead"[1]) was, in February 1937, "living in a state of suspense and never knows when he might find himself in trouble with the Japanese, which amounts at best to being put in jail, and at worst just disappearing overnight."[2] As Japanese armies swept south and Swires' river traffic along the Yangtze dried up, there was one last great marshaling of networks to probe alternative routes to the interior. Wong Pao Hsie and C. T. Feng of Swires' southern freight broker, Kwei Kee, were sent to Haiphong to scout rail, road, and forwarding connections north to Yunnan province. In their wake followed F. R. Lamb, armed with Kwei Kee introductions to the eight Chinese forwarding hongs that controlled overland shipments through Haiphong port. E. James Tandy went to Burma armed with a letter of introduction from T. V. Soong, Chiang Kai-shek's brother-in-law and brother of the head of the Chinese trucking firm charged with hauling Nationalist supplies into China. Mansfields made inquiries with the Irrawaddy Flotilla Company. Two more Swires agents traveled to Hsia-Kwan (Xiaguan) to establish contact with "leading old-style Chinese business firms" trading by caravan between Bhamo and southwestern China. But nothing came of any of these ventures.[3]

[1] See Chapter 2.
[2] SOAS/JSSI/Box 17/24 February 1937.
[3] SOAS/JSSII 2/17/Box 53/19, 30 January (quoted), 3, 7, 14, 20, February, 16 March, 21 November 1939; SOAS/JSSIII 1/18/Box 77/19 August, 8, 31 October, 19, 30 November

Conditions deteriorated over the next two years, until in the first days of December 1941 all ships north of Hong Kong concentrated in Hong Kong harbor to await "the balloon going up." Key staff were kept ready "to embark for Singapore at short notice."[4] The next reports were unrelievedly bleak. Most ships made it out before the 7th of December, but those that sailed into Manila harbor were bombed, and after "appalling muddle" six made it into port in western Australia. As of April 1942, fifteen China Navigation ships and ten river steamers had been scuttled, seized, or sunk.[5]

Of those men who made it out, many would go on to serve in the Ministry of War Transport. Eastern firm headquarters were reestablished at Bombay, with Shanghai personnel relocating to Chungking. CNCo ships still in British hands were put to use along the Indian coast, in the Arabian Sea, and down the east coast of Africa. In China, however, everything east of Nationalist-controlled territory – docks and dockyards, sugar refineries, offices – was a complete loss. Personnel left behind joined thousands of other Britons streaming into Japanese internment camps, some never to emerge alive from this ordeal. Yet, despite the total fiasco, Swires' top managers, as early as May 1942, were already planning their future return.[6] In March 1944, with the tide in their favor, plans were well underway concerning staffing in eastern ports as they "opened." Then, with Japanese capitulation, Swires, like every other Eastern firm, rushed to get its people in as soon as possible. In the interim, old Chinese employees on the spot were sent instructions to occupy and safeguard company premises. Ready to go, Swires was set to restart operations from where it had left off in December 1941.[7] What it found and what it could do, were, however, other matters.

Even more than the Great War, the Second World War was a global war with global consequences. In this war, land power and air power were as decisive as sea power. But fought as it was across every ocean, and on littorals on both sides of the planet, this war could not be engaged – let alone won – without maritime resources, knowledge, and connections, or the

1938; SOAS/JSSIII 1/19/Box 79/19 January 1940; JSSIII 1/20/Box 80/18 January 1941; SOAS/JSSI/ Box 17/24 March 1939, 2 August 1940.

4 SOAS/JSSXI 1/9/Box 523/4 December 1941.

5 SOAS/JSSIII/1/20/Box 80/23 December 1941, 6 February 1942 (quoted); Havilland, *China*, 116–117.

6 SOAS/JSSXI 1/9/Box 523/1 May 1942.

7 SOAS/JSSI/Box 18/28 August, 20 November 1942, 31 March 1944; SOAS/JSSII 2/19/Box 205/4, 14 September 1945. See also Cain and Hopkins, *Crisis*, 275, on general British plans.

expertise and means to organize logistical flows by sea. Once again, maritime systems and culture made history on a world scale. But as they did so they too were caught up and reworked by six years of bi-hemispheric combat. The impact was most dramatic in the East, where reconquest was neither sufficient to repair the damage of defeat and humiliation, nor to withstand the pressure for European retreat. In the years after the war the very meaning of globalization was cut loose from its former imperial base. Elsewhere, it was possible to entertain the illusion that the old machinery of capital, goods, installations, networks, and culture, once refurbished, could re-create seaborne flows as they had existed in the best of times. For a brief period this is exactly what happened. But here too there was instability, and a slide toward a Schumpeter future. The preludes of the interwar years thus continued, refracted now through the experiences of a far more thoroughly global war, its destructions, and its reconstructions. The 1940s, 1950s, and the first half of the 1960s consequently began with maritime mastery, but then hovered between a "remaking" in both senses of that word.

WORLD WAR II

On the surface of things, the maritime history of World War II has all the appearances of a retread. The Allies secured sufficient ships, prevented submarine slaughter, managed port congestion, and effected the successful carriage of whatever was necessary by sea to assure survival and victory. Yet the differences were also glaring. This was, to begin with, a global war on a completely different scale. Military fronts stretched across the Atlantic, Pacific, and Indian Oceans. Some sense of the global reach can be gathered from the havoc in ports along Africa's western, southern, Red Sea, and Mediterranean coasts, the consequence of carrying hundreds of thousands of troops to the Middle East and with them their ammunition, their guns, their tanks, their food, and all the heavy equipment to construct their bases and logistical systems. On the west coast, Freetown was a modest way station accustomed to anchoring one or two ships on any given day during peacetime. The closure of the Mediterranean and the positioning of armies in the Western Desert of Libya and Egypt transformed it into possibly the largest staging point of convoys in the world. By 1941 as many as fifty ships were sailing each day into a harbor with no deep-water berths, no dry dock, insufficient reservoirs or piping for water supplies (despite torrential rainfalls), and insufficient storage for bunkering coal.[8] The *Domby*, arriving in Freetown on 4 May 1941 with 7,000 tons of coal, required two months to discharge. The *Ashbury*, sailing in a week later with a little more than 5,000 tons, did not begin to discharge until 11 June.[9] Cape ports, although accustomed to larger traffic, were no less overloaded.[10] Around the Cape and up through the Red Sea, the small port of Suez, never designed for this degree of world attention, was receiving tens of thousands of crates and boxes, and heavy lifts such as tanks, for which it was ill-equipped. According to shipowner Charles Hill, dispatched in May 1941 to report on conditions from Port Sudan to Haifa, "The whole of the shipping position in the Middle East was in a most ghastly muddle." Repeating himself, Hill labeled Suez "the most appalling muddle I have ever seen in any port." Hogg of Mackinnon Mackenzie, sent out to Suez to assist Hill, stuck at the same point on the record: "Conditions were simply ghastly." At the time of Hill's arrival at Suez, 117 ships were in the process of discharging or waiting to commence.[11]

Farther east, supply lines to Russia through Persia clogged Gulf harbors. One ship capable of seventeen knots and thus highly desirable for use on the open seas languished seventy-three days in these congested waters. At one point in May 1942, 171 vessels filled Bombay harbor, many of them ships that had fled India's east coast under threat of Japanese attack or comprising the arrival of survivor shipping from Singapore and the East Indies.[12] So dispersed were fronts that at the time of the Japanese surrender, the British had assembled 150 deep sea freighters to support amphibious landings to retake Penang and Singapore.[13] The engulfment of this conflict at all dimensions of shipping and trading were sweeping. KPM ships accustomed to shuttling along sleepy coastlines at the outer edges of world streams were suddenly operating at the front lines of battle.[14] Between 1914 and 1918, Harrisons & Crosfield had shipped out large

[8] Behrens, *Merchant*, 206–209.
[9] PRO/MT 63/277/25 June 1941.
[10] PRO/MT 63/253/16 December 1942.
[11] Behrens, who saw all the relevant documents, brilliantly describes the scene at Suez: *Merchant*, 210–214, 241. For Hill and Hogg quotes, PRO/MT 62/27/Report on the Shipping Position in the Middle East by Mr. Charles Hill.
[12] PRO/MT/63/338/6 December 1942; PRO/MT 63/317/22 June 1942; PRO/MT 63/256/ November 1941; PRO/MT 63/415/November 1942; PRO/MT 63/259/27, 28 October 1943.
[13] PRO/MT 40/117.
[14] H. Th. Bakker, *De K.P.M. in oorlogstijd: Een overzicht van de verrichtingen van de Koninklijke Paketvaart-Maatschappij en haar personeel gedurende de wereldoorlog 1939–1945* (Amsterdam: N.V. Koninklijke Paketvaart-Maatschappij, 1950).

tonnages of rubber and tea from safe havens and moved into timbering on Sandakan. In January 1942, reports from agents in the heart of rubber country described strafings and bombings, frantic efforts to load rubber onto last ships, demolitions and evacuations, and the chaos that accompanied breakdown of civil authority.[15]

Against this background economic warfare was thus bound to play out differently than in the last war, although the fall of France and the rise of air power wrought even greater changes. The Allies did reproduce much of the machinery of blockade and blacklists from the First World War with some success.[16] In this war, however, German occupation of Europe vitiated the full effects of blockade by sea, and victory in Europe rendered German seaborne capacity far more effective than in the First World War. For long into this war, Germany and Italy made use of Mediterranean and Black Sea waters, largely by deploying occupied or neutral fleets. Even world connections, if thin, were sustained for a time. Until the invasion of the Soviet Union, the trans-Siberian railroad was available for shipments across Asia to Europe. When it closed, German blockade runners carried plant equipment, machinery, and chemicals to Japan, and brought back desperately needed supplies of rubber, tin, wolfram, and vegetable fats. Progressively, Allied countermeasures interrupted nearly all of this traffic, but even one ship getting through managed to bring in vital quantities of materials.[17] Ironically, the greatest Allied victories came in the Pacific and in the southeastern reaches of the Indian Ocean where initially Japanese freighters and tankers dominated the sea lanes. U.S. submarines and bombers sent large numbers to the bottom of the ocean, while air strikes on ore ships moving down the Yangtze cut the Japanese off from essential iron, coal, and oil supplies.[18] There was then a distinct reversal from the economic warfare waged in the First World War. In the Second, the decisive impact came in the Pacific, not the Atlantic, and it came through the denial of seaborne resources in the one theater where Axis sea power was initially hegemonic. In that fact nestled harbingers of

---

[15] Guildhall/Harrisons/Correspondence/Kuala Lumpur/Box 4/1940–1946, 17 January 1942.

[16] W. N. Medlicott, *The Economic Blockade*, 2 vols. (London: Her Majesty's Stationery Office, 1952–1959); HAPAG/447/13 August 1940; Hauschild-Thiessen, *Zwischen*; Trümper, *Kaffee*, 76.

[17] Medlicott, *Blockade*, vol. 2, 166–172, 438–453; HAPAG/456/17 November 1942; Witthöft, *HAPAG*, 86; Gerhard L. Weinberg, *A World at Arms: A Global History of World War II*, 2nd ed. (Cambridge: Cambridge University Press, 2005), 400–403; PRO/ADM/1283/French Shipping Intelligence Report No. 13, 5 May 1941.

[18] Medlicott, *Blockade*, vol. 2, 405–408.

growing Asian centrality, the global presence of America, and of an even tighter drawing of world linkages.

Besides, air power was now the strategic weapon of strangulation. Air attack in the Second World War introduced a completely new order to the threat that supply lines might choke at harbor's point. In combination with mines and torpedo boats, aerial strafing and bombing along the North Sea approaches or over ports forced massive diversions. By July of 1940 major London trades with the Baltic, North Sea, and Mediterranean had "vanished," and large freighters were reassigned to the other side of the island. Then, on the 7th of September 1940, and for fifty-six days consecutively, waves of bombers struck at London. The port was shut to all but coastal shipping. For considerable stretches to come in the war, the port remained either closed or open to but a fraction of its peacetime capacity.[19] In December 1940 Liverpool was hit by intensive air raids that leveled warehouses, damaged berths, and reduced the port temporarily to 50 percent of working capacity. Only the failure of the Germans to persist prevented far more serious immobilization. In May the bombers returned, blitzing city and harbor over eight consecutive nights. Docks were littered with ships damaged, sunk, or gutted by fire. In Bootle, adjacent to the northern docks, 14,000 out of 17,000 houses were damaged or destroyed, and harbor board managers scoured the countryside in search of dock laborers who had evacuated or fled. So many forwarding firms had lost their offices and were improvising services out of hotels, that basic reception and dispatch work was seriously impaired. When the skies at last cleared of planes, port working capacity was down 70 percent.[20] If the Allies managed to counter this life-and-death threat, once their own, far more powerful air fleets concentrated bombing on the transport network of the Ruhr, they "had the capacity to halt assembly lines across Germany."[21]

Vichy's strange role in this war highlights another critical difference with the first one: Where were the needed ships to come from once Europe had fallen to the Axis? French shipping has often been the forgotten chapter in the maritime history of the Second World War, but Vichy's history throughout intertwined with the sea. The pretense to sovereignty without the substance of sovereign power led, in the matter of ships,

[19] PRO/MT 63/28/18 July 1940 (quoted); PRO/MT 63/99; Behrens, *Merchant*, 126, 152.
[20] MMM/MDHB/Liver PEC/vol. 2/c. 1946, pp. 61–63; PRO/MT 63/214/7, 13, 16 May 1941; PRO/MT 63/140/4, 8, 14 May 1941; PRO/MT 63/375/23 May 1941.
[21] Adam Tooze, *The Wages of Destruction: The Making and Breaking of the Nazi Economy* (New York: Viking Penguin, 2007), 596–602 (quoted 598).

to the same compromises, surrenders, and collaboration with the occupiers that Robert Paxton unmasked, decades ago, in nearly every other sphere of Franco-German relations.[22] The severe deprivation at home that undermined Vichy's legitimacy was worsened by the stripping of French overseas transport. Despite stalls, conditions, legalisms, and the impeccably logical rationales in which French education excelled, by the beginning of 1943 practically all but 50,000 tons of the French merchant marine had been surrendered to the Germans, along with most Greek, Danish, and Norwegian ships stranded in French harbors at the time of the armistice.[23]

For the Allies, Vichy also portended calamitous consequences in the ability to sustain supply lines at sea. In the First World War, the French merchant marine had been the Allies' second fleet. With the fall of France, theoretically several million tons were severed, at one blow, from Allied carrying capacity. The Second World War consequently introduced a completely new twist to the struggle for control of Europe's "non-combatant" shipping, particularly as roughly 10 million tons of Norwegian, Dutch, Danish, and Greek shipping were additionally at stake.[24] As with Vichy, outcomes were initially ambiguous. Hundreds of thousands of tons of Norwegian and Dutch shipping each were captured or sunk during the German invasion.[25] There were dramatic contests – competing radio broadcasts and telegrams for mastery of Norwegian ships at sea,[26] brawls and intrigues waged in Lisbon and New York over control of Belgium's CMB assets[27] – that were sui generis to this war.

Thus the familiar history of war at sea between 1914 and 1918 replayed between 1939 and 1945, but in very different keys. If there were great constants, they came in the solutions. In one way or another, the bulk of the world's shipping came over to the Allied side. Bolstered by a Norwegian government in exile in London, the British won the

[22] Robert O. Paxton, *Vichy France: Old Guard and New Order, 1940–1944* (NY: Alfred Knopf, 1972; reprint, NY: Norton, 1975).

[23] There are substantial materials on French wartime shipping in SHM/TT B10 and B11; AN/AJ/706, 709, 2091, and 2092. See also Medlicott, *Blockade*, vol. 2, 343–378.

[24] Sturmey, *British*, 139.

[25] L. L. Von Münching, *De Nederlandse koopvaardijvloot in de tweede wereldoorloog. De lotgevallen van Nederlandse koopvaardijschepen en hun bemanning* (Bussum: De Boer Maritiem, 1978), 43–48, 207; J. W. De Roever, *De Nederland in de Tweede Wereldoorlog* (Amsterdam: N. V. Stoomvaart Maatschappij "Nederland," 1951), 39; Petersen, *Saga*, 118.

[26] Behrens, *Merchant*, 93–94; Petersen, *Saga*, 118–158.

[27] CMB/D 16/1/17 December 1940; Greta Devos and Guy Elewaut, *CMB 100: Een eeuw maritiem ondernemersschap 1895–1995* (Tielt: Lannoo, 1995), 130–135.

greater part of Norway's ships. If anything, German invasion of Holland made it easier for the Allies to secure the use of the free Dutch fleet. Through conquest or progressive rallying of imperial territories, a very large part of the French fleet was Allied by May 1944.[28] France's merchant marine did have a wartime history, even if it occurred largely for the Germans, Italians, Japanese, Americans, and British. American entry was once again critical in closing the gap between carrying capacity and demand. The United States lent tonnage, but more important, American shipyards, employing standardized models, prefabrication, and new welding techniques, were primarily responsible for the production of 50 million tons dwt of new ships that, by war's end, more than replaced losses at sea.[29]

Those losses totaled 4,786 Allied merchant ships, or 21 million tons grt, so that the same epic battle to keep sea lanes open, and survive, was fought in the first half of this war just as it had been in 1917 and 1918. The weapon of massacre was still the submarine, now able to operate from bases along Europe's Atlantic coast, which made it even more lethal. Submarines accounted for 70 percent of tonnage sunk.[30] For a long time, perhaps the most dangerous duty in the West was to man merchant ships at sea. Novel means such as sonar or escort carriers were used to win this fight. The most effective countermeasures, however, were those learned from the First World War. A "Masters and Officers Handbook," issued by the Admiralty in 1938, specified techniques for avoiding discovery, capture, or destruction: Disperse tracks by widening out customary sea lanes by hundreds of miles. Depart harbors just before dark and arrive at dawn. Zigzag to complicate the ability of the enemy to home in. Sail in convoys. This last one was the key tactic learned from 1917, and it proved as critical a quarter century later.[31]

The salient, and probably decisive, repeat factor was the marshaling of maritime expertise. As in the First World War, the vital issue was less getting ships than knowing how to use them. The records of the Military Cargo Branch (MCB) give the clue. This organ, responsible for "the programming, booking, and loading" of anything from ammunition to locomotives, likened itself to "a gigantic Cargo Liner Company in respect

[28] SHM/TT B11/Étude sur la situation de la flotte commerciale au 1er mai 1944.
[29] H. Duncan Hall and C. C. Wrigley, *Studies of Overseas Supply* (London: Her Majesty's Stationery Office, 1956), 5–6; Harlaftis, *Greek*, 235.
[30] Von Münching, *Nederlandse*, 150.
[31] PRO/FO 371/21457/"Defense of Merchant Shipping, Masters and Officers Handbook," March 1938.

of its operating and cargo handling activities."[32] The allusion – from an agency so masterful that it could assure that when amphibious forces hit the beaches their weapons would be unloaded from support ships "in the precise order required by the Force Commander in relation to his plan of action"[33] – caught the line of continuity between logistical victory at sea in the First and Second World Wars. Shipping, port, and trading figures from nearly every major line or firm served in one capacity or another to move armadas of men and cargo where they were needed. Indeed, Charles Hill's scathing report from Suez condemned the Sea Transport Division for not employing professional experts.[34]

Perhaps nowhere else was the contribution so stark as in the alleviation of port congestion in home base Britain. Even before Merseyside or Swansea, Bristol, Plymouth, and the Clyde were bombed, west coast ports strained to keep up with diverted traffic.[35] Planners before the war, contemplating air attack and closure of east coast ports, had warned that "congestion at any one point has widespread effects and when it once starts it increases in geometric rather than arithmetic progression and is increasingly difficult to overcome."[36] The saga of the *Argos Hill*, to be found in an aptly named file on "Delays in Clearance of Goods from Ports," highlighted the vexations brought on by massive diversions to ports designed for specific trades. Sailing from New York via Halifax, the *Argos Hill* headed for London in September 1940, but was diverted to Glasgow where it arrived on 6 October. Discharge of its general cargo was held up by blockage from heavy lifts in the same hold, by heavy congestion at the berth, and by difficulty arranging transfer to consignees in London. At the mineral wharf, there were insufficient cranes to lift the steel, and even when they could get the steel out, there were not enough rail carriages of the right size available for off-loading. Removal of the heavy lifts was delayed for lack of proper equipment; the port possessed no floating crane. In all, the ship was required to move ten times from berth to berth, and not until 26 November, fifty-one days after unloading had begun, was the ship turned around and ready to sail back to New

---

[32] PRO/MT 40/117/Resumé of the Operations of Military Cargo Branch during the War Period September, 1939–August 1945 (quoted foreword).

[33] Ibid., 16.

[34] PRO/MT 63/290/17 July 1941; PRO/MT 62/27/Report on the Shipping Position in the Middle East, 1941.

[35] PRO/MT 63/48/Weir Report, n.d. (c. November 1940); PRO/MT 63/213/14 March 1941.

[36] PRO/MT 63/94/Committee of Imperial Defence, Diversion of Shipping to West Coast Ports, April 1939 (316-A), p. 7.

York. Its next voyage was essentially a repeat.[37] Air attacks then threatened to bring the whole system down.

The solution came from mobilizing the experts. Representatives of the nation's nine major ports, along with shipping, Admiralty, and other wartime officials, gathered into what became known as the Diversion Room, where they assembled every morning the necessary pieces of information – convoys and cargoes in route, approaches threatened, conditions in ports, desired destination of specific goods – to assign ships to ports.[38] The government also appointed regional port directors to coordinate, authorize, and, when required, rewrite operational procedures. Robert Letch, assistant general manager at London's PLA, went to the Clyde where he worked wonders with a port overwhelmed by traffic diverted to it. His report on "Traffic Arrangements at the Glasgow Docks" was circulated to other ports as a template, and Letch himself was sent on to Merseyside. Before his assignment to Glasgow, Letch brought his London experience in unloading waterside to the creation of an emergency port farther down the Clyde to relieve some of the pressure already building up at the Glasgow docks. There he was seconded by the London stevedore firm Scruttons, which saw much of its business dissolve with the closing of London and was critical in selling the idea of transferring London know-how to the far side of the kingdom. Within a week of the first air raids on the capital, Scrutton managers, foremen, leading clerks, tally clerks, dock departmental staff, and seventy-five dockers were on a special overnight train from Euston Station to Gourock. Within a day they were at work discharging a BI steamer from India. Eventually Scruttons assembled 500 of its men at the Emergency Port; over the remainder of the war they were to turn around 1,885 ships.[39]

The achievements of Letch and Scruttons repeated in every sphere of global logistics. The head of the Ministry of War Transport (MOWT), the equivalent to the First World War's shipping controller, was Frederick Leathers, a coal and shipping man who had served with the Ministry of Shipping in the previous war. Like his predecessor, Leathers staffed the MOWT with men who had made a career of moving ships and cargoes around the world. Chief representative in South and East Africa between 1942 and 1944 was Charles Wurtzburg, who had run Mansfields and the

[37] PRO/MT 63/177/24 February 1941, 11 March 1941; PRO/MT 59/1826, 10 February 1941.

[38] Behrens, *Merchant*, 32–33; PRO/MT 63/94/316-A; PRO/MT 63/96/5 April 1939.

[39] Behrens, *Merchant*, 132–137; PRO/MT 63/69/6 March 1941; MMM/MDHB/Liver PEC/ vol. 2, c. 1946, pp. 112–113; Jeffrey, *Scruttons*, 66–73.

Straits Steamship Co., had served on the Singapore Harbour Board, and had then been named managing director for the Glen Line. Elder Dempster's G. H. Avezathe represented MOWT in West Africa and oversaw all the shipping between Dakar and the Congo. Swires' J. R. Masson and Holts' Stewart MacTier and John Nicholson (who would become senior partner in 1957) were all forwarded by their firms to work with MOWT or Sea Transport. Sir William Currie, head of P & O, became MOWT's director of the liner division. Cunard's Percy Bates (director 1910; chairman 1930) served on MOWT's Advisory and Liner Committees; in the First World War he had served as well in the Ministry of Shipping. Ben Line's Douglas Thomson worked for MOWT, as did Blue Star's S. V. Jones. As a result of the inquiry into Sea Transport Organisation's botch-ups in the Middle East, Glen Line's Herbert McDavid (later Glen's chairman) was appointed deputy director of Sea Transport with the brief "to advise and assist generally on all matters concerning its commercial shipping problems." The Prince Line's Robson was brought in to assist him. Furness Withy's Ernest Murrant was sent out to Egypt as MOWT's special representative. Earlier, in response to the awful congestion in the canal zone ports, the ministry dispatched Colonel Sadler ("in civil life … an executive of one of the dock ports in the United Kingdom"), and seconded him with Lieutenant Colonel Gentry, a PLA manager before the war. The two went out with "a number of trained dock supervisors with Army rank" to clean up the mess at quayside. Ashley Sparks, who had headed the Ministry of Shipping's New York operations at the end of the First World War, ran MOWT's New York organization. Holts' John Hobhouse was appointed deputy regional commissioner for the Merseyside area in 1939 and then regional shipping representative. All this, moreover, was replicated in the shipping groups that came over to the Allies. Birger Gran, who would build Norwegian shipbroker Fearnley and Eger's postwar tanker business into its biggest profit center, spent four years in New York with Nortraship, Norway's umbrella shipping organization in exile or, effectively the largest shipping company in the world at the time of its founding. For all these men, moving ships and goods came as second nature. The result was that once again a maritime community that had put together the structures and mastered the techniques of global flows in peacetime did no less for global flows in wartime.[40]

---

[40] Francis Keenlyside, "Leathers, Frederick James, First Viscount Leathers (1883–1965)," rev. Mark Brodie, in *Oxford Dictionary of National Biography*, eee online ed. H. C. G. Matthew and Brian Harrison (Oxford: Oxford University Press, 2004), online edition, ed. Lawrence Goldman, January 2011, http://www.oxforddnb.com/view/article/34457

In larger terms, similitudes and disparities in the two world wars infiltrated the meanings and outcomes of the Second. The planetary spread of the war again underscored how globally connected the world had become by the twentieth century. Transnational systems, despite warring blocs, reappeared in the way the war reasserted local-to-global identities. Rarely before had local affinities been so fiercely embedded as in the waging of total war at sea; but rarely too had those identities been mobilized for such global projects. Throughout the twentieth century a local-global continuum would predominate; only the form it took would vary as the century progressed. Yet the return in 1945 of the same expansive globalizing forces announced in 1918 – American power in the West, challenge in the East, and a reconstruction of world integration through global decentralization – now came with a vengeance. The sheer breadth of fighting and destruction in World War II produced a cracking apart of empires rather than their preservation, thus a clearing away of older forms of connectedness. Precisely because this war was so global it would reconfigure the very foundations of globalism.

At more direct levels of networks and culture, the interplay of encore and departure was just as pronounced. Again world war expanded network possibilities. Shipbroker Birger Gran built an extraordinary circle of future contacts during his four years among the shipping exiles that flocked to New York. Gibsons' shipbroking firm in the City did practically no business during the war, but its brokers, who worked for government ministries "made jolly good contacts" for the future. For the younger generation of men who served at ground or sea level in the army and navy, there emerged a cohort experience and way of communicating that was to serve in good stead in the 1960s when they came together, across company lines, to create the first container consortia.[41] But the

(accessed 16 February 2012); Bates, Sir Percy Elly Fourth Baronet (1879–1946), Alan G. Jamieson, in *Oxford Dictionary of National Biography*, eee online ed. Lawrence Goldman (Oxford University Press, 2004), http://www.oxforddnb.com/view/article/30638 (accessed 16 February 2012); MMM/OA/4A/284/1 May 1952/Lloyds List obituary (Wurtzburg); Davies, *Trade*, 257 (Avezathe); Falkus, *Blue*, 242, 290; SOAS/JSSII 2/ 9/ Box 205/24 January 1945; SOAS/JSSI/Box 18 (these three on Holts and Swires people); Howarth, *P & O*, 146 (Currie); PRO/MT 63/ 290/3 April, 17 July 1941 (Thomson; Jones), 3 April 1941 (Sadler and Gentry); PRO/MT 62/27/ September 1941 (McDavid through Murrant); Liverpool, University of Liverpool/Cunard Steam-Ship Company Archives/Frederick A. Bates Papers/C4/ 8/ 20 February 1950 (Sparks); MMM/OA 4A/671/*Bulletin*, January 1962 (Hobhouse); Fischer and Nordvik, "Economic," 22–23 (Gran); Petersen, *Saga*, 124 (Nortraship). See also Behrens, *Merchant*, 213–215, 220, 406, 451.
[41] Fischer and Nordvik, "Economic," 22–23; Shawyer (interview); P & O/OCEL/K. St. Johnston – Recollections (P & O Recollections).

implications of such possibilities – the primacy of oil and the coming of supertankers, container transport – also opened on a very different world of shipping. After World War I, the effects of epic shipbuilding was to produce a glut of ships on the market. After World War II, the availability of Liberty Ships and T-2 tankers provided the springboard from which new men – Onassis, Niarchos, McLean – would vault to shipping prominence and, in the case of the latter, remake entirely maritime practice. In the First World War, economic warfare had been waged primarily at sea. In the Second World War, it was waged with air power as much as sea power, and this too presaged a closure of core trades in the future. Even more, the logistical triumphs of this war potentially undermined, as well as affirmed, the extraordinary investment in installations, ships, networks, local-global identities, knowledge, and expertise that enabled maritime mastery of the seas. All the pioneering ways of moving cargo after the war had roots in logistical experiments during the conflict: RoRo (suggested by landing craft); palletization (widely adopted by U.S. supply services); and containerization, the great vitiator of traditions (implied in the lashing of boxes to the decks of ships to maximize carrying capacity to global theaters). The expertise and culture that, in a certain sense, won the war was, in another sense, to end up its victim. But that would still be several decades into the future. First came the end of empire, the initial step in redoing globalization and the maritime world.

THE REVOLVING DOOR

The Remains of War

For three and a half years, Japanese occupation of perhaps the greatest commodity-producing region of the world had meant, for Europeans, humiliation, expropriation, brutalization, and destruction. In 1945, grass eighteen inches high grew in the wharves of Hong Kong. Shanghai appeared beat up and "shabby." Two months into the surrender, Holts still wanted Japanese military protection of its waterfront holdings in the city. Of the 350 lighters in Swatow harbor from before the war, only 50 remained, "including old and damaged ones." Practically all of Holts' property was damaged or looted, including all company books and records. Reports from Singapore in 1946 were like an echo. Sixty-five percent of the port's transit godowns, 49 percent of its storage godowns, and all quayside cranes were either in ruins or looted. Wrecks littered the harbor. Most of the trained labor force had been carted off (and disappeared) for the construction of the Burma-Siam railroad. Rangoon, on its recapture, lacked electricity, public transport, and even clothing. Damage to the port was extensive. What had not been destroyed by bombing in Sandakan was set alight by the Japanese.[42]

Up-country, the damage was extensive. Estates suffered from neglect, theft, or conversion to food production. On some, trees had been cut down. Machinery and record books (including carefully planned schedules for rotational tapping, weeding, replanting, and eradication of root disease) were gone or wrecked. Gone too were laborers, more victims of the Burma-Siam railroad. Those who remained, perhaps down to one-third, were ridden with malaria or disease as a result of malnutrition. Overgrowths of lalang, a long jungle grass, plagued rubber plantations. Serious damage had occurred to oil installations. Timberland leases had been suppressed or confiscated. Getting commodity production running again would be a staggering task, particularly as planters and engineers, many of them specialists, had also disappeared in the course of the war.[43] Simply trying to start up was going to be challenging. As one Harrisons & Crosfield man noted in a dispatch from the west coast of Borneo more than a year after war's end, "Correspondence is not easy from a small tent in the midst of a coconut swamp. Your properties can easily be reported on because there is nothing left to report on. Office buildings and godowns completely *non est* – also residential properties. Not a brick or board left. This town [Labuan] is obliterated."[44]

In human terms the losses were higher. The fall of European colonial Asia had brought with it the internment of several hundred thousand prisoners of war and civilians, and maritime people were to be found in both groups. Nearly all internees – men and women – suffered horribly. Exceptional cases aside, beatings, unending punishment lineups under the tropical sun, forced labor, lack of medicine, crowded housing, and malnutrition were sufficient to wear people down and sweep thousands away. Estimates for the approximately hundred thousand civilian internees in the East Indies suggest a death rate of one in six. The great killers were

---

[42] SOAS/JSSXI 1/9/Box 523/4 September (Hong Kong), 3 October 1945; SOAS/JSSII 2/19/Box 205/30 November 1945 (Shanghai); SOAS/JSSIII 1/21/Box 408, 27 August 1945, 10 March 1946 (on Swatow); PRO/MT 73/12/September 1946 (Singapore); Christopher Bayly and Tim Harper, *Forgotten Armies: The Fall of British Asia, 1941–1945* (Cambridge, MA: Harvard University Press, 2004), 437–438; Pugh, *Great*, 140–142 (Sandakan).
[43] ICHVR/71/Verslag over de periode 1940/1947, 18 June 1948, pp. 13–17, 34; Guildhall/Harrisons/Correspondence/Kuala Lumpur/Box 4/1940–1946, 19 June 1946; Allen and Donnithorne, *Western*, 73–74, 128, 144, 179; Longhurst, *Borneo*, 96, 99.
[44] Pugh, *Great*, 140–141.

malaria, jaundice, and dysentery, but most of all the human-imposed conditions that made these so lethal. Prisoners of war suffered worse. Sixty thousand worked on the infamous Burma-Siam railroad, with death rates approximating one in five (probably still worse for Asians; far more were worked to death or died of disease and hunger). Thousands more died on slow, horribly crammed Japanese transport ships picked off by Allied submarines and bombers unaware of their human cargo.[45]

So scattered and contused were the survivors that a special Allied organization was created at the end of the war to locate and evacuate the tens of thousands still languishing in camps. Surprisingly, a fair number were in good enough health to take up where they had left off three and a half years previously. Large numbers were not, however, and required medical care and long periods of leave. Every expatriate company had its list of losses, among these some of its most experienced people. Eighteen members of the Borneo Company did not survive the war. Dodwells lost twelve. Of Mansfields' European staff in Singapore, only fourteen out of forty had escaped, and of those that did not, seven perished, as did four Chinese employees.[46] In early 1946, half a year after war's end, a list of Harrisons & Crosfield's Singapore staff included such items as "N. G. Cumming, not yet passed as fit, probably leaving in June"; "W. B. Cruickshank, not yet fit – probably leave end April"; "W. L. Kitersow, in Australia. We are suggesting early return" (but subsequent correspondence indicated that he was not fully recovered and turning fifty-nine, had decided to leave the firm); "R. R. Broom, Still unfit."[47]

In the East Indies, now proclaimed the Republic of Indonesia, where perhaps 80,000 to 90,000 Dutch internees were still alive, plus British civilians who had fled Singapore before its fall and assorted Allied troops imprisoned along the archipelago, the situation was dire. Following three and a half years of Japanese entombment came the *bersiap*, a quasi-revolutionary terror that targeted Dutch, Eurasians, and Ambonese (likely Christian and a source of recruitment for the Dutch colonial army). British troops did what they could to evacuate the endangered to

[45] L. de Jong, *Het koninkrijk der Nederlanden in de Tweede Wereldoorlog*, Deel 11b, tweede helft (The Hague: Staatsuitgeverij, 1985), 561–733 (on prisoners of war), 734–843 (on civilian internees); De Roever, *Nederland*, 358–384; Bayly and Harper, *Forgotten*, 147–148, 336–343, 405–408.

[46] Longhurst, *Borneo*, 99; *Dodwell*, 139; MMM/OA 4/1801/21 March 1945; A. Jackson, C. E. Wurtzburg, and A. McLellan, *The History of Mansfield & Company*, vol. 2, 1953, 9.

[47] Guildhall/Harrisons/Correspondence/Kuala Lumpur/Box 4/1940–1946, 15 February 1946.

collection points in coastal cities, and then to safe havens in the region. But there were frightful incidents of torture and murder. A Dutch journalist flying into Batavia in December 1945 found tens of thousands of Europeans huddled in quarters akin to pig sties – "It all seems so hopeless" – desperate to get out to somewhere quiet and safe.[48] The casualty rolls of companies on the islands thus compounded. Approximately 100 Internatio people perished in the war and terror. Totaling up their losses in late 1945, the conclusion was that they must expect half their eastern staff to be evacuated for medical reasons.[49]

For evacuation en masse to Holland, the government turned to the shipping companies, which were well versed by this point in the century in organizing mass flight. Ships scattered across the world were summoned for the enterprise. The full dimensions of the exodus clarified midway in the voyage when the ships called at Adabya in the Gulf of Suez. Evacuees were offloaded, put on a train, and taken several kilometers to Ataka, where the Dutch had established a clothing depot in a hangar. The scene must have bordered on the surreal. Here in the Egyptian desert men and women who had spent nearly the last four years of their lives subsisting in some sort of primitive camp, many of whom had left nearly everything behind, arrived before a structure decked out in Dutch flags. They were greeted by an orchestra of German prisoner-of-war musicians (the reverse symbolism is palpable). At the entrance stood buffets stacked with rolls, baked goods, and cups of coffee. Inside were women from the leading Dutch fashion houses and clothing stores, or experts in sizing up measurements, to staff makeshift counters and racks, as internees were handed a duffel bag and moved from "department" to "department" to collect the warm clothing they would need for the remainder of their voyage. A return to another time, yet a reminder of what was left behind.[50]

[48] De Jong, *Koninkrijk*, 12, *Epiloog*, second half (The Hague: SDU, 1988), 692–708, 718–730; Wim Willems, *De uittocht uit Indië 1945–1995* (Amsterdam: Bert Bakker, 2001), 19–30 (quoted 23); H. W. van den Doel, *Afscheid van Indië. De val van het Nederlandse imperium in Azië* (Amsterdam: Prometheus, 2001), 99–103. Christopher Bayly and Tim Harper, *Forgotten Wars: The End of Britain's Asian Empire* (London: Allen Lane/Penguin, 2007), 168–189.

[49] ICHVR/71/18 June 1948, p. 2; H. Stout, "Van de Toko uit Rotterdam en van wat daarna kwam," in H. Baudet, *Handelswereld en wereldhandel. Honderd jaren Internatio* (Internatio: Rotterdam, 1963), 39; GAR/Stout Papers/135/Notities, 12 January 1946. Almost certainly Indonesians were counted in these numbers.

[50] GAR/Lloyd 1/487/20 December 1945; GAR/Lloyd 1/500/1 November 1945, 31 January, 5, 22 February, 23 May 1946; Willems, *Uittocht*, 43–51. In one Lloyd report the musicians were Italian.

Yet the most striking thing about this period immediately following the war was not the exodus but the alacrity with which the expatriate companies went back in. The determination to return dated almost from the moment of their expulsion. Like Swires, Harrisons as early as 1942 did "not know how long it will be before we can start operations again in Malaya, but we are laying plans to do so at the earliest moment after the Japs are cleared out." Internatio, Scarlett O'Hara-like after the "burning" of Java, defiantly proclaimed it was going back in as soon as the war ended: "It will be difficult, it will go slowly, but it will go, of that we are convinced."[51] So they came, practically in the baggage trains of military forces. Probably no one was as quick as G. L. Oostergo, a Hagemeyer agent, who had been locked up in the Changi camp on Singapore Island. Oostergo managed to make his way into the city and to renew contact with Anthony P. K. Wee, his Chinese staff assistant from before the war. Through Wee he was able to round up all the prewar Chinese personnel, and to renew as well old network connections with Chinese businessmen who advanced him the money to jump-start the business. Through a Chinese connection he bought a prewar Morris "for a song," then traded this for a ticket to Australia where he could get something, anything (he began with foodstuffs for Japanese POWs) to sell in Singapore.[52] The old transnational connections, built up over decades, proved invaluable for many of these firms. Within a week of British liberation of Penang, Nicholas Ponnudurai, an ex-staff member with twenty years of experience with Borneo Company, was writing the home office about the measures he was taking to protect property, reassemble staff, and get business going again.[53]

Rather quickly, then, most of these firms were up and running again. If there was a symbolic moment it must certainly have occurred on the 13th of December 1945 at the first board meeting in four years of the tiny Sarawak Steamship Company, one of those back-of-beyond links in the old global chains, as the four Chinese and one European director gathered in their chairman's home, and "without commenting in any way on what had elapsed [war, occupation, cessation of operations, bombing, loss of the entire four-ship fleet] merely began business ... by noting, 'Minute One: The Minutes of the Meeting held on Thursday 4 December 1941 were read and confirmed.'"[54] The return of Harrisons & Crosfield

[51] Guildhall/Harrisons/837.4 LHS/Kemlo Correspondence, 8 May 1942; ICHVR/168/June 1944.
[52] Huizinga, "*Take*," 172–174; Jonker and Sluyterman, *At Home*, 273.
[53] Guildhall/BCL/MS 27,274.
[54] Tregonning, *Home*, 135.

to its estate and trading activities in Malaya gives a clear picture of how this was done. By the end of November 1945, rubber broker and dealer Freddie Kemlo was back in the colony and touring by jeep every major rubber-producing area in Malaya, save along the peninsula's east coast. In Singapore he gathered up his prewar Asian staff. Beng Saik Lwi, company storekeeper who had kept Chinese connections open through the occupation, was promoted to compradore. Choi Young, head produce clerk, reconstituted from memory all the necessary business forms and worked alongside Kemlo, "doing the work of a senior European assistant." Hock Seng, a thirty-three-year veteran with the firm re-created the forwarding business. As Europeans then filtered back in, Kemlo was already to go. Houses, godowns, and lorries were repossessed. Goods on consignment were ordered from Australia. Rubber-buying units were restarted up-country. Everything was short. In Singapore seven men were sleeping in a two-room house. But by the summer of 1946, Harrisons & Crosfield was again widely established in Malaya.[55] Across all the reoccupied territories, a comparable resurrection of shipping and trading interests was occurring, firm by firm.

Facts Change

But facts change. The power, property, and culture of colonial enterprise had always advanced in tandem with colonial authority, and that authority was nearing its end. Indonesia was a very troubled place in the late 1940s. The Dutch fought two "police actions," yet abandoned all but New Guinea at the close of 1949. During those years violence was rampant and directed toward multiple populations: Europeans, Chinese, Communists, Islamic separatists, but also Indonesians at the hand of Dutch troops. Many of the expatriate firms came to realize that there could be no stability under continued Dutch rule, and were among those who figured in the decision to withdraw. Until then, however, shipping, trading, and harvesting companies were plagued by disruption, spoilation, murder, and guerilla warfare. In 1948, business enterprises were employing, collectively, 18,000 security guards, a number that rose to 23,000 in 1949.[56]

In counterpoint then to Harrisons & Crosfield regrouping in Malaya was Michiels-Arnold's experience on Java. Much of the colonial history

---

[55] Guildhall/Harrisons/Correspondence/Kuala Lumpur/Box 4/1940–1946, 29 November, 12 December 1945, 16 August 1946 (quoted); Pugh, *Great*, 155–168.
[56] De Jong, *Koninkrijk*, 12, *Epiloog*, second half, 883.

of the Dutch on the island could be traced through a study of the property rights, tropical plantings, trading networks, planter culture, and
estate architecture of this old-line plantation house whose origins dated
back to the VOC. In the fall of 1946, this company was still engaged
in tentative efforts to reclaim its plantations on Java. In some cases the
conditions of estates remained a mystery or were available only through
aerial photographs, which showed gutted houses, offices, and godowns.
Planters making reconnaissance voyages did so in the company of armed
escorts. Work in the capital, if less vulnerable, was scarcely tolerable.
Office space was tight. There were long waits for telephone service. Water
and electricity were erratic. Trams were running, "but as far as I know
no European has yet dared to climb on."[57] Even after Dutch withdrawal
disturbances continued. Disorganization and chaos governed the ports.
Life in the countryside was far from secure, punctuated with burnings,
arrests, and murders.[58]

For Michiels-Arnold there was no real going back. Plantations were
taken up again, but under completely altered conditions. The house itself
went through a down-the-rabbit-hole existence. Forced to sell off most
of its lands in 1949, the two-century estate company reinvented itself as
a trading house. Somehow it managed to win the Batavia representation
for the mighty Deli My on Sumatra, probably the most powerful plantation company in the entire archipelago. None of this made any sense.
In the spring of 1949 Michiels-Arnold had a skeletal staff of a mere ten
people in its Batavia office, if one counted the two typists and the care-
taker. It was desperately scrounging around to set up a commodities trading department. "We don't even have a commodity man," head manager
in the Indies, G. J. W. Koolemans Beijnen, frantically wrote Holland in
April of that year.[59] All of this produced what must have been one of the
great awkward moments in the history of trading when, three months
later, Koolemans Beijnen, traveling to Deli My headquarters at Medan
and riding back from the airport with Secretaris Holtkamp, the Deli My's
number-two man on the island, was told that the news of the representation had caught the top administrators in Sumatra *een beetje* short, since
they knew little about Michiels-Arnold except that they were planters

---

[57] NA/MA/63/Stroeve, September 1946; ibid., Rapport No. 5, 22 October 1946; ibid., 16
December 1946 (quoted).
[58] NA/MA/43/13 April, 11 May, 15 June 1951; NA/MA/77/"Rubberonderneming
Klapanunggal," September 1955.
[59] NA/MA/43/12 April (quoted), 14 April 1949.

and wondered what planters could do for them in Batavia. And then "came off hand the question: 'Just how much staff do you have, really, in Batavia?'"

Now [as Koolemans Beijnen wrote in his letter back home several days later, describing this moment] I don't know if you know Medan and the place the Deli My occupies there.... One comes, in the center of the city, upon a great way, the Cremer Way [named for Deli My's J. T. Cremer] from which an avenue, the Deli My Avenue, leads to grounds where a great building stands, like the theater in Batavia, with a number of large homes grouped around it. In the great building is established the head office of the Deli My and in the houses, when they are not set aside for the delegate of the High Representative of the Crown, the Territorial Commander for Sumatra East Coast, and so forth and so forth, live the Head Administrator and his staff. Rounding off the whole is a large hospital. So certainly you will understand that when I had gone over our staff there was, in the car, a painful silence.

But what Koolemans Beijnen also discovered in Medan was that the Deli My, like nearly every other expatriate enterprise in the former East Indies, was plunging down the same rabbit hole. Describing his stay he reported on the large security forces that patrolled the estates and elaborate warning systems that had been set in place. His impression was that every night a drying shed went up in flames. During his stay guerillas ambushed a platoon of troops, sending two men stark naked back with the news, and carrying off the rest and their weapons. "Even for Java," he remarked, "this would be a very serious event." As he prepared to leave, Holtkamp made a first agency request: to arrange the transport home of a murdered assistant's widow and children.[60]

This experience could be generalized for all the archipelago. Political tensions, labor reforms, high taxes, remittance restrictions, and rapid deforestation, which led to silting up of river mouths and flooding of estates, created sufficiently hostile conditions for companies to revisit their visions of return in 1944–1945. Harrisons & Crosfield managed to restart an estate on Sumatra but the chief engineer, Rovenkamp, was shot and killed in the middle of his Sunday morning coffee. In 1952 Harrisons & Crosfield sold the plantation off to the state. Other investments on the islands turned over little in these years, and in the 1960s, for a time, all the company's estates were confiscated. Internatio was still gathering 70 percent of its profits from its Indonesian operations in 1956, but it had

[60] NA/MA/73/12–15 July 1949 (written in Medan on 14 July; Koolemans Beijnen was almost certainly the author).

already begun to invest elsewhere and in 1957 it, and other Dutch enterprises, were taken over.[61]

Across a rapidly decolonizing world, the pattern turned similarly hostile. Many of the measures new states adopted were less overt than in Indonesia but no less inhospitable: high taxes, remittance restrictions, commodity marketing and buying boards, and demands to share out equity.[62] Burma took over the Irrawaddy Flotilla Company and Steel Brothers' and Wallace Brothers' vast teak concessions in 1948, and in the early 1960s all of Steel Brothers' investments in the country. Sri Lanka nationalized tea estates in 1975. A winding down of older investments and activities thus became inevitable. There was a wholesale abandonment of India by British agency firms.[63]

One by one, trading houses in China shut down or lost their business. French estate owners soldiered on in Vietnam and Cambodia through colonial and civil war, but began to leave by the mid-1960s.[64] For a time there was a trend to seek greener pastures in Africa. Yet few transplants of this order paid off. Conditions that had driven them out of Asia repeated in Africa, and in certain areas there was an even worse unraveling. "Don't," warned a Compagnie Maritime Belge official describing the infrastructural decay, widespread poverty, run-down equipment, and pervasive climate of fear and edginess in the Congo ports of Matadi and Boma in 1967, "send out beginners, and certainly not any high-strung types."[65] The romantic promises of going back in, forged in the midst of a titanic struggle, had had the same outcome as that namesake. Something new, instead, was going to take shape.

The Coming Shape of Things

At the very close of the war, the Bretton Woods agreements, followed shortly by GATT, or the General Agreement on Tariffs and Trade, created a new world order for the exchange of money and goods. Together

[61] Allen and Donnithorne, *Western*, 74–87, 134–136; Stoler, *Capitalism*, 111–130; ICHVR/71/18 June 1948, pp. 13–16; ibid., 1949, pp. 33–38; ibid., 1956, p. 32; Jonker and Sluyterman, *Home*, 261–270; Pugh, *Great*, 143–145, 185–187.

[62] Jones, *Merchants*, 117–157; Fieldhouse, *Merchant*, 229–280, 425–448.

[63] McCrae and Prentice, *Irrawaddy*, 128, 141–148, 170 (photo opposite), 186; Jones, *Merchants*, 122, 127, 137; Pugh, *Great*, 212–213; Goswami, "Marwaris," 244–247.

[64] MMM/OA 4C/1148/22 July 1949, 8 June, 13 July 1950; Falkus, *Blue*, 280; Jones, *Merchants*, 137; Dodwell, 50, 139; Jackson, *Sassoons*, 264–272; Coates, *Commerce*, 358–359.

[65] CMB/C 7/17/Voyage à Matadi & Boma, 8–18 December 1967.

they provided for rapid recovery from the appalling destruction, a basis for return to world economic stability, and the platform for an enormous surge in world trade that would occur over the next two-and-a-half decades. Globalization, as it was referred to at the end of the century, would come out of the further restructuring of world capital flows when the Bretton Woods system unraveled in the early 1970s, but also out of lowering trade barriers set in motion by GATT, and which continues to the present day. This was the framework within which all world movements would operate in the postwar years. But at sea level, where maritime bases, identities, and networks had been founded on colonial trades, another reordering occurred when set against the abandonment of empire. That change can be tracked along three lines. First, what became of trading companies in a postcolonial world. Second, the emergence of a more assertive non-Western presence in global trades. Third, the redesignation of shipping identities when severed from home-colonial termini. All three pointed backward toward decolonization and its dissolutions, but also forward, toward the new look in maritime culture and action at the end of the century. All three, moreover, reaffirmed the transnational, networked character of connectedness by sea, even in the midst of major scission.

Overseas trading companies had never been static enterprises. But for those located in Asia or Africa, two conditions had held constant: They were overseas companies in imperial lands, primarily engaged in the exchange of European manufactured products for tropical produce; and they were maritime companies, closely attached by function and geography to the sea. By the 1960s, both of these had changed. A model that had stood at the center of global capitalism in 1900 looked old-fashioned and uncomfortably out of its element half a century later.

Internatio's company trajectory illustrated the mutations that occurred. Its last people departed Indonesia in May 1958, and by this time it was closing down offices throughout the old imperial word. Roughly by the early 1960s, four-fifths of the company's operations had relocated to Europe, mostly the Netherlands. A 1954 brochure, "Some Facts about Internatio," paraded still the old Internatio, heavily concentrated in Southeast Asia and dealing in long lists of tropical goods. There was a produce department (teas, coffees, spices), a gums department, a hides and skins department, a rattan department (*djahabs, kooboos, pulut, segas,* and so on), a reptile department (crocodiles, karungs, lizards, and pythons from Indonesia, Malaya, and Thailand), a rubber department, a shells department, and a timber department. Eleven years later the

1965 brochure referred to the "Internatio Group," and featured installation, industrial production, insurance, and trade in manufactured and
semi-manufactured goods, alongside trade in produce as "main sectors
of activity." Increasingly, the weight of activities gravitated toward engineering, distributive trades, manufacturing, pharmaceutical wholesaling,
and information and communication technology, even after a merger in
1970 with Wm H. Müller (creating Internatio-Müller) pushed it back to
some extent in the direction of port terminals and shipping.[66]

Others, including Harrisons & Crosfield, held out much longer. Here
too, however, there was a long-term shift, in Harrisons & Crosfield's case
deeper and deeper into chemical manufacturing in North America and
Europe, or from timber leasing in the tropics to building supplies in the
UK. Still others went through so many permutations of mergers, acquisitions, and disinvestment that they had little in common with their former imperial or maritime selves. John Holts of Liverpool kept trading
interests in West Africa, but it diversified into French vineyards and wine
shops, launderettes, and dry-cleaning outlets in Britain.[67] This seemed a
retreat from older local-global commitments. But was it? These firms had
always been transnational as well as imperial enterprises. If by the 1960s
the older imperial platform was crumbling, other transnational markets –
the Common Market, a more accessible American market[68] – were beck-
oning. The way of the future would be circulation between developed
trading blocs, a pattern these companies were prepared to assume.

And what of the companies that did not fall back? CFAO refused to
budge from Africa. But it also extended buying to China and Pakistan,
relocated back to Europe as a hedge, and in Africa diversified into mono-
prix stores or cold drink manufactures. Absorbed in 1990 by the Pinault
Group, which also controlled FNAC and Printemps, it renewed concentration on Africa, but now as a provider of sophisticated and high-tech
manufactures and services. Swires meanwhile converted its transport
know-how into one of Asia's most successful airlines (Cathay Pacific), its
sugar refining and sales know-how into Coca-Cola bottling franchises,
its Hong Kong insider know-how (along with its valuable waterfront
property) into real estate development, and its century of cross-national
Chinese connections into effecting all three. These firms too underwent

[66] ICHVR/172/1954, 1965; ICHVR/71/1948; Stout, "Toko"; Jonker and Sluyterman,
    Home, 295, 304–305, and 271–325 on Dutch trading company experience, 1950s–1970s;
    Annual Report: Internatio-Müller NV 1996.
[67] Pugh, *Great*, 121–122, 152–155, 186–253; Jones, *Merchants*, 145–151.
[68] Frieden, *Global*, 268, 279, 283.

mutation, but emerged, if anything, as still greater globalizers purveying Western leisure drinks, electronic and computer technology, and tropics-erasing climatizing systems to an increasingly consumerist world.[69]

The most dramatic change, therefore, was less at the older trans-national level than in company culture and expertise. By the 1960s Internatio's old Indies hands, back in Rotterdam, were a minority within the company, surrounded by new men who were university trained, pos-sessed no colonial past, saw no value in it, and performed very different functions. Even in what remained of the older commodity trades, there were new men who traded on the commodity exchanges rather than peo-ple who had long years of handling a physical product. Internatio, which had once lived on the seas, increasingly lived without them. At the turn of the new century even the name was abandoned for Imtech NV, because "Internatio-Müller ... has become a European technology group. All other non-central activities have been hived off." Harrisons & Crosfield, one of the last to divest of plantations, nevertheless mutated at the end of the century completely into a chemical company, and rebaptized itself Elementis. The company logo, long a sailing ship with H & C embla-zoned on its sails to recall the company's tea-trading origins, was now an abstract design.[70] Such cultural dissonances first adumbrated, then reflected, the reordering of identities and knowledge across the entire maritime community that would follow conversion to containers.

As Westerners "retreated," moreover, the others advanced toward a multicentered global capitalism. The seafaring Hajj trade, situated at the imperial-transnational interface, and which Muslims had surrendered to Europeans a century earlier, signaled this change when it was retaken by Muslims in the 1960s. Everywhere the organization of the flows continued as a large, capitalistic, and complex logistical venture, only now it was non-Westerners who were responsible for the lion's share of initiatives and services.[71] A still larger step was the construction of broad, cross-oceanic networks that rivaled the power of Western ones. The Japanese had done this for a half century. In the 1950s and 1960s, former colonial subjects increasingly began to do so as well. These were the pivotal years when Singapore Chinese dealers, having made initial

---

[69] Bonin, *C.F.A.O.*, 316–406; idem, *CFAO (1887–2007). La réinvention permanente du commerce outre-mer* (Saint-Denis: SFHOM, 2008), 633–708; Jones, *Merchants*, 148, 155, 297–298, 330–331.

[70] Brouwershaven (interview); "Internatio-Müller N.V. Continues as Imtech N.V.," http://www.imtech.eu/eCache/DEF/1/659.bGFuZz1FTg.html (quoted); Pugh, *Great*, 265–272.

[71] Miller, "Pilgrims," 218–228.

advances in the 1930s, truly broke onto the international rubber scene. Producers and packers began to integrate vertically, bringing together within one concern cultivation, transport, packing, port handling, and overseas selling. Postcolonial politics were far from coincidental to this development. When Indonesia embargoed rubber exports to Singapore in retaliation for the formation of a Malaysian state, a massive smuggling business invariably followed. Seagoing vessels loaded for Hong Kong sailed for a symbolic twenty-four hours into the South China Sea, and then steamed for Singapore. Big Chinese companies with the financial means to fund such ventures, took advantage of the economic fallout to seize still greater control of regional sources of supply.[72]

Lee Rubber Company, set up by Lee Kong Chian in 1927, was in the postwar years well on its way to becoming the giant firm through whose hands perhaps one-quarter of all Malayan and Indonesian rubber exports passed in the 1980s. In the 1950s it was a sign of Lee's growing importance that foreign shipping lines were assigning shipping agencies to Lee Rubber "in order to find a way for securing better support from them."[73] Across South and Southeast Asia, Asian companies were becoming prime competitors in commodity markets. Buan Lee Seng was Singapore's largest copra exporter in 1956. In the same period, Teck Guan was the largest copra exporter from the resource-rich region of North Borneo. His closest competitors were no longer British but Chinese traders. Most of their exports were, moreover, being shipped not to Europe or America, but Japan.[74]

This too was a sign of the times. Whereas import substitution still ruled in a large part of the non-industrialized world, something else began to take shape in Asian maritime territories where export economies were given the preference.[75] Trade patterns broke with older colonial models and began to reflect a newfound regional cohesiveness. In certain ways this was a continuation of intra-Asian exchanges between Japan and China that had been going on since the late nineteenth century and that spurred the economic development of each.[76] But it also reflected wider opportunities and dislocations opened up by decolonization. Australian exports

[72] Coates, *Commerce*, 336–346.
[73] Brown, *Capital*, 111; Huff, *Economic*, 219–222, 311–312; Coates, *Commerce*, 311, 336–337; GAR/Lloyd 1/1545, 19 July 1952, attached to 1 August 1952 (quoted); in 1985, Lee Rubber was the world's largest rubber merchant: Chalmin, *Négociants*, 272–273.
[74] ICHVR/69/20 August 1956; GAR/Lloyd 2/S2032/#433/25 October 1958.
[75] Frieden, *Global*, 319.
[76] Sugihara, *Japan*, 1–8.

flowed more toward Japan than Britain. The wool market became totally decentered, with Japan buying nearly twice as much wool as its closest competitor.[77] It was still too early for this to be generalized worldwide, but West African exports that before the war had been directed primarily to Europe were also decentering. In the 1950s and 1960s, Scindia Line had services to India, Japanese lines had services to East Asia, other lines services to Australia, New Zealand, and South America.[78] The great harbor outposts – Singapore, Hong Kong – held on to their role as global hubs; only by the 1960s they did so primarily as rising Asian centers. Even import substitution never excluded world trade altogether because there was always a need to import machines and to export commodities to pay for these. Meanwhile, behind trade barriers loomed the prospect of reentering trade flows, but this time as an exporter of manufactures.

And shipping companies? Future Asian giants, the Malaysian International Shipping Corporation and Neptune Orient Lines, were founded in the late 1960s, Hong Kong's Orient Overseas Container Line (later OOCL) even earlier. On the other hand, where European companies had grown comfortable operating within protected trades – as was the case of French lines – with their heavy state involvement, the response to decolonization in one place was often to cleave more closely to such traffic in another. After the retreat from Algeria, the CGT, whose North African and West Indies business outweighed in passengers and cargo all of its noncolonial services combined, fell back on the Antilles in the 1960s as an even more crucial profit center.[79] This experience, however, was not universal. Where national shipping traditions were more transnational, and better networked, the responses were more creative. P & O, whose history was inseparable from the stream of British administrators and troops and merchants and planters back and forth to India, recognized that these trades had gone forever and made the necessary conversions to freight. The company expanded into tanker lines so aggressively that by the mid-1960s it possessed the largest British tanker fleet shy of the majors. Through buyouts and consolidations, it repositioned itself as a far more global line than ever before.[80]

Others, British India and the Dutch, went even further in prefiguring the global operators of the future. Probably no steamship company was harder hit by decolonization than British India. Partition ejected it

[77] NMM/P & O/4/81/Agents' Reports/Sydney, 1967.
[78] Davies, *Trade*, 311.
[79] AAFL/CGT/5195/Conseil d'administration/4 October 1967; Frémont, *French*, 62–65, 103.
[80] Howarth and Howarth, *P & O*, 153–160.

from the Indian coasting trades, which BI had dominated for more than a century. State quotas for Indian lines slashed off a large part of its trunk trades. In 1964 a manager on an inspection tour remarked on the extraordinary rupture with the past: During his fortnight in Calcutta not one British India ship had visited the harbor. The recourse was to reorient toward the cross trades – those operating routes that lay completely outside national spheres and that had been largely the purview of trampers. Here was a detachment not only from colonial but national bases and identities. Harboring within was a coverage predicated solely on sea flows, or the prospect of greater global extension. BI's steps were still partial, but it opened a new operations center in Hong Kong and pioneered routes such as the one it sailed between the Persian Gulf and Japan and Australia, growth trades of the future. Aggressive in developing new markets, the company evolved a culture of adaptation that filtered toward a deeper restructuring. When OCL, the British consortium that containerized eastern traffic was assembled in the second half of the 1960s, BI men would form part of the nucleus that put it together.[81]

The Dutch too were cast out of their imperial paradise. No national fleet was so dislodged by decolonization. Excepting Holland Amerika and the KSMN, all the principal Dutch lines focused in one way or another on the East Indies, and at the end of the 1950s all were expelled. What they did then was instructive. Thinking ahead, the Java-China-Japan Line and the KPM had already merged their overseas lines into a new company, officially the Koninklijke Java-China Paketvaart Lijnen, but renamed, for international purposes, Royal Interocean Lines, or RIL. Following expulsion its energy too was directed into the cross trades. Symbolically, RIL removed itself from an East Indies identity (just as its name signaled nothing Dutch), and set up its eastern headquarters in Hong Kong. From there it reinforced older connections to Japan, but also to ports and countries with little if any linkage to the old Dutch imperial shipping systems. The career trajectory of one of its leading figures, Ru van Osselen, indicated how easily older transnational experience could effect the transition. Van Osselen's time in the East went back to 1928, and he had worked with JCJL in Surabaya, Batavia, Hong Kong, and Kobe. Back in Hong Kong in 1960 when the Indonesians threw them out of the archipelago, he saw no need to "wail over the fact that it was over," because he was already reoriented in other directions and knew that he could use his

---

[81] Adams (interview); NMM/BIS/9, 10/business trip reports (quoted 9/2/ 13 March 1964); P & O/OCEL.

ships better on the new routes. This rough-and-ready attitude, but even better, the ability to reinvent, made RIL one of the true postwar success stories within European shipping circles. RIL, too, would provide much of the drive when the Dutch shipping companies banded together to containerize as Nedlloyd.[82]

The two great trunk lines, the Dutch Mails, did the same. Like van Osselen, the Rotterdamsche Lloyd's Bernard Ruys, when tossed out of Indonesia, was not about to cry over spilled milk. "Oh, is that so," he said. "Then we will just have to do something else with our ships." At first they fought like cats and dogs to force their way into conference berths in East Asia. But their greater effort was to build out what, to reflect their two names, they had come to call their Nedlloyd trades. These included a service between the U.S. and South and East Africa, and a more focal route that tied together the two postwar centers of the world's oil trade, the Gulf of Mexico and the Persian Gulf. Agents who went out to the latter in the late 1940s found an inhospitable land, but one on the verge of a boom that would have to import just about everything it needed. For years to come there would be huge imports of machinery and oil field materials, which would suffer under the harsh climate and require constant replacement. There would in addition be the construction materials for refineries, and then all the secondary and tertiary trades in materials for water systems, lighting systems, and housing. Money would flow almost as thick as the oil, and this would produce still further needs (so that by the late 1960s Nedlloyd agents were canvassing for business in pleasure boats, refrigerators, air conditioners, and big American cars, even though Bedouins had a habit of disappearing from both car and car payments after crashing their Chryslers in the desert). As the Mails plowed resources into the Nedlloyd trades they increased services to the Persian Gulf and added more cross trade services between the United States and South Asian harbors, eventually with Caribbean and South American calls added in.[83]

Ironically, just as Europeans elsewhere were being squeezed out of older trades by nationalistic demands for a greater share of the carrying trade – what Europeans branded as "flag discrimination"[84] – the old

---

[82] NA/KPM/371/20 July 1946; Brugmans, *Chinavaart*, 169–195; Oosterwijk, *Op*, 126–138, 146–149 (quoted 149); Delprat, *Reeder*, 279–280; Van den Wall Bake (interview).

[83] Oosterwijk, *Op*, 36, 48 (quoted); Leeman, *Barkschip*, 290–308; Brugmans, *Tachtig*, 214; Reuchlin, "Handelsvaart," 256–257; GAR/Lloyd 2/S2024/#231/November–December 1947; ibid., #258/November–December 1949; GAR/Lloyd 2/S2039/#634.

[84] Seiler, *Südamerika*, 230–232.

imperial Dutch, who had begun to pioneer round-the-world routes in the 1930s, stood squarely at the center of a local-global reordering. They were still local, *Dutch* companies, embedded in home identities; when containerization came, all the former imperial lines joined in a national consortium under the Nedlloyd imprimatur. Certainly they were still global companies, even more so than ever before. But neither side of the equation represented what it once had. Royal Interocean Lines took Hong Kong as its home base. The Mails, which since the second half of the nineteenth century had operated a relay between the Netherlands and the East Indies, with subsequent routes radiating out of their Indonesian trades, now sailed the world with large numbers of ships that never called at either of these termini. Maritime globalism, as a conflux of flows and identities, was as yet only beginning to change. But here too a metamorphosis was underway.

PHOENIX REPRISED

One company, however, that stayed put and flourished was Gray Mackenzie, Mackinnon Mackenzie's branch in the Persian Gulf. This somewhat sleepy firm, wedded to truly backwater trades even by non-Eurocentric standards, suddenly found itself after 1945 at the center of the greatest commodity trade in the world. As the majors stormed into Gulf oil fields, where little in the way of port infrastructure preceded them, Gray Mackenzie's fleet of tugs, barges, and lighters hauled their rigs and everything else they required to pump oil out of the ground. Despite its own postcolonial troubles – Saudi Arabia and Iraq pushed it out in the 1960s – Gray Mackenzie prospered. Its expatriate workforce magnified tenfold as the firm turned itself into a provider of essential services for one of the greatest growth regions in the world.[85] Oil shipments grew explosively after the war and are a reminder that paralleling the throes of decolonization was a still larger story of spectacular recovery in the industrial and consumer heartlands. This too shaped maritime history after the war, to the point that it fairly burst at the seams.

Growing up in Hamburg in the 1930s, Franz Wooge's life mapped out in traditional Hanseatic fashion. He would finish *Gymnasium*, do his military service, take up an apprenticeship with a Hamburg import firm, go to London for a year of work with a cargo-surveyor friend of his father,

---

[85] Guildhall/Gray Mackenzie/MS 27,734A/Noble Typescript.

and then enter the family cargo-surveying business his grandfather had established two generations earlier. Instead he went to war in Poland in 1939 and did not return until a half decade later. Years after, a successful brokering career behind him, he entered Albrecht & Dill, the big Hamburg chocolate importing firm, as a partner. Yet the apprenticeship he did serve was one neither he nor his father could possibly have imagined: with a company dealing right after the war in any unrationed goods it could get its hands on, "No questions asked." Their greatest coup came at Christmastime in 1947 when they bought a damaged lot of toys, dolls, teddy bears, and "little things moving on four wheels but there were not four wheels there were only three of them." They then nailed notices on the trees that there would be a sale of toys on Saturday from nine to four, and set up tables on the side of the road. "There was a railway line. They stopped! They stopped in front of our tables! And the people came out and bought! It was unbelievable! And we had so much that we had been selling for five days or so." In 1949, now an import broker of dried fruits, Wooge found himself traveling into the city by tram every morning through kilometers of empty lots, not ruins anymore because these had been cleared away, but "not parking lots because there were no cars to park, so it was nothing."[86]

What Allied traders found on their reentry to Shanghai or the East Indies paled in comparison to conditions in Europe, especially in Germany. In Hamburg and Bremen, home offices, warehouses, and archives had gone up in flames. At Alter Wall 10, Wille's bombed-out headquarters, only the cellar was protected from the elements. To clear out a working space, employees scraped away with shell casings, spades, and coffee pots.[87] Shipping too was back at scratch. HAPAG's fleet right after the war consisted of one boat formerly used to ferry passengers to North Sea seaside resorts. NDL's water services consisted of tugboats in Bremen and Bremerhaven harbors.[88] Once the greatest shipping company in the world, HAPAG was reduced to distributing care packages, an apt trade since Christian Ahrenkiel (who had been running the company at war's end) and his wife were living in one small, unheated room and surviving largely on care packages sent by old HAPAG connections abroad. Other money came in from hotel and restaurant services that both HAPAG and NDL opened to hold on to kitchen and service personnel. The grand

---

[86] Franz-Albert Wooge, Albrecht & Dill, interview with author, Hamburg, 2 July 1996.
[87] Zimmermann, *Wille*, 166–167, 211.
[88] Wiborg and Wiborg, *Unser*, 310–316.

headquarters building on the Alster had survived the bombings, but British military officials occupied all except two floors, which HAPAG shared with twenty other tenants.[89] Not much was left of the port. There was a quay wall standing here, a shed or crane there, but so widespread was the destruction, including a harbor jagged with wrecks, that even where it was possible to unload goods, the means of sailing in and out, or removing them, was practically nil. For years the harbor would be preoccupied with clearing and rebuilding.[90]

Damage to infrastructure in Europe was nearly universal. London and Liverpool had been heavily bombed. Harbors along the Le Havre-Hamburg range, the world's greatest agglomeration of overseas switching points, were, with one exception, largely a composite of wreckage and ruins. From Rouen to Dunkirk, two-thirds of berths, two-thirds of bridges, two-thirds of sheds and entrepots, and nearly three-quarters of dredging equipment were gone. Rotterdam had been terror-bombed by the Nazis and then, because it was used as a German naval base and repair station, further bombed by the Allies. In the last years of the war, most services in the city were coming to a standstill. Directors of the Holland Amerika Line, who needed to travel to the Hague, were lucky if they could catch a seat in the two-horse carriage that Heineken still operated between the two cities. Before it was all over, German demolition crews demolished much of the remaining harbor installations, an action they repeated all along the coast. Only Antwerp was captured essentially intact.[91]

Yet, very rapidly, all were rebuilt and surpassed their best years in the past. By the 1960s London's turnover was half again what it had been on the eve of the war, and Rotterdam had crossed the 100 million ton threshold. All the big liner companies were back, including the Japanese and the Germans, and continued to dominate traditional trades. World tonnage, despite all the war losses, was already a third larger in 1948 (81 million tons) than in 1939, and shot up to 130 million tons in 1960, 268 million tons in 1972.[92]

[89] HAPAG/431; Wiborg and Wiborg, *Unser*, 317–321.
[90] Klugmann and Seeler, *Hafen*, 34, 43; Hamburg, Staatsarchiv/BWV I/1897/6 June 1947, 9 January 1948, 7 July 1950.
[91] Vigarié, *Grands*, 563–565; Havenbedrijf der Gemeente Rotterdam/Jaarverslag/1945; Leo Ott, "Rotterdam during the Years of War," in Schraver, *Rotterdam*, 71–80; Van de Laar, *Stad*, 410–411, 435–447; Wentholt, *Brug*, 242; F[rans] Posthuma, "Het havenbedrijf der gemeente Rotterdam, 1945–1965," in G. E. van Walsum, ed., *Rotterdam Europoort* (Rotterdam: A. D. Donker, 1972), 16–19.
[92] Sturmey, *British*, 138; Klugmann and Seeler, *Hafen*, 10, 46; Devos and Elewaut, *CMB*, 198, 217; Havenbedrijf der Gemeente Rotterdam/Jaarverslag/1952, 1963.

The same networked, clubby, trust-laden maritime culture continued to prevail. Just as after the First World War, the road to resurrection was traveled via the old cross-national cosmopolitan networks. The war may have been fought to obliterate the enemy, but right after it, old working relationships with Rowntree enabled Albrecht & Dill to restart operations.[93] Overseas, Wille was never able to regain its former position in world coffee markets, and Melchers' rebuilding plans in China were dashed by Communist takeover.[94] But Buschmann's trading house, flattened in the war, was back in contact with client networks thanks in part to critical support from English connections. Illies' long-developed close relations with Japanese firms sustained its return to Japan. Japanese trading relations then opened a channel to Samsung, and this led to a flourishing business association, more South Korean contacts and clients, and the establishment of a branch office in Seoul. HAPAG used insider connections to rebuild its coffee carrying business with Central America, and its conference memberships renumbered in the dozens.[95]

There was then a vintage quality to the look and sound of maritime life by the 1960s, but only just. The paradox was that whereas Europeans in the East had gone in like gangbusters to restore their prewar world, had failed, and thus had settled on a major transition, elsewhere they had succeeded spectacularly only to produce what would turn into a comparable dismantlement. The reason was oil. From the late 1940s to the early 1970s, the stars were perfectly aligned for the world of shipping. During those two-and-a-half decades, world trade volumes multiplied more than sixfold.[96] Three-quarters of this tonnage was carried by sea.[97] The conjunctural causes were many: a sharp demographic rise; GATT and Bretton Woods; the Common Market, which stimulated growth and export-oriented industry; and full employment welfare systems. But on the oceans the driver was the two billion tons of petroleum that were being extracted from the earth by 1968, sixty percent of which was crossing some body of water by ship. Oil transport accounted for sixty percent of the enormous expansion in seaborne trade, to the point that more than half of the goods shipped over the world's oceans at the beginning of the

[93] Hauschild-Thiessen, *Albrecht*, 90–101.
[94] Zimmermann, *Wille*, 171; *150 Jahre Melchers*, 19.
[95] Molsen, *C. Illies*, 88; Wilhelm Michels, Hamburg, written report to the author, 6 May 2002; Krieg, *Buschmann*, 66–71; HAPAG/3142/Liste der Konferenz-Mitgliedschaften, 1955.
[96] Harlaftis, *Greek*, 247; Frieden, *Global*, 289.
[97] Cassagnou, *Grandes*, 113.

1970s was, in metric tonnage, black, filmy mineral oil. Oil tankers, only 16 percent of the world's fleet in 1938, were rapidly approaching the 50 percent mark. More than any other form of shipping, it was tankers that accounted for the enormous increase in world tonnage. And with that preponderance came far-reaching consequences.[98]

To understand these, it is first necessary to understand the scaling-up dynamics that were overtaking bulk transport, especially given the volume and value of oil on the seas. One giant tanker was cheaper to build and man than several smaller ones adding up to its total. Geography compounded that advantage, because the longer the voyage, the greater the paying freight on one ship carrying more oil and costing less to operate. And, as one person put it, "one would be hard pressed to find an area more remote from both Western Europe and Japan than the Persian Gulf." In 1970, Japan was importing 213 million tons of oil, nearly all brought in by ship over seven thousand sea miles from the principal source in the Middle East. European oil imports between 1950 and 1970 progressed tenfold. When Suez closed twice, forcing a thousands of miles increase in sea mileage around the Cape, the economic argument for supertankers was driven home. In the 1960s, the size of tankers was approaching 200,000 tons, and in 1971 an order was placed for a tanker of 373,400 tons.[99] Bulk carriers, or dedicated vessels constructed for the specifications of one particular bulk commodity such as ore or grain, spread the same scaling-up dynamics to the dry bulk trades. Like tankers, their arrival was favored by an increasing demand for primary materials whose chief source lay many thousands of miles distant, and by the economics of running big ships full over very large sections of the sea.

Together they began to alter shipping and ports profoundly, although in nearly every case the effects were double edged because as shipping and terminal operators reconfigured for supersized ships, they simultaneously paved the way for a new stage of world economic exchange and development. Another, more comprehensive dynamic thus kicked in. Marine communities made possible a wider, new kind of globalism, but as they did so they also subverted who they were and what they did. The full effects would only come with the container revolution, but already in the 1950s and 1960s the impact of oil and bulk shipping set the process on its way. A first stage was the eradication of distance as an economic

[98] Ibid., 115, 145; Harlaftis, *Greek*, 247; Sturmey, *British*, 75.
[99] Cassagnou, *Grandes*, 143–144; Atle Thowsen and Stig Tenold, *Odfjell: The History of a Shipping Company* (Bergen: Odfjell ASA, 2006), 283–84 (quoted 283); Van Driel and de Goey, *Rotterdam*, 68; Rotterdam, Havenbedrijf Archief (HA)/ 39/ 5 February 1969.

factor. Tankers brought oil to consumer centers in heavy, even, and relatively cheap quantities from fields as remote as imaginatively possible.

Bulk carriers rearranged world supply lines in iron ore. What had once been mined largely at home or transported over short seas from Sweden or Spain, now came from distant sources, especially when strip mining techniques applied with ruthless disregard for the land on the other side of the planet substantially lowered the cost of extraction. The amount of ore moving across oceans in 1960 exceeded the amount carried by sea in the late 1930s by at least a factor of four. The two leading export nations became Australia and Brazil.[100]

These developments then had an internal impact on the world of shipping because just at the moment that decolonization was drawing traditional liner companies into cross trades, bulk carriage, on regular runs, was converting to liner-like service. Older categories of shipping thus began to dissolve toward new definitions. Moreover the profits of tankers and bulk carriers encouraged liner companies to enter these businesses, further skewing who they were. There was also the rise of new specialty trades like chemical transport that rode a worldwide demand for chemicals in basic manufacturing processes but also in postwar synthetic production of plastics, fabrics, fertilizer, and pharmaceuticals. When innovative shipping designs permitted transport of corrosive and dangerous materials in scaled-up volumes, the distribution of chemicals for global production enlarged along a North American–European–East Asian axis. But this also enlarged the mutable categories of shipowning and shipping, and turned ports into big chemistry production centers.[101]

The interchange carried over to levels of leadership. The movers and shakers in tankers were new men, especially Greeks. Ready to move at the end of the war, they gobbled up what they could of surplus war shipping at bargain prices, and they contracted with oil companies for long-term charters that then served as security for more construction loans. In the boom years of the 1950s and 1960s, it was not difficult to pay off mortgages with one year's round of voyages and then to plow profits back into new ship orders. Pacesetters were Aristotle Onassis and Stavros Niarchos, both only minor shipowners before the war and, in the case of Onassis in particular, someone on the outer edge of even Greek shipping circles, although he had experience in running tankers.

[100] Devos and Elewaut, *CMB 100*, 197–199; Harlaftis, *Greek*, 251–257; Cassagnou, *Grandes*, 118–120. Figures vary by source; I have chosen the lowest of these.
[101] Thowsen and Tenold, *Odfjell*, 268–309; Loyen, *Haven*, 143, 269, 277, 303–306.

Their profits were also very high because they registered their ships offshore under the Panama flag of convenience. Although hardly new, this too was partially an oil phenomenon. After the war, American oil companies and other shipowners saw in Panamanian registry a means of building a sizable tanker and tramping fleet despite noncompetitive American labor costs. The American government saw in such vessels a strategic reserve they could call in during times of international crisis. As a fail-safe measure, another American clientele-state registry – Liberian – was introduced in 1948. The advantages were obvious. Regulations were fewer, taxation slight or nonexistent, and manning requirements minimized. Flagging out took off, and by the end of the 1980s, one-third of the world's shipping in deadweight tonnage was registered as Panamanian or Liberian, or under the flags of such shipping superpowers as Honduras, Cyprus, the Cayman Islands, and Bangladesh. The Greeks had plenty of company, but they were especially keen practitioners, and would use flags of convenience, along with their new ships, to catapult themselves to the very top of world shipowning.

If then, on the surface, the shipping world had returned to its traditional order, the reality was that momentum had passed to new men, largely upstarts such as Onassis and Niarchos, the poor club man Douglas Thomson, or the Odfjells of Norway, who were not even in Norway's top forty for the first half century of their shipping lifetime, but who pioneered the new methods of chemical transport. With them came a new transnationalism, more fluid and less fixed to a home base, as had characterized local-global connections through the first half of the century. Onassis was a perfect example. He was Greek, but from his hometown of Smyrna (Izmir), made his start in Buenos Aires and held Argentinian citizenship, cultivated Scandinavian shipping circles, ordered ships in Germany, took his financing from New York, lived in the United States or in Europe, sought partnerships with the Saudis, sent his ships all around the world, and registered them in offshore countries on third or fourth continents. Whether he was any more a man of the world than Richard Holt, or Kerry St. Johnston, or Marius Böger was questionable; but there was a different kind of worldliness here. Certainly one of the great ironies from this period was that as decolonization advanced globalization in one sense, the rise of the American imperium did so in another.[102]

---

[102] Fraser, *Onassis*; Doris Lilly, *Those Fabulous Greeks: Onassis, Niarchos, and Livanos* (New York: Cowles, 1970); Rodney Carlisle, *Sovereignty for Sale: The Origins and Evolution of the Panamanian and Liberian Flags of Convenience* (Annapolis, MD: Naval

Probably the greatest impact of oil flows and supersized ships was the one on ports. From Marseille to Hamburg, Europe's main ports had rebuilt and outfitted with state-of-the art installations. But the new leviathans posed challenges never before encountered. Not only were drafts too great for most river ports, but the dangers of bringing in ships of several hundred thousand tons, especially those loaded with inflammable substances, were considerable.[103] Major dredging operations occurred all through this period, but far more auspicious, ports began to extend their terminals way downriver, or, in the case of Marseille, northwest to deep-water basins in the Golfe de Fos. Rotterdam, the bellwether for all other port development programs in these years, underwent a history of unrelenting expansion until, with the huge Europoort project, it reached the ocean. In the 1960s more Europoort basins and plant sites were laid down, this time practically out into the North Sea on the Maasvlakte. Each stage of planning sought to keep pace with the extraordinary increase in tanker size. The nautical challenges the port had taken on were so great that it had to carve a separate channel to separate inland barge traffic from big ship movements on the New Waterway.[104] All of this occurred under relentless pressure and blackmail from the oil companies. Letters to port authorities were little less than ultimatums about ship size and access requirements.[105] Modern Rotterdam, to a certain degree, was a creation of big oil.

The scaling-up of ships triggered a scaling-up along every other bulk phase of the harbor chain: giant oil storage complexes, huge grab cranes, push tugs on inland waterways.[106] Port industrialization intensified. From the producer's end it made economic sense to locate refineries or factories at the point of massive delivery, and from the port's end the reward was to capture industrial traffics for the harbor. It was at this time that big steelworks began to locate in ports along Europe's littoral.[107] Particularly sought after were chemical and petrochemical plants.

Institute Press, 1981), 34–115, 193–203; Harlaftis, *Greek*, 226–227, 235–245, 262–268; Bauchet, *Transport*, 210; Sturmey, *British*, 218–225; Pedraja, *Rise*, 133–136.

[103] BWV II/10043/Schiffsliegeplätze: Grosseschiffe 1966–1970/28 November 1967, 2 April, 18 July, 25 August 1969, 19 November 1970.

[104] Posthuma, "Havenbedrijf"; De Goey, *Ruimte*, 70–133; Van de Laar, *Stad*, 464–465, 485–498.

[105] GAR/Havenbedrijf 1945–1963/48 (2) doos 15/7 February 1956; ibid., doos 14, 19 March, 31 August 1959.

[106] Van de Laar, *Stad*, 512–513; Devos and Elewaut, *CMB 100*, 199; Suykens, *Antwerp*, 465; Lederer, *Histoire*, 290.

[107] Devos and Elewaut, *CMB 100*, 199.

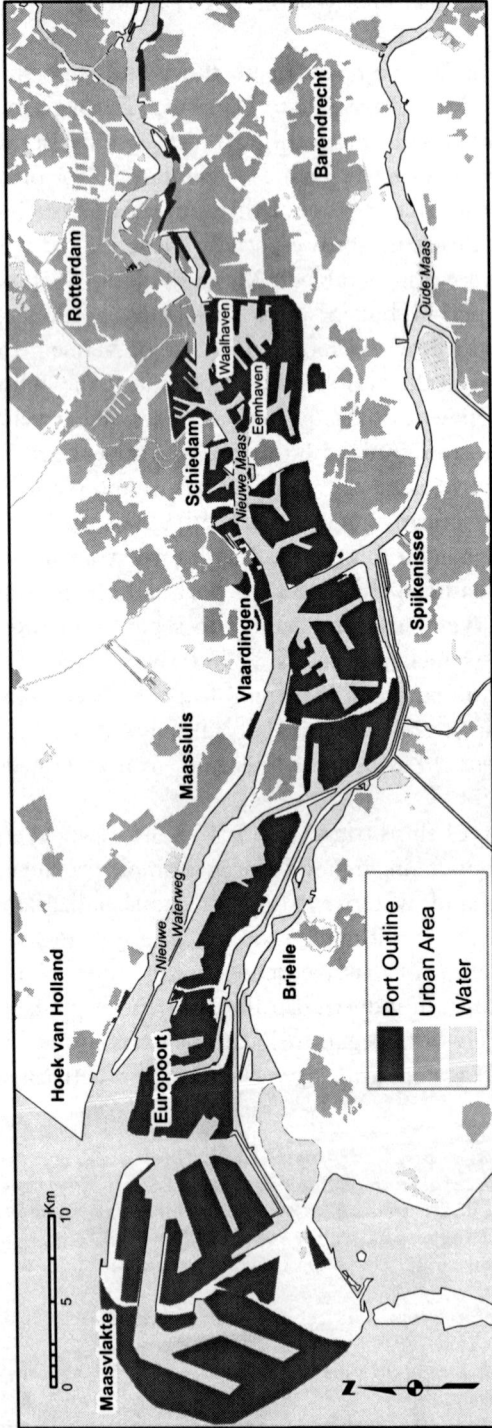

MAP 4. Rotterdam's extension to the sea.

Antwerp beat out Rotterdam in a tough fight to bring BASF to its harbor, drawing subsequent investment by DEGUSSA and Bayer.[108] Thirty years later, refineries, and gas, chemical, and petrochemical complexes ran along the entire right bank of the Scheldt, from the city to the Dutch border. In all ports the rationale for the vast expansion downriver was not only to provide deep-water access for bigger ships, but terrains for industrial investment.

The big consequences then were that ports became industrial as well as water-station complexes, they extended miles downriver from the old city centers, and they made a mockery of earlier turnover figures. Oil was again the big driver. Rotterdam, which became Europe's top oil port, began, by the 1960s, to move beyond main port status to a category all its own: world leader, continental behemoth, and standard for the future. In 1962 the city displaced New York as the world's greatest port in seaborne cargo handled. In 1963, Rotterdam crossed the magical 100 million mark, turning over 103.3 million tons. New York moved 92.6 million tons in that year, with London a distant third at 61.3 million tons. Next in line was Antwerp, handling 20 million tons higher than its best prewar totals, but 56.7 million tons shy of the city it had always regarded as its principal competitor. Almost all of this spectacular rise was built out of oil. In the early 1960s, Rotterdam was one of the three great pipeline termini for the continent. Shell, Esso, Caltex, and Gulf had refineries in the port, with BP constructing another major refinery in 1966. Oil accounted for nearly three-fifths of Rotterdam's turnover totals, or approximately 13 million tons more than *all* of the freight moving in and out of the port of Antwerp. Transit was still a major function of the port, but vast quantities of goods were now off-loaded for harbor industries established on the new harbor lands and that drove homeland industrialization. What had been a mass of twisted debris in 1945 now drew delegations from Japan and America to study what appeared the beacon to the future. Within Rotterdam there were plans to function as the distribution center for northwestern Europe. The very name Europoort, whose deep-water harbors and industrialized environs were the most obvious symbol of the port's success, spoke volumes. Having lost one empire, the Dutch began to contemplate another.[109]

---

[108] De Goey, *Ruimte*, 134–138.
[109] HA/3238/11 February 1964; Posthuma, "Havenbedrijf," 39, 53; Havenbedrijf der Gemeente Rotterdam/Jaarverslag/1963; HA/39/Stukken betreffende lezingen van directeur Posthuma 1969–1972 [Stukken], 5 February 1969.

Typically, nothing occurred in the above narrative outside port networks; this is one thing that did not change. Caltex and Shell may have made modern Rotterdam, but so too did port directors N. Th. Koomans and Frans Posthuma, who rallied port users and city authorities around the raw figures of port turnover. Both men were committed to an oil flow strategy. Posthuma, who worked on plans for Europoort as Koomans's assistant director and succeeded him in 1959, had traveled to the United States in 1952 where he saw firsthand the coastal spread of petrochemical complexes and decided that this too would be Rotterdam's future. From the 1950s through the 1960s, the two men enjoyed the almost unqualified backing of local government for their vision that city and port destiny were inextricably linked, and that harbor growth and expansion were the highest priority. Home shipping companies, stevedore firms, barge operators, local banks and business figures, and representatives of the Transport Workers Union, brought together in informal advisory committees to consult on infrastructural matters with port and city officials, all cohered behind that vision. As the port expanded downriver, a representative from the chamber of commerce, then a former Unilever director with good contacts abroad, traveled to America to drum up investors for the new industrial terrains.[110]

The power of networks to make and break port destinies carried over to geopolitics. Cold War divisions cut Hamburg off from potentially one-third of its prewar traffic to the east (although when those barriers eventually came down old Hamburg connections to the now powerful economies of East Asia brought considerable rebound and enrichment).[111] In western Europe, the formation of the Common Market reaffirmed old peripheries and centralities. More than ever Marseille was cast to the margins of European production and consumption. Meanwhile, modernization of transport networks in the new spirit of economic cooperation – electrification of railroads, new canals, superhighways – routed traffic heavily toward the northwestern ports of Antwerp and Rotterdam. These were the two big winners of European economic union. As an engine for growth, the Common Market accounted in good part for the massive shipments pouring through Rotterdam. Antwerp, if dwarfed by its neighbor's turnover figures, retained its preeminence in general cargo trades

---

[110] Van de Laar, *Stad*, 485–493; De Goey, *Ruimte*, 69, 75; Posthuma, "Havenbedrijf," 30; HA/39/Stukken, 5 February 1969.
[111] Klugman and Seeler, *Hafen*, 18–20.

and more than held its own in terms of port-generated wealth. Besides, in an era of cooperation, Rotterdam interests at last were obliged to relent and accept a Scheldt-Rhine connector.[112]

Here too port networks made all the difference in the step from "cooperation" into investment. Rotterdam interests quickly moved to orchestrate planning and financing of waterway projects beneficial to their harbor. In the Union of Rhine Chambers of Commerce, whose permanent secretariat located in Rotterdam, and in the Dutch Rhine-Main-Danube-Union, they had two organizations through which they could elaborate programs and succeed in placing their strategic goals on the priority list of Common Market objectives. Antwerp-led planning organizations, with Belgian government sponsorship, infiltrated "competent, sound men, 'oceanics' capable of interpreting problems through the perspective of harbors," into Common Market technical commissions. By contrast, in France, where continental outlooks predominated, other priorities were pursued. In fact lobbying efforts by powerful French barge interests desirous of better access to Antwerp were as responsible as new spirits of partnership in linking the Rhine to the Scheldt.[113]

Ports too, by the 1960s, had consequently a vintage look: the same powerhouses concentrating on the Rhine and the Scheldt, the same reliance on networks, the same massive flows of seaborne trade carrying on as they always had. Yet these highly industrialized harbors running down to the sea had not altogether been remade as the harbors of the past. Oddly, the most subversive force working on ports was not big oil, nor geopolitics, but the one that did not occur. Despite restoration, then reordering in other trades, no rationalizing process had redefined the way general cargo, whose volumes also broke records, moved through harbors after the war. Cargoes of tea, coffee, tobacco, rubber, cotton, textiles, cement, steel, meat, fruit, processed food, machines, spare parts, hardware, durables, musical instruments, animals – the whole infinite range of goods that added the greatest value to human exchange and were the vital center of maritime life still required, as they had always

---

[112] Roncayolo, *L'imaginaire*, 227–228; Rolf Oldewage, *Die Nordseehäfen im EWG-Raum, Fakten und Probleme: Hamburg, Bremen, Wilhelmshaven, Emden, Amsterdam, Rotterdam, Antwerpen, Gent, und Dünkirchen* (Tübingen: J. C. B. Mohr, 1963), 54–75; Vigarié, *Grands*, 612–630; Posthuma, "Havenbedrijf," 34–37; Loyen, *Haven*, 281–282; Suykens, *Antwerp*, 463–468.

[113] Vigarié, *Grands*, 612–630 (quoted 622); Cassagnou, *Grandes*, 618–621; Suykens, *Antwerp*, 465.

done, winches, and cranes, and lots of human muscle to get from one part of the world to another. The result was that as ports filled up and labor costs rose, they collided head-on with port tradition. No matter how modern the rebuilding process had been, it could not keep pace with the future. Ports turned into bottlenecks, and only a revolution could force these narrows, which is why absence of change placed ports, in effect all the maritime world, on the verge of the greatest remaking of all. René Borruey, observing Marseille's reconstruction at this moment in time, caught the oxymoronic reality of such up-to-the-minute custom when he described the perfection of the mid-century harbor and transport system, all the links in the transport chain – ships, railroads, trucks – operating at levels of high efficiency, ports organized for "conditions of fluidity," in ways that the past century's engineers "would not have dared to imagine," as nothing but "an image in black and white," soon to be passé, rephrased as merely "conventional" when set against a coming new world, the one that we would see in colors, if far from radiant ones.[114]

Thus it is fitting to end with London. This was still Europe's greatest port, if the full-bloodedness of activity, as much as volume, is what we mean by that term. Before the war it had surrendered statistical leadership to New York, and by the 1960s Rotterdam had shot by as well. But turnover in London in the early 1960s was still more than 60 million tons, 15 million tons higher than Antwerp, and an astonishing number by any exercise of prewar memory. Not even Rotterdam's prodigious march to the sea could equal London's thirty-six miles of quays.[115] This majestic old port had been badly beaten up in the war. A third of the port's infra- and superstructure had been destroyed from the skies. So extensive was the damage that the restoration period lasted until the mid-1950s. Five years alone were required to remove all the sunken ships or heavy pieces of equipment that had fallen into the shipping channels. With the port closed or off-limits to all but certain categories of ships for long periods during the war, and after the great fire raids on the East End in 1941, much of the trade on which it fed had evacuated.[116]

[114] Borruey, *Port*, 290–291.

[115] Havenbedrijf der Gemeente Rotterdam/Jaarverslag/1963; Ministry of Transport, *Report of the Committee of Inquiry into the Major Ports of Great Britain* (Rochdale Report) (London: Her Majesty's Stationery Office, 1962), 174; Bird, *Major*, 366. Bird gives 34.75 miles of quays for the PLA's docks alone.

[116] NMM/P & O/4/62/Freight Department, 30 September 1947; Rochdale, 174; Brown, *Port*, 111–112, 117–118.

FIGURE 6. London's Royal Albert Dock, 1958. Courtesy Museum of London, PLA Collection.

The port's comeback, for these reasons, was all the more remarkable. Very quickly shipping and tonnage totals began to approach the best years before the war and then to surpass them. Large investments were made to modernize as well as rebuild. Docks were re-equipped. A deeper channel was dredged to receive supertankers. As in Rotterdam or Marseille, oil refineries dotted the port. But, in the main, "The port was rebuilt in its pre-war image." London, in the early 1960s, was not much different from its heyday years of the past. The fabulous complex of docks ran miles down-river. Each continued to serve its designated trades: timber at the Surrey docks; grain at Millwall; meat, fruits, tobacco at the Royals; passenger liners at Tilbury. Wharfingers, in the hundreds, still lined the Thames. Barges and lighters in the thousands plowed along the wending river, carrying goods from ship to shore or to the wall of warehouses in the oldest tight-water docks closest in to the city. Every good imaginable still found its way from any distant point on the globe to London; people and goods of nearly any manufactured kind still sailed out of this harbor.[117] Rotterdam's huge

---

[117] Brown, *Port*, 116–118 (quoted 117), 120–130; HA/4849/Havens aan de Thames, February 1975; Hyde, *Liverpool*, 182–183; Jackson, *History*, 159.

lead in tonnage aside, this was still in many ways Europe's glory port, redolent of maritime life as it had existed in the best of modern times. But this, like everything else that had seemed reset for reprise, was also an illusion, because London and the maritime world were on the cusp of momentous change that would alter nearly everything about them, including the displacement of this city, once the world's greatest water magnet, to the outer regions of main port status, if still that.

9

Transformation

From perhaps time immemorial people had traveled the oceans by ship, but by the end of the twentieth century such travel was limited to ferry crossings, pleasure cruises, or the odd crossing on freighters. Probably the only steady flow of passengers across the seas was the unscheduled and hazardous voyage of illegal immigrants on unsound vessels or inside containers. In that sense time had reversed by four or five centuries to the days of lone and adventurous crossings, or of human cargo stuffed into holds. Even then, it was the disappearance more than the repetition of history that pummeled the imagination. Since the voyages of discovery, the conquest, administration, exploitation, and trans-population of distant lands by Europeans had been inseparable from human passage by sea. Scores of millions of people had then crossed the oceans, among these Europeans, but also Africans, Indians, Japanese, and Chinese. The opening of new lands and the dispersal of demand had been as central to global economies as had been the exodus of capital or power. Surface flows of people and goods had moved in tandem, the one occasioning and enabling the other. The history of ports and shipping companies had consequently been inextricably bound to the massive outpouring of people overseas in modern times. Change, when it came, was therefore abrupt and encompassing. Decolonization phased out one rationale for overseas passenger travel, but the more sweeping effect came when air travel turned routine and hegemonic. After the 1970s the era of sailing across oceans for business, migration, pilgrimage, or invasion was completely gone, replaced by a new culture of pleasure cruising that mimicked the abandonment of nearly all other maritime verities.

Strangely, the death knell – Pan Am's introduction of transatlantic jet service – sounded only thirty months to the day after the *Ideal-X*, a converted T-2 tanker from the Second World War, sailed on 26 April 1956 from Newark to Houston with fifty-eight truck trailers on board and loosed a still greater revolution on the seas. Containerization would require another decade or two to settle in as the rule in general cargo shipping, but when it did it would change nearly everything. Ports would look different, rank different, and do business differently. Within harbors, older hierarchies and job designations would rearrange or crumble. Shipping companies would merge or disappear, and newcomers would rise, until only a few of the most venerable names remained, passed by lines that were inconsequential or nonexistent a few decades earlier. Britain, which opened the century with nearly half the world's ships, would close it in eighth place, even after real ownership was computed.[1] Placing freight in boxes, of a unitary size and shape, would substitute "intermodality" and "logistics" for the conventional way of doing things. Ships would become more important than ever to how the world economy operated but, ironically, would also figure in a larger transport chain in which ocean freight costs were often the least consequential. Reconfiguration of identities, expertise, hierarchies, and port-city space would ravage maritime culture. "Maritime" itself would have an unstable meaning, as sea and land integrated. In the last three decades of the century, everything would thus become mutable. Not even ships would look the same.[2]

Containerization's power to transform stemmed from its targeting of general cargo. Here lay the high-value end of the freight trades, the most extensive user of port services, and the center of the shipping establishment. To revolutionize all of these, as containerization did, was to revolutionize ports and shipping – and practically everything in between – in ways that preceding changes in bulk could never have done. Only the transformative impact of the steamship a full century earlier was comparable in its effect.

But that power also derived from the ways globalism changed toward the end of the century. Some of this change, pointing towards decentered

---

[1] Broeze, *Globalisation*, 223. Based on 1996 figures and includes foreign-flagged ships.

[2] For general studies: Broeze, *Globalisation*; Brian J. Cudahy, *Box Boats: How Container Ships Changed the World* (New York: Fordham University Press, 2006); Arthur Donovan and Joseph Bonney, *The Box That Changed the World: Fifty Years of Container Shipping – an Illustrated History* (East Windsor, NJ: Commonwealth Business Media, 2006); Marc Levinson, *The Box: How the Shipping Container Made the World Smaller and the World Economy Bigger* (Princeton, NJ: Princeton University Press, 2006); Hans Jürgen Witthöft, *Container. Transportrevolution unseres Jahrhunderts* (Herford: Koehlers, 1977).

world systems and new forms of transnationalism, was a long time in the making and has been traced in preceding chapters. Two new generators, however, also altered profoundly global connectedness. First, there occurred a deregulation of markets, including the crumbling of trade and investment barriers, that took off after 1980 and accounted for unprecedented outflows, especially in capital. Between 1980 and 2000 the amount of capital invested in other lands is estimated to have multiplied by a factor of ten, while foreign assets accounted for perhaps as much as 92 percent of world Gross Domestic Product.[3] Accompanying the deregulation of capital was the entry of China into world markets, the collapse of Cold War economic divisions, and the discrediting of import substitution. Second, there occurred a technological revolution in communications. In some respects this simply intensified the world-binding effects introduced by telegraphs, cables, telephones, and radio generations earlier. Yet the computer revolution was also astonishingly new and enabled circulation of capital and goods at unprecedented volumes and levels of complexity. Electronic breakthroughs so greatly lowered the cost of international communications and sped up the power and facility of computing, that trading and sourcing on a global scale became both manageable and affordable. The jet plane was another time-space disintegrator and again demonstrated the dramatic impact global connectedness in the late twentieth century would have on the seas.

These generators did not create globalization, nor re-create it, both common myths about globalization by the turn of the twenty-first century. But they did so rewrite local-global relations that, along with developments such as decolonization or American and Asian world prominence, they introduced a new phase in global connectedness. What this meant in its totality has far surpassed any consensus, but in relationship to maritime affairs four elements did constitute a fundamental change. First, what had once been largely a Eurocentric globalism decentered into exchanges within and between three great trade blocs – North America, Europe, and East/Southeast Asia. The decentering accentuated regionalism, witness the European Union, but such regionalism also offered a platform for wider global connectedness. Second, with markets so unfettered it was often just as easy to trade or invest half a world away as it was to do so next door. Volumes of circulation magnified so considerably that, as one set of authors put it, the intensity, extensity, velocity, and impact of transnational exchange was greater than ever

[3] Cassis, *Capitals*, 244.

before.[4] Third, new global supply chains created new vectors and flows. In these chains, multinationals dispersed production to the "cheapest" sites per component, shipped these components to another site for assemblage, and then shipped again to points of distribution. Components or semi-finished products, as well as manufactured goods, thus circulated through trade lanes, with production, assembly, and distribution potentially global in their composite. Companies (or importers and exporters) decentralized geographically not only by markets but by operations, and they expanded networks to include smaller, more flexible independent producers regardless of their location. World sourcing thus lowered costs, but in so doing it also realigned and expanded global connectedness. Fourth, and as a consequence of the preceding three, all maritime sectors increasingly established a "global" presence. Under these circumstances, transnational firms and careers could not be quite as they had been before. In particular there was less embedment at the local end of the spectrum, more detachment from home communities and identities. Toward the end of the century, shipping companies were routinely operating round-the-world services, and ports were multinational enterprises. Intermediaries who had always engaged in global transport from one base now felt the need to ship from others. As one Antwerp agent put it, "We are thinking more and more worldwide."[5]

This new stage of globalization, dependent on high volume flows of general cargo swinging back and forth across the globe, was the framework within which the container revolution occurred and the driving force for carrying it through. But as always the relationship was reciprocal, because out of containerization came dropping freight rates and fast and reliable worldwide logistics that, in effect, made global supply chains and surging volumes possible. If globalization remade the maritime world, then the maritime world, as the container transformed it, also remade globalization. The exchanges between world history and the sea that had existed from the beginning of the century lasted through to its end.

AIR AND SEA

Jet air transport killed off the traditional passenger trades, but equations of change and consequence were never so simple as that. If the roots

---

[4] Held et al., *Global*.
[5] Herman Reynaerts, Overseas Maritime Transport N.V., interview with author, Antwerp, 11 December 1997.

of the wreckage went back decades, shipping companies had initially parented fledgling airlines, and for years envisioned a transport world where air and sea passage would complement as much as rival each other. Eventually the airplane triumphed at the expense of the passenger liner. Even then, air transport made it possible to reimagine the cruise industry, while shipping companies diversified into air tourism as a potent source of revenues. Ted Arison, who would build Carnival Lines into the world's leading cruise company, made his first fortune out of air cargo. The relationship between sea and air was thus a complex one, as was the relationship between the demise of one passenger business and the rise of a newer one. Cruises too had a long history, longer than air travel, and as established companies such as P & O or Holland Amerika pulled out of the ocean-crossing business, they also converted their passenger divisions into full-time cruise operations. Nearly all the new cruising companies, including those that would come to dominate, like Carnival or Royal Caribbean, were founded by men with shipping backgrounds and in some cases traditional formations. Yet the cruise business of the late twentieth century bore little resemblance to its past, and instead repeated the three deepest changes of its times: in identities, in hierarchies, and in the nature of transnational or global enterprise. The leading figures were new men, with very different conceptions of the culture and business of shipping. They revolutionized cruises and, when useful, expropriated older names for their new business purposes. They displaced traditional rivals, but also the center of operations – from Europe to South Florida. If shipping had always been cosmopolitan, they and their companies took transnationalism to a new level in ownership and management, in flag registration, and in the composition of officers and crews. This was therefore more than a simple story of death and reincarnation. Still, as one era ended and another began, the dynamic between history and the maritime continued. Older passenger trades had cross-populated the world and had thereby advanced global connectedness. Newer passenger trades carried people nowhere, but that vulgarization of leisure was congruent with virtual global worlds that permeated the present, and it turned sea travel once again into a constituent of modern life.

Very early into the history of flying, shipping lines concluded that air travel could evolve into a serious competitor for passengers and mail. Yet few if any lines felt mortal peril, and practically from its infancy most welcomed and promoted civil aviation. Having long organized and operated transoceanic services, they were confident of their role, even right, as partners in all transoceanic ventures. Their response to aviation therefore was to participate jointly with the airlines. The CGT invested in airframe construction companies, and in 1928, using a catapult from the rear deck of the *Ile de France,* launched a seaplane with mail 400 miles off the U.S. coast to demonstrate the possibilities of combining sea and air travel connections. When the Popular Front government set up the Compagnie Air-France-Transatlantique in 1937 to prepare for cross-Atlantic travel with Latécoère seaplanes, the understanding was that there would be close collaboration between the air and sea lines. In these same years, Percy Bates, chairman of Cunard, entered into discussions with Imperial Airways to associate his company with the inauguration of British transatlantic service. Germany's NDL formed its own air company, while HAPAG participated in the creation of Deutsche Luft-Reederei, Germany's first regular air service, and collaborated in the commercial development of zeppelin flights across the North and South Atlantic. In 1923 NDL and HAPAG interests merged, with both shipping companies exhibiting a strong sense of proprietary rights over transoceanic carriage of passengers and mail. Holland Amerika contemplated a syndicate with Fokker and KLM to operate over the Atlantic.[6] Where distances were greatest, between metropole and empire, air travel began to cut seriously into passage by ship.[7] But here too ship companies were first movers, and initially there were close interchange arrangements between air and sea lines.[8]

Yet, in nearly every instance, resistance by governments and airlines produced the same result: exclusion of shipping lines from the principal air routes. All the shipping companies were left out in the cold when Air France, British Airways (later merged with Imperial into BOAC), Lufthansa, and KLM inaugurated transatlantic service.[9] Within the first decade or two after the war, little remained of the earlier collaboration between air and sea, although the occasional initiative was still possible. In 1948 Swires took control of Cathay Pacific, then a tiny organization run by Americans and Australians to airlift freight into Shanghai, and turned

[6] Barbance, *Histoire,* 230, 239, 321–324; Hyde, *Cunard,* 268–270; Wiborg and Wiborg, *Unser,* 242–249; Wentholt, *Brug,* 213.

[7] AAFL/MM/4662/Agence de Saigon/Résultats globaux du trafic "passages" 1937; Guildhall/Smith Mackenzie & Co. Ltd./MS 28,124, 1938.

[8] Davies, *Trademakers,* 249–253; Daumalin, *Marseille,* 328–329.

[9] Hyde, *Cunard,* 270–279, 296–301; Gordon Boyce, "Transferring Capabilities across Sectoral Frontiers: Shipowners Entering the Airline Business, 1920–1970," *International Journal of Maritime History* 13 (June 2001): 6–19; Barbance, *Histoire,* 321–324; Wiborg and Wiborg, *Unser,* 249–251; Wendt, *Kurs,* 290–292; Delprat, *Reeder,* 102–120; Brugmans, *Tachtig,* 157–160; Leeman, *Barkschip,* 206, 226; Wentholt, *Brug,* 276. A second effort of Cunard to invest in BOAC was also short-lived.

this into a leading regional carrier.[10] Nevertheless, the operative relationship between ships and planes was one of rivalry and portentous doom.

For a decade, perhaps longer, after the war, good money could still be made off of sea passage and the emigration trades. Repatriating colonials brought in additional revenue. Yet the incursion of air travel was inexorable. In 1957 air and sea passage nearly balanced out on the heavily traveled transatlantic route (1,010,000 by air, 1,027,000 by sea), and thereafter, with the introduction of jet planes, the number of air passengers climbed from one to four million by 1965, while the number of sea passengers declined to 650,000. At the beginning of the 1970s, over 13 million people crossed the Atlantic, but less than 1 percent of these (100,000) did so by sea.[11]

Once the unraveling began, it proceeded at almost breakneck pace. Passenger liners declined to less than 6 percent of the world's fleet by 1966.[12] In the years that followed, one great passenger ship after another was retired from service. The last holdouts, the *United States* and the *Leonardo da Vinci*, were gone before the close of the 1970s. During these years there were no new constructions save the *QE2*. Conceived to function as a "resort hotel," it benefited from technical innovations that permitted construction of a massive ship (65,000 grt) capable of sailing through the Panama Canal and accessing many cruising ports of call, with half the fuel consumption of its predecessors. The *QE2* could have a future, but only because its builders knew that traditional identities had hit a dead end.[13] At some time in the 1970s, the millennia-long era of purposeful travel by sea from one point to another came to an end.

The sea travel business, however, did not. Instead, it turned itself into a purely tourist operation and flourished. Since the late nineteenth century steamship companies had run cruises, built hotels, introduced tourist class passage – in short had been one of the central actors in the creation of a global tourist industry. When the older passenger trades died, it was thus a logical step to reinvent themselves as mass tourist operators. Already in the late 1960s, P & O identified itself as "a holiday operator." By the 1970s, it was no longer carrying passengers in the traditional way but was still transporting large numbers of people through channel ferry and cruise operations. Having purchased Princess Cruises in the early 1970s, it became the third largest cruise operator in the world. NDL and

[10] Havilland, *China*, 4; Boyce, "Transferring," 21–33.
[11] Hyde, *Cunard*, 296; Wentholt, *Brug*, 298; Cassagnou, *Grandes*, 128.
[12] CAC/810740/57/8 September 1967.
[13] Hyde, *Cunard*, 285–295, 302–303 (quoted).

HAPAG had both made their names carrying passengers across the North Atlantic. Merged into Hapag-Lloyd by the 1970s, they had completely abandoned that trade, but ran cruise ships, possessed a wide array of travel bureaux, and expanded into the air charter business. In the mid-1990s, 40 percent of turnover was coming from the tourist side of the company, and even, for a moment before reorganization, Hapag-Lloyd qualified as Europe's largest tourism combine.[14]

But the real instigators of new tourist markets at sea were other types, parvenus in the world of passenger shipping whose innovations reflected their own non-orthodox derivations. Changers of shipping culture, so too would they change the culture of its products. Paradoxically, the catalyst that made them leaders was once again the jet plane, which reoriented the center of cruising on the Caribbean and the once-preposterous port of Miami. Air travel could fly in passengers, in great numbers, to sail out of Florida into a sea that was calm and sunny the whole year round and was studded with tropical ports of call. The imagination to exploit this potential came from an Israeli with shipping ties but an improbable maritime past, and an American with no shipping history at all.

The former was Ted Arison, whose Carnival Line at its start in 1972 consisted of one ship, the *Mardi Gras*, which Arison billed as the "Flagship of the Golden Fleet." The billion-dollar industry giant that emerged thirty-five years later out of these carnivalesque origins all but guaranteed an overturning of cruising culture. Arison came from a European and Israeli shipping family, but his professional life bore little resemblance to the patterns of traditional shipping men. At the beginning of the 1950s he sold off the family firm and made his first fortune shipping air cargo out of New York. Practically on a lark he dove into the cruise business with a fly-by-night manner that would characterize his operations for some time to come. Starting in the mid-1960s with a marketing operation but no ship (his charter disappeared when the ship's owner went bust), Arison formed a joint cruising venture with Norwegian shipowner Knut Kloster, who had a car ferry but was without passengers. Together they ran Norwegian Caribbean Lines, the first of a series of companies to demonstrate the drawing power of the jet-age Caribbean. As the partnership soured, Kloster retained control of the company, which he renamed Norwegian Cruise Lines, but Arison made off with the advance sales receipts, which he used to purchase the *Empress of Canada*, the Canadian

[14] NMM/P & O/4/81/Passenger Department, 1967 (quoted); Arnold Kludas, *Vergnügungsreisen*, vol. 2, 184–188; Wiborg and Wiborg, *Unser*, 367–369, 396, 417–421.

Pacific's last ocean liner, just recently withdrawn from service and placed up for sale. Renamed the *Mardi Gras*, a changeover symbolic of the mockeries to come, the ship's first voyage reflected the birthing pains of a new era. Sailing out of Miami's harbor it ran aground on a sandbar where it sat awkwardly for a full day before breaking free. Unable to convince anyone in San Juan to sell him fuel, Arison was only able to get the ship home after he had raided every cash register on the vessel.

What kept Carnival afloat in these early years was the backing Arison received from a wildcatting financier, Meshulam Riklis, an old Israeli school friend. To ride herd on his investment, Riklis insisted that Arison take on Bob Dickinson, a Duquesne University MBA whose previous experience had been at Ford and RCA. Surrounded by such figures, and with his own shambolic beginnings, Arison was thus free to reinvent the cruising industry. Out of financial necessity, but also unbound to received wisdom, he and Dickinson aimed for a completely new market: younger, first-time cruisers uninhibited by a traditional image of life aboard ship. Carnival billed its vessels as "fun" ships. Whereas older generations of passengers had cruised to sightsee or to enjoy a long, leisurely and recuperative voyage at sea, Carnival ran short vacation cruises for which the ship became the primary destination. There were to be no dress codes or other barriers to "fun," and certainly no image that suggested that cruises were for people of high status and distinction. Vulgarity was practically welcomed. On-board spending was encouraged in every way. Mocked by its competitors as "the Kmart of the Caribbean," Carnival turned cruising into a mass leisure market. In 1970, half a million people had voyaged on cruises. Twenty years later, 2.8 million Americans (and another nearly half million Europeans) were taking cruises, and the largest share of these sailed on Carnival ships.[15]

After Carnival's breakthrough, leisure at sea equated with nearly every other facet of contemporary consumerism. Although lines catering to traditional markets continued to do well, the trend clearly was elsewhere. There was a clear rupture with the codes of distinction, exclusivity, rights and wrongs, or the belief that leisure should be identified with

---

[15] Bob Dickinson and Andy Vladimir, *Selling the Sea: An Inside Look at the Cruise Industry*, 2nd ed. (Hoboken, NJ: John Wiley and Sons, 2008), viii, 20–30, 106–126, 254–260; Kristoffer A. Garin, *Devils on the Deep Blue Sea: The Dreams, Schemes, and Showdowns That Built America's Cruise-Ship Empires* (New York: Viking, 2005), 21–54, 64–88, 141; "Robert H. Dickinson, CTC, President, Carnival Cruise Lines," http://www.floridaoceanalliance.org/bios/bio_dickenson.htm (accessed 23 February 2008); Kludas, *Vergnügungsreisen*, vol. 2, 52, 123, 127.

moral formation inbred into an older bourgeois culture. The Carnival way was to incline sea travel toward self-indulgence with as little self-consciousness as possible. Lavish and spectacular entertainment mimicked the two premier tourist sites in America: Las Vegas and Orlando. Just as containerization was fusing ship and truck carriage, land and sea leisure culture converged, to the point that Disney entered the cruise ship business. The same symbiosis occurred with popular culture's foundation medium. Television's *Love Boat*, whose ten-year run exactly paralleled the industry's growth years, drew its inspiration from the new, democratized format of cruising.[16] The cruise industry engorged on the show's popularity, but also Hollywood's blurring of artifice and reality. Cruise lines too learned to master illusion. They engineered their own tropical beaches and orchestrated market tours to reproduce a Caribbean as perfect, and self-contained, as a studio set.[17]

How completely the Carnival model refashioned the cruise business can be seen in the history of its closest competitor, Royal Caribbean Cruise Lines, where outsiders were just as prominent. Royal Caribbean began with a very different vision for the air age: a cruising line that would combine the lure of old-fashioned sea voyages with the potential of a mass American market. Its ships were to be purposely built for year-round cruising in the Caribbean, and with drafts sufficiently shallow to permit entry and docking at most island harbors. The profile of these ships was to be "sleek, yacht-like," with a long clipper-like prow. Their signature feature would be a covered observation deck projecting out from the funnel; the idea was taken from the Seattle Space Needle. Everything was to be custom designed, down to the uniforms for crews and officers. The top decks were to be open and sunny, surrounding swimming pools, but the accent would be as much on elegance as it would be on pleasure. Volume was vital to this conception. Cabins were kept small to increase the number of passengers while encouraging them to spend their time, and money, in public rooms. Royal Caribbean applied the same economies of scale pioneered by supertankers to the cruise sector: Run fewer, bigger ships with lower crew costs per passenger, especially at the higher salary positions of captains or officers. Like Carnival, it too lived by the airplane, flying passengers in from California to Miami

[16] Garin, *Devils*, 93–101; Dickinson and Vladimir, *Selling*, 138.
[17] Bård Kolltveit and John Maxtone-Graham, *Under Crown and Anchor: Royal Caribbean Cruise Line: The First Twenty-five Years, 1970–1995* (Miami Beach, FL: Royal Caribbean Cruises, 1995), 126–130; Garin, *Devils*, 276.

or arranging special rates with British Air to stream in passengers from Britain. Together, with Arison, Royal Caribbean invented a mass cruising market, only it stressed the "Royal" in its name, and sought to distinguish itself from Arison's "fun" ships, which it considered as the bargain basement of the industry. If it too was Norwegian in origin, assembled by a combine of three Norwegian shipping lines, by the 1960s these were blue-bloods in the Norwegian shipping community.

Yet Royal Caribbean in one respect was remarkably similar to Carnival: Its guiding genius was another maverick – Ed Stephan – and new men would continue to remake Royal Caribbean until eventually there was little difference from Carnival. An even greater upstart than Arison, Stephan, from the American interior, migrated to Miami after the Korean War, attended hotel school on the G. I. Bill, and started his career in the Miami Beach hotel business. Later he drifted into managing one of the early Miami cruise lines, all the while working out designs for a new kind of cruise ship and company, which he sold to Skaugen and Wilhelmsen, two of the founders, via contacts he had made with shipbrokers Fearnley and Eger. Stephan was responsible for nearly all of Royal Caribbean's marketing innovations. The Norwegians, realizing what they had, made him president of the company and placed him in charge of Miami-based operations. He too, then, was an outsider who could reimagine cruising as a mass market leisure business. In 1984, Royal Caribbean and Carnival held, between them, one-quarter of the cruise business, with Royal Caribbean's share slightly larger than Arison's.

Stephan was only the first of a string of outsiders to infiltrate Royal Caribbean. He was followed by Jack Seabrook, the CEO of a Canadian utilities company, which came to control Gotass-Larsen, the third of the Norwegian founding lines. Seabrook was prepared to sell out its share to Carnival until he was prevented by another outsider, Jay Pritzker, a Chicago-based billionaire-investor and owner of the Hyatt hotel chain, who joined Arne Wilhelmsen, of another of the founding lines, in thwarting Carnival's bid to swallow Royal Caribbean wholesale. But in the wake of this fight, Richard Fain, a Wharton MBA and Seabrook lieutenant, came over to Royal Caribbean via the Gotass-Larsen connection and stayed to run the company after Pritzker and Wilhelmsen saved it from Arison. Under Fain, the Royal Caribbean "brand" still claimed distinction from Carnival, but increasingly the company was run to compete with Carnival in the same market. Over time even Stephan was marginalized and finally replaced in 1997 by an executive recruited, in a last coup de grace, from American Airlines. Together Carnival and Royal Caribbean then devoured a large part of the industry. Carnival alone acquired eleven companies, including Cunard and P & O's Princess Cruises. Although traditional forms of cruising remained available, many of the companies running these were controlled by Carnival, while the Carnival concept of "fun" ships had, by the 1990s, firmly penetrated even the German cruise market, the world's third largest.[18]

Over a span of fifty years passenger travel, therefore, underwent a metamorphosis, reinvented as a new consumer-culture version of sailing. Embodying this "sea change" was the transfer of cruising's center from Europe to Miami, a city built on speculation and mass tourism. Before the 1960s, the port of Miami figured on few shipping companies' charts. Under Carnival, Royal Caribbean, and Norwegian Cruise Lines, it became the largest cruise/passenger port in the world. This city of leisure and flamboyance thus rode the crest of the new wave of shipping. But it was also the perfect breeding ground for interlopers like Arison and Stephan to rethink the practice of cruising.

The new cruise lines represented as well a new, free-floating brand of transnationalism, well removed from cross-world seaborne ties of the past. Carnival's identity from the start was uncertain, a Norwegian-Israeli-American operation. The nationality of its owner, Ted Arison, was itself ambiguous: first Israeli, then American, then Israeli at the end of his life in a failed attempt to leave his estate unburdened by inheritance taxes.[19] The Vorwerks of Hamburg and Chile had possessed dual identities, but also deep roots in the business communities of each. Arison's identities, like Onassis's, seemed to depend on the opportunities of the moment. Royal Caribbean was another such hybrid. Its ownership was Norwegian but its management and home base American. After it parried Carnival's takeover bid, ownership spread to Jay Pritzker, an American, but also Sammy Ofer, an Israeli born in Romania but who had grown up in his father's shipping business after their migration to Palestine, a resident of London in the 1960s where he created and ran the Zodiac Shipping Agency, and by the 1990s a joint citizen of Austria and Israel, but a resident in Monaco. Acting as go-between in the deal that brought Wilhelmsen, Pritzker, and Ofer together was the French Banque

---

[18] Kolltveit and Maxtone-Graham, *Under*, 21–66, 88, 96–97, 134–136, 154–170; Garin, *Devils*, 55–63, 148–179, 209–243, 296–335; Dickinson and Vladimir, *Selling*, vii–viii, 22 (quoted on profile), 131–132; 156–166; Kludas, *Vergnügungsreisen*, vol. 2, 7–8, 124, 174–175, 203.

[19] Garin *Devils*, 180–181.

Indo-Suez.[20] This confusion of identities, in one form or another, eventually spread to the rest of the cruise business.[21] In the passenger trades of the late twentieth century, home identity depended on whether one was referring to cruise company, tour organizer, charterer or owner, crew and officers, or registry. But then changing identity was also one of the selling features that drove the industry, as life on shipboard allowed passengers to assume, or flee, whatever persona they wished. The experience of a week of travel from one island nation to another, but sleeping every night in one's shipboard cabin, created a process of crossing borders without clear definition or commitment. Miami, perhaps the most cosmopolitan city in North America by the turn of the century, the southern tip of the North American continent but nonetheless the hub of Latin America, and its bolt-hole, was again the perfect site for a business tending toward such random identities.

The demise of the Holland Amerika Line symbolized how radically the culture of shipping was changing. Over the course of a century it had carried nearly 4 million passengers between Europe and America,[22] but in 1971, just shy of its centenary, it terminated all regular transatlantic service and converted its liners to all-season cruise ships. In 1975, the cargo division was sold off to Swedish American Lines. The passenger business remained afloat on a reputation for quality cruises developed in the interwar years. But in the 1970s, Holland Amerika bought out Westours, an Alaskan cruise company, and at the end of the decade the company packed up its bags and moved its headquarters to the United States.[23]

By the 1980s, then, Holland Amerika was a Dutch company based in America, running ships registered in the Dutch Antilles, and crewed by Indonesians. A product of one global age, its identity completely altered in another. This was most glaring in the break with the port of Rotterdam. Rotterdam investors founded Holland Amerika and they had rallied in the 1930s to save the company, known in the city as "The Line." After the 1970s, those connections to the world's largest seaport were

---

[20] Kolltveit and Maxtone-Graham, *Under*, 167, 206–207; Simon Clark, "Israeli Tycoon Idan Ofer: Joint Business – A Way of Fostering Peace," 1 May 2007, http://www. blomberg.com/apps/news?pid=20101119&sid=abNkP3XU808M&refer=news (accessed 29 February 2008).

[21] Kludas, *Vergnügungsreisen*, vol. 2, 8, 15–16, 90–119, 185, 188.

[22] Wentholt, *Brug*, 339.

[23] Lels (interview); GAR/HAL/Wentholt/W A-51/H. N. Dutilh Passage memorandum, 3 February 1965; GAR/HAL/Viamar/MMPH 2; Wentholt, *Brug*, 298, 309–348; Dickinson and Vladimir, *Selling*, 25–26; De Goey, "De Holland Amerika Lijn," 29–32.

only a memory.[24] For Royal Caribbean to move from Oslo to Miami was one thing. For Holland Amerika to abandon Rotterdam for Stamford, Connecticut, and then Seattle, was another kind of switch altogether. Nor did the mutations stop there. At the end of the 1980s, Holland Amerika sold out to Carnival, the epitome of the raucous cruise industry that had evolved out of the crushing of the traditional passenger lines. Holland Amerika as an enterprise continued, but from this point on it was completely divorced from the world of shipping and operated strictly as an investment company; the name Holland Amerika was now the property of the Arisons. The final irony came at the end of the 1990s, when the old headquarters building on the Wilhelminakade, dating from the turn of the century and a monument to a time when European shipping lines covered the seas, was refurbished and resurrected as Hotel New York.

Obviously what constituted shipping, maritime business or culture, or even a port and its community, was subject in late twentieth-century global economies to redefinition. Europe's maritime world had always been transnational, but both the content and inference of what that entailed were shifting after the mid-1960s. The effect of technological change and a new form of globalism, but also business initiatives at sea level, was to destabilize nearly every facet of that world: identities, methods, purposes, networks, flow patterns, and hierarchies. Aviation set off sweeping changes in the movement of people. Still more encompassing were those that came with containerization.

THE CONTAINER REVOLUTION

Containerization, the defining feature in maritime transport in the final third of the twentieth century, was both simple and complex. Effectively, it began as nothing more than packing cargo into metal boxes known as containers, about as obvious as placing wheels on suitcases. But, if harmonized into standard units of one or two basic sizes, these boxes could then be handled with such ease and rapidity that port costs could diminish to a fraction of their former levels. Stowage could be simplified. The heroic but time-consuming efforts of an Otto Brix, loading the *Brasilia* in Antwerp harbor during a snowstorm in the 1920s could be reduced to folklore, the need for men like Brix likewise rendered obsolete. Once packed into the metal box, cargo could be all but impregnable from quayside theft. Freight insurance could therefore also be lowered.

[24] Wentholt, *Brug*, 340–341.

If harmoniziation fit with tractor-trailer dimensions, and was suitable for flatcars, the metal boxes could then travel by land and sea with minimal interchange or manipulation, or what was called intermodality. There had always been a transport chain, even if this only meant carrying goods on pack animals down to the sea. Metal boxes and intermodality could make that chain all but seamless and move goods in greater volume, at higher speeds, with superior regularity, and less cost than ever before. Thus, as computerization, air travel, and massive and deregulated capital flows created possibilities for a next level of global interconnectedness, containers could add the essential link by realizing a comparable order of change in the transport of manufactured or processed products. Mechanically, the container was certainly far less complicated than building a printing press or assembling a steam engine, but its long-term effects on shipping, and how we organize our lives, could be just as revolutionary.

That was the simple side, the great imaginary of shipping goods within a box. The complexity was turning transformative possibilities into reality. For containers would matter only when every other facet of the transport chain was systematically calibrated to handle them. This meant ports and ships designed for carriage and transit of metal boxes alone. Conventional cargo, as the old style of packing bags or crates was henceforth to be known, could still possess a life of its own. Yet there was no advantage to containerization if only some goods aboard ship were loaded into metal boxes or if conventional facilities were charged with loading or off-loading containers. Port labor too would have to collaborate, or at least be battered into its own near obsolescence. There would have to be a means for tracking the position of millions of containers around the world, and for planning their distribution and return. To achieve intermodality, there would have to be standardization of norms among three very different forms of transportation: ships, railroads, and trucks. Shipping companies, but also port authorities, stevedores, agents, forwarders, importers, and exporters, would have to adjust to the organizational and logistical consequences of packing and moving goods in boxes, even if this meant accepting the eradication of what they had always been and done. Despite massive investments that had been made in the past, containerization was going to require starting over from scratch in operational levels, but ultimately in those of identity, power, and influence. The complications of so simple a concept were going to leave their revolutionary imprint on maritime business, maritime cities, maritime culture, and late twentieth-century globalism. What follows will show how containerization came about, and then how these great fissures occurred.

The Process

For the first two-thirds of the twentieth century, the bulk cargo trades led the way in rationalizing the transport of goods. They were the first to mechanize, to scale-up, and to pioneer bargain basement global supply links. Even when the bulk shipping trades spun into crisis in the oil-led slumps of the 1970s and 1980s, with more than 50 million tons dwt of tankers laid up in 1983, the effect was to push out globalization by shifting investment and operations to countries with lower costs, especially in East and Southeast Asia.[25] Containers were about general cargo, however, and even in 1960, when they were still in their infancy, manufactured goods constituted half the value of world trade, a figure that, with containerization, would grow to more than two-thirds in the 1980s and nearly three-quarters by 1995.[26] As valuable as oil or bulk ore shipments were to world shipping and the world economy, cutting the knot in turn-around time of general cargo was what made the difference in the last third of the century.

Driving that impact was the paradoxical fact that in the sector where time most equated with money, the passage through ports was at its slowest. For years, shipping people had been preoccupied with moving general cargo more cheaply and fluidly. The problem had always been how. Best-practice "sea stations"[27] could eliminate the worst of bottlenecks, but would hit ceilings far below anything revolutionary. Roll-on/Roll-off (RoRo), or driving loaded trucks onto ships and then driving them off at port of arrival, was encouraged by landing craft use in World War II. But full trucks on ships were wasteful of space and too valuable to idle on ships for long voyages. With a few exceptions, shipping companies restricted RoRo to short hauls or ferry services, such as cross-Channel shipping.[28] Pallets were more promising. The pallet was simply a wooden or metal platform onto which packages could be stacked and strapped

---

[25] Stig Tenold, *Tankers in Trouble: Norwegian Shipping and the Crisis of the 1970s and 1980s*, Research in Maritime History 32 (St. John's, Newfoundland: International Maritime Economic History Association, 2006), 1–3, 89–103; Broeze, *Globalisation*, 74.

[26] Cassagnou, *Grandes*, 111, 748; Bauchet, *Transport*, 52, 69; idem, *Les transports mondiaux, instrument de domination* (Paris: Economica, 1998), 48.

[27] CMB/E 27/66/Historique de la Gare Maritime; Devos and Elewaut, *CMB 100*, 167–170.

[28] Jackson, *History*, 153–154; P & O/OCEL/Administrative Staff College Case Study on Innovation; CMB/C7/11/Voyage aux USA. Etude Containers, 22 December 1965; Witthöft, *Container*, 29.

General cargo handling the old way

FIGURE 7. Men, muscle, and sacks. Rotterdam Harbor, c. 1920. Collection Municipal Archives of Rotterdam.

FIGURE 8. Crates, hoists, and lighters. Rotterdam Harbor, 1948. Collection Municipal Archives of Rotterdam.

to create something approaching a unit load manipulable by forklifts. U.S. Army use in the Second World War had awakened shipping people to their wider possibilities, and for a time in the 1940s and 1950s palletization appeared the miracle means of breaking through port congestion and rising port costs. But from the start, even the most enthusiastic proponents of pallets had recognized their limitations. Too much time was lost leveling the stacking for optimal packing. Pallets in holds often wasted storage space, and stevedores often preferred to unpack them so that they could stuff more cargo into unused areas. Pallets were best for loads of ten tons or less, but not much use for heavier freight. Most of all, pallets did not lend themselves to intermodality between one transport system and another. As containers began to come on line, much cargo traveling by pallet was still being packed or unpacked within the port rather than transiting door-to-door. By the 1980s palletization was useful for loading goods into containers. As a system, however, it had been relegated to the designation of conventional (read: old-fashioned) practice.[29]

Curiously, containers, which would be the solution and sweep all other methods before them, had been around for a very long time. But always there were problems. In the United States, Interstate Commerce Commission rulings vitiated any economic advantage to interwar railroad initiatives to ship in containers. Europeans went further in these years, but balked at any major remaking, as in ship design, to proceed very far. When, in World War II, the U.S. Army lashed heavily tarred crates to ship decks in desperate attempts to stretch shipping capacity to the limit, new life was injected into the concept. More favorable ICC rulings after the war then induced American railroad companies to introduce what they called piggyback services, or flatcar carriage of truck trailers, and these were picked up and used by a short haul company called Seatrain. Elsewhere container usage crept into shipping practice: on shipping lines between Seattle and Anchorage, or on KPM interisland services in Indonesia. In 1954, the KPM was lining up major shippers to extend container shipments between the archipelago and the Netherlands.[30] But there was nothing inexorable in this progression to produce what later became containerization. It is quite possible to imagine other scenarios

[29] MMM/MDHB/Management Files 1, American trips May–June 1945, June–July 1947; NMM/BIS/10/7, 1959; NMM/NZS/15/16/Unitisation, 12 March 1970; CMB/C7/4/ Etude ... palletisation; Van Driel and de Goey, *Rotterdam*, 53, 88–91; Van Driel, *Samenwerking*, 105–106, 257.

[30] Levinson, *Box*, 29–32, 153–159; Donovan and Bonney, *Box*, 5–8, 26–30; Borruey, *Port*, 295–309; Jackson, *History*, 154; P & O/OCEL/Narrative; NA/KPM/86/9 June 1954.

in which containers, pallets, and RoRo so greased old choke points as to resolve any further urgency for change.

Two things, however, determined otherwise. The first was that by the 1960s, when containers first really took hold, shipping people were looking for something truly all encompassing. There would be hesitations and resistance, but once containers began to prove their promise, containerization would spread like wildfire. That hunger for a clear breakthrough should not be missed. Shipping companies in the 1960s were caught between two unrelenting pressures. One was the surge in world trade to unprecedented levels with no corresponding reduction in port clearance time. Congestion in ports was approaching unsustainable levels. Expensive liner ships were spending on average only about 40 percent of their time on the open sea, where they could make money. At the same time, wage rates for harbor workers were rising.[31] Only containerization could slice cleanly through both of those Gordian knots. Thus like it or hate it, and many did hate it, containerization was embraced with a passion and little looking back, even if few visualized just how far-reaching the changes would turn out to be.[32] The results were simply too compelling. In 1967, still the infancy of containers, Rotterdam stevedore costs for containers were dropping to one-fifteenth those of handling conventional cargo. Where conventional turnaround of a ship would take a week, Sea-Land, one of the pioneering companies, was turning its ships around in a day. Belgian shipping observers of Sea-Land operations in Port Elizabeth thought containerization differed from traditional practice as did "the Thunderbird from the Model A." The British consortium OCL's container ship, *Encounter Bay*, logged in 300 sea-days during its first year of operation.[33] Containers, once properly understood, were not a better method. They were a completely different method.

The second was the appearance, simultaneously, of advocates who brought to containers a big-picture vision. Like Onassis and Arison, these were outsiders, men positioned to rethink completely the business of shipping. One was Foster Weldon, a Johns Hopkins professor with years of experience in operations research and part of the team that developed the Polaris submarine. Matson Lines hired him to standardize general cargo shipments on their routes between the Hawaiian Islands and the

---

[31] Levinson, *Box*, 10; Cudahy *Boats*, 9; Havenbedrijf der Gemeente Rotterdam/Jaarverslag 1966.
[32] Broeze, *Globalisation*, 28.
[33] Van Driel, *Samenwerking*, 106; Witthöft, *Container*, 67; CMB/C7/11/Voyage aux USA, December 1965, quoted p. 39; Cudahy, *Boats*, 104.

U.S. West Coast. Arriving in the mid-1950s, Weldon set up a research department and used computer models to plan traffics and services. His conclusions – stuff cargo into containers, design new equipment for handling these, redesign ships for exclusive container carriage, and merge container shipping by sea with truck carriage by land – remarkably paralleled what containerization in fact turned out to be. If it had not been for the fact that Weldon, proceeding methodically, was beaten to the punch by Malcom McLean, Matson Line would have enjoyed the reputation as the founder of the container revolution. But by the time Matson got around to hiring Weldon, McLean's *Ideal-X* was already taking to the sea and making history.[34]

McLean was also a total outsider, a trucker in the process of reinventing himself as a "transportation" man who "saw the ship as just another piece of highway to transport goods on."[35] Born in 1913 to a North Carolina farming family, he had, by the early postwar years, assembled one of the largest trucking companies in America. Later speculation on why Americans were the first to containerize shipping found the logical answer in especially prohibitive labor costs in America, forcing a radical turn toward standardization.[36] McLean, however, had more specific incentives. In the early 1950s his operating costs were rising not only from labor expenses, but also highway fees and heavy road congestion. He was concerned too that piggyback would cut into his trucking business. At some point in the early 1950s, he therefore began to toy with the idea of hauling trailers by low-cost water transport along the coast to bypass traffic jams and reassert his competitive position.

Once launched along this line of line of thinking, he pushed the envelope as far as he could. Lacking Weldon's methodical approach, McLean's gift was to invent everything anew as he went along, feeling his way until he arrived at containerization. His drive and commitment were relentless. Convinced that shipping would be the pivotal component in his new scheme, he abandoned trucking altogether when ICC regulations forced him to choose between land and sea. Beginning with the idea of some sort of RoRo service, he tossed this aside and instead lashed the storage units of trucks alone to the spar deck of a T-2 tanker – the *Ideal X* – when it

[34] Levinson, *Box*, 59–67, 187–192; Donovan and Bonney, *Box*, 73–78; 127–128.
[35] Donovan and Bonney, *Box*, 46. The words were those of Walter Wriston, Malcom McLean's banker. Extensive discussions of McLean can be found here, and in Cudahy and Levinson. I have relied on these in my discussion of McLean, most heavily on Levinson.
[36] MMM/OA 4A/1911 Box 1/Report by McKinsey & Company, London for British Transport Dock Board (McKinsey Report), 20 July 1966.

made its historic voyage in 1956. Then he immediately abandoned this and converted a freighter into a "container ship" with cellular interiors, which he accomplished by 1957, still a year before the first containers were lashed to the deck of a Matson Line steamer. In 1960 he renamed his company Sea-Land, which more suitably captured what he was doing. By 1964, with service to Puerto Rico, the U.S. West Coast, and up to Alaska, he was making preparations to take containers across the Atlantic, and soon after, into the Pacific.

To the extent he could, he anticipated problems and planned his way around them. At a very early stage he dispatched his brother, James, to a Teamsters executive board meeting in Miami Beach to win support for his project. Before opening his service to Europe he carefully lined up a network of truckers and agents. But mostly he improvised every new step along the way. This style would characterize containerization all through its formative years. Everyone who became a part of building a container service would later remark on the effort to work everything out anew. Rolf van den Wall Bake, working for Nedlloyd in Australia as containers came in, had to figure out how to pack coffee in them without it being ruined by dampness and temperature drops, or how to pack fishmeal without the heat causing it to ignite. The same kind of problems haunted Tabaknatie's shipments of tobacco, which had a high humidity content. Tobacco could not just be packed into unventilated boxes, because otherwise water would come gushing out at the end. "Slowly, slowly, slowly everybody had to adapt themselves to new systems of shipping."[37] Eventually, this incessant reinvention seeped into every core sphere – ports, shipping company size and shape, the culture of intermediaries – and thoroughly remade them as well.

From nearly the beginning, Europeans paid close attention to what McLean was doing. Some were unpersuaded or hesitant.[38] Still, in 1965, before any containers had moved across the Atlantic, a Swedish-Dutch consortium was planning a joint container service,[39] and a Belgian Lines delegation was poring over every facet of American container operations with the conclusion that "containers and container ships are going to enter the North Atlantic whether one likes it or not," and to opt out would mean "*to abandon all pretension of transporting general cargo to and from New York.*"[40] The British studied and spied on

[37] Van den Wall Bake (interview); de Maeyer (interview, quoted).
[38] See the discussions among companies in CMB/D 13/38 and CMB/D 13/39.
[39] Atlantic Container Line. Cunard and CGT later joined it.
[40] CMB/C7/11/Voyage aux USA, December 1965, p. 67.

FIGURE 9. Unloading the first all-container ship to dock in Rotterdam, May 1966. Collection Municipal Archives of Rotterdam.

McLean,[41] and even sought his blessing.[42] American companies, beginning with Moore-McCormack in 1966, were the first to ship containers across the Atlantic, but Europeans followed in short order. Within four years, 70 percent of general cargo on the North Atlantic run was voyaging in containers.[43]

Americans were also the first across the Pacific, but here Europeans matched them toe-to-toe, and were meticulously planning how to do so at a time when Sea-Land was still confined to coastal routes and Matson was simply shuttling between California and Hawaii. The instrument was Overseas Containers Limited (OCL), a British consortium set up by four companies to containerize the long-distance routes to Australia and East Asia, and led by the biggest blue-bloods in the business, P & O and Holts. Typically the preliminary plans were sketched out over dinner or discussions at Brooks' Club in St. James. The men delegated were old shipping hands, Kerry St. Johnston from Holts and also Ronald Swayne, who had read history at Oxford, played rugby, had taken part in the St. Nazaire

---

[41] P & O Recollections.
[42] P & O/OCEL/Malcolm Maclean–Sealand, Note by Sir Andrew Crichton.
[43] CAC/840626/17/Plan du Rapport, August 1971.

raid in the war, and was a superb club man – "they all loved Ronny." One of the great paradoxes of this entire transformation was how a revolution that would subsequently erase European shipping superiority and drive many from the sea was initially taken up by Europeans and advanced by the tremendous resources they could mobilize from their shipping experience and know-how, and their culture of collaboration. But nearly all the men seconded to OCL had also served in the war and brought with this an easy informality that could reach across company lines. They were not unlike Weldon in their methodical planning, nor McLean in their readiness to improvise. "The early phase," St. Johnston recollected, was "heady stuff, we were inventing as we went along." What joined all three was the vision to rethink wholly the transport experience. OCL worked out the practical details of packing cargoes into containers in a cold climate and shipping these through the tropics. But it also schematized integrated land and sea transport, new ship and terminal design, and computerized documentary controls.[44]

Once underway, the process then was a very rapid one: containerization of the North Atlantic in the second half of the 1960s, Asia and Australia just a few years later, the remaining dominoes falling into place throughout the 1970s, followed by application on land of intermodality, and with practically everyone, old and new, coming on board. But once it did become inexorable, "inventing as we went along" also turned into a ride on a tiger. Bounding forward, there was no certainty where they were going to end up, or what was going to be devoured along the way. There was, however, very early on a clear sense that they were crossing a line and entering some brave new world. In 1966 a McKinsey & Company report prepared for the British Transport Dock Board stated flatly that "containerization represents a fundamental and world-wide process of change," of global consequence and not controllable from the UK, and that its eventual outcome would be "*a few very large organizations with world-wide interests in international transport*," and routes "*served by a greatly reduced number of ports*,"[45] a prediction that turned out to be far from fanciful. As the tiger ride sped on, strange new phenomena popped up along the way – shipping companies running their own dedicated trains across the North American landmass; "non-vessel

---

[44] P & O Recollections (quoted on inventing); P & O/OCEL/Narrative; MMM/OA 4A/1582, 4, 6, 7, May 1965, 21 October 1977; MMM/OA/4A/554/Press Release, n.d.; MMM/OA 4A/1911/Box 1/15 March 1966; MMM/OCL/C/29/Feasibility Study; Bott (interview, quoted on Swayne).

[45] MMM/OA 4A/1911/Box 1/20 July 1966.

operating carriers" that bought container slots on others' ships – each a reminder of how pitilessly they had launched themselves into a dynamic of change. Even at purely seafaring levels there was a sense of having left all comfort zones behind. Whereas the first container ships had carried several hundred containers, capacity several generations later surpassed 6,000 TEU,[46] and there was talk of going still higher. Toward the close of the century, with the conquest complete and container ships "the pre-eminent sector of the world's deep-sea merchant fleet,"[47] the points of arrival began to clarify, starkly. The leading container company, by far, was Denmark's Maersk, an outlier only a few decades earlier, and the leading container ports were neither Rotterdam nor New York, but Hong Kong and Singapore. Whether brave or not, containerization did produce a very new world.

Effects: Globalization

One striking thing about the agencies of world connectedness at the end of the century was how they potentiated each other. The hugely expensive conversion to container ships, and the easy entry of newcomers, could not have occurred without the roaring flow of Eurodollars, petrodollars, or other novel financial instruments made available by the deregulation of capital markets.[48] Deregulation too permitted intermodality. The computer was indispensable to containerization. It made simple the complex problem of how to stow thousands of TEUs not only in a logical order for unloading and distribution, but also how to prevent uneven weight distribution and capsizing at sea. Information technology managed the logistics of routing, tracking, and recovering several hundred millions of container shipments distributed over the planet. The compression of all maritime activities into the rubric of logistics, as occurred in late century, was a computer-generated outcome. The jet airplane facilitated global management of world logistical shipments, and it forced shipping to produce a sea-land equivalent to rapid on-schedule world coordination. But the container also circulated the world's goods in such new ways, and with such new effects, that it combined with the other three to push globalization into a new stage.

---

[46] Twenty-foot Equivalent Unit, or equal to a twenty-foot container, one of the two standard sizes (forty was the other), and the new gauge for measuring turnover.

[47] Broeze, *Globalisation*, 1.

[48] On Eurodollars, petrodollars, and new ship construction, see Tenold, *Tankers*, 39, 55–60; Broeze, *Globalisation*, 73–74.

The salient example of how this occurred was global sourcing, or how global supply chains were redrawn under containerization. In the past, world supply lines largely functioned as a linear progression from source of material to point of usage. At the end of the twentieth century, what turned up in Nancy, Leeds, or Atlanta was likely to be far more globally constructed, made of materials from the cheapest sources of the world that shipped to the cheapest semi-finishing plants in other parts of the world, whose components then shipped to the cheapest assembly plants in yet other parts, whose manufactured goods then shipped across the ocean to a port in Europe or America before carried by truck or train to retail outlets in urban areas of consumption. The oft-cited example was that of the Barbie doll created out of hair from Japan, plastic from Taiwan, clothes from China, molds from America or Europe, and assembled in Indonesia, Malaysia and China, all the components moving across the seas to Hong Kong where they were gathered together and then ultimately shipped back to America.[49] But there were also instances of fish farmed in the Western Hemisphere, shipped to Asia for deboning, slicing, and packaging, and then shipped again across the Pacific for sale to American consumers.[50]

Containerization made "global sourcing" imaginable because it was cheap and logistically manageable. The world markets in goods, capital, and services that were so lauded or detested at century's end thrived on instantaneous means of communication, but just as much on cheapness. Computer power enabled complex global systems at breakneck volumes, but it was also decisive because its costs fell so dramatically. Containers, by cutting theft and turnaround and other overhead costs, accomplished the same price plummet on the seas, indeed to the point that ocean freight rates were all but meaningless in economic decisions about sourcing and selling. According to one set of authors, shoes manufactured in Asia and retailing for 45 dollars in America cost perhaps 34 cents to transport.[51] Under these conditions, multinationals could indulge in multiple shipments to attain cheapest sourcing, while world markets opened to small and intermediate suppliers of goods and services. Anyone, practically anywhere in the world, could enter the chain. Asian export economies with

---

[49] Frieden, *Global*, 417; Levinson, *Box*, 264.

[50] Larry Rohter, "Shipping Costs Start to Crimp Globalization," *The New York Times*, 3 August 2008.

[51] Donovan and Bonney, *Box*, xxiii. For a reevaluation of the impact on ocean freight rates, Yrjö Kaukiainen, "The Container Revolution and Liner Freights," *International Journal of Maritime History* 21 (December 2009): 43–74.

access to low-cost inputs like labor all profited from the deep fall in ship-ping costs, but so too did Chilean fruit farmers and farmers of salmon. As containers lowered costs, volume and geographical spread magnified.[52]

Global sourcing, with millions of containers circulating the globe, however, would have spun out of control without the logistical means to manage the system. From the start, then, methodical planners such as Weldon began to think of themselves as much as logisticians as men run-ning a shipping company. McLean was more seat-of-the-pants, but he too understood the logistical imperatives and by 1965 was using computers to manage his shipments.[53] Global sourcing thus emerged as much from containerization's conversion of the shipping business into the logistics business, as it did from containerization's cutting of costs. Critical to this turn was yet another infiltrator, Bruce Seaton, who trained as a CPA, not as a shipping man, and who had worked for years in the oil indus-try before joining American President Lines, a transpacific carrier. It was Seaton who, in the 1980s, introduced the idea of dedicated container trains across the continental United States, composed of APL leased cars, operating on APL schedules, passing through APL terminals, and carrying containers brought in on APL ships. Seaton, with no shipping traditions behind him, saw himself less as the head of a shipping company than as a logistician managing world flows. His aim was to create a system by which goods packed in boxes could circulate in endless automated streams between as many points of the world as desirable. He described this using a new containerese vocabulary, the need to "correlate multiple variables," or the need to make a "marginal analysis." As the Seaton view conquered shipping, the systematizing as well as pricing means became available to operate global supply chains that swung components around the world.[54] It also made global sourcing still cheaper, by making possi-ble just-in-time worldwide delivery, or the squeezing down of inventory costs. Big box retailers who were among the biggest utilizers of contain-ers thrived on just-in-time. By the twenty-first century, America's, and probably the world's, largest shipper of containers was retail's premier logistician, Wal-Mart, which understood how the logistical turn of con-tainerization not only lowered transport costs but provided built-in effi-ciencies to every dimension of global sourcing.[55]

[52] Frieden, *Global*, 395–396, 415, 425.
[53] Levinson, *Box*, 74.
[54] Donovan and Bonney, *Box*, 166–175 (quoted 170); Broeze, *Globalisation*, 102–103; Cudahy, *Boats*, 162–167.
[55] Nelson Lichtenstein, ed., *Wal-Mart: The Face of Twenty-first Century Capitalism* (New York: The New Press, 2006); Levinson, *Box*, 264–267.

To understand the difference from global shipping of the past, it is only necessary to exhume the 1930s tribulations of the Edward L. Eyre Company, an American West Coast importer that relied on the ships of the Silver-Java-Pacific Line (SJPL), one of the first experiments in running a round-the-world service. Booking 400 bales of gunnysacks on the SJPL's *Saparoea*, Eyre was forced to cancel most of the order when the *Saparoea* sailed into Colombo seven days late, made three berth shifts to discharge its various cargoes, and then moved to a fourth berth to load its export freight. A few days later Eyres was caught even shorter when the SJPL's *Hoegh Merchant* was slotted in to cover the route of another SJPL ship run aground in the Philippines. On board the *Hoegh Merchant* was an Eyre shipment of hop yarn due in San Francisco on 4 March and needed for immediate inland transfer to farmers "as it must be in the fields to string up the hop vines at a certain time." The SJPL planned to transfer the cargo to the *Marken*, but when the *Hoegh Merchant* arrived too late to make the connection, the hop yarn was transferred to still another SJPL vessel, the *Silverwillow*, which in turn was delayed leaving the Philippines and would not arrive in California until 30 March. This was twenty-six days later than originally promised and too late for Eyre, who lost its sale, lost the goodwill of its buyers, and was forced to "carry this hop yarn over until next year," with resultant storage and inventory costs adding insult to injury.[56] Performance like this would have made a mockery of the global supply networks and just-in-time scheduling of the late twentieth century. Container ships could still arrive behind schedule and road congestion might cause further delays, but containerization's rapid turnaround times, smooth interchanges through intermodality, and logistical management provided a level of exactitude that the SJPL, even at its best moments, could only have dreamed of in precontainer days.

Containerization had other effects on global interchange in the late twentieth century. It facilitated entry of Asians on world markets, and its reinvention of sea transport paved the way for construction of new Asian fleets. By the 1970s all shipping companies, in a sense, were starting from scratch, and all that was necessary to enter shipowning was seafaring know-how and capital. The latter, moreover, was in plentiful supply, thanks to Eurodollars and petrodollars or shipyards hard up from the crash in the tanker market and prepared to offer seductive rates. Westerners had begun containerization, but fairly rapidly it was taken up by non-Americans and non-Europeans. Decentered vectors, but also

[56] GAR/Lloyd 1/274/20 (two letters), 22 March, 6 April 1939.

command centers, characterized global shipping in this new stage. At the
end of the century, not only Japan, but Hong Kong, Taiwan, South Korea,
Singapore, and China were important shipping nations, the preeminent
traffic in the world was Asian,[57] Asian shipping lines dominated this trade,
and Asian shipping lines led the carrying trade between North America
and Europe.[58] Taiwan's Evergreen within two decades of its founding
inaugurated the first successful container round-the-world service. In
1998 it took over Lloyd Triestino, once Italy's premier shipping line, and
in 1999 it was the world's second largest container shipping company.
Little in this story was anomalous. Before Evergreen swallowed Lloyd
Triestino, Hong Kong's Orient Overseas Container Line (OOCL) had
shocked the shipping world by taking over one of the most venerable (if
shaky) British titans, Furness Withy, in 1980. Singapore's Neptune Orient
Line (NOL) acquired American President Lines. Korea's Hanjin bought
out the Bremen-based DSR-Senator Line. In 1999, when Evergreen had
climbed to number-two rank among container companies, Hanjin was
fourth, China Ocean Shipping Company (COSCO) was fifth, NOL was
eighth, and Japan's NYK was ninth, with six more Asian lines, an Israeli
line, and a Gulf State line all but rounding out the next top ten (see
Table 5).[59]

   A third basic change in late twentieth-century globalism was therefore greater global presence at all maritime levels. Global sourcing and
just-in-time delivery led multinational shippers to search for "one shop"
transporters. What they wanted were global transport companies capable of handling all their shipments, regardless of whether these were in
America, Europe, Singapore, or China, or simply passing through these
regions.[60] In the past, global shipping had been the aggregate of multiple
shipping networks, nearly all confined to one or two oceans with interchange points at main ports in between. Round-the-world service was
exceptional and often patched together within the shipping lines that ran
it. In the 1980s, all that changed as container companies became global
mega-carriers. P & O, synonymous with Eastern imperial trades for nearly

---

[57] Frémont, *French*, 171; Wiborg and Wiborg, *Unser*, 415.
[58] Broeze, *Globalisation*, 161.
[59] CAC/930149/30/Etude du développement des armements d'Asie du Sud-Est, December
    1981; Gilbert Wong, "Business Groups in a Dynamic Environment: Hong Kong, 1976–
    1986," in Gary Hamilton, ed., *Business Networks and Economic Development in East
    and Southeast Asia* (Hong Kong: University of Hong Kong, 1991), 142–143; Broeze,
    Globalisation, 151–152.
[60] Bott (interview, quoted); Broeze, *Globalisation*, 107, 115–116.

TABLE 5. *The World's Twenty Largest Container Companies, January 1999*

Rank	Company	Country	TEU Capacity
1	Maersk	Denmark	378,205
2	Evergreen	Taiwan	297,030
3	P & O Nedlloyd	UK/Netherlands	263,248
4	Hanjin/DSR Senator	Korea/Germany	232,911
5	COSCO	China	227,137
6	Sea-Land	USA	209,226
7	Mediterranean SC	Switzerland	199,226
8	NOL/APL	Singapore	198,163
9	NYK	Japan	164,311
10	CP Ships/TMM	Canada/Mexico	139,085
11	Mitsui OSK	Japan	129,210
12	CMA/CGM	France	115,843
13	Zim	Israel	113,673
14	Hyundai	Korea	109,192
15	K-Line	Japan	105,643
16	Yang Ming	Taiwan	101,094
17	Hapag-Lloyd	Germany	100,216
18	OOCL	Hong Kong	90,944
19	USAC	Arab Gulf states	68,553
20	Wan Hai	Taiwan	56,194

Source: Broeze, *Globalisation*, 151. Reprinted with the kind permission of the International Maritime Economic History Association.

all its existence, sent ships into the North Atlantic. Where the reach into a third or fourth ocean strained, companies formed "global" or "grand" alliances. The design was to keep all containers in motion, delivering and loading full ones on the way while carrying the empties to where they were needed. Economies of scale, it was hoped, would increase, as round-the-world services drew traffic from all the sea lanes.[61]

The bid for global presence spread across sectors. Ahlers, an Antwerp shipping agent, opened offices in Riga, St. Petersburg, Tashkent, Shanghai, and employed an international workforce of Europeans, Asians, and Africans. Clarksons, a big London shipbroking firm, possessed overseas branches in the United States, South Africa, Hong Kong, Shanghai, and Singapore.[62] Tabaknatie's Jules de Maeyer, when asked what difference

[61] Broeze, *Globalisation*, 79–100, 138; Levinson, *Box*, 239–244; Mitsui O.S.K. Lines, "Corporate Profile," 1997, 4, 21–22; Frémont, *French*, 171.
[62] Weynen (interview); McCoy (interview).

present globalization made answered, "We are obliged to think global," and when prodded, "But weren't you always thinking global?" he answered, "No. Till ten years ago we were thinking Antwerp.... There's only four or five left [big multinational cigarette companies].... And they think global so we must think global with them." To keep pace, Tabaknatie invested in state-of-the-art tobacco warehouses and equipped itself to handle container shipments from Brazil, America, Zimbabwe, Turkey, the Philippines, Thailand, and Malawi. At dealer's behest they now organized the transshipment of tobacco from Africa to Antwerp with further shipment to any point in the world. A once very local intermediary, it too had expanded to think and act globally, emblazoning on its brochures, "Global strategy. Local activity."[63]

In a sense, then, as containerization progressed it too, like Nedlloyd, Onassis, and Arison, rewrote the meaning of transnationalism. The transnationalism of a Holts, Vorwerks, or Bunge had been overt, but in each case transnational identity divided between distinct overseas foci and home commitment; for instance, Liverpool and East Asia for Holts, Hamburg and Chile for the Vorwerks, and Antwerp and Argentina for Bunge. Once companies went truly global, there was far less fixity to transnational identities, much as shipping ownership so submerged beneath flags of convenience that in 2000 the top five world fleets, in descending order, were, preposterously, those of Panama, Liberia, the Bahamas, Malta, and Greece.[64] In shipping the consequence was to abandon preserves for world systems. Attachment to former home identities wore so thin that absorption into foreign lines was not out of the question. Even P & O, despite moving headquarters to Pall Mall, just buildings down from St. James's Palace, was not above merging its container networks with Holland's Nedlloyd and then, shortly into the twenty-first century, selling these out to Denmark's Maersk, just as it had its cruise line division to Americans in Miami. For ports, the thinning out of local-global distinctions accompanied a transformation from global nodes to global operators. Expanding global presence in this sector meant not simply wider foreland networks, but investing in other world ports or selling management services abroad. Asian ports were among the most aggressive venturers, to the point of reversing older transnational lines of direction. The Port of Singapore (PSA), Hong Kong's Hutchison's Port

[63] Jules de Maeyer (interview, quoted) and Eric van Nueten, who gave me a tour of Tabak Natie's harbor facilities.
[64] Theotokas and Harlaftis, *Leadership*, 27. The top five national owners were Greece, Japan, Norway, the United States, and China.

Holdings (Chinese owned), and Dubai Ports Authority – renamed, appropriately, DP World – operated terminals and management contracts on several continents.[65] Whereas previously Europeans had developed ports in imperial lands, by the start of the twenty-first century former imperial harbors were running terminals in Britain, Rotterdam, and Antwerp, and were behaving not altogether unlike the managing agencies that had sallied forth from London or other great Western cities to found or administer commodity plantations worldwide in the past. The effect was also to confuse older senses of place and connection. Since the late nineteenth century Antwerp had received and sent ships to and from all points of the world and had been a most cosmopolitan harbor, but the port was also clearly Belgian, and local in its identification. At the end of the twentieth century, that identification had destabilized. Whole chunks of Antwerp port, including traditional entities like *naties*, were foreign owned or operated, just as ports themselves, physically, or juridically, spread parts of themselves across the seas. Under containerization, not only were ports coming to look, interchangeably, like one another, they were becoming bits and pieces of each other.

Finally, although many of the changes in globalization appeared to have sprung up overnight, or were attributable to contemporary innovations in technology and management, it must be recalled that they were in fact the fruition of forces set in motion with the First World War. The impact of global conflict had not only been to rent and contract, but to open possibilities for wider global participation. To interruption and rebirth can be posited an alternative paradigm of progression, but scarcely a linear one, because new opportunities were seized on by new men from new places with corresponding mutations in the globalizing process. Perhaps it is a dialectic of action and reaction that best captures how globalization moved across the century. But move it did, with features at century's end that were not those at century's beginning.

Effects: Maritime Power and Culture

A central contention of this book has been the reciprocity between maritime and wider histories. Containerization rewrote this dynamic, because

---

[65] *Fairplay*, 15, 22, March 2001; Wong, "Business Groups," 142–143; Broeze, *Globalisation*, 191–193. Liverpool also sold advising and operating services to ports in Latin America, the Persian Gulf, West Africa, the former Soviet Union, and South and Southeast Asia: Furlong (interview); *The Port of Liverpool: Handbook and Directory 1998*, 116–117; *The Mersey Docks and Harbour Company: Annual Report and Accounts*, 1997, 11.

in the last third of the twentieth century the principal motor and orchestrator of maritime change came from within rather than from without. A contrast can be drawn with the earlier blows that had been delivered to trading companies. Once integral to maritime networks, these enterprises had less and less, and often nothing, to do with the seas. Internatio had turned into Imtech, Harrisons & Crosfield into Elementis – a global specialties chemical company so far removed from seaborne trade that it had abandoned its sailing ship logo in favor of an abstract design. Theodor Wille in the early twenty-first century was still close in name – TWI, or Theodor Wille Intertrade – but this once quintessential Hamburg-Brazilian trading house was now American owned, had converted to a contractor of distribution services for the U.S. military, and was headquartered in Zug, Switzerland, with offices in Frankfurt, Dubai, the UAE, and the United States. Institutional memory had largely disappeared, along with ties to either Brazil or the coffee trade.[66] Those still engaged in traditional activities, such as Swires or Illies, were the exception. Many others had gone through so many permutations that they had little in common with their former imperial or maritime selves. For nearly all the big moment of change had been the war and the break up of empire, and all further evolution built on these sources of rupture.[67]

Containerization, a self-generated instigator, was different, although its impact on nearly every other aspect of maritime life and culture after 1970 was no less profound. Two careers from these years provide an entrée into what that revolution entailed. Rolf van den Wall Bake's began in Sydney in 1977, after studies in naval architecture and business administration. Joining Nedlloyd, his first assignment was as a line manager, or agent, for services where conventional methods still obtained, so that even though his shipping career began on the cusp of change, the early years in Sydney taught him the business in the old way. From this experience he developed a lifelong pleasure in fixing things: "You were always a 'Mr. Fix-it.'" Like Diedrich Döhle, he learned to drink like a lion. "It was still a fairly rough sort of environment, I mean the idea of a sale in those days was still you go to the pub and try to get pissed together and the sale was on the back of ... the coasters ... that was your booking." He got his first tallow contract by drinking the client under the table.

---

[66] Correspondence between Patrick Malcor, Managing Director, Theodor Wille Intertrade GMBH, and author, 11 August 2009.

[67] Jones, *Merchants*, 325–342; *Swire Group*, company brochure, n.d., c. 1996. I am indebted to the written reports sent me by Wilhelm Michels, in response to questions I put to him on Illies.

Summing up those early years several decades later, he remarked that "I think the biggest pleasure was simply fixing things ... nothing was routine basically. Nowadays, I mean, a lot of it is very much routine and there are so many elements of shipping that you don't get involved with anymore. You really felt you were right in the middle of everything." Yet even as the services containerized and the old methods disappeared, the love of fixing things stayed with him. Still in the infancy of containers, he struggled with how to pack commodities such as coffee into metal boxes without their spoiling by the time of arrival. Later, as he moved up the company chain, in Hong Kong and Tokyo, he moved on to applying computer programming to shipping. To the amusement of his colleagues he bought an Apple II, but he learned how to use it to improve voyage calculations. The spreadsheets he developed became Nedlloyd standards for operations across the globe – quite a jump from getting contracts by drinking clients under the table. In the 1990s, now managing director for Mitsui OSK lines in the Netherlands, his Sydney days were a distant memory. Rarely going to the port, he concentrated on the logistics of container flows and how to minimize empty container movements. His life work, therefore, spanned two eras in the history of shipping; but there remained the satisfaction in making things work.[68]

Herman Reynaerts, general manager of a ship agency in Antwerp, told a very different life story. The son of a financial manager for British Petroleum, he had no interest in going to university, and when a neighbor offered him a job with a forwarding company, he accepted. Beginning in 1981 as a courier shuttling documents to liner offices, he took on more forwarding duties, moved on to agency and shipping companies, and then back into agency work. The constant in his life was the discovery of his love for working in the shipping trades, but only of the traditional or conventional sort, by now a minor part of general cargo transport. "Working in shipping is a kick, I guess.... Because there you are talking about *cargo*." But he would not touch the container trades with a ten-foot pole because "whenever you are in the container trades everybody is talking about boxes ... and nobody cares what is transported inside, nobody cares. You are just moving quantities of boxes.... A box is a box, and that's it."[69]

The contemporaneity of van den Wall Bake and Reynaerts was roughly the same, but the dichotomy in how each regarded containerization could

[68] Van den Wall Bake (interview).
[69] Reynaerts (interview).

not have been greater. For van den Wall Bake, the kick was the challenge. He was at home in the old days, but when his trades containerized it was still a kick: "I mean there was still so much to do. So much improvements to be made.... The industry was really changing in those days and it was fantastic to be part of them, to be involved in them." If a box was a box, shipping nonetheless "all of a sudden became a much more sophisticated industry.... The past was maybe experience and now it became into the stage where thinking and analyzing was becoming more important." He felt fortunate to be part of a generation where such a transition was taking place. Containerization took away the quays and pubs, and replaced them with computers and logistics, but that meant nothing to him except new opportunities to transform and perfect a business. At the end of the interview I summed up what he had told me as "a lifetime of seeking innovation," to which he responded, "That's right." Reynaerts saw things wholly differently. Containerization was the Antichrist, a dumbing-down and ultra-routinization of shipping. It had broken open bottlenecks, and clearly there was no turning back. But its power had been as destructive as constructive. Where Van den Wall Bake was content to find his way in the container world, Reynaerts opted for marginality. Yet both men did agree on one thing. Containerization had ruptured the past from the present, and that rupture had governed their professional lives: "The biggest change has to be the container and the way it has really controlled our whole business."[70] What then did containerization mean for maritime companies, cities, and people?

First, it revolutionized the shipping industry. When containerization took hold, it was scarcely possible for shipping companies to go it alone. Not only were the investment costs in new container ships daunting; what could not be imagined was how one company could sustain weekly services across multiple routes when each new container ship could lift several times the cargo of conventional liners. From the late 1960s into the early 1970s there occurred an era of national consolidations, building on an older culture of cooperation as well as competition. The major Dutch shipping companies, save Holland Amerika, merged into Nedlloyd. HAPAG and NDL merged into Hapag-Lloyd. The CGT and the Messageries merged into CGM. The British formed OCL and other British consortia. But the pressure for bigness became unrelenting. New generations of container ships raised the investment ante. Round-the-world services and over tonnage forced increasing pursuit of economies

---

[70] Van den Wall Bake (interview, final quote); Reynaerts (interview).

of scale. There was therefore a need for still larger, international combines, the way again paved by older cosmopolitan traditions. These proved unstable, however, and were accompanied by an equally strong trend in mergers and buyouts until ultimately there emerged a new dog-eat-dog world. Newcomers like Evergreen, moreover, operated outside conferences and, unable to co-opt rising shipping stars or contain freight rates, this system too collapsed.

The fallout was that little remained of traditional shipping identities. Large numbers of shipping companies disappeared or dropped out along the way, lacking the resources and even the heart to continue in a business world that was not only unfamiliar and unchartered, but required surrendering independence and a sense of oneself. Many of these were old-line companies, with a century or longer in their trades, and among them some of the best known in the shipping world, such as Holland Amerika or the Chargeurs Réunis. The most stunning reversal occurred in British shipping, which had once commanded the sea lanes. Practically all the great companies went, including icons like Cunard and Holts, either swallowed up by others or disengaging from deep-sea shipping altogether.[71] Peter Warwick, who, like his father, had been associated with Houlder, once prominent in the South American meat trades but now vanished, remarked on how there had been about a hundred British Companies on the Baltic Exchange when he had become a member in the early 1950s: "They've virtually all gone now." Eric Shawyer, head of E. A. Gibson Shipbrokers Ltd., and a Baltic chairman, pulled out an old directory of British shipping companies after his interview and intoned "gone" as he flipped through the pages.[72] At the turn of the new century the only substantial British liner company left standing was P & O, another iconic charter member, for many years the largest shipping company in the world, and still towering over all but a few of its international competitors. But it too had passed through the kaleidoscopic universe of shipping since the onset of containerization, and in 2005, out of the cruise business, it sold its container division to Maersk. This left Denmark's Maersk, which also engorged Sea-Land, at the top of the heap. But this was a firm only founded in 1928, and for years it had been rather marginal in shipping circles. Indeed, among the top ten container lines in 1999, only two or three – P & O/Nedlloyd and NYK – were leading lines (or combinations of these) before the Second World War.

---

[71] Carnival, after buying Cunard, retained the name.
[72] P. J. Warwick, Hadley Shipping Company Limited, interview with author, London, 26 August 1998; Shawyer (interview).

The next tier included only Mitsui OSK, the K-Line, Hapag-Lloyd, and CGM (see Table 5).

What these companies could possibly represent in relation to the past was an abiding question. Traditions only partially survived the first round of national mergers. Established ties to old bases in Bremen, Amsterdam, and Liverpool were strained or severed altogether. As Holts phased out shipping and retreated into other marine-related activities, the redefinition of this once-defining shipping line was "such that those attending the annual dinners for retired seafarers must have felt as if they had gate-crashed on an alien host; 'it is obvious that Ocean is no longer a shipping company,' they were told at one dinner by the head of the Shipping and Marine Services Division."[73] Survivors like CGM or Hapag-Lloyd fell into the hands of previous unknowns or corporations with no shipping connections whatsoever. Flags of convenience, but also slot agreements, nonvessel operators, and cross-national mergers and acquisitions gutted previous firm, national, or even functional identifications. A major European newcomer was the Mediterranean Shipping Company, founded in 1970 by an Italian ferryboat captain, headquartered in landlocked Switzerland, closely allied to nonvessel operators, and absent from any regular service to the Mediterranean for the first thirty-two years of its existence. In 2005, it ranked second only to Maersk among the world's container shipping lines.[74] Regardless of power, or who was in and who was out, these were not the same companies as before.

A major catalyst in this process was the advent of new men with no previous connection to shipping. The great innovators, McLean and Bruce Seaton, came from trucking and accounting trades. Seaton's business formation was with oil. Containerization was thus initiated and carried through by outsiders with no sense of boundaries and untethered to traditions. Joining them were waves of business managers and financiers, useful for an industry increasingly complex in its logistics and costs, but who brought with them backgrounds and outlooks that bore no resemblance to the biographies and apprenticeships described earlier in this volume, and who could not have cared a whit for the loss of good club men. The replacement of Jack Kruse by Bernd Wrede at the head of Hapag-Lloyd in 1993 represented a sea change in the history of that firm. Kruse was an old-line shipping man who had grown up professionally within Hapag-Lloyd. Wrede, "to the contrary a business school graduate

[73] Falkus, *Blue*, 376.
[74] Donovan and Bonney, *Box*, 183–186.

and financial expert, saw himself from the beginning as the manager and strategist of a transport and tourism group to which, as the sector with the greatest weight, shipping also belonged."[75] Such a transition was becoming commonplace at the head of shipping firms. Jeffrey Sterling, a City financier, brought into P & O in the early 1980s to safeguard it from predators, performed brilliantly in preserving the company as the one great British survivor until he sold off at the turn of the century. But under Sterling, P & O also was changing: "It became much more business oriented and shipping was not thought of as a peculiar and extraordinary thing by most people. It was another series of assets which were being exploited as well as they could for the benefit of shareholders."[76] Others pointed out how "you might find people who are in the container shipping company [and] have never been on board a ship.... They could sell today insurance covers, or bonds, or containers, or whatever."[77] Jérôme Seydoux, a "professional manager" who got control of the Chargeurs Réunis in the 1980s, lost interest after several years of losses and sold off most of the company to concentrate on media investments with Silvio Berlusconi.[78] Even where new men such as Evergreen's Chang Yung-fa or Mediterranean Shipping Company's Gianluigi Aponte were as schooled in the sea as erstwhile competitors,[79] they climbed very different ladders under containerization, with no incentive to adhere to the old rules of engagement. Evergreen, Maersk, and other new giants ignored conferences and went their own way, forcing nearly all the others to follow.

The net effect of this influx, as with Arison and Stephan, was to dissolve the bonds that held precontainer shipping together. Their influence showed up in the pitiless world of shipping in the last third of the century, but also in the internal language of companies. Identities and professional formation, or the definition of expertise, simply severed from older signifiers; the contrasts were very stark. Lawrence Holt, for instance, had made it a habit in prewar days to meet with every master, chief officer, and chief engineer on their appointment. The interview would begin with Holt explaining that he could simply put his advice to paper, but "we try to keep up this personal charge in order to preserve as fully as possible the human touch in our relations with the fleet." Holt would then run

[75] Wiborg and Wiborg, *Unser*, 407.
[76] Bott (interview, quoted); Broeze, *Globalisation*, 109–111; Howarth and Howarth, *P & O*, 200–207. Bott, despite the different background, had enormous respect for Sterling.
[77] Ehrhardt (interview).
[78] Cassagnou, *Grandes*, 872–875.
[79] Donovan and Bonney, *Box*, 145, 184.

through his instructions and counsel. Masters were to report "by word of mouth" at the end of each voyage. They were to watch the drink. They were to set the right tone in off-duty social hours, "but in any case it is imperative that you should require a high standard of keenness on duty." It was the captain's role to train up his officers. "This is necessary for the Company's existence.... You and I and everyone else here have received most of what we know from those who have gone before us, and it is our business to pass it on unimpaired, and, if possible, improved by our own exertions.... Never teach anyone anything which he could easily find out for himself ... but teach him all your own experience." They were to know everything there was to know about cargo. "It is not sufficient to be the chauffeur of the ship. It is the whole job that really matters.... Encourage [your officers] ... to study all about stowage.... Encourage them to read books, the Company's books, and pass on to them what more you can from your own experience." Log books were to be kept "truthfully.... It is vital that we should have a first-class reputation in all courts of law, and that we shall be trusted in all respects." In the event of an accident, Masters should think things through and then sleep on it before committing words to paper. "And if you still hold to it after that sleep, stand by it. If you want to alter it, alter it, but do not write the entry in the log until you have slept on it, because sleep is the proof that you have your nervous system in respectable order." Agents were to be worked with closely, but masters should also remember that "you go with our complete confidence. We entrust the ship to you." And the master should "know all about the port you are coming to." "Money can be saved by slowing down and arriving at the right moment, instead of twelve hours too soon. On the other hand money can also be saved by putting on more speed and clearing a port before a holiday."[80]

Set Holt's remarks alongside K. St. Johnston's long letter of advice to Julian Taylor,[81] and the two would fold into each other. Both were about a lifetime in the shipping business. Both stressed experience and expertise and reeked of common sense. Both emanated from a culture built on networks, trust, and reputation. Both were about authority, but also face-to-face relations and the personal touch. Both were the product of old hands. Both were chatty, the work of letter writers. Both came right out of the codes, right out of the world of conventional shipping.

---

[80] MMM/OA/4C/913/Appointment of Capt. Dugdale as Master: Mr. Lawrence Holt's Interview/21 February 1936.
[81] See the opening to Chapter 5.

By the 1970s, both were also ceding to another world of professional management consultants or management training sessions. In December 1969, P & O held a Supervisory Management Program for supervisors, middle, and top management. At it a Mr. Taylor "introduced us to the 'Mechanistic' and 'Organic' systems of Management and talked about 'effective work groups.'" Mr. A. Cowling, lecturer in human aspects of management at the Polytechnic School of Management Studies, "introduced his subject by analysing in detail the 'communication process.'" Mr. J. Oreton, lecturer in quantitative aspects of management studies, "asserted that Management exists to select from available alternatives the best route towards 'chosen objectives.'" According to Oreton, effective decision making "is more than just sifting facts with dynamic precision; it involves three deliberate activities," an "Intelligence Activity," a "Design Activity," and a "Choice Activity."[82] The planet had not changed, but either Holt or these people were in a different orbit. Holt had warned his captains that "it is not sufficient to be the chauffeur of the ship." At the end of the 1990s, Hamburg shipping agent Diedrich Döhle, who remembered the old days with captains in port as "super times," said they had been reduced to just that: "a taxi driver." And Jean Lerbret, a French shipbroker, said the same thing: They were no better than "a bus driver." "The poor wretch. He has gone through splendid studies ... he is responsible." But for what, since the orders were now in a computer plan and the position determined by a satellite?[83]

Not a little of the difference was owed to wider trends in business practice and culture; for instance the hegemonic conception of management as a profession learned in business schools and applicable across industry and sector, or the extraordinary opportunities offered by electronic data systems for modeling and massaging information, which put a premium on new kinds of expertise. Yet there was also plenty in the container revolution to structure a new kind of company culture and morph shipping houses into logistics specialists. Intermodality, plus the transition to "transport," displaced shipping from being trade specific and sufficient to itself: "The shipowner went like [an] amphibian. He crawled on land."[84]

[82] NMM/NZS/15/16/Report on P & O Supervisory Management Programme, December 1969. Alan Bott noted that at one time OCL contemplated sending everyone off to the Harvard Business School. He, however, was immersed in freight negotiations and pleaded off: "And Ronny Swayne called me in and he said, 'I think we really ought to go to this Harvard thing. He said, 'Wait a minute, you've got a history degree from Oxford don't you. Oh.... You don't need to go." Bott (interview).

[83] Döhle (interview); Lerbret (interview).

[84] Seiler (interview).

That evolutionary move was not baggage-free. Containers stripped contents and former expertise of meaning. Acute attention to flow systems guaranteed the primacy of logistics in function and identity. Dutch shipping has filled the pages of this history, but in the 1980s Nedlloyd abandoned the ascription of liner shipping for "containerlogistic[s] on a world-wide scale." A Lloyd's List International celebration of 650 years of Rotterdam's history had to remind readers, after discussing Nedlloyd's reorientation toward "the entire transport chain," that "its commitment to liner trades remains."[85] Once hatched into an environment of global firms, new men, new companies, and old conference lifeboats rotting away, house cultures of the past had little likelihood of surviving.

The reverberations of these new company cultures on the remainder of the maritime world would be trenchant. How that occurred, however, requires first an understanding of how containerization also remade port cities.

Since the 1950s and 1960s oil and bulk carrier trades had drawn port installations farther downriver, until, as in the case of Rotterdam, they were all but astride the sea. But general cargo and with it the physical structures and hurly-burly of dock life remained in the center, or adjacent to it. Containerization blotted as much of that traditional world out as it could to clear the way for the efficient movement of cargo through the harbor. Ironically, the desire to reduce ports to pure and minimalist transit zones was to result in a revival of the entrepot activities of the past, which had been winnowed down over the course of the first two-thirds of the century. Yet in the process, containerization changed the look of ports and completed the massive spatial transition initiated by supertankers. Containers required of ports only two things. One was a new design of crane. The other was open space by fairly deep water. A traditional quay required approximately one and a half hectares, early container berths ten, and as container ships scaled-up, terminals doubled to twenty hectares per berth, and then well beyond that.[86]

Those facts produced four subsequent effects. The first was the conversion of port receiving and loading areas into parking lots. The contemporary container port was a fascinating mix of minimalist modern design: machine-like, futuristic, and randomly yet geometrically colored. It was also thoroughly banal. About all there was quayside consisted of cranes, boxes, and trucks. There were scarcely any buildings. There

---

[85] Van Driel, *Samenwerking*, 163 (quoted on containerlogistics); Lloyd's List International, *Rotterdam*, 32.

[86] Suykens, *Antwerp*, 516–517.

FIGURE 10. Containers, cranes, trucks – but where are the people? Rotterdam Harbor 1972. Collection Municipal Archives of Rotterdam.

were scarcely any people. This was the second effect: the disappearance of longshoremen from harbors, save those skilled operators of container cranes, EDP systems, and, where they were not replaced by automatically guided systems, drivers of forklifts and weird container movers called straddle carriers. There were also truck drivers and a man at the gate. Dockers and stevedores, however, in the numbers that had once typified ports, had gone the way of crates, barrels, and bales or any other sign of human production and consumption. Ports that dropped out of the running, like London and Liverpool, saw the most precipitous decline. There were 28,722 registered workers in the port of London in 1960, but only 7,537 left in 1979, and a mere 1,759 at the end of the 1980s. Yet Antwerp, despite a doubling of tonnage figures, also experienced a dwindling of its workforce from around 14,500 in the 1950s to less than half that in the mid-1990s.[87] Gluttons for pavement, container ports were teetotalers when it came to humans.

The third effect was the further distancing of harbor activities from old port areas. General cargo followed bulk cargo downstream toward

[87] Mankelow, "Effects," 73, 86; Van Isacker, *Afscheid*, 128; Stad Antwerpen, *Identiteitskaart Antwerpen*, 1997.

open water. There were few alternatives, as the flat open space necessary for container handling was only to be had in virgin port territory.
Rotterdam concentrated early container traffic in the Eemhaven and
the Waalhaven, but subsequent terminals were sited all the way out in
the Maasvlakte, essentially into the North Sea. A drive out Antwerp's
Noorderlaan, bordered by functional buildings with familiar names of
forwarders, *naties*, or other harbor services, reveals the hugeness of this
port complex as it extends farther and farther away from the city. In the
past, ships would have lined the river berths alongside the city – "these
were the best berths."[88] A view from a tenth floor in the downtown area
overlooking the cathedral now shows little river traffic, whereas a view
downriver catches the immense number of cranes that signal the port in
the distance.

Such pursuit of open territory led to the fourth effect: the creation of entirely new ports, or the enlargement of previously minuscule
ports into substantial container harbors. New sites offered open land,
but also better access to superhighway networks or the absence of
"history," that is, difficult or expensive labor relations. The harbingers of
this development were the ports of northern New Jersey and Oakland,
each at the expense of neighboring New York and San Francisco,
respectively.[89] The obvious European instance was the ascent of tiny
Felixstowe, just north of Harwich on the eastern English coast, to the
status of Britain's first container port. But the world was filled with
such gazetteer places, including Gioia Tauro, Marsaxlokk, Yantian, and
Tanjung Pelepas.[90]

Displacement by space carried over to function. Container ships that
concentrated cargo in greater quantities on fewer vessels and were all
about rapid turnover time could not follow the old, slow progression
from port to port. Under containerization, containers – not ships – would
chase after cargo. Ports had always divided between hubs and feeders, but
now former main ports were bypassed by the big consortia whose ships
stopped perhaps only twice or thrice along the northwestern European
littoral. No port was excluded altogether, but containers threatened to
rewrite main port status.

As a result, ports came to look on themselves as distribution centers or logistical command posts in the supply chain. This strategy

---

[88] Durot (interview).
[89] Levinson, *Box*, 78–100; 191–197.
[90] Broeze, *Globalisation*, 173.

was accompanied by a fair amount of business speak, with references to "service culture" and "stakeholders" and other word-inflation that dressed up features that had long defined what ports did. But language also expressed central truths about changing port functions and identities in the container age. In the container version of hub and feeder systems, distribution radii exceeded older hinterlands to encompass container flows potentially anywhere, outward on the seas as well as inland. Warehousing revived, but this was because short distances in Europe encouraged the storage of big vessel shipments in harbor areas with port services managing just-in-time flow to inland centers. Late-century warehousers no longer identified themselves in the old entrepot sense. Instead they were links in efficient flow management and were coupled to container-age logistical services: stuffing and stripping of containers, sophisticated information control systems, intermodal arrangements, and supply chain management, all of which were replacing older value-added services in dock labor, tallying, weighing, sorting, and reception.[91] Some flavor of this could be culled from Hamburg's elaborate port brochure from the mid-1990s that described the port as a "European distribution center," and vaunted its "extensive computer-based management and information systems ... [that] play an important role in supply chain management." Compared to port publicity literature from 1930, self-presentation was repackaged to represent services demanded by container logistics. Port systems and companies – witness the Buss Logistik Terminal – had taken on new, complex responsibilities, and the intensification of global connectedness, recast as global interface, was indicative of how globalization had progressed over sixty-plus years, as was another boast, repeated several times, that Hamburg possessed "the largest Asian business community in Europe."[92]

All these changes played out on the terrain of power. In one sense containerization reinforced earlier trends toward *l'horizon terrestre*.[93] Command posts often located with the great retail chains or multinationals who assembled the supply chains. The integration of sea and land transport into a single transport chain, and one in which sea freight

[91] B. S. Hoyle and D. A. Pinder, *European Port Cities in Transition* (London: Belhaven Press, 1992), 52–53; Suykens, *Antwerp*, 525–530; Reginald Loyen, "Functional Shifts in the Port of Antwerp: A Throughput Model," *International Journal of Maritime History* 13 (December 2001): 85–88; De Maeyer (interview).

[92] Port of Hamburg, *The Port of Hamburg, 1995/1996* (London: Charter International, 1996), 7, 23–29, 34–37.

[93] CAC/840626/17/Les ports français et le conteneur, August 1971; Roncayolo, *L'imaginaire*, 247–248.

accounted for only a quarter of total transport costs, diluted still further any paramountcy of "the maritime." Perhaps most damaging were the dynamics of containers and intermodality, where boxes off-loaded in a day on great slabs of concrete often far downstream, transferred to trucks or block trains, and headed inland, bypassing what had once constituted ports in the traditional sense. Yet the power dynamics of containers were far more complex, and were just as likely in the present stage of globalization to reaffirm as diminish the significance of seaports. Access to high-end container flows, and incorporation into transport and supply chains, dictated massive investments in seaport infrastructures. It was no coincidence that Hong Kong and Singapore ascended to the rank of the world's greatest container ports as Asian exports flooded across the world.[94] Besides, as ports and port companies repositioned themselves as logistical service providers, they retained an intermediary role in transport chains, regardless of how unitary these became. Indeed, in terms of raw power, it was not at all clear that the basic power brokers were not what they had always been: the shipping companies. Ports had always run after shipping companies, but the power of the new behemoths such as Sea-Land to deliver 500,000 TEUs as a starting figure raised their authority to a new order.[95] The difference following containerization was the evisceration of home fleets and their replacement in large part by new global giants, mostly of nontraditional or non-Western origins yet in command of massive container shipments. To assure greater control over their intermodal flows, these companies began to purchase terminals in ports or even to attain management control over ports altogether. Their rival bidders were other ports or international terminal operators such as Port of Singapore Authority or Dubai's DP World.[96] Ports thus lost local power, but following containerization the shift was global, and in any event seaward, as much or more as it was inland.

Where power shifts were undeniable was in port hierarchies, and in the most severe instances, main port discontinuity. At the broadest level, port power had shifted to Asia. In 1996, Rotterdam was still the world's largest port in turnover tonnage, but the next five ports were Asian. Three Asian ports topped the list of containers handled, and the first two, Hong Kong and Singapore, were far ahead of the rest of the pack. In 1999 and 2003, European main ports slid still further down the scale (see Tables 6, 7).

[94] Levinson, *Box*, 269–270.
[95] Antwerp, Port of Antwerp Technische Dienst Archives/7281/30 December 1987.
[96] Broeze, *Globalisation*, 186–194.

TABLE 6. *The World's Ten Largest Ports in 1996;*
Tonnage in Million Metric Tons

Rank	Port	Tonnage
1	Rotterdam	292
2	Singapore	242.5
3	Shanghai	164
4	Hong Kong	125.8
5	Yokohoma	124.9
6	Nagoya	118.3
7	Antwerp	106.5
8	Long Beach	97.7
9	Busan	97.6
10	Marseille	90.7

Source: Gemeentelijk Havenbedrijf Rotterdam, *Haven in cijfers*,
1997. Reprinted with the permission of the Havenbedrijf Rotterdam.

TABLE 7. *The World's Largest Container Ports Measured*
in Thousands of TEUs

Rank	1996	1999	2003
1.	Hong Kong: 13,280	Hong Kong: 16,200	Hong Kong: 20,800
2.	Singapore: 12,950	Singapore: 15,900	Singapore: 18,400
3.	Kaohsiung: 5,063	Kaohsiung: 7,000	Shanghai: 11,400
4.	Rotterdam: 4,936	Rotterdam: 6,300	Shenzhen: 10,700
5.	Busan: 4,684	Busan: 6,300	Busan: 10,400
6.	Long Beach: 3,067	Long Beach: 4,400	Kaohsiung: 8,800
7.	Hamburg: 3,065	Shanghai: 4,200	Rotterdam: 7,100
8.	Los Angeles: 2,683	Los Angeles: 3,800	Los Angeles: 6,600
9.	Antwerp: 2,654	Hamburg: 3,700	Hamburg: 6,100
10.	Yokohama: 2,400	Antwerp: 3,600	Antwerp: 5,400
11.		NY/NJ: 2,900	Dubai: 5,100
12.		Dubai: 2,800	Port Klang: 4,800
13.		Tokyo: 2,700	Long Beach: 4,700
14.		Felixstowe: 2,600	Qingdao: 4,200
15.		Port Kelang: 2,600	NY/NJ: 4,000
16.		Gioia Tauro: 2,300	Tanjung Pel: 3,500
17.		Bremerhaven: 2,200	Tokyo: 3,300
18.		Manila: 2,100	Bremerhaven: 3,200
19.		Yokohama: 2,100	Laem Chabang 3,200
20.		San Juan: 2,100	Gioia Tauro: 3,000

Sources: 1996: Gemeentelijk Havenbedrijf Rotterdam, *Haven in cijfers*; 1999: Broeze,
Globalisation, 169; 2003: Levinson, *The Box*, 273.

The fall was cruelest in some of Europe's once-greatest harbors. The contrast between Rotterdam's and London's fortunes showed the container's impact in the sharpest light.

Rotterdam in the 1960s had risen to world port supremacy on the basis of two things: oil, and the commitment of city and port authorities to the port as Rotterdam's motor. In the 1970s, both these supports shattered on OPEC's price increases and environmental concerns that disconnected city priorities from the harbor. The turnover in 1973 of 310 million tons represented a peak that would still not be rescaled twenty years later. Within this context, the container was something of a saving grace. Recognizing its potential, Port Director Posthuma, as early as 1963, met with McLean during a visit to America. Determined to bring Sea-Land's transatlantic service to Rotterdam, Posthuma brokered the creation of what would become Europe's largest container terminal operator – the joint stevedore venture Europe Container Terminus (ECT) – and won the contract for his harbor. Rotterdam, long known for its bulk cargo trades, quickly emerged as Europe's leading container destination. Containerization was thus a boon to the city at the very moment oil revenues were on the wane. Moreover, containerization, more than any other port traffic, fit snugly into new city plans to reinvent Rotterdam as a postindustrial, high-tech information and logistics European center. By the early 1970s, the industrialization of the harbor came to a screeching halt. But in its place on the Massvlakte was to rise a massive ECT expansion.[97]

Across the channel the container's effect was precisely the opposite, although scarcely for lack of foresight or preparation. Like Posthuma, the Port of London Authority's Dudley Perkins had traveled to America and, with OCL, readied new berths at Tilbury twenty miles down the Thames for the coming of transoceanic container shipping.[98] Yet by the early 1970s, London port was collapsing and container traffic was hemorrhaging to Felixstowe, heretofore just a blip by the sea. At the center of that extraordinary demise lay a history of labor militancy and poor productivity that undercut London's competitive position at the critical, and vulnerable, moment of changeover. This was a complex story, one that surpasses this narrative, and where a destructive dynamic emerged

---

[97] Van de Laar, *Stad*, 485–521; Van Driel, *Samenwerking*, 183–194, 229, 237–238, 324; *NRC Handelsblad*, "Afbouw raffinage-capaciteit in Rotterdam onvermijdelijk," 19 August 1978 (in HA/2661); HA/2660/12 October 1967; Lloyd's List International, *Rotterdam*, 36.

[98] Geoffrey Ennals, Port of London Authority, interview with author, London, 2 June 1998; Brown, *Port*, 138–143.

between a series of landmark reforms that decasualized port labor and abolished restrictive practices, but clashed with a deeply masculine dockers' culture that responded to the challenge of strong-man feats and "the ability to con the governor; the ability to screw that extra bit of money out of the shipping company by blackmail or coercion.... They loved it; it was the spice of life." Strikes, militancy, and deep distrust between management and labor, despite a pathbreaking deal that had been negotiated with unions at Tilbury, thus crippled London's ability to compete with its continental rivals.[99] On the other side of the channel, long spells of labor peace followed reforms in the 1960s or a longer history of progressive labor relations.[100] Nothing from London's swan song days would compare to a letter sent to the Port of Rotterdam Authority in 1980 (following a strike that did occur in that harbor) from an importing company, asking for an official letter stating the commencement and ending days of the strike to win a claim over late weighing due to the strike, because "our sellers refuse to believe [it] ever happened."[101]

Containerization, a boon for Rotterdam, thus turned into a bust for London. With its full implementation, Hays's Wharf had gone, the Royal docks had gone, and Scruttons had gone, as OCL reassigned its Far Eastern services to Southampton, and other container ships found more welcoming quarters in Felixstowe. True, the latter port had better tidal conditions and roadway access was superior, but as John Hovey, who ran a well-regarded stevedore company in London, put it, it was successful for one reason only: "because it had no history."[102] PLA figures in the late 1990s were less than what they had been in the 1960s.[103] Still a large, active port, compared to Rotterdam London had been relegated to the minor leagues.

---

[99] Mankelow, "Effects of Modernisation," especially strong on what happened; Ennals (interview, quoted on conning); DLA/PLA/Chief Docks Managers Files/Box S; DLA/ London Ports Employers Association/130/Devlin Stage II/Talk Given by Director-General, 26 February 1971; Brown, *Port*, 157–175; Hovey, *Tale*, 36, 81.

[100] Isacker, *Afscheid*; Suykens, *Antwerp*, 533–535; HA/4849/February 1975, pp. 10–11; Stéphane Hoste, Reginald Loyen, and Stephan Vanfraechem, "New Perspectives on Port Competition: Antwerp and Rotterdam, 1945–1975," in Tapio Bergholm, Lewis R. Fischer, and M. Elisabetta Tonizzi, eds., *Making Global and Local Connections: Historical Perspectives on Ports*, Research in Maritime History 35 (St. John's, Newfoundland: International Maritime Economic History Association, 2007), 73–75; Vanfraechem, "Why"; Nijhof, "Dock."

[101] HA/2973/10 September 1980.

[102] Mankelow, "Effects," quoted from his interview with Hovey.

[103] DLA/Trade of the Port of London figures – this sheet was provided to me by Robert Aspinall, archivist at the time of my research.

Labor militancy alone only partially explains the fall of London. The collapse of networks was also fundamental. Even before the advent of the container, London's port networks were under stress from the weakening of former imperial trades and from poor highway connections. If in the 1960s Britain realigned its trading toward Europe, short-sea RoRo links leached business toward ports like Dover. Worse, other networks failed to materialize or simply faded away. In a state with the ruling presumption that shipping and goods would have to come through one harbor or another, no government was going to staunch the bleeding.[104] The most fateful network, however, turned out to be the one that should have been the strongest: the linkage with the City. The maritime powers in the square mile or so that governed Britain's financial, commercial, and shipping fortunes, practically within walking distance of the port, appear to have been indifferent to where shipping went, as long as it was efficient and profitable. In the era of empire and conventional trades, the overlap had been very strong and London port had prospered. With containers, old rationales disappeared. Eric Shawyer and Hugh McCoy, each a president of the Baltic Exchange at the end of the century, reveled in London's maritime market power but felt little identity with London's port. London's river was a tired river, "an old river," its port "redundant," its docks "tombstones." Bad labor relations were also a problem, and management "should have sorted it out."[105] That they did not is the nagging question in London's decline. The answer, it appears, is that they were not adverse to going elsewhere.

Port history at the end of the century was thus just as much about networks as it had been at the beginning. Hamburg remained a great port city because historical currents, which since the First World War had abraded old networks, reversed course toward the century's close. Hamburg thrived on the collapse of communism and the revival of old hinterland connections. Long tied commercially to the East, it reaped a large share of the boom in Asian container traffic. As one Hamburg shipping agent told it, companies that manufactured shirts in Munich and sold in Hamburg shipped nothing through the port, but textile factories that moved production offshore shipped materials and machinery out of Hamburg and manufactured products back in again.[106] Home fleet connections also held firm. In contrast, Liverpool's networks broke

[104] Ennals (interview); Brown, *Port*, 180–182.
[105] Shawyer (interview); McCoy (interview).
[106] Von Pfeil (interview).

under the combined assault of containerization and the new shape to globalism. An imperial port with great home fleets and worldwide connections, it possessed none of these by the late twentieth century. Imperialism had gone, the fleets had gone, and the port was on the wrong side of the island to receive container ships from Asia that would make one stop in Britain. Holts' demise was the perfect example of what went wrong. Britain's premier shipping line to the East and the epitome of global network building, its persona had been that "Liverpool led the world and they led Liverpool." After the 1960s, however, neither Holts nor Liverpool led anyone. Once Holts joined OCL it filtered its eastern trades through London. At no point in its planning did OCL contemplate utilizing Liverpool, even though one of the two founders was a Liverpool house. By 1980, Holts had moved its headquarters to London and was disengaging from deep-sea shipping altogether. Bereft of home fleets, and world trades, and with labor relations as notoriously atrocious as in London, Liverpool's glory days faded fast and deep.[107] Marseille, off the main east-west container routes, limited in its hinterland, and still counting West Africa as its top trading partner as late as 1980 (with Asia far down the list), likewise remained imprisoned in the wrong network system. Massive oil shipments kept it within the top ranks of world ports when measured by turnover, but it was not a major container destination.[108]

All this remaking of shipping companies and ports carried over into port city life and culture. The prime example was the fall of ship agents. This was a profession without whom the maritime past was inconceivable. Ship agents had founded shipping companies, constituted networks, acted as nodes, and had been local powers within port cities. All this world was turned inside out by the container. First came mergers of principals into national companies: the Hapag-Lloyds and Nedlloyds and so forth, followed by subsequent rounds of international alliances and consortia, that at each stage shred traditional networks and forced a consolidation of agencies. Then, in the race to proffer global services, liner companies did away with independent representations altogether

---

[107] Furlong (interview); Mankelow, "Effects," 44, 53, 79; Falkus, *Blue*, 333, 376; Hyde, *Liverpool*, 209–210; P & O/OCEL/Narrative; Nicholas J. White, "Liverpool Shipping and the End of Empire: the Ocean Group in East and Southeast Asia, c. 1945–73," in Sheryllynne Haggerty, Anthony Webster, and Nicholas J. White, *The Empire in One City? Liverpool's Inconvenient Imperial Past* (Manchester: Manchester University Press, 2008), 165–187.

[108] CAC/870385/33/Port autonome de Marseille. Activités 1980; Roncayolo, *L'imaginaire*, 249–253.

and reinvented themselves as "one-shop" transporters. Either agents were internalized into company divisions or simply let go. For traditional agents, accustomed to acting as fulcrums, the process was brutal. For many who remained, the recourse was to flee into the "niche" trades of conventional cargo, or to the less competitive north-south routes, but this drove them out of the loop and cost income to boot, since the container's downward pressure on freight rates depressed agent commissions. "If I had been a liner agent, I probably would have committed suicide two, three, or five years ago. Because what happened to ship agents was murder. Absolute. Absolute," confided a French shipbroker whose own business was immune from the carnage.[109]

Compounding the fall was a comparable reversal within the harbors. Ship agents, "men of the world," had, before containers, ruled at the top of their roost. They were representatives of shipping lines, the ones who ordered the gangs and formed the decisive power on the quays when ships came in. In some harbors the berth leases were in the ship agents' names. Courtly, residing in mansions, they were local kingpins, and if their work world coincided with stevedores their social world did not. They entertained forwarders in their homes, but stevedores were not invited. "No, the ship agents went to manicure their nails and the stevedores never did. Let's put it that way."[110] But that status world also came crashing down with containers, which promoted the stevedores to men of great power and even respectability. The costs of container terminals accelerated a trend underway since the Second World War for stevedores and *naties* to concentrate into firms of considerable size.[111] A wave of mergers and acquisitions swept over nearly every port as stevedores and *naties* converted to capital intensive terminal operators. In Rotterdam, Pakhuismeesteren and Blaauwhoed merged into Pakhoed, and Müller took over Thomsen.[112] Hessenatie in Antwerp was so large by the 1980s that negotiations to bring Sea-Land's traffic to the Scheldt, and plans to construct a riverside container harbor – formerly something only the city would have undertaken – were largely managed through its own initiatives.[113] At the beginning of the 1970s there had been about thirty

---

[109] Lerbret (interview).

[110] Noorduyn (interview).

[111] Asaert, Devos, and Suykens, *Naties*, 259–264, 288–297; Van Isacker, *Afscheid*, 161–163.

[112] Van Driel, *Samenwerking*, 172–233, 310–319; Theo Notteboom, "Thirty-five Years of Containerization in Antwerp and Rotterdam: Structural Changes in the Container Handling Market," in Loyen, Buyst, and Devos, *Struggling*, 130.

[113] Antwerp, Port of Antwerp Technische Dienst Archives/7281/27 April 1992.

stevedore companies in Hamburg; at century's end this number was down to a handful, including the giant HHLA and Gerd Buss, which was now a "group," and was expanding its terminal capacity to potentially a million TEU throughput.[114] Swallowed up in these mergers was also the rough, competitive culture that had colored stevedore life in the past. Twenty-seven years old in 1959, Frans Swarttouw of Quick Dispatch had no intention of "being tied to the apron strings of Thomsen [then the leading stevedore firm in Rotterdam] ... I wanted my place in the sun." Thomsen, a pure-blood stevedore firm, had little time for Blaauwhoed, which it dismissed as a real estate company; nor, as the "best stevedore in Rotterdam harbor," was Thomsen thrilled about working together with Müller.[115] But none of these animosities could hold out forever against the container, and as stevedores combined into bigger, more powerful units they also turned themselves into respectable figures.

Thus as the gorillas in suits climbed to the top, the shipping agent slid further down the poles of prestige, power, and income. The quays became the stevedore's quays, *their* terminals where they had the decisive say: "Today the agent is almost completely out of that picture." One of the telling moments in this exchange came in 1966 when Thomsen bought out Wambersie & Zoon, a Rotterdam broker but also agency firm that dated back to the early nineteenth century and represented such carriers as HAPAG and Holland Amerika. Thomsen wanted Wambersie's quay holdings in Rotterdam, but also its hinterland connections. Once, Wambersie people would have had only business relations with stevedores, whom they looked on as "rough customers." Now they worked for them.[116]

This cracking apart of older relationships was inseparable from the drift of ports farther downriver. Containers physically reordered ports but also their urban social geography and rent still further traditional port culture. Offices followed terminals out of the center. A few ports retained harbor activities fairly close in; Hamburg was perhaps the best example, although even here port businesses divided between the city and the outskirts. Elsewhere, ships in port cities were as much a rumor as a manifest fact. In Antwerp a fair number of agents, forwarders, and *naties* remained within older city quarters, but others colonized the functional buildings that lined the Noorderlaan as it wound its way out toward the

[114] Ehrhardt (interview).

[115] Van Driel, *Samenwerking*, 232–233 (quoted 232), 306–307.

[116] Durot (interview, quoted on picture); Velge (interview); Weynen (interview); Van Driel, *Samenwerking*, 210–211; Van de Laar, *Stad*, 163 (quoted on "customers").

Dutch border. In Rotterdam port services followed ships away from the city, often not only downriver but across to the south bank, in distant districts like Barendrecht or Poortugaal. Complicit in the diaspora was new technology – computers, faxes, and cell phones – which kept businesspeople intensely in touch, despite distance, and replaced city exchanges with electronic communications. The displacement was cultural as well as physical because much of the practice and custom of maritime people was inseparable from the daily, dense interaction that transpired within city business centers. Bourses, pubs, restaurants, and close-in city quarters where business was conducted and information exchanged provided the sort of hothouse milieu in which trust, face-to-face relations, and networking luxuriated. Philip Durot, the Antwerp ship agent who started in shipping the day he was born, identified how that milieu had worked and, by implication, what was gone when it dissipated:

We had in Antwerp the Exchange where people went ... every day so to say between two and four o'clock where you would have the shippers, the forwarders, lighterage people, naties, stevedores, and where all kinds of business would be discussed or even just in and out and to the café next door for some drink and even a game of dice. That doesn't exist any more. There is no more time for that personal contact. And that meant also that all shipping agents were more or less in easy reach of this Exchange if you like so that it would be in the region of the Exchange, the Meir if you like, where most shipping offices were located. Today that has changed to some extent and shipping agents have moved out into the port area even so that the exchange is non-existent. There is no real 100 percent shipping center in Antwerp.[117]

Out of this erosion there emerged a new business culture suspiciously like the one that took over in shipping companies. Trust and personal relations remained a necessary bedrock on which to do business, but nearly all port businesspeople agreed that business life was tougher, more demanding, and considerably more ruthless. Traditional boundary lines between professions disappeared with networks and city milieus. Stevedores, *naties*, forwarders, and agents all trespassed on each other's territory for what business remained, and all felt the long hand of the big shipping companies, most of whom had little or no historical connection to the port. The unwritten codes that had been so determinative in the search for a head manager in Brazil in the 1940s would have been risible in the 1990s. Poaching was a practice, not a taboo. Long lunches and pub life faded into the background not simply because offices had dispersed

---

[117] Durot (interview). The Baltic Exchange was also a shadow of its former self: Warwick (interview); Shawyer (interview).

but because the pace was so furious that no one any longer had time. The Durot family's relationship with the Johnson Line had been very old school, but companies like the Johnson Line were gone and so was that style. Again Durot expressed the difference. Whereas in his day the principal would take the train to Antwerp and ask, "Are you happy?," today an agent's principal would fly in and ask "Why are you costing me so much money?"[118]

Expertise and identities were also different. The advice to Julian Taylor had been to listen to the men on the docks who had spent a lifetime in the harbors. By the 1990s that would have made no sense since few agents, forwarders, or brokers bothered any longer to spend much time at the port. J. J. Hordijk said that he never visited foreign ports on his travels, not even in Singapore and Hong Kong, because they all looked the same.[119] But a deeper rationale was that there was little need to do so. Ships came and went in twenty-four hours, they were loaded and unloaded by computer, and aside from the conventional trades they all carried the same thing: boxes. The conquest by container was occasioned by caustic and weary comments: "I belong to the very old guys who had really fun at the time you had general cargo because you had to work with your brains…. [Now] it's all container stupidity, it's a box"; and, "It's terribly dull … it's almost … like sort of just putting bricks one on top of the other."[120] Like Herman Reynaerts, few, if anyone, got a kick from loading containers, and the refrain "a box is a box" was the biggest cliché in the business. But it was also a dirge for the interment of their past. Under the reign of the container, expertise and identities disassociated from knowledge of commodities and harbors and attached to knowledge of logistics. Apprenticeship gave way to university training. The ability to compute rates by commodity and destination in one's head was replaced by keystrokes on the computer. Information migrated from personal contacts at the exchanges to the telephone and software. When asked how containerization had changed his agency business, Hamburg's Bolko Graf von Pfeil explained that "sea transportation … has by now practically become the smallest part of our business. The biggest part is logistic, is positioning the container, doing the container

[118] Yves van Doosselaere, Van Doosselaere & Achten, interview with author, Antwerp, 17 November 1997; Durot (interview); the comment on "Are you happy?" was made over lunch at La Rade restaurant, 5 February 1998. Many interviewees discussed the pressurized environment.

[119] Hordijk (interview).

[120] Damster (interview); Adams (interview).

control."[121] Kühne & Nagel, the global forwarding giant, insisted on their transformation into "*logistiker*."[122] Port businessmen thus reintegrated back into container networks, but at the cost of their previous identities. Expertise still mattered, but a lifetime in the harbors did not.

So there remains the lingering question of what had been lost in the great transition. Standing out on Hamburg's Tollerort pier and waiting for the water ferry, Buss' Lutz Ehrhardt and I watched the river traffic pass by, until Ehrhardt, who worked for one of the victors, remarked that containerships lacked the romance of the past. Whether ports or shipping were still romantic was an omnipresent theme, expressed by ship agent Diedrich Döhle when he complained that cargo in boxes no longer smelled, or by P & O's Richard Adams when he said that there was nothing "like seeing something, an elephant or something, being swung on board your ship." Hans Jürgen Witthöft, who wrote the first major study of containerization, pointed out the irony that ports had once smelled of the world, but that in this moment of globalization there was no world fragrance, just technology.[123] This was, implicitly, the same question posed at the beginning of this section in the biographies of van den Wall Bake and Reynaerts – what did it all mean? – and the resolution can be found, perhaps, in one last career. Dirk Dhondt, who managed the Antwerp office of Sea-Land, the great instigator, spent his professional life outside the old-fashioned independent agencies, nor did he see much need for them. Buying up agencies was in his opinion simply an investment decision, not much different from building a championship basketball team in the United States: You just bought the best people to work for you. In his background there was no maritime history. The son of a baker, and trained in civil engineering, he had joined Sea-Land in a bottom-level position with the intention of getting out as soon as he could; he just needed some time to tide himself over because there were no jobs in his profession. Yet he stayed. Because "it grew … shipping is like, how can I say this, it's like a drug, once in your blood … you can't get rid of it anymore." He stayed and rose within the company. He too decried the increased pressure and end to personal touches, but he loved the challenges that persisted, the old Mr. Fix-it role, the daily headaches that forced him to work out a solution. A truck has a collision. A vessel leaves early with a client's cargo still aboard. A client commits more cargo out of Italy and suddenly the railroad goes on strike and it is necessary

[121] Von Pfeil (interview).
[122] *Wir setzen Alles in Bewegen. Kühne & Nagel 100 Jahre* (Bremen: 1990), 44.
[123] Döhle (interview); Adams (interview); Witthöft, *Container*, 56.

FIGURE 11. Nothing "like seeing something, an elephant or something, being swung on board your ship." Here swung off at London Docks, 1946. Courtesy Museum of London, PLA Collection.

to scramble for trucks. "And then you get this stupid phone call where the client says 'my production is a little bit late, it will not be loading for tomorrow but it will be for Monday.'" What gave him satisfaction from shipping was that each day was different. "That's ... the drug."[124]

At the belly of the beast, Dhondt understood Reynaerts, but he understood van den Wall Bake even better. The kick was in the challenge, and this did not disappear with containerization. The truth was that most

[124] Dirk Dhondt, Sea-Land, interview with author, Antwerp, 20 January 1998.

port businessmen were pretty much like the Dutchman who began by drinking people under the table and then became a logistics computer whiz. Nearly all agreed that containerization had to happen. Döhle, even, said that when he first saw containers in New York he too thought that this was the future, and he took the lead in introducing electronic data systems to his agency. Agents too produced their Arisons, McLeans, and Sterlings, even if the range for innovation was considerably smaller. The answer to what it all meant, then, was that maritime business culture at century's close was no less about moving ships and goods around the world than it had been when clubbiness and all the older networks and connections had served that purpose at the century's start. Identities and practice simply adjusted to new ways of doing so. The historical significance was not in the loss, but in just how revolutionary containerization had been, and how fundamentally meaningful the sea remained.

Afterword

This book may provoke some discussion of our understanding of globalization in the past century. Those who argue that globalization occurs when there are capacious, integrated flows of capital, trade, people, and information across the world distinguish "globalization" from mere world exchange itself. The attractiveness of such a definition is its ability to identify precise processes and effects that come from nearly full levels of world integration, and to separate, as well, current levels of exchange from all previous periods, save the half century that preceded the First World War. Focused and presumably dynamic – in the sense that the particularity of the present world is explained – this perspective has become the "master narrative" of how we speak and write of globalization today.

My instincts as a historian, however, tell me that globalization cannot be simply this. Trained to think in terms of continuity and change, and of history in all its multiformity, I find more rewarding a looser definition that ascribes to globalization a process of world connectedness that goes back at least 500 years and that has varied in intensity and consequence since those first voyages of discovery. In this perspective, an event with such world momentum as the Russian Revolution scarcely fits within a definition of "deglobalization," no matter how catastrophic it may have been for global market integration. In this book I did not set out to prove the market integrators wrong – my initial interest in maritime history lay elsewhere. But my research uncovered a world of unrelenting linkages across the seas, and it pointed to a more genuine dynamic to explain globalization's progress across the twentieth century than the tightly-argued paradigm of market integration. In this dynamic three things occurred. First, retrenchment in one sphere was balanced by global outreach in

375

another. Second, ruptures with the world order before 1914 prepared a more decentered globalism after 1945. Third, globalization, while continuous, thus also evolved, until a new, different phase emerged in the final decades of the twentieth century. These ideas do not stand alone. Others have challenged the idea that globalization reduces to market integration, or that world business ties severed altogether in the Depression years, or that the world was not becoming a more integrated place in the middle years of the twentieth century. I must also acknowledge that my own thinking on globalization could scarcely have advanced without the work that has been done by the market integrators themselves. But we do differ, and this book should be read in that light.

The difference is the right place to begin these final words, but it is not what has driven my decision to write maritime history as the history of globalization, nor is it the leading idea I would like readers to take from this volume. More meaningful to me has been the exposition of how local and global actually did come together by sea. My argument has been that coexistence of cosmopolitanism with local identity and commitment in all sectors of the maritime world produced connectedness. Individuals and companies so well linked into local and global networks, and so at home in either, provided a mechanism by which global exchange could be rendered routine.

This book is then better understood as an investigation into how the modern world has worked. If the topic has been large, the pleasures have come from figuring out the mechanics – in this case maritime ones – turning and meshing behind the sophisticated encasements of European lives and society. The historian's tinkering – either poring over the pieces and then fitting them together, as I have done with the networks of ports and shipping companies, or acquiring, vicariously, the expertise of the ship agent – has been the basis by which everything else in this book has been assembled into a picture of world flows, or what I have called globalism. I began this book by arguing that the seas have mattered, and have revealed how through a history of world coordination and circulation, in times of war as well as peace. But in reality I have shown it through the professional and social slog of business trips, or through port competitiveness, or through what the Hansen & Tidemann agency could do for its principals, or through Otto Brix loading the *Brasilia* in a snowstorm. Much of the pleasure of the research has been turning open the files and learning what shipping and trading companies actually did day to day. Catching globalization, or world coordination, in action, is largely what this book has been about.

My other satisfaction has been the opportunity to write about change across the entire twentieth century, and what this meant for both lives and city spaces. At an early interview at Hamburg's Elysée Hotel, Diedrich Döhle commanded my attention, and probably a good part of the room, as he told me how cargo smelled, or at least did until containers altered that and nearly everything else that had defined the shipping world in his generation's formative years. This theme echoed through nearly all the interviews I conducted: the tremendous change these men had witnessed in their professional lifetimes. It was certainly not possible, unless armed with the powers of historical recollection, to walk through Liverpool, or to ride the Docklands Light Railway in London, with any sense of passing through what had been the site of two of the world's greatest ship gatherings not that many years ago. Even in Antwerp and Rotterdam there was little physically in the city to recall port life a mere thirty years gone by. By the time I began the research for this project, an era that had lasted a century in shipping and port life had gone forever.

Historical imagination thus required not only comprehending how things had worked, but articulating what had disappeared, and why this mattered. This is why culture has held a central place in this narrative. The chapter on business culture, preceded by the portrait of intermediaries, was intended to show how things held together, but even more to serve as a prelude for what fell apart as the century ended. To capture that change I have pursued several paths. One was to observe how decolonization ended one set of maritime histories and inaugurated new ones in ways that bore little semblance to how things had worked in the past, but a great deal of verisimilitude to how they would look in the future. Another was to write about new men. Aristotle Onassis is perhaps the household name among contemporary maritime figures, but my interest in him was drawn less by his flamboyance and accumulated power than by how he rose with big oil transport after the Second World War, and, even more, by the peculiarities of his transnational trajectory when set alongside those of the Vorwerks or the Braunds. Identities and commitments and consequently actions, and representations, were bound to differ among men of such divergent backgrounds and moments in time. The flooding in later of many new men, the Arisons, McLeans, Seatons, and Chang Yung-fas, none with any special tie to the past, none of whom would have figured even remotely as "the *right* man" several decades earlier, caught the ripeness of conditions for thoroughgoing change, and how completely the maritime world was consequently remade. It was with some amusement that I juxtaposed Lawrence Holt's instructions to ship captains with the business-speak gurus of a generation later, but this too allowed me to set, in dramatic form, the casualness with which traditions were simply wiped away.

Mostly, however, it was only necessary to wander through the cities and to talk to people – former ship company directors, port authorities past and present, ship agents and brokers, and freight forwarders – to gather the profundity of the transformation. The rest was simply the work of historical reconstruction. It cannot be said that the sociability of this milieu has completely died away. Certainly this is one research project I would gladly begin again. In a work that has stretched across the planet, and from one end of a century to another, the center has remained the lives of individuals and their firms. This book has been about the world they created and changed and from which they have drawn their own sense of purpose. For many who write about globalization, identity has become a problematical matter. What is often forgotten is how profoundly identity lies at the heart of how globalization has happened.

Bibliography

ARCHIVAL AND SPECIAL LIBRARY COLLECTIONS

I. Belgium

Antwerp

Bibliotheek Havenbedrijf
Compagnie Maritime Belge Archives (CMB)
Stadsarchief Antwerpen (SA)
  Series Haven
  Series Havenbedrijf
  Series Politie
  Series Politieke Gebeurtenis
Technische Dienst Archives/Havenbedrijf

II. France

Fontainebleau

Archives nationales/Centre des archives contemporaines (CAC)
  Series Ministère de l'équipement, du logement, de l'aménagement du territoire,
    et des transports
  Series Ministère de la marine marchande
  Series Ministère de la mer
  Series Ministère des transports

Le Havre

Archives de l'association French Lines (AAFL)
  Collection Compagnie Générale Transatlantique (CGT)
  Collection Compagnie des Messageries Maritimes (MM)

Paris

Archives nationales (AN)
  Series AJ 41/Organismes issus de l'armistice
  Series F 12/Commerce
  Series F 14/Travaux Publics
Ministère des affaires étrangères (MAE)
  Series Amérique 1918–1940
  Series Asie 1918–1940
  Series Guerre 1939–1945
  Series Levant 1930–1940
  Series Nouvelle série/Turquie
Service historique de la marine (SHM)
  Series 1 BB 3/Correspondence reçue
  Series SS/Première Guerre mondiale
  Series TT/Seconde Guerre mondiale

III. Germany

Hamburg

Commerzbibliothek der Handelskammer Hamburg
Staatsarchiv Hamburg
  Series Bureau für Wirtschaft und Verkehr (BWV)
  Series Deputation für Handel, Schiffahrt, und Gewerbe (DHSG)
  Collection Firma HAPAG-Reederei (HAPAG)

IV. Great Britain

Liverpool

Liverpool Record Office
  Collection London and Kano Trading Company
Merseyside Maritime Museum (MMM)
  Collection Edward W. Turner & Son
  Collection Mersey Docks and Harbour Board (MDHB)
  Collection Ocean Steam Ship Co./Blue Funnel (OA)
  Collection Thomas and John Brocklebank Ltd. (BROC)
University of Liverpool Archives
  Cunard Steamship Co. Ltd. Archives

London

Docklands Library and Archive (DLA)
  Collection Port of London Authority (PLA)
  Collection London Port Employers Association (LPEA)
Guildhall Library/London Metropolitan Archives (Guildhall)
  Collection Anglo-Thai Corporation
  Collection Antony Gibbs & Sons Ltd.

Collection Binny & Co. Ltd.
Collection Borneo Company Ltd. (BCL)
Collection Gray, Dawes & Co.
Collection Gray, Mackenzie & Co. Ltd.
Collection Harrisons & Crosfield Ltd.
Collection Rivers Steam Navigation Co. Ltd.
Collection Steel Brothers and Company Ltd.
National Archives/Public Record Office (PRO)
   Series Admiralty (ADM)
   Series Board of Trade
   Series Colonial Office
   Series Foreign Office
   Series Ministry of Reconstruction
   Series Ministry of Transportation (MT)
National Maritime Museum (NMM)
   Collection British India Steam Navigation Company (BIS)
   Collection New Zealand Shipping Company Ltd. (NZS)
   Collection Peninsular & Oriental Steam Navigation Company (P & O)
Peninsular & Oriental Steam Navigation Company/Peninsular House (P & O)
School of Oriental and African Studies (SOAS)
   John Swire and Sons Ltd. Papers

V. The Netherlands

Amsterdam

Stadsarchief Amsterdam
   Collection Firma H. G. Th. Crone

The Hague

Nationaal Archief/Algemeen Rijksarchief (NA)
   Collection Koninklijke Java China Paketvaart Lijnen (JCJL)
   Collection Koninklijke Paketvaart Maatschappij (KPM)
   Collection Michiels-Arnold, Cultuur-en Handelmaatschappij te Amsterdam
     (MA)
   Collection Nederlandsche Handelmaatschappij
   Collection N.V. Deli Maatschappij
   Collection N.V. Handel-Maatschappij v/h G. Hoppenstedt (Hoppenstedt)
   Collection N.V. Maatschappij tot Exploitatie van de Suikeronderneming
     Tjomal

Rotterdam

Archieven van de Internationale Crediet- en Handelsvereeniging "Rotterdam"
   (ICHVR)
Gemeentearchief Rotterdam (GAR)
   Bibliotheek

Series Gemeentelijk Havenbedrijf Rotterdam
Collection Holland Amerika Lijn (HAL)
Collection H. Stout, directeur N.V. Internationale Crediet-en Handelsvereniging
    Rotterdam
Collection Rotterdamsche Lloyd (Lloyd)
Havenbedrijf Archief

Interviews

(Firms or services are current with time of interview or represent past associations, if retired.)

Antwerp:

Jean-Pierre Bosteels, Ziegler, 12 January 1998
Jacques Damster, Compagnie Générale Maritime Benelux, N.V., 13 January 1998
Jan de Bie, De Keyser Expeditions, 25 November 1997
Jules de Maeyer, Tabaknatie, 23 December 1997
Dirk Dhondt, Sea-Land, 20 January 1998
Philip Durot, A. Durot N.V./Boekmans N.V., 18 November 1997
Theo Marischal, Overseas Maritime Transport N.V., 11 December 1997
J. W. Noorduyn, Ruys & Co., Belgium, 11 February 1998
Herman Reynaerts, Overseas Maritime Transport N.V., 11 December 1997
Leon Rijckaert, General Maritime Services N.V., 18 November 1997
Fernand Suykens, Port of Antwerp, 17 February 1998
Yves Van Doosselaere, Van Doosselaere & Achten, 17 November 1997
Eric Van Nueten, Tabaknatie, 23 December 1997
Maurice Velge, Grisar & Velge, 8 January 1998
Tony Vuylsteke, Belgo-Ruys N.V., 2 January 1998
Albert Weynen, Ahlers Bridge N.V., 2 December 1997

Hamburg:

Klaus Bültjer, German Shipbrokers Association Hamburg, 21 June 1996
Diedrich Döhle, Paul Günther, 4 July 1996
Lutz Ehrhardt, Gerd Buss (AG & Co.), 6 August 1996
Peter Hüpeden, Hüpeden & Co., 27 June 1996
Hans H. Killinger, FA. Aug. Bolten Wm. Miller's Nachfolger, 11 June 1996
Wolfgang Piehler, Bachmann, 22 July 1996
Otto J. Seiler, HAPAG, 6 August 1996
Walter Stork, Navis, 22 July 1996
Bolko Graf Von Pfeil, Detjen Schiffahrtsagentur, 13 June 1996
Franz-Alfred Wooge, Albrecht & Dill, 2 July 1996

Liverpool:

P. T. Furlong, The Mersey Docks and Harbour Company, 15 July 1998

London:

Richard B. Adams, British India/P & O, 24 September 1998 (Henley-on-Thames)

Alan J. Bott, New Zealand Shipping Company/P & O, 16 September 1998 (Milford)

Geoffrey Ennals, Port of London Authority, 2 June 1998

H. O. McCoy, Baltic Exchange/Clarksons, 20 April 1998

Eric F. Shawyer, Baltic Exchange/E. A. Gibson Shipbrokers Ltd., 21 April 1998

P. J. Warwick, Hadley Shipping Co. Limited, 26 August 1998

Paris:

Edouard de Clebsattel, G. Feron-E. de Clebsattel S.A./FONASBA/FACAM, 5 March 1999

Jean Lerbret, Lerbret et Cie S.A.M., 29 January 1999

Rotterdam:

Rolf H. De Boer, Lehnkering Montan Nederland B.V., 9 July 1997

Charley L. M. Dietvorst, Internationale Expediteurs Alfons Freriks Rotterdam B.V., 15 July 1997

Hans Hentzen, Henk Hentzen Beheer B.V., 29 July 1997

J. J. Hordijk, Vinke & Co., B.V., 16 July 1997

H. H. Horsting, Holland Amerika, 2 September 1997

A. M. Lels, Holland Amerika, 24 July 1997

B. E. Ruys, Rotterdamsche Lloyd, 5 August 1997 (Wassenaar)

F. A. van Brouwershaven, Internatio, 4 September 1997

Rolf H. A. van den Wall Bake, Mitsui O.S.K. Lines (Nederland) B.V., 23 July 1997

Han van Os, FENEX, 15 July 1997

Printed Sources

(For multiple contributions to edited works, I have cited only the authors of the edited volumes unless only a single article was consulted.)

Abernethy, David B. *The Dynamics of Global Dominance: European Overseas Empires, 1415–1980*. New Haven, CT: Yale University Press, 2000.

À Campo, J. N. F. M. *Koninklijke Paketvaart Maatschappij. Stoomvaart en staatsvorming in de Indonesische archipel, 1888–1914*. Hilversum: Verloren, 1992.

A Century of Ship Agency and Brokerage: The Story of Funch Edye & Co., Inc. 1847–1947. New York: Business Biographies, c. 1947.

1890–1965: Kühne & Nagel 75 Jahre. Bremen, 1965.

Adriaens, Mathieu. *Le commissionnaire-expéditeur au port d'anvers*. 3rd edition. Anvers: Editions Lloyd Anversois, c. 1940.

Agence Maritime Internationale S.A. AMI: Anvers, 1939.

Akveld, L. M. and J. R. Bruijn, eds. *Shipping Companies and Authorities in the 19th and 20th Centuries: Their Common Interest in the Development of Port Facilities*. Den Haag: Nederlandse Vereniging voor Zeegeschiedenis, 1989.

Allen, G. C. and Audrey G. Donnithorne. *Western Enterprise in Indonesia and Malaya: A Study in Economic Development*. First published 1954. Reprint, New York: Augustus M. Kelley, 1968.

Antrobus, H. A. *A History of the Assam Company, 1839–1943*. Edinburgh: T. and A. Constable, 1957.

Armstrong, John. "Coastal Shipping: The Neglected Sector of Nineteenth-Century British Transport History." *International Journal of Maritime History* 6 (June 1994): 175–188.

Armstrong, John and Andreas Kunz, eds. *Coastal Shipping and the European Economy, 1750–1980*. Mainz: Philipp von Zabern, 2002.

Asaert, Gustaaf, Greta Devos, and Fernand Sukyens. *De Antwerpse Naties. Zes eeuwen actief in stad en haven*. Tielt: Lannoo, 1993.

Augé-Laribé, Michel and Pierre Pinot. *Agriculture and Food Supply in France during the War*. New Haven, CT: Yale University Press, 1927.

Backx, J. Ph. *De haven van Rotterdam. Een onderzoek naar de oorzaken van haar economische beteekenis, in vergelijking met die van Hamburg en Antwerpen*. Rotterdam: N.V. Nigh & Van Ditmar's, 1929.

Baetens, R., Ph. M. Bosscher, and H. Reuchlin, eds. *Maritieme geschiedenis der Nederlanden. Tweede helft negentiende eeuw en twintigste eeuw, van 1850–1870 tot ca. 1970*. Bussem: De Boer Maritiem, 1978.

Bailey, J. D. *A Hundred Years of Pastoral Banking: A History of the Australian Mercantile Land & Finance Company, 1863–1963*. Oxford: Clarendon Press, 1966.

Bakker, H. Th. *De K.P.M. in oorlogstijd: Een overzicht van de verrichtingen van de Koninklijke Paketvaart-Maatschappij en haar personeel gedurende de wereldoorlog 1939–1945*. Amsterdam: N.V. Koninklijke Paketvaart-Maatschappij, 1950.

Banerjee-Dube, Ishita. *Divine Affairs: Religion, Pilgrimage, and the State in Colonial and Postcolonial India*. Shimla: India Institute of Advanced Study, 2001.

Baranowski, Shelley. *Strength through Joy: Consumerism and Mass Tourism in the Third Reich*. Cambridge: Cambridge University Press, 2004.

Baranowski, Shelley and Ellen Furlough, eds. *Being Elsewhere: Tourism, Consumer Culture, and Identity in Modern Europe and North America*. Ann Arbor: University of Michigan Press, 2001.

Baratier, Edouard, ed. *Histoire de Marseille*. Paris: Privat, 1973.

Barbance, Marthe. *Histoire de la Compagnie Générale Transatlantique. Un siècle d'exploitation maritime*. Paris: Arts et Métiers Graphiques, 1955.

Barber, Richard W. *Pilgrimages*. Woodbridge, Suffolk: The Boydell Press, 1991.

Barnard, A., ed. *The Simple Fleece: Studies in the Australian Wool Industry*. Carlton: Melbourne University Press, 1962.

"Wool Brokers and the Marketing Pattern, 1914–1920." *Australian Economic History Review* 11 (1971): 1–20.

Barty-King, Hugh. *The Baltic Exchange: The History of a Unique Market*. London: Hutchinson Benham, 1977.

Barzman, John. *Dockers, métallos, ménagères. Mouvements sociaux et cultures militantes au Havre (1912–1923)*. Rouen: Presses Universitaires de Rouen et du Havre, 1997.

"Port Labour Relations in Le Havre, 1928–1947." *International Journal of Maritime History* 9 (December 1997): 83–106.

Bauchet, Pierre. *Le transport international dans l'économie mondiale*. 2ème édition. Paris: Economica, 1991.

Les transports mondiaux, instrument de domination. Paris: Economica, 1998.

Bauer, P. T. *The Rubber Industry: A Study in Competition and Monopoly*. Cambridge, MA: Harvard University Press, 1948.

Bayly, C. A. *The Birth of the Modern World, 1780–1914*. Oxford: Blackwell, 2004.

Bayly, Christopher and Tim Harper. *Forgotten Armies: The Fall of British Asia, 1941–1945*. Cambridge, MA: Harvard University Press, 2004.

Forgotten Wars: The End of Britain's Asian Empire. London: Allen Lane/ Penguin, 2007.

Beaugé, Jean and René-Pierre Cogan. *Histoire maritime des Chargeurs Réunis et de leurs filiales françaises*. Paris: Barré et Dayez, 1984.

Becker, Ursula. "Entwicklung und Organisation des Hanseatischen Kaffeehandels im 19. und 20. Jahrhundert." Ph.D. diss., Westfälischen Wilhelms-Universität Münster, 1995.

Beckert, Sven. "Emancipation and Empire: Reconstructing the Worldwide Web of Cotton Production in the Age of the American Civil War." *American Historical Review* 109 (December 2004): 1405–1438.

Behrens, C. B. A. *Merchant Shipping and the Demands of War*. London: Her Majesty's Stationery Office, 1955.

Bell, A. C. *A History of the Blockade of Germany and of the Countries Associated with Her in the Great War, Austria-Hungary, Bulgaria, and Turkey, 1914–1918*. London: Her Majesty's Stationery Office, 1937.

Bell, Alan. *Port of London, 1909–1934*. London: Port of London Authority, 1934.

Bell, H. S. *Wool: An Introduction to Wool Production and Marketing*. London: Pitman & Sons, 1970.

Berneron-Couvenhes, Marie-Françoise. "Le naufrage de la marine marchande française au XXe siècle." *Entreprises et Histoire* 27 (June 2001): 23–43.

Bes, J. *Liner and Tramp Shipping: Practical Guide to the Subject for All Connected with the Shipping Business*. New York: W. S. Heinman, 1966.

Bessell, Georg. *Norddeutscher Lloyd 1856–1957. Geschichte einer bremischen Reederei*. Bremen: Carl Schünemann, c. 1957.

Biechler, Michael J. "The Coffee Industry of Guatemala: A Geographic Analysis." Ph.D. diss., Michigan State University, 1970.

Bird, James. *The Major Seaports of the United Kingdom*. London: Hutchinson & Co., 1963.

Birks, J. S. *Across the Savannas to Mecca: The Overland Pilgrimage Route from West Africa*. Totowa, NJ: Frank Cass, 1978.

Blake, George. *B.I. Centenary, 1856–1956*. London: Collins, 1956.

Gellatly's, 1862–1962: A Short History of the Firm. London: Blackie & Son, 1962.

Blomme, Jan, Greta Devos, Mandy Nauwelaerts, Werner van Hoof, and Kathelijne
    Verlinden. *Momentum: Antwerp's Port in the 19th and 20th Century*.
    Antwerp: Pandora, 2002.

Bois, Paul. *Armements marseillais. Compagnies de navigation et navires à vapeur
    (1831–1988)*. Marseille: Chambre de Commerce et d'Industrie Marseille-
    Provence, 1988.

    Le grand siècle des Messageries Maritimes. Marseille: Chambre de Commerce
    et d'Industrie Marseille-Provence, 1991.

Bonin, Hubert. *C.F.A.O. Cent ans de compétition*, Paris: Economica, 1987.

    CFAO (1887–2007). La réinvention permanente du commerce outre-mer.
    Saint-Denis: SFHOM, 2008.

Bordo, Michael D., Alan M. Taylor, and Jeffrey G. Williamson. *Globalization in
    Historical Perspective*. Chicago: University of Chicago Press, 2003.

Borruey, René. *Le port moderne de Marseille du dock au conteneur (1844–
    1974)*. Marseille: Chambre de Commerce et d'Industrie Marseille-Provence,
    1994.

Bousteads. C. 1960s.

Boyce, Gordon. "Edward Bates and Sons, 1897–1915: Tramping Operations
    in Recession and Recovery." *International Journal of Maritime History* 23
    (June 2011): 13–50.

    *Information, Mediation, and Institutional Development: The Rise of Large-
    Scale Enterprise in British Shipping, 1870–1919*. Manchester: Manchester
    University Press, 1995.

    "Transferring Capabilities across Sectoral Frontiers: Shipowners Entering the
    Airline Business, 1920–1970." *International Journal of Maritime History* 13
    (June 2001): 1–38.

Brandt, Karl. *Management of Agriculture and Food in the German-Occupied and
    Other Areas of Fortress Europe: A Study in Military Government*. Stanford,
    CA: Stanford University Press, 1953.

Braudel, Fernand. *The Mediterranean and the Mediterranean World in the Age
    of Philip II*. 2 vols. First published 1966; reprint, Berkeley: University of
    California Press, 1995.

Braund, H. E. W. *Calling to Mind: Being Some Account of the First Hundred
    Years (1870 to 1970) of Steel Brothers and Company Limited*. Oxford:
    Pergamon Press, 1975.

Brendon, Piers. *Thomas Cook: 150 Years of Popular Tourism*. London: Secker &
    Warburg, 1991.

Broeze, Frank. "Albert Ballin, the Hamburg-American Line and Hamburg:
    Structure and Strategy in the German Shipping Industry (1886–1914)."
    Deutsche Schiffahrtsarchiv 15 (1992): 135–158.

    "Albert Ballin, the Hamburg-Bremen Rivalry, and the Dynamics of the
    Conference System." *International Journal of Maritime History* 3 (June
    1991): 1–32.

    *The Globalisation of the Oceans: Containerisation from the 1950s to the
    Present*. Research in Maritime History 23. St. John's, Newfoundland:
    International Maritime Economic History Association, 2002.

    *Mr. Brooks and the Australian Trade: Imperial Business in the Nineteenth
    Century*. Carlton: Melbourne University Press, 1993.

"The Political Economy of a Port City in Distress: Hamburg and National Socialism, 1933–1939." *International Journal of Maritime History* 14 (December 2002): 1–42.

"The Ports and Port System of the Asian Seas: An Overview with Historical Perspective from c. 1750." In *Puertos y sistemas portuarios (siglos XVI–XX): Actas del Coloquio International el sistema portuario español, Madrid, 19–21 October 1995*. Madrid: 1996, 99–120.

Brown, Rajeswary Ampalavanar. *Capital and Entrepreneurship in South-East Asia*. New York: St. Martin's Press, 1994.

Brown, R. Douglas. *The Port of London*. Lavenham: Terence Dalton, 1978.

Brugmans, I. J. *Tachtig jaren varen met de Nederland, 1870–1950*. Amsterdam: N.V. Stoomvaart Maatschappij "Nederland," 1950.

Van Chinavaart tot oceaanvaart. De Java-China-Japan Lijn, Koninklijke Java-China-Paketvaart Lijnen, 1902–1952. KJCPL, 1952.

Butel, Paul. *The Atlantic*. London: Routledge, 1999.

Cabantous, Alain. *Les citoyens du large. Les identités maritimes en France (XVIIe–XIXe siècle)*. Paris: Aubier 1995.

Cain, P. J. and A. G. Hopkins, *British Imperialism: Crisis and Deconstruction, 1914–1990*. London: Longman 1993.

British Imperialism: Innovation and Expansion, 1688–1914. London: Longman, 1993.

Campbell, Persia Crawford. *Chinese Coolie Emigration to Countries within the British Empire*. London: Frank Cass & Co., 1971. First published 1923.

Campbell, Reginald. *Teak-Wallah: A Record of Personal Experiences*. London: Hodder and Stoughton, 1935.

Campbell, Wallace J. *The History of CARE: A Personal Account*. New York: Praeger, 1990.

Cangardel, Henri. *La Marine marchande française et la guerre*. Paris: Les Presses Universitaires de France, 1927.

Carlisle, Rodney. *Sovereignty for Sale: The Origins and Evolution of the Panamanian and Liberian Flags of Convenience*. Annapolis, MD: Naval Institute Press, 1981.

Carour, Roger. *Sur les routes de la mer avec les Messageries Maritimes*. Paris: Editions André Bonne, 1968.

Cassagnou, Bernard. *Les grandes mutations de la Marine marchande française (1945–1995)*. 2 vols. Paris: Comité pour l'histoire économique et financière de la France, 2002.

Cassis, Youssef. *Capitals of Capital: A History of International Financial Centres, 1780–2005*. Cambridge: Cambridge University Press, 2006.

Casson, Mark. "Entrepreneurship and Business Culture." In Jonathan Brown and Mary B. Rose, eds., *Entrepreneurship, Networks, and Modern Business*. Manchester: Manchester University Press, 1993, 30–54.

Castells, Manuel. *The Rise of the Network Society*. 2nd edition. Oxford: Blackwell, 2000.

Caulier-Eimbcke, Franz Guido. *Schiffsmakler-Kompass*. Hamburg: Cram, De Gruyter, 1954.

Cecil, Lamar. *Albert Ballin: Business and Politics in Imperial Germany, 1888–1918*. Princeton, NJ: Princeton University Press 1967.

Chalmin, Philippe. *Négociants et chargeurs. La saga du négoce international des matières premières*. Paris: Economica, 1983.

Chandler, Alfred D. Jr., Franco Amatori, and Takashi Hikino, eds. *Big Business and the Wealth of Nations*. Cambridge: Cambridge University Press, 1997.

Chapman, Stanley. *Merchant Enterprise in Britain: From the Industrial Revolution to World War I*. Cambridge: Cambridge University Press, 1992.

Chernow, Ron. *The Warburgs: The Twentieth-Century Odyssey of a Remarkable Jewish Family*. New York: Random House, 1993.

Chickering, Roger. *Imperial Germany and the Great War, 1914–1918*. 2nd edition. Cambridge: Cambridge University Press, 2004.

Clarence-Smith and William Gervase. "Middle Eastern Entrepreneurs in Southeast Asia, c. 1750–c.1940." In Ina Baghdiantz McCabe, Gelina Harlaftis, and Ioanna Pepelasis Minoglou, eds. *Diaspora Entrepreneurial Networks: Four Centuries of History*. Oxford: Berg, 2005, 217–224.

Clarence-Smith, William Gervase, and Steven Topik, eds. *The Global Coffee Economy in Africa, Asia, and Latin America, 1500–1989*. Cambridge: Cambridge University Press, 2003.

Coates, Austin. *The Commerce in Rubber: The First 250 Years*. Singapore: Oxford University Press, 1987.

Cochran, Sherman. *Encountering Chinese Networks: Western, Japanese, and Chinese Corporations in China, 1880–1937*. Berkeley: University of California, 2000.

Cohen, Deborah and Maura O'Connor, eds. *Comparison and History: Europe in Cross-National Perspective*. New York: Routledge, 2004.

Commonwealth Economic Committee. *Vegetable Oils and Oilseeds: A Summary of Figures of Production, Trade, and Consumption*. London: Her Majesty's Stationery Office, 1952.

Conrad, Joseph. *The Heart of Darkness*. 1902. Reprint, London: Penguin Books, 1989.

Constantine, Stephen. "Migrants and Settlers." In Judith Brown and W. M. Roger Louis, eds., *The Twentieth Century*. Vol. 4 of *The Oxford History of the British Empire*, edited by W. M. Louis. Oxford: Oxford University Press, 1999, 163–187.

Cook, Christopher. *The Lion and the Dragon: British Voices from the China Coast*. London: Elm Tree Books, 1985.

Coons, Lorraine and Alexander Varias. *Tourist Third Cabin: Steamship Travel in the Interwar Years*. New York: Palgrave Macmillan, 2003.

Cotter, Edward P. *The Port of Liverpool*. Washington, DC: U.S. Government Printing Office, 1929.

Coudurié, Marcel and Jean-Louis Miège. *Marseille colonial face à la crise de 1929*. Marseille: Chambre de Commerce et d'Industrie Marseille-Provence, 1991.

Course, A. G. *The Deep Sea Tramp*. London: Hollis and Carter, 1960.

Cox, Howard, Huang Biao, and Stuart Metcalfe. "Compradors, Firm Architecture, and the 'Reinvention' of British Trading Companies: John Swire & Sons' Operations in Early Twentieth-Century China." *Business History* 45 (April 2003): 15–34.

Cudahy, Brian J. *Box Boats: How Container Ships Changed the World.* New York: Fordham University Press, 2006.

Curtin, Philip D. "Migration in the Tropical World." In Virginia Yans-McLaughlin, ed. *Immigration Reconsidered: History, Sociology, and Politics.* New York: Oxford University Press, 1990, 21–36.

Daumalin, Xavier. *Marseille et l'Ouest africain: l'Outre-mer des industriels (1841–1956).* Marseille: Chambre de Commerce et d'Industrie Marseille-Provence, 1992.

Davenport-Hines, R. P. T. and Geoffrey Jones, eds. *British Business in Asia since 1860.* Cambridge: Cambridge University Press, 1989.

Davies, Peter N. *Fyffes and the Banana: Musa Sapientum: A Centenary History, 1888–1988.* London: Athlone Press, 1990.

    Henry Tyrer: A Liverpool Shipping Agent and His Enterprise, 1879–1979. London: Croom Helm, 1979.

    The Trade Makers: Elder Dempster in West Africa, 1852–1972, 1973–1989. Research in Maritime History 19. St. John's, Newfoundland: International Maritime Economic History Association, 2000. First published 1973 by George Allen & Unwin.

Davis, Belinda. *Home Fires Burning: Food Politics and Everyday Life in World War I Berlin.* Chapel Hill: University of North Carolina Press, 2000.

De Boer, M. G. and J. C. Westermann. *Een halve eeuw paketvaart, 1891–1941.* Amsterdam: Koninklijke Paketvaart-Maatschappij, 1941.

De Goey, Ferry, ed. *Comparative Port History of Rotterdam and Antwerp (1880–2000): Competition, Cargo, and Costs.* Amsterdam: Aksant, 2004.

    "De Holland Amerika Lijn, Carnival Cruises en de cruise-industrie in de twintigste eeuw." *Tijdschrift voor zeegeschiedenis* 26 (2007): 17–38.

    Ruimte voor industrie. Rotterdam en de vestiging van industrie in de haven, 1945–1975, Delft: Eburon, 1990.

Dehne, Phillip. *On the Far Western Front: Britain's First World War in South America.* Manchester: Manchester University Press, 2009.

De Grazia, Victoria. *Irresistible Empire: America's Advance through Twentieth-Century Europe.* Cambridge, MA: Harvard University Press, 2005.

De Jong, L. *Het koninkrijk der Nederlanden in de Tweede Wereldoorlog.* Deel 11b, tweede helft. The Hague: Staatsuitgeverij, 1985.

    Het koninkrijk Der Nederlanden in de Tweede Wereldoorlog. Deel 12. Epiloog, tweede helft. The Hague: SDU, 1988.

De Kesel, L. *Het Tienjaren plan.* 1962–1967.

De Keuster, J. *La concurrence entre les trois grands ports nord-européens: Hambourg, Rotterdam, Anvers.* Antwerp: Groll, 1930.

De La Pedraja, René. *Oil and Coffee: Latin American Merchant Shipping from the Imperial Era to the 1950s.* Westport: Greenwood, 1998.

    The Rise and Decline of U.S. Merchant Shipping in the Twentieth Century. New York: Twayne, 1992.

Delprat, D. A. *De reeder schrijft zijn journaal. Herinneringen van Mr. D. A. Delprat.* Gravenhage: Martinus Nijhoff, 1982.

Dertilis, Georges B., ed. *Banquiers, usuriers et paysans. Réseaux de crédit et stratégies du capital en Grèce (1780–1930).* Paris: Editions de la Découverte, 1988.

De Roever, J. W. *De Nederland in de Tweede Wereldoorlog.* Amsterdam: N. V. Stoomvaart Maatschappij, "Nederland," 1951.

De Schaepdrijver, Sophie. *De Groote Oorlog. Het koninkrijk België tijdens de Eerste Wereldoorlog.* Amsterdam: Atlas, 1997.

Detlefsen, Gert Uwe. *1891–1991. Paul Günther. A Century of Dedicated Service.* Translated by Norbert Bellstedt. Hamburg: Paul Günther, 1991.

Devos, Greta. "German Ocean Shipping and the Port of Antwerp, 1875–1914: An Introduction." In C. Koninckx, ed., *Proceedings of the International Colloquium "Industrial Revolutions and the Sea.* Brussels: Collectanea Maritima V, 1991, 217–227.

Devos, Greta and Guy Elewaut. *CMB 100: Een eeuw maritiem ondernemersschap 1895–1995.* Tielt: Lannoo, 1995.

Devos, Greta and Hugo van Driel. "Local Government and Port Business in Antwerp and Rotterdam in the 19th and 20th Century." In Anne-Marie Kuijlaars, Kim Prudon, and Joop Visser, eds. *Business and Society: Entrepreneurs, Politics, and Networks in a Historical Perspective, Proceedings of the Third European Business History Association (EBHA) Conference.* Rotterdam: 2000, 79–89.

Dick, H. W. *The Indonesian Interisland Shipping Industry: An Analysis of Competition and Regulation.* Singapore: Institute of Southeast Asian Studies, 1987.

Dickinson Bob and Andy Vladimir. *Selling the Sea: An Inside Look at the Cruise Industry.* 2nd edition. Hoboken, NJ: John Wiley and Sons, 2008.

Doig, Jameson W. *Empire on the Hudson: Entrepreneurial Vision and Political Power at the Port of New York Authority.* New York: Columbia University Press, 2001.

Donovan, Arthur and Joseph Bonney. *The Box That Changed the World: Fifty Years of Container Shipping – An Illustrated History.* East Windson, NJ: Commonwealth Business Media, 2006.

Dunning, John H., ed. *Regions, Globalization, and the Knowledge-Based Economy,* Oxford: Oxford University Press, 2000.

Du Plessis, A. F. *The Marketing of Wool.* London: Pitman & Sons, 1931.

Eickelman, Dale and James Piscatori, eds. *Muslim Travellers: Pilgrimage, Migration, and the Religious Imagination.* Berkeley: University of California Press, 1990.

150 Jahre C. Melchers Co. China. Bremen, 1956.

175 Jahre J. H. Bachmann Bremen, 20 August 1775–1950. 1950.

Eng, Robert Y. "The Transformation of a Semi-Colonial Port City: Shanghai." In Frank Broeze, ed. *Brides of the Sea: Port Cities of Asia from the 16th–20th Centuries.* Honolulu: University of Hawaii Press, 1989, 129–151.

Engelsing, Rolf. *Herm. Dauelsberg Schiffsmakler, 1857–1957.* Hamburg: Verlag Hanseatischer Merkur, 1957.

Evans, Nicholas J. "The Role of Foreign-Born Agents in the Development of Mass Migrant Travel through Britain, 1851–1924." In Torsten Feys, Lewis R. Fischer, Stéphane Hoste, and Stephan Vanfraechem, eds. *Maritime Transport and Migration: The Connections between Maritime and Migration Networks.* Research in Maritime History, 33. St. John's, Newfoundland: International Maritime Economic History Association, 2007, 49–61.

Evans, Richard. "Family and Class in the Hamburg Grand Bourgeoisie, 1815–1914." In David Blackbourn and Richard J. Evans, eds. *The German Bourgeoisie: Essays on the Social History of the German Middle Class from the Late Eighteenth to the Early Twentieth Century.* London: Routledge, 1991, 115–139.

Falkus, Malcolm. *The Blue Funnel Legend: A History of the Ocean Steam Ship Company, 1865–1973.* London: Macmillan, 1990.

Faroqhi, Suraiya. *Herrscher über Mekka. Die Geschichte der Pilgerfahrt.* München: Artemis, 1990.

Fayle, C. Ernest. *Seaborne Trade.* 3 vols. New York: Longmans, Green & Co., 1920–1924.

A Short History of the World's Shipping Industry. London: Allen & Unwin, 1933.

The War and the Shipping Industry. London: Humphrey Milford/Oxford University Press, 1927.

Featherstone, Mike. *Undoing Culture: Globalization, Postmodernism, and Identity.* London: Sage, 1995.

Feinstein, Charles H., Peter Temin, and Gianni Toniolo. *The European Economy between the Wars.* Oxford: Oxford University Press, 1997.

Ferguson, Niall. *Paper and Iron: Hamburg Business and German Politics in the Era of Inflation, 1897–1927.* Cambridge: Cambridge University Press, 1995.

The House of Rothschild, Vol. 2, *The World's Banker 1849–1999.* New York: Viking Penguin, 1999.

The Pity of War. New York: Basic Books, 1999.

Feys, Torsten. "A Business Approach to Transatlantic Migration: The Introduction of Steam-Shipping on the North Atlantic and Its Impact on the European Exodus, 1840–1914." Ph.D. diss., European University, 2008.

Fieldhouse, D. K. *Merchant Capital and Economic Decolonization: The United Africa Company, 1929–1989.* Oxford: Clarendon Press, 1994.

Unilever Overseas: The Anatomy of a Multinational, 1895–1965. London: Croom Helm, 1978.

Fischer, Lewis R. and Helge W. Nordvik, "Economic Theory, Information, and Management in Shipbroking: Fearnley and Eger as a Case Study, 1869–1972." In Simon P. Ville and David M. Williams, eds. *Management, Finance, and Industrial Relations in Maritime Industries: Essays in International Maritime and Business History.* Research in Maritime History 6. St. John's, Newfoundland: International Maritime Economic History Association, 1994, 1–29.

"The Growth of Norwegian Shipbroking: The Practices of Fearnley and Eger as a Case Study, 1869–1914." In Lewis R. Fischer and Walter Minchinton, eds. *People of the Northern Seas.* Research in Maritime History 3. St. John's, Newfoundland: International Maritime Economic History Association, 1992, 135–155.

eds. *Shipping and Trade, 1750–1950: Essays in International Maritime Economic History.* Pontefract, West Yorkshire: Lofthouse, 1990.

Fletcher, Max E. "The Suez Canal and World Shipping, 1869–1914." *The Journal of Economic History* 18 (1958): 556–573.

Forrest, Denys. *Tea for the British: The Social and Economic History of a Famous Trade*. London: Chatto & Windus, 1973.

Fox, Edward Whiting. *History in Geographic Perspective: The Other France*. New York: Norton, 1971.

Fraser, Nicholas, Philip Jacobson, Mark Ottaway, and Lewis Chester. *Aristotle Onassis*. Philadelphia: J. B. Lippincott, 1977.

Frémont, Antoine. *La French Line face à la mondialisation de l'espace maritime*. Paris: Anthropos, 1998.

Friedemann, Claus. *Der Speditions-Fachmann*. Hamburg: Verlag Hans A. Blum, 1932.

Frieden, Jeffry A. *Global Capitalism: Its Fall and Rise in the Twentieth Century*. New York: W. W. Norton, 2006.

Friedman, Walter. *Birth of a Salesman: The Transformation of Selling in America*. Cambridge, MA: Harvard University Press, 2004.

Furlough, Ellen. "*Une leçon des choses*: Tourism, Empire, and the Nation in Interwar France." *French Historical Studies* 25 (Summer 2002): 441–473.

Fussell, Paul. *Abroad: British Literary Traveling between the Wars*. Oxford: Oxford University Press, 1980.

Gardiner, Robert and Ambrose Greenway. *The Golden Age of Shipping: The Classic Merchant Ship, 1900–1960*. London: Brassey, 1994.

Garin, Kristoffer A. *Devils on the Deep Blue Sea: The Dreams, Schemes, and Showdowns That Built America's Cruise-Ship Empires*. New York: Viking, 2005.

Garside, Alston Hill. *Cotton Goes to Market: A Graphic Description of a Great Industry*. New York: Frederick A. Stokes, 1935.

Wool and the Wool Trade. New York: Frederick A. Stokes, 1934.

Gemeentelijk Havenbedrijf Rotterdam. *Haven in cijfers*. Rotterdam, 1997.

Gipouloux, François. *La Méditerranée asiatique. Villes portuaires et réseaux marchands en Chine, au Japon, et en Asie du Sud-Est, XVIe–XXIe siècle*. Paris: CNRS, 2009.

Giszas, Heinz. "Die Zukunft des Hamburger Hafens." *Hansa. Zentralorgan für Schiffahrt – Schiffbau – Hafen* 8 (1989): 528–534.

Godée Molsbergen, E. C. *Maatschappij tot exploitatie van rijstlanden op Java "Michiels-Arnold" N.V. 'S-Gravenhage, 1887–23 Juli–1937*. 'S-Gravenhage: Mouton, 1937.

Goswami, Omkar. "Then Came the Marwaris: Some Aspects of the Changes in the Pattern of Industrial Control in Eastern India." *The Indian Economic and Social History Review* 22 3 (1985): 225–249.

Government of India. *Report of the Haj Enquiry Committee*. Calcutta: Government of India, 1931.

Great Britain/Empire Marketing Board. *Oilseeds and Vegetable Oils: A Summary of Figures of Production and Trade*. 1933.

Greenhalgh, Elizabeth. *Victory through Coalition: Britain and France during the First World War*. Cambridge: Cambridge University Press, 2005.

Greenhill, Robert G. "Investment Group, Free-Standing Company or Multinational? Brazilian Warrant, 1909–1952." *Business History* 37 (1995): 86–111.

Griffiths, Percival. *A History of the Inchcape Group*. London: Inchcape & Co. Limited, 1977.

A History of the Joint Steamer Companies. London: Inchcape & Co. Limited, 1979.

Grosvenor, J. *The Port of London.* London: Staples Press Limited, 1957.

Guichard, Louis. *Histoire du blocus naval (1914–1918).* Paris: Payot, 1929.

Haasse, Hella S. *Heren van de thee.* Amsterdam: Querido, 1992.

"Hadj, Hadji." In P. A. van der Lith, A. J. Spann, and F. Fokkens, eds., *Encyclopaedie van Nederlandsch-Indië.* Vol. 2. S'Gravenhage: Martinus Nijhoff, 1895–1905, 4–6.

Hall, H. Duncan and C. C. Wrigley. *Studies of Overseas Supply.* London: Her Majesty's Stationery Office, 1956.

Halpern, Paul. *A Naval History of World War I.* Annapolis, MD: Naval Institute Press, 1994.

Hamilton, Gary, ed. *Business Networks and Economic Development in East and Southeast Asia.* Hong Kong: University of Hong Kong, 1991.

Hanna, Martha. "A Republic of Letters: The Epistolary Tradition in France during World War I." *American Historical Review* 108 (December 2003): 1338–1361.

Hao Yen-P'ing. *The Comprador in Nineteenth Century China: Bridge between East and West.* Cambridge, MA: Harvard University Press, 1970.

Harcourt, Freda. "Black Gold: P & O and the Opium Trade, 1847–1914." *International Journal of Maritime History* 6 (1994): 1–83.

Harlaftis, Gelina. *A History of Greek-Owned Shipping: The Making of an International Tramp Fleet, 1830 to the Present Day.* London: Routledge, 1996.

Harris, J. R., ed. *Liverpool and Merseyside: Essays in the Economic and Social History of the Port and Its Hinterland.* London: Frank Cass, 1969.

Harvey, David. *The Condition of Postmodernity: An Enquiry into the Origins of Cultural Change.* Cambridge, MA: Blackwell, 1990.

Hauschild-Thiessen, Renate. *Albrecht & Dill, 1806–1981. Die Geschichte einer Hamburger Firma.* Hamburg: Hans Christians, 1981.

   Zwischen Hamburg und Chile. Hamburg: Vorwerk y Cía.: 1995.

Havilland, Charlotte. *The China Navigation Company Limited: A Pictorial History, 1872–1992.* N.p.: John Swire and Sons, 1992.

Hayes, Peter. *Industry and Ideology: I. G. Farben in the Nazi Era.* Cambridge: Cambridge University Press, 1987.

Headrick, Daniel. *The Tools of Empire: Technology and European Imperialism in the Nineteenth Century.* New York: Oxford University Press, 1981.

Heaton, P. M. *Lamport & Holt.* Risca, UK: The Starling Press, 1986.

Held, David, Anthony McGrew, David Goldblatt, and Jonathan Perraton. *Global Transformations: Politics, Economics, and Culture.* Stanford, CA: Stanford University Press, 1999.

Helfferich, Emil. *Behn, Meyer & Co. – Arnold Otto Meyer.* 2 vols. Hamburg: Hans Christians Verlag, 1957–1967.

Hinterland. "Speciaal nummer aangeboden aan Oscar Leemans." 13, 1964.

Hirst, Paul and Grahame Thompson. *Globalization in Question: The International Economy and the Possibilities of Governance.* 2nd edition. Cambridge, UK: Polity Press, 1998.

Hodgson, Godfrey. *Lloyd's of London.* New York: Viking, 1984.

Hohenberg, Paul M. and Lynn Hollen Lees. *The Making of Urban Europe, 1000–1950*. Cambridge, MA: Harvard University Press, 1985.

Honderjarig bestaan van de firma John P. Best & Co., 1865–1965. Antwerpen, 1965.

Hook, F. A. *Merchant Adventurers, 1914–1918*. London: A. & C. Black, Ltd., 1920.

Hopkins, A. G., ed. *Globalization in World History*. London: Pimlico, 2002.

Hoste, Stéphane. *Bunge in de Lage Landen. Twee eeuwen maritieme handel vanuit Amsterdam, Antwerp en Rotterdam. Bunge in the Low Countries: Two Centuries of Maritime Trade from Amsterdam, Antwerp, and Rotterdam*. Tielt, Lannoo, 2006.

Hoste, Stéphane, Reginald Loyen, and Stephan Vanfraechem. "New Perspectives on Port Competition: Antwerp and Rotterdam, 1945–1975." In Tapio Bergholm, Lewis R. Fischer, and M. Elisabetta Tonizzi, eds. *Making Global and Local Connections: Historical Perspectives on Ports*, Research in Maritime History 35. St. John's, Newfoundland: International Maritime Economic History Association, 2007, 57–84.

The House of Dodwell: A Century of Achievement, 1858–1958. London: Dodwell & Company, 1958.

Hovey, John. *A Tale of Two Ports: London and Southampton*. London: the Industrial Society, 1990.

Howard, Deborah. *Venice & the East: The Impact of the Islamic World on Venetian Architecture, 1100–1500*. New Haven, CT: Yale University Press, 2000.

Howarth, David and Stephen Howarth. *The Story of P & O*. Revised edition. London: Weidenfeld and Nicholson, 1994.

Hoyle, B. S. and D. A. Pinder. *Cityport Industrialization and Regional Development: Spatial Analysis and Planning Strategies*. Oxford: Pergamon Press, 1981.

European Port Cities in Transition. London: Belhaven Press, 1992.

Hoynck Van Papendrecht, A. *De zeilvloot van Willem Ruys Jan Danielszoon en de Rotterdamsche Lloyd*. Rotterdam, 1933.

Huff, W. G. *The Economic Growth of Singapore: Trade and Development in the Twentieth Century*. Cambridge: Cambridge University Press, 1994.

Hughes, Quentin. *Seaport: Architecture and Townscape in Liverpool*. London: Lund Humphries, 1964.

Huizinga, Leonhard. "*Take Your Jacket Off: The Chronicle of a Merchant House as Seen against 75 Years of World History*. Hagemeyer N.V., 1975.

Hunt, Wallis. *Heirs of Great Adventure: The History of Balfour, Williamson and Company Limited*. 2 vols. 1951–1960. Norwich: Balfour Williamson, 1960.

Hyde, Francis E. *Blue Funnel: A History of Alfred Holt and Company of Liverpool from 1865 to 1914*. Liverpool: Liverpool University Press, 1956.

Cunard and the North Atlantic, 1840–1973: A History of Shipping and Financial Management. London: Macmillan, 1975.

Liverpool and the Mersey: An Economic History of a Port, 1700–1970. Newton Abbot (Devon): David & Charles, 1971.

Shipping Enterprise and Management, 1830–1939: Harrisons of Liverpool. Liverpool: Liverpool University Press, 1967.

Imperial Economic Committee (Intelligence Branch). *Wool Production and Trade, 1928–1934.* London: His Majesty's Stationery Office, 1935.

International Institute of Agriculture/Bureau of Statistics. *Oleaginous Products and Vegetable Oils: Production and Trade.* Rome: International Institute of Agriculture, 1923.

International Institute of Social History. *Port Reports Prepared for the Conference Comparative International History of Dock Labour, c. 1790–1970.* 2 vols. Amsterdam: International Institute of Social History, 1997.

Iriye, Akira. *Global Community: The Role of International Organizations in the Making of the Contemporary World.* Berkeley: University of California Press, 2002.

Jackson, A., C. E. Wurtzburg, and A. McLellan. *The History of Mansfield & Company.* 1952–1953.

Jackson, Gordon. *The History and Archaeology of Ports.* Kingwood, Tadworth Surrey: World's Work Ltd., 1983.

Jackson, Stanley. *The Sassoons: Portrait of a Dynasty.* London: Heinemann, 1989.

James, Harold. *The End of Globalization: Lessons from the Great Depression.* Cambridge, MA: Harvard University Press, 2001.

Jamieson, Alan G. "Bates, Sir Percy Elly, Fourth Baronet (1879–1946)." In *Oxford Dictionary of National Biography,* online ed., edited by Lawrence Goldman. Oxford: Oxford University Press, 2004, http://www.oxforddnb.com/view/article/30368 (accessed 16 February 2012).

Jarvis, Adrian. *Docks of the Mersey.* London: Ian Allan 1988.

In Troubled Times: The Port of Liverpool, 1905–1938. Research in Maritime History 26. St. John's, Newfoundland: International Maritime Economic History Association, 2003.

"The Members of the Mersey Docks and Harbour Board and Their Way of Doing Business, 1858–1905." *International Journal of Maritime History* 6 (June 1994): 123–139.

Jeffery, A. E. *The History of Scruttons: Shipbrokers and Shipowners, 1802–1926: Stevedores, Master Porters, and Cargo Superintendents, 1890–1967.* London: Scruttons, 1967.

Jerchow, Friedrich. *Knöhr & Burchard NFL. Hamburg, 1814–1989.* Hamburg: Hanseatischer Merkur, 1989.

Jog, N. G. *Saga of Scindia: Struggle for the Revival of Indian Shipping and Shipbuilding.* Bombay: Scindia Steam Navigation Co. Ltd., 1969.

Jones, Geoffrey. *Beauty Imagined: A History of the Global Beauty Industry.* Oxford: Oxford University Press, 2010.

British Multinational Banking, 1830–1990. Oxford: Clarendon Press, 1993.

Merchants to Multinationals: British Trading Companies in the Nineteenth and Twentieth Centuries, Oxford: Oxford University Press, 2000.

Jones, Geoffrey and Judith Wade. "Merchants as Business Groups: British Trading Companies in Asia before 1945." *Business History Review* 72 (Autumn 1998): 367–408.

Jones, Geoffrey and Jonathan Zeitlin, eds. *The Oxford Handbook of Business History.* Oxford: Oxford University Press, 2008.

Jones, Stephanie. *Trade and Shipping: Lord Inchcape, 1852–1932.* Manchester: Manchester University Press, 1989.
   Two Centuries of Overseas Trading: The Origins and Growth of the Inchape Group. Houndmills, Basingstoke: Macmillan, 1986.
Jonker, Joost and Keetie Sluyterman. *At Home on the World Markets: Dutch International Trading Companies from the 16th Century until the Present.* The Hague: SDU, 2000.
Kaukiainen, Yrjö. "The Container Revolution and Liner Freights." *International Journal of Maritime History* 21 (December 2009): 43–74.
Keeling, Drew. "The Transportation Revolution and Transatlantic Migration." *Research in Economic History* 19 (1999): 39–74.
Keenlyside, Francis. "Leathers, Frederick James, First Viscount Leathers (1883–1965)," rev. Marc Brodie, in *Oxford Dictionary of National Biography*, eee ed. H. C. G. Matthew and Brian Harrison. Oxford: Oxford University Press, online ed., ed. Lawrence Goldman, January 2011, www.oxforddnb.com/view/article/34457 (accessed 16 February 2012).
Kettle, Russell. *Deloitte & Co., 1845–1956.* Oxford: Deloitte, Plender, Griffiths & Co. 1958. Reprint, New York: Garland Publishing, 1982.
King, Frank H. H. *The History of the Hongkong and Shanghai Banking Corporation.* 4 vols. Cambridge: Cambridge University Press, 1987–1991.
Kludas, Arnold. *Die Geschichte die deutschen Passagier-Schiffahrt.* 5 vols. Augsburg: Weltbild, 1994.
   Vergnügnungsreisen zur See. Eine Geschichte der deutschen Kreuzfahrt. 2 vols. Hamburg: Convent Verlag, 2001–2003.
Kludas, Arnold, Dieter Maass, and Susanne Sabisch. *Hafen Hamburg. Die Geschichte des Hamburger Freihafens von den Anfängen bis zur Gegenwart.* Hamburg: Ernst Kabel, 1988.
Klugman, Werner and Walter Steeler. *Hafen Hamburg, 1945–1965. Zwanzig Jahre Afbau und Entwicklung.* Hamburg: Verlag Okis, 1965.
Knap, Ger. H. *A Century of Shipping: The History of the Royal Netherlands Steamship Company, 1856–1956.* Amsterdam: 1957.
Kolltveit, Bård and John Maxtone-Grahm. *Under Crown and Anchor: Royal Caribbean Cruise Line: The First Twenty-Five Years, 1970–1995.* Miami Beach, FL: Royal Caribbean Cruises, 1995.
Korver, H. J. *Koninklijke boot. Beeld van een Amsterdamse Scheepvaartonderneming 1856–1981.* Amsterdam 1981.
Krieg, Hans. *Bernhard Buschmann. Die Geschichte eines Ostasienhauses.* Hamburg: Verlag Hamburgische Bücherei, 1952.
Küsel, Ernst-Günther. *Die Kaffeehandelsorganisation in Zentralamerika und Kolumbien.* Hamburg: Friederichsen, De Gruyter, 1939.
Kynaston, David. *The City of London.* 4 vols. London: Pimlico, 1995–2000; Chatto & Windus, 2001.
La maison de Denis Frères à l'occasion de son centenaire. Histoire depuis sa fondation en 1862 jusqu'à nos jours. Denis Frères: Bordeaux, 1963.
Lang, Michael. "Globalization and Its History." *The Journal of Modern History* 78 (December 2006): 899–931.

Lederer, André. *Histoire de la navigation au Congo.* Tervuren (Belgique): Musée Royal de l'Afrique Centrale, 1965.

Leeman, F. W. G. *Van barkschip tot "Willem Ruys." 120 jaar zeevaart.* Rotterdam: Willem Ruys & Zonen, 1961.

Legoy, Jean. *Le peuple du Havre et son histoire. Du négoce à l'industrie, 1800–1914.* Le Havre: Le Cadre de Vie, 1982.

Lenoble, Jean. *Les frères Talabot. Une grande famille d'entrepreneurs au XIXe siècle.* Limoges: CCSTI Lucien Souny, 1989.

Levinson, Marc. *The Box: How the Shipping Container Made the World Smaller and the World Economy Bigger.* Princeton, NJ: Princeton University Press, 2006.

Lichtenstein, Nelson. *The Retail Revolution: How Wal-Mart Created a Brave New World of Business.* New York: Metropolitan Books, 2009.

ed. *Wal-Mart: The Face of Twenty-first Century Capitalism.* New York: The New Press, 2006.

Lilly, Doris. *Those Fabulous Greeks: Onassis, Niarchos, and Livanos.* New York: Cowles Book Company, 1970.

Lindemann, Mary. *Patriots and Paupers: Hamburg 1712–1830.* New York: Oxford University Press, 1990.

Link, Paul. *Sheep Breeding and Wool Production in the Argentine Republic.* Buenos Aires, 1934.

Lissone's Gazette. Jubileumnummer, 1876–1926. Amsterdam: N.V. Lissone & Zoon's Reisbureau, 1926.

Littler, Dawn, ed. *Guide to the Records of Merseyside Maritime Museum, Volume 2.* Research in Maritime History 17. St. John's, Newfoundland: International Maritime Economic History Association, 1999.

Lloyd's List International. *Rotterdam 650 Years.* Colchester: Lloyd's of London Press, 1990.

Löbe, Karl. *Seeschiffahrt in Bremen. Das Schiff Gestaltete Hafen und Stadt.* Bremen: H. M. Hauschild, 1989.

Long, David Edwin. *The Hajj Today: A Survey of the Contemporary Makkah Pilgrimage.* Albany: State University of New York Press, 1979.

Longhurst, Henry. *The Borneo Story: The History of the First 100 Years of Trading in the Far East by the Borneo Company Limited.* London: Newman Neame, 1956.

Loyen, Reginald. "Functional Shifts in the Port of Antwerp: A Throughput Model." *International Journal of Maritime History* 13 (December 2001): 73–93.

Haven in de branding. De economische ontwikkeling van de Antwerpse haven vanaf 1900. Leuven: Universitaire Pers Leuven, 2008.

Loyen, Reginald, Erik Buyst, and Greta Devos, eds. *Struggling for Leadership: Antwerp-Rotterdam Port Competition between 1870–2000.* Heidelberg: Physica-Verlag, 2003.

Lynn, Martin. "From Sail to Steam: The Impact of the Steamship Services of the British Palm Oil Trade with West Africa, 1850–1890." *Journal of African History* 30 (1989): 227–245.

Macfadyen, Violet S. *Eric Macfadyen, 1879–1966.* Barnet, Hertfordshire: Stellar Press, 1968.

Macmillan, Allister. *Seaports of the Far East: Historical and Descriptive Commercial and Industrial Facts, Figures, and Resources.* 3rd edition. London: W. H. & L. Collingridge, 1926.

MacMurray, Charles D. and Malcolm M. Cree. *Shipping and Shipbroking: A Guide to All Branches of Shipbroking and Ship Management.* 3rd edition. London: Sir Isaac Pitman & Sons, 1934.

Maier, Charles S. "Consigning the Twentieth Century to History: Alternative Narratives for the Modern Era." *The American Historical Review* 105 (June 2000): 807–831.

Malon, Claude. *Le Havre colonial de 1880 à 1960.* Mont-Saint-Aignan: Publications des Universités de Rouen et du Havre/Caen: Presses universitaires de Caen, 2006.

Mankelow, Roy. "The Effects of Modernisation and Change in the London Docks: With Particular Reference to the Devlin Reforms and Events since 1967." Ph.D. diss., Cambridge University, 1994.

Markovits, Claude. *The Global World of Indian Merchants, 1750–1947: Traders of Sind from Bukhara to Panama.* Cambridge: Cambridge University Press, 2000.

Marriner, Sheila and Francis E. Hyde. *The Senior John Samuel Swire, 1825–98: Management in Far Eastern Shipping Trades.* Liverpool: Liverpool University Press, 1967.

Maude, W. *Merchants and Bankers: A Brief Record of Antony Gibbs & Sons, 1808–1958.* London: Anthony Gibbs & Sons, 1958.

Maurette, Fernand. *Les grands marchés des matières premières.* Paris: Armand Colin, 1922.

McCoy, O. L. *History of THE SYNDICATE Group of Australian Agents.* Sydney: 1954.

McCrae, Alister and Alan Prentice. *Irrawaddy Flotilla.* Paisley, UK: James Paton, 1978.

McDonnell, Mary Byrne. "The Conduct of Hajj From Malaysia and Its Socio-Economic Impact on Malay Society: A Descriptive and Analytical Study, 1860–1981." Ph.D. diss., Columbia University, 1986.

McKeown, Adam. *Chinese Migrant Networks and Cultural Change: Peru, Chicago, Hawaii, 1900–1936.* Chicago: University of Chicago Press, 2001.

  "Conceptualizing Chinese Diasporas, 1842 to 1949." *The Journal of Asian Studies* 58 (May 1999): 306–337.

  "Global Migration, 1846–1940." *Journal of World History* 15 (June 2004): 155–190.

McPherson, Kenneth. *The Indian Ocean: A History of People and the Sea.* Delhi/Oxford: Oxford University Press, 1993.

Medlicott, W. N. *The Economic Blockade.* 2 vols. London: Her Majesty's Stationery Office, 1952–1959.

Mees, A. C. N. V. *Internationale Crediet-en Handels-Vereeniging "Rotterdam". Gedenkboek uitgegeven bij het vijf-en-zeventig jarig bestaan op 29 Augustus*

1938. Rotterdam: N.V. Internationale Crediet- En Handelsvereeniging "Rotterdam," 1938.

"Mekkagangers." J. Paulus, *Encyclopaedie van Nederlandsch-Indië*. Tweede Druk, vol. 2. S'Gravenage: Martinus Nijhoff, 1917, 695–697.

Mersey Docks and Harbour Board. *The Port of Liverpool*. 4th edition. Liverpool: Littlebury Bros., 1923.

Meuleau, Marc. *Des pionniers en Extrême-Orient. Histoire de la Banque de l'Indochine, 1875–1975*. Paris: Fayard, 1990.

Meyer, David R. *Hong Kong as a Global Metropolis*. Cambridge: Cambridge University Press, 2000.

Meyer, Han. *City and Port: Urban Planning as a Cultural Venture in London, Barcelona, New York, and Rotterdam: Changing Relations between Public Urban Space and Large-Scale Infrastructure*. Translated by D'Laine Camp and Donna de Vries-Hermansader. Rotterdam: Han Meyer, 1999.

Meyer, Heinrich. *Hamburg als Güterumschlagsplatz vor und nach dem Kriege*. Hamburg: Schroedter & Hauer, 1930.

Miller, Michael B. "Pilgrims' Progress: The Business of the Hajj." *Past and Present* 191 (May 2006): 189–228.

Miller, Rory. "Latin American Consumers, British Multinationals, and the Merchant Houses, 1930–1960." MS, 2004.

Milne, Graeme J. *Trade and Traders in Mid-Victorian Liverpool: Mercantile Business and the Making of a World Port*. Liverpool: Liverpool University Press, 2000.

Milward, Alan. *The European Rescue of the Nation-State*. 2nd edition. London: Routledge 2000.

Ministry of Labour. *Final Report of the Committee of Inquiry under the Rt. Hon. Lord Devlin into Certain Matters Concerning the Port Transport Industry* (Devlin Report). Presented to Parliament by the Minister of Labour by Command of Her Majesty, August 1965. London: Her Majesty's Stationery Office, 1965.

Ministry of Transport. *Report of the Committee of Inquiry into the Major Ports of Great Britain* (Rochdale Report). Presented to Parliament by the Minister of Transport by Command of Her Majesty. September 1962. London: Her Majesty's Stationery Office, 1962.

Mintz, Sidney W. *Sweetness and Power: The Place of Sugar in Modern History*. New York: Penguin Books, 1986.

Misra, Maria. *Business, Race, and Politics in British India c. 1850–1960*. Oxford: Clarendon, 1999.

Molsen, Käthe. *C. Illies & Co., 1859–1959. Ein Beitrag zur Geschichte des deutsch-japanischen Handels*. Hamburg: Verlag Hanseatischer Merkur, 1959.

Monzel, Jürgen. *Die Änderung des Wettbewerbsverhältnisses im Stückgutumschlag des Seehäfen. Eine Untersuchung des Antwerpen-Hamburg-Range unter besonderer Berücksichtigung des Containerverkehrs*. Hamburg: Stiftung Europa-Kolleg Hamburg, 1974.

Morgan, Dan. *Merchants of Grain*. Harmondsworth: Penguin Books, 1980. First published 1979.

Möring, Maria. *A. Kirsten, Hamburg*. Hamburg: Wirtschaftsgeschichtliche Forschungstelle, 1952.

Das Lebenswerk Carl Wilhelm Uhlmanns. Hamburg: Hambürgische Bücherei, 1953.

H. W. Pott & Körner. 175 jahre Schiffsmakler un Reederei-Agenten zu Hamburg. Hamburg: Verlag Hamburgische Bücherei, 1952.

Munro, J. Forbes. *Maritime Enterprise and Empire: Sir William Mackinnon and His Business Network, 1823–93*. Woodbridge, Suffolk: Boydell Press, 2003.

Munz. H. *The Australian Wool Industry*. Melbourne: F. W. Cheshire, 1964.

Murphey, Rhoads. *Shanghai: Key to Modern China*. Cambridge, MA: Harvard University Press, 1953.

Nickalls, Guy. "Macfadyen, Sir Eric (1879–1966)." In *Oxford Dictionary of National Biography*, online ed., edited by Lawrence Goldman Oxford: Oxford University Press, 2004, http://www.oxforddnb.com/view/article/34722 (accessed 1 March 2009).

Noer, Deliar. *The Modernist Movement in Indonesia, 1900–1942*. Singapore: Oxford University Press, 1973.

North, Douglass. "Ocean Freight Rates and Economic Development, 1750–1913." *The Journal of Economic History* 18 (1958): 537–547.

Norval, A. J. *The Tourist Industry: A National and International Survey*. London: Sir Isaac Pitman & Sons, Ltd., 1936.

Nuhn, Helmut. "Der Hamburger Hafen. Strukturwandel/und Perspektiven für die Zukunft." *Geographische Rundschau* 41 (1989): 646–654.

Offer, Avner. *The First World War: An Agrarian Interpretation*. Oxford: Clarendon Press, 1989.

Oldewage, Rolf. *Die Nordseehäfen im EWG-Raum, Fakten, und Probleme: Hamburg, Bremen, Wilhelmshaven, Emden, Amsterdam, Rotterdam, Antwerpen, Gent, und Dünkirchen*. Tübingen: J. C. B. Mohr, 1963.

Oosterwijk, Bram. *Op één koers. Nedlloyd*. Rotterdam: Koninklijke Nedlloyd Groep N.V., 1988.

O'Rourke, Kevin H. and Jeffrey G. Williamson. *Globalization and History: The Evolution of a Nineteenth-Century Atlantic Economy*. Cambridge, MA: MIT Press, 1999.

Osterhammel, Jürgen. *Die Verwandlung der Welt. Eine Geschichte des 19. Jahrhunderts*. Munich: C. H. Beck, 2009.

Osterhammel, Jürgen and Niels P. Petersson. *Globalization: A Short History*. Princeton, NJ: Princeton University Press, 2005.

Owen, D. J. *The Port of London Yesterday and Today*. London: Port of London Authority, 1927.

Paxton, Robert O. *Vichy France: Old Guard and New Order, 1940–1944*. New York: Alfred Knopf, 1972. Reprint, New York: Norton, 1975.

Pearson, M. N. *Pious Passengers: The Hajj in Earlier Times*. New Delhi: Sterling Publishers, 1994.

Peters, F. E. *The Muslim Pilgrimage to Mecca and the Holy Places*. Princeton, NJ: Princeton University Press, 1994.

Petersen, Kaare. *The Saga of Norwegian Shipping: An Outline of the History, Growth, and Development of a Modern Merchant Marine*. Oslo: Dreyers, 1955.

Phillips, Carla Rahn and William D. Phillips, Jr. *Spain's Golden Fleece: Wool Production and the Wool Trade from the Middle Ages to the Nineteenth Century.* Baltimore, MD: The Johns Hopkins University Press, 1997.

Phillips, Gordon and Noel Whiteside. *Casual Labour: The Unemployment Question in the Port Transport Industry, 1880–1970.* Oxford: Clarendon, 1985.

Pieterse, Jan Nederveen. *Globalization and Culture: Global Mélange.* 2nd edition. Lanham, MD: Rowman & Littlefield, 2009.

Platt, D. C. M., ed. *Business Imperialism, 1840–1930: An Inquiry Based on British Experience in Latin America.* Oxford: Clarendon Press, 1977.

Latin America and British Trade, 1806–1914. London: Adam & Charles Black, 1972.

Porter, Andrew. "Gentlemanly Capitalism and Empire: The British Experience since 1750." *The Journal of Imperial and Commonwealth History* 18 (1990): 265–295.

The Nineteenth Century. Vol. 3 of *The Oxford History of the British Empire,* edited by Wm. Roger Louis. Oxford: Oxford University Press, 1999.

Port of Antwerp. *The Metamorphosis of a Seaport over the 25 Year Period, 1950–1977.* Antwerp: S. P. R. L. Publitra, c. 1979.

Port of Hamburg. *The Port of Hamburg, 1995/1996.* London: Charter International, 1996.

Post, Peter, "Chinese Business Networks and Japanese Capital in South East Asia, 1880–1940: Some Preliminary Observations." In Rajeswary Ampalavanar Brown, ed., *Chinese Business Enterprise in Asia.* London: Routledge, 1995, 154–176.

Posthuma, F. "Het havenbedrijf der gemeente Rotterdam, 1945–1965." In G. E. van Walsum, ed. *Rotterdam Europoort, 1945–1970.* Rotterdam: A. D. Donker, 1972, 15–82.

Pugh, Peter et al. Edited by Guy Nickalls. *Great Enterprise: A History of Harrisons & Crosfield.* Harrisons & Crosfield, 1990.

Rabson, Stephen and Kevin O'Donoghue. *P & O: A Fleet History.* Kendal, Cumbria: The World Ship Society, 1988.

Randier, Jean. *Histoire de la marine marchande française des premiers vapeurs à nos jours.* Paris: Editions Maritimes & d'Outre-Mer, 1980.

Read, Gordon and Michael Stammers, eds. *Guide to the Records of the Merseyside Maritime Museum.* Research in Maritime History 8. St. John's, Newfoundland: International Martime Economic History Association, 1995.

Records of the Hajj: *A Documentary History of the Pilgrimage to Mecca.* 10 vols. Slough: Archive Editions: 1993.

Rees, Graham L. *Britain's Commodity Markets.* London: Paul Elek Books, 1972.

Ritchie-Noakes, Nancy. *Liverpool's Historic Waterfront: The World's First Mercantile Dock System.* London: Her Majesty's Stationery Office, 1984.

Ritter, Jean. *Le Rhône.* Paris: Presses Universitaires de France, 1973.

Roche, Julian. *The International Wool Trade.* Cambridge: Woodhead, 1995.

Roff, William R. "Sanitation and Security: The Imperial Powers and the Nineteenth Century Hajj." *Arabian Studies* 6 (1982): 143–160.

"The Meccan Pilgrimage: Its Meaning for Southeast Asian Islam." In Raphael Israeli and Anthony H. Johns, eds. *Islam in Asia*. Vol. 2. Jerusalem: Magnes Press, 1984, 238–245.

Rogge, J. *Het handelshuis van Eeghen. Proeve eener geschiedenis van een Amsterdamsch handleshuis*. Amsterdam: Nederlandsche Boekenimport, 1949.

Roncayolo, Marcel. *L'imaginaire de Marseille. Port, ville, pôle*. Marseille: Chambre de Commerce et d'Industrie de Marseille, 1990.

Roseberry, William, Lowell Gudmundson, and Mario Samper Kutschbach, eds. *Coffee, Society, and Power in Latin America*. Baltimore, MD: The Johns Hopkins University Press, 1995.

Roskill, S. W. *A Merchant Fleet in War: Alfred Holt & Co., 1939–1945*. London: Collins, 1962.

Rowe, J. W. F. *Primary Commodities in International Trade*. Cambridge: Cambridge University Press, 1965.

Rübner, Hartmut. *Konzentration und Krise der deutschen Schiffahrt. Maritime Wirtschaft und Politik im Kaiserreich, in der Weimarer Republik und im Nationalsozialismus*. Bremen: H. M. Hauschild, 2005.

Salter, J. A. *Allied Shipping Control: An Experiment in International Administration*. Oxford: Clarendon Press, 1921.

Sanmann, Horst. *Die Verkehrsstruktur der nordwesteuropäischen Seehäfen, Antwerpen, Rotterdam, Amsterdam, Bremen, und Hamburg und ihre "Wandlungen von der Jahrhundertwende bis zur Gegenwart*. Hamburg: Shiffahrts-Verlag "Hansa," 1956.

Sassen, Saskia. *The Global City: New York, London, Tokyo*. 2nd edition. Princeton, NJ: Princeton University Press, 2001.

ed. *Global Networks, Linked Cities*. New York: Routledge, 2002.

Saunier, Pierre-Yves. "Globalization." In Akira Iriye and Pierre-Yves Saunier, eds. *The Palgrave Dictionary of Transnational History*. Houndmills, Basingstoke: Palgrave Macmillan, 2009, 456–462.

Schoonhoven, Etienne. *Anvers son fleuve et son port. Coup d'oeil sur les principales étapes de son histoire économique et maritime*. Antwerp: Lloyd Anversois, 1958.

Schraver, J., ed. *Rotterdam: The Gateway to Europe: History of the Port and Trade of Rotterdam*. Rotterdam: A. D. Donker 1948.

Schück, Walter. *Organisation und Betrieb des Brasilianischen Importhandels*. Stuttgart: C.E. Poeschel, 1926.

Scranton, Philip and Janet F. Davidson. *The Business of Tourism: Place, Faith, and History*. Philadelphia: University of Pennsylvania Press, 2007.

Seberechts, Frank. "Le port d'Anvers et le trafic des potasses d'Alsace, 1920–1950." *Revue Belge d'histoire contemporaine* 29 (1999): 91–143.

"The Political Influences on the Port of Antwerp in the Twentieth Century." In Blomme, *Momentum*, 33–47.

Seiler, Otto J. *A Century of the Far East Service, 1886–1986*. Translated by Peter Alexander. Hamburg: Hapag-Lloyd, 1986.

Südamerikafahrt. Deutsche Linienschiffahrt nach den Ländern Lateinamerikas, der Karibik und der Westküste Nordamerikas im Wandel der Zeiten. Herford: E. S. Mittler & Sohn, 1993.

Siegfried, André and Jérome et Jean Tharaud. *Le centenaire des services des Messageries Maritimes (1851–1951)*. Paris, 1952.

Sipos, G. E. "Expansie, crisis, en aanpassing. De geschiedenis van het handelshuis Internatio in Nederlands-Indië voor de Tweede Wereldoorlog en de mate waarin de aanpassing aan de crisis van de jaren dertig effectief was." Ph.D. diss., Rijksuniversiteit Leiden, 1992.

Smith, Michael Stephen. *The Emergence of Modern Business Enterprise in France, 1800–1930*. Cambridge, MA: Harvard University Press, 2006.

"Unlikely Success: Chargeurs Réunis and the Marine Transport Business in France, 1872–1914." *Entreprises et Histoire* 6 (1994): 11–27.

Smith, Richard. "Britain and the Strategy of the Economic Weapon in the War against Germany, 1914–1919." Ph.D. diss., University of Newcastle upon Tyne, 2000.

Snodgrass, Katharine. *Copra and Coconut Oil*. Stanford, CA: Stanford University Press, 1928.

Starkey, David J. and Alan G. Jamieson, eds. *Exploiting the Sea: Aspects of Britain's Maritime Economy since 1870*. Exeter, UK: University of Exeter Press, 1998.

Starkey, David J. and Gelina Harlaftis, eds. *Global Markets: The Internationalization of the Sea Transport Industries since 1850*. Research in Maritime History 14. St. John's, Newfoundland: International Maritime Economic History Association, 1998, 355–383.

Staveacre, F. W. F. *Tea and Tea Dealing*. London: Pitman & Sons, 1933.

Stearns, Peter N. *Consumerism in World History: The Global Transformation of Desire*. 2nd edition. New York: Routledge, 2006.

Steinweg, Gunther. *Die Deutsche Handelsflotte im Zweiten Weltkrieg. Aufgaben und Schicksal*. Göttingen: Otto Schwartz, 1954.

Stewart, Gordon T. *Jute and Empire: The Calcutta Jute Wallahs and the Landscapes of Empire*. Manchester: Manchester University Press, 1998.

Stoler, Ann Laura. *Capitalism and Confrontation in Sumatra's Plantation Belt, 1870–1979*. New Haven, CT: Yale University Press, 1985.

Stout, H. "Van de Toko uit Rotterdam en van wat daarna kwam." In H. Baudet, *Handelswereld en wereldhandel. Honderd jaren Internatio*. Internatio: Rotterdam, 1963, 17–74.

Straits Settlements Trade Commission. *Report of the Commission Appointed by His Excellency of the Governor of the Straits Settlements to Enquire into and Report on the Trade of the Colony, 1933–1934*. 5 vols. Singapore: Government Printing Office, 1934.

Sturmey, S. G. *British Shipping and World Competition*. London: Athlone Press, 1962.

Sugihara, Kaoru, ed. *Japan, China, and the Growth of the Asian International Economy, 1850–1949*. Oxford: Oxford University Press, 2005.

Suykens, Fernand, Gustaaf Asaert, Alex De Vos, Alfons Thijs, and Karel Veraghtert. *Antwerp: A Port for All Seasons*. 2nd edition. Translated by R. Legreve. Antwerp: MIM, 1986.

Tate, D. J. M. *The RGA History of the Plantation Industry in the Malay Peninsula*. Kuala Lumpur: Oxford University Press, 1996.

Taylor, James. *Ellermans: A Wealth of Shipping*. London: Wilton House Gentry, 1976.

Taylor, L. G. *Seaports: An Introduction to Their Place and Purpose*. Glasgow: Brown, Son & Ferguson, 1974.

Tenold, Stig. "The Harder They Come ... Hilmar Reksten from Boom to Bankruptcy." *The Northern Mariner/Le marin du nord* 11 (July 2001): 41–53.

  Tankers in Trouble: Norwegian Shipping and the Crisis of the 1970s and 1980s. Research in Maritime History 32. St. John's, Newfoundland: International Maritime Economic Association. 2006.

Thede-Ottowell, Anne-Marie. *Hamburg vom Alsterhafen zur Welthafenstadt*. Hamburg: Otto Heinevetter, 1988.

Theotokas, Ioannis and Gelina Harlaftis. *Leadership in World Shipping: Greek Family Firms in International Business*. Houndsmills, Basingstoke: Palgrave Macmillan, 2009.

Thompson, Kristin. *Exporting Entertainment: America in the World's Film Market, 1907–1934*. London: British Film Institute, 1985.

Thowsen, Atle and Stig Tenold. *Odfjell: The History of a Shipping Company*. Bergen: Odfjell ASA, 2006.

Tomlinson, B. R. *The Political Economy of the Raj, 1914–1947: The Economics of Decolonization in India*. Houndmills, Basingstoke: Macmillan, 1979.

Tomlinson, John. *Globalization and Culture*. Chicago: University of Chicago Press, 1999.

Tooze, Adam. *The Wages of Destruction: The Making and Breaking of the Nazi Economy*. New York: Viking Penguin, 2007.

Topik, Steven C. "Coffee." In Steven C. Topik and Allen Wells, eds., *The Second Conquest of Latin America: Coffee, Hennequen, and Oil during the Export Boom, 1850–1930*. Austin: University of Texas Press, 1998, 37–84.

Tregonning, K. G. *Home Port Singapore: A History of Straits Steamship Company Limited, 1890–1965*. Singapore: Oxford University Press, 1967.

Treue, Wilhelm. "Die Geschichte des Bremer Handelshauses C. Melchers & Co. von seiner Gründung bis zum Ende des Ersten Weltkrieges." In Friedrich Prüser und Wilhelm Treue, eds. *Beiträge zur bremischen Firmen-Geschichte*. München: F. Bruckmann, 1966, 33–46.

Trümper, Katharina. *Kaffee und Kaufleute: Guatemala und der Hamburger Handel 1871–1914*. Hamburg: Lit Verlag, 1996.

Turnbull, C. M. *A History of Singapore, 1819–1988*. 2nd edition. Singapore: Oxford University Press, 1989.

Tyson, Geoffrey. *Forgotten Frontier*. Calcutta: W. H. Targett, 1945.

Ukers, William H. *All About Coffee*. 2nd edition. New York: The Tea & Coffee Trade Journal Company, 1935.

Van Acker, Jan. *Anvers d'escale romaine à port mondial*. Translated by Bénédicte Evard. Antwerp-Brussels: Editions Mercurius, 1975.

Van Cauwenbergh, George. *Antwerp: Portrait of a Port*. Antwerp: Uitgeverij Ontwikkeling s.v., 1970.

Van de Laar, Paul. *Stad van formaat. Geschiedenis van Rotterdam in de negentiende en twintigste eeuw*. Zwolle: Waanders, 1999.

Van den Doel, H. W. *Afscheid van Indië. De val van het Nederlandse imperium in Azië.* Amsterdam: Prometheus, 2001.

De stille macht. Het europese binnenlands bestuur op Java en Madoera, 1808–1942. Amsterdam: Bert Bakker, 1994.

Van der Meulen, D. "The Mecca Pilgrimage and Its Importance to the Netherlands East Indies." *The Muslim World* 31 (1941): 48–60.

Van Doorn, J. A. A. *De laatste eeuw van Indië. Ontwikkeling en ondergang van een koloniaal project.* Amsterdam: Ooievaar, 1996. First published 1994.

Van Driel, Hugo. "Collusion in Transport: Group Effects in a Historical Perspective." *Journal of Economic Behavior & Organization* 41 (2000): 385–404.

Four Centuries of Warehousing: Pakhoed, The Origins and History, 1616–1967. Rotterdam: Royal Pakhoed N.V., 1992.

"Innovation and Integration in Mineral Bulk Handling in the Port of Rotterdam." *Business History* 44 (July 2002): 63–90.

Samenwerking in haven en vervoer in het containertijdperk. Delft: Eburon, 1990.

"Uitschakeling van de Nederlandse koffiehandel in de negentiende en de twintigste eeuw?" *NEHA-jaarboek voor economische bedrijfs-en techniekgeschiedenis* 60, 1997, 159–203.

Van Driel, Hugo and Ferry de Goey. *Rotterdam: Cargo Handling Technology, 1870–2000.* Eindhoven: Stichting Historie der Techniek, 2000.

Van Driel, Hugo and Greta Devos. "Path Dependence in Ports: The Persistence of Co-operative Forms." *Business History Review* 81 (Winter 2007): 681–708.

Van Driel, Hugo and Irma Bogenrieder. "Memory and Learning: Selecting Users in the Port of Rotterdam, 1883–1900." *Business History* 51 (September 2009): 649–667.

Vanfraechem, Stephan. "The Antwerp Docker between Militantism and Pragmatism, 1900–1972." *International Journal of Maritime History* 14 (December 2002): 167–180.

"Why They Are Tall and We Are Small! Competition between Antwerp and Rotterdam in the Twentieth Century." Work in progress.

Van Isacker, Karel. *Afscheid van de havenarbeider, 1944–1966.* Antwerp: De Nederlandsche Boekhandel, 1967.

De Antwerpse dokwerker, 1830–1940. 2nd edition. Antwerp: De Nederlandsche Boekhandel, 1966.

Vigarié, André. *Les grands ports de commerce de la Seine au Rhin. Leur évolution devant l'industrialisation des arrière-pays.* Paris: S.A.B.R.I., 1964.

Ville, Simon. *The Rural Entrepreneurs: A History of the Stock and Station Agent Industry in Australia and New Zealand.* Cambridge, Cambridge University Press, 2000.

Von Marchtaler, Hildegard. *Geschichte der Kaffee-Import und Reederei-Firma H. H. Eggers, Hamburg.* Hamburg: 1953.

Von Münching, L. L. *De Nederlandse koopvaardijvloot in de tweede wereldoorlog. De lotgevallen van Nederlandse koopvaardijschepen en hun bemanning.* Bussum: De Boer Maritiem, 1978.

Vredenbregt, J. "The Haddj: Some of Its Features and Functions in Indonesia." *Bijdragen tot de taal-, land- en volkenkunde* 118 (1962): 91–154.

Wäänänen, Ilmari. *Rotterdam als Seehafen unter besonderer Berücksichtigung des Konkurrenzkampfes mit Antwerpen.* Weida i. Thür: Thomas & Hubert, 1930.

Wardle, Arthur C. *Steam Conquers the Pacific: A Record of Maritime Achievement, 1840–1940.* London: Hodder and Stoughton, 1940.

Wasserstein, Bernard. *Britain and the Jews of Europe, 1939–1945.* Oxford: Clarendon Press, 1979.

Weinbaum, Alys Eve, Lynn M. Thomas, Priti Ramamurthy, Uta G. Poiger, Madeleine Yue Dong, and Tani E. Barlow. *The Modern Girl around the World: Consumption, Modernity, and Globalization.* Durham, NC: Duke University Press, 2008.

Weinberg, Gerhard L. *A World at Arms: A Global History of World War II.* 2nd edition. Cambridge: Cambridge University Press, 2005.

Weinhauer, Klaus. *Alltag und Arbeitskampf im Hamburger Hafen. 1933: Sozialgeschichte der Hamburger Hafenarbeiter 1914–1933.* Paderborn: Ferdinand Schöningh, 1994.

Wendemuth, L. and W. Böttcher. *The Port of Hamburg.* 2nd edition. Translated by Wilhelm Eggers. Hamburg: Meissner & Christiansen, 1932.

Wendt, Herbert. *Kurs Südamerika. Brücke zwischen zwei Kontinenten.* Bielefeld: Ceres-Verlag, 1958.

Wentholt, A. D. *Brug over den oceaan. Een eeuw geschiedenis van de Holland Amerika Lijn.* Rotterdam: Nigh & Van Ditmar, 1973.

White, Nicholas J. "Liverpool Shipping and the End of Empire: The Ocean Group in East and Southeast Asia, c. 1945–73." In Sheryllynne Haggerty, Anthony Webster, and Nicholas White, *The Empire in One City? Liverpool's Inconvenient Imperial Past.* Manchester: Manchester University Press, 2008, 165–187.

Wiborg, Susanne and Klaus Wiborg. *1847–1997. Unser Feld ist die Welt. 150 Jahre Hapag-Lloyd.* Hamburg: Hapag-Lloyd AG, 1997.

Wickizer, V. D. *Coffee, Tea, and Cocoa: An Economic and Political Analysis.* Stanford, CA: Stanford University Press, 1951.

Wiedenfeld, Kurt. *Die nordwesteuropäischen Welthäfen: London – Liverpool – Hamburg – Bremen – Amsterdam – Rotterdam – Antwerpen – Havre in ihrer Verkehrs- und Handelsbedeutung.* Berlin: Ernst Siegfried Mittler und Sohn, 1903.

Wilkins, Mira. *The Emergence of Multinational Enterprise: American Business Abroad from the Colonial Era to 1914.* Cambridge, MA: Harvard University Press, 1970.

   The History of Foreign Investment in the United States, 1914–1945. Cambridge, MA: Harvard University Press, 2004.

   The Maturing of Multinational Enterprise: American Business Abroad from 1914 to 1970. Cambridge, MA: Harvard University Press, 1974.

Wilkins, Mira and Harm Schröter. *The Free Standing Company in the World Economy, 1830–1996.* Oxford: Oxford University Press, 1998.

Willems, Wim. *De uittocht uit Indië, 1945–1995*. Amsterdam: Bert Bakker, 2001.

Williams, D. M. "Liverpool Merchants and the Cotton Trade, 1820–1850." In J. R. Harris, ed., *Liverpool and Merseyside: Essays in the Economic and Social History of the Port and Its Hinterland*. London: Frank Cass, 1969, 182–211.

Williamson, Oliver. *The Economic Institutions of Capitalism: Firms, Markets, Relational Contracting*. New York: Free Press, 1985.
  Markets and Hierarchies: Analysis and Antitrust Implications. New York: Free Press, 1975.

Wilson, Charles. *The History of Unilever*. 2 vols. London: Cassell & Company, 1954–1968.

Withey, Lynne. *Grand Tours and Cook's Tours: A History of Leisure Travel, 1750–1915*. New York: William Morrow, 1997.

Witthöft, Hans Jürgen. *Container. Transportrevolution unseres Jahrhunderts*. Herford: Koehlers, 1977.
  HAPAG: Hamburg Amerika Linie. Herford: Koehlers Verlagsgesellschaft, 1973.

Wir Setzen Alles in Bewegung. Kühne & Nagel 100 Jahre. Bremen, 1990.

Wolfe, Tom. *The Right Stuff*. New York: Farrar, Straus & Giroux, 1979.

Wray, William D. *Mitsubishi and the N.Y.K., 1870–1914: Business Strategy in the Japanese Shipping Industry*. Cambridge, MA: Harvard University Press, 1984.

Wrenn, John Edwin. *World Trade in Vegetable Oils and Animal Fats*. Washington, DC: U.S. Government Printing Office, 1923.

Yen Ching-Hwang. *Coolies and Mandarins: China's Protection of Overseas Chinese during the Late Ch'ing Period (1851–1911)*. Singapore: Singapore University Press, 1985.

Yonekawa, Shin'ichi. *General Trading Companies: A Comparative and Historical Study*. Tokyo: United Nations University Press, 1990.

Yui, Tsunehiko and Keiichiro Nakagawa, eds. *Business History of Shipping: Strategy and Structure*. Tokyo: University of Tokyo Press, 1985.

Zhongli Zhang, Chen Zengnian, and Yao Xinrong. *The Swire Group in Old China*. Shangahi: The Shanghai People's Publishing House, 1990.

Zimmermann, Siegfried. *Theodor Wille, 1844–1969*. Hamburg: Hanseatischer Merkur, 1969.

Index

Lightning Source UK Ltd.
Milton Keynes UK
UKOW01f1456090915

258337UK00005B/184/P

9 781107 659629